A Feminist Companion to
the New Testament Apocrypha

Feminist Companion to the New Testament
and Early Christian Writings, 11

Other titles published in this series:
A Feminist Companion to Matthew
A Feminist Companion to Mark
A Feminist Companion to Luke
A Feminist Companion to John, volume 1
A Feminist Companion to John, volume 2
A Feminist Companion to Paul
A Feminist Companion to the Deutero-Pauline Epistles
A Feminist Companion to the Catholic Epistles and Hebrews
A Feminist Companion to the Acts of the Apostles
A Feminist Companion to Mariology

Forthcoming:
A Feminist Companion to Early Christian Apocalyptic Literature
A Feminist Companion to Patristic Literature
A Feminist Companion to the Historical Jesus

A Feminist Companion to

the New Testament Apocrypha

edited by

Amy-Jill Levine

with Maria Mayo Robbins

T&T CLARK INTERNATIONAL
A Continuum imprint
LONDON • NEW YORK

Published by T&T Clark International
A Continuum imprint
The Tower Building, 11 York Road, London SE1 7NX
80 Maiden Lane, Suite 704, New York, NY 10038

www.tandtclark.com

British Library Cataloguing-in-Publication Data
A catalogue record for this book is available from the British Library

Typeset by Fakenham Photosetting Limited Fakenham Norfolk
Printed on acid-free paper in Great Britain by MPG Books Ltd, Bodmin, Cornwall

ISBN   0826466877 (hardback)
        0826466885 (paperback)

CONTENTS

PREFACE

A Feminist Companion to the New Testament Apocrypha, along with its sister volumes on the other documents of the New Testament and early Christian literature, signals the extent to which feminist critique has become a core element of biblical, historical and theological study.

Letters of invitation to contribute to this series went well beyond scholars known from their contributions to explicitly feminist or women-identified collections, such as the two volumes of *Searching the Scriptures*[1] and the *Women's Bible Commentary*,[2] or from books and articles with 'feminist' in the title. Authors already established as having feminist interests were asked to suggest additional voices, and so interpreters at the beginning of their academic careers joined their senior colleagues in the pages of the volumes.

Invitations went beyond North America and Western Europe to East and South Asia, Africa, Eastern Europe, Central and South America, and Australia/New Zealand. Along with an intentional focus on cultural diversity, we targeted as well authors who might speak explicitly from two perspectives sometimes overlooked even in feminist biblical collections, namely, sexual identity (e.g. lesbian critique) and religious tradition (e.g. Evangelicals, Jews). Some chose to write explicitly from their social location, and some did not. For either new or previously published work not in English, Vanderbilt Divinity School/The Carpenter Program in Religion, Gender, and Sexuality provided funds for translation.

Not all those invited were able to contribute, but readers should be able to hear echoed in the footnotes – and by extension in the sources those notes utilize – numerous and diverse feminist voices speaking in other volumes and venues.

In addition to publishing select 'classics' in feminist analysis, the series invited numerous senior scholars to reconsider their earlier approaches and conclusions. Through their revisions, changes in feminist thought can be tracked. The series also sought contributions from biblical experts not known for feminist interests or even, in some cases, sympathies: 'Write a "feminist" piece', we exhorted; when a few demurred ('I don't "do" feminist critique'; 'I don't know what feminist critique is'), we responded: 'You should find out about it; you should engage it; if you don't like it, explain why, for all disciplines can profit from engaged critique; if you do find it helpful, use it.'

We wish to thank Marianne Blickenstaff for help with editing. We also wish to thank the Carpenter Program in Religion, Gender, and Sexuality at the Vanderbilt Divinity School for financial and technical support.

1 Elisabeth Schüssler Fiorenza (ed.), *Searching the Scriptures: A Feminist Introduction and Commentary* (2 vols.; New York: Crossroad, 1993, 1994).

2 Carol A. Newsom and Sharon H. Ringe (eds.), *The Women's Bible Commentary* (Louisville, KY: Westminster/John Knox Press, 1992; rev. edn, 1998).

It is our hope that this new series will quickly establish itself as a standard work of reference to scholars, students and also to others who are interested in the New Testament and Christian Origins.

Amy-Jill Levine and Maria Mayo Robbins
Vanderbilt Divinity School and Graduate Department of Religion

ACKNOWLEDGEMENTS

The editors and publisher are grateful to the following for permission to reproduce copyright material: Stanford University Press for 'Thinking with Virgins: Engendering Judeo-Christian Differences' by Daniel Boyarin, from *Dying for God: Martyrdom and the Making of Christianity and Judaism* (Stanford, CA: Stanford University Press, 1999); The Johns Hopkins University Press for '"Her Own Proper Kinship": Marriage, Class, and Women in the Apocryphal Acts of the Apostles' by Andrew S. Jacobs, originally published as 'A Family Affair: Marriage, Class, and Ethics in the Apocryphal Acts of the Apostles' in the *Journal of Early Christian Studies* 7.1 (1999), pp. 105–38; Peeters Publishers for 'The Erotic Asceticism of the *Passion of Andrew*: the Apocryphal *Acts of Andrew*, the Greek Novel, and Platonic Philosophy' by Caroline T. Schroeder, originally published as 'Embracing the Erotic in the *Passion of Andrew*: the Apocryphal *Acts of Andrew*, the Greek Novel, and Platonic Philosophy', in Jan N. Bremmer (ed.), *The Apocryphal Acts of Andrew* (Leuven: Peeters, 2000), pp. 110–26; and Sheffield Academic Press for 'Construction of Culture Through the Construction of Person: the *Acts of Thecla* as an Example' by Johannes Vorster, in Stanley E. Porter and Thomas H. Olbricht (eds.) (1997), *The Rhetorical Analysis of Scripture: Essays from the 1995 London Conference* (JSNTSup 146; Sheffield, UK: Sheffield Academic Press), pp. 445–73.

Abbreviations

ANRW	Hildegard Temporini and Wolfgang Haase (eds.), *Aufstieg und Niedergang der römischen Welt: Geschichte und Kultur Roms im Spiegel der neueren Forschung* (Berlin: W. de Gruyter, 1972–)
BJS	Brown Judaic Studies
CCSA	Corpus Christianorum Series Apocryphorum
CCSL	Corpus Christianorum Series Latina
CH	*Church History*
EvTh	*Evangelische Theologie*
HTR	*Harvard Theological Review*
JBL	*Journal of Biblical Literature*
JECS	*Journal of Early Christian Studies*
JFSR	*Journal of Feminist Studies of Religion*
JRS	*Journal of Roman Studies*
JSNT	*Journal for the Study of the New Testament*
JSNTSS	Journal for the Study of the New Testament Supplement Series
JTS	*Journal of Theological Studies*
LCL	Loeb Classical Library
LXX	Septuagint
NHS	Nag Hammadi Studies
NovT	*Novum Testamentum*
NPNF	*Nicene and Post-Nicene Fathers of the Christian Church* (14 vols.; Edinburgh: T&T Clark and Grand Rapids, MI: Eerdmans, 1980–89)
NRSV	New Revised Standard Version
NTS	*New Testament Studies*
RE Suppl.	*Paulys Real-Encyclopädie der classischen Altertumswissenschaft. Supplement* (15 vols.; Stuttgart: J.B. Metzler, 1903–1980)
RSV	Revised Standard Version
SBL	Society of Biblical Literature
SBLDS	SBL Dissertation Series
SBLSP	SBL Seminar Papers
TDNT	Gerhard Kittel and Gerhard Friedrich (eds.), *Theological Dictionary of the New Testament* (trans. Geoffrey W. Bromiley; 10 vols.; Grand Rapids: Eerdmans, 1964–76)
TU	*Texte und Untersuchungen*
TZ	*Theologische Zeitschrift*
VC	*Vigiliae Christianae*
ZKG	*Zeitschrift für Kirchengeschichte*
ZNW	*Zeitschrift für die neutestamentliche Wissenschaft*

LIST OF CONTRIBUTORS

Daniel Boyarin, University of California, Berkeley, USA
Jan N. Bremmer, University of Groningen, The Netherlands
Susan A. Calef, Creighton University, Omaha, NE, USA
Jill C. Gorman, Rollins College, Winter Park, FL, USA
Cornelia B. Horn, St Louis University, St Louis, MO, USA
Andrew S. Jacobs, University of California, Riverside, USA
Dennis R. MacDonald, Clarement School of Theology and Claremont Graduate University, Claremont, CA, USA
Magda Misset-van de Weg, Radboud University, Nijmegen, The Netherlands
Caroline T. Schroeder, Stanford University, Stanford, CA, USA
Gail P.C. Streete, Rhodes College, Memphis, TN, USA
Richard Valantasis, Candler School of Theology, Emory University, Atlanta, GA, USA
Johannes N. Vorster, University of South Africa, Pretoria, South Africa

INTRODUCTION

AMY-JILL LEVINE

Feminist New Testament scholarship in the early 1970s optimistically argued for the existence of an initially egalitarian movement in which there was 'not male and female' (Gal. 3.28) and for which women served as disciples, apostles, prophets, teachers and leaders. But whereas women's discipleship (Dorcas, Acts 9.36), apostolic recognition (Junia, Rom. 16.7), teaching authority (Priscilla, Acts 18.26), leadership activities (Phoebe, Rom. 16.1), and other prominent roles certainly marked the nascent church, the canon did not yield evidence of an egalitarian movement. The feminist scholars were, appropriately, not deterred by this evidentiary gap, for one of the strengths of their approach was to broaden the historical horizons to look not only behind the canonical texts but also beyond them. Not constrained by the borders of the New Testament, feminist scholars and fellow travellers interested in women's history found what seemed to be proof not only of women's leadership but also of women's communities in the Apocryphal Acts.

In 1980, Stevan Davies published the ground-breaking *The Revolt of the Widows*[1] which claimed that the Apocryphal Acts were written by and for groups of celibate women. Davies's thesis received immediate approbation from a number of feminist scholars: the concept of a women's community, an alternative to the dreaded and dreadful 'patriarchy', a literature of our own; the Acts provided for women role models in the host of apocryphal women who asserted control over their own bodies, intellects and religious identifications. The self-baptized, resilient Thecla became in a number of classrooms and more liberal churches just as popular as Paul, and infinitely more likeable. Even more appealing for some: the Acts offered some readers 'proof' that the Church had engaged in a conspiracy to remove women from positions of power, but there were women who resisted. The 'True Church' was not that of 1 Timothy or Tertullian, but of Drusiana, Maximilla and Tryphaena. While these women were converted by apostles and so initially dependent on male leadership, conveniently, the apostles either disappear or die at the end of the stories, and so the image of the free, celibate and saved woman remains.

Twenty-five years later, the Apocryphal Acts remain the site of vibrant feminist study, but the optimism that marked Thecla's academic debut has substantially abated. Today scholars are less sanguine not only about the origins of the texts in women's communities but also about their potential to liberate. The early thesis had projected onto the past concerns derived in good measure from early feminist consciousness (with its generally privileged advocates), and it was probably far too optimistic in its claim that it could recover the actual voice of women. As a number

---

1 Stevan L. Davies, *The Revolt of the Widows: The Social World of the Apocryphal Acts* (Carbondale: Southern Illinois University Press, 1980).

of the contributors to this volume propose, the heroines of the Apocryphal Acts are less representative of women's voices than they are reflections of male authors who expressed their concerns via the figures of women. Similarly, the burden of the narratives becomes less the surface promotion of celibacy and more about creating a new social order, in which class and family, gender and the body, are redefined from the prevailing pagan values to the new 'Christian' ideals. From reconstructions of an anterior gynocentric utopia, the Acts now prompt interpretations that emphasize the patriarchal reinforcing of women's self-abnegation. Ostensive evidence of women's social roles now yields to theories of female figures as constructs by which men work out their views of sexuality and gender. The heroines of the Acts may be figures worthy of emulation; they may also be prizes in the contest between the Apostle and the Husband, between Church and World.

Yet whatever the texts were, their legacies remain. Despite the attempts of the Church to domesticate the heroines of the Apocryphal Acts, the models these women offer of female autonomy, the levelling of class status, the recuperation of the language of the erotic and the reconfiguration of the family shifted social attitudes. Moving from prescriptive to descriptive, the Acts emerge as formative in the shaping of Christian identity in Antiquity. The figures of these fascinating documents – Thecla, Xanthippe, Polyxena, Cleopatra, Drusiana, Petronilla, the 'chaste prostitute', and the apostles Paul, Andrew, John, Thomas and a host of others – provide insight into Christian imagination and information for reconstructing the Christian past. By analysing the Apocryphal Acts, by extending the borders of the genre to encompass the *Martyrdom of Perpetua and Felicity* and by invoking the Christian Old Testament, Hellenistic Romances and Rabbinic literature, the essays in this volume explore both the influences upon and the fate of the Apocryphal stories. In so doing they also consider the fate of the women and men influenced by them.

Andrew S. Jacobs' study of 'apostolic homewreckers' nuances the earlier view that the Apocryphal Acts reveals a feminist manifesto that rebels against patriarchal marriage and women's sexual servitude. For Jacobs, the heroines of the Acts represent neither historical reality nor empty rhetoric but rather serve as 'discursive construction' by which women could 'reconceptualize their own moral agency'. Because symbolism, metaphor and other rhetorical moves serve to inspire rather than erase women, they could, and did, prompt the auditors of the Acts to transform their own worldviews. The prescriptive texts thus become descriptive. Women readers could, and did, use Drusiana and Cleopatra to 'think with': Macrina, Melania (Elder and Younger), Paula and other upper-class women from the third and fourth centuries demonstrate how the prescriptive Acts became descriptive.

Following his well-taken caveats against projecting modern conceptions of marriage onto Antiquity, Jacobs demonstrates how Augustus's attempts to inculcate marriage and morality among the senatorial class eventually disseminated into the lower classes, a dissemination facilitated by philosophical writings and the Hellenistic romance. As the new ideals spread, the conception of marriage shifted from a mechanism for the transmission of property between elite families to a mode for determining moral character. In like manner, it also shifted from a private to a public concern: marriage was both mechanism and model for maintaining the (elite-controlled) state. Finally, the familial ideal shifted from the top-down model privileging the father/husband/master (as in the household codes of 1 Peter,

Colossians and Ephesians) to a model of loving partnership between husband and wife. In modern terms: Rome shifted from the 'Father Knows Best' model to 'The Simpsons'.

Jacobs then demonstrates how second- and third-century Christians rejected this 'elite conjugal union of husband and wife' and replaced the power of the *paterfamilias* and his attendant upper-class ethics with that of the Christ and his 'declassed' albeit still hierarchical kinship group. The focus shifts from husband and wife to apostle and convert, whether male or female, with the apostle standing as proxy for the Christ; similarly, the goal shifts from partnership (κοινωνία) to kinship (συγγένεια). Putting the matter succinctly, he states: 'we can now frame the Apocryphal Acts as a deliberate form of narrative resistance to this ethical family configuration centered on marriage'. Using the *Acts of Andrew* as his example, Jacobs demonstrates how the apostle converts Maximilla's bedroom not into a Plutarchian ethical schoolhouse, but into a Christian meeting house. Maximilla's husband, the Greek proconsul Aegeates, echoes Juvenal's marital model of partnership: he regards sexual intercourse as representing 'a higher union' of fellowship. From a non-Christian perspective, he's the ideal husband. But Maximilla has been seduced by Andrew's offer of moral superiority not in marriage but in Christian kinship.

This kinship model remains, however, the choice of the elite. Whereas the romances do speak to and sometimes of non-elites such as slaves achieving connubial ethical partnership, the Acts offer an alternative class-configuration. In the Acts, slaves do not ascend to the ethical heights of the chaste elite; rather, male and female Christian aristocrats join the humble and subservient 'brethren' within the newly configured family. The same dropping down appears, as Jacobs notes, in the *Acts of John*. Again, the apostle becomes the 'father' to his 'children' and 'servants', who include elite couples along with their servants and a 'chaste prostitute'. The upper-class Thecla rejects not only her fiancé but also her wealth and status (symbolized by the bracelets and silver mirror she gives to Paul's jailers). According to the *Acts of Peter*, the apostle sells the property bequeathed to his paralysed daughter and distributes the proceeds to the poor. The *Acts of Thomas* depicts continent royal newly-weds who meet together with a 'Hebrew slave girl' and 'many of the brethren', and also recount the conversion to chastity and so status renunciation of the royal family of India. Such solidarity appears as well in Perpetua's *Diary*. Virtue is thus gained by rejecting class as a marker of ethical superiority.

Confirming Jacobs' point that the Apocryphal Acts offer an alternative to the marital-partnership model and extending it to reveal a partial subversion of gender roles, Caroline T. Schroeder demonstrates how the *Acts of Andrew* replaces the deity Eros, who begins most of the Hellenistic novels, with Christ or his proxy. In like manner, the Christianized Platonic *Eros* – the love of beauty, the one, the divine – replaces the novels' *Eros* of sexual desire. The ascetic agenda is, as Schroeder demonstrates, 'couched in a recognizable discourse', namely, that of the philosophic school.

The language of the romance is also recognizable even as it subverts marital, heterosexual and gender-determined norms. Maximilla's servants and husband suspect her secret nightly visits to Andrew to be sexual, and she does confirm to Aegeates, 'I am in love' (φιλῶ). Despite her insistence that her love is 'not of this world' and despite her withdrawal from 'filthy intercourse' and 'disgusting pollution', the erotic codes are not lost. Andrew describes Stratocles as 'the one I sought ... the one I desired ... the one I loved' (ἠγάπων), and Stratocles describes Andrew as his true love. Andrew is the new Socrates who both inseminates his elite converts Maximilla and Stratocles and then serves as their midwives as they give birth to their 'new perfected selves' from their union with their 'inner husband'. Gender constructions fall as Andrew impregnates Stratocles even as he calls Maximilla a 'man' (ἀνδρός).

Yet as Schroeder astutely notes, the gendered concerns of the romance and the philosophic schools are not fully absent. Andrew also compares Maximilla to a 'repenting Eve' and so positions her as the 'iconic female'. Further, unlike Stratocles, Maximilla does not converse with Andrew about theological or philosophical matters. Despite Andrew's role as midwife and Stratocles's labour, these images appear in the context of the masculine roles of 'teacher' and 'disciple'. The feminized imagery does not undercut Stratocles's masculine nature. Therefore, Schroeder concludes that the 'gender boundaries are fluid but not transcended'; the cultural categories are challenged but not erased.

In both issuing their challenges to cultural norms and in attempting to define themselves, Christian writers provide several early, and prescient, examples of what today is termed 'identity politics'. Claiming to be a third 'race' or 'gender' (*genos, genea*), they saw themselves as distinct from the received binary categories of Jew and Pagan, male and female, married and single, even human and divine. By analysing the variations on this self-definitional strategy in Paul's Epistle to the Galatians, the *Gospel of Thomas* and the *Acts of Paul and Thecla*, *Peter*, *John* and *Thomas*, Richard Valantasis demonstrates how from the mid-first through the third century the followers of Jesus explored the erasure of prior identity, the unification of opposites and finally the redefining of social categories. Valantasis also remarks on the political implications of these exercises, for while the strategies function as the survival mechanisms a sectarian movement requires in order to face internal rivalries and external persecution, the same strategies threaten to become tools of oppression when the Church becomes the majority and proceeds to label the 'left behind' groups as fallen, subhuman, or 'unworthy of life'.

According to Valantasis, Paul refuses to subordinate Christian identity to accommodationist models that seek to retain or impose circumcision if not other Jewish practices. Instead, Paul favours a 'new creation' (Gal. 6.15) based on a gospel of freedom and novelty rather than law (νόμος) and custom. Baptism 'replicates the experience of revelation and inaugurates the freedom from social and religious categories' (Gal. 3.27–28); the baptized individual no longer belongs to, or is defined by, normative categories of ethnicity/race, social status, or gender, ideally if not necessarily in practice. The new identity, which is premised upon revelation rather than tradition or human agency, secures itself by means of negatively defining its alternatives: Judaism is slavery; Paganism is sin.

The *Gospel of Thomas* does not erase traditional characteristics of identity in the context of sectarian polemic; rather, it unifies them and so reconstructs them both spiritually and physically in the context of universal wisdom: the third *genos* is created by having all genders become male. When in Logion 114 Jesus states he will 'lead [Mary Magdalene] in order to make her male ... for every woman who will make herself male will enter the kingdom of heaven', he renders gender categories fluid. The same fluidity marks Logion 22, which speaks of making 'the male and the female one and the same, so that the male not be male and the female female'.

Conversely, the four Apocryphal Acts retain the categories male and female. Yet they too promote a socially disruptive message, namely, an intrusive argument for continence. Speaking of the *Acts of Paul and Thecla*, Valantasis summarizes: 'Christian identity, while maintaining society's dominant categories, changes the content so that whatever one's social status "chastity" remains determinative' for identity. 'Chastity' here as well as in the *Acts of Thomas* provides identity to males as well as females, animals as well as humans. For the *Acts of Peter*, the narrative intrusion of the Pauline 'gospel of purity' and not the contest of power that otherwise dominates the story motivates the apostle's martyrdom. The *Acts of John*, combining themes of new identity and power, problematizes the category 'human' (ἄνθρωπος): 'humans' are those who lack faith and so lack power. Epitomizing this shift in the defining characteristics of the ἄνθρωπος is Jesus himself, whose own nude body, by appearance and by its polymorphic abilities, defies the definition of 'human'. He *and his followers* who both return from the dead and have the power to raise the dead are no longer constrained by human physicality, including sexual differentiation. Thus, for the Christian, appearance does not reliably mirror actuality. The external modality of Christians in these Acts conforms to the status quo; internally, according to Valantasis, it is completely different.

Jan N. Bremmer's detailed analysis of the *Acts of John* focuses less on its potential for prompting social or familial change and more on possible evidence for change that had already occurred. Bremmer begins with a helpful survey of earlier work on the Apocryphal Acts, in which theories of resistance to 'patriarchy', liberation from marriage, women's communities and women's oral tradition optimistically attempted to rewrite the history of early Christianity. While appreciating the sociological questions and while agreeing that the Acts offer evidence of 'liberation' from gender-determined social barriers, Bremmer calls for a more cautious approach that looks at each Act individually to determine the place of women not only in the narrative, but also in its production and reception.

The plot summary confirms the observations made by Jacobs, Schroeder and Valantasis: traces of the Hellenistic romances remain attached to the elite, beautiful protagonists; eroticism is rechannelled into celibacy; social groupings are dismantled. For example, John encounters the young, beautiful, rich, noble and politically powerful Lycomedes, who seeks a healing for Cleopatra, his equally young, beautiful, noble and rich, albeit paralysed wife. The husband, distraught over his wife's illness and despite John's protestations, first announces that he will commit suicide and then – going the hero of the romance one better – drops dead. Conveniently, John heals Cleopatra, who then resurrects her husband.

The fate of the next aristocratic couple is less appealing. Andronicus and Drusiana appear in John's socially diverse company, along with the recent widow Aristobula, Aristippe and Xenophon, and the oxymoronically identified 'chaste prostitute'. Drawing upon an allusion to their story in the Manichaean *Coptic Psalter*, Bremmer recounts how Andronicus, less than thrilled with his wife's conversion, entombs her together with Andrew. Two weeks later, the husband relents, releases his prisoners and agrees to a celibate marital life. Then Drusiana, distressed at causing grief to her suitor Callimachus by not responding favourably to his amorous advances, also drops dead. But, this being an Apocryphal Act, not only is she resurrected, she then resurrects Andronicus's steward, who had been killed by a snake when he had attempted to aid Callimachus in committing necrophilia (a charming scene matched later by the self-castration of a parricide whose father John resurrects). Meanwhile, Andronicus – whose name ironically suggests masculine virtues – cries so much that even John commands his silence. Clearly we are not in Kansas.

Nevertheless, Bremmer displays a certain optimism in moving from the narrative to social history. For example, he locates in John's specific compassion for old women – which is also characteristic of the titular figures of the *Acts of Peter* and the *Acts of Paul* – the Church's concern for this despised and oppressed social group. Bremmer thus finds the Church's 'revolution in the ancient value system' (nevertheless, the old women remain only the objects of charity). Bremmer, like Jacobs, also finds the protagonists offering a more inclusive community than indicated either in the Romances or in society writ large. Whereas the married couples in the *Acts of John* are, in terms of class, appearance and wealth comparable to the heroes and heroines of the Greek novels, their lives are more inclusive. Cleopatra shares faith and friendship with the apostle, her husband and other men. While she and Lycomedes are not described as renouncing sexual intercourse (then again, parts of the text are missing), Drusiana and Andronicus clearly are. The *Acts of John* thus confirms the impression given in the correspondences between Church Fathers and elite women that Christian life provided at least upper-class women, celibate and otherwise, opportunities for developed friendships and intellectual discussion. Whether we can conclude from this text and others of its genre that Christian women 'could occupy influential positions to a degree unheard of in contemporary pagan religions or Judaism' may be too optimistic. The text itself does suggest a partial dismantling of social class, but the women do not appear to advance in leadership per se. Instead, the upper-class women cede their status-privilege, but there is no indication that the lower-class women gain. The basis of power for women in both the Acts and the correspondences remains an economic one. Perhaps Drusiana and Cleopatra are liberating in the same way that Catwoman and Lara Croft are liberating: they have power over men, miraculous strength and amazing intelligence; they are the Judiths of their age. They are figures of fantasy, but they should not be dismissed, for the fantastic can also inspire.

Focusing on the 'chaste prostitute', one of the more obscure figures in the *Acts of John*, Dennis R. MacDonald reveals another of the mechanisms by which these early Christian narratives respond to and adapt prevailing cultural tropes. Among John's entourage, the prostitute is anomalous: other characters are paired (husband and wife; slave and owner; friends), while she stands alone; other characters are named while she remains identified only by (what are at least) sexual categories. Nor is she simply 'a' chaste prostitute; she is 'the' chaste prostitute: thus MacDonald proposes not only that her identification likely occurred in a part of the Apocryphon which is now lost, but also that an even earlier identification may be found together with those of her fellow travellers Aristippus and Xenophon in Xenophon's *Memorabilia* and Plato's *Phaedo*.

In the *Memorablia*, Socrates, who 'praised the rigorous avoidance of the delights of Aphrodite', fails to convince Aristippus to exercise self-control; in the *Acts*, John convinces his Aristippus to eschew sexual intercourse. In the *Memorablia*, Socrates advises Xenophon himself – who would have enjoyed 'kissing the beautiful son of Alcibiades' – to 'flee at full speed' from the sight of a beautiful boy; perhaps in the missing section of the Acts, John similarly convinced his Xenophon to avoid the company of young boys. Turning to prostitutes, both philosopher and apostle advise restraint, but with different reactions and for different ends. Socrates seeks to gaze upon the beautiful prostitute Theodote ('gift of God') and he advises her that playing 'hard to get' will help her ensnare men. John, for whom 'even staring at a woman was burdensome', plausibly provided in the section of the *Acts of John* now lost an even stronger message of restraint: be impossible to get.

The *Acts of John* does offer additional evidence for a challenge to gender roles. For example, in the *Phaedo*, Socrates has dismissed his wife Xanthippe and is, at the end of his life, surrounded by his male friends. Both men and women surround John. Whereas Socrates does not want his followers to cry 'like women', the narrator of the Apocryphon acknowledges, 'we wept'. Yet although John is surrounded by men and women, free and slave, married and single, and although class distinctions have been surrendered as all these converts become 'slaves of God', the narrative nevertheless continues to mark the free and the rich. Included in this contingent are also animals, and so the *Acts of John* confirms Valantasis' point about the third *genos*. Along with the chaste prostitute, the narrative offers the 'obedient bedbug' or even 'faithful cockroach' that 'stayed where it was in silence and did not overstep'. Yet the prevailing categories remain: bugs are still bugs; the prostitute is still a prostitute; the apostle even in death remains the dominant figure.

This depiction of characters who both resist cultural norms and participate in them involves more than just questions of marriage, celibacy and power. In his study of the 'Construction of Thecla', Johannes Vorster explores the relationship between the body, language and culture, and so determines 'the extent to which a culture may affect the body' as well as how the body informs an understanding of a specific culture. According to Vorster, the body produces language on the one hand, and on the other it is produced by, or fabricated by, language and known only through the process of symbolization. The body is understood through, and incarcerated by, cultural codes; concurrently, a person is constituted substantially by the impression the body makes and the activities in which the body engages. For the *Acts of Thecla*, the construction of the body by means of an ascetic discourse creates counter-cultural possibilities.

The dominant culture the *Acts of Thecla* challenges constructs the 'person' linguistically as 'androcentric, sociocentric and futuristic'. To be a 'person' is to be male, and a woman becomes a 'person' only when associated with a male. Betrothed and, according to Vorster, likely having begun to menstruate, Thecla is 'becoming a person'; she will not become a γυνή until she gives birth, and that act requires her body's subjugation to male social control. Despite the fact that certain cults required priestesses to remain virgins and others mandated periods of celibacy, and despite Soranus having advocated 'lifelong virginity' for women, the prevailing culture naturalized the necessity of marriage and childbirth. Thus Thecla is understood in terms of her relationship to Thamyris and then to Paul: her construction as a 'person' cannot be independent of Paul's (male) facilitation as 'donor'. In this reconceptualization of their relationship, the narrative's erotic signals need not be attributed to the Hellenistic novel or a redefined *Eros*; they 'may be regarded as traces of a dominant culture emphasizing the necessity of the female body to attach herself in one way or the other to the male body'. When Thecla does begin to travel by herself, she adapts her body to that of the male.

Society's androcentric focus may also provide Theocleia one motive for her seemingly extreme reaction to her daughter's decision, namely, the demand that she be burned alive. The loss of a son-in-law (especially one as elite as Thamyris) could have resulted in her 'societal marginalization and a diminishing of her status as a person'. Vorster views Theocleia as a widow, and so already having suffered 'loss of identity'. He similarly locates Tryphaena, the queen who saves Thecla's purity and then adopts her, as 'helpless because she is a widow'; her social power resides in her affiliation with Caesar, not in her own 'person'. Whether the status of the biological and the proxy mothers decreased because, according to Vorster, they no longer had 'regular impregnation and insemination' (a problematic argument, since the same physical state would apply, e.g. to menopausal women or to women who used birth control), or whether the concern was more cultural than biological remains open for discussion.

Theocleia's motives may also extend to sociological concerns, given that for the dominant culture, the body of the person affects the body politic. Marriage controlled the woman sociosexually and harnessed her body to civic demands even as it functioned to preserve the social hierarchy (a concern also manifested in the philosophic and legal literature as well as the Romances, as Jacobs indicates). Here Thecla's elite body creates the problem, for by refusing to submit to marriage and so setting a possible example for other 'young men and virgins', it threatens the community and so must be eliminated. But Thecla's body cannot be eliminated. As Vorster states, 'Putting the body into an alternative discourse, whether oral and/or written, should in itself be seen as a powerful strategy to obtain social empowerment'. This symbolic body, which attempts but does not fully succeed in separating androcentrism from personhood, can be imitated; Thecla becomes a role model who calls into question and moves towards abrogating the sociocentric and androcentric codes. Paul's refusal to baptize her provides her the opportunity to baptize herself; his initial pre-eminence in Iconia is replaced by her teaching him. Simultaneously, God replaces Paul, and androcentrism is trumped by theocentrism. With this shift, Thecla's body becomes as Vorster puts it, 'the locus of supra-natural power'.

But this female body is more than just a locus of power and a means of constructing gender. As Cornelia Horn's analysis of the suffering daughters in the *Acts of Paul and Thecla*, the *Acts of Peter* and the *Epistle of Pseudo-Titus* reveals, the bodies of female *children* (i.e. non-married girls under parental control) are also contested sites. Her study contributes to both the understanding of the ancient Christian family and the means by which some girls could break away from parental control and achieve some sense of autonomy.

Horn, like Vorster, identifies Thecla as 'a girl at the transition from child to young teenager', a conclusion she draws from several textual hints. The virgin Thecla is betrothed to Thamyris, who eagerly anticipates the date they will wed (likely when she is old enough); still a child (τέκνον) under parental control (from her mother Theocleia to her patroness Tryphaena). Whereas Vorster insists that the betrothal marks Thecla as having begun menstruation and therefore in the process of becoming a socially constructed 'person', Horn does not and need not. Rather, by locating Thecla as a 'child' rather than a proto-woman, she grants Thecla a more subversive position. Thecla's paradigmatic value now doubles: she escapes submission to both parent and husband; she becomes a role model not only for women, but also for children; she eschews all markers of becoming a 'person' as the prevailing culture constructs the idea. More, as Horn demonstrates, she becomes an *exemplum* not only for women seeking a life of chastity but also for women who desire greater independence. She may even provide a model for slaves, especially those exploited for sexual purposes.

This focus on children's roles also provides new insight into the narrative's social subversion. Children, present in the amphitheatres, watch the bloody executions of Christians. 'Boys and girls' spread the wood on which Thecla is to be burned, and 'women with their children' stand near the place where the wild beasts enter the arena. Thecla's near-executions may function as cautionary tales to children, but given her divine protection and the casting of her willing executioners as evil, the same story may have encouraged children to adopt her way of life, regardless of the earthly consequences. Thus she functions conventionally as the exceptional child – like Augustus the *puer senex* or the boy Jesus in the Temple (Lk. 2.41–51) – whom other children are encouraged to follow.

As Horn points out, such girls who fought familial and social expectations to remain virgins improve on Jesus' exhortation that his followers 'become like little children'; because they never make the transition, via marriage and/or sexual experience, from girl to woman, they never lose the identity as 'child'. Conversely, Thecla's chastity takes on the connotation of a state not only of 'purity' but also of 'inexperience'. Thecla will never, as her mother fears, make the transition from 'girl' (παρθένος in Patristic Greek is synonymous with 'girl') to (married and so sexually experienced) 'woman'. The connection between the female virgin and the 'child' risks infantilizing any woman who chooses the celibate life. Horn states, 'In such a worldview, females who did not share in this experience were forever to be grouped alongside children.'

This grouping underlies the multiple repressions of Peter's daughter, who remains under her father's control and suffers because of it. According to the Coptic fragment of the *Acts of Peter*, on the day of his daughter's birth, Peter receives a vision instructing him that 'if her body remains healthy ... this (girl) will wound many souls'. When she turns ten years old, a rich man sees her bathing with her mother and determines to marry her. Following a two-page lacuna, the fragment picks up with the girl left outside her parents' home; 'one whole side of her body' is 'paralysed and withered'. Augustine's *Against Adimantus* suggests that Peter had prayed that his daughter's virginity be preserved, but whether he left the means up to Heaven or specifically prayed that her body be afflicted remains unknown. The message in either case is that it is better to be paralysed than penetrated, just as Thecla's story indicates that death by torture is preferable to marriage. The daughter's paralysis saved her suitor's soul, her parent's honour and her own virginity.

The paralysis also helps Peter's reputation. When the crowds ask the apostle to heal his daughter, he does so: he enables her, 'crippled there in the corner', to walk, but then he sends her back to her place, for it was 'beneficial for her and me that she become paralysed again'. Like Thecla, Peter's daughter is a model; she is also, for the reader today if not in Antiquity, a warning of what happens when the roles of apostle and *paterfamilias* combine. For Peter's daughter, unlike Thecla, there is no escape.

Horn documents four possible responses to such paternally and divinely inflicted suffering. First, Augustine highlights Peter's prayer. Second, the copyist of the Nag Hammadi codex *Papyrus Berolinensis 8502*, which includes the *Acts of Peter*, may have wanted to highlight the story's encratite message or, less likely, to present the girl as an allegory for the fallen Sophia. Perhaps, suggests Horn, because the papyrus begins with the *Gospel of Mary*, wherein the female apostle bests Peter, the copyist wanted the codex to end on a story of Peter's complete control, physically and spiritually, of a woman. 'Peter's daughter could become an embodiment of the community of believers as child of the one who was apostle, father, and representative of God.' Third, the daughter can be complicit with her father's concerns. In the *Acts of Nereus and Achilleus*, which names the daughter Petronilla, paralysis is not a sufficient disincentive to suitors. Petronilla chooses to preserve her own virginity, and, conveniently, she dies before her suitor forces his case. Hailed in this text as one whose suffering brings healing and salvation, she becomes a saint in service to the Church. Finally, according to the *Epistle of Pseudo-Titus*, an old gardener asks Peter to offer prayers for his daughter's well-being; the apostle does so, and the daughter dies. Horn laconically notes, 'That was not quite what the father had had in mind.' The father begs Peter to restore his child and the apostle agrees. A few days later, a male guest 'ruins' the girl (*perdiditque puellam*), and she leaves with him. In the lower classes, the father's concern leads to the daughter's ruination (at least from Peter's perspective); for Peter's daughter, there is only paralysis and death; for the upper-class Thecla, there are multiple tortures and yet there is divine protection.

The investigation of children is but one of a number of hermeneutical keys that unlock the mysteries Thecla and her sisters reveal. Magda Misset-van de Weg explores two others: patronage and magic, and these two themes then provide detail to the subjects of marriage and celibacy. Matters of patronage begin in the opening scene of the *Acts of Paul and Thecla*, when Paul is received by an Iconian Christian named Onesiphorus, his two children and his wife Lectra. Misset-van de Weg suggests that Lectra represents 'the category of women who are indispensable but invisible'; nevertheless, the fact that she is named gives her a certain prominence. Indeed, she may be seen as a foil to the other 'mothers' of the narrative: unlike Theocleia, who rejects her daughter and who is never depicted as associated with any husband, and Tryphaena, another whose husband is missing and whose daughter is dead, Lectra has both husband and children. Misset-van de Weg classifies their marriage as indicating that Iconia's Christian community rejected neither marriage nor procreation, and the point may be developed. Other Apocryphal Acts, such as those of *Andrew* and *John*, require not marital dissolution but celibacy (or 'self-control') within the marital relationship. Then again, that Onesiphorus and Lectra have done so in the past does not indicate that they are continuing to engage in sexual relations. And, as Misset-van de Weg notes, Paul's beatitude does presume that celibacy is the prerogative of the male: 'Blessed are those who have wives as not having them; they shall be heirs of God.'

A concern for patronage may surface again in Theocleia's extreme reaction to her daughter's decision to follow Paul. Absent a *paterfamilias*, Thecla is her mother's responsibility, and it was her mother's job to maintain the social norms, including, as Horn demonstrates, making the transition from 'virgin' to 'wife'. Were she to fail, the family – including Thecla's fiancé Thamyris – would be shamed; the loss of honour and concurrent social death could easily lead to a fiscal plight. Calling for her daughter's execution puts Theocleia therefore in the role of both good mother and good citizen.

Paul too serves as Thecla's patron (as Vorster suggests, albeit with 'donor' terminology). This patronage can be read positively, in that Paul recognizes that Thecla will ultimately achieve on her own the 'seal' of baptism and will survive the tortures with which she is threatened, or negatively. Misset-van de Weg notes the problems with the positive reading: Paul refuses Thecla's request that she accompany him because she is 'beautiful' and perhaps will not be able to resist temptation. Ironically, he fears she will succumb to intercourse; Theocleia feared that she would refuse it. Paul's failure to protect her, or to give her the seal of protection, also places him in Theocleia's role, for his inaction leads to the second threat on Thecla's life. When Alexander, a prominent Antiochene citizen, offers Paul money for Thecla, the apostle responds: 'I do not know the woman of whom you speak, nor is she mine.' Misset-van de Weg notes: 'the apostle fails her'.

Onesiphorus and his family are at best underdeveloped patrons; Paul is in this reading a failed patron; Alexander is a bad patron (at least from a Christian perspective). He is, as Misset-van de Weg puts it, 'the wrong kind of benefactor': he uses his patronage position for revenge and restoring his honour. Conversely, Tryphaena is the right kind of patron: she uses her influence to protect women from rape, torture and death, and she uses her financial resources to minister to the poor. Thus the *Acts of Thecla* not only may have encouraged young women to choose the celibate life, it may have encouraged wealthy women to serve as Christian patrons.

Concerning the role of magic, which Vorster also adduces, Misset-van de Weg begins with the notice that 'Christians translated social concerns and problems into miracle stories': by using accounts of healing, rescue and resurrection performed by and for Jesus and his followers to reconfigure social problems – from the canonical debates over Sabbath healings to the Apocryphal concerns for celibacy – Christians developed a form of propaganda. The problem, however, remained one of definition. The same act could be classified as miracle (if one approved of the facilitator), magic or the work of demons (if one disapproved of the facilitator), or even medicine (if one, typically, paid the facilitator). For the *Acts of Paul and Thecla*, accusations that Paul is involved with 'magic' serve to reveal both the extent of negative social pressure facing those who would follow his gospel of celibacy and ultimately to reveal his, and his followers' heavenly sanction. Thecla, bound between two bulls, sees 'the Lord sitting there in the shape of Paul'. A visionary and recipient of miracles that protect both her modesty and her life, Thecla begins to work her own miracles. Like Cleopatra and Drusiana, she and her new patron Tryphaena save others. Thecla prays successfully for the salvation of Tryphaena's deceased daughter Falconilla, and Tryphaena prays successfully, 'God of Thecla, my child, help Thecla.' In both cases, the women's prayers serve to help not fainting husbands or felonious lovers, but daughters. The protection of both daughters in turn can be seen as an alternative to the fate of Peter's daughter and the gardener's daughter: Thecla and Falconilla are neither reduced to paralysis nor completed by a male.

Susan Calef's approach to the 'trials and ordeals' Thecla faces is informed by the anthropological category of 'interpretive convention', that is, a narrative pattern that provides cultural guidelines for negotiating diverse circumstances. For the Romances, the test involves male and female upper-class lovers who must preserve their mutual fidelity by overcoming numerous obstacles (shipwreck, pirates, rival suitors, lusty queens, annoying legal experts, meddling gods, mistaken identities and the like). Only after enduring their ordeals and so proving their loyalty, can the marriage be consummated. The biblical narratives offer a similar concern for both fidelity and morality, although the ordeals faced by Abraham, Job, the people Israel, the Maccabean martyrs, Jesus, Paul, the Church, etc. are much more theological and much less erotic. Calef finds in Thecla both a subversive alternative to marriage and family and a recapitulation of the ancient worthies.

Thecla more than proves her fidelity in her tests. Condemned first to death by fire, one of the *summa supplicia* reserved for those guilty of the most heinous crimes and usually meted out to slaves and *humiliores*, she is to serve as deterrent to other women who might be attracted to Paul's message. The government, and the crowds, expect to see the woman evince penitence and then fear as she faced her death; her carefully scripted humiliation in the spectacle was designed to objectify her and so reduce audience sympathy. Thecla disappoints. Showing no fear and voicing no protest, she manifests her power, and so her fidelity. And faithfully, heaven rewards her – as the gods reward the heroines of the Romances and God rewards Shadrach, Meshach and Abednego – by protecting her from the flames and then arranging for a convenient rainstorm.

Following her brief reunion with, and then apparent rejection by Paul, Thecla once again rejects the advances of an elite man and so once again finds herself condemned to the arena. Here the stakes are higher. Thamyris was the ideal fiancé, but Alexander, the second suitor and a priest of the imperial cult, physically assaults Thecla and so prompts her to rip his cloak and knock off his crown. The violence has spilled from the arena to the street; Thecla's challenge is now not merely to the institution of marriage, but to elite men and the system they maintain. First eschewing the male, she now symbolically castrates him. Alexander, less than pleased, charges her with 'sacrilege'; Thecla, more than stalwart, boldly confesses that she is guilty as charged and so is condemned to the beasts. Still the Romantic heroine, she expresses fear not at the certain death, but at the possibility that she would not be able to remain 'pure'.

Thecla maintains her purity through both human and divine effort. The Queen Tryphaena protects her between the sentence and its execution, so she is not molested in prison. In the arena, 'the lioness grappled with the lion', and so both animals perish while Thecla remains untouched. When Thecla, recognizing that the time for her baptism was at hand, hurls herself into a pool filled with carnivorous seals, lightning hits the pool and kills the seals. The heroine again remains pure: 'there was about her a cloud, so that neither could the beasts touch her nor could she be seen naked'. Finally, Alexander has Thecla bound by the feet between two bulls and orders red-hot irons to be placed against the bulls' genitals: as Calef remarks: 'the bulls, goaded to gore Thecla's body are proxy for the enraged Alexander whose sexual advances this woman had dared to reject'. He of course again proves impotent, as again divine aid frees the heroine.

When Thecla reunites with Paul, she receives his apostolic commission. Because she has withstood her trials and received the baptismal seal, he need no longer worry about her fall into temptation. She goes off not into marriage and childbirth, but to the begetting of children through missionary activity. Her success is proved by the cult that developed in her name and, as Calef concludes, 'In preserving her story the tradition affords contemporary women an encouraging exemplar for their own aspirations to ministry of the Word'. Thus, Calef's study counters several negative readings the *Acts of Paul and Thecla* has received: that her story is a pornographic spectacle reducing the heroine to an untouched, unpenetrated, objectified sexually desirable body; that Thecla functions primarily as a token of exchange in the male struggle for power both in the narrative and in the broader Christian world; that as God's 'slave' who achieves her goals only by rejecting her female attributes and appearance, Thecla is at best only heroic because she 'can do what men do'; that as a figure of fantasy, Thecla cannot seriously challenge the social order. Calef acknowledges these points, and yet she still is able to recuperate Thecla via her own 'feminist gaze'.

The numerous thematics revealed by previous studies of the *Acts of Paul and Thecla* – the construction of the body and the definition of the person, the role of the child, matters of patronage and magic, the trials of the saints, the religious exemplar who both serves the purposes of the culture and critiques it, the impossible model who yet encourages others to follow – unite in Gail P.C. Streete's study of Thecla and her less-well-protected counterpart, the early third-century North African martyr Vibia Perpetua along with her equally faithful slave Felicity.

Streete begins not with antiquity but with the all-too-recent stories of Cassie Bernall and Rachel Scott, the 'martyrs' who perished among several students shot by two classmates in 1999 at Columbine High School in Littleton, Colorado. Like the stories of Thecla and Perpetua, these modern martyrologies prompt questions of historical accuracy, for as several credible sources indicate, it was not the dead girls but a girl who lived who confessed to the teenage killers her belief in God. She is not celebrated, because she lived. Thus Streete finds an excellent analogue to the ancient Christian women: the preferred martyr is a female, and she serves as the vehicle for conveying cultural values as a 'marginal', 'liminal' or 'threshold' figure. But whereas Cassie and Rachel's stories support the 'family values' agenda of the Christian right and so validate popular social and religious ideals (if not norms), Perpetua and Thecla challenge the prevailing Roman worldviews.

The *Acts of Thecla* and Perpetua's *Diary* and *Martyrdom* sound the same themes. Both women exemplify the masculine virtues of 'courage' (ἀνδρεία) and self-control (ἐγκρατεία), and both adopt a masculinized identity (Thecla by cutting her hair and wearing men's clothes; Perpetua by imagining herself a victorious gladiator). Yet both retain female codes, from the emphasis on the sexuality of their bodies and their modesty to their being matched with female beasts; Thecla finds her partner in God, and Perpetua is the 'wife' (*matrona*) of Christ. Already liminal by having ceded family and status, they successfully plead on behalf of the beloved dead: Thecla for Tryphaena's daughter Falconilla and Perpetua for her brother Dinocrates. Even the slave Felicity, appropriately given the Apocryphal Acts' interest in collapsing although not fully erasing class status, 'overcomes' her role's limitations. Yet unlike Thecla, Perpetua and Felicity only achieve their new status in martyrdom.

It would be the martyrs, Perpetua, Felicity and their sisters, rather than the independent apostle Thecla, to whom the Church turns for its exemplars. Tertullian had condemned Thecla's story as a forgery even as he condemned women who appealed to it by sanctioning their teaching, preaching and baptizing. Whereas Perpetua and her fellow martyrs are still regarded as saints, the Roman Catholic

Church (but not Eastern Orthodoxy) removed Thecla from the canon in 1969. Streete observes, 'A rejection of this world and its social norms may all be very well when the world is defined as anti-Christian, but when it becomes defined as a Christian world in which the norms being rejected are Roman social norms that have been Christianized, it is a very different story.' As Boyarin's contribution to this collection also discusses, Ambrose and Jerome prefer the martyr Agnes to Thecla as the model for virgins, and Pseudo-Basil of Seleucia transforms Thecla from counter-cultural heroine into advocate of Christian orthodoxy.

Streete observes that the *Acts of Xanthippe and Polyxena* (also called the *Acts of Xanthippe, Polyxena and Rebecca*) refers to Thecla as an example; given Christian orthodoxy's appropriation as well as marginalization of Thecla, her connection to Xanthippe is particularly apt. Like Thecla, Xanthippe harnesses her body against penetration; like Thecla, her autonomy needs to be constrained. Yet as Jill Gorman's study reveals, the threat Xanthippe poses by her fasting may be even greater than the threat posed by Thecla's celibacy.

Fasting, like chastity, guards the body: as long as the lips remain closed, nothing enters that will create more of an earthly as opposed to heavenly nature. Galen had remarked on the perceived link between a woman's diet and her sexual desire. But if food, women and sex are inseparable, it may follow that if a woman gives up both food and sex, she gives up being a 'woman' or even being a 'human'. Gorman explains how female chastity and fasting link the corporeal and the spiritual and how this linkage leads to power, purity and transcendence. Both also endanger the practitioner: the power vested in the disciplined female body functions as a sign of her autonomy and so as a challenge to familial and civic values. Here fasting reveals its truly subversive effect (as today's studies of anorexia nervosa also demonstrate). A highly individualistic practice, fasting can both empower and corrupt. According to Evagrius, fasting enabled ascetics to experience visions of God. But Melania the Younger warned that while moderate fasting leads to holiness, excessive fasting leads to pride. Pseudo-Chrysostom, Cyril of Jerusalem and others echo Melania's cautions. Whether as a means of controlling women, of solidifying institutional and economic power, of protecting the practitioner from death, or of combating the sin of pride, the Church's interest in and regulation of female fasting would continue. Xanthippe's sisters such as Catherine of Siena, Claire of Assisi, Veronica Guiliani and any number of elite women whose only means of *excelling* spiritually and gaining religious authority was through fasting revealed the power of her threat.

Melania and her associates might also have noted that excessive fasting leads to death. For the Apocryphal Act, the power of Xanthippe's fast leads not to pride, but both to visions of the Christ and to protection by proxy: her forty-day regimen protects the kidnapped Polyxena's virginity. Such power cannot be let loose on the world, and so it is finally regulated by Xanthippe's death. In protecting her 'true sister's' body, she destroys her own.

The *Acts of Xanthippe and Polyxena* begins with Xanthippe's acceptance of Paul's teaching of chastity and her consequent renunciation of her marriage. Tormented by demons that seek to reawaken her sexual desire, she drives them off with 'manly' force. But this force is spiritual, for she herself immediately begins 'wasting herself away with waking and abstinence and other austerities'. The imagery in her prayers confirms her physical displacements. She insists that the Eucharist both 'inflames and sweetens [her] within', and her references to 'the ever-living and abiding seed' have both sexual and alimentary connotations.

Her fasting, rather than her chastity, prompts her husband Probus's concern. A new Christian himself, he is not bothered by his wife's chastity. But as Xanthippe is 'seized with great faintness from lack of food', Probus recognizes that something is amiss: he asks his friends to see if Xanthippe is still alive, given that 'it's been twenty-nine days since she has tasted anything'. But only at the end of the narrative do readers learn the purpose of her fasts. Xanthippe's reunion with Polyxena, who has been through her own series of unfortunate events, is a Christianized climax familiar from the Hellenistic Romance. The truth is revealed as Xanthippe explains that she had secluded herself in prayer and fasting in Polyxena's defence. Xanthippe then dies, and Polyxena spends her remaining days in Paul's company, 'in fear of her temptations'.

Gorman suggests that the narrative undercuts the power of women's prayer, chastity and fasting; certainly it is at best ambivalent. Polyxena recognizes that only God can protect her virginity. Unaware of Xanthippe's efforts, she regards Paul's prayers on her behalf as likely to carry some weight: he is the 'proper intercessory'. Paul confirms this point when he informs Xanthippe that Polyxena's virginity will be protected, and even Probus remarks both that Polyxena's fate is in divine hands and that through suffering one comes to recognize God as the true protector. By rejecting Paul's assurance, by substituting her prayers and fasting for his, and by refusing Probus's understanding of Polyxena's circumstances, Xanthippe manifests the very pride against which Melania cautioned. Gorman describes this scenario as 'the textual admonition of Xanthippe's ascetic performance'. It is confirmed when Xanthippe herself acknowledges that her reunion with Polyxena was 'unexpected': the men, displaying a healthy moderation, fully trusted in divine providence; the woman, extreme in her practice, did not.

The constraints upon autonomous women promoted by the *Acts of Polyxena and Xanthippe* became the normative reading of Thecla and her sisters. As several of the essays in this collection intimate, the Christian woman's ideal would become not the independent Thecla and her equally independent sisters from the *Acts of Andrew* and the *Acts of John*, but the martyrs Perpetua and Agnes, the dependent Polyxena and the obedient Petronilla. This domestication is matched in the rabbinic corpus. Daniel Boyarin details in his study how the Rabbis also used virgins to 'think with' and how stories of threatened Jewish virgins also lead to constraints upon women's public presence and autonomy.

Boyarin's essay shows not only that Jews of Late Antiquity also had heroic male teachers and their virgin exemplars, but it also demonstrates how both early rabbinic Judaism and early Christianity resisted Roman culture by depicting 'gender-bending' males who renounced masculine markers of power and sexuality. As symbolic women (the men of) both Church and Synagogue defined themselves in resistance to the masculine Rome. The differences appear when discussion shifts away from the increasingly dominant Church to the always minority rabbinic culture, and away from the always dominant men to the always marginal women. Unlike the apostles or the Church Fathers, the Rabbis do not seek converts; their troubles with authorities arise when they are themselves attracted to Christianity or when they teach Torah in public. Unlike the virilized Theclas, Maximillas and Perpetuas, the Jewish women in the parallel stories are destined neither for celibacy nor for martyrdom but for the marriage bed.

And unlike the Apocryphal Acts or the Hellenistic Romances, the chaste Jewish male rather than the female virgin is the protagonist. The enticer is a female-identified, sexy Christianity. Ironically but not illogically, the feminized Rabbi/Israel is in the best position to resist the feminized lures of Christianity. In like manner, Ambrose found 'self-feminization' the ideal response to late Roman masculine codes even as he rewrote Thecla's story to eliminate female subjectivity and appeal to a male audience. For Boyarin, this transformation lends some credence to the optimistic view that the Apocryphal Acts promote female autonomy and even indicate female authorship.

Using the Talmudic story of the martyr Rabbi Hanina and his family as his example, Boyarin demonstrates how the Rabbis qualified Torah study in the hostile Roman (Christian) environment through sexualized, feminized metaphors: just as the proper woman should not display herself to the public, so too the Torah must be taught in private. The Rabbis are advised to act as women, to flee from rather than court the martyr's death; they take the opposite role from the masculinized Thecla and Perpetua, who willingly enter the arena. Hanina's refusal of the rabbinic model and so his teaching Torah in public is matched by his daughter's appearance in the market: they are each exposing themselves to the 'predatory male gaze'. Both are then punished, he by martyrdom and she by sentence to a brothel. Yet unlike Perpetua and Thecla, Hanina's daughter neither defends her virtue by masculine assertion nor bravely seeks her own death. Rather, she tricks her way out of unwanted intercourse and then tricks her way out of the brothel. Boyarin bluntly states, 'In the rabbinic world, there can be no virgin martyrs.' The Christian virgin becomes the admired martyr; the Jewish virgin becomes the silenced wife. Ironically, the rabbinic texts recapitulate the plots of the Hellenistic Romances: following an adventure of test and trial prompted by a perceived theological transgression, the protected Jewish virgin finds her husband (another Rabbi, much like her father). There is no rejection of marriage and family, no desire for suffering and death. Autonomy may be foreclosed, but life goes on.

Despite its popularity in the classroom today, Thecla's story and those of her super-human sisters do not usually encourage young women to choose the celibate life. Today the women of the Apocryphal Acts are no more and no less a threat to 'family values' than the canonical Jesus, who advises his male followers to leave 'your father and mother and wife and children and homes for my sake'. But Thecla and her sisters continue to suggest (with varying degrees of approval) to many women, as well as a number of men, that women's roles in the Church could be – and perhaps for some Christians in Antiquity were – equal to that of their fathers and brothers, husbands and sons. Although the earlier optimism of women's communities has been tempered, the Apocryphal Acts nevertheless inspired women and children as well as men to challenge the status quo, to recognize and then reject the import of wealth and class, to attain an intellectual and theological status that transcended gender roles. That their stories comport with those of the martyrs Perpetua and Felicity as well as with rabbinic stories of virgins condemned to brothels prove the thesis that men used women to 'think with'. At the same time, those stories were both influenced by and provided an influence for women's own concerns. Perhaps, were the stories of Thecla and Drusilla, Cleopatra and Maximilla, even Xanthippe and Polyxena, told today along with those of Perpetua, Petronilla and their rabbinical sisters, readers would recognize new aspects of Christian history, new possibilities for women's ecclesial roles, and new means by which 'family values' could be configured.

'HER OWN PROPER KINSHIP':
MARRIAGE, CLASS AND WOMEN
IN THE APOCRYPHAL ACTS OF THE APOSTLES*

ANDREW S. JACOBS

For the domus *need not be a family's own space*
Even for Rome's upper classes;
Commercial apartments comprise part of the place
And the courtyard invites in the masses.[1]

Introduction: Apostolic Homewreckers

It is a tale that became familiar to most early Christians: A well-born young woman of a prominent house in Asia Minor is causing her family some distress. When the woman's fiancé comes to woo, her mother greets him with chagrin. A 'strange man' has come to town and started preaching a disastrous message. 'My daughter also, like a spider hanging at the window bound up by his words, is conquered by a new desire and a fearsome passion. She hangs upon his sayings and the maiden has been taken captive' (*Acta Pauli et Theclae* 8–9).[2] It becomes clear that the young woman no longer wants anything to do with her fiancé or her mother, and she turns from them in silence. At once the whole house becomes terrified: 'And they wept bitterly: Thamyris for losing a wife, Theocleia a daughter, and the maidservants a mistress' (*Acta Pauli et Theclae* 10). The young lady whose defection fractures a household from top to bottom is Thecla, heroine of early Christian 'romance' and a symbol of sexual renunciation.[3] Her 'captor' is Paul, apostle of Jesus, whose message twice leads Thecla to capital condemnation

* A previous version of this essay appeared as 'A Family Affair: Marriage, Class, and Ethics in the Apocryphal Acts of the Apostles', *JECS* 7 (1999), pp. 105–38 (reprinted with permission of The Johns Hopkins University Press). I thank Amy-Jill Levine for her invaluable editorial suggestions in the revision of this piece.
1 Amy-Jill Levine, 'Theological Education, the Bible, and History: Détente in the Culture Wars', in D.L. Balch and Carolyn Osiek (eds), *Early Christian Families in Context* (Religion, Marriage, and Family series; Grand Rapids: Eerdmans, 2003), pp. 327–36 (335).

2 All texts of the Apocryphal Acts (except the *Passio Andreae*; see below n. 25) are cited from R.A. Lipsius and M. Bonnet (eds.), *Acta Apostolorum Apocrypha* (2 vols.; Hildesheim: G. Olms, 1959), with translations adapted from J.K. Elliott, *The Apocryphal New Testament: A Collection of Apocryphal Christian Literature in an English Translation based on M.R. James* (Oxford: Clarendon Press, 1993).

3 On the legend and veneration of Thecla, see Stephen J. Davis, *The Cult of St Thecla: A Tradition of Women's Piety in Late Antiquity* (Oxford Early Christian Studies; Oxford: Oxford University Press, 2001). See also Averil Cameron, *Christianity and the Rhetoric of Empire: The Development of Christian Discourse* (Berkeley: University of California Press, 1991), pp. 89–119, on the appeal of these 'Christian romances' in the second and third centuries.

and who himself leads a life of harassed itinerant preaching.[4] Echoing and expanding the call of Jesus, who enticed his disciples away from jobs and families (e.g. Mt. 4.18–22, Mk 1.16–20, Lk. 14.26),[5] the *Acts of Paul* preaches radical renunciation: 'Blessed are they who have renounced this world, for they shall be pleasing to God! … Blessed are they who through love of God have gone out of the form of the mundane for they will judge angels and be blessed at the right hand of the Father!' (*Acta Pauli et Theclae* 5–6).

This disruption of households by some early Christians struck at the perceived building block of civilized society, the family.[6] As some Christian circles became more institutionalized, such social disruption became untenable: witness the household codes in the deutero-Pauline letters to the Colossians and Ephesians, and the careful theological mapping of Christian piety onto conservative values in the Pastoral epistles (Col. 3.18—4.1, Eph. 5.21—6.9, Tit. 2.1–10). Yet in other spheres the apostles were still wielded rhetorically and socially as initiators not of household order but disorder. The so-called Apocryphal Acts of the Apostles, circulating from the second century onward, replicated this narrative of apostolic homewreckers, often centered on the choice for sexual abstinence and family renunciation made by an inspired heroine, like Thecla. In this essay, I make two arguments out of the narrative richness of these texts of family despoliation. First, I argue that a very specific form of family configuration – the elite conjugal union of husband and wife – is rejected in order to position Christian virtue in opposition to the upper-class morality becoming dominant in the later Roman Empire. Second, I suggest that the female heroines, renouncing status and marital union, should be interpreted neither as simple historical reality nor as historically meaningless symbolic rhetoric, but rather as the discursive construction of a charged new space in which women could (and, eventually, did) reconceptualize their own moral agency. It will be helpful to provide context for each of these two arguments before engaging with the ancient sources.

We must begin by attending more carefully to types of families in the ancient world. It is my contention that we witness in these tales of apostolic homewrecking and female renunciation more than merely a blanket condemnation of this world, symbolized by the

---

4 For an analysis of the elements of ascetic renunciation and itinerancy in the *Acts of Paul and Thecla*, see Davis, *Cult of St Thecla*, pp. 18–26.

5 See Gerd Theissen, *Sociology of Early Palestinian Christianity* (trans. John Bowden; Philadelphia, PA: Fortress Press, 1978), pp. 11–12 and 61, on the sociological implications of these statements; Elizabeth A. Clark, 'Antifamilial Tendencies in Ancient Christianity', *Journal of the History of Sexuality* 5 (1995), pp. 356–80 and Andrew S. Jacobs, '"Let Him Guard *Pietas*": Early Christian Exegesis and the Ascetic Family', *JECS* 11 (2003), pp. 265–81.

6 For a survey of 'Graeco–Roman' philosophical attitudes towards family, society and marriage in particular, see Suzanne Dixon, *The Roman Family* (Oxford: Clarendon Press, 1997); Susan Treggiari, *Roman Marriage: Iusti Coniuges from the Time of Cicero to the Time of Ulpian* (Oxford: Clarendon Press, 1991), pp. 185–228; Beryl Rawson (ed.), *Marriage, Divorce, and Children in Ancient Rome* (Oxford: Clarendon Press, 1991). On the Christian appropriation and manipulation of familial structures, see Halvor Moxnes (ed.), *Constructing Early Christian Families: Family as Social Reality and Metaphor* (London and New York: Routledge, 1997); Geoffrey S. Nathan, *The Family in Late Antiquity: The Rise of Christianity and the Endurance of Tradition* (London and New York: Routledge, 2000); Balch and Osiek, *Early Christian Families in Context*; and the secondary literature cited in Andrew S. Jacobs and Rebecca Krawiec, 'Fathers Know Best? Christian Families in the Age of Asceticism', *JECS* 11 (2003), pp. 257–63.

basic social unit of the family. The impact of the apostles is registered specifically in the marital bond in these texts, a choice I suggest is both deliberate and meaningful in the context of early Christian social and cultural constructions of religious identity. We are conditioned to think of marriage as the time-honoured and traditional ethical location of sexual desire and family loyalty, the core of the nuclear family structure. Yet the far more traditional understanding of family in the ancient world centred not on the union of a husband and wife, but on the exertion of power by a male head of household (*paterfamilias*) over his subordinates (wife, children, slaves). Other Christian groups in the second and third centuries, coeval with the producers and consumers of the Apocryphal Acts, expressed their dissatisfaction with the structures of 'this world' by opposing Christian virtue to the power of the *paterfamilias*. One example of such a paternal narrative of family disruption can be reviewed briefly in the story of another 'homewrecking' Christian female, the third-century North African martyr Vibia Perpetua.[7]

Like Thecla, Perpetua is a 'woman of good family and upbringing' (*Passio Perpetuae* 2) brought to face public punishment for her disruptive adherence to Christian belief.[8] Also like Thecla, Perpetua renounces her family in order to embrace a new Christian identity. The family structure overturned by Perpetua, however, is somewhat different from that of Thecla. Instead of a jilted fiancé we have a grey-haired father pleading for mercy:

> 'Daughter,' he said, 'have pity on my grey head – have pity on me your father, if I am worthy to be called father by you; if I have brought you with these very hands into the bloom of life … do not now surrender me to the reproaches of men. Think of your brothers, think of your mother and your aunt, think of your own son who will not be able to live after you. Set aside pride lest it overturn all of us!' (*Passio Perpetuae* 5; cf. *Passio Perpetuae* 3)

Perpetua appears as the well-born *matrona* who sets aside the authority of her *paterfamilias*, and in so doing breaks apart the entire extended family. She abandons her father's will and seeks to follow the will of another Father instead.[9] Thecla, by contrast, abandons a potential husband to follow another man who has 'captured' her in a 'new desire and fearsome passion' (*Acta Paula et Theclae* 9).[10] There is no father in Thecla's tale, no *patria potestas* to overturn, just as there is no (explicit) husband to whom Perpetua is (even metaphorically) unfaithful.[11]

If Perpetua's familial drama is set squarely in the context of paternal (dis)loyalty,

---

7 The comparison between Thecla and Perpetua is drawn for different reasons by Peter Brown, *The Body and Society: Men, Women, and Sexual Renunciation in Early Christianity* (Lectures on the History of Religions, 13; New York: Columbia University Press, 1988), p. 158 and Davis, *Cult of St Thecla*, pp. 28–29. See also the essay by Gail P.C. Streete in this volume.

8 Text and translation in Herbert Musurillo, *The Acts of the Christian Martyrs* (Oxford: Clarendon Press, 1972), pp. 106–31.

9 Note the visual parallel between the description of Perpetua's earthly father (*canis meis*: *Passio Perpetuae* 5) and the 'heavenly father' in one of Perpetua's visions (*hominem canum*: *Passio Perpetuae* 4).

10 'Capture' or *raptus* was one way in which a woman in Antiquity could be claimed by a husband: see Antti Arjava, *Women and Law in Late Antiquity* (Oxford: Clarendon Press, 1996), pp. 37–41.

11 Perpetua is described in *Passio Perpetuae* 2 as *matronaliter nupta*, but her husband is not in evidence. Scholars have often attempted to find the husband (or, at least, father of Perpetua's child) between the lines of the narrative: see, most recently, Carolyn Osiek, 'Perpetua's Husband', *JECS* 10 (2002), pp. 287–90.

then Thecla's story – and the general narrative pattern of the Apocryphal Acts – focuses explicitly on the familial configuration of marriage. The reasons for this, I suggest, have to do with developing notions of family ethics and class in Late Antiquity. Far from being the default state of sexual and ethical union in Antiquity, marriage (*matrimonium*) was a legally and morally regulated state designed to promote the ethical union of upper-class families. Christians attacking 'marriage' in the Apocryphal Acts were therefore levelling charges against a very specific familial configuration, the conjugal family, as a way of demeaning a distinctly upper-class ethics and replacing it with a declassed (and yet still hierarchalized) ideal of common Christian 'kinship'. My first goal, therefore, will be to elicit from these powerful texts of family disjunction one early Christian pattern of moral virtue as a mode of class-based resistance.

My second goal is to elucidate how this struggle over ethics and class in the Apocryphal Acts can also give helpful nuance to our understanding of both ancient women's history, and the production of 'feminist histories' from the Apocryphal Acts.[12] These two goals are not unrelated, as scholars have traditionally assumed that these texts' attention to the conjugal family structure can be explained by theories about the feminist nature of early Christian asceticism. Social historians once attributed the Apocryphal Acts' focus on women's sexual renunciation to the identity of their original authors and readers: with such interest in the 'liberation' of women from a repressive marriage bond into the freedom of an egalitarian Christianity, it was argued that these texts must have originated from and for various women's groups who would 'naturally' embrace such a message. In 1980, Stevan Davies came to the 'rather startling' conclusion that 'many of the apocryphal Acts were written by women', due both to the subject matter (the choice of chastity over marriage) and the woman's 'point of view' found therein.[13] Dennis R. MacDonald curtailed Davies's conclusions a bit by suggesting female 'storytellers' and (later) male 'writers', while Virginia Burrus drew on both scholars to examine the 'folkloristic' nature of these 'women's chastity stories'.[14]

More recent scholarship has called into question the relation between the Apocryphal Acts' apostolic homewrecker and the notion that eradication of the

---

12 I understand 'feminist history' as it has been described by Joan Wallach Scott, *Gender and the Politics of History* (rev. ed.; New York: Columbia University Press, 1999), p. 27: 'Feminist history then becomes not the recounting of great deeds performed by women but the exposure of often silent and hidden operations of gender that are nonetheless present and defining forces in the organization of most societies.'

13 Stevan Davies, *The Revolt of the Widows: The Social World of the Apocryphal Acts* (Carbondale: Southern Illinois University Press, 1980), p. 95; he also characterizes this conclusion as 'rather startling' on p. 50. The 'women's point of view' is discussed on pp. 105–107.

14 Dennis R. MacDonald, *The Legend and the Apostle: The Battle for Paul in Story and Canon* (Philadelphia, PA: Westminster Press, 1983), pp. 33–53; Virginia Burrus, *Chastity as Autonomy: Women in the Stories of the Apocryphal Acts* (Studies in Women and Religion, 23; Lewiston, NY and Queenston, Ont.: The Edwin Mellen Press, 1987). The development of this historiographic narrative is reviewed by Davis, *Cult of St Thecla*, pp. 8–18. See also Elisabeth Schüssler Fiorenza, 'Word, Spirit and Power: Women in Early Christian Communities', in Rosemary Ruether and Eleanor McLaughlin (eds.), *Women of Spirit: Female Leadership in the Jewish and Christian Traditions* (New York: Simon & Schuster, 1979), pp. 29–70 (37–39).

socially conservative family emanated from a context of historical female resistance.[15] Simply focusing on the liberatory aspects of the Acts (such as they are) may not be as fruitful as was once imagined.[16] In addition to being wary of projecting modern conceptions of marriage and feminist liberation into Antiquity,[17] recent studies have been less optimistic about recovering a female (or feminist) point of view. For Peter Brown, these texts 'reflect the manner in which Christian males of that period partook in the deeply ingrained tendency of all men in the ancient world, to use women "to think with" '.[18] Similarly, Kate Cooper contends that 'the challenge posed here by Christianity is not really about women or even about sexual continence, but about authority and the social order'.[19] Cooper analyses 'the apostle's proposal of sexual abstinence' in the Apocryphal Acts as a means to a countercultural and subversive end: the political disruption of 'this world' by the Christian message.[20] Marriage is a conservative metaphor, and continence a countermetaphor discharged from the camp of the Christians. Both the reality of sexual renunciation and the solidity of its female proponents dissolve in such metaphorical speculation, leaving historians interested in the lives of ancient women with nothing to hold on to.

Yet the dichotomy of reality and rhetoric in this case might be oversimplified. We need not aver the straightforward historical realism of ancient texts of women's piety in order to illuminate some corner of women's history; nor does attention to symbolism, metaphor and rhetoric necessarily force us to disavow any hope of access to the religious identities of those ancient women.[21] The rhetorical force of these narratives of female renunciation can potentially shape the discursive worlds of future readers and auditors of such stories, reconstruct their worldview and so transform rhetoric into a new reality. Early Christians found the narratives of apostolic homewreckers and their female disciples compelling.[22] Even as metaphor, or code for 'something else', the image of family disintegration, set vividly in the late Roman context of competing models of family ethics – marital *concordia* and paternal *potestas* – continued to gather rhetorical and theological steam throughout

15 For narratological and historical critique of MacDonald's views (among others), see Esther Yue L. Ng, '*Acts of Paul and Thecla*: Women's Stories and Precedent?' *JTS* n.s. 55 (2004), pp. 1–29.

16 See Kate Cooper, *The Virgin and the Bride: Idealized Womanhood in Late Antiquity* (Cambridge, MA: Harvard University Press, 1996), pp. 67–72; and Clark, 'Antifamilial Tendencies', pp. 371–80.

17 See Gillian Clark, *Women in Late Antiquity: Pagan and Christian Lifestyles* (New York: Oxford University Press and Oxford: Clarendon Press, 1993), p. 4: 'There is no certainty that our own dissatisfaction was shared by women of the time, whose experience and expectations were so different from our own.'

18 Brown, *Body and Society*, p. 153.

19 Cooper, *Virgin and the Bride*, p. 55.

20 Cooper, *Virgin and the Bride*, pp. 58–62. Cooper's 'political' reading of ancient novels and Acts is criticized in Judith Evans Grubbs's extensive review '*The Virgin and the Bride: Idealized Womanhood in Late Antiquity*', *Classical Philology* 93 (1998), pp. 201–209.

21 See Andrew S. Jacobs, 'Writings Demetrias: Ascetic Logic in Ancient Christianity', *CH* 69 (2000), pp. 719–48, which draws on the critical insights of Elizabeth A. Clark, 'The Lady Vanishes: Dilemmas of a Feminist Historian after the "Linguistic Turn"', *CH* 67 (1998), pp. 1–31.

22 The popularity of these stories is well attested throughout Late Antiquity, in liturgical and homiletic settings, as well as ascetic texts, hagiography, iconography and pilgrimage: see François Bovon, 'Byzantine Witnesses for the Apocryphal Acts of the Apostles', in François Bovon, Ann Graham Brock and Christopher R. Matthews (eds.), *The Apocryphal Acts of the Apostles* (Harvard Divinity School Studies; Cambridge, MA: Harvard University Press, 1999), pp. 87–98.

Late Antiquity. Stephen Davis has argued that, from the third century through the Islamic conquest, an 'ethic of *imitatio Theclae*' took hold among Christian women, for whom 'Thecla's example was a source of empowerment'.[23] Whatever the origins of these texts, or intentions of their authors, the crafting of narratives in which women stand at the centre of broken conjugal households generated potential models for women's piety, a rhetorical space into which real women could (and, eventually, did) step. The goal of a feminist historical study of the Apocryphal Acts, therefore, might not be so much to authenticate the tenor of the 'woman's voice' within the text, but rather to delineate the potential space in which subsequent ancient voices might echo.

With this goal, we attend to the narrative structure of these texts, and ask anew: Why are apostles presented as 'homewreckers', and why do these aristocratic women, like Thecla, emerge as their heroic counterparts? Why is the conjugal bond, the representative familial structure, to be overturned by apostolic preaching and female resistance? If the canonical Paul chooses to address one of his churches 'like a father with his children' (1 Thess. 2.11),[24] why should Thecla's Paul instead, like a lover, seduce her away from her fiancé with 'deceptive and subtle words' (*Acta Pauli et Theclae* 8)? Or why should a Greek proconsul's wife, who has left the marriage bed to follow the apostle Andrew, be described as having 'so given way to desire for him that she loves no one more than him' and as having 'become intimately involved with that man' (*Passio Andreae* 25)?[25] What does a woman's renunciation of marriage, initiated by this apostolic 'seduction', achieve for readers or auditors that rejection of *patria potestas*, like Perpetua's, does not?

The issue of competing rhetorics of family, class and ethics is deeply intertwined with the role of women in this contest. Below I first survey the ways in which elite authors in the first centuries of the Roman Empire came to promote the conjugal family as a model of social order and stabilization among the upper classes.[26] Legally constituted marriage, historically a question of property transmission, became a matter of public *dignitas*, a gauge of a man's moral character. Simultaneously, it transformed the (theoretically) asymmetrical relation of *man–woman* into the new (theoretically) symmetrical relation of *husband–wife*, creating a new familial economy considered particularly apt for the wealthy, educated elites. Slowly, however, this elite ethics of marital 'couplehood' became transformed into a universalized family ethics. I demonstrate these rhetorical fronts on which this transformation and universalization

---

23 Davis, *Cult of St Thecla*, p. 194; the volume focuses on the emergence of Thecla's saint's cult in Asia Minor and Egypt.

24 On Paul's 'paternal' authority, see Christopher Frilingos, '"For My Child, Onesimus": Paul and Domestic Power in Philemon', *JBL* 119 (2000), pp. 91–104.

25 Text and translation in D.R. MacDonald, *The Acts of Andrew and the Acts of Andrew and Matthias in the City of the Cannibals* (Texts and translations, 33; Christian apocrypha series, 1; Atlanta: Scholars Press, 1990).

26 My use of the term 'class' does not connote the 'high' Marxist readings of antiquity like that of G.E.M. de Ste Croix (*The Class Struggle in the Ancient Greek World from the Archaic Age to the Arab Conquests* [Ithaca, NY: Cornell University Press, 1981], esp. pp. 19–30); I do, however, feel that substitution of 'status' or similar terms for 'class' (as by Wayne Meeks, *The First Urban Christians: The Social World of the Apostle Paul* [New Haven, CT: Yale University Press, 1983], pp. 53–55 and pp. 214–15) masks the very real *monetary* component of senatorial and provincial aristocracy.

were effected through comparison of legal initiatives, philosophical writings and the fanciful Greek 'romances'. Next, I locate the Apocryphal Acts in the stream of this particular familial discourse as a form of class-based resistance. The emergence of woman-as-subject of the Apocryphal Acts can thus be fruitfully contrasted with the construction of woman-as-subject in the new elite ethics of the conjugal family, as I conclude by asking new questions about the female heroine and feminist history of early Christian homewreckers.

'Live Together as Partners': The Institution of Conjugal Ethics

According to the third-century Roman historian Cassius Dio, the Emperor Augustus delivered a public address in the year 9 CE to the men of the equestrian class.[27] Apparently there had been complaints about the severity of a new series of laws penalizing unmarried and childless knights. Augustus first divided the members of the wealthy classes in the forum: unmarried men to one side and married to the other. To the far less numerous married men he addressed words of encouragement and gratitude; to the unmarried his words were 'harsh and bitter'. He concluded his harangue against those negligent bachelors by expressing his ideal of the Roman family:

> My ideal is that we may have lawful homes (ἑστίας ἐννόμους) to dwell in and houses full of descendants, that we may approach the gods together with our wives and children, that a man and his family should live together as partners (ἀλλήλοις ὁμιλῶμεν) who risk all their fortunes in equal measure, and likewise reap pleasure from the hopes they rest upon one another. (*Historia Romana* 56.9)[28]

This retrospective, third-century description of the new Roman family gives important ethical nuance to Augustus's first-century legislative efforts to coerce the upper class into marrying and producing new generations of Roman elites.[29] Through the rhetoric of *dignitas*, a factor upon which a man could establish or diminish his public 'face', Augustus's laws transformed the ideal of marriage: 'Augustus ... turned what had previously been a private family responsibility into a public concern, and established the basis for marriage legislation for the next five hundred years.'[30] This 'public concern' marks a shift in the ancient discourse of social status and families that has been traced on several fronts.

Some scholars in the burgeoning field of the ancient family have observed a transformation of the ideal family from a coherent unit following vertical lines of

---

27 See T.D. Barnes, 'The Composition of Cassius Dio's *Roman History*', *Phoenix* 38 (1984), pp. 240–55.

28 Text in U.P. Boissevain (ed.), *Cassii Dionis Cocceiani Historiarum Romanarum Quae Supersunt* (5 vols.; Berlin: Weidmann, 1895–1931). English translation adapted from Ian Scott-Kilvert, *Cassius Dio: The Roman History. The Reign of Augustus* (London: Penguin Books, 1987). On the rhetorical nature of this speech see Judith Evans Grubbs, *Law and Family in Late Antiquity: The Emperor Constantine's Marriage Legislation* (Oxford: Clarendon Press, 1995), p. 102.

29 The laws in question are the *lex Iulia de maritandis ordinibus* and the *lex Iulia de adulteriis* (both 18 BCE) and the *lex Papia-Poppaea* (9 CE). See Evans Grubbs, *Law and Family*, pp. 96–98.

30 Judith Evans Grubbs, '"Pagan" and "Christian" Marriage: The State of the Question', *JECS* 2 (1994), pp. 361–412 (378).

patriarchal authority (husband-father-master on top, wife-children-slaves on the bottom) to a partnership centred around the affective union of the married couple.[31] Conjugal cooperation and unity seem to replace the model of absolute authority emanating downward from the omnipotent *paterfamilias*. Paul Veyne first described this transformation as the psychological response on the part of elite males to their political emasculation by the new Augustan regime.[32] His historical interpretation has since been challenged or altered on several fronts;[33] some historians, invoking judiciary evidence, deny that the Roman family 'shifted' at all in Late Antiquity, ideally or otherwise.[34] Yet even if there is no 'real' shift in the legal relations of husband and wife, such factors do not obviate the rhetorical manipulation of a marital ideal.[35] This manipulation is precisely where we must locate the variegated literature that attempts to idealize marriage as the defining feature of the correct (upper-class) family and, by extension, the correct microcosm of (aristocratic) society.[36]

One theme that permeates our sources is the moral interiorization of the conjugal bond of *concordia*: marriage is not just a procreative or monetary transaction between families, but an ethical union between individuals. Veyne dubs this 'the birth of the couple'.[37] In the early imperial period, the rhetoric of conjugal ethics went from a charming (if irrelevant) *accoutrement* of marriage to its theoretical underpinning and justification. We can trace this rhetorical shift in legal and philosophical materials as well as in the so-called 'Greek romances', which encapsulate much of the marriage rhetoric of both the jurists and the philosophers into an exciting narrative that could

---

31 On the complexity of charting the structures of Roman families, see Dale B. Martin, 'The Construction of the Ancient Family: Methodological Considerations', *JRS* 86 (1996), pp. 40–60, who challenges the claims of R.P. Saller and B. Shaw, 'Tombstones and Roman Family Relations in the Principate: Civilians, Soldiers, and Slaves', *JRS* 74 (1984), pp. 124–56.

32 Paul Veyne, 'La famille et l'amour sous le Haut-Empire romain', *Annales Economies, Sociétés, Civilisations*, 23 (1978), pp. 35–63.

33 Suzanne Dixon, 'The Sentimental Ideal of the Roman Family', in Rawson, *Marriage, Divorce and Children*, pp. 99–113, places the 'shift' in the late Republic, and Evans Grubbs, ' "Pagan" and "Christian" Marriage', p. 370, attributes it to the 'provincial' Flavians. Veyne's psychology is questioned by Aline Rousselle, 'The Family Under the Roman Empire: Signs and Gestures', in André Burguière *et al.* (eds.), *A History of the Family*. I. *Distant Worlds, Ancient Worlds* (2 vols.; Cambridge, MA: The Belknap Press of Harvard University Press, 1996), pp. 269–310 (275–77).

34 See Antti Arjava, *Women and Law*, p. 127; but Arjava also alludes at other points to 'conflicting ideals for the conjugal relationship ... in the Roman upper classes' (p. 111) without further elaboration. See also p. 57 for changes in the financial arrangement of marriage that might follow the ideological curve of Veyne's discursive 'happy couple'.

35 Cooper, *Virgin and the Bride*, p. 3: 'Philosophers might debate the best view of marriage not because of a change in the structure of the aristocratic family but because of a jostling for position among schools.'

36 For a sociological study of competing family structures, especially in relation to class, see Françoise Lautman, 'Differences or Changes in Family Organization', in Robert Forster and Orest Ranum (eds.), *Family and Society: Selections from the Annales, Economies, Sociétés, Civilisations* (trans. Elborg Forster and Patricia Ranum; Baltimore, MD: The Johns Hopkins University Press, 1976), pp. 251–61.

37 Veyne, 'Famille et l'amour', p. 48: 'Alors naît le couple'. Cooper, *Virgin and the Bride*, p. 38, points out that the *topos* of the non-material 'charms' of marriage can be traced back to the *Odyssey*. See also Treggiari, *Roman Marriage*, p. 185: 'The Greek moral philosophers found in Homer the marriage of Odysseus and Penelope as a recipe for perfection and the marriage of Paris and Helen as the recipe for failure.'

spread the moral discourse of marriage quite far afield.[38] The aim here is to establish how marriage, the ethical union between male and female partners, became the particular ethical emblem of the upper-class family, initiating a new theoretical economy (*oikonomia*) of class and gender relations.

The Augustan legislation was never meant to mobilize the entire citizenry to become married partners with children: the efforts were directed at the senatorial classes, whose sons and daughters were not producing sufficient legitimate progeny to perpetuate the workings of the principate.[39] This series of *leges* was concerned strictly with *matrimonium*, that is, the legal form of marriage between two consenting parties that would result in legitimately conceived heirs:[40] 'In fact, the Augustan legislation was originally designed to promote marriage and child-bearing (and to discourage extramarital sexual activity) among those Romans whose moral and social behaviour was of the greatest importance to Augustus – that is, the Roman senatorial aristocracy, and the wealthier and more socially distinguished classes in general.'[41] Most of the surviving pieces of the *lex Iulia et Papia* (as this conglomeration of laws came to be known) therefore limit any ethical imperatives to their appropriate social sphere. One jurist cites a long passage from the legislation directed squarely at the highest aristocracy:

A senator, his son, or his grandson, or his great-grandson by his son shall not knowingly or fraudulently become betrothed to marry or marry a freedwoman, or a woman who is or has been an actress or whose father or mother are or have been actors. Nor shall the daughter of a senator, his granddaughter by his son, or great-granddaughter by his grandson become

38 Simon Goldhill, *Foucault's Virginity: Ancient Erotic Fiction and the History of Sexuality* (Cambridge: Cambridge University Press, 1995), has to some extent anticipated me in this comparative effort, moving from 'Augustus' legislation on marriage and adultery' (p. 113) to discuss 'ideals of marriage, that key institution of normative sexual discourse' through readings of the ancient romances and Plutarch's other notable text on married love, the *Amatorius*. Goldhill's interest in marriage, however, is as a normative *locus* of desire and sexuality and not as a class-based social and ethical institution.

39 For a concise summary see Evans Grubbs, *Law and Family*, pp. 94–96; for more detailed discussion and bibliography on the laws, see Treggiari, *Roman Marriage*, pp. 60–80; on the difficulties in reconstructing the exact wording and function of these laws, see Arjava, *Women and Law*, pp. 77–78. The main points of the laws were transformation of adultery and *stuprum* (illicit sex) into public crimes tried in court, stricter regulation of divorce, forfeiture of inheritance by unmarried or childless individuals, and prohibition of certain unions based on degree of relation and difference in status.

40 Jurists agree that 'consent' is a central component of *iustum matrimonium*; see, for example, *Digesta* 23.2.3 (Paul). Texts from the *Digesta* cited from Theodor Mommsen and Paul Kruegger (eds.), *The Digest of Justinian* (3 vols.; trans. Alan Watson; Philadelphia: University of Pennsylvania Press, 1985), with the name of the cited jurist in parentheses. Lawmakers assumed consent even when parties later sought annulment: 'If by his father's force (*cogente*) he marries a woman whom he would not have married if left to his own free will (*sui arbitrii*), nevertheless he has contracted legal marriage (*matrimonium*), which could not have taken place between unwilling parties (*invitos*): he seems to have wanted to do it' (*Digesta* 23.2.22 [Celsus]).

41 Evans Grubbs, *Law and Family*, p. 105. The language of jurists commenting on these laws can be generalized, especially when considering the ethics of marriage: 'Marriage is the union of a man and a woman, a partnership for life involving divine as well as human law' (*Nuptiae sunt coniunctio maris et feminae et consortium omnis vitae, divini et humani iuris communicatio*) (Modestinus) (*Digesta* 23.2.1).

betrothed to or marry, knowingly or fraudulently, a freedman, or a man who is or has been an actor or whose father or mother is or has been an actor. (*Digesta* 23.2.44 [Paul])[42]

By labelling such inappropriate unions not only legally void but also morally shameful – *stuprum* – these laws invest marriage with an ethics that lies at the heart of the conjugal union yet is *de facto* (and *de iure*) restricted to a particular social location: there is little or no concern as to whether these restricted lower-class groups themselves ever marry and produce children.[43]

Augustus's legislation was to a large extent framed in moralizing terms, perhaps as a form of *noblesse oblige*: the laws encouraged constant scrutiny of a man's *dignitas* by his upper-class neighbours, even prompting senatorial families to inform on those in violation of marital prescriptions.[44] Thus, we need not discount Cassius Dio's later reconstruction of Augustus's public defence of his legal programme as the fanciful work of a third-century historian.[45] Later second-century sources, both historians and jurists, do suggest a certain senatorial irritation with Augustus's legal efforts, a resistance that perhaps bespeaks the friction generated by this public moralizing.[46] The moralizing tone of the Augustan legislation becomes so hard to hear through

42 The commentator, Paul, softens the legislation by noting that if the freeborn woman's parents take up acting after the marriage 'it would be most unfair to divorce her since the marriage was respectable (*honestate*) when contracted, and there may already be children'. Several other prohibitions centre on senatorial *dignitas*: *Digesta* 23.2.23 (Celsus), 23.2.27 (Ulpian), 23.2.33 (Marcellus), 23.2.43 (Ulpian), 23.2.47 (Paul), 23.2.49 (Marcellus).

43 As Jane F. Gardner, *Women in Roman Law and Society* (Bloomington: Indiana University Press, 1986), p. 57, points out: 'Augustus' legislation on marriage and on adultery had created several categories of women who were themselves free and of citizen status, but either had no *conubium* [i.e. right to marry legally] at all, or no *conubium* with certain categories of citizens.'

44 Reported with irritation by Tacitus, *Annales* 3.25–28 (text in *Tacitus*, volume 3: *Histories 4–5. Annals 1–1–3* [LCL; trans. Clifford H. Moore and John Jackson; Cambridge, MA: Harvard University Press, 1969]), who uses the public disturbance generated by these laws that attempted 'to popularize marriages (*coniugia*) and the rearing of children' to critique the chequered history of invasive Roman legislation. On the moral framing of Augustus's legislation and its coding as 'revival' of purer times, see Catharine Edwards, *The Politics of Immorality in Ancient Rome* (Cambridge, UK: Cambridge University Press, 1993), pp. 35–38 and 53–58.

45 On Cassius Dio's sources and representation of the Augustan period, see Fergus Millar, *A Study of Cassius Dio* (Oxford: Clarendon Press, 1964), pp. 83–102, esp. 100–102. Cassius Dio may be not unreasonably importing senatorial reaction to a revival of the adultery laws by Septimius Severus at the end of the second century: see Cassius Dio, *Historia Romana* 76.16 and the sneering comments of Tertullian, *Apologeticus* 4.8 (text in Dom Eligius Dekkers [ed.], *Tertulliani Opera*, I [CCSL, 1; Turnhout: Brepols, 1953]), both cited by Barnes, 'Composition', p. 243.

46 Ulpian refers often to the *lex Iulia et Papia*, yet only briefly treats the *dignitas*-based restrictions on senatorial marriage while going on at length about the ramifications of these laws on minute aspects of inheritance: *Regulae Ulpiani* 13.1–2 on the marriages of 'senatores ... liberique eorum'; *Regulae Ulpiani* 11.20, 14, 16.1–3, 18, 19.17, 24.12, 24.30, 29.3–5 on dowry, legacy, intestacy and wills. Text in S. Riccobono *et al.* (eds.), *Fontes Iuris Romani Antejustiniani* (3 vols.; Florence: S.A.G. Barbèra, 1968), II, pp. 259–301. Such fiduciary concern (while understandable from a jurist) functions to translate the discourse of marriage from the ethical to financial realms. On the resistance of the aristocracy to Augustus's coercion, see also Suetonius, *De Vita Caesarum: Divus Augustus* 34. Text in *Suetonius: The Lives of the Caesars*, vol. I: *Julius, Augustus, Tiberius, Gaius, Caligula* (LCL; trans. J. C. Rolfe; Cambridge, MA: Harvard University Press, 1969). For a study of similar aristocratic manipulation of marital regulation, see Pierre Bourdieu, 'Marriage Strategies as Strategies of Social Reproduction', in Forster and Ranum, *Family and Society*, pp. 117–44, esp. p. 135.

the barrage of complaints that Michel Foucault even dismissed it as a significant factor in late ancient sexual ethics.[47] Nonetheless, Augustus's legal reconfiguration of the aristocratic family cannot be separated from its broader ethical implications. As Catharine Edwards notes:

> Scholars tend to treat Roman law as a domain independent of what is labeled literature, a series of practical responses to practical problems. It should rather be seen as a symbolic discourse, bearing as much or as little relationship to patterns of behavior in ancient Rome as the effusions of Roman moralists, and in dialogue with, indeed part of, moralistic discourse.[48]

Indeed, it is precisely through the 'effusions of Roman moralists' such as Plutarch of Chaeronea that we see the new ethical economy of the conjugal family embraced and articulated.

Plutarch's *Coniugalia praecepta*, a recondite gift to some newlywed friends to 'swell the nuptial song' in the bridal chamber (*Coniugalia praecepta* preface, 138B),[49] proclaims that the matrimonial state both produces and is produced within a certain elite philosophical ethics.[50] This philosophical shading of the conjugal union echoes the ethical coercion of Augustus's legal reforms, as Plutarch describes moral development as the duty of well-brought up individuals who marry. The gift of this discourse itself symbolizes marriage's philosophical and ethical potential:

> I am sending it as a gift for you both to possess in common, and at the same time I pray that the Muses may lend their presence and cooperation to Aphrodite, and may feel that it is no more fitting for them to provide a lyre or lute well attuned than it is to provide that the harmony which concerns marriage and the household shall be well attuned through reason, concord, and philosophy (διὰ λόγου καὶ ἁρμονίας καὶ φιλοσοφίας). (*Coniugalia praecepta* preface, 138C)

The Muses, whose 'nuptial song' in a traditional way initiated this marriage,[51] are here drafted into a philosophical role of using their 'harmony' to phrase marriage as an ethical and reasonable union of male and female souls. Philosophy becomes the musical 'theme' of marriage, through which it 'chants a spell' over those entering a 'lifelong fellowship' (βίου κοινωνία) (*Coniugalia praecepta* preface, 138C). This high-status couple has a particular responsibility to marriage *because* they have

---

47 Michel Foucault, *History of Sexuality*, vol. 3: *The Care of the Self* (trans. Robert Hurley; New York: Vintage Books, 1986), p. 40.

48 Edwards, *Politics of Immorality*, p. 35.

49 Text and translation in *Moralia, II* (LCL; trans. Frank C. Babbit; Cambridge, MA: Harvard University Press, 1969).

50 On the ethical symbolism of marriage in Plutarch, see Cooper, *Virgin and the Bride*, pp. 5–11; Lisette Goessler, *Plutarchs Gedanken über die Ehe* (Zürich: Buchdruckerei Berichthaus, 1962) examines the *Amatorius*, *Coniugalia praecepta* and several *Lives* to trace Plutarch's marriage theory; Foucault, *Care of the Self*, pp. 193–210; and for a different reading of the treatise's social location, see Cynthia Patterson, 'Plutarch's "Advice on Marriage": Traditional Wisdom through a Philosophical Lens', *ANRW* II.33.6 (1992), pp. 4709–23.

51 Presumably sexually: Plutarch compares his discourse to the 'horse rampant' flute music used to 'arouse ardent desire' (*Coniugalia praecepta* preface, 138B). See Goessler, *Plutarchs Gedanken*, p. 45.

been 'brought up in the atmosphere of philosophy' (ibid.),[52] and it is to the ethics of 'harmony' and 'reason' that they must therefore dedicate their union. Such gross motives as money or even reproduction (standard reasons for marriage in the ancient world) are dismissed as inferior to the glorious commingling of spirits for which matrimony is intended:

> The marriage of the couple in love with each other is an intimate union; that of those who marry for dowry or children is of persons joined together; and that of those who merely sleep in the same bed is of separate persons who may be regarded as cohabiting (συνοικεῖν) but not really living together (συμβιοῦν). (*Coniugalia praecepta* 34, 142F–143A)

Plutarch does retain a notion of hierarchy within this 'symbiosis':[53] it is the husband's duty to 'lead' his wife into a state of higher morality. Marriage is intended to be an 'ethical schoolhouse' (διδασκαλεῖον εὐταξίας) in which the groom teaches his bride about 'virtue, devotion, constancy, and affection' (*Coniugalia praecepta* 46–47, 144F–145A). Nonetheless, the framework of symbiosis creates an economy (*oikonomia*) distinct from the rigorously hierarchical vertical structure of *patria potestas*: even if only theoretically, the wife enters this 'ethical schoolhouse' from which she may emerge as her husband's moral equal.

This schoolhouse replaces more common marriage settings, such as the bedroom. Plutarch insinuates his ethical ideals into the reproductive efforts of husband and wife: 'Man and wife ought especially to indulge in this [procreation] with circumspection, keeping themselves pure from all unholy and unlawful intercourse with others, and not sowing seed from which they are unwilling to have offspring' (*Coniugalia praecepta* 42, 144B). Plutarch nearly supplants physical reproduction altogether when he compares the fatherless uterine growths found in some women with the danger incurred by wives engaging in philosophical rumination without their husbands' guidance: 'Great care must be taken that this sort of thing does not take place in women's minds. For if they do not receive the seed of good doctrines and share with their husbands in intellectual advancement, they, left to themselves, may conceive many untoward ideas and low designs and emotions' (*Coniugalia praecepta* 48, 145E). The husband's role as literal inseminator is replaced with a philosophical insemination, and the product of this intellectual reproduction is, somewhat paradoxically, the wife herself as newly reconstructed philosophical partner (if not equal to her husband, then at least 'sharing' his 'intellectual advancement'). Not only does marriage provide a convenient opportunity for wives to advance in philosophical education and wisdom along with their husbands, it is the very *nature* of marriage to be born from and in turn 'reproduce' a union of 'minds'. As his own version of a 'love-song' draws to a close, Plutarch once again invokes the Muses in the service of 'education and philosophy' (παιδείαν καὶ φιλοσοφίαν) whose 'fruits' the bride Eurydice is to enjoy (*Coniugalia praecepta* 48, 146A).

It is unlikely that Plutarch imagines Pollianus and Eurydice would never have children or fulfil their civic duty to produce a full and prosperous *oikos*, or that

---

52 On the curial status of the recipients' families, see Bernadette Puech, 'Prosopographie des amis de Plutarque', *ANRW* II.33.6 (1992), pp. 4831–93 (4842–43, 4849, 4873, 4879–83).

53 As by Treggiari, *Roman Marriage*, pp. 224–26.

they would create in their homes a sort of egalitarian wonderland in which gender distinction dissolves in the dizzying light of philosophical instruction. At one point Plutarch makes the very conventional observation that 'a man therefore ought to have his household well harmonized who is going to harmonize state, forum, and friends' (*Coniugalia praecepta* 43, 144C). The husband, for all his philosophical partnership and symbiosis with his wife, is still the master of hearth and forum. Plutarch's rhetoric, however, shifts the theoretical underpinnings of marriage in the same direction as the Augustan legislation: from the financially constituted union of variously interested *patresfamilias* to the 'philosophically' oriented union of male and female minds, 'an institution *particularly* able to foster moderation and stability in the participants'.[54] Also similar to the Augustan legislation, Plutarch makes it clear that the ethical internalization of this philosophy remains within a restricted social sphere. Marriage, the ethical *symbiosis* of husband and wife, remains the elevated privilege of an upper-class family. When we turn to the Greek 'romance' novels, we see how the class-specific nature of that conjugal family begins to be camouflaged, even as it retains its reorientation toward male–female 'partnership'.[55]

The world of the Greek romance – a modern designation for a constellation of thematically and generically related texts from the first centuries CE – is a curious mixture of fantasy and reality:[56] while its heroes and heroines participate in adventures that could justly be called swashbuckling, it is clear that their proper place remains the entirely familiar. Their travels may take them to the court of the Great King of Persia,[57] or to the squalid hut of a goatherd,[58] or even to battle on the deck of a pirate ship,[59] but always the final destination is home and hearth, symbolized and actualized by marriage, the '*happy ending*' *par excellence*.[60] The extremities of the social disruption within the novels underscore the cohesion triumphantly restored

---

54 Cooper, *Virgin and the Bride*, p. 11, emphasis mine.

55 For the growing literature on the novels, see the bibliography of David Konstan, *Sexual Symmetry: Love in the Ancient Novel and Related Genres* (Princeton, NJ: Princeton University Press, 1994).

56 The term 'romance' is casually applied to the collection of Greek novels centred on the amorous relationship between a hero and heroine, often with implicit comparisons to the modern 'romance novel': the explicit relation is rejected by Richard Stoneman, 'The *Alexander Romance*: From History to Fiction', in J.R. Morgan and Richard Stoneman (eds.), *Greek Fiction: The Greek Novel in Context* (London: Routledge, 1994), pp. 117–29 (117–18). The comparison, particularly in terms of the socialization of women, might nonetheless prove fruitful: see Janice A. Radway, *Reading the Romance: Women, Patriarchy, and Popular Literature* (Chapel Hill: University of North Carolina Press, 1991).

57 Chariton, *Chaireas and Kallirhoe* 5.8–6.9. Text in Warren E. Blake (ed.), *De Chaerea et Callirhoe Amatoriarum Narrationum Libri Octo* (Oxford: Clarendon Press, 1938); translation by B.P. Reardon in *idem* (ed.), *Collected Ancient Greek Novels* (Berkeley: University of California Press, 1989).

58 Xenophon of Ephesus, *An Ephesian Tale* 2.9–11. Text in Georges Dalmeyda (ed.), *Les Éphésiaques ou Le Roman d'Habrocomès et d'Anthia* (Paris: Editions Belles Lettres, 1926); translation by Graham Anderson in Reardon, *Greek Novels*.

59 Achilles Tatius, *Leukippe and Kleitophon* 3.9–10. Text in Jean-Phillippe Garnaud (ed.), *Le Roman de Leucippé et Clitophon* (Paris: Editions Belles Lettres, 1991); translation by John J. Winkler in Reardon, *Greek Novels*.

60 On 'marriages as happy ending', see Judith Perkins, *The Suffering Self: Pain and Narrative Representation in the Early Christian Era* (London and New York: Routledge, 1995), pp. 41–76.

at their conclusions.[61] Marriage between the protagonists (either celebrated at the beginning and tragically interrupted, or deferred by circumstance until the end of the story) is, as has been frequently noted, 'the social backbone of the romances'.[62] Marriage is in fact so omnipresent in the romances that merely cataloguing its appearances borders on the redundant: to a great extent the novels *are* marriage, conveyed through an exciting narrative.[63]

Brigitte Egger argues that, in comparison with Roman and provincial law, the Greek romances are socially archaizing: they project their heroines into a fictitious legal status more reminiscent of a restrictive Attic past than a Romano-Hellenistic present.[64] She posits that under the thin veil of the erotic and sentimental love story, 'marriage' in the end works to 'factually debilitate ... [the] image of women'.[65] Egger overlooks, however, the distinctly moralizing tenor of the rhetorics of marriage in Late Antiquity. While she may find Heliodorus's legal fiction of adultery as capital crime (for the woman) fanciful and misogynistic (a point I would not dispute), this extreme position on the moral imperatives of marriage does resonate with the ethical coercion exercised by the Augustan legislation.[66] Similarly, the novels' great attention to fidelity and legitimate procreation speaks to the same ethical duties promulgated by Augustus's laws or even Plutarch's 'love-song'.[67]

The threat of feminine disempowerment Egger discerns in the Greek novels must be placed in the context of the overarching ideology of conjugal partnership, that is, the ideal new family promulgated by Augustan jurists and moralists. The romantic protagonists serve as exemplary citizens who freely fall in love and 'live together as partners' in 'reason, concord, and philosophy'. The new *symbiosis* of the

---

61 See Perkins, *Suffering Self*, p. 46: 'These romances filled with travel, adventure, and final union idealize social unity'; also Cooper, *Virgin and the Bride*, p. 34: 'Since love and disruption were linked in the ancient imagination, romance was a narrative form well suited to the exploration of the limits of an established identity.'

62 Brigitte Egger, 'Women and Marriage in the Greek Novels: The Boundaries of Romance', in James Tatum (ed.), *The Search for the Ancient Novel* (Baltimore, MD and London: The Johns Hopkins University Press, 1994), pp. 260–80 (260).

63 See the excellent discussions in Perkins, *Suffering Self*, pp. 41–76 and Cooper, *Virgin and the Bride*, pp. 20–44, which focus more on social institutions and power than, as other modern works, on sexuality per se.

64 Egger, 'Women and Marriage', pp. 266–74: 'Often, the law tends to be more conservative than other aspects of reality and expressions in mentality; but in the case of women in late Hellenistic society, it is not so conservative and constraining a discourse as that of Greek romance' (p. 274).

65 Egger, 'Women and Marriage', p. 273; romances, she believes, are at times 'even more *frauen-feindlich* than Attic law' (p. 270).

66 Egger, 'Women and Marriage', p. 279 n. 48; see Heliodorus, *An Ethiopian Story* 1.11.4 (θάνατον τὸ τέλος τοῦ παρανομήματος ... μοιχᾶται). Text in R.M. Rattenbury and T.W. Lumb (eds.), *Les Éthiopiques: Théagène et Chariclée* (3 vols.; Paris: Edition Belles Lettres, 1935–43); translation by J.R. Morgan in Reardon, *Greek Novels*. Egger also refers to 1.17.5, but it is not clear that Demainete's death there is imagined as commensurate with her legal 'punishment'. For a third- or fourth-century discussion of when husbands and fathers can put adulterers and adulteresses to death based on the *leges Iuliae de adulteris coercendis*, see the *Mosaicarum et Romanarum Legum Collatio* 4.2.1–12.8 (text in Riccobono, *Fontes Iuris*, II, pp. 544–89), discussed with other *Digesta* passages in Treggiari, *Roman Law*, pp. 282–85.

67 Cooper, *Virgin and the Bride*, p. 43, suggests that the novels' eroticism 'should be understood as an encouragement to fertility similar in aim to the Augustan marriage legislation'. Goldhill, *Foucault's Virginity*, p. 113, also makes this connection.

conjugal family did not erase gender distinction; it rather relativized the male–female relationship into an ethical 'partnership' in which the husband still ruled hearth and home, but his symbiotic relationship with his wife was no longer merely another extension of his *potestas*, homologous to his relationship with his children and slaves. It is this reconfiguration of relation and difference that the Greek novels narratavize and dramatically expand.

Marriage is, first of all, construed as the locus of unique ethical and social advancement. Simon Goldhill, whose essays on ancient erotic writings attempt to supplement Foucault's *History of Sexuality*, connects the philosophical significance of Plutarch's *Amatorius* (a middle-Platonic dialogue contrasting the virtues of opposite- and same-sex erotic desire) with the Greek novels: 'Its significance is perhaps better seen as the fullest statement of an ideological or theoretical self-situating that runs in different guises through the various texts I have been discussing and finds its most developed narrative expression in the great sophistic novels of Longus, Heliodorus and Achilles Tatius.'[68] The novels transform the philosophical guise of Plutarch's *Coniugalia praecepta* and *Amatorius* into a romanticized contrast between 'successful' marriages and 'doomed' homoerotic affairs.[69] This contrast does not so much value 'heterosexual' over 'homosexual' desire, but rather juxtaposes types of relationships in which desire may be actuated.[70] The married couple survives extraordinary perils to arrive at a position at the centre of society, the conjugal union, superior and triumphant, while the much less harshly tested relationships of unmarried couples end in tragedy and death. In Achilles Tatius's *Leukippe and Kleitophon*, the hero's cousin Kleinias laments that his 'boyfriend' (μειράκιον) Charikles is being pushed into an arranged marriage. Kleinias, outraged, launches into a diatribe against women and marriage familiar from classical and Hellenistic Greek literature (including the *Amatorius* of Plutarch). As Kleinias is wrapping up, news comes that Charikles is dead, having been thrown by the horse Kleinias gave him (Achilles Tatius, *Leukippe and Kleitophon* 1.7–12). At the funeral, the eulogy of Charikles's father reminds the reader what his son's fate *should* have been: 'O groom and bridegroom (ἱππεῦ καὶ νυμφίε) – unconsummated bridegroom, unlucky chevalier. Your bridal chamber is the grave, your wedlock is with death, your wedding march a funeral hymn, your marriage song this dirge' (*Leukippe and Kleitophon* 1.13.5). Kleinias's own lament makes it clear that their relationship, explicitly counterpoised to legal marriage, is the cause of this tragedy: 'O cruel fate! I bought you your murderer and gave him to you as a gift!' (*Leukippe and Kleitophon* 1.14.3). Later in the same novel, as Leukippe and Kleitophon elope with Kleinias's aid, they encounter an Egyptian named Menelaus, who also tells the story of causing his male lover's death in a hunting accident: 'He died in the embrace of the very arms that had killed him' (*Leukippe and Kleitophon* 2.34.5). This tragedy, set in the context

---

68　Goldhill, *Foucault's Virginity*, p. 144.

69　Konstan, *Sexual Symmetry*, p. 29, calls the affairs 'doomed'; John J. Winkler, translator of Achilles Tatius's *Leukippe and Kleitophon*, in a note also refers to these 'tragic gay subplots' (Reardon, *Greek Novels*, p. 185).

70　See for instance Goldhill, *Foucault's Virginity*, pp. 76–92, where these erotic *logoi* are analysed 'as providing a particular counterpoint to the framing tale – as foreshadowing events … offering thematic focuses, constructing paradigms which help articulate the place of the hero and heroine within the realm of erotic discourse' (p. 81).

of Kleitophon's erotic journey to the marriage bed and reinforced by a retelling of Kleinias's own tale and a mock-Platonic dialogue on the virtues of boy-love versus woman-love (*Leukippe and Kleitophon* 2.35–38), again acts as a negative foil to the properly constituted marital relationship which is the novel's inevitable conclusion.

The novels also echo the legal and philosophical literature on marriage by situating the conjugal union within a new, symbiotic economy of familial gender relations. David Konstan has proposed that the Greek novels alone of Hellenistic amatory literature conform their protagonists' relationships to a model of 'sexual symmetry', in which the male and female partners are socially and romantically matched. The 'pederastic paradigm', characterized by an asymmetry between *erastēs* and *erōmenos*, is set forth as a negative counterpart, 'doomed' to failure.[71] By contrast, the marital union is one of symmetrical 'equals', promoting erotic and familial partnership. The narrative flow makes such conjugal 'happy endings' appear natural and inevitable, in much the same way that Plutarch depicted marriage as the natural site of philosophical progression. To nuance Konstan's potentially optimistic reading of 'symmetry', we might add that the inequalities of gender difference are, as in Plutarch, relativized and reconfigured by the gentle rubric of 'partnership' or *symbiosis*, through a discourse of elite matrimonial harmony.

Yet strikingly absent from the narrative framework of the Greek novels is the insistence on the proper upper-class setting for such *concordia*. Konstan remarks that social status is made symmetrical in a way that masks its significance altogether in the maritally driven novel:

> Divisions of class and status marked ancient society as well as modern, and are reflected in the narrative presuppositions of New Comedy, epic, and other classical genres. But the Greek novelists, uniquely as it seems, elected to portray reciprocal erotic relationships between social equals and thereby defined for the genre a problematic involving love and fidelity that excluded a primary concern with issues of status or rank.[72]

Status and rank are unrealistically 'deproblematized', as if they were not factors in the negotiation of a proper marriage. The class-based restrictiveness of the partnership, emphasized by Augustus and Plutarch, is thus strangely veiled in the novels, as illustrated by the house slaves Leukon and Rhode, companions of the protagonists Habrokomes and Anthia in Xenophon of Ephesus's *Ephesian Tale*. Leukon and Rhode are featured sporadically throughout the novel; they make their first appearance in the second book as 'two slaves' (οἰκέτας δύο), not necessarily sharing a relationship with each other (*Ephesian Tale* 2.2.3). Later, also subject to the misfortunes of their master and mistress, they are sold together in Lycia 'to an old man who gave them every attention and treated them as his own children' (*Ephesian Tale* 2.10.4). We meet this pair next in the last book of the novel where they are described as the 'companions (σύντροφοι) of Habrokomes and Anthia'; their Lycian master has since died and 'left his large estate to them' (*Ephesian Tale* 5.6.3). Leukon and Rhode now play the role of wealthy householders, travelling to Rhodes where they

---

71 Konstan, *Sexual Symmetry*, pp. 14–59.
72 Konstan, *Sexual Symmetry*, p. 218; see also p. 186: '[The Greek novel] abolishes the tension between *eros* and marriage that informs all previous genres.'

make offerings to Helios and erect a 'pillar inscribed in gold' with their own names (*Ephesian Tale* 5.10.6). The erection of such a monument, in normal circumstances, would seem the act of a well-to-do married couple:[73] in fact, Leukon and Rhode's monument stands next to a 'gold panoply' that had earlier been dedicated by Anthia and Habrokomes themselves (see *Ephesian Tale* 1.12.2–3). On Rhodes, Leukon and Rhode are instrumental in reuniting Anthia and Habrokomes after their separation and adventures; upon recognizing Habrokomes they 'made over their possessions to him, took care of him, looked after him, and tried to console him' (*Ephesian Tale* 5.10.12). At this point they stand halfway between their former status as slaves and their recent status as the 'happy couple': their own conjugal bliss acts as a salve for the temporarily solitary Habrokomes. When they discover Anthia mourning next to the offerings at Helios's temple, their exclamation restores the 'real' happy couple to the centre of the narrative while resituating themselves in a position of servitude: 'Mistress Anthia, we are your slaves (ἡμεῖς οἰκέται σοί), Leukon and Rhode, who shared your voyage and the pirate lair … Have courage, mistress; Habrokomes is safe, and he is here, always mourning for you!' (*Ephesian Tale* 5.12.5). That night the protagonists and their entourage break up into what seem to be comparable couples: 'Leukon with Rhode, Hippothous with the handsome Kleisthenes … Anthia with Habrokomes' (*Ephesian Tale* 5.13.6). 'Handsome Kleisthenes', however, is soon after adopted by Hippothous, and Leukon and Rhode give over the rest of their possessions to Anthia and Habrokomes, or, as Xenophon phrases it, 'share everything with their companions' (*Ephesian Tale* 5.15).

What position Leukon and Rhode hold at the end of the *Ephesian Tale* is remarkably unclear. We can assume that they retain their freedom as granted by their Lycian master's will; perhaps they are enjoying conjugal bliss alongside their former owners and masters. Or we could imagine that narratively their own conjugal union, like their wealth, was merely held in trust for the true protagonists during their unfortunate separation; both wealth and marital happiness are then transferred to their rightful owners (Habrokomes and Anthia) to generate a happy ending. This ambiguity inscribes a fluidity into the novel's marital discourse: the happiness of the maritally centered household, the upper-class ethics of the couple, has for a brief moment slipped through the status-oriented cracks that the Augustan legislation and Plutarch's philosophical tracts sought to cement. As Konstan remarked, class and status as issues in proper marriage have been veiled, in a genre that might itself extend deeper into the lower social and economic classes of imperial society.[74] By 'romancing' an ethics of the conjugal family, the Greek novel seems to open up an imaginative ethical space, however small, beyond the

---

73 See Cooper, *Virgin and the Bride*, pp. 38–43, where she analyses the social significance of Daphnis and Chloe's munificence, which frames Longus's novel.

74 Ewen Bowie, 'The Readership of Greek Novels in the Ancient World', in Tatum, *Search for the Ancient Novel*, pp. 435–59, argues with some acuity that the novels were likely *intended* for a sophisticated, educated (*pepaideumenoi*) audience, but concedes that 'a number of points could support the notion that the readership of the novel may have spilled over … to reach a slightly wider circle' (p. 441). See also Christine M. Thomas, *The* Acts of Peter, *Gospel Literature, and the Ancient Novel: Rewriting the Past* (Oxford and New York: Oxford University Press, 2003), pp. 149–50 n. 58.

socioeconomic sphere in which it was fabricated.[75] Here is where we can begin to trace the ethical and narrative intervention of the so-called Apocryphal Acts of the Apostles.

'This Filthy Intercourse': Wives as Homewreckers in the Apocryphal Acts

The so-called Apocryphal Acts of the Apostles, like the Greek novels, attend a great deal to marriage and the ethical advancement of heroines. As we saw above, a previous generation of scholarship found the negative focus on marriage to be the logical counterpart to the positive exhortations to chastity and virginity. Yet, as Kate Cooper notes, the non-specific ascetic language of these Acts stands 'poised between revolution and irrelevance':[76] it is a moral cipher masking a more profound statement about Christian values. Indeed, creating a simple inverse equation between 'marriage' and 'chastity' also ignores the salient fact that the Apocryphal Acts are being composed and disseminated in the wake of a sustained period of pro-nuptial propaganda stretching through the first and second centuries, in which marriage was beginning to attain its familiar configuration.[77]

'Marriage' began to appear, in the first and second centuries, as a *new* ethical model for the family, one that might (through suggestive literary devices) translate beyond its intended upper-class sphere. Often scholars fail to apply this observation to analyses of literary representation of marriage, and so ignore the class-based implications of marital discourses. Generally only the scholars writing 'against the grain' point out the social exclusivity of *iustum matrimonium*: Bernadette Brooten and John Boswell, writing to carve out a historical space for same-sex unions in Antiquity, emphasize the restrictedness of ancient marriage to very particular social classes.[78] Paul Veyne, concerned to 'de-Christianize' the foundations of modern ethics, states it baldly:

> All the transformations of sexuality and conjugality are anterior to Christianity. Two principal shifts come to pass, from a bisexuality of penetration to a heterosexuality of reproduction; and from a society where marriage is in no way an institution designed for all society to a society where it 'goes without saying' that marriage (*'le' mariage*) is a fundamental

---

75 Although my focus remains on literary interpretation, it is notable that the interactive physical spaces of the urban centres of the first centuries might also have encouraged such class slippage: see the important comments of Andrew Wallace-Hadrill, *'Domus* and *Insulae* in Rome: Families and Housefuls', in Balch and Osiek, *Early Christian Families*, pp. 3–18. Amy-Jill Levine's verse, which serves as the epigraph for this essay, nicely conveys the material and ideological significance of Wallace-Hadrill's argument.

76 Cooper, *Virgin and the Bride*, p. 52 and see p. 57.

77 Dixon, 'Sentimental Ideal', p. 99: 'From the late Republic on, it is possible to discern a sentimental ideal of family life at Rome which can be compared with our own cultural ideal. The expectation of affection within marriage and the appreciation of young and youthful children were both part of this ideal.'

78 Bernadette J. Brooten, *Love Between Women: Early Christian Responses to Female Homoeroticism* (Chicago: The University of Chicago Press, 1996), pp. 333–34; John Boswell, *Same-Sex Unions in Premodern Europe* (New York: Villard Books, 1994), pp. 31–38; compare the unsupported statement of Egger, 'Women and Marriage', p. 261: 'To [the novelists] the whole world is married (as most people, we may presume, actually were ...).'

institution of all societies (so one believes) and of society in its entirety. In pagan society, *everyone did not get married* ... One married in one sole case: if one decided to transmit one's fortune to one's children.[79]

Accepting Veyne's proposal that as this new ethics became interiorized it was also universalized, and having traced one route by which this upper-class discourse might have penetrated to lower classes, we can now frame the Apocryphal Acts as a deliberate form of narrative resistance to this ethical family configuration centred on marriage.[80] I attend especially to the dynamic of female agency in this rejection of 'conjugal partnership' to ask how the subversive Christian emphasis on eradication of marital *symbiosis* might translate into new articulations for the possibilities of women's piety.

The generic links between the Greek romances and Apocryphal Acts have been the subject of scholarly enquiry for close to a century.[81] When the novels were seen as a sort of popular literature, intended for women or other 'juvenile' readers, the Apocryphal Acts were similarly regarded as appealing to an analogous audience. Scholars now concede that the novels were intended for a more sophisticated audience, occasionally penetrating to a 'wider' readership; the Apocryphal Acts, however, are often still seen as the province of a lower-class audience,[82] and thus their strange liberties and inversions of 'romantic' themes have been read more and more as incidents of political and social subversion. Judith Perkins, who maintains 'that in the so-called *Apocryphal Acts of the Apostles* signs and strategies of an emerging representational and social challenge are preserved',[83] charts the many examples of class- and status-oriented resistance in the *Acts of Peter*. While Perkins focuses on the subversion of 'public' social institutions and their reconfiguration around a new model of subjectivity, I would like to redirect her enquiry into the reconfigured

---

79 Veyne, 'Famille et l'amour', pp. 39–40, emphasis mine. See also Paul Veyne, 'The Roman Empire', in *idem* (ed.), *A History of Private Life*, I. *From Pagan Rome to Byzantium* (trans. A. Goldhammer; Cambridge, MA: Harvard University Press, 1987), pp. 5–234 (36): 'At some point people began to internalize, as a moral code, what had been a civic and dotal institution ... Note, however, that everything I am about to say applies to only a tenth or a twentieth of the free population, to the class of the wealthy, who also considered themselves cultivated.'

80 Not all scholars read the Apocryphal Acts as uniformly subversive or antisocial: see, for instance, Ann Graham Brock, 'Political Authority and Cultural Accommodation: Social Diversity in the *Acts of Paul* and the *Acts of Peter*', in Bovon *et al.*, *Apocryphal Acts of the Apostles*, pp. 145–69.

81 Rosa Söder, *Die apokryphen Apostelgeschichte und die romanhafte Literatur der Antike* (Stuttgart: W. Kohlhammer, 1932), p. 181: 'Romanhafte Erzählungen – das dürften die vorgelegten Untersuchungen klargemacht haben – sind auch die AGG [apokryphen Apostelgeschichte].' (The preceding investigations clearly show that the Apocryphal Acts are also romance narratives.) Cooper claims of the Greek romance and Apocryphal Acts that 'neither genre can be fully understood without reference to the other' (*Virgin and the Bride*, p. 22). See also Cameron, *Christianity and Rhetoric*, p. 90 n. 1 and now Thomas, *Acts of Peter*.

82 As discussed by Perkins, *Suffering Self*, pp. 124–25, 138–41, drawing mainly on literary style and the various 'sympathies' played out in the *Acts of Peter*.

83 Perkins, *Suffering Self*, p. 124. See also Cooper, *Virgin and the Bride*, pp. 66–67; and Melissa Aubin, 'Reversing Romance? The *Acts of Thecla* and the Ancient Novel', in Ronald Hock, Brad Chance and Judith Perkins (eds.), *Ancient Fiction and Early Christian Narrative* (SBL Symposium Series, 6; Atlanta: Scholars Press, 1998), pp. 257–72.

models of family and kinship, given the deliberate emphasis in many of the Acts on the apostles' disastrous interventions into a conjugally oriented family.[84]

The Acts subvert many of the tropes of 'partnership' or κοινωνία expressed as a marital ethics in the classical literature, and replace them with broader modes of 'kinship', συγγένεια. The *Acts of Andrew*, for instance, distorts the philosophically beneficial 'procreation' lauded by Plutarch: while Plutarch transformed the bedroom into an 'ethical schoolhouse', the *Acts of Andrew* converts the bedroom of the heroine, Maximilla, into a Christian meeting-place (e.g. *Passio Andreae* 13). One of the text's more bizarre moments comes when Maximilla's husband Aegeates, proconsul of Achaea, returns to the palace while the Christians are meeting in his bedroom; as Aegeates sits outside the bedroom on a chamberpot, Andrew 'seals' the Christians so they can pass by unseen (*Passio Andreae* 13–14). After they have all departed, Aegeates rushes into the bedroom and attempts to return it to a place of conjugal union. His words to his wife might come from the *Coniugalia praecepta*: 'Give me your right hand first: I shall kiss her whom I no longer call "wife" (γυναῖκα) but "lady" (δέσποιναν), so that I may find relief in your chastity and affection for me (τῇ σωφροσύνῃ καὶ φιλίᾳ τῇ πρός με)' (*Passio Andreae* 14). Maximilla resists, and once Aegeates has fallen asleep she sends for Andrew so they may meet in 'another bedroom' (*Passio Andreae* 15). Much of this section of the *Acts of Andrew* takes place in various bedrooms of the proconsular *praetorium* in Patras;[85] both the tender speeches delivered by Aegeates to his wife and the sermons delivered by Andrew to his 'brethren' make clear that the locus of elite conjugal *koinōnia* is being actively transformed into a site of sacred *sungeneia*, i.e. kinship. Although Andrew and Maximilla characterize Aegeates's desires as 'filthy intercourse' (μιαρᾶς μίξεως) and a 'foul and sordid way of life' (μυσαροῦ βίου καὶ ῥυπαροῦ) (*Passio Andreae* 14, 37), Aegeates himself echoes the ethical configuration of marriage found in the philosophical and romantic literature. Sex for Aegeates represents a higher union, in which female sexual submission becomes aristocratic, wifely 'fellowship' (as Plutarch might have described it). When Aegeates discovers that Maximilla has been sending a slave-girl to his bed in her place, he does not reproach his wife with threats and *potestas* but beseeches her in language of partnership and union: 'I cling to your feet, having lived with you as your husband (ἀνὴρ συμβίου ... συγγεγονώς σοι) for twelve years, you whom I held as a goddess and now I still hold you as such on account of your chastity (σωφροσύνης) and your generally refined character' (*Passio Andreae* 23). Later, when Maximilla persists in their separation even while Andrew sits in prison, Aegeates again attempts to win her back. His description of

---

84 For generic and textual studies of the 'five main' Apocryphal Acts, see the essays in F. Bovon *et al.* (eds.), *Les Actes Apocryphes des Apôtres: Christianisme et monde païen* (Geneva: Labor et Fides, 1981), especially the useful appendix of date and provenance for each of the Acts (pp. 289–305). See also David Konstan, 'Acts of Love: A Narrative Pattern in the Apocryphal Acts', *JECS* 6 (1998), pp. 15–36, on narratives of 'familial affection and integration' in the Apocryphal Acts.

85 The action in Patras begins in this portion of the *Acts of Andrew* with Maximilla 'leaving her bedroom' to greet her brother-in-law Stratocles (*Passio Andreae* 1); she likewise 'emerges from her bedroom' when Stratocles's servant is possessed (*Passio Andreae* 2); Andrew's conversion speech to Stratocles takes place in Maximilla's bedroom (*Passio Andreae* 6–8); and it is likely that the baptism of the 'brethren' also takes place in this elaborate network of bedrooms (*Passio Andreae* 10–12).

their nuptial bond sets aside the typical worldly concerns of marriage and emphasizes their spiritual and ethical union, even in sexual intercourse:

> Maximilla, because your parents thought me worthy to be your mate (τῆς συμβιώσεώς
> σου), they pledged you to me in marriage without regard to wealth, heredity or reputation,
> considering only the kindness of my soul … If you would be the woman you once were,
> living together with me (συμβιοῦσα μοι) as we were accustomed, sleeping with me,
> consorting with me, conceiving children with me (συγκαθεύδουσά μοι, συγγινομένη,
> συντεκνοῦσα), then I would treat you well in every way. (*Passio Andreae* 36)

Sharing a bed, having sex and bearing children are all subordinate aspects of 'living
together', *symbiosis*, which for Plutarch had been the highest form of companionship
(e.g. *Coniugalia praecepta* 34, 142F–143A).

Maximilla rejects Aegeates's soulful union, however, and is seduced away by a
competing rhetoric of family.[86] This couching of moral superiority in alternative
familial terms appears throughout the Patras episode by means of a repeated
emphasis on *sungeneia*.[87] Andrew's speeches not only refer to the Christian converts
as 'brethren', they reconstruct the diverse body of believers into a family formed by
the apostle: 'If you desire a friend who supplies goods not of this world, I am your
friend. If you desire a father for those who are rejected on earth, I am your father.
If you desire a legitimate brother (ἀδελφὸν γνήσιον) to set you apart from bastard
brothers, I am your brother' (*Passio Andreae* 12). The first time Maximilla refuses
to sleep with Aegeates, and meets instead with Andrew in 'another bedroom', the
apostle commends her choice and prays to God, 'If she has such a firm faith in you,
may she obtain her own proper kinship (τὴν ἰδίαν συγγένειαν) through separation
from those who affect such (τῶν προσποιητῶν) but are really enemies' (*Passio
Andreae* 16).[88] By intervening in what might seem the correct familial context for
the wife of a Greek proconsul and providing instead a 'truer' and morally superior
family life, Andrew demonstrates the deficiency of the conjugally oriented family.
Maximilla is 'freed' from her *symbiosis* and marital *concordia*.

Unlike the Greek novels, the Apocryphal Acts do not mask the particular status of
that conjugal family: the failure of this familial configuration is linked throughout
with its upper-class *milieu*. Compare the ambiguously paired house-slaves Leukon
and Rhode, who enjoy a (perhaps brief?) married family life, with the 'wanton slave-
girl' Euclia in the *Acts of Andrew*. Sent by Maximilla to be 'used' by Aegeates 'as
his wife' (χρώμενος ὡς τῇ ἑαυτοῦ συμβίῳ) and take Maximilla's place in the
marriage bed (*Passio Andreae* 17), Euclia grows boastful and demands both money
and freedom from her mistress (gifts Leukon and Rhode receive easily from their
Lycian master before beginning a life of conjugal bliss). Resented by her fellow-

---

86 Cooper, *Virgin and the Bride*, pp. 46–67, esp. pp. 56–60, demonstrates that the 'rivalry' for the
fidelity of one woman was designed to demonstrate the 'moral superiority' of the apostolic hero over
his pagan (often imperial) counterpart.

87 See MacDonald, *Acts of Andrew*, p. 331 n. 7.

88 MacDonald assumes that the προσποιητῶν are 'masquerading friends', but the emphasis in
the entire work on 'true' and 'false' kin suggests to me instead 'pretend' families. Since Aegeates
is repeatedly referred to as the son or relative of demons (see for example *Passio Andreae* 40), as
Maximilla's husband he is the worst of these pretenders.

slaves, Euclia is betrayed and the 'furious proconsul' cuts out her tongue and casts her outside, where she becomes 'food for the dogs' (*Passio Andreae* 18–22, cf. 2 Kgs 9.34–37). The marriage bed is evidently a dangerous place for slaves. In the novels, class is veiled to the point that a slave could be elevated into the ethically superior family constructed by marriage; in contrast, in the Apocryphal Acts those wealthy aristocrats instead 'drop down' socially into the inferior state of the other 'brethren'.

This inversion of the novels' ethical universalization is represented by the figure of Stratocles, Aegeates's brother. Like Pollianus and Eurydice in the *Coniugalia praecepta*, Stratocles is first distinguished in the *Acts of Andrew* as spiritually and ethically advanced: he is 'Aegeates's brother, who had petitioned Caesar not to serve in the army (μὴ στρατεύευσθαι) but to pursue philosophy' (*Passio Andreae* 1). Furthermore he endures a crisis like those of the heroes' best friends in the Greek novels: Alcman, 'a boy whom Stratocles loved dearly', falls violently ill, and Stratocles blames himself. 'If only I had never come here but perished at sea this would not have happened to me! Friends ... I cannot live without him' (*Passio Andreae* 2). If this were a scene from one of the Greek novels, Alcman would die and Stratocles' brother Aegeates would initiate a brief discourse on the benefits of married life over pederasty; we are far from the land of romance, however. Instead Maximilla fetches Andrew, who promptly heals Alcman and engages Stratocles in a further inversion of the Platonic love-discourse mimicked in *Leukippe and Kleitophon* (*Passio Andreae* 5–6). Andrew, 'no novice at midwifery' (μαιευτικῆς), draws out the embryonic 'new self' trapped inside Stratocles. Andrew recognizes that 'whatever [Stratocles'] former philosophy, he now knows that it was hollow' (*Passio Andreae* 7). Stratocles gives up all his possessions (an act he manages to repeat after his baptism: *Passio Andreae* 8, 12) and through Andrew's care his 'embryos' are 'brought into the open, so that they may be registered by the entirety of the kindred (συγγενῶν) and brought into the donative of saving words, whose associate (κοινωνόν) I found you to be' (*Passio Andreae* 9). Stratocles, like Maximilla, enters into his own 'proper kinship' with his fellow Christian believers, one of whom is his (presumably former) young lover Alcman (*Passio Andreae* 10).[89] Leukon and Rhode had moved 'upwards' into a marital relationship marked by gentility and munificence; Stratocles in contrast moves 'down' into a kinship marked by humility and subservience. One of Aegeates's servants reports to his master that 'even though [Stratocles] owns many slaves, he appears in public doing his own chores – buying his own vegetables and bread, and other necessities and carrying them on foot through the centre of the city – making himself look simply repulsive to everyone' (*Passio Andreae* 25). This Christianized family ethics is again inscribed as 'lower class' at the end of the *Acts of Andrew*; after Andrew has faced martyrdom, Maximilla separates herself from the proconsular household and spends 'her time happily with the brethren'. When Aegeates kills himself in dejection, Stratocles for a third time renounces wealth and station: 'Stratocles ... did not want so much as to

89 Konstan, 'Acts of Love', p. 20, uses this story to argue that the 'apostle does not destroy human bonds of affection, except insofar as they necessarily involve sex'. I find his argument persuasive, but would add that a particular nexus of sex and class represented by marriage is especially to be resisted by Christian fellowship.

touch the property Aegeates left – for the wretch died childless. He said, "May your possessions go with you, Aegeates! May Jesus be my friend!"' (*Passio Andreae* 64). The marital union has failed on all counts – not even children were produced – and this failure signals the breakdown of a markedly upper-class *oikonomia* of status and gender relations.

This eradication of an upper-class familial economy is articulated variously throughout the Apocryphal Acts of the Apostles, sometimes with more subtlety than the devastated family in Patras. In the *Acts of John* the apostle gathers a collection of formerly wealthy married couples into his wandering circle of believers. The text's first extant portion portrays the apostle arriving at Ephesus, where he is greeted by the forlorn general Lycomedes ('a wealthy man') whose wife has fallen ill. Both Lycomedes and John speak of the woman, Cleopatra, as a beloved wife and partner. Lycomedes cries out that if Cleopatra dies he will follow her, and John immediately promises that his 'partner for life' (τὴν αὑτοῦ σύμβιον) will be restored to him (*Acta Ioannis* 19–21). John raises Cleopatra, but not before Lycomedes himself falls down and seems dead. So the scene repeats itself, with Cleopatra threatening to die unless Lycomedes is raised. When both husband and wife are restored, they fall to John's feet and beg him and his 'companions' to stay with them in their house. John's disciples persuade him to transform the house of the married couple into the meeting-place of the Christians in Ephesus, 'so that they [Lycomedes and Cleopatra] remain unsullied (ἀσκανδάλιστοι) before the Lord' (*Acta Ioannis* 24–25; see also *Acta Ioannis* 26, 31). Here there is no need to defeat a male rival in order for a wife to become a continent Christian, and what had been a conjugal union based on affection and reciprocity is neatly subsumed into a larger Christian *sungeneia*. A duplicate story in the *Acts of John* (now lost) seems to have presented a rockier road to Christian kinship, but a similar ending: Drusiana, wife of a wealthy Ephesian named Andronicus, is persuaded by John to remove herself from her husband's bed. Later, other Ephesians recount the tale to the woman's lusty admirer: 'Do you alone not know that Andronicus, who was not the godly man he now is, had locked her up in a tomb, saying, "Either I'll have you as a wife, as I had you before, or you must die?"' (*Acta Ioannis* 63). The situation recalls that of Aegeates and Maximilla; at the point in the *Acts of John* that this story is recounted, however, Andronicus has been 'persuaded to become like-minded' (ἔπεισε τὰ ἴσα τοῦτον φρονῆσαι) (*Acta Ioannis* 63), travels chastely with his wife in John's apostolic entourage (*Acta Ioannis* 59, 105) and, like Lycomedes, offers his house as a meeting-place for John's followers (*Acta Ioannis* 46, 62). Once again, the chaste couple allow their well-off conjugal family to be swallowed up by the more common Christian kinship led by the apostle. Like Andrew, John is a 'father' to the brethren who set aside the things of this world to become his 'children' and his 'servants'; we are even treated to a catalogue of believers who move with John across Asia Minor: 'Andronicus and Drusiana, Lycomedes and Cleobius, and their attendants … Aristobula, who had heard that her husband Tertullus had died on the way, Aristippus with Xenophon, and the chaste prostitute (ἡ σώφρων πόρνη), and many others' (*Acta Ioannis* 59).[90] This

---

90 Some MSS read 'Cleobis' instead of 'Cleobius', perhaps signifying that the two couples, Andronicus and Drusiana, Lycomedes and Cleopatra, were once listed here.

motley crew of nobles, servants, repentant harlots and others are articulated primarily as members of an itinerant Christian 'family'.

Marriage, as in the Greek novels, could also be disrupted before the bride and groom had consummated their nuptial union. Such disruption occurs in the house of Thecla, still affianced to Thamyris when Paul breezes into town. For Thecla, breaking her bond with Thamyris and the validity of the conjugal union itself entails renunciation of wealth and station; at her first visit to Paul in prison, she hands over her bracelets and silver mirror to the jailers in order to gain entry (*Acta Pauli et Theclae* 18). By surrendering these precious items, Thecla symbolically surrenders her gendered social status as a 'cultivated' wife.[91] She who was once 'first' among the Iconians becomes a 'slave of God' (*Acta Pauli et Theclae* 26). Even more dramatic is the treatment of the apostle Peter's own daughter in a Coptic fragment of the *Acts of Peter*. A beautiful young girl, his daughter becomes a 'stumbling-block', and a 'very rich man, Ptolemy by name . . . sent for her to take her for his wife' (*Acta Petri* 132).[92] Although the text is fragmentary, it seems that Peter asked the Lord to paralyse the girl to make her less desirable; Ptolemy, on the brink of suicide (Aegeates's fate in the *Acts of Andrew*), is stopped by a vision and converted to following Christ. Upon his death, he leaves land to Peter's daughter which the apostle promptly sells to give 'the whole sum to the poor' (*Acta Petri* 135–39).[93] Wealth and marriage narrowly avoid colliding with the morally superior (i.e. poor) family of the apostle, here represented by a literal daughter.

The long and involved *Acts of Thomas*, probably composed in Syriac, was quickly translated into Greek and transmitted through the same channels as the other Apocryphal Acts.[94] The affinities of the Greek recension with the rising discourse of marital ethics in the Graeco–Roman world allow us to bring together the different scenarios of marital and familial disruption accomplished by an apostle. Thomas's first intervention occurs at the moment of marital consummation. Having recently been sold by a vision of Jesus (his twin brother) to an Indian merchant, Thomas finds himself attending the wedding of the only daughter of the king of Andrapolis (*Acta Thomae* 4). At the wedding reception he is taken by the king to pronounce a blessing on his daughter and her husband. His words sound innocent enough: 'I beseech you, Lord Jesus, offering you supplication for these young persons, that you may do to them what helps, benefits, and is profitable for them' (*Acta Thomae* 10). Immediately afterwards in the wedding chamber, however, a vision of Jesus 'in the appearance of Judas Thomas' reveals these 'benefits':

---

91 On the class- and gender-specific significations of bracelets and mirrors, see Maria Wyke, 'Woman in the Mirror: The Rhetoric of Adornment in the Roman World', in Léonie J. Archer, Susan Fichler and Maria Wyke (eds.), *Women in Ancient Societies: An Illusion of the Night* (New York: Routledge, 1994), pp. 134–51.

92 Text in D.M. Parrott (ed.), *Nag Hammadi Codices V, 2–5 and VI with Papyrus Berolinensis 8502, 1 and 4* (NHS 11; Leiden: E.J. Brill, 1979), pp. 473–93; translation in Elliott, *Apocryphal New Testament*, pp. 397–98.

93 For a study of the role of wealth and class in the rest of the *Acts of Peter*, see Perkins, *Suffering Self*, pp. 124–41.

94 On the textual history of the *Acts of Thomas*, see A.F.J. Klijn, *The Acts of Thomas: Introduction, Text, Commentary* (Leiden: E.J. Brill, 1962), pp. 1–17 and pp. 18–26 on the parallels and possible literary connections between the *Acts of Thomas* and the other early Apocryphal Acts.

Know that if you refrain from this filthy intercourse (τῆς ῥυπαρᾶς κοινωνίας ταύτης) you will become temples holy and pure, being released from afflictions and troubles ... If you beget many children, for their sakes you will become grasping and avaricious, plundering orphans and deceiving widows ... But if you obey and preserve your souls pure to God, there will be born to you living children, untouched by these hurtful things, and you will be without care, spending an untroubled life, free from grief and care, looking forward to receive that incorruptible and true marriage, and you will enter as groomsmen into that bridal chamber full of immortality and light. (*Acta Thomae* 12)

The 'benefits' of marriage, companionship and procreation, are spiritualized and their corruptible elements eliminated. The next morning the unveiled bride announces proudly to her father the king, 'And that I have set at naught this husband and these nuptials (τοὺς γάμους τούτους) which have passed away before my eyes is because I have been joined in a different marriage (ἑτέρῳ γάμῳ) ... I have been united to the true husband' (*Acta Thomae* 14). The bride passes through the rhetoric of conjugal union into a spiritualized 'union', inverting the ethical superiority of upper-class marriage from within its own terms. Thomas sails away with his master to India, but we are told that a Hebrew slave who had served at the wedding 'rejoiced greatly' upon hearing that the couple had chosen to remain continent: 'And she arose and went to them, and was with them a long time, until they had instructed (κατήχησαν) the king also. And many of the brethren also met there, until the rumour had spread that the apostle had gone to the cities of India and was teaching there. And they went away and joined him' (*Acta Thomae* 16). Although Thomas's intervention was brief (in fact the apostle's role in this conversion is unclear) the scenario is by now a familiar one: a couple turns away from an upper-class marital union upon learning its moral deficiencies, and instead enters into a spiritualized marriage in turn subordinated to their new 'kinship', in which their 'brethren' could as easily be slaves as kings.

In India Thomas performs a series of miracles instigated by the disastrous consequences of love, marriage and status: he heals a woman whose renunciation of sex was abrogated by a demon who chose to live with her 'as man and wife' (*Acta Thomae* 42–49);[95] he cures the withered hands of a man who had slain his lover when she refused to live with him 'in chaste and pure conduct', and then raises the woman herself from hell (*Acta Thomae* 51–59); and he casts out the demons from an Indian captain's wife and daughter, who had been possessed since their unwilling attendance at a wedding (*Acta Thomae* 62–81).[96] These incidents slowly chip at the moral edifice of marriage. Finally the *Acts of Thomas* strikes at the upper-class core when Thomas is heard preaching by Mygdonia, 'wife of Charisius the near relative of the king' (*Acta Thomae* 82; an epithet repeated throughout the text: *Acta Thomae* 87,

---

95 The demon's proposal is quite sentimental: ἐγώ τε καὶ σὺ ἐν μιᾷ ἀγάπῃ ἐσόμεθα, καὶ κοινωνήσωμεν ἀλλήλοις ὡς ἀνὴρ γυναικὶ συμμείγνυται (*Acta Thomae* 43). There might be a possible allusion to Sarah and the demon Asmodeus in the Book of Tobit, with Thomas subverting the role of Tobias.

96 The captain, Siphor, later offers his home to Thomas as a meeting-place, like Lycomedes and Andronicus in the *Acts of John* (*Acta Thomae* 131). The setting of a wedding (γάμον) is more precise than the ambiguous term 'banquet' (*mashtotah*) used in the Syriac (William Wright [ed.], *Apocryphal Acts of the Apostles*, vol. I: *The Syriac Texts* [Amsterdam: Philo Press, 1968], pp. 172–333 [232]; see Klijn, *Acts of Thomas*, p. 255).

89, 93, 95, 102, 134, 135). Like a disease, Thomas's disastrous message of sexual and marital renunciation spreads through the royal family: Mygdonia converts, followed by Tertia, the king's wife, and Vazan and Mnesara, the king's son and daughter-in-law. Like Thecla, Mygdonia finds that renunciation of her married state entails surrendering her wealth and status. Thomas tells her that 'neither the fame of the authority which surrounds you nor the power of this world nor the filthy intercourse (ἡ κοινωνία ἡ ῥυπαρά) of your husband will be of use to you if you are deprived of the true intercourse' (*Acta Thomae* 88). She gives up her finery and wallows on the ground in sackcloth and ashes; her husband Charisius laments 'the madness of the stranger, whose tyranny throws the great and illustrious into the abyss ... her noble soul has been humbled' (*Acta Thomae* 135, 99). Charisius pleads with her time and again, as Aegeates pleaded with Maximilla, to restore not just their marriage bed but their sacred bond: 'You are my riches and honour, you are my family and kindred' (πλοῦτος δέ μοι καὶ τιμὴ εἶ ... γένος δὲ μοι καὶ συγγένεια σὺ εἶ) (*Acta Thomae* 116). Charisius cannot convince his wife, nor later the king his queen, that the noble marriage bond which they believed would be ethically edifying and fulfilling is anything but a pale shadow of the superior kinship found in Christianity.

When the fledgling Christian community gathers on the eve of Thomas's martyrdom, his prayer reconfigures them as a family of harassed, impoverished wanderers, huddling for life and security around the bright light of Christ: 'Companion and associate,' he prays, 'hope of the weak and trust of the poor, refuge and shelter of the weary, voice which came forth from on high, comforter who dwells among us, shelter and haven of those who travel through dark countries ... be with Vazan, Misdaeus's son, and Tertia and Mnesara, and gather them into your fold and unite them with your number' (*Acta Thomae* 156). One might never suspect from such a baptismal prayer that the baptizands being prayed for are of the Indian royal family. The familial configuration which might have marked their noble status, the conjugal union, has been beaten back, and with it disappear notions of worldly hierarchy and class: the mere captain becomes a priest at the end, and the king's son his deacon (*Acta Thomae* 169). Eventually even King Misdaeus of India, after years of resistance, is transformed into merely one of 'the multitude of those who had believed in Christ' (*Acta Thomae* 170).

Conclusions: The Broken Family Circle

The narrative through which the Apocryphal Acts paint their family portraits resembles a twisted, abstracted representation of the romantic ideal of the jurists, philosophers and novelists; they transform the naturalized intersections of gender 'partnership' and elite ethical advancement promulgated in the early Empire. In a doubled gesture of appropriation and renunciation, the Apocryphal Acts enter into and deconstruct the upper-class notion of symbiotic partnership trickling down through society, and replace it with a distinctly un-classed notion of 'kinship', *sungeneia*, through which an entirely different sense of relation and difference might be offered forth. Throughout these Acts women emerge as the focus of marital breakdown: Thecla, Maximilla, Drusiana, Mygdonia, all symbolize the destructive force of the apostles' anti-marriage message. By stepping back to consider how and why women emerge as the heroes of both narratives, that of upper-class *koinōnia* and un-classed *sungeneia*, we can begin to understand the potential impact of this clash of 'family values' among early Christian women.

We might begin, as did a previous generation of social historians, by enquiring after the social location of these narratives. The particularly upper-class notion of ethics put forward in the literature of the first and second centuries takes the strongest blow in the Apocryphal Acts. The well-born heroes and heroines are precisely the figures who must discover the moral and ethical failure of the marital ideal laid before them: Thecla would not have the same impact in the *Acts of Paul* were she not one of 'the first of Iconium'. The king of Andrapolis must be catechized by his (former?) slave-girl, and a new kinship patterned on social renunciation must transform the bedroom into a new and better 'ethical schoolhouse'. Christian auditors and readers learning to internalize this disavowal of society must first, then, learn the lessons of society's failure: the new, high-status ethics of the conjugal union must fail before the better ethics of Christian kinship can succeed.

Yet it would be simplistic and fallacious to assume that a truly gritty lower class produced these texts that celebrate the failure of a dangerously romanticized upper-class family ethics. When analysing early Christian discourse, we must never lose sight of its conscious reliance on rhetoric and representation.[97] Instead we would do well to place these rich narratives in the same stream of Christian rhetoric that permitted the educated author of the third Gospel to celebrate the blessedness of the poor (Lk. 6.20), and the astonishingly well-read third-century exegete Origen happily to accept Celsus's criticism that Christians are 'the most illiterate and bucolic yokels', and turn it to his advantage (Origen, *Contra Celsum* 3.55–60).[98] Judith Perkins has suggested that in the first centuries of Christianity a subjectivity constructed around suffering was deployed to empower Christian communities.[99] Narratives of pain and subjugation do not necessarily tell the historical story of martyrdom and 'real' suffering, but rather construct a resistant and subversive identity. So, too, in the Apocryphal Acts of the Apostles, the family as locus of ethical progression is bifurcated into a failed upper-class family, represented by the increasingly popularized ideal of the conjugal union, and a more successful ethical mode of Christian 'kinship', *sungeneia*: instituted by the homewrecking apostle, embodied by the intransigent wife, and bringing down the swashbuckling heroine of romance into a 'simply revolting' brotherhood of slaves, kings and women. What becomes potentially empowering for a Christian seeking detachment from social norms is not the *reality* of poverty, but the rejection of class as a marker of ethical superiority.

How, then, do we characterize the heroines of the Apocryphal Acts, those renunciatory women – wives, or wives-to-be – who give up both wealth and conjugal

---

97 See the useful remarks of Cameron, *Christianity and Rhetoric*, pp. 36–39.

98 Text in *Origène: Contre Celse* (*Sources chrétiennes* 136; trans. M. Borret; Paris: Éditions du Cerf, 1968); translated in Henry Chadwick, *Origen: Contra Celsum* (Cambridge, UK: Cambridge University Press, 1965), p. 165. See Cameron, *Christianity and Rhetoric*, p. 111: 'The Pauline claim to truth – in contrast to the "wisdom of the world" – could be turned to good effect, converting charges of uncouth lack of refinement into claims of simplicity and truth'. See also Dale Martin, *Slavery as Salvation: The Metaphor of Slavery in Pauline Christianity* (New Haven, CT: Yale University Press, 1990), pp. 147–49.

99 Perkins, *Suffering Self*, pp. 12 and 104–23.

symbiosis in order to embrace their 'own proper kinship'? Although they reject the ostensibly symmetrical husband–wife relation promulgated by philosophers and *littérateurs*, we do not see them returning to a state of paternal surrender, submitting silently to apostolic fathers in lieu of living as partners with aristocratic husbands. To come back to the most famous tale, that of Thecla: her story originally ended with her taking her leave of Paul, as she had earlier left Thamyris, and marching back to Iconium as apostle and preacher in her own right.[100] Even if Thecla's 'liberated' behaviour seems extreme (baptizing herself, dressing as a man), we can still observe the relative novelty of female autonomy (of sorts) in the other Apocryphal Acts by noting that, by the end of all the Acts, the apostolic 'homewrecker' is dead while the converted wives and fiancées live on. Detached from paternal *potestas*, freed from conjugal *symbiosis*, the heroine of the Apocryphal Acts is neither/nor: a fitting symbol of the social deconstruction preached by this form of Christianity. She is not the poor woman preaching poverty, nor is she the single woman preaching celibacy: she is the rich woman who moves outside the rigid class structures of the ancient world; she is the married (or marriageable) woman who transcends the ethics of conjugal union.

In considering the most plausible locus for the profitable consumption of these texts and these heroines, we must then move beyond the facile binaries of 'rich/ poor' and 'man/woman'. The very nature of these categories (class and gender) and the relationship between them is precisely what is problematized by these literary constructions of social and religious ethics and 'family values'. We are not dealing with the simple opposition of 'self' and 'other', but rather the subversion of the 'other' (or the self?) from within: the rich woman, destined for *symbiosis* and conjugal partnership, becomes the emblem of the classless and the unmarried, a source of (potential) empowerment because of her rejection of these twin sources of power: wealth and ethical 'partnership'. This subversion from within perhaps delineates the real power of the narrative of renunciation. If we can sense any space within which women find empowerment through renunciation, it is strangely refracted through the lens of marital *concordia* and the new economy of family ethics through which a woman (as 'wife') can potentially find moral advancement equal to her husband's. The heroine of the Apocryphal Acts moves through this possibility of *symbiosis* and *concordia*, and emerges on the other side now equipped for a radical discipleship.

In the centuries following the circulation of these narratively subversive texts, they came to life in rather public and literal fashion. In the fourth century, generations of wealthy and noble-born 'Theclas', such as Macrina, the sister of Basil the Great, and the famed ascetic grandmother and granddaughter both named Melania, sought to live out these 'strange stories'.[101] From within the structures of an upper-class family, organized around the idealized intertwining of male and female souls, that 'lifelong partnership', these women enacted lives of monetary

---

100 See Ng, *'Acts of Paul'*, pp. 4–8 on ways to read the relationship between Thecla and Paul throughout the story.

101 Gillian Cloke, *This Female Man of God: Women and Spiritual Power in the Patristic Age, AD 350–450* (London: Routledge, 1995), pp. 165–66, who also helpfully points out the continuity of class issues between Thecla and these fourth-century 'Theclae'.

and sexual renunciation. Empowered by the possibilities generated by wealth and station, these women embraced poverty and familial rejection. There is, perhaps, a certain predictable irony that the celebration of non-elite ethics should be so readily available to the elites themselves: spectacular renunciation only becomes spectacle when the ascetic has so much to give up.[102] Rich women became living symbols of holy poverty, and the female scions of famous households became emblems of familial renunciation. Through subversion and inversion they claimed a particular female agency outside the norms of family, or class, or society; they embraced an ethics of renunciation of class and marriage, and became the saintly homewreckers of Christian memory.

102 The ability of a woman like Melania the Younger or Jerome's companion Paula to embrace 'poverty' so ostentatiously is made possible by their incredible wealth: it takes Melania the Younger, for instance, most of her life to manage to give away her vast riches. See Elizabeth A. Clark, 'Piety, Propaganda, and Politics in the *Life of Melania the Younger*' and 'Authority and Humility: A Conflict of Values in Fourth-Century Female Monasticism' both in *eadem*, *Ascetic Piety and Women's Faith: Essays on Late Ancient Christianity* (Studies in Women and Religion, 20; Lewiston/Queenston: The Edwin Mellen Press, 1986), pp. 61–94 and 209–28.

THE EROTIC ASCETICISM OF THE *PASSION OF ANDREW*:
THE APOCRYPHAL *ACTS OF ANDREW*, THE GREEK NOVEL AND
PLATONIC PHILOSOPHY*

CAROLINE T. SCHROEDER

There has been a wave of recent scholarship on the social repercussions of desire in the Greek novels.[1] Classicists and historians alike have argued that in the romances of the first through third centuries, sexual desire is most successfully consummated in heterosexual relationships either within or leading to matrimony. True love itself can be found only within the confines of proper, upper-class marriage, which in turn is required to ensure the equilibrium of the larger community: the *concordia* of the romantic couple parallels the *concordia* of the state.[2]

With marriage comes the production of children, the maintenance of lines of inheritance within a certain social class, and the prosperity of the lovers' communities. Through marriage, Longus's Daphnis and Chloe are restored to their proper heritage and the state is restored to its proper leaders. Through marriage Chariton's Chaereas and Callirhoe reconcile the two leading families of their city-state. As Kate Cooper has argued, the 'ancient romance was designed to mobilize this complicity in desire on behalf of the social order ... The love that aspired to marriage involved the temporary disruption of the social order which led to its reassertion; other forms of love might put the individual's interests against the common good.'[3]

The type of love that dominates the novels and drives desire is *eros*. *Eros* brings the couple together, maintains their fidelity through adventure and tragedy, and expresses itself through the marriage and passionate lovemaking of the couple. The deity *Eros* himself begins most of the novels, either by sparking the relationship or by

---

* An earlier version of this essay appeared as 'Embracing the Erotic in the *Passion of Andrew*: the Apocryphal *Acts of Andrew*, the Greek Novel, and Platonic Philosophy', in Jan N. Bremmer (ed.), *The Apocryphal Acts of Andrew* (Leuven: Peeters, 2000), pp. 110–26. I thank Jan Bremmer and Peeters Press for permission to revise and republish the piece.

1 David Konstan, *Sexual Symmetry: Love in the Ancient Novel and Related Genres* (Princeton, NJ: Princeton University Press, 1994); Jack Winkler, 'The Invention of Romance', in James Tatum (ed.), *The Search for the Ancient Novel* (Baltimore, MD and London: The Johns Hopkins University Press, 1994), pp. 23–38; Kate Cooper, *The Virgin and the Bride: Idealized Womanhood in Late Antiquity* (Cambridge, MA: Harvard University Press, 1996), pp. 20–44; Judith Perkins, *The Suffering Self: Pain and Narrative Representation in the Early Christian Era* (London and New York: Routledge, 1995), pp. 41–76. I rely primarily on the five major Greek novels believed to have been written during the first three centuries CE: Achilles Tatius, *Leucippe and Cleitophon*; Chariton, *Chaereas and Callirhoe*; Longus, *Daphnis and Chloe*; Xenophon of Ephesus, *An Ephesian Tale*; and Heliodorus, *An Ethiopian Story*. English translations of these and additional novels may be found in B.P. Reardon (ed.), *Collected Ancient Greek Novels* (Berkeley: University of California Press, 1989). All English translations cited here are taken from Reardon's volume.

2 Perkins, *Suffering Self*, pp. 48–49.

3 Cooper, *Virgin and the Bride*, pp. 21, 35.

acting as the patron god who stands as a symbol for the story as a whole. In *Chaereas and Callirhoe* Eros decides to find the heroine a match (1.1). In the *Ephesian Tale*, the young Habrocomes's initial refusal to recognize Eros as a god prompts Eros to cause him to fall in love with the young Anthia (1.1–2). The narrator of *Leucippe and Cleitophon* begins with an *ekphrasis* of a mural in Sidon, focusing on the image of Eros (I.1–2). Longus, also remarking on a painting depicting love, dedicates his book 'as an offering to Love (ἔρως), the Nymphs, and Pan' (Prologue).

Historians of early Christianity have directed their analyses of the novel towards comparisons with the Apocryphal Acts. The parallels between the two groups of literature are generally acknowledged: the hero and heroine's mutual desire and fidelity, their subsequent separation from each other, frequent travel narratives, the heroine's high social status, and the eventual reunion of hero and heroine.[4] Although employing the same plot devices as the novels, the Apocryphal Acts centre on an apostle and his convert(s) rather than on a young romantic couple. Cooper and Perkins both argue that the Apocryphal Acts use elements of the Greek novels to subvert that genre's central goal of social stability: '[W]e move from a celebration of sexuality in the service of social continuity to a denigration of sexuality in the service of a challenge to the establishment.'[5] Instead of advocating marriage, the Apocryphal Acts use the relationship between apostle and convert to champion sexual abstinence. Perkins suggests that this promotion of chastity disrupted traditional marriage and implicitly challenged the social structure for which, according to the novels, marriage was the foundation.[6] Cooper regards the specific practice of sexual abstinence as subordinate to this larger, counter-social narrative.[7]

While such analysis has reanimated the study of the Greek novels and the Apocryphal Acts, it tends to neglect the Acts' erotic elements, and in particular the final segment of the *Acts of Andrew* known as the *Passion of Andrew*.[8] For in this

---

4 The most succinct and comprehensive comparison of the novel and Apocryphal Acts can be found in Jean-Daniel Kaestli's response to Virginia Burrus ('Response' to Burrus, *Semeia* 38 [1986], pp. 119–31). Cooper and Perkins also find shared elements in these two literary forms. See Cooper, *Virgin and the Bride*, pp. 45–46, and Perkins, *Suffering Self*, pp. 25–26. One of the earliest arguments for this connection is Rosa Söder, *Die apokryphen Apostelgeschichten und die romanhafte Literatur der Antike* (Stuttgart: Kohlhammer, 1932).

5 Cooper, *Virgin and the Bride*, p. 55.

6 Perkins, *Suffering Self*, pp. 28–29.

7 Cooper, *Virgin and the Bride*, p. 57.

8 The text now called the *Passion of Andrew* circulated independently from other narratives about Andrew and contains an account of the apostle's martyrdom. Much ink has been spilled over the relationship among the *Passion of Andrew*, a presumably longer set of the *Acts of Andrew* which may have included the *Passion of Andrew*, the *Acts of Andrew and Matthias*, and Gregory's epitome of the *Acts of Andrew*. Jean-Marc Prieur has argued that the *Acts of Andrew* and the *Acts of Andrew and Matthias* come from two separate textual traditions, whereas Dennis Ronald MacDonald has argued that the *Acts of Andrew and Matthias* originally formed a part of the text of the *Acts of Andrew*. Additionally, the theory that a lengthy *Acts of Andrew* included the martyrdom account in the *Passion of Andrew* is based solely on the existence of fragments of stories about Andrew that circulated with all or part of the martyrdom account and the existence of Gregory's epitome, which describes a larger *Acts of Andrew* text. No one text incorporating all of these diverse acts of Andrew survives. Since the *Passion of Andrew* circulated separately and is the most widely attested Andrew tradition, I treat it as a somewhat distinct textual unit regardless of its lost origins. For descriptions of the manuscript and textual traditions, see Jean-Marc Prieur and Wilhelm Schneemelcher, 'The Acts

Passion, as in the novels, only the proper expression of love produces positive results. While the *Acts of Andrew* may be characterized as a 'denigration of sexuality', one must be careful not to confuse that with a denigration of love or *eros*.[9] In the *Passion of Andrew,* the *eros* of the novels becomes the Platonic *eros* – the love of beauty, the one, the divine. Eroticism is embraced as an important aspect of Christian identity.

On the surface, the *Passion of Andrew* tells the tale of the necessary renunciation of all things erotic and sexual, especially for Christian female converts. It recounts the apostle Andrew's arrival into the town of Patras, his performance of several miracles, and his conversions of the elite characters Stratocles and Maximilla to an ascetic Christianity. Maximilla's close relationship with Andrew and her new adherence to sexual renunciation enrage her prominent pagan husband, Aegeates, who has Andrew killed and then kills himself. Whereas the novels always end with the lovers' union and the fulfilment of their desire, in the *Passion of Andrew*, the consummation of erotic desire appears permanently deferred. None of the couples – Aegeates and Maximilla, Andrew and Maximilla, and Andrew and Stratocles – achieves sexual union; instead, the text ends with deaths and conversion to asceticism.

Although sex is condemned in the *Acts of Andrew*, love certainly is not.[10] In fact, love, its objects, its expression, and its culmination are central elements. The definition of proper love and the goals of such love, however, diverge greatly from the novels. Neither Maximilla nor Stratocles engages in physical intercourse with a beloved, but their sojourn with Andrew does not end with tragic separation. It closes

---

of Andrew', in W. Schneemelcher (ed.), *New Testament Apocrypha* (2 vols.; trans. R. McL. Wilson; Cambridge, UK: James Clarke & Co., 1992), 2, pp.101–118 (104–110); *idem* (ed. and trans.), *Acta Andreae* (2 vols., CCSA 5–6; Turnhout: Brepols, 1989); Dennis R. MacDonald, *The Acts of Andrew and the Acts of Andrew and Matthias in the City of the Cannibals* (Texts and Translations 33; Christian Apocrypha 1; Atlanta: Scholars Press, 1990), pp. 1–51; A. Hilhorst and P.J. Lalleman, 'The *Acts of Andrew and Matthias*: Is It Part of the Original *Acts of Andrew*?', in Bremmer (ed.), *Acts of Andrew*, pp. 1–14; Laura S. Nasrallah, '"She Became What the Words Signified": The Greek *Acts of Andrew's* Construction of the Reader-Disciple', in François Bovon *et al.* (eds.), *The Apocryphal Acts of the Apostles: Harvard Divinity School Studies* (Cambridge, MA: Harvard University Press, 1999), pp. 233–58. Furthermore, the *Passion of Andrew* is the most widely attested of the apocryphal legends surrounding Andrew. Most of the Greek witnesses to the *Acts of Andrew* include a portion or a complete version of the martyrdom account, the Latin texts attest to the martyrdom story, and an Armenian account of the last part of the *Passion of Andrew* exists as well. See Prieur and Schneemelcher, pp. 104–106 and James K. Elliott, *The Apocryphal New Testament: A Collection of Apocryphal Christian Literature in an English Translation* (Oxford: Clarendon Press, 1993), pp. 232–34. Unfortunately, its date and provenance are in dispute. Both Prieur and MacDonald argue that the *Acts of Andrew* was written between 150 and 200, but the possibilities for its location of origin range from Greece to Syria to Egypt to Asia Minor. See MacDonald, *The Acts of Andrew*, pp. 55–59; Prieur and Schneemelcher, pp. 114–15; now also Bremmer, 'Man, Magic, and Martyrdom in the *Acts of Andrew*', in *idem* (ed.), *Acts of Andrew*, pp. 15–34. On eroticism in Gregory's epitome, see T. Adamik, 'Eroticism in the *Liber de miraculis beati Andrea apostoli* of Gregory of Tours', in Bremmer (ed.), *Acts of Andrew*, pp. 35–46.

9 Cooper, *Virgin and the Bride*, p. 55.

10 David Konstan, also taking to task scholars who have argued that the Apocryphal Acts uniformly critique the institutions of marriage and family, notes that the apostles frequently perform miracles that function to unite family members and loved ones rather than separate them. (David Konstan, 'Acts of Love: A Narrative Pattern in the Apocryphal Acts', *JECS* 6 [1998], pp. 15–36.) Of the *Acts of Andrew*, Konstan writes, 'The apostle does not destroy human bonds of affection, except insofar as they necessarily involve sex' (p. 20).

instead with joyous consummate union of the soul with the divine. The erotic love of the novels is consummated in sexual passion, marriage and procreation. Love in the *Passion of Andrew* does culminate in the heroine's union with her beloved, but the beloved is the figure of the divine, to whom both Maximilla and Stratocles are introduced by their teacher Andrew and with whom they give birth to their new, perfected selves. Andrew is the erotic stand-in for the divine lover. The results of true love and properly oriented desire in the *Passion of Andrew* are Platonic objectives: an understanding of the inner self, a unification with the divine, and a lasting sense of peace and rest.

Maximilla and Stratocles relationships with Andrew are described with language and metaphors reminiscent of the *eros* presented in the Greek novels. Although the *Passion of Andrew* rarely uses ἔρως, preferring terms such as στοργή or ἀγάπη, the context of the relationships parallels the novels' 'erotic' element. In the *Passion of Andrew*, true love becomes the Platonic *eros*, the love of beauty, the one, the divine. Both Stratocles, a man, and Maximilla, a married woman, share erotic relationships with the apostle.

Early in the text, Stratocles encounters Andrew when the apostle heals his servant (*Passion* 4–5).[11] Andrew then tells Stratocles that he will assist him in giving birth to his 'new self'. Of particular interest is Stratocles response to Andrew's gestures. In an oath similar to the oaths of fidelity the novels' lovers swear to one another, Stratocles declares, 'I too will not separate from you', but then adds the philosophical condition, 'until I recognize myself' (*Passion* 8). Stratocles vows to remain with Andrew until Andrew's promise can be fulfilled. Then the story recounts: 'Stratocles was with the apostle night and day and never left him, sometimes examining, learning from, and interrupting him, and other times remaining silent and enjoying himself, having truly become enamoured (φίλος) of saving attentiveness' (*Passion* 8). Stratocles, thus, cultivates a certain affection in Andrew's presence. Although this emotion is not the *eros* of the novel, it is a fondness that strongly parallels the passions of the lovers: Stratocles immediately feels this attachment for Andrew, avows his faithfulness to him, and spends all his time with him. Near the end of the *Passion of Andrew*, Andrew declares his love to Stratocles: 'I have the one I sought. I have found the one I desired (ἐπόθουν). I hold the one I loved (ἠγάπων)' (*Passion* 43). Stratocles responds by naming Andrew his true love (*Passion* 44). Yet Andrew and Stratocles intercourse is not passionate lovemaking but a Socratic dialogue: questioning, examining, learning. They discuss the passion of the soul.

Maximilla, too, experiences an erotic relationship with Andrew, as the other characters in the *Passion of Andrew* testify. They, however, mistake the relationship for a sexually erotic one. Maximilla's servants, aware of her and Stratocles secret nightly visits to Andrew, threaten to tell her husband, presumably because they believe she is having a sexual relationship with the apostle (*Passion* 21). When Aegeates learns of Maximilla's association with Andrew, he asks her if she is having an affair. He extols her chastity and promises forgiveness if she has 'tarnished' it: 'So if you are keeping some secret from me about another man – something I never would have suspected … [O]r if there is something else even more serious than this that separates

11 The edition used throughout can be found in MacDonald, *Acts of Andrew*. All quotations are from MacDonald's English translation, as well.

you from me, confess it and I will quickly remedy the situation...' (*Passion* 23). Maximilla responds that she is in love with another, but that he could not understand such a love: 'I am in love (φιλῶ), Aegeates. I am in love, and the object of my love is not of this world and therefore is imperceptible to you. Night and day it kindles (ἐξάπτει) and enflames (φλέγει) me with love (τῇ στοργῇ) for it' (*Passion* 23). Maximilla confirms Aegeates's fears that she loves another, but she corrects him by telling him that the *eros* of the novels is not the kind of love about which he must worry. Nonetheless, Aegeates remains enraged after his servant reports, 'My mistress ... became acquainted with this stranger. She has so given way to desire for him (τῷ αὐτοῦ πόθῳ) that she loves (στέργειν) no one more than him, including you I would say. Not only has she become intimately involved (συεκράθη) with the man, she has tied up your brother Stratocles with the same passion (τῷ αὐτῷ πόθῳ) for him that has tied her up' (*Passion* 25). As Cooper recognizes, Aegeates and Andrew seem to be in competition against each other for Maximilla's affection, a subject to which I will return.[12] What also requires further consideration is the confluence of Aegeates's explicitly sexual accusations with Maximilla's distinctly philosophic discourse; *her* love is 'not of this world'. Maximilla is playing a doubly charged game of love. That her dalliance with Andrew has been interpreted as sexual by her husband and others in her community is no accident. Though she has reoriented her sexual love into a philosophical one, the erotic overtones of her relationship with the apostle are clear.

Ironically, however, Maximilla's association with Andrew results not in physical intercourse with the apostle but in the cessation of physical intercourse with Aegeates. After baptism, Maximilla prays to be kept from his 'filthy intercourse' (*Passion* 14). Andrew, too, prays for the preservation of Maximilla's purity: 'In particular, protect her, O Master, from this disgusting pollution. With respect to our savage and ever boorish enemy, cause her to sleep apart from her visible husband and wed her to her inner husband (τῷ ἔσω ἀνδρί), whom you above all recognize, and for whose sake the entire mystery of your plan of salvation has been accomplished' (*Passion* 16). Andrew uses the very language of marriage, mimicking the discourse of the novels but at the same time undermining it, to describe Maximilla's new state: she will no longer be married to Aegeates but to another, non-earthly personage. Maximilla's true love is not a human person, but an inner husband. As with a corporeal husband, Maximilla wishes to unite with it: '[Y]ou cannot separate me from it, for that is impossible. Let me have intercourse (προσομιλεῖν) and take my rest with it alone,' she states (*Passion* 23). Maximilla's sexuality is not stifled but rechannelled into an explicitly erotic relationship with the divine.

Andrew serves as the human representative for the divine object of Maximilla's affection, but her husband, mistakenly, assumes that they have become sexual lovers. Eventually confronting Andrew, Aegeates demands, 'Teach me too about your renown and what sort of power you have, such that you have lovers (ἐραστάς), so I hear, who are rich and poor, including infants, even though you appear in this manner like a simple old tramp' (*Passion* 26). Here the connection between Andrew and *eros* is most explicit: Aegeates can understand Andrew's relationships with his converts only as sexually erotic. He appears doubly offended that a man of obviously lower

12 Cooper, *Virgin and the Bride*, pp. 48–49.

social and economic status than he – a man who appears as a 'simple old tramp' – has cuckolded him. He misunderstands the erotic element as sexual; he fails to see that it is philosophic – the Platonic *eros* or love of the divine.

While the interactions between the *Passion*'s main characters resemble those in the novels, they also resemble Platonic writings. Two distinct Platonic dialogues frame the entire narrative. The first dialogue – like most of the scenes involving Andrew, Maximilla and Stratocles in the first third of the *Passion* – takes place in Maximilla's bedroom. In the beginnings of the novels heroines' bedrooms are frequently sites of the consummation, or attempted consummation, of the lovers' desire for each other. Maximilla's bedroom, however, shifts from a site of sexual intercourse to one of philosophic discourse through which Maximilla and Stratocles are not only converted to Christianity but also somehow transformed. At the beginning of the *Passion of Andrew*, Maximilla emerges from her bedroom to greet Stratocles. They enter her bedroom together and remain there for some portion of the evening.[13] When Andrew heals Stratocles' servant, Maximilla leaves her bedroom (*Passion* 2–5). Then she leads her brother, the apostle and their companions back into her bedroom (*Passion* 6), where Andrew begins the first of several dialogues that have been compared to Socrates' philosophic dialogues.[14] Andrew, a Christianized Socrates,[15] tells Stratocles,

> I must bring out into the open the person now latent within you. Your total bewilderment and pondering of the source and cause of what has happened are the greatest proofs that the soul within you is troubled ... Bring to birth the child you are carrying and do not give yourself over to labour pains alone. I am no novice at midwifery or divination. I desire what you are birthing. I love what you are stifling. I will suckle what is within you ... Already your new self speaks to me. (*Passion* 7)

Andrew uses the language of birth to describe the transformative process Stratocles will undergo as a result of his conversion. As Dennis MacDonald has noted, the model for this dialogue seems to be Socrates's speech in Plato's *Theaetetus*. Socrates refers to himself as the son of a midwife, as well, and compares his work in eliciting the birth of the self to a midwife's work eliciting the birth of a child. Later, Andrew compares Stratocles constant questioning of him to labour pains and exhorts him to exhibit them publicly as if giving birth among attending women:

> It is not right for you to conceal your labour pains even from your peers. Take the example of a woman in labour: When the labour pains overcome her and the fetus is pressured by some power to come forth – not to stay within but to be squeezed outside – the fetus becomes obvious and noticeable to the attending women who take part in such mysteries ... Then, postpartum, these initiates at last provide for the newborn whatever care they know,

13 Immediately after reporting that Maximilla 'entered with him' into her bedroom the text reads that Maximilla was alone 'at daybreak' while Stratocles visited his friends (*Passion* 1).

14 Kenneth C. Wagener, '"Repentant Eve, Perfected Adam": Conversion in *The Acts of Andrew*', in Eugene H. Lovering, Jr. (ed.), *Society of Biblical Literature 1991 Seminar Papers* (SBLSP 30; Atlanta: Scholars Press, 1991), pp. 348–56 (352–53); MacDonald, *Christianizing Homer: The Odyssey, Plato and* The Acts of Andrew (New York: Oxford University Press, 1994), p. 252. See also MacDonald's article in this volume.

15 MacDonald, *Christianizing Homer*, pp. 218–20.

so that, insofar as it is up to them, the fetus might be born alive. Likewise, Stratocles my child, we too must not be passive but bring your embryos into the open, so that they may be registered and be brought to the donative of saving words by many kindred … (*Passion* 9)

Just as the recognition of children signifies the stability of family and society in the novel, so does the recognition of Stratocles new self signify salvific effects for him and his companions.[16]

The birthing imagery resonates with both Platonic philosophy and the Greek novels. The dialogue is presented in Maximilla's bedroom, or *koiton*,[17] the same physical space as the sexual act that results in physical birth. The product of Andrew's relationship with Stratocles parallels one of the primary products of true love in the novels: offspring. Before the apostle's martyrdom, Stratocles reveals that it is Andrew who has inseminated him: 'But after this, where and in whom will I seek and find your concern and love? I received the seeds of the words of salvation while you were my sower; for them to shoot up and reproduce requires no one else but you, blessed Andrew' (*Passion* 44). Andrew has impregnated Stratocles, and soon Stratocles will give birth to the true self. Despite the obvious sexual overtones in all these scenes, neither desire nor its effects are of the physical realm. The *Passion of Andrew* reorients love and desire to the Platonic goals of self-knowledge, union with the divine, and the creation of the new self, away from the novels' goals of marriage, children and social stability.

Maximilla's bedroom also becomes the location of spiritual transformation in explicit contrast with Aegeates's view of the bedroom as the location of marital sexual intercourse. Aegeates returns home before Andrew and his companions have left Maximilla's bedroom. Recognizing the impropriety of the situation, Andrew miraculously covers everyone with a shield of invisibility while they exit (*Passion* 13). It is in Maximilla's bedroom that Aegeates approaches Maximilla for sex and is rebuffed (*Passion* 14); it is there that Aegeates threatens to torture Andrew unless Maximilla resumes her marital obligations (*Passion* 36). Finally, it is in her bedroom that Maximilla recruits her slave to sleep with Aegeates in her place (*Passion* 17). Significantly, her slave's sexual encounters with Aegeates never occur in Maximilla's bedroom, but always in Aegeates's bedroom. Her room, a space once devoted to sexual desire, is now transformed. The transformed bridal chamber signifies both Maximilla's conversion to asceticism and her newfound power over her own sexuality.[18] She has confined the physically erotic to her husband's realm.

The *Passion of Andrew* deliberately combines the two themes of Platonic self-knowledge and physical procreation to introduce a decidedly Christian notion of desire: the redeployment of physical love to the divine, resulting in salvation. This theme appears in the *Passion*'s second Platonic dialogue, a rewriting of the *Phaedo*, which appears near the end of the text. As MacDonald notes, both Socrates and

16 The communal aspect of birthing has been noted by Wagener, 'Repentant Eve, Perfected Adam', p. 330.

17 MacDonald acknowledges this as one of the more sexually suggestive words that could have been used to describe her chambers (*Christianizing Homer*, p. 217).

18 Burrus draws attention to the female characters' sexual agency in many Apocryphal Acts in her influential book, *Chastity as Autonomy: Women in the Stories of the Apocryphal Acts* (Studies in Women and Religion 23; Lewiston, NY and Queenston, Ont.: Edwin Mellen, 1987).

Andrew – in jail before their executions – converse with their followers; both laugh in the face of death, and both speak on the nature of death as the separation of soul and body.[19] In Andrew's discourse, love and desire play prominent roles. Consistent with the philosophical tradition, Andrew warns his followers to reorient their desire away from 'immediate pleasures' and towards the divine. He instructs Stratocles not to interfere in his execution and warns him not to become too 'attached to mere appearances' (*Passion* 53).

When the apostle arrives at the cross on which he will be crucified, he addresses all his followers:

> [I]f you suppose this act of dying is the end of ephemeral life, leave this place at once. If you understand the conjunction of the soul with a body to be the soul itself, so that after the separation (of the two) nothing at all exists, you possess the intelligence of animals ... And if you love immediate pleasures and pursue them above all, in order to enjoy their fruits exclusively, you are like thieves ... What benefit is there for you who gain for yourselves external goods but do not gain your very selves? ... And why do we desire pleasure and childbearing, for later we have to separate? ... Follow after my deep-seated love. Learn of my sufferings about which I am now speaking with you ... I greet you with the grace of God and with love which is due him. (*Passion* 56–58)

The speech draws upon Socrates's exhortation to avoid the passions and his description of death as the separation of the soul from the body.[20] For Socrates and Andrew, bodily passions distract the philosopher from the contemplation of the truth.[21] *Philia*, instructs Andrew, must replace other baser forms of love. Attachments formed by bonds of the flesh should be supplanted by a bond with the divine, as he explains immediately before his death, when he chastises his followers for wishing that he would not die: 'Why this excessive fondness for the flesh? Why this great complicity with it? Do you again encourage me to be put back among things in flux? If you understood that I have been loosened from ropes but tied up to myself, you yourselves would have been eager to be loosened from the many and to be tied to the one' (*Passion* 61). Andrew implicitly replaces desires of the flesh with another desire – that of the soul for God. But the sexualized rhetoric and context of the *Passion of Andrew* implicitly invoke those baser desires, suggesting a slippage between the erotic and the sexual on the one hand and the ascetic love of God on the other.

The goal of reoriented desire is also realized through the figure of Maximilla, who strives to replace her sexual, marital relationship with the union she also seeks with 'the one'. Maximilla consults the apostle after Aegeates delivers an ultimatum: if she returns to her husband, resumes having sex with him, and bears his children, he will spare Andrew's life (*Passion* 36). But Andrew encourages Maximilla to orient her love towards its proper object – and thus to resist 'any proposition of sexual intercourse' by Aegeates. He continues,

---

19 MacDonald has written on the similarities in both of these dialogues; for his summary of similarities between the *Phaedo* and the *Passion of Andrew* see his *Christianizing Homer*, p. 274.

20 Plato, *Phaedo* 9, 13 (*Plato*, ed. and trans. Harold North Fowler, LCL, 7 volumes [Cambridge, MA: Harvard University Press, 1914, repr. 1982], vol. 1, pp. 222–25, 236–41).

21 Plato, *Phaedo* 10 (*Plato*, LCL, vol. 1, pp. 227–28).

I rightly see in you Eve repenting and in me Adam converting. For what she suffered through ignorance, you – whose soul (ψυχήν) I seek – must now redress through conversion. The very thing suffered by the mind (νοῦς) which was brought down with her and slipped away from itself, I make right with you, through your recognition that you are being raised up. You healed her deficiency by not experiencing the same passions, and I have perfected Adam's imperfection by fleeing to God for refuge. What Eve disobeyed, you obeyed; what Adam agreed to, I flee; the things that tripped them up, we have recognized. For it is ordained that each person correct his or her own fall. (*Passion* 37)

Andrew here narrates the fall of Adam and Eve in a Platonic framework.[22] The mind, or *nous*, has fallen away from its original unity with the divine into a bodily existence it then seeks to transcend in order to return to the divine.[23] Maximilla's rejection of sexual passion will assist her soul in its return to its true self. Because she refuses to unite her body with her husband's, her soul can unite with the divine.

The philosophy in the *Passion of Andrew* has parallels in the neo-Platonic writings that were composed during the period when the *Passion* began circulating widely.[24] In the *Enneads,* Plotinus writes that the good or virtuous life is 'concerned with the soul and is an activity of the soul' (I.4.14)[25] requiring a 'separation from the body and despising of its so-called goods …' (I.4.14). Plotinus also writes of a system of the fall and redemption of souls similar to the account of the fall of the *nous* or mind in the *Passion of Andrew*. According to Plotinus, the mind has descended from the divine realm, and the soul has settled in the body. The ultimate objective of the individual soul is to become like the 'soul of the All' (IV.8.2), to 'rest in the divine'

22 As Kenneth Wagener has observed, Maximilla and Andrew become the heirs to the first couple, Adam and Eve, whose fall away from God prefigured all others: 'For Andrew, the present scenario is a reenactment of the Paradise drama, with himself and Maximilla as the primal human beings' ('Repentant Eve, Perfected Adam', p 330). For more on the Platonic parallels to this account of the fall, see the discussion of Plotinus below.

23 Soon after, Andrew speaks of escaping his own body. Responding to Maximilla's grief at his impending martyrdom, the apostle retorts, 'So what? Let [Aegeates] destroy this body as he will, for it is only one body and it is akin to him' (*Passion* 39).

24 Plotinus lived from approximately 205 to 270 CE. The *Acts of Andrew* seems to have achieved popularity in the third and fourth centuries. Eusebius has knowledge of a text he calls the *Acts of Andrew*; the Manichaean psalm-book mentions Andrew, his crucifixion and Maximilla; Philaster of Brescia writing around 390 refers specifically to the story of Maximilla and Aegeates from the *Passion of Andrew*; Bishop Innocent of Rome lists the *Acts of Andrew* among heretical books and attributes its authorship to Platonic philosophers in a letter dated to 405. See Wilhelm Schneemelcher and Knut Schäferdiek, 'Introduction, Second and Third-Century Acts of the Apostles', in W. Schneemelcher (ed.), *New Testament Apocrypha* (2 vols.; trans. R. McL. Wilson; Cambridge, UK: James Clarke & Co., 1992), 2, pp. 75–100 (88–89). Knut Schäferdiek argues that the *Apocryphal Acts* of *Andrew, John, Paul, Peter* and *Thomas* circulated together as one unit among Manichaeans. Kaestli refutes the idea that the Apocryphal Acts had canonical status among the Manichaeans in his 'L'utilisation des Actes Apocryphes des apôtres dans le Manichéism', in M. Krause (ed.), *Gnosis and Gnosticism* (NHS, 8; Leiden: Brill, 1977), pp. 107–16. Despite these disagreements, the attestations demonstrate the breadth of circulation of the *Acts of Andrew* in some form. See Prieur, *Acta Andreae,* vol. 1, pp. 91–128, for the most extensive account of the witnesses to the *Acts of Andrew* as well as Elliott, pp. 231–302. A lengthier treatment of the similarities between the philosophy in the *Acts of Andrew* and Plotinus can be found in the original version of this article.

25 All translations come from the English translation in A.H. Armstrong (ed. and trans.), *Plotinus* (7 vols.; LCL; Cambridge, MA: Harvard University Press, 1966–88).

(IV.8.1), and to return to its original union with the divine (IV.8.4). Yet the 'soul's fellowship with the body' (IV.8.2) occurs for an important reason: 'The soul itself would not have known the powers it had if they had not come out and been revealed' (IV.8.5). The revelation of the soul can occur only in embodied existence and in the process of the return to the divine. This anthropology bears a striking resemblance to Andrew's speech on the fall of the *nous*, sexual passion and the separation of the soul from the body. The apostle's disdain for the 'flux' and multitude of this world echoes the Platonic goal of 'rest' achieved in the soul's return to the divine realm.[26]

Most important with respect to the *Passion of Andrew*, however, is Plotinus's treatment of *eros*. He writes, 'Now about the affection of the soul for which we make love responsible, there is no one, I suppose, who does not know that it occurs in souls which desire to embrace some beauty, and that this desire has two forms: one which comes from the chaste who are akin to absolute beauty, and one which wants to find its fulfilment in the doing of some ugly act' (III.5.1). Sexual intercourse constitutes such an ugly act for it remains embedded in a desire for 'the beauty here below' rather than the true beauty of the divine realm (III.5.1). Plotinus, who advocates chastity to avoid the 'error' of sexual intercourse (III.5.1), establishes a hierarchy of lovers: the lowest is one whose desire is directed solely towards procreation; the lover who engages in sexual intercourse but is motivated by a love of beautiful bodies rather than procreation is one step higher; the highest are those who 'venerate that higher beauty, too, and do not treat this earthly beauty, either, with disrespect, since they see in it the creation and plaything of that other. These lovers, then, are concerned about beauty without any ugliness' (III.5.1). Aegeates's love for Maximilla represents the lower form of neo-Platonic *eros*, whereas Maximilla and Stratocles' love for Andrew and God represents the higher, truer form.[27] Where *eros* in the Greek novel is the love expressed in sexual intercourse for the purpose of procreation and family maintenance, true love for the ideal Christian in the *Passion of Andrew* is a Platonic love, directed away from physical bodies and towards the realm of the divine. The eroticism of the *Passion of Andrew* results in childbirth, but it is the birth of the true, inner self, not the physical children and heirs of the Greek novels.

While scholars have noted the Platonic elements of the *Passion of Andrew*,[28] in

---

26 Another frequently recurring Platonic theme in the dialogues that appears in the *Passion of Andrew* is that of rest and motion. When Maximilla confesses her love for another to Aegeates, she wishes both to have intercourse with it and take rest in it. While urging chastity, Andrew exhorts Maximilla 'to pursue things that are stable, and to flee from all that undulates' (*Passion* 47). He recalls that everything in the current life is 'in flux'; if they maintain their faith in God they will be able to find rest (*Passion* 48). Additionally, the disorder of Aegeates's household – the slave's replacement of Maximilla as Aegeates's lover, the subsequent treachery of other servants in the household, and Aegeates's execution of many of those servants (*Passion* 20–22) – and Aegeates's constant anger or lack of control contrasts strongly with the peace and equilibrium in Andrew's presence. The earthly world is connected with motion, disturbance and the desires of the flesh. The world of the divine, in contrast, is characterized by rest, unity and true love – the love for God.

27 The *Passion of Andrew* and Plotinus diverge, however, in that the *Passion* never exhibits a positive valuation of the physical, sexual expression of love.

28 François Bovon mentions Platonism and the importance of self-transformation and self-discovery in the conclusion to his 'The Words of Life in the *Acts of the Apostle Andrew*', *HTR* 87.2 (1994), pp. 139–54 (153–54); Bovon and Eric Junod only mention the Platonic elements in passing in 'Reading the Apocryphal Acts of Apostles', *Semeia* 38 (1986), pp. 161–71 (166); MacDonald's

efforts to characterize the text as ascetic, encratic or 'gnostic'[29] they have overlooked its Platonic formulation of love. The importance of the *Passion of Andrew* lies not in its *degree* of asceticism, Platonism, or gnosticism, but both in the early link between the ascetic way of life and Platonic philosophy and in the highly sexualized framing of this form of asceticism. For all its counter-social tendencies, the *Passion of Andrew* nonetheless places its ascetic agenda within a context that could be identified and understood by Christian and non-Christian readers: the philosophic school.[30] The subversive nature of Christian asceticism is couched in a recognizable discourse.[31]

Ironically, this culturally familiar aspect of the text also led to its suppression. In the West, Platonizing ascetic traditions were deemed heretical as a result of the Origenist controversies of the fourth and fifth centuries. It should not be surprising that at the beginning of the fifth century, Innocent, bishop of Rome, believed the *Acts of Andrew* to be written by philosophers and condemned the work as heretical.[32]

discussion of Platonism in the *Acts of Andrew* is subordinate to his interest in the texts' parallels with Homer, and he does not mention the relationship between its Platonic elements and eroticism.

29 On 'encratism' see Yves Tissot, 'Encratisme et Actes apocryphes', in François Bovon *et al.*, *Les Actes apocryphes des apôtres: Christianisme et monde païen* (Geneva: Labor et Fides, 1981), pp. 109–20. The 'gnostic' problem seems endemic to any study of any text of the Apocryphal Acts, and I have deliberately chosen to sidestep the issue of whether the text is 'gnostic' because that very category of description has been thrown into question recently. Michael A. Williams adroitly demonstrates the problems of using the term to describe a particular philosophy or community in *Rethinking 'Gnosticism': An Argument for Dismantling a Dubious Category* (Princeton, NJ: Princeton University Press, 1996), esp. pp. 29–53. Elliott briefly reviews the positions of various scholars regarding the *Acts of Andrew*'s status as 'gnostic', 'orthodox', or something in between (Elliott, *Apocryphal New Testament*, p. 236). Prieur cleverly describes the *Acts of Andrew* as not 'a gnostic text in the proper sense' but instead as belonging to a 'gnosticising way of thinking' (Schneemelcher and Prieur, 'Acts of Andrew', p. 114).

30 Although James Francis recently has demonstrated that ascetic tendencies in non-Christian philosophical traditions also functioned as fundamentally subversive movements, their form of social protest would have been more familiar than Christian ascetic movements. See his *Subversive Virtue: Asceticism and Authority in the Second-Century Pagan World* (University Park: Pennsylvania State University Press, 1995).

31 Indeed, the relationship between sexual renunciation and Platonic philosophy in the *Passion of Andrew* also may be one of the earliest witnesses outside the Nag Hammadi writings to the existence of Platonizing, ascetic Christian communities. The most notable Christian Platonist of Antiquity is Origen, whose cosmology in *On First Principles* bears striking resemblance to both those of the *Passion of Andrew* and of Plotinus. Origen's philosophy about the redemption of the soul is generally believed to have been introduced into the asceticism and monasticism of Late Antiquity via Platonizing monks in Egypt and Cappadocia such as Evagrius Ponticus and Gregory of Nyssa. Evagrius and Gregory appear to have taken their cosmologies almost wholesale from Origen. The seminal work on Evagrius and later Origenist traditions is Antoine Guillaumont, *Les 'Kephalaia Gnostica' d'Evagre le Pontique et l'histoire de l'Origénisme chez les Grecs et chez les Syriens* (Patristica Sorbonensia 5; Paris: Editions du Seuil, 1962). The most comprehensive work in English on Origenism and asceticism is Elizabeth A. Clark, *The Origenist Controversy: The Cultural Construction of an Early Christian Debate* (Princeton, NJ: Princeton University Press, 1992). The *Passion of Andrew* presents a link between ascetic practice and a Platonic understanding of salvation that predates Origenist monasticism by centuries and Origen himself by decades. Further, Origen's *askesis* is a more intellectual exercise – contemplation and interpretation of Scripture.

32 Innocent of Rome lists the *Acts of Andrew* among heretical books and attributes its authorship to philosophers in a letter dated to 405 (Schneemelcher and Prieur, 'Acts of Andrew', p. 103; Elliott, *Apocryphal New Testament*, p. 231).

What also remains subversive about this recognizable, philosophical discourse is its eroticism. Andrew's relationships with both Maximilla and Andrew are sexually charged and oddly productive, resulting in labour and birthing. To some readers, the sexual tension between Andrew and Maximilla mimics and subverts the *eros* of the Greek novels primarily as a plot device: it serves the Christian text's primary message, that of political critique. For Cooper, the *Acts of Andrew* is a story about political competition between men: Aegeates and Andrew. Maximilla's sexual abstinence functions as a social protest against her husband's treatment of Andrew, a Christian; her celibacy is primarily a narrative device designed to propel a critique against both the 'politically powerful' or imperially connected elite rulers of the second- and third-century city (of which Aegeates is the representative), and the message of the novels, that elite marriages and households promote stable cities.[33] While this reading illuminates important social and political aspects of the text, it privileges one intertextual reference (the Greek novels) over others (philosophical dialogues). It sees the ascetic emphasis of the text as without much 'substance' and primarily as a 'cipher' for the social commentary about power relations in ancient society.[34]

Rereading the text with an eye to its multiple literary heritages draws the eroticized asceticism of the *Passion of Andrew* to the fore. The sexualized language of union and birthing creates an intellectual space in which characters (and possibly readers?) engage in a certain degree of gender-bending. As Rosamond Rodman has argued, Andrew even calls Maximilla a 'man' (both ἄνθρωπε and ἀνδρός) when he exhorts her to remain celibate.[35] Maximilla does not undergo a complete gender reversal, however. In the same speech, Andrew also fixes her gender as female by comparing her to Eve; albeit a 'repenting' Eve, Maximilla is nonetheless positioned as the heir to the iconic female, and thus female herself.[36] There are also limits to Maximilla's participation in the philosophical life Andrew teaches her and Stratocles. While she listens and lives by the teachings of the apostle, she, unlike Stratocles, does not dialogue with him about theological and philosophical issues. She listens, and his words transform her – she becomes 'what the words themselves had signified' – but she does not respond in kind with words of her own.[37] Thus, although Maximilla takes on masculine roles, in certain respects she remains woman – a woman who has embraced yet who has not become fully integrated in a Christianized philosophical ideal traditionally open only to men. The *Passion of Andrew* thus presents to its audience an imagined world in which women engage with philosophers and in which gender boundaries are fluid but not transcended.

The male Christian characters cross, but do not break, gender boundaries, as well. Andrew acts as midwife for a Stratocles in labour. As I have argued, however, these feminized roles – midwife and birthing mother – come within a deeply masculinized

33 Cooper, *Virgin and the Bride*, pp. 51–67.

34 Cooper, *Virgin and the Bride*, p. 57.

35 Rosamond C. Rodman, 'Who's on Third? Reading *Acts of Andrew* as a Rhetoric of Resistance', *Semeia* 79 (1997), pp. 27–44 (38). Rodman also analyses other masculine language that Andrew directs at Maximilla in this speech.

36 Cf. Rodman, 'Who's on Third?', pp. 38–39, for whom Andrew, Stratocles and Maximilla undergo gender inversions – male to female, and female to male.

37 On this transformation of Maximilla, see Nasrallah, 'She Became What the Words Signified'.

context, philosophical dialogue. Andrew remains in a recognized masculine role of philosopher and teacher. Stratocles, while subordinate and somewhat feminized, nonetheless remains a recognizably male figure: that of Socrates'/Andrew's student. Even the erotic overtones to Stratocles and Andrew's relationship fit in the context of their teacher-student relationship. Moreover, the feminine birthing imagery is intellectualized; the strikingly physical language of childbirth and labour pangs is divorced from the physical (and female) body and relocated to the realms of the mind or the soul. Their seemingly transgressive gender performance is situated on a decidedly masculine stage. The men flirt with femininity, but they are not emasculated.[38]

Despite this, the *Passion of Andrew* remains a text open to feminist interpretation, precisely because of its confluence of eroticism and philosophical discourse. The text opens up possibilities for a Christianity in which women and men engage with each other as intellectuals. It also presents an ascetic Christianity that somewhat ironically makes room for eroticism.[39] Although it destabilizes the Greek novels' construction of the ideal elite marriage as foundation for society, it does not remove Christianity from the realm of the sexual or the erotically productive. The sexual eroticism of the Greek novels is displaced, but not elided, in the *Passion of Andrew*, erupting as an explicit and productive eroticism between the Christian and God. Sexuality, and female sexuality in particular, emerges as a complex aspect of early Christian selfhood, something not entirely denied and denigrated, but ascetically reimagined and reconfigured as a positive element of the ascetic life for both men and women. The asceticized sexuality of the *Passion of Andrew* gives birth to the inner 'man' in Christians of both genders.

38 Cf. Rodman, 'Who's on Third?', p. 40, who posits, 'Stratocles goes from military man to pregnant woman.'

39 On eroticism and a 'discourse of Christian desire' in fourth- and fifth-century ascetic literature, see Virginia Burrus, *The Sex Lives of Saints: An Erotics of Ancient Hagiography* (Divinations Series; Philadelphia: University of Pennsylvania Press, 2003).

THE QUESTION OF EARLY CHRISTIAN IDENTITY:
THREE STRATEGIES EXPLORING A THIRD *GENOS*

RICHARD VALANTASIS

Over the past three decades, two kinds of New Testament research have made this present essay possible: the latest quest for the historical Jesus and analyses of religious sectarians who describe themselves as a different race. Recent studies of the historical Jesus[1] have speculated that his social movement revolved about itinerancy (or at least the rejection of the familial οἶκος) with its attendant poverty, renunciation of family and outside social ties with its attendant refashioned kinship group, and a rejection of traditional piety with its attendant alternative religious expression in a radically open meal signifying the Reign of God. Sociology[2] and anthropology[3] inform most of these studies. They have been highly successful and provocative in shaping anew the understanding of formative Christianity.[4]

Correlatively, other scholars have explored the self-description as a distinct *genos* or *genea* – both words signifying race or class or gender (Latin, *genus*) – by various Christian and Gnostic groups. Abraham Malherbe points out that the *Preaching of Peter*, a second-century text, 'is the first Christian writing to demonstrate the church's self-consciousness by dividing humanity into Greeks, Jews, and Christians as three races'. He maintains that 'Christians are said to worship God as a third race in a new way'.[5] Gedaliahu Stroumsa[6] and Michael Williams[7] have explored the concept of

---

1 See the work of the Jesus Seminar and especially the magisterial work of John Dominic Crossan, *The Historical Jesus: The Life of a Mediterranean Jewish Peasant* (San Francisco, CA: HarperSanFrancisco, 1991). See also Burton L. Mack, *The Lost Gospel: The Book of Q and Christian Origins* (San Francisco, CA: HarperSanFrancisco, 1993); Stephen J. Patterson, *The Gospel of Thomas and Jesus* (Sonoma, CA: Polebridge, 1993).

2 Notably Gerd Theissen, *Sociology of Early Palestinian Christianity* (trans. John Bowden; Philadelphia, PA: Fortress Press, 1978; German edition, Munich: Kaiser Verlag, 1977), and see Patterson, *Gospel of Thomas and Jesus*, pp. 158–70. For the sociology of Pauline Christianity the standard still is Wayne A. Meeks, *The First Urban Christians: The Social World of the Apostle Paul* (New Haven, CT: Yale University Press, 1983).

3 Crossan, *Historical Jesus*, pp. xxvii–xxxiv.

4 Two essays by Birger A. Pearson provide critical evaluation of both the trend and the methods of this research: 'The Gospel according to the "Jesus Seminar": On Some Recent Trends in Gospel Research', and 'Some Personal Observations on Scholarly Method' in *The Emergence of the Christian Religion: Essays on Early Christianity* (Harrisburg, PA: Trinity Press International, 1997), pp. 23–57 and 214–25.

5 Abraham Malherbe, 'The Apologetic Theology of the *Preaching of Peter*', *Restoration Quarterly* 13 (1970), pp. 205–23 (220–21).

6 Gedaliahu A.G. Stroumsa, *Another Seed: Studies in Gnostic Mythology* (NHS, 24; Leiden: E.J. Brill, 1984), esp. pp. 71–134.

7 Michael Allen Williams, *The Immovable Race: A Gnostic Designation and the Theme of Stability in Late Antiquity* (NHS, 29; Leiden: E.J. Brill, 1985).

genea within Gnostic mythology and theology respectively and within the classical tradition.

These two areas of research open the way to exploring a related issue: the strategies undertaken in the construction of a specifically Christian identity in the period from 55 CE through the third century.[8] This paper examines three different and yet related strategies. First is Paul's Letter to the Galatians, which exhibits a strategy of erasure of prior identity. Next is the *Gospel of Thomas*, which promulgates a strategy of unification of opposites. Finally I explore four Apocryphal Acts (*Paul and Thecla, Peter, John, Thomas*), which display a strategy of redefining social categories. These three strategies, when viewed together, show a consistent pattern: each attempts to create space for the articulation of Christian identity as a third *genos*, a third race or gender, beyond the received categories normally mapped through the polarities human and divine, male and female, married and single.

Paul and the Strategy of Erasure

Paul's argument for understanding Christian identity in the letter to the Galatians,[9] probably written from Ephesus in the winter of 52–53 CE,[10] functions within an internal Christian disagreement.[11] Paul vigorously defends his gospel from 'the other gospel' (Gal. 1.6) preached by competing evangelist(s) to his congregations in Galatia. The identity that Paul opposes, that is, his opponents' construction which may be determined only obliquely through Paul's writing, revolves about a seemingly accommodationist stance for Christians within Jewish religious practice. His opponents support circumcision and, perhaps, other customs that have come down to them. These accommodationists understand their Christian identity as consistent with and emergent from their past: for them, to be associated with Jesus Christ does not mean the rejection of received tradition.

Contrary to this subjectivity in which Christian identity remains subordinate to the traditional one, Paul advocates something radically new. For Paul, the origin of

8 Gedaliahu A.G. Stroumsa's article '*Caro salutis cardo*: Shaping the Person in Early Christian Thought' (*History of Religions* 30 [1990], pp. 25–50) posed the question for patristic thought from a theological and philosophical perspective. He argues that the reflexive self as it emerged in Late Antiquity results from a uniquely Christian combination of a simultaneous expansion of the self and its interior breakdown. This resulted from three factors: the doctrine of the creation of humanity in God's image; the theology of original sin; and the doctrine of the incarnation of Christ. While Stroumsa emphasizes the Greek and Latin patristic sources, I explore identity from an earlier period and with literary rather than systematic theological writings; he investigates philosophical anthropology while I explore the construction of identity.

9 Two books have influenced significantly my understanding of Paul: Hans Dieter Betz, *Galatians: A Commentary on Paul's Letter to the Churches in Galatia* (Hermeneia Series; Philadelphia, PA: Fortress Press, 1979) and Daniel Boyarin, *A Radical Jew: Paul and the Politics of Identity* (Berkeley: University of California Press, 1994).

10 Helmut Koester, *Introduction to the New Testament* (2 vols.; Philadelphia, PA: Fortress Press, 1982), II, pp. 114–20.

11 Jerome H. Neyrey, *Paul, In Other Words: A Cultural Reading of His Letters* (Louisville, KY: Westminster/John Knox Press, 1990), pp. 192–94.

Christian identity stands under the dual aspects of freedom[12] and novelty. Paul sought to develop a new subjectivity totally independent of the past (although emergent from it) and totally unprecedented and new. He literally underscores this strategy of clearing the way for something new in his personal note at the end of the letter: 'neither is circumcision anything, nor a foreskin, but a new creation' (Gal. 6.15). In one bold stroke Paul erases the cultural marks of both Jew and Roman.

Paul develops freedom as a touchstone by contrasting it with *nomos*, that is, with custom and tradition. His argument simply relates that humans enter a proper relationship with God not through the performance of religious acts, but through a trusting based upon Jesus Christ, and this applies especially to the Jews: 'We ourselves who are naturally Jews and not sinners from among the nations, knowing that a human is not rectified by performing traditional deeds except through trust in Jesus Christ' (Gal. 2.15–16). Ironically, here the sure understanding of freedom arises directly from a proper understanding of the traditional Jewish project. The focus, however, has shifted from custom to trust, from *nomos* to *pistis*. Paul argues this shift consistently throughout the letter, but his most articulate presentation comes in the summary of the allegory of chapter 4: 'therefore we are not offspring of the slave but of the free woman (οὐκ ἐσμὲν παιδίσκης τέκνα ἀλλὰ τῆς ἐλευθέρας), Christ has liberated (ἠλευτέρωσεν) us with freedom (τῇ ἐλευθερίᾳ), so stand firm and do not again bear the yoke of slavery' (Gal. 4.31–5.1). This is strong language. Paul depicts customary religion as enslaving in contrast to the new subjectivity provided by Christ and marked by freedom. Paul's opponents found this freedom so curious that they sent representatives to his Jerusalem meeting 'to scope out the freedom which we possess in Christ Jesus' (Gal. 2.4).

The novelty of this subjectivity and its freedom arise through revelation: 'For I want to explain to you, brethren, that the gospel which was preached by me was not according to a human category (κατὰ ἄνθρωπον), nor did I receive it from a human (παρὰ ἀνθρώπου παρέλαβον), nor was I instructed, but it came through a revelation (δι' ἀποκαλύψεως) of Jesus Christ' (Gal. 1.11–12). Both teaching and human agency detract from the novelty and freedom that characterize the development of the Christian subjectivity articulated in this letter and descriptive of Paul's own apostolic self-understanding. Paul affirms that he was a well-trained, active leader among the Jews who at first persecuted the movement he later joined (Gal. 1.13–14). A revelation from God, however, redirected him to a universal mission (Gal. 1.16). Breaking with the tradition of teaching and training that he himself experienced, Paul did not 'take council with flesh and blood; neither did I go up to Jerusalem to those apostles who preceded me' (Gal. 1.16–17) but set out on a new, universal course.

Paul's experience of revelation patterns the experience of those members of the communities to which he ministered. His description of baptism makes sense only in this context because baptism both replicates the experience of revelation and inaugurates the freedom from social and religious categories. His discussion of baptism in 3.27–29 occurs in the course of arguing that the customs of Judaism provided the teachable environment for something new to develop now through *pistis*, trust, rather

12 For the theme of freedom, see Elisabeth Schüssler Fiorenza, *In Memory of Her: A Feminist Theological Reconstruction of Christian Origins* (New York: Crossroad, 1983), pp. 205–18.

than through obedience as to a schoolmaster. The baptismal formula[13] emergent from earlier tradition speaks in the language of creating a new identity: 'as many of you as have been baptized into Christ have been clothed with Christ' (Gal. 3.27). This clothing in Christ erases the normal marks of prior identity in ethnicity, religious tradition, social status and gender: 'one is neither Jew nor Greek, neither slave nor free, neither male and female' (Gal. 3.28). In place of these social markers,[14] the new subjectivity identifies the practitioner with Christ by means of a strategy that at once erases the marks of Abrahamic identity and gains the full benefit of it: 'for all of you are one in Christ Jesus. If then you are of Christ, then you are the seed of Abraham and inheritors according to the promise' (Gal. 3.28b–29). The universal mission to unite all peoples in Christ mirrors the universal identity of all people in Christ.[15]

This letter articulates two alternative Christian subjectivities: one (advocated by Paul's opponents) in which the Christian remains part of the dominant religious culture, and one (advocated by Paul) that marks a significant break from any dominant religious orientation. Paul's universal subjectivity originates in revelation not in social and religious custom, so freedom and novelty characterize his understanding of identity. Paul argues for a redefinition of identity based upon a common revelation ritually enacted in baptism and upon a new union with Christ. He posits a category outside *anthropos* to characterize his subjectivity, and thereby he establishes a Christian identity as a third *genos* outside those things that mark *kata anthropon*, namely race, social status and gender. The believer enters that new identity and status not by being taught the customs and practices of the past, but rather by a revelation that overturns the very structures of identity and society. The old categories of race, social status and gender are erased so that a new identity may emerge. What that new construction may have looked like is probably reflected by the Corinthian community. It has long been argued that First Corinthians displays the danger, the consequences and the joys of that new identity performed openly within a widely (if not wildly) diverse community. Certainly the congregation evokes the stark redefinition of identity especially related to gender and class in its problems with marriage and celibacy, the multivalent use of the body, and interactions with the higher classes of non-Christian people.[16]

13 Any interpreter of this passage is dependent upon Wayne Meeks, 'The Image of the Androgyne: Some Uses of a Symbol in Earliest Christianity', *History of Religions* 13 (1973–74), pp. 165–208.

14 My emphasis on the construction of identity avoids the problems of identifying this baptismal formula with the question of the role and function of women. Those who look at sexual identity alone miss the point of the letter as a whole; see, for example, Dennis R. MacDonald, *There Is No Male and Female: The Fate of a Dominical Saying in Paul and Gnosticism* (Harvard Dissertations in Religion, 20; Philadelphia, PA: Fortress Press, 1987). I also avoid the problem of orienting such an identity to Gnostic theology or mythology. This is where I would disagree with Meeks ('Image of the Androgyne', pp. 189–97).

15 Paul Bowers ('Paul and Religious Propaganda in the First Century', *NovT* 22 [1980], pp. 316–23) argues that the strategy of geographical missionary activity represents Paul's unparalleled contribution. Such an understanding of Paul's religious propaganda correlates nicely with my description of his theological agenda.

16 Dale B. Martin explores these issues in his *The Corinthian Body* (New Haven, CT: Yale University Press, 1995). See also Schüssler Fiorenza, *In Memory of Her*, pp. 218–36; MacDonald, *There Is No Male and Female*, pp. 72–111; Meeks, 'Image of the Androgyne', pp. 197–206.

The Gospel of Thomas *and the Strategy of Unification*

Paul's strategy revolved about the erasure of traditional characteristics in order to create a new identity. The *Gospel of Thomas*, which minimally gathers material from the earliest traditions of the sayings of Jesus around 50 CE[17] until at least the turn of the first century, moves in other directions: it widens the arena even further than did Paul, and it employs a strategy of unification, that is, of uniting all genders under the male and all people into a single one. Here the third *genos* emerges as a unified and universally available identity through discursive practice.[18] My argument does not explore what constitutes the parameters of Thomistic subjectivity but rather takes up the more general question of how the *Gospel of Thomas* discusses the question of identity.

Unlike Paul, the *Gospel of Thomas* articulates its understanding of identity in relationship not just to other Christians but to all other human beings. The goal in these sayings is not the construction of a Christian identity within a dominant Jewish religious environment, but rather a new identity within the larger society as a whole. Two arguments indicate the wider human context for the gospel's construction of identity: its genre and its correlative portrayal of Jesus as sage.

The oblique character of these arguments concerns the social significance of textual modes, as opposed to the more direct textual interpretations of the gospel that follow later in this paper. The genre of the gospel, a collection of wisdom sayings, points to a universal audience in a number of ways. First, such sayings found wide reception in Antiquity among a wide and diverse group of religious practitioners.[19] John Kloppenborg demonstrates the breadth and depth of this sort of instructional material and documents its wide geographic, linguistic and ethnic dissemination.[20] Based on his exposition, it could be said that this genre of literature easily intersected the religious traditions of Jews, Romans (both Greek and Latin speaking), and most other cultures of the Mediterranean and Near East. The *Gospel of Thomas*, then, participates in a discursive mode that would have been universally recognized. The genre makes the identity promulgated in this gospel accessible to a wide assortment of people, so that it confounds the kinds of divisions normally posited between Eastern and Western, Greek and Jewish writings.

Moreover, the characterization of Jesus as a sage in the tradition of Mediterranean and Near Eastern sages has a universal appeal and hence a broad purview. Jesus' sayings collected in this gospel bear almost no sectarian markings. A few relate

17 See Helmut Koester, *Ancient Christian Gospels: Their History and Development* (Philadelphia, PA: Trinity Press International, 1990), pp. 75–128; Patterson, *Gospel of Thomas and Jesus*, pp. 17–93.

18 My reading of the *Gospel of Thomas* is based upon my commentary (*The Gospel of Thomas* [London: Routledge, 1997]) and upon an article 'Is the Gospel of Thomas Ascetical? Revisiting an Old Problem with a New Theory', *JECS* 7 (1999), pp. 55–81. See also Meeks, 'Image of the Adrogyne', pp. 180–89; MacDonald, *There Is No Male and Female*, pp. 43–48.

19 On the genre of the sayings collection see James M. Robinson, 'LOGOI SOPHON: On the Gattung of Q', in James M. Robinson and Helmut Koester (eds.), *Trajectories through Early Christianity* (Philadelphia, PA: Fortress Press, 1971), pp. 71–113. See also John S. Kloppenborg, 'The Formation of Q and Antique Instructional Genres', *JBL* 105 (1986), pp. 443–62.

20 John S. Kloppenborg, *The Formation of Q: Trajectories in Ancient Wisdom Collections* (Studies in Antiquity and Christianity; Philadelphia, PA: Fortress Press, 1987), pp. 263–316.

specifically to Jewish religious sensibilities (e.g. the Kingdom of heaven, the Pharisees), but these represent minor touches to what is almost completely generic teaching about the way of wisdom. This means that although some elements of Judaism find expression in these sayings, Jesus appears more as a general sage than as a specifically Jewish one. The knowledge promulgated could be used by anyone, as the genre implies, so that Jesus is portrayed simply as a sage, not specifically as a sage in the Jewish tradition; he speaks and teaches a universal wisdom, set free of cultural and religious restrictions.

I begin with the saying that provides the most difficulty. Saying 114, addressed to Simon Peter's request that Mary be expelled from the disciples, takes up the question of gender.[21] Jesus responds to Peter: 'I myself shall lead her in order to make her male, so that she too may become a living spirit resembling you males. For every woman who will make herself male will enter the kingdom of heaven.' The meaning of the saying does not concern me here:[22] what does are the categories that find justification and contestation. The gendered categories male and female stand at the centre of the discourse, and yet they do not stand solidly: Jesus may transform female into male, as can any woman who wishes to enter the kingdom.[23] The saying posits the categories, but in such a way as to render them fluid, ineffective and conditioned.

The much more complicated Saying 22 provides further evidence for the fluidity of categories:

Jesus saw infants being suckled. He said to his disciples, 'These infants being suckled are like those who enter the kingdom.' They said to him, 'Shall we then, as children, enter the kingdom?' Jesus said to them, 'When you make the two one, and when you make the inside like the outside and the outside like the inside, and the above like the below, and when you make the male and the female one and the same, so that the male not be male and the female female; and you fashion eyes in place of an eye, and a hand in place of a hand, and a foot in place of a foot, and a likeness in place of a likeness; then will you enter [the kingdom].'

Here gender joins many other categories in articulating a new subjectivity constituted by a number of elements: unity and duality, interiority and exteriority, spatial location, the eradication of gender, and the transformation of the physical body. The subjectivity here unifies the various parts of the believer: two become one; the sexes become one; opposites become alike and thereby erase the distinction between them. The new identity relates not only to the imagined or imaged body, but also to the physical body refabricated part by part (eye, hand, foot, as well as image).

21 Translations from Thomas O. Lambdin, 'The Gospel of Thomas', in Bentley Layton (ed.), *Nag Hammadi Codex II, 2–7 Together with XIII.2*, Brit. Lib. Or. 4926 (1), and pOxy. 1, 654, 655* (2 vols.; NHS, 20; Leiden: E.J. Brill, 1989), I, pp. 52–93.

22 See my *Gospel of Thomas*, pp. 194–95 and also Jorunn Jacobsen Buckley, *Female Fault and Fulfillment in Gnosticism* (Chapel Hill: University of North Carolina Press, 1986), pp. 84–104, and her 'An Interpretation of Logion 114 in *The Gospel of Thomas*', *NovT* 27 (1985), pp. 245–72; Marvin W. Meyer, 'Making Mary Male: The Categories of "Male" and "Female" in the Gospel of Thomas', *NTS* 31 (1985), pp. 554–70; Patterson, *Gospel of Thomas and Jesus*, pp.153–55.

23 I have earlier argued for a variety of cultural intertextual frames for this saying: see 'The Nuptial Chamber Revisited: The *Acts of Thomas* and Cultural Intertextuality', SBLSP 34 (1995), pp. 380–93 (386–89).

Nonetheless the discourse revolves about a remaking of the person under a variety of different headings strategically effected through a combination of unification and reconstruction.

These two sayings posit the identity effected through processes of unification. A specific set of practices enables the construction of this new identity: interpretation of the sayings (Saying 1); searching and finding (Saying 2); discovery of both the beginning and the end (Saying 18); manifestation of the interior light (Saying 24); being yoked to a singular new path (Saying 47); understanding one's origin in light and destiny in rest (Saying 50); the rejection of parents and siblings (Sayings 55, 101); becoming a solitary (Saying 74), and many others. The sayings set up a discursive mode of living that performs mostly mental tasks; these in turn reconstruct the categories of identity precisely in order to create a space for a new subjectivity. The unification sought emerges from an interactive process of reading, interpreting, searching, rejecting, realizing and many other activities that bring the mind to another place, and the person to another understanding of self and world.

All these elements construct a third *genos*. The believer can no longer understand the self as male or female, above or below, inside or outside, but rather must understand the self as something else, something beyond those categories. Unity marks that third thing, a unity emergent from a prior diversity and plurality, and constituted as something tertiary through textual discursive practices.

Four Apocryphal Acts of the Apostles and the Strategy of Redefinition

In Galatians the strategy revolved about the erasure of categories of race, class and gender as a means of creating a third *genos*; in the *Gospel of Thomas* that strategy attempted to redefine the categories applicable to human identity in order to construct a Christian subjectivity. In the Apocryphal Acts,[24] there is yet another direction for constructing Christian identity as a third *genos*. These acts accept traditional gender constructions and social patterns as normative but change their meaning by transforming their content.[25] For example, sexual identity no longer means sexual actions, but continence and chastity; marriage no longer unites two people to become one flesh, but unites two chaste partners to a heavenly bridegroom, Christ. Categories of identity, gender and social relationships no longer hold the meaning maintained in the dominant society. Moreover, the category *anthropos* itself is displaced so that animals may be numbered among the believers and may be empowered to perform miraculous deeds. This is a bold conclusion to the problem of identity, but one which follows directly upon the strategies observed in both earlier texts. The strategy of redefinition revolves about four different factors that I explore through four different Apocryphal

24 Jan N. Bremmer, 'The Novel and the Christian Acts: Place, Time and Readership' (*Groningen Colloquia on the Novel* 9 [1998], pp. 157–80) provides an important overview of the state of scholarship.

25 Kate Cooper argues for a direct correlation between the ancient novels (Roman and Christian) and social concerns of the elite in *The Virgin and the Bride: Idealized Womanhood in Late Antiquity* (Cambridge, MA: Harvard University Press, 1996), pp. 20–67.

Acts:[26] the promulgation of a gospel of purity and chastity that renounces sexual intercourse; the persistent intrusion of this message even in a text whose narrative is not related to purity; a definite set of principles that at once problematizes the category 'human' and reorients it; and a concerted effort literally to redefine identity by a substitution of continence and purity for sexual intercourse and marriage.[27]

The Gospel of Purity in the Acts of Paul and Thecla

The proclamation of a gospel of purity[28] provides the starting point for redefining the categories of identity. The *Acts of Paul and Thecla*[29] exemplify this aspect of the strategy. Paul's message revolves about continence, virginity and purity, especially, for example, in his version of the beatitudes:

> Blessed are the clean of heart, for they will see God. Blessed are those who preserve their flesh as chaste, for they shall become a temple of God. Blessed are the self-controlled, for God will speak to them ... Blessed are those who have wives as though they did not have them, for they will become heirs of God ... Blessed are the bodies of virgins, for they will be acceptable to God and not dismiss the payment of their chastity (τὸν μισθὸν τῆς ἀγνείας). (*Acts of Paul and Thecla*, 6)

In the apocryphal version of Paul's message the categories stand firm: marriage and gender remain, but their content has been changed so that 'having a wife' is 'as if not having a wife'; purity, holiness and continence replace sexual relations and identity. Thecla hears this message, endorses and adopts it, and the plot of the story unfolds around it: 'A certain Thecla, a virgin whose mother was Theocleia and who was engaged to the man Thamyris, sat at a proximate window of her house listening night and day to the discourse concerning chastity spoken by Paul' (*Acts of Paul and Thecla*, 7). Thecla remains a betrothed virgin fascinated by the discourse of chastity (τὸν περὶ ἀγνείας λόγον) exemplified and preached by Paul. She and Paul become a sort of mirror image of one another in chastity and in apostolic fervour. They both exemplify their status as a third *genos* in purity and in vocation. That status, however,

26 François Bovon and Eric Junod ('Reading the Apocryphal Acts of the Apostles', *Semeia* 38 [1986], pp. 161–71) correctly argue that the Apocryphal Acts ought not to be treated as a corpus but as individual literary pieces (see pp. 164–66). Here, however, I gather them as a collection based on their similarity as fictional narratives indicative of a wide variety of audiences from the late second through the third century CE, that is, as literature representing diverse groups exploring identity after Galatians and the *Gospel of Thomas*.

27 Judith Perkins ('The Apocryphal Acts of the Apostles and Early Christian Martyrdom', *Arethusa* 18 [1985], pp. 211–30) argues for an intentionally socially disruptive agenda in the Apocryphal Acts. The construction of identity explored here displays one more strategy for that social disruption. See also Cooper, *Virgin and the Bride*, pp. 45–67. Both Cooper and Perkins emphasize the social conflict in the texts.

28 Perkins points to the pervasiveness of this 'doctrine of continence' ('Apocryphal Acts of the Apostles', p. 215).

29 Willy Rordorf ('Tradition and Composition in the *Acts of Thecla*: The State of the Question', *Semeia* 38 [1986], pp. 43–52) argues that the *Acts of Thecla* originally formed a part of the *Acts of Paul*.

is not restricted only to chaste humans.[30] The lion Paul baptized, according to a
Coptic text, also remained chaste: 'A lioness met him, and he did not yield himself
to her but ... ran off.'[31] Christian identity, while maintaining society's dominant
categories, changes the content so that whatever one's social status 'chastity' remains
determinative. 'Chastity' also provides identity to males as well as females, animals
as well as humans.

The Intrusion of the Gospel of Purity and the Acts of Peter

The centrality of this apocryphal Pauline message finds confirmation in the place
Paul holds in the *Acts of Peter*. Paul's presence in Peter's *Acts* has long been
considered peculiar (if not problematic).[32] The majority of the *Acts of Peter* portrays
the conflict between Simon and Peter as a discourse on the nature of power as characterized by Simon's magic and Peter's ministry. The figure of Paul, however, intrudes
into this discourse on power and introduces the gospel of chastity. Paul's sermon at
the beginning of the narrative exemplifies the intrusion:

> Then Paul called for silence and said, 'Men and brethren, who have not begun to believe in
> Christ, if you do not continue in your former works, those of the tradition of your fathers (*si
> non permanseritis in pristinis operibus uestris et paterne traditionis*), but keep yourselves
> from all deceit and anger and cruelty and adultery and impurity, and from pride and envy
> and contempt and hostility (*et abstinueritis uos ab omni dolo et iracundia et seuitia et
> moecia et conquinamenta, et a superbia et zelo, fastidio et inimicitia*), then Jesus the living
> God will forgive you what you have done in ignorance'. (*Actus Vercellenses*, 1)[33]

Paul's presence in this Petrine narrative links Peter to the gospel of purity and
chastity. It is as though this gospel is the foundation upon which the narrative rests so
that ministry and power must originate in purity in order to be valid and effective.

Two other scenes underscore this connection. The first is the story contained in
the Berlin Coptic Papyrus 8502[34] about Peter and his deformed daughter. Having
healed her, Peter – told in a vision that 'this (daughter) will do harm to many souls
if her body remains healthy' – returns her to her deformity in order to protect men
from her beauty. He keeps her an invalid in honour of the Lord 'who has preserved
his servant from uncleanness and shame'. When Ptolemaus, who had desired her, is
converted, Christ tells him, 'Ptolemaus, God has not given the vessels for corruption

---

30 Richard I. Pervo argues that 'animal fables were time-honored modes for the pleasant
expression of didactic wisdom ... in learned and philosophical circles' of the second and third
centuries CE (*Profit with Delight: The Literary Genre of the Acts of the Apostles* [Philadelphia, PA:
Fortress Press, 1987], p. 128). My argument addresses the significance of such an interest in the
ancient novels and Apocryphal Acts.

31 This story is taken from an (as yet) unpublished Coptic papyrus. Hennecke and Schneemelcher
include a preliminary translation which I use here: *New Testament Apocrypha* (2 vols.; trans. R.
McL. Wilson; rev. ed.; Louisville, KY: Westminster/John Knox Press, 1992), II, pp. 75–86.

32 Bremmer, 'Correspondences Between the Ancient Novel', dates the *Acts of Peter* later than the
Acts of Paul precisely because of this inclusion. Pervo, 'Ancient Novel', provides a similar sequence
for these two *Acts* and for the same reasons.

33 Translation from Hennecke and Schneemelcher (eds.), *New Testament Apocrypha*, II, p. 288.

34 'Acts of Peter', translated by J. Brashler and D.M. Parrott in Hennecke and Schneemelcher
(eds.), *New Testament Apocrypha*, II, pp. 271–321 (285–86).

and shame; nor is it right for you, a believer in me, to defile my virgin, one whom you are to know as your sister, since I have become for both of you one spirit.' Peter's daughter remains chaste, Ptolemaus converts to chastity, and their union is their spiritual relationship to Christ. Again, Peter's narrative relates tales of power, but all around it sounds the gospel of purity.

The second story relates the decision by Agrippa's concubines to remain continent, as well as Xanthippe's (Ablinus's wife) similar decision. These two conversions to chastity become the narrative occasion for Peter's martyrdom (*Acts of Peter* 34). In the end, it is not the question of power that leads to his death, but the intrusion of the gospel of purity.

These three elements (the presence of Paul, the disfigurement of Peter's daughter, and the conversions of the women to chastity) have an important role in Peter's narrative, even though they are not related to its central plot (the contest of power). I suggest that the theme of power remains subordinate to that of chastity as the defining element of Christian identity. The intrusion of Paul locates the manifestation of power among the apostles as contingent upon a gospel of chastity. Apostolic power cannot be understood apart from that gospel of purity, nor can martyrdom have meaning apart from it.

The Principal Elements of Identity in the Acts of John

The *Acts of John* carefully explains the principles of Christian identity as a third *genos* by problematizing the category of 'human'. Human bodies die and are raised with regularity to live a converted life, and they symbolize graphically the defeat of one identity and the inauguration of another. For example, in chapters 19–25, John receives a revelation to raise Cleopatra from the dead; Cleopatra in turn raises her lover Lycomedes. Life and death no longer constrain true followers. Here the themes of new identity and power are merged (as in the *Acts of Peter*), and they apply not just to the apostles, but to any believer – even a converted priest of Artemis (chapter 46) – who can show the power to raise the dead. The clear implication of the newly converted raising the dead is that even new followers become as powerful as Jesus. The new person, raised from the dead category *anthropos*, manifests the power appropriate to a new identity no longer in any way linked to the former one, the one that preceded death. It could be said that the human being died so that a totally new person might emerge.

This characterization of the power of the new person suggests that Christians (raised from the dead and empowered to raise others from the dead) both emerge from and live in a world distinct from the human world. They no longer function as humans. Even John (the character in the *Acts*) confesses that his lack of faith resulted from being merely human, in the category *anthropos*; when he attempts to observe Jesus surreptitiously, this is what follows: 'And then when I was feigning sleep, I saw a certain other like him sleeping, whom I heard saying to my lord, "Jesus, those whom you have selected still do not believe in you (ἔτι σοι ἀπιστοῦσιν)". And my lord said to him, "You are right, for they are human (ἄνθρωπος γὰρ εἰσιν)"' (*Acts of John* 92). The person who resembles Jesus specifically identifies 'lack of faith' with being *anthropos*. The category 'human being' receives negative valuation because 'human' refers only to those who do not have faith. This implies, of course, that those who do have faith fit into some other category that would not be called 'human'. Power as manifested in the ability to live beyond death, and faith as the marker of those who live beyond the grave go together, but neither relates to the status of being 'human'. A third category, marked by both faith and power, emerges to describe the followers of Jesus.

Jesus embodies and models this new identity. When John, James and Peter went up on the mountain with him, John peeked when Jesus was naked and discovered thereby that Jesus was not at all like one in the category *anthropos*: 'Then since he loved me, I approached him quietly so that he would not see and I stood watching him toward his hinter parts (εἰς τὰ ὀπίσθια αὐτοῦ), and I saw him not at all in clothes and he was seen naked by me (γυμνὸν δὲ τούτου ὀρώμενον), and he was not at all a human (ἄνθρωπον δὲ οὐδὲ ὅλως)' (*Acts of John* 90). The body of Jesus itself does not operate in the category *anthropos* even when closely inspected by the beloved disciple. This recalls the strategy of the *Gospel of Thomas* regarding gender and Paul's theology in Galatians. Jesus now symbolizes in his body the emergent body of the believer no longer constrained by sexual differentiation. It is a third thing, neither male nor female, neither human or animal or angel, but something tertiary. The traditional characteristics of those in the category 'human' simply cannot stand either for Jesus or for his followers.

In yet another way Jesus models the third *genos*: his polymorphic capacities. Jesus exemplifies the fluidity of categories of identity held out as the ideal for believers. Frequently in this text (and in other apocryphal and extracanonical texts as well), he appears in different forms,[35] as different people, sometimes with a solid and material body and sometimes not.[36] Jesus does not appear consistently as only one person or as at a consistent age; his identity remains changeable according to the circumstances and needs of the moment.[37] This models as well what happens to those who follow him: people become 'other'; firm categories of identity become fluid and transformed. David Cartlidge argues in reference to the *Acts of John* (Chapter 21) that 'the protean character of Jesus is a grace to the church in that everyone can see Jesus as he or she is able to understand'.[38] This polymorphism underscores the question of identity as a primary category while also displacing the effectiveness of the broad category 'human' from its hegemony.

35　David R. Cartlidge, 'Transfigurations of Metamorphosis Traditions in the *Acts of John, Thomas*, and *Peter*', *Semeia* 38 (1986), pp. 53–66.

36　Lynne C. Boughton ('From Pious Legend to Feminist Fantasy: Distinguishing Hagiographical License from Apostolic Practice in *Acts of Paul/Acts of Thecla*', *Journal of Religion* 71 [1991], pp. 362–83) argues that 'this kind of transformation is appropriate to pantheistic religious systems in which the deities are not eternal in nature or personality' (p. 377). The Apocryphal Acts categorically disprove such an understanding: there is no question that both Jesus and the apostles are divine and relate to a heavenly realm. She also argues (more successfully) that 'the idea of transitory personalities would also be acceptable to Montanism' because it 'emphasized possession and uses of human personality by God and relied on prophets and prophetesses who claimed that Christ appeared in different forms and identities' (p. 377). The polymorphism may indeed relate both social information and a theology of divine embodiment.

37　Cartlidge ('Transfigurations of Metamorphosis Traditions', p. 55) suggests that these transformations relate to a docetic Christology. If the function of the transformation of Jesus' body addresses more the community and its identity as a 'body of Christ', then these transformations have social as well as theological significance.

38　Cartlidge, 'Transfigurations of Metamorphosis Traditions', p. 59.

The most dramatic description of this identity, both of Jesus and his followers, relates to the Cross (chs. 97–102). Jesus explains that he has been misinterpreted by many: 'they thought I was what I am not, but what they will say of me is lowly and not worthy of me since I am not that which I was for the many' (*Acts of John* 99).[39] Many people consider Jesus to be something base and unworthy, and he emphasizes for John that what he is remains ineffable and greater than the categories in which he has been placed. Rather than articulating a docetic Christology, this text makes space for understanding mysteriously different modalities of existence: Jesus was not merely human and therefore subject to death, but he was the archetype of the new person whose life in the body after dying in the body created a new subjectivity beyond what could be comprehended and articulated.

What argues against a solely Christological reading of Chapter 99 is the description of the new *genos* among Jesus' followers.[40] Jesus explains that 'human nature' when it is taken up onto the Cross will advance to a new race: 'When human nature is taken up, and they come over to a race won over by my voice, then the one who now hears me will become this yourself and no longer be what you now are' (*Acts of John* 100).[41] The new person 'shall no longer be what he now is', but will become as Jesus is. These statements consistently deny the status of normatively functioning categories about humans. Since people are not what they seem to be, the content of the categories has changed; appearances no longer describe reliably what actually occurs; neither Jesus nor his followers function as humans, but as something different and more mysterious.

The Redefinition in the Acts of Thomas

The *Acts of Thomas* illustrates the complete redefinition of categories that has taken place among these Christians. That redefinition has three foci: the problematizing of sexuality in the gospel of chastity; a continued construction of a class of being as a third *genos*; and the redefinition of marriage in the nuptial chamber.

The problematizing of sexuality in the gospel of chastity finds its most dramatic expression in the account of the young man who killed the woman he loved because she was unwilling to enter into a chaste relationship:

> An evil deed was performed by me, even though I thought I was doing something good. I
> loved a certain woman who lived outside the city in an inn; she also loved me. But when I
> heard you and believed that you preach the living God, I came forth and received the seal

39 The Greek text reads: ὅ οὐκ εἰμὶ ἐνομίσθην, μὴ ὦ ὃ ἄλλοις μολλοῖς ἀλλ' ὅ τι με ἐροῦσιν ταπεινὸν καὶ οὐκ ἐμοῦ ἄξιον.

40 Some scribes, noticing the problematic nature of the recategorization, changed the manuscripts to *melos* ('limb') rather than *genos*, seemingly to underscore that the person was a 'limb' of an *anthropos* or only a portion of a corporate body. The editors substituted *meros* ('share; portion; part') suggesting that believers remain part of the larger category, but their frequent question marks indicate that they do not understand the text. See Richard Lipsius and Maximilian Bonnet (eds), *Acta Apostolorum Apocrypha* (2 vols; Darmstadt: Wissenschaftliche Buchgesellschaft, 1959), Vol. II, part 1, p. 210 *loc. cit.*

41 The Greek text reads: ὅταν δὲ ἀναληφθῇ φύσις καὶ γένος προσχωροῦν ἐπ'ἐμὲ φωνῇ ᾖ πειθόμενον, ὃν νῦν ἀκούον με σὺ τοῦτο γενήσεται, καὶ οὐκέτι ἔσται ὃ νῦν ἔστιν. I have emended ὃν νῦν ἀκούω με to ὃν νῦν ἀκούον με with other textual witnesses. See Lipsius and Bonnet, *Acta Apostolorum Apocrypha*, Vol, II, pt. 1, p. 201.

from you together with the others. You said: 'Whoever might participate in the impure union, and most of all in adultery, this one shall not have life with the God whom I preach'. Since, therefore, I loved her exceedingly, I entreated her and prevailed upon her so that she would become my housemate (σύνοικός μοι) in chastity and clean living which you yourself are teaching, but she did not wish to do so. Since, therefore, she was unwilling, I took a sword and killed her; for I did not wish to see her live adulterously with another. (*Acts of Thomas* 51)

The young man interprets the message as a call to live as consort and spouse (σύνοικός μοι), but without sexual relationships. The gospel upholds the dominant social patterns but redefines their content. And although murder is not part of the plan for those who refuse (Thomas will eventually raise the woman from the dead), nevertheless her experience of death compels her to live in chaste marriage. The foul deed of sexual expression repeatedly finds condemnation, while purity and chastity mark the most intimate relationships of the newly converted. Thomas summarizes his gospel to this couple:

> So believe in Christ Jesus, and he will forgive for you the sins that you have committed before this time, and he will cleanse you from all your bodily desires which live on earth, and he will heal you from the failures which shall follow after you, since he will go out with you and will be found before you. Therefore each one of you strip off your old humanity and be clothed with the new; leave behind your former way of life and conduct (ἀναστροφὴ καὶ πολιτεία). (*Acts of Thomas* 58)

The constellation of elements has been carefully assembled so that the new identity, the new 'way of life and conduct' (ἀναστροφὴ καὶ πολιτεία) no longer means a relationship marked by sexual intercourse. The union remains, but the content has been replaced with the gospel of chastity.

This redefined gospel also articulates a category of believers that continues to problematize the category *anthropos*. Here, animals recognize the power of God, are capable of being agents in salvation (*Acts of Thomas* 39), and even instruct the apostle Thomas on behalf of Christ (*Acts of Thomas* 78). One characteristic of those who as believers become a third *genos* and also of the animals who are a part of this new identity is a kind of transcendent understanding. The inability of people to see him because of the crowd becomes in one of Thomas's sermons an example of the necessity for followers to be lifted up to another level, freed from the bondage of human existence (*Acts of Thomas* 37). Followers live in a different modality marked by freedom from 'the former way of life' (προτέρα πολιτεία) with all its attendant practices, desires, wealth, possessions and clothing (*Acts of Thomas* 37). Baptism inaugurates it:

> Then he began to speak about baptism: 'This baptism is for the forgiving of trespasses. It regenerates (ἀναγεννᾷ) light that is poured about; it births anew (ἀναγεννα) the new human (τὸν νέον ἄνθρωπον) and mixes together humans and spirit while renewing the mind (τοὺς ἀνθρώπους μειγνύον πνεῦμα καινοῦν ψυχήν);[42] it raises up threefold the new human and is a participant in the forgiving of trespasses. (*Acts of Thomas* 132)

---

42 The text is corrupt. See Lipsius and Bonnet, *Acta Apostolorum Apocrypha*, Vol. II, pt. 1, p. 239.

The nuptial chamber illustrates at once this new humanity and the mode of redefinition of social and religious categories. Thomas's preaching of chastity forces the redefinition of the nuptial chamber: 'if you desist from this foul intercourse, you become holy temples' (ἐὰν ἀπαλλαγῆτε τῆς ῥυπαρᾶς κοινωνίας ταύτας, γίνεσθε ναοὶ ἅγιοι) (*Acts of Thomas* 12). The new marriage Thomas advocates to Gundaphorus's daughter and her groom will produce another kind of children that will not bring parental grief (*Acts of Thomas* 12); it will be an eternal marriage that can never pass away (*Acts of Thomas* 13). The bride explains to her upset father: 'I have rejected (ἐξουθένισα) from before my eyes this husband (τὸν ἄνδρα τοῦτον) and his marital practices which pass away, since I am joined (ἡρμόσθην) in another marriage ... I have no intercourse with a temporary husband, whose goal is lasciviousness and bitterness of soul, since I am yoked (συνεζεύχθην) to a true husband' (*Acts of Thomas* 14).

Mygdonia provides her newly spurned earthly husband with the following comparison between the heavenly and the earthly nuptial chamber:

> That time demanded its own things and this (time) things appropriate to it; that time concerned beginnings, but this one endings; that time was about temporary life, but this one of eternal; that was of temporary delight, but this one that remains for ever; that one of day and night, this of day without night. You have seen that elusive marriage that remains here alone, but this marriage remains to eternity; that intercourse was of destruction, but this of eternal life; the bridal attendants were temporary men and women, but these now remain until the end. (*Acts of Thomas* 124)

This comparison (which goes on for several more lines) clearly distinguishes different understandings of the same phenomenon. Marriage, coitus, delight and every other dimension remain in both instances, but with radically different understandings of their content.

These four Apocryphal Acts take up the question of Christian identity with energy. Marked by purity, chastity and remarkable power, joined by animals and even babies speaking divinely inspired words, the Christian nobility in these narratives affirm the identities and social relationships of their class even while they change the meaning of them. To all outward appearances they continue to exercise the freedom of their status, to marry, to relate to one another as patron and client, to bear children, but these life-situations have been spiritualized. Outward appearances have not changed; inwardly, however, everything has changed.

Two factors underscore the significance of these internal changes. First, many of these Christians are raised to a new life during their earthly life. Death and the grave become parts of their earthly experience through which they pass in order to enter a new phase of existence. Second, their new life forms part of a community in which now even animals may participate. Although nothing externally appears different, these Christians live as people no longer 'human' by any stretch of the imagination, no longer constrained by death, no longer restricted by class and gender, and even no longer estranged from community with animals. They are a third *genos*, people living like humans, and yet not; people living in the world, and yet not.

The Question of Christian Identity

These texts that I have proposed as exemplifying strategies for articulating identity have very wide and divergent interests. Each struggles to make space for a new identity to emerge, and the novelty of that identity could not function in the already established categories of their particular religious context. At one level these texts are part of a larger attempt to create a specifically 'Christian' culture inhabited by a strictly 'Christian' people who form an unprecedented 'Christian' society. The texts do not necessarily represent communities, but their strategies reveal attempts to create an alternative way of living. The old ways, like old wineskins, simply could not be transformed without ruining the new identity, and the new identity would be ripped apart like a new cloth patched with old.

Modern ears, however, do not hear this struggle to articulate something decidedly new. Perhaps the description of early Christianity as a third gender will resensitize perceptions to the radical identity projects present in formative Christianity: a new gender; new people for a new world order; new social relationships outside family and religion; new understandings of time and eternity; different conceptions of the body individual and social; and new energy for exploring the extremities of human existence.

Each of these texts in its own way directs attention to the struggle about the articulation and formation of a new person. In the end, as Gedaliahu Stroumsa[43] has argued, that new anthropology takes deep root in philosophy and theology, but in the beginning the new anthropology began in narrative and in wisdom sayings, in rituals of initiation and renewal, in conflicting visions of human life and the community of faith. The practices, it seems, preceded the theological reflection. Paul erased the presence of markers of identity in a pneumatic body of Christ. The *Gospel of Thomas* attempted to unify the parts into a new single and divine identity for the believer. Some of the Apocryphal Acts attempted to redefine identity by retaining the same elements of identity and yet altering their meaning. Thus, attempts to articulate a new identity persisted without resolution and satisfaction. None of these strategies could prevail; none could survive in the catholic Church as it became more and more established.

The strategy of defining Christian identity promulgated by the Apocryphal Acts brings the process full circle by realigning identity with the categories of the dominant culture. Paul attempted in Galatians to forge a new identity by erasing the traditional categories of Jewish religion as well as the marks of race, class and gender. He opposed accommodating Christian identity to either Graeco–Roman or Jewish models so that through baptism a new kind of being could emerge. Baptism inaugurated a subjectivity beyond the dominant cultural patterns, and this subjectivity revolved about its novelty and its freedom.

The *Gospel of Thomas* began with the same discomfort with dominant models of identity. The culturally available categories of identity were not effective, so the sayings attempt to recreate new social and religious identity. However, this new identity remained ambiguous. On the one hand, Saying 114 affirms the superior status of the male while expanding its referent to include females. On the other hand,

---

43 Stroumsa, '*Caro salutis cardo*', pp. 25–50.

Saying 22 advocates the refabrication of the body beyond sexuality and duality. Here the *Gospel of Thomas* retains the categories while uniting opposites (male, female; above, below; interior, exterior) and positing them as the origin of a new and unified subjectivity. The categories ultimately remain unstable, fluid and redefined under the aegis of singularity and reformation. By uniting the divisive and distinctive elements of human identity into a singular being, the *Gospel* creates a third *genos* whose renegotiated identity both participates in and redefines the categories. The *Gospel of Thomas* still works in the same vein evident in the Pauline letter to oppose accommodationist identity, but that opposition results in categories still in some logia connected to gender.

The four Apocryphal Acts, abandoning the attempt to create a third *genos* through erasure and unification, adopt an accommodationist strategy of redefinition. The categories of identity erased in Galatians and unified in the *Gospel of Thomas* emerge as the primary categories in these Acts. Women and men get engaged, marry, cohabit and have children, but now these activities have only a theological meaning: the nuptial chamber and spiritual marriage replace the dominant culture's meanings with alternative and subversive ones. The third *genos* status of the believer displays no difference in modality from the lifestyles of non-believers, but the interior modality differs radically. This tertiary status forces the orientation from a practical question of lifestyle to a psychological and theological question of disposition. In appearance and even in practice Christian believers are free to live out the life appropriate to their social station; but interiorly, intellectually and spiritually their minds and wills have been conformed to a new being, a different order, a spiritual disposition and a religious sensibility significantly at variance from their non-believing neighbours.

Although the social categories (including gender, race and class) were contested sites for the new Christian identity, the problematization of the category 'human' remained constant through these first 250 years of Christian development. All these texts make Christians something 'other' than mere humans. Paul erases the marks of sexual, ethnic and social differentiation and makes the Christian in some way a 'member' of Christ's body through baptism. The follower of Jesus Christ has taken on a new identity beyond that of 'human' and not yet that of 'divine'. The *Gospel of Thomas* does not address the category 'human' directly, but it does offer a post-gendered, singular and dominant personality that is withdrawn from the mundane world. This subject lives not only in the world, but also simultaneously in a super-natural light, unscathed and unconcerned about it, and yet somehow still connected to it. The Apocryphal Acts also problematize the 'human' not only by allowing animals to enter the category 'Christian believer', but also in elevating Christians to participation in the polymorphic and so 'non-human' body of Christ.

Christianity inaugurated an identity as a third *genos*. When establishment came, that new identity could only be preserved on the fringes – by ascetics who under-stood themselves (even into modern times) as living the 'angelic life' on earth. The impulse to create an identity as a third race or gender became a sign of a more perfect life withdrawn from the mundane world. That perfection at once marginalized these seekers and made them the ideal. They were (and in some cases still are) understood as taking the difficult road, the narrow path, while those in the world live out their faith in mixed, highly problematized and conflicting environments. The strategies for

Christian identity as a third gender or race documented during the time of Paul, the *Gospel of Thomas*, and the Apocryphal Acts continue to influence the understanding of true Christianity, even when Christianity itself became the dominant religion of the Empire and so implicated itself in the power and status of the world.

DRUSIANA, CLEOPATRA AND SOME OTHER WOMEN IN THE *ACTS OF JOHN*

JAN N. BREMMER

At the beginning of the 1980s, feminism began to influence the study of the Apocryphal Acts.[1] Stevan Davies suggested that they were conceived and read by a community of Christian women; Dennis MacDonald attributed the origin of the *Acta Pauli* to oral traditions deriving from women opposed to the ruling patriarchal order; and Virginia Burrus stated that the Apocryphal Acts were originally oral stories told by women in female communities, while the focus on chastity reflected their desired or experienced liberation from the patriarchal order.[2] But towards the end of the decade a reaction set in. While in principle approving of this sociological approach, Jean-Daniel Kaestli argued strongly that the Apocryphal Acts are unlikely to have had an oral background or origin in a female community, and Peter Dunn has seriously questioned the degree of liberation that they offered to women.[3]

Considering these differences in opinion it is hard to disagree with Kaestli that we now need a study of each of the individual treatises in order to appreciate their contribution as a whole to our knowledge of ancient Christianity and to understand the role women played in that movement.[4] It is the aim of this paper to contribute to

---

1 This chapter is the abbreviated, but revised and updated version of my contribution to J.N. Bremmer (ed.), *The Apocryphal Acts of John* (Kampen: Kok Pharos, 1995), pp. 37–56. For the position of early Christian women see also my contributions in J.N. Bremmer (ed.): *The Apocryphal Acts of Paul and Thecla* (Kampen: Kok Pharos, 1996); *The Apocryphal Acts of Peter* (Louvain: Peeters, 1998); *The Apocryphal Acts of Andrew* (Louvain: Peeters, 2000) and *The Apocryphal Acts of Thomas* (Louvain: Peeters, 2001).

2 S.L. Davies, *The Revolt of the Widows: The Social World of the Apocryphal Acts* (Carbondale: Southern Illinois University Press, 1980); D.R. MacDonald, *The Legend and the Apostle. The Battle for Paul in Story and Canon* (Philadelphia, PA: Westminster Press, 1983); *idem*, 'The Role of Women in the Production of the Apocryphal Acts', *The Iliff Review* 41 (1984), pp. 21–38; V. Burrus, *Chastity as Autonomy: Women in the Stories of the Apocryphal Acts* (Studies in Women and Religion, 23; Lewiston, New York and Queenston, Ont.: Edwin Mellen Press, 1987), who first expounded her views in an article with the same title in *Semeia* 38 (1986), pp. 101–17; S.L. Davies, 'Women in the Third Gospel and the New Testament Apocrypha', in A.-J. Levine (ed.), *'Women Like This': New Perspectives on Jewish Women in the Greco-Roman World* (Early Judaism and Its Literature, 1; Atlanta: Scholar's Press, 1991), pp. 185–97 simply ignores the critique by Kaestli (note 3).

3 J.-D. Kaestli, 'Response' (viz. to preceding article by Burrus), *Semeia* 38 (1986), pp. 119–31; *idem*, 'Les Actes apocryphes et la reconstitution de l'histoire des femmes dans le christianisme ancien', *Cahiers bibliques de Foi et Vie* 28 (1989), pp. 71–79; *idem*, 'Fiction littéraire et réalité sociale: que peut-on savoir de la place des femmes dans le milieu de production des actes apocryphes des apôtres?', *Apocrypha* 1 (1990), pp. 279–302; P.W. Dunn, 'Women's Liberation, the *Acts of Paul*, and other Apocryphal Acts of the Apostles', *Apocrypha* 4 (1993), pp. 245–61.

4 Kaestli, 'Fiction littéraire', p. 302.

the current debate through a detailed study of the place of women in the *Acts of John*, which was probably written in southwestern Asia Minor around 150 CE.[5]

Lycomedes and Cleopatra (19–29)

The beginning of the *Acts of John* has been lost, and our text starts *in medias res* with the information that John, prompted by a vision,[6] hurried to Ephesus. His companions only with difficulty prevail upon him to rest one day in Miletus. These companions are mentioned by name, except for 'the wife of Marcellus'. Neither Marcellus himself nor his wife plays a role in the surviving parts of the *Acts*, but the particular reference might indicate that previous chapters described her conversion or a miracle performed by John on her behalf. It is interesting to note that we find both males and females among these companions. This is already an indication of the importance of women in the spread of early Christianity. In the Greek novel the world of the women is highly limited, and the only friends of a female protagonist are usually slaves. The situation is different in the Apocryphal Acts, where women and men regularly mingle.[7] Admittedly, one could think that this is only a fictional reality, but there are abundant testimonies that leading Christian males taught, mixed and corresponded with upper-class women,[8] just like their Gnostic counterparts.[9]

Unfortunately, we are unable to reconstruct the precise route of the apostle. Yet his journey from Miletus via Ephesus to Smyrna, and subsequently via Laodicea (58–59) back to Ephesus, suggests that he first toured the coastal cities before visiting those inland, just like the Roman governor on his yearly visits to the assize

---

5 Cf. my 'The Novel and the Apocryphal Acts: Place, Time and Readership', in H. Hofmann and M. Zimmerman (eds.), *Groningen Colloquia on the Novel* IX (Groningen: Egbert Forsten, 1998), pp. 157–180 (place); P.J. Lalleman, *The Acts of John: a two-stage initiation into Johannine Gnosticism* (Louvain: Peeters, 1998), pp. 268–70 (date). A. Jakab, '*Actes de Jean*: État de la recherche (1892–1999)', *Rivista di Storia e Letteratura Religiosa* 36 (2000), pp. 299–334 reviews recent work on the *Acts of John*. I have used the standard edition of the *Acts of John* by E. Junod and J.-D. Kaestli, *Acta Iohannis* (2 vols; CCSA, 1–2; Turnhout: Brepols, 1983). Parts of the episode *Acts of John* 63–86 and 106–15 have since been discovered in a Manichaean library at Kellis, Egypt, cf. G. Jenkins, 'Papyrus 1 from Kellis. A Greek text with affinities to the Acts of John', in Bremmer, *Apocryphal Acts of John*, pp. 197–216, re-edited by I. Gardner and K. Worp, 'Leaves from a Manichaean Codex', *Zeitschrift für Papyrologie und Epigraphik* 117 (1997), pp. 139–55.

6 This is a recurrent motif in the *Acts*, cf. R. Söder, *Die apokryphen Apostelgeschichten und die romanhafte Literatur der Antike* (Stuttgart: Kohlhammer, 1932; repr. Darmstadt: Wissenschaftliche Buchgesellschaft, 1969), pp. 171–75; J.N. Bremmer, 'Marginalia Manichaica', *Zeitschrift für Papyrologie und Epigraphik* 39 (1980), pp. 29–34 (29).

7 For women in the Greek novel see the perceptive study of B. Egger, 'Zu den Frauenrollen im griechischen Roman. Die Frau als Heldin und Leserin', in H. Hofmann (ed.), *Groningen Colloquia on the Novel* I (Groningen: Egbert Forsten, 1988), pp. 33–66.

8 See J.N. Bremmer, 'Why Did Early Christianity Attract Upper-class Women?', in A.A.R. Bastiaensen *et al.* (eds.), *Fructus Centesimus, Mélanges offerts à Gérard J.M. Bartelink* (Steenbrugge and Dordrecht: S. Pietersabdij and Kluwer, 1989), pp. 37–47.

9 For gnostics and women see J.E. Goehring, 'Libertine or Liberated: Women in the So-called Libertine Gnostic Communities', in K.L. King (ed.), *Images of the Feminine in Gnosticism* (Philadelphia, PA: Westminster Press, 1988), pp. 329–44, repr. in D.M. Scholer (ed.), *Women in Early Christianity* (New York and London: Garland, 1993), pp. 183–98; H. Havelaar, 'Sofia en Maria Magdalena. Twee vrouwenfiguren in gnostische teksten', in D. van Paassen and A. Passenier (eds.), *Op zoek naar vrouwen in ketterij en sekte* (Kampen: Kok, 1993), pp. 25–40.

districts.[10] However, the focal point of the surviving part of the *Acts of John* is clearly Ephesus and all non-Ephesian parts have been lost.[11] When John and his followers approach Ephesus, they are met by a certain Lycomedes, who requests the apostle to come to his house and to heal his paralysed wife Cleopatra. Lycomedes is still young and one of the Ephesian *strategoi*, a member of the executive council of Ephesus.[12] Moreover, he is 'a wealthy man': the reader is not left with any uncertainty about his importance. Cleopatra is equally young and although according to her husband she is now 'a withered beauty', she had once been so beautiful that the whole of Ephesus had been ecstatic about her. It is not difficult to recognize in these descriptions *topoi* of the Greek novel, which also regularly details the youth, beauty and noble birth of the hero and heroine.[13]

After this appeal John immediately goes to his house, where Lycomedes kneels before him and begins to lament his fate. He blames his wife's illness on the evil eye of his enemies and, as often happens in pagan novels, he announces his suicide – a frequently occurring narrative ploy designed to enhance the dramatic character of the situation.[14] Despite the exhortations of the apostle to control himself, Lycomedes falls to the ground and dies. The apostle then heals Cleopatra who in turn resurrects her husband, as converts do more often in the Apocryphal Acts.[15] After Lycomedes recovers, he charges a painter with making a portrait of John, which he installs in his bedroom in front of an altar, surrounded by candles and wreathed with garlands. Irenaeus, a contemporary of the *Acts of John*'s author, informs us that Carpocratian gnostics wreathed and worshipped portraits of Jesus, Pythagoras, Plato, Aristotle and other philosophers (*Adv. haer.* 1.25.6). According to Augustine, a certain Marcella from the same sect worshipped Homer, Pythagoras and Jesus as well as burned incense in front of their images (*De haer.* 7).[16] Lycomedes's altar will have served a similar purpose.

In this episode the difference in behaviour between husband and wife is striking.

10 Cf. J. den Boeft and J.N. Bremmer, 'Notiunculae Martyrologicae III', *VC* 39 (1985), pp. 110–30 (119), overlooked by E. Plümacher, 'Apostolische Missionsreise und statthalterliche Assisetour. Eine Interpretation von Acta Iohannis c. 37.45 und 55', *ZNW* 85 (1994), pp. 259–78.

11 As is observed by L. van Kampen, *Apostelverhalen* (Diss. Utrecht: Merweboek, 1999), p. 101.

12 Unfortunately, the discussion by W. Schwahn, 'Strategos', *RE* Suppl. 6 (1954), pp. 1112–13 is totally out of date, cf. H. Engelmann, H. Wankel and R. Merkelbach, *Die Inschriften von Ephesos* (8 vols; Bonn: Habelt, 1979–84), index.

13 Cf. Xen. *Eph.* 1.1 and F. Letoublon, *Les lieux communs du roman. Stéréotypes grecs d'aventure et d'amour* (Leiden: Brill, 1993), pp. 114–17 (young: this element is not mentioned in Junod and Kaestli, *Acta Iohannis* I, 165, 441–42), pp. 119–26 (beautiful, noble).

14 B. Wesseling, *Leven, Liefde en Dood: motieven in antieke romans* (Ph.D. diss. Groningen, 1993: privately printed), pp. 73–119.

15 In addition to this passage see also *Acts of John* 24, 47, 82–3; *Acts of Andrew* (Latin version) 19; *Acts of Thomas* 54.

16 This worship of portraits is clearly of Greek origin and was introduced by the Epicureans, cf. B. Frischer, *The Sculpted Word* (Berkeley, Los Angeles and London: University of California Press, 1982). In the course of time the custom seems to have merged with the Roman ritual of worshipping important 'gurus' in a *lararium*, cf. A.D. Nock, *Essays on Religion and the Ancient World* II (ed. Z. Stewart; 2 vols.; Oxford: Oxford University Press, 1972), p. 669 (where this passage is absent); S. Settis, 'Severo Alessandro e i suoi Lari (S.H.A., S.A., 29, 2–3)', *Athenaeum* 50 (1972), pp. 237–51; J.D. Breckenridge, 'Apocrypha of Early Christian Portraiture', *Byzantinische Zeitschrift* 67 (1974), pp. 101–109.

Lycomedes is weak, grovels at the feet of the apostle, and dies from grief. On the other hand, Cleopatra is firm, and the apostle sees her 'neither raging from grief nor being outside herself', although she also grieves for her partner. In fact, it is explicitly said that because of her controlled behaviour the apostle had pity on Cleopatra and prayed to Christ on her behalf. Moreover, he allowed her to resurrect her own husband,[17] and she did not relapse into pagan practices. Clearly, the author of the *Acts of John* pictures Cleopatra both as more in control of herself and as a firmer follower of Christ than her husband. In this episode, then, we see the reflection of the development that 'the ability passively to hold out, often in the hope of better, became the cardinal virtue of Christians under threat'.[18]

Fortunately, the chapters about the relationship between Lycomedes and Cleopatra have survived almost completely,[19] unlike those about Andronicus and Drusiana, the other married couple who appear as protagonists in the *Acts of John*.

Andronicus and Drusiana (63–86)

When John returns to Ephesus for the last time, he is accompanied by Andronicus and Drusiana, Aristobula, 'who had learnt that her husband Tertullus had died in the Way (of Christ)', Aristippe and Xenophon, and the 'chaste prostitute' (59). Allusions in later literature strongly suggest that they all played a role in the original *Acts of John*,[20] but only some episodes about Andronicus and Drusiana survived the abbreviations and censorship of previous centuries. As Gregory of Tours' Latin edition of the *Acts of Andrew* shows, succeeding centuries cut out speeches considered to be too long or tedious, but why certain episodes have disappeared from our text but others not remains totally unclear.[21]

The introduction of Drusiana has been lost, but we may assume that she, like Cleopatra, was a young woman, since Callimachus, who has fallen in love with her (below), is described as a young man (71, 73, 76); love for an older woman is hardly probable in these novels. Andronicus's age is not mentioned, but he is described as a στρατηγός, like Lycomedes, and he is 'πρῶτος' of the Ephesians at that time' (31).[22] Junod and Kaestli translate this qualification with 'un notable', but this insufficiently brings out the agonistic flavour of the term: Andronicus is a 'leading citizen' (*Schäferdiek*) of the town. The terminology of 'the first' or 'the first of the city' (fatherland) as an aristocratic self-designation is typical of Aphrodisias and northern Lycia. In addition, it is found in eastern Phrygia, Bithynia and Pisidia

---

17 P. Schneider, *The Mystery of the Acts of John* (San Francisco, CA: Mellen Research University Press, 1991), p. 24 curiously states that 'Lykomedes had only fainted'. This contradicts the explicit testimony of the text that he had died (23: νενεκρωμένον).

18 See the excellent discussion by B.D. Shaw, 'Body/Power/Identity: Passions of the Martyrs', *JECS* 4 (1996), pp. 269–312 (297).

19 But see Junod and Kaestli, *Acta Iohannis*, on 25.3, 29.10, 19.

20 Junod and Kaestli, *Acta Iohannis*, I.94–6.

21 For an excellent discussion of the problem of the size of the original *Acts of John* and the extent of our losses see Lalleman, *Acts of John*, pp. 5–24.

22 For this designation see my 'The Novel and the Apocryphal Acts'.

where Antiochene Jews stirred up 'the first of the city' against the apostle Paul (Acts 13.50)[23]. It was in this area, then, that the *Acts of John* was probably written.

From allusions in the *Manichaean Coptic Psalter* it appears that after Drusiana's conversion Andronicus had locked her up together with John in a tomb.[24] After two weeks they are released, the husband also converts, and the couple start to live together as brother and sister (63).[25] Does this relationship to some extent reflect contemporary events? It is clear that an ascetic trait runs through all the Apocryphal Acts, but contemporary notices about ascetic couples are unfortunately lacking. The negative influence of conversion on pagan–Christian marriages, however, can be paralleled in real life: Justin relates the story of an anonymous Roman *matrona* who after her conversion divorced her husband for his 'sinful' life and whose Christian teacher was subsequently executed (*Ap.* 2.2).

In the surviving parts of the *Acts of John* we are told that Callimachus, also a 'πρῶτος' of the Ephesians', falls in love with Drusiana. But as he does not succeed in winning her favours, he lapses into a state of melancholy. This distresses Drusiana to such an extent that she becomes ill and, rather improbably, dies 'because of the bruising of the soul of that man'. Andronicus also grieves too much, if not to the same degree as Lycomedes. He regularly bursts into tears in the company of others so that John repeatedly has to silence him.

After her burial, Drusiana is not yet free from her 'lover'. On the contrary, together with Fortunatus, the corrupt steward of Andronicus, Callimachus breaks into her tomb in order to commit necrophilia. They are on the point of removing the last garment, the rather expensive *dikrossion*,[26] when suddenly a huge snake appears, fatally bites the steward, and remains on Callimachus after he falls to the ground. The next day Andronicus, John and some other brothers go to the tomb. As they had forgotten the keys, the apostle opens the doors by a simple order. The motif of automatically opening doors derives from pagan literature,[27] as does another detail in this scene. When they enter the tomb, they see an attractive, smiling young man. The same smiling figure is also encountered both in the *Acts of Paul*, where a smiling youth of great beauty loosens Paul's bonds (7), and in the *Acts of Peter*, where Jesus appears smiling to Peter in his prison (16). The motif is well known from pagan

23 See most recently F. Quass, *Die Honoratiorenschicht in den Städten des griechischen Ostens* (Stuttgart: Steiner, 1993), pp. 51–55; S. Sahin, *Die Inschriften von Arykanda* (Bonn: Habelt, 1994), nn. 42, 49, 50; M. Adak, 'Claudia Anassa – eine Wohltäterin aus Patara', *Epigraphica Anatolica* 27 (1996), pp. 127–42; N.P. Milner, *An Epigraphical Survey in the Kibyra-Olbasa Region Conducted by A.S. Hall* (Ankara: British Institute of Archaeology at Ankara, 1998), n. 1; *Supplementum Epigraphicum Graecum* 31.1316 (Lycian Xanthus); 41.1343, 1345–46, 1353 (Lycian Balboura); 42.1215 (Pisidian Etenna); 46.1524 (Lydian Sardis).

24 Junod and Kaestli, *Acta Iohannis* I, p. 549, rightly point to the novel for this motif; add Letoublon, *Lieux communs*, pp. 74–78.

25 Junod and Kaestli, *Acta Iohannis* I, pp. 86–91.

26 The discussion by Lalleman, *Acts of John*, pp. 258–59 has now to be corrected in the light of the very full collection of references to this type of garment by F.R. Adrados (ed.), *Diccionario Griego-Español* V (5 vols; Madrid: Consejo Superior de Investigaciones Científicas, Instituto 'Antonio de Nebrija', 1997), s.v. *dikrossion* and *dikrossos*.

27 The classic study is O. Weinreich, *Religionsgeschichtliche Studien* (Darmstadt: Wissenschaftliche Buchgesellschaft, 1968), pp. 45–290. For more passages and the most recent bibliography see J.J. Smolenaars, *Statius Thebaid VII: a commentary* (Leiden: Brill, 1994), pp. 40–41.

epiphanies where the god traditionally smiles to reassure anxious mortals.[28] Erik Peterson has argued that when Christ appears as a youth, he appears as the child Adam was before the fall.[29] This explanation, however, is hardly persuasive, and the motif deserves further attention.

Andronicus considers Fortunatus unworthy of being saved but asks John to resurrect Callimachus in order that he should confess exactly what had happened, not – we may observe – so that he should convert. But Drusiana generously asks the apostle to resurrect Fortunatus as well, even though Callimachus opposes her request. When John charges her to do so she performs the resurrection with enthusiasm, but not before uttering a prayer in which she mentions Andronicus's earlier violence towards her. As in the case of Cleopatra, then, Drusiana is represented in a more favourable light than her husband.

Old Women and Widows (30–37)

In addition to the two couples we have discussed, the surviving part of the *Acts of John* also depicts John actively engaged on behalf of old women. He orders Verus to bring to him all the old women of Ephesus in order that he might care for them. When he hears how many of them are in ill health, he instructs Verus to bring them to the theatre so that he could heal them there and thus also convert some of the spectators through these healings.

When the masses of Ephesus hear of John's plan, they queue up during the night in order not to miss the spectacle. In the Apocryphal Acts the 'crowd' is a recurrent *topos* in descriptions of miracles and serves to enhance the dramatic character of many scenes.[30] Yet these crowds are not only a literary phenomenon; they also reflect contemporary behaviour, as is well illustrated by a scene in the *Martyrdom of Pionius*. When Pionius and his fellow Christians, wearing chains, are led off after their arrest, 'quickly, as if for an unexpected spectacle, a crowd rushed up so that they jostled one another. And when they arrived at the agora, at the eastern stoa and the double gate, the whole of the agora and the upper porticoes were filled with Greeks and Jews, and even women.'[31] Söder has drawn attention to the prominence of the theatre in these descriptions. This motif, too, reflects a contemporary phenomenon, viz. the enormous popularity of the theatre in Imperial times which gradually replaced the agora as the public meeting-place.[32]

---

28 Many parallels: O. Weinreich, *Antike Heilungswunder* (Giessen: Töpelmann, 1909), p. 3 n. 2; M. Puelma, 'Die Dichterbegegnung in Theokrits Thalysien', *Museum Helveticum* 17 (1960), pp. 144–64 (149).

29 E. Peterson, *Frühkirche, Judentum und Gnosis* (Freiburg: Herder, 1959), pp. 189–96.

30 For the place of the crowd see G. Theissen, *Urchristliche Wundergeschichten* (Gütersloh: Gerd Mohn, 1974), pp. 78–81; R.I. Pervo, *Profit with Delight: The Literary Genre of the Acts of the Apostles* (Philadelphia, PA: Fortress Press, 1987), pp. 34–39.

31 *Mart. Pion.* 3, cf. L. Robert, *Le martyre de Pionios, prêtre de Smyrne* (Washington, DC: Dumbarton Oaks, 1994), pp. 54–55, who does not comment upon the remarkable presence of the women.

32 Söder, *Apokryphen Apostelgeschichten*, pp. 158–62; S. Saïd, 'The City in the Greek Novel', in J. Tatum (ed.), *The Search for the Ancient Novel* (Baltimore, MD: The Johns Hopkins University Press, 1994), pp. 216–36 (221–22); F. Kolb, 'Die Sitzordnung von Volksversammlung und Theaterpublikum im kaiserzeitlichen Ephesos', in H. Friesiner and F. Krinzinger (eds.), *100 Jahre*

When the old women and the crowd are assembled, John harangues his audience with a long sermon, in which he threatens them with the last judgement. The threat was apparently such a stock-in-trade of early Christian preaching that even Celsus notes that Christians 'threaten others with these punishments' (*C. Cels.* 8.48). According to Lane Fox, 'there was an ample place ... for plain fear in Christian conversions, and Christian authors did not neglect it: their martyrs' words on hell and the coming Judgment were believed to be an advertisement every bit as effective as their example at the stake'.[33] Although Lane Fox is probably right that the threat was intended to support the plea for conversion, he provides not a single example to support his statement that the threat actually worked. Yet there can be no doubt that the early Christians internalized the fear of the last judgement to an extent unthinkable today, as the following example may illustrate. The Carthaginian group of martyrs around Perpetua threatened those pagans who had come to their prison to jeer at them 'with God's judgement, stressing the joy they would have in their own suffering, and ridiculing the curiosity of those that came to see them'. John's words, then, clearly reflect contemporary Christian thinking in this respect.[34]

Finishing his sermon, the apostle heals the illnesses, but, unfortunately, the conclusion of the episode has been lost. Presumably, the old women and many spectators accept the new faith. Curiously, Junod and Kaestli pay no attention to the fact that the apostle cures *old* women, although this is a most remarkable feature of the episode. Old women had joined the Christian movement from the very beginning, as the pseudo-Pauline *Letter to Titus* shows (2.3), but in Greek and Roman society old women were in many ways at the bottom of the social scale. They were the butt of Attic comic mockery; Hellenistic sculptors frequently represented them as drunks; and Romans typically represented witches as old women.[35] In concentrating on old women, then, the early Christians showed compassion for members of a social category who were despised and who must have often been in dire circumstances. Even contemporary pagans note this concern for old women. In a book written *ca.* 165 CE about the self-immolation of the philosopher Peregrinus,[36] the satirist Lucian mentions 'old crones' among his visitors in prison (12). Lucian clearly satirized their prominent position among the Christians, but he did not realize that he was witnessing a revolution in the ancient value-system.

Old women also play a small role in an episode of the *Acts of John* that has only

Österreichische Forschungen in Ephesos (Vienna: Verlag der Österreichischen Akademie der Wissenschaften, 1999), pp. 101–105.

33 R. Lane Fox, *Pagans and Christians* (Harmondsworth: Allen Lane, 1986), p. 326; see also R. MacMullen, *Changes in the Roman Empire* (Princeton, NJ: Princeton University Press, 1990), p. 136.

34 *P. Perp.* 17; see also *Mart. Pol.* 11.2; *Mart. Ptolemaei et Lucii* 2; *Mart. Lugd.* 26; *Mart. Agape* etc. 4.

35 Cf. J. Bremmer, 'The Old Women of Ancient Greece', in J. Blok and P. Mason (eds.), *Sexual Asymmetry. Studies in Ancient Society* (Amsterdam: Gieben, 1987), pp. 191–215; S. Pfisterer-Haas, *Darstellungen alter Frauen in der griechischen Kunst* (Frankfurt: Peter Lang, 1989); P. Zanker, *Die trunkene Alte* (Frankfurt: Fischer, 1989); H. Wrede, 'Matronen im Kult des Dionysos', *Römische Mitteilungen* 88 (1991), pp. 164–88; G. Dönni, *Der alte Mensch in der Antike* (Bamberg: Difo Druck, 1996), pp. 175–94.

36 Cf. C.P. Jones, *Culture and Society in Lucian* (Cambridge, MA: Harvard University Press, 1986), pp. 117–32.

recently been recovered from an Old Irish text. According to the fourteenth-century *Liber Flavus Fergusiorum*, 'very many pious nuns, widows, and such holy persons following John' lived on the alms the apostle received from his fellow Christians. When they complained continuously about their small portions and accused the apostle of embezzling charitable donations, he changed hay into gold that he subsequently threw into the sea. In this way he showed the 'hypocritical widows' that he did not need any wealth and had given them every penny of the alms he had received.[37]

Charity towards widows was an important activity in second-century Christianity. In the *Acts of Peter* we hear of a certain Marcellus who was the 'refuge' of all the widows in town (8). Peter heals some blind, old widows (21), and after he resurrects the son of a senator and the mother decides to distribute some of her property to her newly freed slaves, the apostle tells her to distribute the remainder among the widows (28). In the *Acts of Paul* a father sold his possessions and 'brought the price to the widows' after Paul had resurrected his son (4). In Rome in the first half of the second century some Christians even tried to profit from this charity: Hermas saw in his visions a mountain with snakes and other wild animals meant for those deacons who embezzled money destined for widows: some of the deacons, who did the day-to-day work of charity while the bishop had the final responsibility, clearly lived in style at the expense of the congregational funds.[38] In fact, charity must have been reasonably 'big business' since around 250 Bishop Cornelius proudly mentioned that the congregation supported 1500 widows and other needy persons.[39] The organization involved in charity must have been an important factor in the overall strength of the early Church.[40]

Not every Christian, though, was pleased with the special treatment of widows, which so strongly contradicted prevailing values. The anonymous author of the popular *Apocalypse of Peter*, which perhaps originated in Egypt about 135, understood this negative feeling well and therefore included in his description of Hell the following warning:

> In another place situated near them, on the stone a pillar of fire (?), and the pillar is sharper than words – men and women who are clad in rags and filthy garments, and they are cast

---

37 M. Herbert and M. McNamara, *Irish Biblical Apocrypha. Selected Texts in Translation* (Edinburgh: T&T Clark, 1989), p. 93, whose translation slightly differs from that in Junod and Kaestli, *Acta Iohannis* I, 114.

38 Cf. *Sim.* IX.26.2 (deacons) and 27.2 (bishops); Just. *Ap.* 67.7 (deacons); M. Leutzsch, *Die Wahrnehmung sozialer Wirklichkeit im 'Hirten des Hermas'* (Göttingen: Vandenhoeck & Ruprecht, 1987), pp. 73–74, 135, 161.

39 Eus. *HE*. 6.43. For the importance of charity for the development of the Christian church in Late Antiquity see Peter Brown, *Power and Persuasion in Late Antiquity: Towards a Christian Empire* (Madison: University of Wisconsin Press, 1992), pp. 78–103.

40 For the widows see more recently J.-U. Krause, *Witwen und Waisen im Römischen Reich* (4 vols; Stuttgart: Steiner, 1994–95); C. Methuen, 'Widows, Bishops, and the Struggle for Authority in the *Didascalia Apostolorum*', *Journal of Ecclesial History* 46 (1995), pp. 197–213; J.N. Bremmer, 'Pauper or Patroness: the widow in the early Christian Church', in J. Bremmer and L. van den Bosch (eds.), *Between Poverty and the Pyre. Moments in the History of Widowhood* (London and New York: Routledge, 1995), pp. 31–57; C. Schlarb, 'Die (un)gebändigte Witwe', in M. Tamcke *et al.* (eds.), *Syrisches Christentum weltweit* (Münster: LIT, 1995), pp. 36–75.

upon it, to suffer the judgment of unceasing torture. These are they who trusted in their riches and despised widows and the woman (with) orphans ... in the sight of God. (9)

The wealthy that despised widows were not alone in their contempt. As in the case of the old women (above), Lucian also mentions, presumably with a sneer, the presence of widows among the visitors to Peregrinus. It seems not improbable that the above-mentioned scene from the Irish *Liber Flavus* also reflects something of the ambivalence upper-class Christians must have felt towards the prominence of widows in the early Church.

Conclusion

What have we learned, then, about the place of women in the production, reception and text of the *Acts of John*? It would not be impossible for a woman to have been the author, since many women in the Roman period could read and write,[41] but very few women in antiquity are known to have written prose fiction.[42] The simple fact of a sympathetic treatment of women in a piece of writing does not necessarily make the author a woman.[43] Moreover, the treatment of women in the *Acts of John* is rather varied. Whereas upper-class women play an active role, old women are only objects of the apostle's actions, and widows are even severely reproached. Clearly, the *Acts of John* reflects in this respect the normal hierarchical views of the Graeco–Roman upper classes and, thus, can hardly be the product of a community of egalitarian 'sisters'. Similarly, Burrus's idea of an oral background for some of the stories, notably that about Drusiana, will not stand a critical test, since the stories are too poorly informed about Ephesus for such an origin to be credible.[44]

If female authorship, then, is not immediately probable, what about readership?[45] In the study of the Greek novel, the thesis of female readership has lost much of its earlier popularity.[46] Yet female readership cannot be excluded, since throughout the Greek novel women are represented as literate and, for example, in Chariton's

41 Cf. S.G. Cole, 'Could Greek Women Read and Write?', in H. Foley (ed.), *Reflections of Women in Antiquity* (New York and London: Gordon and Breach, 1981), pp. 219–45; add the Christian examples in Bremmer, 'Why Did Christianity Attract Upper-Class Women?', pp. 42–43; R. Lane Fox, 'Literacy and power in early Christianity', in A.K. Bowman and G. Woolf (eds.), *Literacy and Power in the Ancient World* (Cambridge: Cambridge University Press, 1994), pp. 126–48.

42 Cf. E. Bowie, 'The Readership of Greek Novels in the Ancient World', in Tatum, *The Search for the Ancient Novel*, pp. 435–59 (438).

43 See the objections to Davies's thesis in M. Lefkowitz, 'Did Ancient Women Write Novels?', and R. Kraemer, 'Women's Authorship of Jewish and Christian Literature in the Greco-Roman Period', in Levine, *'Women Like This'*, pp. 199–219 and pp. 221–42.

44 Persuasively argued by K. Schäferdiek, 'Herkunft und Interesse der alten Johannesakten', *ZNW* 74 (1983), pp. 247–67. H. Engelmann, 'Ephesos und die Johannesakten', *Zeitschrift für Papyrologie und Epigraphik* 103 (1994), pp. 297–302 is not convincing.

45 For a much fuller discussion of the readership of the ancient novel and the Apocryphal Acts see now J.N. Bremmer, 'The Novel', pp. 171–78. For an updated and slightly expanded version, see 'The Apocryphal Acts: Authors, Place, Time and Readership', in *idem* (ed.), *The Apocryphal Acts of Thomas* (Leuven: Peeters, 2001), pp. 149–70.

46 Cf. B. Wesseling, 'The Audience of the Ancient Novel', in Hofmann, *Groningen Colloquia* I, pp. 67–79; S.A. Stephens, 'Who read ancient novels?', in Tatum, *The Search for the Ancient Novel*, pp. 405–18.

Callirhoe they also form part of the internal audience.[47] In the case of the *Acts of John* a female readership certainly seems to have been one of the author's target audiences,[48] if only since the readership of the *Acts of Paul* included women. But there are other indications as well. For example, the two heroines are clearly depicted as far superior to their husbands: Cleopatra, unlike Lycomedes, does not relapse into pagan practices, and Drusiana is not only more in control of herself but also resurrects her husband, not vice versa. The *Acts of John*, then, allows upper-class women clear possibilities for identification, and this strongly points to female readership; considering the nature of Graeco–Roman literacy, such readers were by definition members of the middle and upper classes.[49] Indeed, it would be strange if it had been otherwise, since in the first centuries women seem to have constituted the majority of Christian membership.[50]

Did the *Acts of John* also suggest a 'liberated' lifestyle to women?[51] Whereas Cleopatra and Lycomedes presumably lead a normal married life, Drusiana and Andronicus renounce sexuality. Apparently, the author leaves both possibilities open to married couples. In this connection there is a further scene we should consider (48–55). Before he departs Ephesus for Smyrna, John meets a young man who had fallen in love with his neighbour's wife.[52] Irritated by his father's warning against this liaison, the young man kicks him to death. Junod and Kaestli insufficiently bring out the evil character of this deed. For Greeks and Romans parricide was the most appalling crime imaginable – witness the myth of Oedipus, whose parricide led to incest with his mother.[53] The story therefore has a strong moralistic flavour. Moreover, the parricide subsequently leads to the self-castration of the young man, since after John resurrects the father the man cuts off his testicles and throws them before his former girlfriend.[54] Although John disapproves of this act, nevertheless he does not heal the youth but accepts him as he is. In other words, if the *Acts of John* offers an alternative lifestyle to women, it also suggests a life of continence for men.

Finally, the prominent position of the women will also have had a certain missionary appeal among Greek and Roman women. It is important to stress the

47 Cf. B. Egger, 'Looking at Chariton's Callirhoe', in J.R. Morgan and R. Stoneman (eds.), *Greek Fiction. The Greek Novel in Context* (London and New York: Routledge, 1994), pp. 31–48 (35).

48 As was already observed long ago for the Apocryphal Acts in general by F. Pfister, in E. Hennecke (ed.), *Neutestamentliche Apokryphen* (Tübingen: Mohr, 1924), p. 169.

49 Contra P. Lampe, *Die stadtrömischen Christen in den ersten beiden Jahrhunderten* (Tübingen: Mohr, 1989), p. 102.

50 A. von Harnack, *Die Mission und Ausbreitung des Christentums* (1902; Leipzig: Hinrich, 1924), pp. 589–611; Lane Fox, *Pagans and Christians*, p. 310.

51 For the contemporary life of upper-class married women see M.Th. Raepsaet-Charlier, 'La vie familiale des élites dans la Rome impériale: le droit et la pratique', *Cahiers du Centre G. Glotz* 5 (1994), pp. 165–97.

52 Considering the hostile attitude towards the country in most Greek novels, we may notice that the young man is explicitly described as coming from the χώρα (48), cf. E. Bowie, 'The novels and the real world', in B. Reardon (ed.), *Erotica Antiqua* (Bangor: University College of North Wales, 1994), pp. 91–96 (94).

53 Cf. Bremmer, 'Oedipus and the Greek Oedipus Complex', in *idem* (ed.), *Interpretations of Greek Mythology* (London: Routledge, 1988), pp. 49–51.

54 For the connection between youth and castration see Nock, *Essays* I, 476.

inclusion of the latter in the *Acts of John*, since in the Greek novel the Roman world is mostly carefully eliminated. The *Acts of John*, however, mentions a proconsul (31) and contains a number of Roman names: Marcellus, Tertullus, Fortunatus, and Drusiana, a most unusual but unmistakably Roman name.[55] In the earliest stages of Christianity, these women could occupy influential positions to a degree unheard of in contemporary pagan religions or Judaism,[56] as still sometimes today in modern Africa,[57] although a reaction against this more active role set in at an early stage.[58] If we can trust the transmitted text of Tertullian's *De baptismo* (17.5),[59] certain Carthaginian women invoked the *Acts of Paul* to claim the right to instruct and to baptize. A certain 'liberating' effect of the Apocryphal Acts thus cannot be denied.[60]

55 I have been able to find only one other instance of this name, viz. Drusiana, the daughter of M. Flavius Drusianus (*Corpus Inscriptionum Latinarum* 6.1414: *c.* 200 AD). Dio Cassius 57.13.1 mentions that the sharpest swords were called 'Drusiana', but this does not seem relevant in our case. Note, however, its frequent occurrence in Manichaean circles as a testimony to the success of the *Acts of John* in those circles: I. Gardner *et al.*, *Coptic Documentary Texts from Kellis* I (Oxford, 1999: Oxbow), nn. 19.62,73; 21.20; 28.31.

56 Pagan religions and Christianity: Bremmer, 'Why Did Christianity Attract Upper-class Women?'; J. Hidalgo de la Vega, 'Mujeres, carisma y castidad en el cristianismo primitivo', *Gerión* 11 (1993), pp. 229–44; A. Bielman and R. Frei-Stolba, 'Les flaminiques du Culte impérial: contribution au rôle de la femme dans l'empire romain', *Études de Lettres* 2 (1994), pp. 114–26. Judaism: see the balanced view by P.W. van der Horst, *Hellenism-Judaism-Christianity. Essays on Their Interaction* (Kampen: Kok Pharos, 1994), pp. 73–95, although women were perhaps not as important as leaders of synagogues as he suggests, cf. T. Rajak and D. Noy, '*Archisynagogoi*: Office, Title and Social Status in the Greco-Jewish Synagogue', *JRS* 83 (1993), pp. 75–93; see now also Van der Horst, 'Images of Women in Ancient Judaism', in R. Kloppenborg and W.J. Hanegraaff (eds.), *Female Stereotypes in Religious Traditions* (Leiden: Brill, 1995), pp. 43–60.

57 G. Kosack, 'Christianisierung – Ein Schritt zur Emanzipation? Die Bedeutung der Religion für die Mafa-Frauen (Nordkamerun)', *Anthropos* 90 (1995), pp. 206–17.

58 Cf. R. Nürnberg, 'Non decet neque necessarium est, ut mulieres doceant. Überlegungen zum altkirchlichen Lehrverbot für Frauen', *Jahrbuch für Antike und Christentum* 31 (1988), pp. 57–73; K.J. Torjesen, 'Tertullian's "Political" Ecclesiology and Women's Leadership', *Studia Patristica* 21 (1989), pp. 277–82; E.M. Synek, 'In der Kirche möge sie schweigen', *Oriens Christianus* 77 (1993), pp. 151–64.

59 Tert. *De baptismo* 17.5, cf. A. Hilhorst, 'Tertullian on the Acts of Paul', in Bremmer, *The Acts of Paul and Thecla*, pp. 150–63; G. Poupon, 'Encore une fois: Tertullien, *De baptismo* 17.5', in D. Knoepfler (ed.), *Nomen Latinum. Mélanges A. Schneider* (Neuchâtel and Geneva: Faculté des Lettres and Droz, 1997), pp. 199–205.

60 For help, observations and the correction of my English in the two versions I would like to thank Ken Dowden, Ton Hilhorst and Ilse Roos.

WHO WAS THAT CHASTE PROSTITUTE?
A SOCRATIC ANSWER TO AN ENIGMA IN THE *ACTS OF JOHN*

DENNIS R. MACDONALD

Acts of John 59 is a travel note providing a transition from the apostle's activities in Laodicea to his second visit to Ephesus. What concerns us here is the curious list of his travel companions.

> With him were Andronicus and Drusiana, who had been with him when he left Ephesus, as well as those who were with Lycomedes and Cleobius. Others who followed him included Aristobula, who learned that her husband Tertullus had died en route, Aristippus together with Xenophon, and also the chaste prostitute [ἡ σώφρων πόρνη] and a throng of others whom he always advanced toward the Lord Jesus Christ, a throng who wanted never to be apart from him.[1]

This passage names eight of the characters and clusters them in groups of two: only the oxymoronic 'chaste prostitute' stands alone and nameless.[2] The surviving witnesses to the *Acts of John* at first glance would seem to provide no additional information about her, but a closer look at this list of names allows reasonable speculation about her role in the original work.[3]

- 'Andronicus and Drusiana, who had been with him when he left Ephesus.' These characters appear earlier in the book. Andronicus is a prominent Ephesian. His wife, Drusiana, converts to Jesus Christ and thereafter refuses to have sex with her husband. Finally, he, too, converts. Both characters continue to play significant roles in the narrative after John returns to Ephesus.[4]
- 'those who were with Lycomedes and Cleobius'. Earlier in the *Acts* the reader learns that Lycomedes is 'commander-in-chief of the Ephesians' and that

---

1 *Acts of John* 59; all translations are my own unless otherwise indicated.

2 The adjective σώφρων, translated here as 'chaste' can also mean 'prudent', even 'wise'. In favour of the translation 'chaste' is its obvious oxymoronic connection to 'prostitute', although the ambiguity of the term may be intentional. For example, Homer's Penelope became a metaphor for the cognate σωφροσύνη, often translated 'self-control', but with the connotation of 'wise'. Thus, she was an exemplar of both chastity and wisdom. Σώφρων can also be used of men, but σωφροσύνη is understood as a female virtue, while the complement (and compliment) for men would be ἀνδρεία.

3 Scribal transmission has not been kind to the *Acts of John*. The beginning of the book is missing, as are other major sections. The best-preserved sections, those pertaining to the apostle's death, survive in several recensions. The best discussion of this vexing problem is that of Eric Junod and Jean-Daniel Kaestli in *Acta Iohannis* (2 vols.; CCSA 1–2; Turnhout: Brepols, 1983), 1, pp. 1–70 ('La tradition manuscrite des Actes de Jean') and 71–107 ('Reconstitution du contenu des Actes de Jean').

4 *Acts of John* 31 and 62–86.

Cleobius is a plutocrat from Miletus, both of whom convert through John's preaching.[5] Among 'those who were with' them is Lycomedes's slave Verus (61).[6]

- 'Aristobula, who learned that her husband Tertullus had died en route.' Unlike the four names treated thus far, neither Aristobula nor Tertullus appears elsewhere in surviving passages from the *Acts of John*, but surely both did in the original. The beginning of the book does not survive, and content is missing from other parts as well. The name Aristobula appears in the *Manichaean Psalm-Book* among other women of the Apocryphal Acts, including Drusiana, who rejected sex with men and suffered for it,[7] but it is unclear if the Manichaean text refers to this Aristobula or to the wife of the wicked proconsul Varianus in the *Acts of Andrew*; she too rejected sex with her husband and may have been named Aristobula ('Best-plan').[8] The editors of the most thorough edition of the *Acts of John*, Eric Junod and Jean-Daniel Kaestli, propose that, like Andronicus, Tertullus ultimately converted and was 'on the way' to be reconciled with his wife but died before he caught up with her.[9] It also is possible that he did not convert, like the frustrated, libidinous Varianus and Aegeates in the *Acts of Andrew*, and died en route as divine punishment. The very fact that Aristobula, a married woman, is travelling with the apostle without her husband may imply her alienation from Tertullus. Be that as it may, it is likely that John's *Acts* once contained an account of Aristobula's battle with Tertullus about their bedroom.

- 'Aristippus together with Xenophon.' Like the previous two characters, these men appear nowhere else in our witnesses to the *Acts*, but they, too, probably were introduced earlier.

- 'and also the chaste prostitute'. Insofar as both Drusiana and Aristobula, the only named women in this list of apostolic associates, were noted for their sexual abstinence, the oxymoronic 'chaste prostitute' seems to have been a sex worker who converted to Christ and thereafter found another means of employment.[10] The use of the article suggests that the reader should know by now who '*the* chaste prostitute' is. Because the episode about her earlier in the *Acta* now seems to be missing, one can speculate that she was named there, but then one may ask why some of the men and women named are here, but she is not. A plausible answer is that the author is playing on her oxymoronic designation and so reducing her to this role.

---

5 *Acts of John* 18–19.

6 Pairs of men (the motif is called 'twinning') are unusually common in the Apocryphal Acts (as well as in folk narratives) for minor characters.

7 The *Manichaean Psalm-Book* does not mention 'prostitutes'.

8 See my *Christianizing Homer:* The Odyssey, *Plato and* The Acts of Andrew (New York: Oxford University Press, 1994), pp. 134–41.

9 *Acta Iohannis,* I, p. 95.

10 Other prostitutes appear in the Apocryphal Acts (e.g. *Acts of Andrew* GE 23 and 28), however, in the *Acts of Andrew* they seem to be special cases: one is ironically mimetic of Atalanta, the Greek tomboy who eschewed sex and men; the other is mimetic of Helen of Troy. It is difficult to generalize from them to this *Acta*.

I will argue that these last three characters are strategic imitations of characters in Xenophon's *Memorabilia*, his recollections of Socrates. The author of John's *Acts* hinted at this classical ancestry not only by naming one of his characters Xenophon, but also by including 'a throng of others whom he always advanced [προέτρεπεν] towards the Lord Jesus Christ, a throng who wanted never to be apart from him'. The verb προτρέπω is a technical term, common in philosophical texts for progress towards some favourable end.[11] For example, the last paragraph in the *Memorabilia* reminds the reader how dearly Socrates was missed by his friends and praises the man for 'reproving sinners and advancing [προτρέψασθαι] them towards virtue and the doing of the good and the beautiful'.[12] By investigating this book for what it says about Aristippus and Xenophon we gain purchase on the identity of the chaste prostitute.[13]

Here is what we learn about a man named Aristippus from Xenophon: 'It seemed to me that he [Socrates] also spoke such things to advance [προτρέπειν] those who were with him to the exercise of self-control in the desire of food, drink, copulation, sleep, cold, heat, and labour. He knew that one of those who were with him was quite undisciplined in such things and said, "Aristippus, tell me ..." '[14] In the dialogue that follows, Socrates demonstrates the folly and inconsistency of hedonism as a way of life, but he failed to convince Aristippus to change his ways.[15] We should imagine that John did Socrates one better: whereas the philosopher failed to convince Aristippus to abandon hedonism, the apostle convinced his Aristippus to become chaste. This is the sex objective throughout John's *Acts*.

Xenophon also states that Socrates 'praised the rigorous avoidance of the delights of Aphrodite; he said, "It is not easy for one who has tasted such things to be chaste [σωφρονεῖν]." '[16] He then asked Xenophon himself what he thought about Critobulos kissing the beautiful son of Alcibiades. He answered that he saw nothing wrong with it; in fact, he would have enjoyed kissing the gorgeous lad himself. Socrates warned him that such kisses might reduce a man to slavery. 'Xenophon, I would advise you that whenever you see a beautiful boy that you flee at full speed.'[17]

Socrates even gave advice to a prostitute concerning how to ensnare men. He had heard about Theodote (God's-gift), a spectacular beauty, and wanted to see her for himself while she posed naked for a painter. After drinking in her beauty for some time, he thanked her for giving him such pleasure and advised her that the trick to making men her slaves was to play hard-to-get, to withhold her affections until they

11 The nominal form of the word appears as the title of Clement of Alexandria's so-called 'Exhortation to the Greeks' (*Protreptikos pros Ellenas*). The verb is ubiquitous in Platonism and Stoicism.

12 *Mem.* 4.8.11.

13 A developed feminist analysis of Xenophon is far beyond the concerns of this essay. However, one observation may be instructive. Xenophon's Socrates does not invite women to become philosophers or join his circle; he merely wants to show that critical thinking can make a woman more seductive and therefore successful. This is unlike Plato's treatment of Diotima in the *Symposium*; she is a philosopher in her own right. The *Acts of John* is rather better on this score: the prostitute follows the apostle and apparently renounces sex in favour of a philosophically Christian *modus vivendi*.

14 *Mem.* 2.1.

15 See *Mem.* 4.6.12.

16 *Mem.* 1.3.8.

17 *Mem.* 1.3.9–13.

burst with desire.[18] The advice is both ironic and strategic when compared with John's preaching, which would make the prostitute chaste, not more 'effective'. If earlier sections of the *Acts of John* contained episodes related to Aristippus, Xenophon and the prostitute, they may have involved the following: John would have taught Aristippus self-control, urged Xenophon to resist beautiful boys, and promoted chastity for the prostitute.[19]

Although the prostitute is not explicitly mentioned later in the *Acts*, John's prayer just before he dies may refer to the missing episode about her. The beginning of the prayer addresses Christ as the one who on three occasions thwarted John's wedding plans.[20]

> You who to the present time have preserved me pure and untouched by union with a woman,
> you who in my youth, when I wanted to marry, appeared to me and said, 'John, I need you',
> you who gave me a bodily ailment just as I was about to marry,[21]
> you who a third time, when I wanted to marry, checked me and did not allow it, and then,
> at the third hour of the day on the sea, said to me, 'John, if you were not mine I would have let you marry.'[22]

The apostle then addresses Christ as the one who blinded him for more than two years apparently to cure his lust.[23]

> [Y]ou who deprived me of eyesight for two years and allowed me to suffer and entreat you,
> you who in the third year opened the eyes of my mind and granted me also to my physical eyes …

This temporary blindness achieved its goal.

---

18 *Mem*. 3.11.14. Two other prostitutes appear in Socrates's circle. Diotima was a woman experienced in love who taught Socrates about love according to the *Symposium* of Plato (201d–212c). Pericles's mistress Aspasia, according to Xenophon, was an associate of Socrates (*Mem*. 2.6.36), and Plutarch calls her a woman of ill-repute, actually a madam (*Per*. 24–25) who 'supported young courtesans' (ἑταιρούσας). All three prostitutes in the Socratic circle were aristocrats and certainly not 'street women'.

19 It would appear that the *Acts of Andrew* opposed male homoeroticism at two points, all of which are classically mimetic. Unfortunately, both of the texts in question survive only in a Latin epitome by Gregory of Tours who disguises the issue, probably out of embarrassment. One story criticizes the homoeroticism of Achilles and Patroclus, one that of Heracles and Hylas. The author seems to have taken a position much like that of the apologists with respect to Hadrian and Antinoos. The *Acts of Andrew* is not unique in this respect, but it is somewhat unusual.

20 Our text is not unique in this respect either. In the *Acts of Paul*, *John*, *Andrew* and *Thomas* the apostles preach total sexual abstinence

21 See *Codex Berol.* 8502.4, 128–32 and 135–41, often considered part of the *Acts of Peter*, in which Peter's daughter is paralysed to keep her from having sex. Such physical ailments are not common in the Graeco–Roman texts.

22 *Acts of John* 113. The threefold prevention of the apostle's nuptials suggests that his sexual desires blazed and needed divine extinguishing. It is impossible to know why John was sailing.

23 Cf. Mk 9.47 and Mt. 18.9: 'If your eye causes you to stumble, gouge it out.'

[Y]ou who, after I regained my sight, spelled out for me that even staring at a woman was burdensome,
you who rescued me from transitory appearance and led me to that which endures forever,
you who separated me from the filthy madness of the flesh …[24]

In this last episode there is no mention of a desire to marry; what is at stake is lustful leering at a woman. It is reasonable to suppose that early in the *Acts* John saw a beautiful woman, the prostitute mentioned in chapter 59. Because of divine intervention, he had no desire for her and, having changed his own attitudes, he preached chastity also to the woman, who seems to have been convinced and later travelled in the apostle's entourage. She thus would be a Christianized Theodote and John an ersatz Socrates. As we have seen, Socrates took great pleasure in watching Theodote pose – he even wanted to 'touch' her – but this was out of character. Elsewhere in the *Memorabilia* one reads 'that Socrates had prepared himself so that he could resist the most beautiful and gorgeous more easily than others resist the most ugly and repulsive'.[25]

I have argued for a Socratic solution to this enigma in the *Acts of John*, but one may reasonably object that the few texts I have investigated are insufficient to establish the author's indebtedness to Xenophon. Although I cannot address this objection fully here, it deserves a partial response.

The *Acts of John* repeatedly and strategically depicts John, among other things, as a Christianized Socrates (minus a nagging Xanthippe); Plato's depiction of him is even more influential than Xenophon's. Here I will focus attention on two other enigmas in the *Acts*, both of which indirectly pertain to the identity of the prostitute: the use of the first-person narration and the episode of the obedient bedbugs.

Strewn throughout the *Acts* are references to 'we' and 'us' and once 'I'. A similar phenomenon appearing in the Pauline half of the canonical Acts in connection with the apostle's shipboard exploits has received detailed and vigorous scholarly attention. Proposals for these 'we-voyages' include the following: (1) the author of Acts was an actual participant in the events narrated, (2) the author used a source written in the first person without making the narrative voice consistent with the rest of the book, (3) the author wrote in the first person to give an appearance of historical veracity, and (4) the author wrote to express his or her solidarity with the apostle and his mission. I have argued that the we-voyages in Acts were modelled after Odysseus's first-person narration of his voyages in *Odyssey* 9–12. Luke apparently expected his readers to be sufficiently jarred by the change in the narrator's voice from the omniscient third to the first plural to view Paul's first voyage to Europe as a Christian *nostos*, or 'return', from Troy. Each of these voyages relates to the Troad.[26]

---

24 *Acts of John* 113.

25 *Mem.* 1.3.14. This is an apparent contradiction in Xenophon. In ancient Greek and Roman literature, prostitutes of both genders not only were beautiful, they went to extraordinary lengths to become more so. This is true also in the story of Theodote, but she was not just a gorgeous body. In fact, Socrates's point is to keep the men watching before they start acting. The author of the *Acts of John* wanted to portray the apostle as a Christianized Socrates in several respects and as sexually more virtuous, at least after his conversion.

26 'The Shipwrecks of Odysseus and Paul', *NTS* 45 (1999): pp. 88–107. Here I also discuss other explanations of the 'we-voyages'.

But this Homeric explanation for the 'we-voyages' in the canonical Acts does not explain what is happening in the *Acts of John*. Eckhard Plümacher suggested that the use of the first person in the Apocryphal Acts generally is an imitation of the we-passages in the canonical Acts and is used to establish the reliability of the narrative as though it came from an eyewitness.[27] Junod and Kaestli doubt that the we-passages imitate Luke's Acts but concur that the use of we intimates that the author was a participant in some of the events narrated.[28] Eduard Norden thought that the *Acts of John* originally was a Gnostic work written in the first-person plural: a catholic redactor removed most, but not all, of the first-person references.[29]

It is my view that the use of the first person in the *Acts of John* notifies the attentive reader that the book resembles the memoirs concerning Socrates that Xenophon and Plato wrote in the first person. Xenophon used the first person to refer to himself; Plato used the first person for his narrator Phaedo in his account of Socrates' death.

Phaedo narrates to his friend Echecrates how the philosopher died. Ironically, Socrates's last day with his friends was anything but pitiable; those who were present sometimes even laughed.[30] Phaedo also names the fourteen men, other than himself, who were with him at the end, as well as 'some other of his fellow-citizens', much as *Acts of John* 59 names eight of John's associates and adds, 'and a throng of others'. While Socrates was surrounded by men in the *Phaedo* (he told Xanthippe to leave), John is surrounded by women as well as men.

Here is Phaedo's description of the beginning of Socrates's last day.

> On the previous days I and the others had always been in the habit of visiting Socrates. We used to meet at daybreak in the court where the trial took place, for it was near the prison; and every day we used to wait about, talking with each other, until the prison was opened, for it was not opened early; and when it was opened, we went in to Socrates and passed most of the day with him. On that day we came together earlier ... We agreed to come to the usual place as early in the morning as possible. And we came, and the jailer who usually answered the door came out and told us to wait and not go in until he told us ... So after a little delay he came and told us to go in. We went in then and found Socrates just released from his fetters. [31]

This passage may have been the model for the first extended first-person narrative in the *Acts of John*. The chaste prostitute is among the people referred to as 'we'.

> On the first day we arrived at an isolated inn, and while we were at a loss about what to do for a bed on which the blessed John might rest, we saw his little skit [παίγνιον, a rare

---

27 'Wirklichkeitserfahrung und Geschictsschreibung bei Lukas. Erwägungen zu den Wir-Stücken der Apostelgeschichte', *ZNW* 68 (1977), pp. 1–22.

28 For a discussion of these various explanations, see Junod and Kaestli, *Acta Iohannis,* I, pp. 530–33.

29 Eduard Norden, *Agnostos Theos. Untersuchungen zur Formgeschichte religiöser Rede* (Leipzig: Teubner, 1913; reprint Darmstadt: Wissenschaftliche Buchgesellschaft, 1974), pp. 313–14.

30 *Phaed.* 59a. Laughter plays a significant role in the passion of Andrew in the *Acts of Andrew*, where that apostle, too, imitates the laughing and dying Socrates. Notice that Jesus himself laughs in the *Acts of John* when he watches the cross!

31 *Phaed.* 59d–60a (LCL).

term that could also be translated 'game', 'trifle', or even 'joke']. Somewhere there was an unmade cot, so we spread over it the cloaks we had been wearing and called him to lie down and rest, while the rest of us slept on the floor. But after he lay down, he was pestered by a swarm of little bugs. Then they became increasingly annoying; midnight had already arrived, and all of us heard him tell them, 'I tell you, all you bugs, be considerate: leave your house this very moment, be quiet in one place, and be far from the slaves of God.' As we were laughing and talking somewhat longer, John went to sleep. We, however, spoke quietly and did not disturb him.[32]

Laughter is unusual in early Christian narratives; its appearance here may be due to the significance of laughter in the *Phaedo*. As Phaedo expressed it at the beginning of the dialogue, 'All of us who were there were in much the same condition, sometimes laughing and sometimes weeping' [γελῶντες ... δακρύοντες].[33] Compare this with the expression in the *Acts of John*: 'As we were laughing' [ἡμῶν γελώντων] ...

Phaedo's description of events at daybreak the day of Socrates's death resembles what happened the next morning in the *Acts of John*. Notice that the narrator shifts to the first-person *singular*, 'I', perhaps under the influence of Plato's individual narrator. Furthermore, the episode takes place at daybreak and involves characters waiting at the door until they are permitted to enter.

At daybreak, I rose first, and with me were Verus [one of Lycomedes's slaves] and Andronicus. We saw that there was a swarm of little bugs at the door of the house. While we were astonished at the sight of their sheer numbers and even though all the brethren [ἀδελφοί; the women of course woke as well] woke up because of them, John kept sleeping. After rousing him we told him what we had seen. Then he sat up in bed, saw them, and ... said to the bugs, 'Because you so prudently heeded my warning, return to your places.' No sooner had he said this and gotten out of bed than the bugs made a mad dash from the door to the bed, clambered up the legs of the bed, and crawled into the joints. John again spoke: 'On hearing the voice of a mortal, this animal stayed where it was in silence and did not overstep, but when we hear the voice of God, we violate the commandments and are lazy. For how long?'[34]

Insects play an unusual and famous role also in the *Phaedo*. In Socrates' discussion of the soul, he stated that people who during their lifetimes were violent and gluttonous were likely to return to life as asses or other beasts; those who lived lives of tyranny and robbery would inhabit the bodies of wolves and hawks; those whose souls were pure through philosophy would not have to undergo reincarnation; but as for the masses who were not wicked but 'moderate and just', they would 'pass again into some such social and gentle species as that of bees, wasps, or ants, or into the human race again'.[35] In other words, bugs contain the souls of people who were gentle and just in a former life and who thus have an affinity with humans. This notion was ridiculed in Antiquity, and the author of our *Acts* seems to have composed

---

32　*Acts of John* 60.
33　*Phaed*. 59a (LCL).
34　*Acts of John* 61.
35　*Phaed*. 82b. Many ancients believed in reincarnation, but the notion that some people became bugs was too much for some. It does appear in Lucian, for example.

a moralistic parody of it. Surely it is no accident that the other extended 'we-passage' in the *Acts of John* echoes the episode of the bedbugs.[36]

Another shift from the third person to the first appears in chapter 110: 'And after breaking the bread, he passed it out to us.' The first-person voice dominates until the end. The name Verus, Lycomedes' slave, appears in both stories, and in both stories the apostle lies down on strewn garments. Compare the following.

Acts John 60	*Acts John* 111 and 115
Somewhere there was an unmade [ἄστρωτος] cot, so we spread over it the clothes [περιβόλαια ἐν αὐτῷ στρώσαντες] we had brought and called him to lie down and rest, while the rest of us slept on the floor. But after he lay down [κατακλιθείς], he was pestered by a swarm of little bugs.	And when the young men had completed the ditch according to the specification he wanted, we had no idea why he took off his clothing [ἱμάτια] that he was wearing and laid them out at the bottom of the ditch as though it were a bed spread [στρωμνήν] ... He lay down in the ditch where his clothing had been strewn [κατεκλίθη ἐπὶ τοῦ σκάμματος ἔνθα τὰ ἱμάτια αὐτοῦ ὑπέστρωσεν].

The story of the bedbugs speaks of John's followers looking for a place for him to rest (ἀναπαύσει) and urging him 'to lie down ... and rest himself' [ἀναπαύεσθαι].[37] Just before John dies he asks Christ to consider him worthy of his rest (ἀναπαύσεως), that is, peace in the hereafter.[38] Earlier in this same speech the apostle praises Christ for having revealed himself in all of nature, 'you who preach yourself even among animals [ζῴων]'. John uses the same word when speaking of the obedient bedbugs: 'On hearing the voice of a mortal, this animal [ζῷον] stayed where it was in silence and did not overstep'.[39] The use of the first-person narration links the two passages; the end of the *Acts of John* again invites the reader to view John as a Christian Socrates.

A detailed comparison of the deaths of John and Socrates would take us far from our quest for the identity of the chaste prostitute, but a few observations are in order. First, John and Socrates both make advanced preparations for their burials: Socrates bathed and dressed himself; John had a pit dug for him and placed his clothing at the bottom.[40] Thus, the apostle went Socrates one better, that is, by preparing even further for his burial and relieving others from looking after it. In fact, Socrates did not care how he was to be buried

The *Phaedo* and the *Acts of John* use precisely the same word in the same tense, voice, mood and person to describe the hero's lying down to die: κατεκλίθη.[41] Second, as we have seen, the voice of the narrator for both deaths is in the first person. Third, John's prayer before he dies lists the many things Christ has done for the soul. He tamed it, gave himself to it, revealed himself to it, conquered its adversary, and raised

---

36 The Greek word for the insect is extremely obscure and seems to be related to young girls. Even the gender of the word is unclear. I speak of them as bedbugs only because that is where they reside; the reference to bed is not lexical, only contextual. They could be cockroaches – and probably were.

37 *Acts of John* 60.

38 *Acts of John* 113.

39 *Acts of John* 61.

40 *Phaed.* 115a; *Acts of John* 111.

41 *Phaed.* 117e; *Acts of John* 115.

it from the works of Hades. Three expressions in this list are particularly Socratic. The apostle addresses Christ: 'You did not allow it [the soul] to conduct its life in a body, you showed it what is inimical to it, you have made its knowledge of you pure.'[42] He then prays, 'receive the soul of your John which is certainly considered worthy by you'. He is worthy because Christ protected his soul from defilement, 'established a spotless friendship with you, traced out a knowledge of you that is pure ... and have oriented my soul to have no more valuable possession than you'. Finally, the apostle asks to receive the promises given to those who have 'lived purely'.[43] The pure knowledge of God, the purging of the soul, and its alienation from the body and one's possessions are dominating concerns also of Socrates in the *Phaedo*.[44]

In the edition of the *Acts of John* by Junod and Kaestli the last sentence is this: 'Having said to us, "Peace to you, brethren [ἀδελφοί; women are included]", he handed over his spirit with joy.' But in many manuscripts this is not the end of the book. For example, several versions add 'and he was still cheering us up. We all saw it and with him were bewailing his departure.' Eight manuscripts add after 'with joy' the words 'in the Lord, while we wept [κλαιόντων ἡμῶν]'. Six other manuscripts read that before the apostle died, 'as we were weeping and grieving [ἡμῶν δὲ κλαιόντων καὶ ὀδρυμένων]', John scolded them for weeping for him. After all, the apostle was going to his kingdom.

Here is how Phaedo describes the sorrow of Socrates's friends:

> We felt that he was like a father to us and that when bereft of him we should pass the rest of our lives as orphans ... [W]hen we watched him drinking and saw that he had drunk the poison, we could do so [hold back their tears] no longer, but in spite of myself my tears rolled down in floods, so that I wrapped my face in my cloak and wept [ἀπέκλαιον] for myself for it was not for him that I wept, but for my own misfortune of being deprived by him. Crito ... could not restrain his tears. But Apollodorus, who had been weeping [κλαίων] all the time before, then wailed and made us all break down.[45]

By using 'we wept' the author of the *Acts of John* seems to be alerting his readers to see the apostle's death as an imitation of Socrates's. In Homer's world crying is not stigmatized, but becomes more so later. In the *Phaedo* itself Socrates does not want his followers to cry 'like women'. Crying men are common in the Apocryphal Acts; even the occasional apostle weeps. It might, however, be inappropriate to conclude, that 'real men weep'; rather, men and women who have transcended gender roles through purity and chastity are those who weep without stigma.

At least one ancient reader of the *Acts of John* seems to have recognized similarities between the deaths of John and Socrates. The author of the *Acts of Andrew* borrowed from the *Acts of John*, and this is how he describes the death of that apostle: 'When he had said these things and further glorified the Lord, he handed over his spirit, while we wept [κλαιόντων ... ἡμῶν] and everyone grieved his

---

42 *Acts of John* 112.

43 *Acts of John* 113.

44 E.g. *Phaed.* 66b–67c. Socrates surely is not commending celibacy, but ethical uprightness – the virtue he spoke of endlessly.

45 *Phaed.* 116a and 117c–d (LCL).

departure.'[46] This is the only instance in the entire *Acts of Andrew* that the voice of the narrator switches from the third-person omniscient to the first-person plural, and it is precisely the same construction as in several manuscripts of the death of John. Surely the congruence is genetic, and it would appear that the author stole from John to pay Andrew.[47]

So who was that chaste prostitute? She is a Christianized Theodote whose conversion appeared earlier in the *Acts of John*. It would appear that near the beginning of the book one would have read that three times the apostle had wanted to marry, but Christ intervened, the last time by blinding him for more than two years. When he regained his sight, he no longer found women sexually desirable, not even a beautiful prostitute whom he converted to chastity just as he had Drusiana and Aristobula. He also may have promoted sexual abstinence to Aristippus and Xenophon. John thus emulates Xenophon's Socrates, who 'reproved sinners' and 'advanced them toward virtue and the doing of the good and beautiful'. The chaste prostitute joined others who had attached themselves to John, travelled with him to Ephesus, and, manifesting not only chastity but also wisdom, steadfastness and fidelity, apparently was with him until the end.

---

46 *Acts of Andrew*, Pass. 63 (9).

47 In my book *Christianizing Homer* I argued that the author of the *Acts of Andrew* modelled the passion after Plato's depiction of the death of Socrates in the *Phaedo* (218–73). Andrew's followers throng to the prison where he is being held for having introduced a new religion into Patras and for having corrupted the wife of Aegeates, charges similar to those against Socrates: he introduced new gods and corrupted the young. While hanging on the cross Andrew addressed the crowds standing nearby and instructed them on the nature of the soul and of death, namely that death does not represent the end of existence but the beginning of a life for the soul far better than its life in the body. This is the very topic that Socrates discussed with his friends the day of his death. Both martyrs begin their speeches with a statement concerning the immortality of the soul, then turn to the pleasures of eating, sex, possessions and finally the concern for the body instead of the soul. When the reader of the *Acts of Andrew* reads 'we wept' – the only change of the narrator's voice in the body of the entire work – she or he might well have recalled the *Phaedo*, where this character narrates the death of Socrates in the first person.

CONSTRUCTION OF CULTURE THROUGH THE CONSTRUCTION OF PERSON: THE CONSTRUCTION OF THECLA IN THE *ACTS OF THECLA**

JOHANNES N. VORSTER

Burke recounts the bodily experience of an anthropologist during a feast given by 'Esquimaux'.[1] Being a good anthropologist he decided to understand from 'within' by sharing their dinner. Their dinner, however, had the appearance of blubber. Despite his good intentions, his stomach revolted and he had to rush outside. As he was recovering, an Esquimau woman approached him in conversation. When she heard that blubber had been served, she felt offended for not being told that blubber was on the menu. She went in, only to appear a moment later in disgust: the diners were not having blubber, but dumplings, something she loathed, but which the anthropologist's body should have appreciated.

Rebhorn, following Mikhail Bakhtin, indicates how the body functioned as a criterion for the distinction between upper and lower classes during the Renaissance.[2] The nobility is identified with the classical body as a finished and completed object; the lower classes stand in a homologous relationship with the grotesque body and are consequently seen as being in process, transgressing their limits and being open to the universe. According to this distinction the courtier's body should be an appropriate size, neither too big nor too small. It should be a size that lends itself to agility, suppleness, lightness, quickness and dexterity, reflecting social mobility and self-control. On the other hand, the grotesque body can be characterized by its stiffness, rigidity and lack of control, reflecting the ridiculousness and powerlessness of a lower social position.

These examples provide us with a glimpse of the complicated relationship between the body, language and culture, and they serve to illustrate the extent to which a culture may affect the body. If the relationship between body and culture is so close as to affect the body physically, investigating perceptions of and attitudes towards the body may help us in understanding the way in which cultures are constructed. In reviewing a number of major studies on the relationship between the body and culture, Sullivan indicates how the body can provide us with an understanding of a specific culture. He

* This essay is a revision of an earlier article, entitled 'Construction of Culture Through the Construction of Person: The *Acts of Thecla* as an Example', published in Stanley E. Porter and Thomas H. Olbricht (eds.), *The Rhetorical Analysis of Scripture: Essays from the 1995 London Conference* (JSNTSS, 146; Sheffield: Sheffield Academic Press, 1997), pp. 445–73. I would like to express my appreciation to Professor A.-J. Levine for the helpful critical comments in the process of revision. The remaining flaws, inaccuracies and open problems are all on my account.

1 K. Burke, 'Definition of Man', in *idem* (ed.), *Language as Symbolic Action* (Berkeley: University of California Press, 1966), pp. 3–24 (7).

2 W.A. Rebhorn, 'Baldesar Castiglione, Thomas Wilson, and the Courtly Body of Renaissance Rhetoric', *Rhetorica* 10.6 (1993), pp. 241–74.

comes to the conclusion that 'all of these studies, whether of Aztec, Chinese, Tamil, Japanese, medieval European, or ancient Mediterranean communities, insist that the body lies at the center of the cultural worldview, especially at the heart of religious experience and practice'.[3] And Rouselle claims that an understanding of ancient morality and ethics (and one could add, politics) presupposes an understanding of the ways and means 'male citizens' made 'customary use ... of the bodies of others'.[4]

The problem I wish to address concerns the complex relationship between an object of reality, the body and its functions, and its interaction with language. On the one hand the body grants materiality to language; language is constituted from an interplay among sensory experiences, cognitive processes and a flow of air issued from the respiratory organs. When the body dies, this ability ceases. On the other hand the body may be seen as something fabricated by language. That which the body has produced, namely language, acts back upon the body, controlling its inlets and outlets. Such is the power of the linguistic structures acting back upon the body that even when the body dies, these structures pretend to maintain some kind of hold on the body. The concern is, therefore, to see how the body was put into discourse and to determine why it received its specific discursive character contingent to a situation.

The body is formed, or fabricated, by the processes of symbolization within a society. However, since the body can be drawn into processes of symbolization, it also functions as a locus of political interaction and may serve to affect societies. If human beings create and use symbols to induce cooperation and if the body is known only through the process of symbolization, the symbolizations of the body can be seen as rhetorical strategies. The body as rhetorical strategy explains why rhetoric has always emphasized the *topos* of person. If the notion of personhood refers to the manner in which the body has been integrated by processes of societal symbolization, an analysis of the construction of 'person' may provide us with access to the construction of culture. Using the apocryphal *Acts of Thecla* as an example,[5] I demonstrate how the construction of person can effect the construction of culture and, specifically, how a different understanding of the body and bodily activities could lead to the construction of a counterculture. Since the *Acts of Thecla* may be regarded as ascetic discourse, its analysis helps us to understand why asceticism played such an important and powerful role in Late Antiquity.

---

3 L.E. Sullivan, 'Body Works: Knowledge of the Body in the Study of Religion', *History of Religions* 30.1 (1990), pp. 86–99 (99).

4 A. Rouselle, 'Personal Status and Sexual Practice in the Roman Empire', in M. Feher *et al.* (eds.), *Fragments for a History of the Human Body*, I (New York: Urzone, 1989), pp. 300–33 (302).

5 The *Acts of Thecla* should by no means be regarded as representative of early Christian discourse; it is selected because the body is here very clearly at the centre. This essay forms part of a larger project in which the analysis of a more representative corpus of texts is undertaken. Textual references to the *Acts of Thecla* are from R.A. Lipsius, *Acta apostolorum apocrypha* (Hildesheim: Georg Olms, 1972), pp. 235–72.

The Body and Culture

Symbolization and Reality

The interaction between body and culture may be approached from the interaction between the human body's potential to symbolize and reality. To interact with reality by means of highly complex processes of symbolization is unique to the human body.[6] As a matter of fact, human bodies need to interact with reality by means of symbols in order to create viable circumstances for survival. Both the complexity of humanity's social organization and its biological development not only require but also facilitate the use of symbols.[7] For that very reason Kenneth Burke also defines a human being as 'a symbol-using animal' or in a more extended form as a 'symbol-using, symbol-making, symbol-misusing animal'.[8] In later years he becomes more specific and defines human beings as 'Being bodies that learn language thereby becoming worldlings ...'[9] It is from this ability to symbolize that culture originates.

Symbolization should not only be understood in a one-dimensional sense as if symbols are created representing and reflecting reality.[10] Reality can, however, never be reflected; nature cannot be created, it simply is. This view has slowly but surely ingrained itself in the study of language.[11] Language as a function of symbolic action is no longer seen as merely representational of reality, but is seen as interactional. Thus, language is not only *agency*; it is an act – with language we *do*. The power of symbolizing through language lies at the root of creativity. By means

---

6 Although it could be argued that other animal species also interact by means of symbolization, the level of sophistication can in no way be compared to that of human beings. See K. Burke, '(Nonsymbolic) Motion/(Symbolic) Action', *Critical Inquiry* 4 (1978), pp. 809–38 (810).

7 Cf. R. Andersen, *The Power and the Word: Language, Power and Change* (London: Paladin Grafton Books, 1988), pp. 43–55.

8 Burke, 'Definition of Man', p. 6. Burke's definition of a human being leads him to dichotomize a person into two components, namely that of animality and symbolicity. Although this duality is unfortunate to the extent that it could be misconstrued as a Cartesian dichotomy, it should be seen in the wider framework of Burke's insistence on life as social drama. He does not claim ontological validity for this distinction; it should rather be seen as a playful epistemological distinction with which to address the power of people's symbolicity.

9 Cf. F.K. Foss and C.L. Griffin, 'A Feminist Perspective on Rhetorical Theory: Toward a Clarification of Boundaries', *Western Journal of Communication* 56 (1992), pp. 330–49 (342). The reference to Burke is juxtaposed to a definition by Starhawk, yet retained. Foss and Griffin argue that a Burkeian type of Rhetoric is more appropriate to discourses in which hierarchy and domination are operative. It is this 'power-over' type of Rhetoric which is more suited for an analysis of the *Acts of Thecla*, since its structuring principles were generated by a culture steeped in and pervaded by social hierarchy.

10 From the sphere of language studies G. Lakoff, *Women, Fire and Dangerous Things* (Chicago: University of Chicago Press, 1987) exposes the myth of representationalism with his outright attack on objectivism. He locates the problem of representationalistic symbolism in the process of categorization. From the sphere of anthropology, see F. De Boeck and R. Devisch, 'Ndembu, Luunda and Yaka Divination Compared: From Representation and Social Engineering to Embodiment and Worldmaking', *Journal of Religion in Africa* 24.2 (1994), pp. 98–133.

11 Lakoff (*Women, Fire*) claims that linguistic structures were largely dominated by an objectivist philosophy of meaning. Within such a philosophy meaning is constituted in the representational relationship between objects of reality and symbols. 'Symbols get their meaning via correspondences to things in the external world' (p. xii).

of the 'word' things can be called into existence; by naming something we evoke something else.

Owing to the ability to symbolize social realities are created, making reality appear structured and ordered. Such is the power of our processes of symbolization that we experience these created social realities as objective, as factual, as the reality; to a certain extent, in a kind of extended way, they are real. Since these processes of symbolization are social, members of social groups are in agreement on its factuality. Scholars refer to this process in different ways. Berger speaks of objectification,[12] Burke of 'context of situation',[13] and Perelman and Olbrechts-Tyteca's remarks on 'facts and truths' would also be applicable.[14]

The formulation 'context of situation' does not refer to a physical setting or to a specific rhetorical situation. 'Context' here refers to those discursive practices in a society that are encountered as factual and objective. Burke uses the analogy of an 'unending conversation'. This is the conversation that has been conducted within that society long before the birth of the individual and which will proceed after his/her death. Contexts of situation consist of, *inter alia*, 'the material interests ... that you symbolically defend or symbolically appropriate or symbolically align yourself with in the course of making your own assertions'.[15] These contexts determine how human beings in their various situations think, talk and act. They are created linguistically, and their power is such that 'things' can become the signs for 'words'. The culture-creating role of language is already becoming clear.[16]

'Languaging' the Body and 'Embodying' Language

Against the backdrop of language as function of symbolic action, body and culture consistently interact. Just as all our knowledge of reality should be seen as

12 P. Berger, *The Social Reality of Religion* (Harmondsworth, UK: Penguin Books, 1967).

13 K. Burke, *The Philosophy of Literary Form* (Berkeley: University of California Press, 1973 [1941]).

14 C. Perelman and L. Olbrechts-Tyteca, *The New Rhetoric: A Treatise on Argumentation* (Notre Dame, IN: University of Notre Dame Press, 1969). For Perelman and Olbrechts-Tyteca (pp. 67–70) the Burkeian 'context of situation' would be 'facts and truth' as objects of agreement. It comprises what amounts to those structures that are accepted by the audience as factual reality.

15 Burke, *Philosophy of Literary Form*, p. 112.

16 Language as a function of humankind's symbolic action is at this state recognized as the most important factor in the creation of culture. L.E. Sullivan, '"Seeking an End to the Primary Text" or "Putting an End to the Text as Primary"', in F.E. Reynolds and S.L. Burkhalter (eds.), *Beyond the Classics? Essays in Religious Studies and Liberal Education* (Atlanta: Scholars Press, 1990), pp. 41–58, downplays the importance of language, especially the written text, in the creation of culture. He notes that besides language various other means give expression to the symbolicity of humankind: weeping, weaving, pottery, etc. He indicates that the textualization of all symbolic actions reduces cognitive processes to linguistic prescriptions, excluding the problems the imagination has with the sheer materiality of language. Furthermore, he argues that the linguistic turn brought about by the emphasis on the arbitrariness of the sign neglects the insight that 'meaning is *a priori* given in the cultural situation through primordial appearance, revelation or spontaneous insight' (p. 46). Although Sullivan does not always clearly distinguish between spoken and written language, his contention seems to be with texts. His warnings should be heeded – language should undoubtedly not be seen as the only function of symbolic action. However, the role of language in the formation of culture cannot be denied. A tribe may symbolize by means of dancing, weaving or weeping, but the meaning of these symbolic actions finds its expression in language.

expressions of our symbolicity, so also our knowledge about the body. Few things may strike human beings as so objective, so given and real, as the body. Yet few areas illustrate the power of language better than where the body is concerned. Naming the body, entitling its activities, happens from the discursive practices in a society, from its context of situation. The body is 'languaged' from the discursive practices of social groups. Putting the body into discourse does not reveal, expose or reflect what the body is, but it incarcerates the body in the value-system of a society. Providing the 'body' with a linguistic sign does not tell us what the body is, but what a community deems it should or ought to be. Cultures become disciplines that prescribe codes for the domestication of the body.[17] Knowledge about the body is therefore always culturally constituted.

Culturally transmitted knowledge of the body should be seen in a very physical sense. Scott remarked that culture or our traditions are not entities at a distance; culture is lived.[18] The implication is that we live the bodies of our cultures. As the body begins its lifelong journey within a cultural system, its growth, intakes, excretions or secretions, its passages, orifices and appendages all acquire their meaning within culturally designated moments in time, mores, customs and habits. Lock and Scheper-Hughes claim such an intimate interaction between the body and society that societal threats also threaten conceptions of the body; the boundaries between the individual body and the body politic blur.[19] They see within Western society's insistence on lean, healthy, strong bodies, the cultural values of autonomy, independence, competitiveness and discipline. A society's discursive practices concerning the body thereby form a screen through which partial knowledge of the body is filtered and certain attitudes towards the body, its parts and its activities are created.

The censuring system thus created provides society with the possibility of social control over the body's functions and activities. By means of language the body is inscribed into the hierarchies, inequalities, loci of powers and structures that are already in existence within society, and thus it becomes the locus of political meaning. The body disappears behind the political 'body', and it is in terms of the latter that we think about ourselves.

Censuring should not be misunderstood as if it is only a filtering system that provides us with the categories in terms of which we seek knowledge of the body. Societies' censuring discursive practices are extremely creative in exerting control over the body. Owing to the way in which they categorize bodies, authority or status can be assigned to certain types of bodies, while others are deprived; while certain types of bodies are included in a class, others can by virtue of discursive practices be excluded. As noted above, during the Renaissance the body functions as one of the ways by which the nobility defines itself and distinguishes itself from artisans and peasants. Rebhorn indicates how ugliness was related to the lower orders of

17 M. Lock and N. Scheper-Hughes, 'A Critical-Interpretive Approach in Medical Anthropology: Rituals and Routines of Discipline and Dissent', in T.M. Johnson and C.F. Sargent (eds.), *Medical Anthropology: Contemporary Theory and Method* (New York: Praeger, 1990), pp. 47–72 (66).

18 R.L. Scott, 'On Viewing Rhetoric as Epistemic', in B.L. Brock *et al.* (eds.), *Methods of Rhetorical Criticism: A Twentieth-Century Perspective* (Detroit, MI: Wayne State University Press, 1989), pp. 134–43 (138).

19 Lock and Scheper-Hughes, 'Critical-Interpretive Approach', p. 66.

society, while virile beauty and graciousness, agility and lightness, balance and symmetry were prescribed for the body of the courtier.[20] Excluded from this class of the nobility are bodies that can be described as grotesque or deformed, bodies that appear stiff, rigid and lack control. Foucault indicates in similar fashion that the languaging of bodily activities does not only comprise prohibition. By virtue of the creative potential of language sexual activities that were marginalized until the eighteenth century started to receive attention. The linguistic embodiment of sexual activities such as sex with children gave it the power of presence, thereby achieving permanent reality – it was as if they were 'implanted in bodies'.[21]

Personhood and the Body

Person can be constructed in a variety of ways. Lock and Scheper-Hughes remind us that the notion of person had first theoretically be considered by John Locke. Following Mauss they indicate that 'person' refers to the 'uniquely Western notion of the individual as a quasi-sacred, legal, moral, and psychological entity whose rights are limited only by the rights of other equally autonomous individuals'.[22] The juridical influence on the construction of person can also be seen in Perelman and Olbrechts-Tyteca.[23] Although they emphasize that the construction of person would vary according to time and metaphysical system, person is to a large extent constituted by their acts. And while stability is necessary for the notion of person, there is a kind of fluidity in the notion. The structure of a person may become more rigid as time goes by, but even death does not preclude an ongoing process of person-construction. Various alternative ways of person-construction in different societies can be indicated.[24]

My concern is, however, with the way in which body and person are related. The problem is that the body in Western tradition has always been regarded with some kind of dualism. Although some assign the origins of bodily dualism to Graeco–Roman philosophy,[25] it was Descartes who very deliberately dichotomized person into 'body' and 'mind'. The dualism in the notion of person has received added impetus with the Cartesian 'I think, therefore I am'. The person became fragmented into mind vs. body. Since the mind got the upperhand in the struggle between body

20 Rebhorn, 'Baldesar Castiglione', pp. 244–46.
21 M. Foucault, *History of Sexuality* I (3 vols.; Harmondsworth, UK: Penguin, 1978), pp. 42–44 (44).
22 Lock and Scheper-Hughes, 'Critical-Interpretive Approach', p. 56.
23 Perelman and Olbrechts-Tyteca, *New Rhetoric*, p. 293.
24 Cf. Lock and Scheper-Hughes, 'Critical-Interpretive Approach', p. 57.
25 Cf. G.A.G. Stroumsa, '*Caro salutis cardo*: Shaping the Person in Early Christian Thought', *History of Religions* 30 (1990), pp. 25–50. Various objections can be lodged against Strousma's proposal. Early Christianity is treated as a rather uniform tradition. When the 'Gnostics' (if we can use this term), with their insistence on the corruptible body, are portrayed, it happens from the perspective of traditional early Christianity. It is also problematic to give equal status to body and soul when these aspects are mentioned in early Christianity. Furthermore, the resurrection of the body does not enhance bodily status, but emphasizes the body as a problem since it always refers to an improvement in the condition of the body. Finally, the incarnation of Christ does not necessarily mean an ennobling of the body – it could just as well also illustrate a frustration of human bodies to cope with their realities.

and mind, the body was excluded from scientific activity; only the mind acquired epistemological status. Since only the mind, as the higher essence of a human being, played a role in the acquisition of knowledge, nature can be objectively studied if the body is successfully inhibited.[26] On the other hand, with this dichotomy firmly entrenched also within the developing medical sciences, the association of the body with nature, that which can be objectively studied, has led to a materialistic view of the self. The real self lies in the body. Lock and Scheper-Hughes indicate how this dichotomy influenced the medical sciences to locate pain, for example, as either 'physical or mental, biological or psychological – never both, or something quite either'.[27]

Conversely, anthropological studies across cultures have shown that personhood need not be dualistically divided and that the individualistic person is a Western creation. Alternatives could also be a sociocentric construction or a personhood that is divided into a multiplicity of selves.[28] Whichever way personhood is constructed within different societies, the body always seems to form at least a part of such a construction.

Indeed, a body comes into existence within social relations. Jung describes it aptly: 'Others in fact give us to ourselves.'[29] From our birth we exist in relationship to others, that is, as social beings. Human existence is always in interaction with 'an-other' and the survival of the human body depends on the success of that inter-action. Sociality is therefore necessarily given with embodiment.[30] However, it is this sociality that constitutes personhood because in the social interaction of the body the person is formed. It is clear that the body cannot be simply identified with the person, but it is in the interaction with its social environment that the person is constructed. As the body, as a sensory centre, develops, sociality or relationality intensifies and is also extended. The sensory centre also becomes centre of meaning, centre of values. Tribby quite correctly maintains: 'Bodies, objects, comportments ... do not "have" meanings, they *acquire* them, and those meanings are contested in social space and social time.'[31] The process of acculturation is therefore responsible for the construction of person, or put differently: acculturation of the body fabricates the person.

A few implications can be drawn. First, if the acculturation of the body consti-tutes the person, our focus should be on the interaction of the body with its social environment. Second, the body is and should always be part of the notion of person. The notion of person expresses the sociality of the body which is indicative of the body's social moulding. Third, personhood can never be rigid and permanent; on the contrary, the person is continuously, differently constructed. As the body exter-nalizes itself in reaching out to the other and as society enforces the internalization of the other, the person is formed. However, this is an unending process. If the body

26 Cf. Lock and Scheper-Hughes, 'Critical-Interpretive Approach', p. 52.

27 Lock and Scheper-Hughes, 'Critical-Interpretive Approach', pp. 52–53.

28 Lock and Scheper-Hughes, 'Critical-Interpretive Approach', pp. 58–59.

29 L.S. Jung, 'Autonomy as Justice: Spatiality and the Revelation of Otherness', *Journal of Religious Ethics* 14.1 (1986), pp. 157–83 (159).

30 Jung, 'Autonomy as Justice', p. 159.

31 J. Tribby, 'Body/Building: Living the Museum Life in Early Modern Europe', *Rhetorica* 10.2 (1992), pp. 139–62 (140).

acquires rather than possesses social meaning, personhood changes consistently according to time and space. Fourth, if the person is subject to constant change, personhood is necessarily pluralistic. This implies that there is no real self, no essence to a person. The social embodiment of the body requires that certain roles have to be selected appropriate to the variety of the social situations in which the body comes to find itself. Fifth, the way in which the body is acculturated influences self-awareness. If the body is negatively or under unfavourable circumstances acculturated, a negative personhood is most likely. Fragmenting the body by culturally maintaining a favourable disposition towards certain body parts or bodily functions, while negativizing others, leads to the production of fragmented personhood.

The Rhetoricity of the Body in the Acts of Thecla

Various writings or groups of writings could have been chosen for a rhetorical analysis. I have decided on the apocryphal *Acts of Thecla* because, whether or not one opts for female authorship, the *Acts of Thecla* provides us with a glimpse into the circumstances of womanhood in the second century.[32] Furthermore, the *Acts of Thecla* can be seen as 'ascetic discourse', providing us with what can be termed a 'counterculture'. As an expression of rhetorical dissent, ascetic discourse contributes to the construction of an alternative society by redefining bodily behaviour. The degree of dissent or alternativity may differ, but the body functions as a locus of potential social empowerment. As such the *Acts of Thecla* can function as an example of how culture is constructed through the construction of a person.

Since the rhetoricity of the body crystallizes in the notion of person, its construction would be our point of departure. In the *Acts of Thecla* we have to look at the construction of person on two levels. The first would be the *context* part of the 'context of situation', i.e. the way in which the construction of person had taken place according to the discursive practices of society – or to put it differently, the culture against which the drama is to take place. The context of the 'context of situation' would constitute the society's dominant culture. The second level functions as the *situation* part of the 'context of situation' or in more familiar terms the 'rhetorical situation', that is the situation the originators of this discourse wished to create. The repeated emphasis and recipience of discourses such as these would at a later stage in Antiquity again form the 'context' level, illustrating the fluidity of the relationship between 'context' and 'situation'. For example, the problem of continence we encounter in the *Acts of Thecla* has by the time of Pseudo-Chrysostom's *Panegyric*[33]

32 Female authorship would have provided us with what can be seen as a more 'direct recovery' of a female perspective as A.S. Jacobs, 'A Family Affair: Marriage, Class, and Ethics in the Apocryphal Acts of the Apostles', *JECS* 7.1 (1999), pp. 105–38 (124) has argued (see his article in this collection). He quotes Peter Brown who has indicated that the Christian Apocrypha should be seen as a reflection of the way men used 'women to think with' (see P. Brown, *The Body and Society: Men, Women and Sexual Renunciation in Early Christianity* [Lectures in the History of Religions, 13; New York: Columbia University Press, 1988], p. 153).

33 For a translation and brief introduction, see D.R. MacDonald and A.D. Scrimgeour, 'Pseudo-Chrysostom's *Panegyric* to Thecla: The Heroine of the *Acts of Paul* in Homily and Art', *Semeia* 38 (1986), pp. 151–59.

more or less during the fifth and sixth centuries already been institutionalized and formed as part of that time's discursive practices.

The kind of 'person' linguistically constructed within the dominant culture, and of which we find traces in the *Acts of Thecla*, can be depicted as androcentric, sociocentric and futuristic. Since the futuristic component requires more extensive treatment, I will restrict myself only to the androcentric and sociocentric components. Suffice it to mention that the futuristic component concerns the notions of the incomplete body, the body in a process of becoming, the possibility of being more than oneself and the possibility of the 'super-body'.

The Androcentric Person

Although the nebulous diversity of ancient culture, the changes in attitudes towards women between the first and second centuries, the difference in perspectives on women in urban or rural areas, and the difference in attitudes towards women in Rome or the provinces caution us against generalization, the dominant culture seems to have advocated androcentric notions of person. Traces of this culture abound in the *Acts of Thecla*. The focus will be mainly on the role of Thecla herself.

Within Antiquity, to be a person is to be a male. To be a woman is to be a person only when associated with a man. This is clearly the discursive setting against which the social drama of the *Acts of Thecla* unfolds. Although Thecla is first defined in terms of her mother, which is obviously subversive, she is then 'termed' in terms of a man, Thamyris, her betrothed, and in terms of her premarital status (*Acts of Thecla* 7.8). Although not married she is consequently referred to as his (cf. 8.1; 9.2; 10.12; 14.3). In Antioch, Paul, rather than Thecla, is consulted as if she belonged to him (26.1), the assumption being that male accompaniment means male control.

Ripe for marriage, but not married, Thecla typifies a stage of 'becoming a person'. The stage of 'becoming a person' may be differently described in variations of legal codes. The concern here is how discursive practices,[34] formed over an extensive period of time, were inscribed upon bodies. In processes of symbolization in Antiquity blood flowing from the bodies of women was given social significance and provided the possibility of becoming socially accepted as 'person'. The stages of menstruation, defloration and procreation therefore signified growth in becoming a person. In the triad of menstruation, defloration and procreation, menstruation may appear out of place since a man need not have been involved. Yet menstruation signified the beginning of a process that was to end in the birth of the first baby. It signified the transition from a παρθένος to a γυνή, that is, from a girl to a woman. King writes: 'To be classified as a mature woman, a γυνή, it was necessary to have given birth: the birth of the first baby ends the process of becoming a woman which started with the first menstrual period demonstrating the readiness of the body, in

---

34 Discursive practices constitute the *context* of the Burkeian context of situation. They function on the level of the assumed, the factual, the taken for real and for granted. These practices originate from various social spheres of life, such as medical and health, cultic, the securing of shelter and safety or the demarcation of space and time, the organization of a group and its striving towards security, solidarity and continuance. The body, its constitution and functions, provides a *locus* for the integration and organization of social meaning given to these practices. It therefore stands to reason that the discursive practices deriving from a 'medical' contextualization of the body cannot but function as a social register allowing the emergence of varieties of appropriate discourses.

terms both of the availability of blood from which a fetus can be formed, and the possibility of male semen gaining entry to the womb.'[35] The attitude was paradoxical. On the one hand, defloration and the flow of blood during childbirth conferred social status upon women, since these events implied that they had been allowed 'inside' male society. Owing to the association with procreation, blood spilled as the result of defloration and childbirth signified maturation into personhood. By virtue of male control the παρθένος has become γυνή.[36] Where the flowing of blood was associated with procreation, social status was conferred upon the body of a woman.

On the other hand, even within the realm of marriage and procreation, the personhood of a woman was constituted by virtue of male association, since the blood of men and women was symbolically differently evaluated. Sissa makes the important observation that certain models of procreation are in themselves models of filiation. According to Aristotle, conception should be understood from the relationship between form and matter, the former being provided by the male in the form of semen and the latter by the female in the form of superfluous blood. The blood from the female body is, however, simply matter, whereas the semen provides the matter with identity; it constitutes what it is going to be. In order to maintain patrilineality, semen is relieved of materiality, becoming the power necessary to shape the identity of the father into the matter. Procreation as such is, therefore, no guarantee for the personhood of a woman. Within ideologies of patrilineality procreation has to happen within the ambit of male control to ensure personhood.[37] From a wide variety of sources, mythological and ritual, King shows how female maturation is seen as a process of taming and ripening. She writes: 'All women start their lives as outsiders to male society; through maturation they are taken "inside" to reproduce it.' Male intervention is considered necessary to bring this transition about.[38]

Having entered only the first stage of womanhood, namely that of menstruation, yet being betrothed to a man, Thamyris, Thecla is in the process of becoming a person.[39] To advocate continence, however, meant to dissociate the sexes. The implication for Thecla was loss of personhood which brought shame upon her, as can be seen in Thamyris' admonition (10.12). Self-imposed virginity or continence was not

35 H. King, *Hippocrates' Woman: Reading the Female Body in Ancient Greece* (London & New York: Routledge, 1998), p. 23. The general age for commencement of this transitional age was 14 years, which explains why this age validated entry into matrimony. It stands to reason that in certain cases menstruation would not have occurred at this age. Where menstruation did not occur at this age and the girl appeared to be 'ripe for marriage', male intervention was the solution, whether that be the husband or the healer (King, 'Hippocrates' woman', p. 77).

36 E.g. King, 'Hippocrates' woman', p. 111.

37 G. Sissa, 'Subtle Bodies', in M. Feher *et al.* (eds.), *Fragments for a History of the Human Body*, vol. 3, pp. 132–56 (154).

38 King, 'Hippocrates' woman', pp. 76–77.

39 Neither Thecla's blood nor menstruation is mentioned in the *Acts of Thecla*, but it need not be mentioned. Thecla is portrayed as a 'virgin' (παρθένος) and also portrayed as 'betrothed to a man' (7.7, 8). The hierarchically engendered assumption, evoked by these terminologies, would have been that she has entered a process of bleeding. A configuration of meaning surrounds her portrayal. Her conduct suggested a threat posed to the city (9.1, 15.10) – a body symbolism functioned, associating the life of the city and the bleeding female body in the reproductive process (e.g. King, 'Hippocrates' woman', p. 76, and also p. 88 where an association between menstrual and sacrifical blood as public blood is made).

a completely foreign idea towards the beginning of the second century CE. It was practised within various Graeco–Roman cults, such as Demeter's priestesses, as well as those of Athena, Artemis and Hera, and in the cult of Isis sexual abstinence was required of both women and men for certain periods. Perhaps the best-known form of required virginity was that of the Vestal virgins, who had to dedicate themselves for a period of thirty years.[40] Furthermore, at the beginning of the second century CE we find ourselves in the midst of a 'medical' debate stretching from the Hippocratics via Aristotle to Soranus and Galen. The issue is whether excessive sexual activity may be harmful to the body. Whereas the Hippocratic tradition emphasized frequent sexual intercourse for the woman, Aristotle argued that too much sex can be harmful to her health. Soranus, however, was apparently the first to advocate 'lifelong virginity' for women based on the assumption that loss of female seed[41] may result in a loss of the body's vital forces, as evidenced in the body's state of relaxation and fatigue after sexual intercourse.[42] However, Pinault argues that neither the existence of cultic oriented obligatory virginity nor the debate concerning female lifelong virginity should be taken as evidence of the actual social practice during this period, despite the fact that Christians have already practised it by this time. As a matter of fact, Soranus's viewpoint should be taken as theoretical. Pinault concludes: 'Despite the greater freedom that Roman women enjoyed compared to Greek women, I have found no evidence to date to show that daughters of well-born Roman families in the early second century CE could – or would have wanted to – disdain marriage and live all their lives as virgins. Family and state still upheld the ideal of the *matrona*, and the goal of marriage still remained the production of children.'[43] Therefore, by opting for continence, Thecla rejected what was regarded by the dominant Graeco–Roman culture as fundamental to the identity of 'being woman'.

One of the probable motivations for Theocleia's extremely aggressive attitude towards her own daughter (20.6) also lies in the loss of a prospective son-in-law. Societal marginalization and a diminishing of her status as a person stared her in the face.[44] As a widow Theocleia must have already suffered loss of identity. Although the children of a widow implied that she must have had status, that status no longer applied to the widow, because there were no regular inseminations and

---

40 G.P. Corrington, 'The "Divine Woman"? Propaganda and the Power of Chastity in the New Testament Apocrypha', *Helios* 13.1 (1986), pp. 151–62 (151–59).

41 The notion of female semen was widespread in Antiquity as can be seen by Hippocrates, *De Semine*, 1.2, Galen, *De Usu Partium* 14.6. Cf. also A. Rouselle, *Porneia: On Desire and the Body in Antiquity* (Cambridge & Oxford: Blackwell, 1988), p. 29; see also M. Foucault, *The History of Sexuality. 2. The Use of Pleasure* (3 vols.; Harmondsworth: Penguin Books, 1985), p. 132, on Aristotle who denied women the ability to produce semen.

42 J.R Pinault, 'The Medical Case for Virginity in the Early Second Century C.E.: Soranus of Ephesus, "Gynecology" 1.32', *Helios* 19 (1992), pp. 123–39 (125).

43 Pinault, 'The Medical Case for Virginity', pp. 130–31.

44 A rather similar situation in which the child may be a cause of shame for the parent in the household can be seen in the *Martyrdom of Perpetua and Felicitas* 6.4 (text in H. Musurillo, *The Acts of the Christian Martyrs* [Oxford: Clarendon Press, 1972]); also J.N.Vorster, 'The Blood of the Female Martyrs as the Sperm of the Early Church', *Religion and Theology* 10.1 (2003), pp. 66–99 (85, 96).

impregnations.[45] Although she might have had status by virtue of her husband, that disappeared with his death and she again became marginalized. This can also be seen in Tryphaena's outcry. Despite the fact that she must have had some power, she is helpless because she is a widow (30.7). Her social power does not reside in her 'self', but in her affiliation to Caesar (36.2). MacDonald also indicates that the economic status of single women was precarious.[46] Although this may not have been applicable in the case of Tryphaena, the financial support Thecla provided Theocleia should not go unnoticed (43.4).

The need to be associated with a male can also be seen in Thecla's relationship with Paul. Despite the subversive nature of the narrative, the fact that it might have been folklore among women's communities,[47] despite the low profile and even negative perspective on Paul, the fact that the narrative is concerned with continence ... Thecla somehow had to be associated with Paul. Jensen disagrees and disputes the necessity of dependency on Paul.[48] She claims that the integration of the *Acts of Thecla* within the *Acts of Paul* tarnished and diminished Thecla's role in the early Christian communities. Instead of being the female apostolic representative, a female symbol, lauded by the martyr tradition, she has been rehabilitated to become '*der Jungfrau*'.[49]

Despite an admirable concern for the historical contingency of this discourse, Jensen's argument concerns to a large extent only the religious status of the relationship between Paul and Thecla. This aspect obviously has to play an important role, but taking the 'context of situation' seriously reminds us to consider the socio-sexual roles of the actors in this drama. Although the second century in Asia Minor

---

45 In the Hippocratic tradition, the womb was a wandering organ in search of moisture that could have been provided by male insemination; Galen again disagreed, but assigned hysterical symptoms especially to 'widows, and particularly those who previously menstruated regularly, had been pregnant and were eager to have intercourse, but were now deprived of all this', quoted in King, 'Hippocrates' Woman', p. 232.

46 D.R. MacDonald, *The Legend and the Apostle: The Battle for Paul in Story and Canon* (Philadelphia, PA: Westminster Press, 1983), p. 50.

47 Although the origins of the *Acts of Thecla* are by no means certain, various voices argue for female originators. S.L. Davies ('The Social World of the Apocryphal Acts', [Ph.D. diss., Temple University, Ann Arbor, MI: University Microfilms Int., 1978], pp. 140, 151–54) offers the probability that the Apocryphal Acts of the Apostles were written by continent Christian women, but that particularly the *Acts of Paul* was written from a woman's point of view. MacDonald (*Legend and the Apostle*, p. 35), identifying typical folklore elements in the *Acts of Thecla*, argues that women originally told the stories behind these discourses. The 'written text is a veneer laid over narrative structures and techniques taken over from oral tradition' (p. 26). While Burrus ('Chastity as Autonomy: Women in the Stories of the Apocryphal Acts', *Semeia* 38 [1986], pp. 101–17) denies literary dependency on the Hellenistic novel, she likewise argues for female folkloric influence. J. Kaestli ('Response to Burrus', *Semeia* 38 [1986], pp. 119–31) opts for female writers instead of female storytellers and disputes the origins of these narratives within exclusive female communities. Although W. Rordorf ('Tradition and Composition in the *Acts of Thecla*: The State of the Question', *Semeia* 38 [1986], pp. 43–52 [43, 52]) concedes a folklore tradition among celibate women behind the *Acts of Thecla*, he remains convinced that the *Acts of Paul* 'once contained' the *Acts of Thecla* (p. 43).

48 A. Jensen, *Thekla – Die Apostolin: Ein apokrypher Text neu entdeckt* (Frauen-Kultur-Geschichte, 3; Freiburg: Herder, 1995).

49 Jensen, *Thekla-Die Apostolin*, p. 110.

seems to have been a period in which women reached out for more power over their own lives,[50] it is most unlikely that their 'persons' would have been constructed independent of the male population.[51] Owing to views of the body pervading the fabric of ancient culture, a relationship of subordination to men is more plausible. As a male, and not only as a religious leader, Paul could have fulfilled that role.[52] The erotic overtones pervading the narrative (e.g. 7.3; 8.12–15; 18.10–14; 19.6; 20.9; 25.4–5; 40.1) may be regarded as traces of a dominant culture emphasizing the necessity of the female body to attach herself in one way or the other to the male body. Although it has to be conceded that if the *Acts of Thecla* has been integrated into the *Acts of Paul* the status of Thecla would be less than if taken on its own, the entextualization of Paul into the *Acts of Thecla* does not function to diminish but functions rather to enhance Thecla's status.

Yet another example that the 'person' was constructed in terms of the male was the spatial restriction of the female body. The space of the female body was that of the 'household', whereas the male functioned in the public domain. Although the distinction between the household and the public arena should not been seen in a rigoristically, physical manner,[53] the seclusion of women to their homes was not an unfamiliar event. The motivation for the seclusion of women can again be found in patrilineal descendancy. Especially in the case of wealthy or powerful public families the seclusion of women secured the transfer of wealth, property and citizenship from generation to generation.[54] Owing to the dreary and unendurable circumstances of housing in lower socioeconomic strata of society, impoverished women were more likely to appear on the streets and therefore were also more vulnerable to exploitation by the male population.[55]

In the *Thecla* narrative the spatial restriction of women can be seen when we encounter Thecla for the first time, sitting and staring from the window of her mother's home. Despite the various other women attending Paul's meeting, she is depicted as a young woman of virtue, adhering to the code of her society (7.6, 10; 8.7, 12; 9.5; cf. also 8.15 where modesty is mentioned). When she finally transgresses the boundaries of her spatial restriction, it has to happen by means of a bribe (18.1). Travelling outside the boundaries allocated to the bodies of women constitutes a problem for

---

50 E.g. Davies, 'Social World', pp. 142–55; MacDonald, *Battle for Paul*, pp. 37–40; Burrus, 'Chastity as Autonomy', pp. 107, 112–13; T.K. Seim, 'The Gospel of Luke', in E.S. Schüssler Fiorenza (ed.), *Searching the Scriptures* II: *A Feminist Commentary* (2 vols.; New York: Crossroad, 1994), pp. 728–62 (753).

51 E.g. also G.P. Corrington, 'The "Divine Woman"?', p. 154.

52 See R.S. Kraemer, 'The Conversion of Women to Ascetic Forms of Christianity', *Signs: Journal of Women in Culture and Society* 6 (1980), pp. 298–307 (303); Burrus, 'Chastity as Autonomy', p. 115.

53 Kraemer, 'Conversion of Women', p. 302; Seim, 'Gospel of Luke', p. 752.

54 The underlying assumption again discloses the androcentrism of the ancient world. Women were perceived as more susceptible to loss of bodily control and therefore more exposed to seduction. Therefore, they had to be 'protected' by seclusion.

55 P. Veyne ('The Roman Empire' in P. Veyne, Philippe Ariès and Georges Duby (eds.) *A History of Private Life I: From Pagan Rome to Byzantium* [Cambridge and London: The Belknap Press of Harvard University Press, 1987], pp. 5–234 [73]) reminds us that even the 'vast Roman houses' such as those in Pompeii did not imply free, unrestrictive space for their owners, since 'they were more densely occupied than today's low-rent apartment houses'.

Thecla. McGinn indicates that Thecla's offer to cut her hair (25.3) can be interpreted not only as a disguise to safeguard her as a woman, but also as a token of 'taking up a "manly" way of life'.[56] Moving into the space allocated to the bodies of men requires imitation of their bodies. Even after she has acquired sociopolitical status, she still needs to dress like a man (40.3) on her journey in search of Paul. Despite Paul's refusal to allow her to 'go public' (25.5) she needs his accompaniment in the public sphere of Antioch.[57] However, his denial that she belongs to him renders her powerless in the domain of men and therefore vulnerable to sexual advances. Since a woman's place was restricted to the household, Alexander mistakenly took her to be sexually free (26.1).[58]

The Sociocentric Person
The body of a person does not belong to the person, but can be seen as a political centre on which the values of the community consistently interact. Therefore, whether a person is good or bad, modest or immodest, moral or immoral, depends on the social code into which the body has been drawn. Where a sociocentric perception of the body prevails, personhood is constructed relative to the 'good' a body may bring the society. The bodily behaviour of the individual person is seen to affect society as a whole. What is perceived and socially encoded to be 'defilement' of the body is consequently a contamination of the city and could lead to the loss of citizenship. For example, Rouselle indicates how certain sexual acts could reduce a person to the status of infamy, a class of people comprising prostitutes and those participating in the games or theatre, all of which were excluded from citizenship.[59] Personhood, therefore, becomes dependent on the successful integration of the body into the social hierarchy. To be a person means to be a good citizen.[60]

In ancient society the personhood of a woman was constituted by her sociosexual role, and marriage was the mechanism by which society orchestrated its control and power over the female body. Within the environment of marriage a woman achieved status and honour; as Kraemer has stated aptly: '[T]o be woman is to be wife.'[61] Outside marriage the female body was perceived to have the potential of chaos, a

56 S.E. McGinn, 'The Acts of Thecla', in E. Schüssler Fiorenza (ed.), *Searching the Scriptures* II: *A Feminist Commentary* (2 vols.; New York: Crossroad, 1994), pp. 800–28 (827).
57 Veyne, 'The Roman Empire', p. 73, aptly refers to this accompaniment as a 'mobile prison' and indicates that 'decency and concern for station required that ladies of rank never go out without maids, companions (*comites*), and a mounted servant known as a *custos* ...' See in this respect also Thecla's response to Alexander at 26.4 indicating her social status.
58 Burrus, 'Chastity as Autonomy', p. 110; McGinn 'Acts of Thecla', pp. 816, 827.
59 Rouselle, 'Personal Status', pp. 315–22.
60 Personhood need not always be an integration of the body into a social *hierarchy*, but personhood will always be qualified by the forces of the social environment in which the body develops. Despite the traces of resistance issuing from early Christianity, some of which can be seen in the Apocrypha, the notion of 'person' did not differ radically from its social environment. The confession 'I am a Christian' uttered by the martyrs of early Christianity apparently demolished social hierarchies as it simultaneously claimed superiority and voluntary self-destruction. Yet the *context* of the 'context of situation' did not construct equal identities with respect to females and males. Embedded within an engendered social hierarchy, the construction of the persons of male and female martyrs differed. See in this regard, Vorster, 'The Blood of the Female', p. 84.
61 Kraemer, 'Conversion of Women', p. 302.

source of disorder and a possible threat to the social fabric. An unmarried woman has the potential to occupy the same role as the magician and can be described, therefore, as 'spirit possessed' or 'mad'.[62] For that very reason, a woman deformed or dead was preferable to a woman not fulfilling her sociosexual role.[63] To defy her sociosexual role was tantamount to a betrayal of the 'citizenbody as a collectivity'.[64] Brown formulates: 'the married couple were presented less as a pair of equal lovers than as a reassuring microcosm of the social order'.[65]

Within marriage the personhood of women could be actualized simply because it provided the context within which the sociosexual role could be fulfilled. Owing to the unreliability of the body, the inability to effectively cure and consequently the short lifespan of the average citizen in Graeco–Roman society, procreation had to be ensured.[66] And marriage was the mechanism by which procreation was promoted, irrespective of the immense stress frequent pregnancies and the desirability or non-desirability of pregnancy could have caused the bodies of women. Furthermore, as procreation within a patrilineal society was also a means to ensure the continuity of the family or tribal honour, its wealth and status, marriage guaranteed legitimate offspring. Finally, as women were biologically regarded as 'failed males', as 'wild' and untamed, marriage functioned to 'domesticate' or 'tame' a woman; it functioned as the context within which a woman could enter the controlled world of men.[67]

Besides the sociosexual role a woman could fulfil in marriage, the person of the married woman also signified a particular class and status – it formed part of a deliberate political strategy to maintain social hierarchy. Unlike contemporary family life, marriage during the second century CE was a status symbol, an emblem of upper-class aristocracy in Roman societies. It was the social and moral product of a process that had already commenced with legislation promulgated by Augustus and directed at the senatorial classes. From a union based on a vertical, patriarchal hierarchy which had to ensure procreation and financial stability, a transformation gradually took place which established an ethical union between partners within the family structure of the aristocracy. Jacobs has indicated how this change in the configuration of the family catapulted 'marriage from the realm of financial transactions between propertied families into the sphere of *dignitas*, a factor upon which a man could establish or diminish his public "face"'.[68] The ethical union that came about by this transformed notion of marriage was infused by the *concordia* ideology.[69] And Veyne distinguishes between an old and a new moral code that shifted into position with the change from a Roman Republic to an Empire. The old moral code offered marriage as one of the civic duties with which a man of the aristocracy may have availed himself – it was not taken for granted, but an option that a citizen of the upper class could decide to accept or reject. The new moral code specified the duties of the married man: In order to be 'a good man, one must make love only in order to have

62 Kraemer, 'Conversion of Women', p. 304.
63 Kraemer, 'Conversion of Women', p. 303.
64 Rouselle, 'Personal Status', p. 307.
65 Brown, *Body and Society*, p. 17.
66 Brown, *Body and Society*, p. 6.
67 Corrington, 'Divine Woman', p. 153; Brown, *Body and Society*, pp. 9–17.
68 Jacobs, 'A Family Affair', p. 110.
69 Jacobs, 'A Family Affair', p. 111.

children. Marriage is not a means to sexual pleasure.'[70] The new moral code still did not establish the notion of the 'happy couple', but it acknowledged affection and lifelong companionship as constituents of marriage. The harmonious union became an added incentive to the requirements of having children and running households.[71] However, although friendship, lifelong friendship, now became a possibility, the relationship within marriage was still hierarchical and the husband was seen as the cultural inseminator.

During the first two centuries of the Common Era, marriage functioned, therefore, as a political mechanism, a strategy to stabilize and strengthen upper-class Roman society by the interiorization of a new moral code that did not really supplant the old one, but infused it with a different quality. Situated within the elite levels of Roman society, it acquired immense public power. The married person signified class and status; marriage served to construct a personhood constituted by noble birth, wealth, education, stability and good balanced citizenship. Refusing to get married could therefore be taken as a deliberate strategy of resistance against authority and the structuring of civic power relations, as an attempt to dismantle social hierarchy. It is in this respect that Jacobs's argument should be taken seriously. He argues that the Apocryphal Acts should be seen as 'a deliberate form of narrative resistance to this ethical family configuration on marriage'.[72]

The portrayal of Thecla's person in the *Acts of Thecla* represents a certain ambivalence. The sociocentric notion of personhood in the Graeco–Roman world in which the individual body was subsumed into the social body and its interests forms the undercurrent for the construction of Thecla's person. Sociocentrism was the dominant determinative constituent, and although an 'alternative' quality was also built in the construction of her person, sociocentrism provided the terminologies.

The requirement for the members of the Roman aristocracy to marry finds its echoes in the references to class which function in the construction of Thecla's person. She is portrayed as a 'mistress' in a household (10.3) to be married to Thamyris, who is depicted as the 'first man of this city' (11.13). The setting in Iconia in the first part of Thecla's story is that of the elite, as can be seen in the sumptuous banquet Thamyris offered Demas and Hermogenes in exchange for information (13.5–8) and the issue at stake is his deprivation of marriage (13.12). This blow to his *dignitas* acquires public indignation, and the authorities of the city are summoned to prevent its effect on the social body (15.3). Thecla's status as part of the upper class is again confirmed in the Antiochean scene in which she portrays herself as 'one of the first among the Iconians' (26.4).

Sexual abstinence and the rejection of marriage are portrayed as serious concerns, not only for Thecla and her partner, but for the citizen body as such. The potential threat continence could entail for the city can be seen in the references to the possible influence this 'doctrine' might have on 'young men and virgins' (e.g. 9.2; 11.10; 15.13; 22.1). The veiled threat to the community can also be seen in the allegation against Paul; as champion of continence he triggers the fear of loss of social control and thereby relegates himself to the category of magician (15.12; 20.1). Thecla is

70 Veyne, 'The Roman Empire', p. 37.
71 Veyne, 'The Roman Empire', p. 40.
72 Jacobs, 'A Family Affair', p. 126.

initially portrayed as someone who manifests symptoms of illness (cf. 8.11; 10.11, 12), thereby relegating herself to the sphere of 'abnormalcy'.[73] That the denial of marriage with its possibility of procreation was regarded as likely to disrupt social control can clearly be taken by the governor's questions posed to both Paul and Thecla. The charge of teaching that effects an aversity to marriage is seen as a serious allegation (16.7), and Thecla's response to Paul's teaching is seen as a transgression of Iconian law (20.4).

The 'no' of society to non-marriage can nowhere better be seen than in Thecla's mother herself, condemning Thecla in anaphoric outcry. The similarly ἄνομος and ἄνυμος by the apanaphoric κατακαίω emphasizes the social antagonism against those exposing the fragility of the social body (cf. 20.6). In the cry from the Theocleia's lips, the anguished lament of the social body against its own mortality can be heard. The sociocentric body, obediently formed and cultivated by the discursive practices of its day, prefers the violent elimination of its own produce in order to safeguard the continued existence of the social body. The public destruction of this social 'disease' corresponds with the publicity of the threat: it is regarded as contagious and may spread. As such the theatre forms the 'scene' in which the 'act' of removal has to take place.

The 'Alternative' Person

Thus far the attempt was to demarcate what could have been the notion of person of the dominant culture within which the *Acts of Thecla* circulated and to illustrate its traces in the construction of Thecla's person. However, the *Acts of Thecla* should be seen as a subversive writing, undermining the value-system of the dominant culture, intending to modify its social values by proposing an alternative construction of person.[74] By a redefinition of personhood, the possibility of an emerging alternative culture appeared. But a redefinition of personhood has several implications, because it meant the dismantling of the androcentric component of person and yet, that dismantling need not necessarily be total. Taking the 'man' out of a 'man-centred' notion of person implied loss of status and identity for a woman.[75] The possibility of achieving personhood within the dominant culture, of acquiring social identity within the household and therefore also the possibility of achieving social power, disappears with the rejection of marriage and the consequent acceptance of sexual abstinence. If personhood is no longer constituted by its sociosexual requirement in an environment where the personhood (of a female) completely coincided with male-association, what functions as its replacement? What were the mechanisms employed to resist social rejection and assist social empowerment?

Putting the body into an alternative discourse, whether oral and/or written, should in itself be seen as a powerful strategy to obtain social empowerment. By 'languaging' the body it became a locus of political interaction. The discursive body acquired a

73 McGinn ('Acts of Thecla', p. 814) indicates that the refusal to follow social convention was seen as a sign of insanity or demon possession.

74 See also Jacobs, 'A Family Affair', p. 126.

75 See G. Clark, 'Women and Asceticism in Late Antiquity: The Refusal of Status and Gender', in V.L. Wimbush and R. Valantasis (eds.), *Asceticism* (Oxford: Oxford University Press, 1995), pp. 33–48 (39).

power that the real body did not possess, because the process of symbolization (or in this case, the 'languaging' of the body) enabled the body to engage and transcend the boundaries imposed by the discursive practices of society. It became a construct of power, inviting identification. Since the discursive body became a body in terms of which a society could perceive their real bodies, possibilities arose that could move the social group beyond the objective 'here-and-now' of their situation, without letting go of real life. Cameron correctly refers to the mimetic quality of ascetic writings. Being biographies they implied that the protagonists should function as role models. Putting the body into discourse also opened the possibility for dissemination of information, thereby widening the possibilities of influence.[76]

As construct of power the alternative discursive body functioned in varying degrees of opposition to the notion of personhood within the dominant culture. That means instead of outright rejection, the notion of personhood is modified. In describing the duality within which the ascetic exists, Valantasis writes: 'The rejection of the dominant culture's forms of subjectivities marks the basis for the embracing of a culturally different subject, an alternative subjectivity.'[77] As such the discursive body of ascetic discourse is always in suspense in its process of emerging into an alternative personhood.

This duality manifests itself in the *Acts of Thecla* in divorcing androcentrism from personhood. In the construction of person the necessity of male association is undermined. It cannot, however, be completely excluded. This can perhaps best be illustrated by briefly examining the role of Paul. Paul plays the role of a 'donor' figure.[78] As such he seems to form part of a strategy of compliance. Needed to legitimate the destruction of household boundaries, the teaching of continence is assigned to him. Despite the erotic overtones abounding in the narratival interaction of Paul and Thecla, her progressive self-empowerment emphasizes a reversal of roles. Her autonomy is depicted in the absence of any assistance from his side. Not only is her body subjected to a much higher degree of suffering (21.1, 2), but Paul is portrayed as completely absent during her times of anguish (21.13, 1–4). During the confrontation with Alexander in the Antioch scene (26.14), Paul's betrayal leads to the ensuing ordeals she has to suffer. Taking personhood within the Graeco–Roman background into consideration, Paul actually 'depersonated' Thecla by his denial of acquaintance. Yet in a strange, ironic manner his actions confirmed her autonomy. Despite her request to be baptized by Paul (25.7), this never happened and she eventually baptized herself (34.10); despite his refusal to allow her to accompany him (25.5), she did (26.11) and eventually journeyed with her own followers (40.3); despite the fact that the beginning of the narrative commences with Paul teaching in the house of Onesiphorus (chs. 4–6), in the end Thecla tells her story in the house of Hermias with Paul and others listening (41.1–4).

I have already indicated that power is invested upon the body by 'languaging' the

76 A. Cameron ('Ascetic Closure and the End of Antiquity', in V.L. Wimbush and R. Valantasis [eds.], *Asceticism* [Oxford: Oxford University Press, 1995], pp. 147–61 [154]) indicates the various ways in which ascetic discourse could have affected society.

77 R. Valantasis, 'Constructions of Power in Asceticism', *Journal of the American Academy of Religion* 58 (1995), pp. 775–821 (802).

78 See Burrus, 'Chastity as Autonomy', p. 107.

body. Against the backdrop of this duality of the body within ascetic discourse this aspect needs to be pursued a little further. Within ascetic discourse the 'languaging' of the body seems strangely paradoxical. On the one hand it seems to propagate bodily denial as can be seen by typical ascetic performances, such as sexual abstinence, fasting, restrictions on bathing, voluntary poverty and so on. On the other hand, it is exactly by these ascetic performances that the body received its power, since it became associated with bodily possibilities exceeding those of the dominant culture. Within the Graeco–Roman world, asceticism invited to what was regarded as the full realization of bodily potential. It approximated the superhero.

The body became the locus of supranatural power. It transcended the ordinary restrictions of the body. It is in this sense that the relationship between resurrection and continence should also be understood. We do not seem to encounter in the *Acts of Thecla* strong tendencies of an urgent apocalypticism motivating continence. The body acquired undoubtedly a futuristic dimension as can be seen in the beatitudes of Paul (chs. 5, 6) where future blessings motivate specified present behaviour. It is even more strongly expressed in the disclosure of Demas and Hermogenes (Paul's two rather dubious travelling companions, 1.2; 12.1) to Thamyris (12.3), where the resurrection of the body is directly linked to sexual abstinence. Although the body acquired a futuristic dimension, future bodily resurrection has to be understood within the wider context of the body as locus of supernatural power. For the discursive body, bodily resurrection became a possibility; the promise of emerging into a 'superbody', of actualizing the full potential of the body, became a possibility. As such future bodily resurrection functioned as an incentive to relativize the household structure.

The body became the locus of supranatural power via its association with God. Instead of a personhood constituted by association with a male, personhood is constructed in association with God. Because God functioned as an omnipresent helper,[79] sexual abstinence has become an attractive possibility.[80] The alternative to the household system is God's household. Access to power could be gained by deliberately avoiding association with the male body; in association with God and with the support of each other, the female body became a locus of power successfully resisting the most brutal attempts of male citizens to make 'customary use' of their bodies.[81]

The possibility that the female body can resist the onslaught of the dominant culture's bodily discursive practices and the promise of self-empowered personhood

---

79 Cf. Paul's absence and God's presence in crises (21.2; 22.11; 30.9), Thecla's confession (37.7), the grounds of her release (38.9–10), Thecla's prayers (31.3–5; 42.4–7), assurance to Theocleia (43.3–4).

80 One would have expected that if resurrection of the body functioned as primary motivation for continence a more detailed presentation of its contents would have been given. Perelman and Olbrechts-Tyteca (*The New Rhetoric*) remind us that in sequential type of argumentation, the values of the end (resurrection) have to persuade to acceptance of the means (continence). However, except for Paul's beatitudes, the resurrection is simply mentioned, not in the least elaborated. Bodily resurrection is therefore part of the package, but definitely not that prominent.

81 Cf. again Rouselle, 'Personal Status', p. 302.

are vividly illustrated by Thecla's consistent, successful resistance of her society's punishment mechanisms, despite the fragility of the body.[82]

Conclusion

The notion of 'person' gives expression to the rhetoric of the body. If 'person' refers to the rhetoricity of the body, it becomes operative in the process of persuasion. Its construction is, therefore, a construction of power. As such its construction releases an energy or constitutes a catalyst for the construction of culture. However, since personhood is constituted by the various discursive practices into which the body has been drawn, an analysis of its construction can be an epistemological tool enabling us to understand why cultural patterns have been formed in a specific manner. In the *Acts of Thecla* the beginnings of an alternative culture were stimulated by an alternative construction of person. In order to launch an alternative culture, validating mechanisms within the ambit of personhood have been created. By means of the construction of person, the *Acts of Thecla* prompts a revision of the social hierarchies during the second century CE. On the one hand, it served as a critique of the political strategy to entrench and stabilize upper-class power via the propagation of marriage; on the other hand, the construction of Thecla's person enabled a social hierarchy independent of male control. There is an ironic twist to this, since the alternative radicalized the engendered terminologies available at the time. Although it may sound strange to twenty-first-century ears, it offered a possibility to women that might have come as a relief to their overburdened bodies, liberating them from the status of being the reproductive containers, from an incarceration in an ideology of 'shedding blood' and from being passive recipients of male cultural insemination.

---

82 The power of woman is disclosed in the weakest moment of the body. This can be seen in the following cases: when Thecla is brought in naked to be burned (22.6–7); her body in the form of a cross on the pyre (22.9); in the embrace of a powerful man (26.1) whom she subsequently humiliated; again stripped with only a girdle in the stadium with the wild beasts (33.1); when she threw herself in the water with the seals (34.4); the power of collective womanhood over the beasts (35.5–7); tied between two symbols of male power, two bulls (35.1–5). The consistent insistence on the support of the women of Antioch, the challenges they direct at the official power structures, as well as the role of Tryphaena, are suggestive of a demand for independence.

Suffering Children, Parental Authority and the Quest for Liberation?: A Tale of Three Girls in the *Acts of Paul (and Thecla)*, the *Act(s) of Peter*, the *Acts of Nerseus and Achilleus* and the *Epistle of Pseudo-Titus**

Cornelia B. Horn

Children as agents, children as participants in events, or even only a concern for children as such are not typically recognized as core elements of any of the πράξεις ἀποστόλων or *acta* of apostles, whether canonical or apocryphal.[1] Conversely, the canonical Gospels of Matthew and especially Luke do attend to the infancy and childhood of Jesus, and a significant subset of apocryphal texts – the so-called infancy gospels – portray traditions regarding the birth and youthful years of holy children, Jesus and Mary.[2] This article will show, however, that also in the Apocryphal Acts of Apostles (AAA), children are a theme worth exploring.

While studies of the broader category of 'family' or 'families' continue to be published,[3] only a few focus specifically on the material and social conditions of

* I am grateful to Robert Phenix, Frederick McLeod, James Kelhoffer and Inta Ivanovska for valuable feedback on earlier drafts of this article, as well as to Amy-Jill Levine for probing questions that aided in sharpening individual points of the discussion. Working with Maria Mayo Robbins on carefully editing this article was a joy. This article is dedicated in friendship to Cheryl Bower Morgan.

1 On the literary genre of the Aprocryphal Acts of the Apostles, see Wilhelm Schneemelcher, 'XV. Apostelgeschichten des 2. und 3. Jahrhunderts. Einleitung', in *idem* (ed.), *Neutestamentliche Apokryphen in deutscher Übersetzung, II. Band: Apostolisches, Apokalypsen und Verwandtes* (Tübingen: J.C.B. Mohr [Paul Siebeck], 1989), pp. 71–93 (72, 74–79). See also David E. Aune, *The Westminster Dictionary of New Testament and Early Christian Literature and Rhetoric* (Louisville, KY: Westminster/John Knox Press, 2003), pp. 2–3.

2 Particularly the *Infancy Gospel of Thomas* and the *Protevangelium of James*. For convenient access to Greek texts and English translations of both the *Protevangelium* (primarily addressing Mary's childhood and youth up to the birth of Christ), and the *Infancy Gospel of Thomas* (stories about deeds Jesus is said to have performed as a young boy), see Ronald F. Hock, *The Infancy Gospels of James and Thomas* (The Scholars Bible, 2; Santa Rosa, CA: Polebridge Press, 1995), with helpful initial further bibliography. Essential to any study of the *Protevangelium of James* is the critical edition and the discussion by Émile de Strycker, *La Forme la Plus Ancienne du Protévangile de Jacques* (Subsidia Hagiographica, 33; Brussels: Société des Bollandistes, 1961). See also Edouard Cothenet, 'Le Protévangile de Jacques: origine, genre et signification d'un premier midrash chrétien sur la Nativité de Marie', in *ANRW* II.25.6 (1988), pp. 4252–69. For the *Infancy Gospel of Thomas*, see Stephen Gerö, 'Infancy Gospel of Thomas: A Study of the Textual and Literary Problems', *NovT* 13.1 (1971), pp. 46–80.

3 Recent books on aspects of the Jewish/Christian family in the New Testament and patristic world include Shaye J.D. Cohen (ed.), *The Jewish Family in Antiquity* (BJS, 289; Atlanta: Scholars Press, 1993); Halvor Moxnes (ed.), *Constructing Early Christian Families. Family as Social Reality and Metaphor* (London and New York: Routledge, 1997); Carolyn Osiek and David L. Balch, *Families in the New Testament World: Households and House Churches* (The Family, Religion, and Culture

children as well as their literary representations.[4] The present work cannot comprehensively examine the role of children in apocryphal literature,[5] or even in the genre of Apocryphal Acts.[6] Rather, this article limits its goal to investigating the different models of how ancient authors addressed the intersection of the themes of children and liberation by focusing on the stories of three girls found in the Apocryphal Acts: Thecla in the *Acts of Paul (and Thecla)*, the apostle Peter's unnamed daughter in the *Act(s) of Peter*, and the daughter of the gardener in the apocryphal *Epistle of Pseudo-Titus*. This article employs an examination of literary fiction to tease out details illustrating ancient social history.

For the purpose of this article, 'children' refers to individuals either characterized by virtue of their pre-teen age, or adolescents not yet having reached full physical maturity, a status that in ancient and early Christian society mostly preceded legal maturity.[7] To take the onset of puberty as the demarcation line for a girl's transition from childhood to adulthood is at least somewhat arbitrary. In the Roman world, the model age for a girl's marriage was between 12 and 15,[8] although especially in

---

series; Louisville, KY: Westminster/John Knox Press, 1997); David L. Balch and Carolyn Osiek (eds.), *Early Christian Families in Context. An Interdisciplinary Dialogue* (Religion, Marriage, and Family series; Grand Rapids, MI and Cambridge, UK: Eerdmans, 2003); and Geoffrey S. Nathan, *The Family in Late Antiquity: The Rise of Christianity and the Endurance of Tradition* (London and New York: Routledge, 2000).

4 Monographs on children in the New Testament, Graeco–Roman, and patristic world include Thomas E.J. Wiedemann, *Adults and Children in the Roman Empire* (New Haven, CT: Yale University Press, 1989); W.A. Strange, *Children in the Early Church: Children in the Ancient World, the New Testament and the Early Church* (Carlisle, UK: Paternoster Press, 1996; repr. Eugene, OR: Wipf and Stock, 2004); Odd M. Bakke, *When Children Became People. The Birth of Childhood in Early Christianity* (trans. Brian McNeil; Minneapolis, MN: Fortress Press, 2005); and Cornelia B. Horn and John W. Martens, *'Let the Little Ones Come to Me': Children in the Early Christian Community* (Baltimore, MD: The Johns Hopkins University Press, forthcoming).

5 See also Cornelia B. Horn, 'The Depiction of Children and Young People as Literary Device in the Canonical and Apocryphal Acts', in Pierluigi Piovanelli (ed.), *Proceedings of the Apocrypha and Pseudepigrapha Section of the SBL International Meeting Held in Groningen, The Netherlands, July 25–28, 2004* (Turnhout: Brepols, forthcoming).

6 Thus far, neither the realities of children's lives as depicted in the Apocryphal Acts nor the literary portrayal of children in those texts has received much attention. Among the few exceptions are James H. Charlesworth, 'From the Philopedia of Jesus to the Misopedia of the Acts of Thomas', in Hugh Nibley, John M. Lundquist and Stephen David Ricks (eds.), *By Study and also by Faith: Essays in Honor of Hugh W. Nibley on the Occasion of his Eightieth Birthday, 27 March 1990* (Salt Lake City and Provo, UT: Deseret Book and the Foundation for Ancient Research and Mormon Studies, 1990), pp. 46–66, and Horn, 'The Depiction of Children and Young People'. In conjunction with this earlier work, the present article is part of a project investigating the place and use of children as real children and as literary motif in apocryphal literature.

7 The leading male head of a given Roman household, the *paterfamilias*, held legal power over all members of his household, even power over life or death. See Antti Arjava, 'Paternal Power in Late Antiquity', *JRS* 88 (1998), pp. 147–65.

8 See M.K. Hopkins, 'The Age of Roman Girls at Marriage', *Population Studies* 18 (1965), pp. 309–27 (319); for age patterns among lower classes see also Brent D. Shaw, 'The Age of Roman Girls at Marriage: Some Reconsiderations', *JRS* 77 (1987), pp. 30–46. See also Jan N. Bremmer, 'Aspects of the Acts of Peter: Women, Magic, Place and Date', in *idem* (ed), *The Apocryphal Acts of Peter: Magic, Miracles and Gnosticism* (Leuven: Peeters, 1998), pp. 1–20 (2), who sees fifteen as the age at which Greek girls married.

the upper classes, marriages could occur earlier.[9] Further, sexual intercourse with a girl who had not yet reached puberty could, and did, occur. The boundaries of the childhood of such girls were violated, and they participated or were forced to participate in the world of sexually experienced adult women, even though their own bodies had not reached the state of maturity for that. Yet despite that disruptive experience of their childhood world, were such girls no longer children? In a given instance a girl's prepubescent status did not allow for pregnancy to occur. Thus pregnancy and the accompanying adult responsibility for offspring were not available as markers of the violated girl's entrance into adulthood. It is unfortunate that we have no evidence for whether prepubescent girls who were married off regarded themselves as still being children or whether they perceived premature sexual intercourse as violation of their bodies. However problematic this may be for the modern reader, the ancient world seems to have thought of them as adults once they were married.[10] Conversely, girls who may have reached puberty several years before marrying at age 15, or even later, and who were not, and were not supposed to be, sexually active but who continued under paterfamilial control were regarded as dependent children. At the least the level of physical development and sexual activity were only two of several factors in determining whether a given individual was to be regarded as a child. The transition from childhood to adulthood is a gradual process, and even in the light of the scarcity of data, relative rather than absolute judgement regarding a person's progress along that continuum is the approach to be preferred in analysing cases. At times, this article will also speak of 'children' to designate a given person's offspring, a case in which age may play a role. Finally, while the Apocryptal Acts of the Apostles do employ the designations 'child' (τέκνον), 'children' (τέκνα), 'little children' (τεκνιά, παιδία), 'little ones' (*parvuli*), and similar terms in a metaphorical sense to speak of Christian believers, these cases do not constitute material for this discussion.[11]

For the Apocryphal Acts of the Apostles, where there are children, often parents are not far off. Many scenes that feature children portray them in situations in which both the children and at least one adult in a parental or quasi-parental role participate. For developments in the west of the Roman Empire from the first to the fifth century, Brent Shaw notes that with regard to 'the empirical phenomenon of "family"', 'the dominant centre of family relationships, in terms of primary duties, obligations and affections, was that of the nuclear family'.[12] The pronounced child–parent

---

9 See the discussion in Hopkins, 'Age of Roman Girls at Marriage'. On the concerns of ancient medical writers, see Gillian Clark, *Women in Late Antiquity. Pagan and Christian Lifestyles* (New York: Oxford University Press, and Oxford: Clarendon Press, 1993), pp. 80–81; and *eadem*, 'The Fathers and the Children', in Diana Wood (ed.), *The Church and Childhood: Papers Read at the 1993 Summer Meeting and the 1994 Winter Meeting of the Ecclesiastical History Society* (Studies in Church History, 31; Oxford and Cambridge, MA: Blackwell, 1994), pp. 1–27 (9–10).

10 See Horn and Martens, *'Let the Little Ones Come to Me'*, Chapter 1 with discussion based on Hellenistic Jewish and Mishnaic sources.

11 On the literary structures in which these expressions occur, see Horn, 'Depiction of Children and Young People'. For some discussion of terminology used for children and youth in the early Christian period, see Horn and Martens, *'Let the Little Ones Come to Me'*, Chapter 1.

12 Brent L. Shaw, 'The Family in Late Antiquity: The Experience of Augustine', *Past and Present* 115 (1987), pp. 3–51 (3).

relationships that emerge from the AAA fit in well with this picture and merit closer attention.

Given the manifold possible, probable and actual inequalities inherent in child–parent relationships, as for example those of age, size, capabilities and competencies, this discussion approaches child–parent constellations through the lens of a critique of power or authority and dependence. This article is interested in elucidating to what extent children, and particularly girls, were able to achieve liberation from their dependence on parental authority. To that end, certain questions guide the following investigation. To what extent are relationships between children and parents reflected in the AAA characterized by the exercise of power or authority on the part of one of the constituents? To what extent does such power or authority create dependence? Are there instances where customary expectations of the influence of a given constituent's exercise of power or the display of authority are frustrated? What new definitions of the child–parent relationships are made possible? It will become manifest that while in some cases the AAA reinforce and even divinely sanction the ordinary exercise of power or authority over children or the experience of dependence on the part of children, in a few cases the AAA also provide encouraging examples of how young girls managed to break out of such absolute parental control and achieve a level of liberation that allowed them to direct their own course of life.

Thecla as a Child: a Model of Liberation?

The representative, 'classic' set of Apocryphal Acts, which forms the larger basis of this investigation and from which initially examples were selected, namely the *Acts of Andrew*, the *Acts of Paul (and Thecla)*, the *Acts of Peter*, the *Acts of John* and the *Acts of Thomas*,[13] constitutes a collection gathered into a whole and transmitted under the influence of adherents of Manichaeism.[14] Within Manichaean mythology as reflected for example in the *Hymn of the Pearl* in the *Acts of Thomas*, children play a central role.[15] Yet this corpus of Apocryphal Acts also includes a direct reference to a child, and a female one at that. The name of a young girl, Thecla, appears in what can be argued is an appropriate title of one of these five texts.[16] By including Thecla's name

13 For a summary and evaluation of current consensus on questions of authorship and chronology as well as geographical and social location of these five Apocryphal Acts, see Jan N. Bremmer, 'The Apocryphal Acts: Authors, Place, Time and Readership', in *idem* (ed.), *The Apocryphal Acts of Thomas* (Leuven: Peeters, 2001), pp. 149–70.

14 See Schneemelcher, 'XV. Apostelgeschichten. Einleitung', p. 72. Photios also considered these texts together. See Photios, *Bibl. cod.* 114 (René Henry [ed.], *Photius. Bibliothèque. Tome II ('Codices' 84–185)* [Collection Byzantine; Paris: Société d'Édition 'Les Belles Lettres', 1960], pp. 84–86). See also Chapter 8, 'La notice de Photius et la question de Leucius', in Eric Junod and Jean-Daniel Kaestli, *L'Histoire des Actes Apocryphes des Apôtres du IIIe au IXe Siècle: Le Cas des Actes de Jean* (Cahiers de la Revue de Théologie et de Philosophie, 7; Genève, Lausanne, and Neuchâtel: Fonds National Suisse de la Recherche Scientifique, 1982), pp. 133–45.

15 For further discussion, see Horn, 'The Depiction of Children and Young People'.

16 See also Jan N. Bremmer (ed.), *The Apocryphal Acts of Paul and Thecla* (Studies on the Apocryphal Acts of the Apostles; Kampen: Kok Pharos, 1996), who chose to print 'and Thecla' in the title in smaller-sized letters.

in the title of the whole work, commonly known as the *Acts of Paul*,[17] in the form of the *Acts of Paul (and Thecla)*[18] the present study reveals a major aspect of the story: the prominent place it accords Thecla, a girl at the transition from child to young teenager.[19] Quantitatively, Thecla's story comprises a smaller part of the redacted text than does the narrative describing Paul's activities;[20] nevertheless, a third of the narrative's eleven sections (including the *Martyrdom of Paul*) clearly relegates Paul to a supportive role, whereas Thecla claims centre-stage. Given the whole of the composition, it is fitting to list Thecla's name in the main title, following that of Paul. Brackets surrounding her name help distinguish the title *Acts of Paul (and Thecla)* from the title *Acts of Paul and Thecla*, a designation that often is chosen to refer only to the *acta* of Thecla.[21]

Among the dimensions that ground appropriations of Thecla as model and inspiration for women in Antiquity[22] and that partially seem to motivate scholarly interest

17 For a discussion of the compositional structure of the *Acts of Paul (and Thecla)*, see Wilhelm Schneemelcher, 'Paulusakten', in *idem* (ed.), *Neutestamentliche Apokryphen*, pp. 198–211, who identifies the text as a whole as 'Paulusakten' (*Acts of Paul*) and names only section three (of eleven) 'Taten des Paulus und der Thekla' (*Acts of Paul and Thecla*). References to the Greek text in the present discussion are based on R. A. Lipsius, *Acta Apostolorum Apocrypha* (= *ActaAA*), vol. 1 (repr. Hildesheim: Georg Olms Verlagsbuchhandlung, 1959), pp. 23–44, 104–117 and 235–72.

18 The figure of Thecla has received much attention both in Antiquity and in modern scholarly literature. Yet thus far, only her gender seems to have been of interest, not her age. For recent discussions of the *Acts of Paul (and Thecla)* with regard to the historiography of women, see on opposite ends of the spectrum, for example, Shelly Matthews, 'Thinking of Thecla: Issues in Feminist Historiography', *JFSR* 17.2 (2001), pp. 39–55; and Esther Yue L. Ng, '*Acts of Paul and Thecla*: Women's Stories and Precedent?' *JTS* 55 (2004), pp. 1–29. For a very helpful study, see also Sheila E. McGinn, 'The Acts of Thecla', in Elisabeth Schüssler Fiorenza (ed.), *Searching the Scriptures. II: A Feminist Commentary* (2 vols.; New York: Crossroad, 1994), pp. 800–28.

19 Recent scholarship dates its composition between 185 and 195 CE, and sees Asia Minor as the likely region of origin. See also Bremmer, 'The Apocryphal Acts: Authors, Place, Time and Readership', p. 153.

20 Yet, from the perspective of the work's literary structure, one may characterize it as a redaction developed on the basis of at least two sets of *acta*, those of Paul and those of Thecla.

21 The narrative concerning Thecla's deeds may have come to the attention of the author of the *Acts of Paul (and Thecla)* either in oral or less likely in written form and subsequently may have been integrated by that author into the composition of the *Acts of Paul*. On the compositional and redactional aspects of the *Acts of Thecla/Acts of Paul and Thecla*, see Willy Rordorf, 'Tradition et composition dans les Actes de Thècle. Etat de la question', *TZ* 41 (1985), pp. 272–83; and Willy Rordorf, 'Tradition and Composition in the *Acts of Thecla*: The State of the Question', *Semeia* 38 (1986), pp. 43–52.

22 See, for example, Ruth Albrecht, *Das Leben der heiligen Makrina auf dem Hintergrund der Thekla-Traditionen. Studien zu den Ursprüngen des weiblichen Mönchtums im 4. Jahrhundert in Kleinasien* (Forschungen zur Kirchen- und Dogmengeschichte 38; Göttingen: Vandenhoeck & Ruprecht, 1986), pp. 239–319. See also the recent study of the cult of Thecla in Asia Minor and Egypt by Stephen J. Davis, *The Cult of Saint Thecla: a Tradition of Women's Piety in Late Antiquity* (Oxford Early Christian Studies; Oxford and New York: Oxford University Press, 2001). For the development of traditions surrounding Thecla, see also the account of miracles ascribed to her in Gilbert Dragon with the assistance of Marie Dupré la Tour, *Vie et miracles de sainte Thècle, texte grec, traduction, et commentaire* (Subsidia hagiographica 62; Brussels: Société des Bollandistes, 1978). Depictions of Thecla in art made her available as *exemplum* to an even broader audience. For the visual reception of Thecla, see Claudia Nauerth and Rüdiger Warns, *Thekla. Ihre Bilder in der frühchristlichen Kunst I* (Göttinger Orientforschungen 2/3; Wiesbaden: Otto Harrassowitz, 1981);

in her today is her characterization as having authority and control as well as her achieving liberation from social expectations of marriage. Thecla frees herself from parental, societal and legal definitions of and expectations for her life by taking charge of her situation as well as by following through on acts of liberation worked on her behalf by God, by human participants, and even by (female) animals. As her story tells, not only did Thecla face societal limitations by being a female person, thus being expected to submit to a husband in marriage, she also had to overcome restrictions placed upon her as a young person who was expected to be submissive to the will of her parents. Thus, to understand Thecla's decisions and adventures, it will be important to attend to the double repression of gender and age which she faced. To understand her paradigmatic function, it is imperative to see her as a role model not only for women but also for children.

When she first encounters Paul, Thecla is still a virgin. Although her age is never specified, the narrative assumes that she has not yet reached but is nearing marriageable age. Details regarding Thecla's relationship to her fiancé Thamyris support this picture: Thamyris eagerly anticipates the day when he would finally marry her, likely the day on which she would be old enough to wed.[23] The text further reaffirms Thecla's identity as child by replacing her physical mother Theocleia, who had rejected her, with the patroness Tryphaena, who functions in a parental role.[24] That she is identified as 'child' (τέκνον) in relationship to her mother Theocleia can serve to reinforce this identification,[25] as can her mother's reference to her as 'my daughter' (ἡ θυγάτηρ μου).[26] However, throughout the AAA, the terminology of childhood is used relatively frequently to describe relationships that have nothing in common with physical parent–child constellations, and thus these two designations alone do not permit conclusions to be drawn regarding the age of the characters involved.[27]

Thecla is introduced as 'a certain virgin' (παρθένος) who day and night sat by a window and listened to Paul's preaching and who watched 'many women and virgins'

Claudia Nauerth, 'Nachlese von Thekla-Darstellungen', in Guntram Koch (ed.), *Studien zur spätantiken und frühchristlichen Kunst und Kultur des Orients* (Wiesbaden: Otto Harrassowitz, 1982), pp. 14–18; and Rüdiger Warns, 'Weitere Darstellungen der heiligen Thekla', in Guntram Koch (ed.), *Studien zur spätantiken und frühchristlichen Kunst und Kultur des Orienst II* (Wiesbaden: Otto Harrassowitz, 1986), pp. 75–131. To what extent awareness of Thecla's age and her identity as a child guided her representations in Christian art requires further investigation. Claudia Nauerth, 'Zweifelhafte Isaak-Bilder in der koptischen Kunst', in *Studien zur frühchristlichen Kunst II*, pp. 1–5 (3), for example, notes the immediate proximity of Thecla-depictions to those of the sacrifice of Isaac in El-Bagawat, Egypt. For reproduction of that image, see also Nauerth and Warns, *Thekla*, plate IV, fig. 5, and discussion on pp. 15–16.

23 *Acts of Paul and Thecla* 8 (Lipsius [ed.], *ActaAA*, vol. 1, p. 241, ll. 8–9): ὡς ἤδη λαμβάνων αὐτὴν πρὸς γάμον; and *Acts of Paul and Thecla* 10 (Lipsius [ed.], *ActaAA*, vol. 1, p. 243, l. 2): Θάμυρις μὲν γυναικὸς ἀστοχῶν.

24 See Magda Misset-van de Weg ('A wealthy woman named Tryphaena: patroness of Thecla of Iconium', in Jan N. Bremmer [ed.], *The Apocryphal Acts of Paul and Thecla* [Kampen: Kok Pharos, 1996], pp. 16–35), who argues for subsuming into the patronage conception the usage of mother–child language used to describe the relationship between Thecla and Tryphaena.

25 *Acts of Paul and Thecla* 10 (Lipsius [ed.], *ActaAA*, vol. 1, p. 242, l. 13 and p. 243, l. 3).

26 *Acts of Paul and Thecla* 9 (Lipsius [ed.], *ActaAA*, vol. 1, p. 242, ll. 4–5).

27 For discussion, see Horn, 'Depiction of Children and Young People'.

(πολλὰς γυναῖκας καὶ παρθένους) going to Paul.[28] In contrast to the married women (γυναῖκας), Thecla is identified as unmarried. In the following chapter her mother describes her to her soon-to-be-rejected fiancé Thamyris as 'such a modest virgin' (ἡ τοιαύτη αἰδὼς τῆς παρθένου).[29] Theocleia appears to be concerned about changes in behaviour of both the 'women and young men' (γυναῖκες καὶ οἱ νέοι)[30] who, in the full bloom of their lives, being energetic and sexually active, learn from Paul to live a life of purity (ζῆν ἁγνῶς).[31] The use of the verbs ἁγνεύω (to purify, to cleanse) and ἁγνέοω (to be ignorant of) may well signal that Paul's 'life of purity' means 'a life of [sexual] ignorance', sexual chastity taking on connotations of a state of inexperience. The reference to 'young men' indicates that age is a factor when considering a person's potential for sexual activity. Since this passage groups together married or at least sexually experienced women and 'young men' and identifies the males as of relatively young age, it is not unreasonable to assume that at least some of the 'women' were young as well. Consequently, when the text later speaks of 'women and virgins', not only their level of sexual experience but also their respective age must be considered.[32]

Theocleia fears that her daughter, who 'like a spider at the window' was 'bound by his [i.e. Paul's] words', might undergo the very same change that the 'women and young men' were experiencing. In fact, she observes that already 'the virgin (ἡ παρθένος) is conquered' by this new message.[33] When Theocleia refers to her daughter as παρθένος, she is concerned, perhaps even afraid, that Thecla would remain not only a 'virgin' but also a 'girl', that she might not mature into the next stage of life, that of a married, sexually experienced woman.

The word παρθένος is most often rendered into English as 'virgin', a translation that hides the often relatively young age of the females so designated. Whereas dictionaries of classical Greek provide sufficient support for a translator's choice between 'virgin' or 'girl' when rendering παρθένος,[34] dictionaries of patristic Greek do not include 'girl' as an option.[35] Bettina Eltrop demonstrates that many ancient sources primarily identified as παρθένος a relatively young girl or teenager who was not married and who had not experienced sexual intercourse.[36] She also makes

---

28 *Acts of Paul and Thecla* 7 (Lipsius [ed.], *ActaAA*, vol. 1, p. 240, l. 7 and p. 241, l. 2).

29 *Acts of Paul and Thecla* 8 (Lipsius [ed.], *ActaAA*, vol. 1, p. 241, l. 15).

30 *Acts of Paul and Thecla* 9 (Lipsius [ed.], *ActaAA*, vol. 1, p. 242, ll. 2–3).

31 *Acts of Paul and Thecla* 9 (Lipsius [ed.], *ActaAA*, vol. 1, p. 242, l. 4).

32 Claudia Janssen (*Elisabet und Hanna – zwei widerständige alte Frauen in neutestamentlicher Zeit. Eine sozialgeschichtliche Untersuchung* [Mainz: Matthias-Grünewald Verlag, 1998]) highlights the need to consider age as a critical factor in analysing women in the biblical texts, here from the perspective of women of older age. Old age also is a factor that determines the life circumstances of some women in the AAA, especially in the cases of the widows.

33 *Acts of Paul and Thecla* 9 (Lipsius [ed.], *ActaAA*, vol. 1, p. 242, ll. 5–7).

34 See Henry George Liddell and Robert Scott, *A Greek–English Lexicon* (Oxford: Clarendon Press, 1996), p. 1339; and Frederick William Danker, *A Greek–English Lexicon of the New Testament and other Early Christian Literature* (3rd edn; Chicago and London: University of Chicago Press, 2000), p. 777, col. B.

35 See G.W.H. Lampe, *A Patristic Greek Lexicon* (Oxford: Clarendon Press, 1961), pp. 1037–40.

36 Bettina Eltrop, *Denn solchen gehört das Himmelreich. Kinder im Matthäusevangelium. Eine feministisch-sozialgeschichtliche Untersuchung* (Stuttgart: Ulrich E. Grauer, 1996), pp. 38–47; and Bettina Eltrop, 'Kinder im Neuen Testament: Eine sozialgeschichtliche Nachfrage', in Martin

a case for understanding some identifications of παρθένοι in the New Testament as references to girls under the age of twelve and a half, who were unmarried, dependent on their fathers for decisions regarding marriage, who were biologically virgins, and who might or might not have eventually married.[37] Certainly, not all virgins (then or now) fall into the category of 'girls' with regard to age. Yet a rereading of early and late ancient Christian texts, particularly those dealing with questions of virginity, while being sensitive to the question of age, could reveal many more 'girls' than have hitherto been acknowledged.

The *Acts of Paul (and Thecla)* poignantly emphasize that a female's sexual experience, preferably in marriage, was part of both the law of nature and the law of society. Theocleia clearly articulates such a view when she called her own child 'a lawless one' (τὴν ἄνομον) who ought to be burned (κατακαίω) since she is 'unmarried' or, more literally, 'not a bride' (τὴν ἄνυμφον).[38] The alliteration in ἄν – between the two accusative objects in the parallel construction of κατάκαιε τὴν ἄνομον, κατάκαιε τὴν ἄνυμφον – highlights the identification the mother perceives between her daughter's refusal to marry and lawlessness. Theocleia recognizes that her daughter is not behaving along expected lines of child-development precisely at a point when the transition from childhood to adult life ought to have taken place. The threat of irregularities in the child's development causes maternal anxiety, and so Thecla's mother is presented as the driving force behind Thecla's death sentence. The 'woman' is cast into the role of the primary persecutor. Education of girls rested primarily in the hands of mothers, or in better-off families in those of nurses.[39] Education in the ancient world also readily involved recourse to various forms of physical punishment. That a mother who feels responsible for the proper education and conduct of her daughter, a mother who fears that her daughter's misconduct would bring shame on the family, would agree to and even promote her daughter's death instead of being willing to endure such shame is not an unreasonable explanation for Theocleia's behaviour. The classical model of Lucretia, seeking death after having been raped and thus having brought shame onto her household, serves as an example of a normative case in the Graeco–Roman world where female life was clearly seen as subordinate to family honour, and where women themselves agreed with this subordination.[40] Certainly, Lucretia's case is different insofar as she was a

Ebner *et al.* (eds.), *Jahrbuch für Biblische Theologie: Gottes Kinder*, vol. 17 (Neukirchen-Vluyn: Neukirchener Verlag, 2002), pp. 83–96 (85), on further methodological and philological factors that 'hide' children in the texts.

37 Bettina Eltrop, 'Problem Girls: A Transgressive Reading of the Parable of the Ten Virgins (Matthew 25.1–13)', in Claudia Janssen, Ute Ochtendung and Beate Wehn (eds.), *Transgressors: Toward a Feminist Biblical Theology* (trans. Linda M. Maloney; Collegeville, MN: Liturgical Press, 2002), pp. 163–71 (165).

38 *Acts of Paul and Thecla* 20 (Lipsius [ed.], *ActaAA*, vol. 1, p. 249, l. 7).

39 For a discussion of the education of Christian children in the ancient world, see Horn and Martens, *'Let the Little Ones Come to Me'*, Chapter 4, as well as comments in Chapter 8. Texts like Gregory of Nyssa's *Life of Macrina* (Pierre Maraval [ed. and trans.], *Grégoire de Nysse. Vie de Sainte Macrine* [Sources Chrétiennes 178; Paris: Les Éditions du Cerf, 1971]) clearly show mothers in their roles of educators of young daughters.

40 See Livy, *Historiarum ab urbe condita* 1.57–58 (Robert Seymour Conway and Carolus Flamstead Walters [eds.], *Titi Livi Ab Urbe Condita, t. 1, libri I–V* [Oxonii: E typographeo Clarendoniano, 1914]); Ovid, *Fasti* 2,725-852 (E.H. Alton, D.E.W. Wormell and E. Courtney [eds.],

married woman, while in Thecla's case her mother insists on her daughter's getting married to fulfil societal expectations. Yet the lesson is the same: women are to subject their bodies to societal and familial expectations. The emphasis on Theocleia as primary persecutor also highlights that enforcement and reinforcement of such behaviour was expected to be passed on from one generation of women to the next.

The quest for the transitional point in Thecla's developmental process from 'girl/virgin' to 'woman' which is at stake here continues to play a crucial role for Thecla's identity. Within the confines of ancient expectations of girls getting married to become women, she may never make that transition. Her continued identity as 'girl/virgin' is one of the scandalous and thus challenging messages of the whole story. She does not have to 'become like little children'; she continues to be one. Yet we are getting ahead of the story here.

For Theocleia, engaging in sexual intercourse is part of her daughter's normal and expected process of growing up.[41] It functions as a marker of leaving behind 'girlhood' and entering the realm of 'womanhood'. In such a worldview, females who do not share in this experience are forever to be grouped alongside children. That such an understanding appears to have been widely accepted is signalled by a comment made in the context of describing preparations for Thecla's public execution. Depending on how one translates the phrase οἱ δὲ παῖδες καὶ αἱ παρθένοι in chapter 22, 'children and virgins' or 'boys and girls' 'brought wood and hay' to burn Thecla.[42] Either translation expresses an association of παρθένοι with the realm of children. That with reference to her mother Thecla is described more often as a 'child' (τέκνον) or a 'girl/virgin' (παρθένος) and only once by Theocleia herself as 'my daughter' (ἡ θυγάτηρ μου)[43] is further support. The text suggests that as long as Thecla is called παρθένος, she is to be seen as a child.

The reference to 'boys and girls' carries further significance as supporting the characterization of Thecla as a relatively young virgin herself. Although the text does not say that the 'boys and girls' watched the attempted burning, there is no reason to assume that children were absent from amphitheatres when wild animals fought with gladiators or martyrs. Rather, grammatically the 'boys and girls' continue to be

---

P. Ovidi Nasonis Fastorum Libri Sex [Leipzig: BSB B.G. Teubner Verlagsgesellschaft, 1978], 48–52). For a helpful discussion of Lucretia that highlights Ovid's interest in showing her beauty to have been the main cause that led to her rape, see A.G. Lee, 'Ovid's Lucretia', *Greece and Rome* 22 (1953), pp. 107–18.

41 For another example of parents resisting the ascetic, sexually renunciatory life desired by their children, see Gerontius, *Life of Melania the Younger* 6–7 (Denys Gorce [ed.], *Vie de Sainte Mélanie* [Sources Chrétiennes 90; Paris: Les Éditions du Cerf, 1962], pp. 136–40); Elizabeth A. Clark, *The Life of Melania the Younger. Introduction, Translation, and Commentary* (Studies in Women and Religion, 14; New York and Toronto: Edwin Mellen, 1984), pp. 30–31. Melania's and seemingly also her young husband Pinianus's 'parents … were wary of peoples' reproaches and would not agree to their children's wishes', but continued to exert 'compulsion' and for fear of 'the abuses of blasphemous men … pained [the young couple], by keeping [them] from [their] heavenly calling of a life of renunciation'.

42 *Acts of Paul and Thecla* 22 (Lipsius [ed.], *ActaAA*, vol. 1, p. 250, l. 5).

43 *Acts of Paul and Thecla* 9 (Lipsius [ed.], *ActaAA*, vol. 1, p. 242, ll. 4–5). Thecla's mother twice calls her 'virgin', once she calls her 'child', and once refers to her as 'lawless one'. In addition, the narrator identifies her as Theocleia's 'child'.

the subject of the verb ἐδάκρυσεν,[44] and thus, by spreading out the wood onto which Thecla climbed, the 'boys and girls' stay intimately involved in the scene. A later scene in Antioch which depicts 'women with their children' (αἱ δὲ γυναῖκες μετὰ τῶν τέκνων)'[45] who are seated or standing on an elevated place before which wild beasts are paraded, presumably in the arena, only strengthens the assumption that children were present also at bloody scenes in the theatres.

Details of Thecla's condemnation to burning and the attempt to carry out this sentence offer further proof of the narrative's interest in Thecla's young age. Theocleia's exclamation that her daughter's execution may serve to create fear in 'all the women instructed by this one' [i.e. Paul] (πᾶσαι αἱ ὑπὸ τούτου διδαχθεῖσαι γυναῖκες),[46] the comment that 'many women and virgins/girls' had been listening to Paul,[47] and the notice that 'boys and girls' were bringing the 'wood and hay' into the theatre all emphasize the public spectacle of Thecla's situation, and thus serve to set an educational example for women, and particularly for young virgins or girls. Thecla's sentencing and execution are also meant to warn the young to conform to the established mould that was set up, time-tested and proven as the proper course of life of a female person, and so to move through marriage and sexual intercourse from girlhood to womanhood. The 'boys and girls' are to see one of their own being burned to death as a warning against following Thecla's path.

Thecla, as both female and young, functions as an *exemplum* for women and children exceptionally well with regard to both the inner logic of the story and the author's literary intent. The greater the potential similarity, the greater the hope on the part of the imitator to reach the ideal modelled by the *exemplum*. The greater the similarity, the greater also the possible distracting effect, in cases where *exempla* are used to dissuade someone from a given course of action. Theocleia wants her daughter to become a warning *exemplum* of the kind of punishment young members of the female sex who refuse to comply with social and more specifically parental expectations concerning marriage and procreation should expect to receive. Given the overt message of sexual renunciation in Paul's preaching and evidenced in the behaviour of those who accepted this message, the fact that Thecla survives the persecution effectively turns her into an *exemplum* not only for women who desire to live a life of renunciation, but also for women who desire greater independence and self-determination.[48]

From the viewpoint of the story's narrative logic, initially the girl Thecla burning in the theatre could function as a negative example for children; up to the point when she climbs on to the stack of wood and hay, her example indicates what would happen to children who made decisions against their parents' will. Then, however, the valuation of Thecla's 'negative' characterization as that of a disobedient girl is clearly turned around, given that divine protection even seems to justify her disobedience. The children who see what happened to her, or who later hear about her story, may

---

44 *Acts of Paul and Thecla* 22 (Lipsius [ed.], *ActaAA*, vol. 1, p. 250, l. 6).
45 *Acts of Paul and Thecla* 28 (Lipsius [ed.], *ActaAA*, vol. 1, p. 255, l. 9).
46 *Acts of Paul and Thecla* 20 (Lipsius [ed.], *ActaAA*, vol. 1, p. 249, l. 8).
47 *Acts of Paul and Thecla* 7 (Lipsius [ed.], *ActaAA*, vol. 1, p. 241, l. 2).
48 See Albrecht, *Das Leben der heiligen Makrina*, pp. 316–17, with brief comments on Thecla's role as *exemplum* for women who were not ascetics.

very well be attracted by the success of her adventurous disobedience, which God ultimately rewards.

Both in classical and in early Christian literature one readily encounters the theme that the example of young persons engaging in exceptional deeds or being confronted with extraordinary circumstances has the power to attract the attention not only of adults but also of children. In his biography of Emperor Augustus, Nikolaos of Damascus (born *ca.* BCE 64) depicts the future leader already during his youth as a *puer senex*.[49] Although only 9 years old, Augustus displays advanced oratorical skills that attract the attention of the Romans; it also led many youths and boys his age to accompany him, for example when he practises on horseback for the military service,[50] both in admiration and in hopes of career advancement. The effectiveness of the example of a young child for purposes of instructing 'boys and girls' is also acknowledged in early Christian authors from the eastern Mediterranean. Assuming a moderate continuation in general educational principles in the same area over two to three centuries within Christian communities, we can note John Chrysostom's recommending to parents that if their 'free-born boy ... yearn[s] after the pleasure to be found there [i.e. in the theatre], let us point out any of his companions who are holding back from this, so that he may be held fast in the grip of emulation'.[51] Chrysostom, who in the same treatise recommends that parents and children talk with one another at home about the stories from the Scriptures which they heard at church, including those of biblical brothers like Cain and Abel, here advises parents to recall to their children as examples the positive, exemplary behaviour displayed by children from the neighbourhood who were of the same age. Chrysostom expresses a conviction that children are most ready to imitate examples set by other children.

Although his *On Vainglory and the Right Way for Parents to Bring Up Their Children* was written around 393/394, about 200 years after the *Acts of Paul (and Thecla)*, the region of origin for both texts is the same.[52] Furthermore, as in the *Acts of Paul (and Thecla)*, also in Chrysostom's comment the theatre is the context for the intersection of the themes of children and their imitation of *exempla*. For Chrysostom, reference to the theatre is both a topos and describes part of the real

---

49 For the motif of the *puer senex*, see Ernst Robert Curtius, *European Literature and the Latin Middle Ages* (trans. Willard R. Trask; Bollingen Series, 36; New York: Bollingen Foundation, Inc. by Pantheon Books, 1953; repr. Princeton, NJ: Princeton University Press, 1990), pp. 98–101. Curtius also discusses the connection between the images of girl and old woman in early Christian literature (pp. 101–105). Elena Giannarelli, 'L'infanzia nella biografia cristiana', *Studia Patristica* 18.2 (1989), pp. 217–21 (217–18); Christian Gnilka, *Aetas spiritalis. Die Überwindung der natürlichen Altersstufen als Ideal frühchristlichen Lebens* (Theophaneia 24; Bonn: P. Hanstein, 1972), *passim*.

50 Nikolaos of Damascus, *On the Life and Education of Caesar Augustus* III.3–5 (Jürgen Malitz [ed. and trans.], *Nikolaos von Damaskus. Leben des Kaisers Augustus* [Texte zur Forschung, 80; Darmstadt: Wissenschaftliche Buchgesellschaft, 2003], p. 28).

51 John Chrysostom, *On Vainglory and the Right Way for Parents to Bring Up Their Children* 77b (Anne-Marie Malingrey [ed. and trans.], *Jean Chrysostome. Sur la vaine gloire et l'éducation des enfants* [Sources Chrétiennes, 188; Paris: Les Éditions du Cerf, 1972], pp. 178–80; English translation, M.L.W. Laistner, *Christianity and Pagan Culture in the Later Roman Empire together with An English Translation of John Chrysostom's Address on Vainglory and the Right Way for Parents to Bring Up Their Children* [Ithaca, NY: Cornell University Press, 1951, reprinted 1967], p. 117).

52 On the date of John Chrysostom's work, see Malingrey, *Jean Chrysostome. Sur la vaine gloire et l'éducation des enfants*, p. 47.

context of experience for early Christian children.[53] In the *Acts of Paul (and Thecla)* it likewise fulfils both functions. The arguments are not quite the same: Chrysostom speaks to children's imitation of the example of other children who do not go to the theatre; conversely, the *Acts of Paul (and Thecla)* features the sufferings of the young girl Thecla, displayed in the theatre, intended by her mother to set a negative example, while the author turns around her example into one that could provide a role model for children. No critique of children's presence in the theatre as such is voiced. The point of clear comparison, however, is that both instances appreciate that children observed the behaviour of, and were understood to draw conclusions from what happened to, a person of their own age.

The actual scene of Thecla's attempted burning, of course, turns out differently from what those in power intended. Although 'a great flame blazed, the fire did not touch her'.[54] Instead, rain and hail extinguish the fire, and Thecla's life is saved. To the extent that Theocleia and the governor of Iconium, who had sentenced Thecla to death, intended to reeducate 'women' and 'boys and girls', part of their goal is fulfilled. Yet while their choosing an *exemplum* proves effective, it does not function in the direction they had planned. The girl Thecla experienced God's liberating work on her behalf and, if we assume the presence of the 'boys and girls' in the theatre, her experience becomes for them an example of their own possible liberation. The girls who are present even have another level of identification with Thecla, namely through gender. To some of the 'boys and girls' (οἱ δὲ παῖδες καὶ αἱ παρθένοι) inspired by Paul to 'live a pure life', Thecla's example may have given hope in their struggle for asceticism. As she overcomes expectations of the state and of her family, her dedication to celibacy continues to be recommended to young girls; Ambrose of Milan would later advise young female virgins: 'If you conquer [your] home, you [are also able to] conquer the world.'[55]

A further struggle that affected many children's lives was their exploitation as slaves for purposes of work or pleasure.[56] In the present context, παῖδες can be rendered either as 'boys' or as 'children', but the word also carries the connotation of

53 For a recent study of Chrysostom on Christians and the ancient theatre, see Blake Leyerle, *Theatrical Shows and Ascetic Lives: John Chrysostom's Attack on Spiritual Marriage* (Berkeley: University of California Press, 2001). For a helpful discussion of Chrysostom's view on how to raise children, see also Blake Leyerle, 'Appealing to Children', *JECS* 5.2 (1997), pp. 243–70.

54 *Acts of Paul and Thecla* 22 (Lipsius [ed.], *ActaAA*, vol. 1, p. 250, l. 10).

55 Ambrose of Milan, *De virginibus* I.11.63 (PL 16.217; Egnatius Cazzaniga [ed.], *S. Ambrosii Mediolanensis Episcopi De virginibus libri tres*, Corpus Scriptorum Latinorum Paravianum 1 [Aug. Taurinorum Mediolani, Patavii, Florentiae, Romae, Neapoli, Panormi: In Aedibus Io. Bapt. Paraviae et Sociorum, 1948], p. 32, ll. 4–5 and 11–12): *Contradicunt parentes, sed volunt vinci ...Vince prius, puella, pietatem: si vincis domum, vincis et saeculum.* See also Elizabeth A. Clark, 'Antifamilial Tendencies in Ancient Christianity', *Journal of the History of Sexuality* 5 (1995), pp. 356–80 (367).

56 For a reconsideration of the use of children acquired by and incorporated into families through means other than procreation, for purposes of entertainment and at times sexual pleasure, see Christian Laes, 'Desperately Different? *Delicia* Children in the Roman Household', in Balch and Osiek (eds.), *Early Christian Families*, pp. 298–324. For discussion of various aspects of the experience of slave children in the early Christian world, see Horn and Martens, *'Let the Little Ones Come to Me'*, Chapter 6 and *passim*.

'slave' and at times is used to speak of a slave.[57] While not all children were slaves, and not all slaves became slaves in childhood, the two could and did intersect. The multiple meanings of παῖς thus always colour the notion of a 'child' as a person who was just as much without rights as a 'slave'.[58] The *Acts of Paul (and Thecla)* lacks any further precision regarding the social status of the παῖδες, or παρθένοι for that matter, who carried the wood and hay. They may have done so of their own will; perhaps they were told to do so. Whether the latter is the case, or whether some of the παῖδες come from lower classes or were slave-children, Thecla's liberation functions for them as a sign of hope: liberation from their bondage is a possibility.

The narrative gives no indication to the reader from which she or he might conclude that during her initial years of travelling with Paul, Thecla left behind the age of youth, or even childhood.[59] The concern for investigating the representation of children in the AAA, therefore, could certainly be grounded in the observation that a youthful girl appears as one of the key figures of at least one of these texts. The *Acts of Paul (and Thecla)* reveals that as a young person Thecla experiences liberation of herself as much as she provides a model that could encourage the hope of liberation for other young persons. Yet certainly not all girls that appear on the pages share the same liberation as Thecla did. The case of the apostle Peter's daughter demonstrates this.

Multiple Repressions as 'Beneficial for Her and Me'? – Peter's Daughter

The story of the daughter of the apostle Peter seems diametrically opposed to that of Thecla. Whereas Thecla overcomes repressions of gender determination and age, empowers others to find their own liberation, and serves as a role model both for women and children, Peter's daughter at best elicits pity in the one who beholds her fragmented literary image. She functions as an example of the multiple and seemingly insurmountable repressions affecting children's lives in the ancient world. If her story does manifest any traces of liberation, it may not be sufficient to offset the tragedy of her life.

---

57 See Liddell and Scott, *Greek-English Lexicon*, p. 1289; Lampe, *Patristic Greek Lexicon*, p. 997, prefers 'servant' as a gloss. See also Mark Golden, '*Pais*, "Child," and "Slave"', *L'Antiquité Classique* 54 (1985), pp. 91–104.

58 On the intersection of slavery and family life, see, for example, Peter Garnsey, 'Sons, Slaves – and Christians', in Beryl Rawson and Paul Weaver (eds.), *The Roman Family in Italy. Status, Sentiment, Space* (Oxford: Clarendon Press; Canberra: Humanities Research Centre, 1997), pp. 101–21; Dale B. Martin, 'Slave Families and Slaves in Families', in Balch and Osiek (eds.), *Early Christian Families*, pp. 207–30; Laes, 'Desperately Different?'; and Bernadette J. Brooten, 'Der lange Schatten der Sklaverei im Leben von Frauen und Mädchen', in Frank Crüsemann, Marlene Crüsemann, Claudia Janssen, Rainer Kessler and Beate Wehn (eds.), *Dem Tod nicht glauben. Sozialgeschichte der Bibel. Festschrift für Luise Schottroff zum 70. Geburtstag* (Gütersloh: Gütersloher Verlagshaus, 2004), pp. 488–503.

59 Scholarship is divided on the question of whether or not the category of 'youth' constituted a distinct period of life in the ancient world. See Emiel Eyben, *Restless Youth in Ancient Rome* (London and New York: Routledge, 1993); Pierre Ginestet, *Les organizations de la jeunesse dans l'Occident Romain* (Brussels: Latomus Revue d'Études Latines, 1991); and Marc Kleijwegt, *Ancient Youth. The Ambiguity of Youth and the Absence of Adolescence in Greco-Roman Society* (Amsterdam: J.C. Gieben, 1991). The study that considers the question from the perspective of female teenagers has yet to be written.

The apocryphal *Acts of Peter* does not exist any longer in a complete whole. About two thirds of the original text are witnessed to in the Latin text of the *Actus Vercellenses*, preserved in the sixth- or seventh-century Codex Vercelli.[60] A few additional scenes can be supplemented on the basis of the account of Peter's martyrdom in a Coptic fragment that introduces Peter's daughter.[61] This fragment was identified as part of the *Acts of Peter*[62] and subsequently labelled *Act of Peter*. Andrea Molinari called into question the literary connection between the *Act of Peter* and the *Acts of Peter*,[63] but Christine Thomas successfully demonstrates that Augustine's identification of the episode concerning Peter's daughter as an apocryphal text establishes a greater likelihood for that scene to have been part of the original *Acts of Peter*.[64] Attempts at complementing this material with stories that feature Peter in Slavonic, Coptic or Syriac texts have been judged unsuccessful.[65]

Neither the canonical Acts nor any other New Testament text mentions Peter's daughter. Yet Mk 1.29–31 speaks of Simon Peter's mother-in-law (ἡ δὲ πενθερὰ Σίμωνος), who lived at Simon's house and whom Jesus healed from fever.[66]

60 For recent observations on that text, see A. Hilhorst, 'The Text of the *Actus Vercellenses*', in Jan N. Bremmer (ed.), *The Apocryphal Acts of Peter: Magic, Miracles and Gnosticism* (Leuven: Peeters, 1998), pp. 148–60; see also in that same volume Christine M. Thomas, 'Revivifying Resurrection Accounts: techniques of composition and rewriting in the *Acts of Peter* cc.25–28', pp. 65–83.

61 See Walter C. Till and Hans-Martin Schenke, *Die gnostischen Schriften des koptischen Papyrus Berolinensis 8502*, in *TU* 60 (2nd rev. and enlarged ed.; Berlin: Akademie Verlag, 1972), pp. 296–321 and 333. This text with minor modifications is reprinted in James Brashler and Douglas M. Parrott (eds. and trans.), 'The Act of Peter, BG, 4: 128,1–141,7', in *Nag Hammadi Codices V, 2–5 and VI with Papyrus Berolinensis 8502,1 and 4*, NHS XI (Leiden: E.J. Brill, 1979), pp. 473–93 (478–92).

62 See Carl Schmidt, 'Die alten Petrusakten im Zusammenhang der apokryphen Apostellitteratur nebst einem neuentdeckten Fragment', in *TU* 24.1, N.F. 9.3 (Leipzig: J.C. Hinrichs'sche Buchhandlung, 1903), pp. 3–7 as well as his 'Studien zu den alten Petrusakten'.

63 Andrea Lorenzo Molinari, 'Augustine, *Contra Adimantum, Pseudo-Titus*, BG 8502.4 and the *Acts of Peter*: Attacking Carl Schmidt's Theory of an Original Unity Between the *Act of Peter* and the *Acts of Peter*' (SBLSP 38; Atlanta: Society of Biblical Literature, 1999), pp. 426–47; and more recently Andrea Lorenzo Molinari, *I Never Knew the Man: the Coptic Act of Peter (Papyrus berolinensis 8502.4): Its Independence from the Apocryphal Acts of Peter, Genre and Legendary Origins*, (Bibliothèque copte de Nag Hammadi. Section 'Etudes' 5; Québec: Presses de l'Université Laval; and Louvain: Editions Peeters, 2000).

64 Christine M. Thomas, *The Acts of Peter, Gospel Literature, and the Ancient Novel: Rewriting the Past* (Oxford and New York: Oxford University Press, 2003), pp. 18–20. For references to Augustine's *Adversus Adimantum* see below.

65 For a description of the state of affairs of the attempts at reconstructing the original *Acts of Peter*, see Gérard Poupon, 'Les "Actes de Pierre" et leur remaniement', *ANRW* II.25.6 (1988), pp. 4363–83 esp. 4364.

66 On Simon Peter's mother-in-law and the purpose surrounding her healing, see Mary Ann Tolbert, 'Mark', in Carol A. Newsom and Sharon H. Ringe (eds.), *Women's Bible Commentary; Expanded Edition with Apocrypha* (Louisville, KY: Westminster/John Knox Press, 1998), pp. 350–62; John Granger Cook, 'In Defence of Ambiguity: Is There a Hidden Demon in Mark 1.29–31?' *NTS* 43 (1997), pp. 184–208; W. Barnes Tatum, 'Did Jesus Heal Simon's Mother-in-law of a Fever?' *Dialogue* 27 (1994), pp. 148–58; Monika Fander, 'Frauen in der Nachfolge Jesu: die Rolle der Frau im Markusevangelium', *EvTh* 52 (1992), pp. 413–32 (414–18); Sister Philsy, 'Diakonia of Women in the New Testament', *Indian Journal of Theology* 32 (1983), pp. 110–18; and Deborah Krause, 'Simon Peter's Mother-in-Law—Disciple or Domestic Servant? Feminist Biblical Hermeneutics and the Interpretation of Mark 1.29–31', in Amy-Jill Levine (ed.), *A Feminist*

Concluding that as a married man Peter likely had children seems to have sufficed for ancient narrators to claim that Peter had a daughter. Of immediate interest for the characterization of Peter's daughter is that the Apocryphal Acts tradition provides the young girl with little cousins in addition to the uncle known via the Gospels (Mt. 4.18; 10.2; Mk 1.16; Lk. 6.14; Jn 1.40-41; 6.8). Indeed, Peter's brother Andrew, whom the canonical texts do not identify as either married or a father, in a Coptic fragment (likely part of the *Acts of Andrew*) is characterized as both married and as a parent. John Barns, the editor of the Bodleian Coptic fragment, convincingly reconstructs a statement by Andrew that when following Jesus, he had left not only father and mother, but also his wife and his little children.[67] For Barns, leaving 'wife and little children' fits in with encratite tendencies of the *Acts of Andrew*.[68] It can be understood as a derivative of Lk. 14.26. The line of text can also be regarded as an elaboration on the words of the disciples to Jesus: 'We have left everything (ἀφήκαμεν πάντα) to follow you!' (Mk 10.28; Mt. 19.27; cf. Lk. 5.11, 28); it simply spells out what that 'everything' meant in Andrew's case. To what extent the picture of Andrew as husband and parent may have influenced the characterization of Peter as married man and father cannot be decided here.[69] Yet he left behind his children for the sake of the gospel. In the same manner in which Andrew seems to have ceded care for his children, so also is Peter portrayed as unconcerned about his daughter's well-being, at least as not concerned about his daughter's physical well-being.

The Coptic fragment of the *Act of Peter* mentions Peter's daughter at two different stages of her life, once at the age of ten and again some time later, perhaps only months, possibly years. The account of her sufferings from which she gained only momentary release functions as the framework for a flashback to what had happened to her during her childhood.

On the day of his daughter's birth, the Lord informs Peter in a vision that 'if her body remains healthy ... this (girl) will wound many souls',[70] that is, her body would

---

Companion to Mark (Feminist Companion to the New Testament and Early Christian Writings, 2; Sheffield: Sheffield Academic Press, 2001), pp. 37–53. On the Aramaic background connecting Mk 1.29–31 with Mt. 8.15, see Günther Schwarz, '"Er berührte ihre Hand"? (Matthäus 8,15)', *Biblische Notizen* 73 (1994), pp. 33–35.

67 John Barns, 'A Coptic Apocryphal Fragment in the Bodleian Library', *JTS* n.s. 11 (1960), pp. 70–76 (71–72) for edition of Coptic text. Following p. 72, Barns prints plate I with a photographic reproduction of the fragment. Jean-Marc Prieur, *Acta Andreae. Praefatio—Commentarius*, (CCSA 5; Turnhout: Brepols, 1989), pp. 22–23, reprints Barns's edition and provides a French translation.

68 Barns, 'Coptic Apocryphal Fragment', p. 75, and following him, Prieur, *Acta Andreae. Praefatio*, p. 24. For a discussion of encratite tendencies in Apocryphal Acts, see also Yves Tissot, 'Encratisme et Actes Apocryphes', in François Bovon *et al.* (eds.), *Les Actes Apocryphes des Apôtres: Christianisme et Monde Païen* (Publications de la Faculté de Théologie de l'Université de Genève Nº 4; Genève: Editions Labor et Fides, 1981), pp. 109–19, esp. 115 and 117–18 for the *Acts of Andrew*. Tissot does not refer to the passage in question here.

69 See Bremmer, 'Apocryphal Acts: Authors, Place, Time and Readership', pp. 152–53, on the relative dating of the *Acts of Andrew* to perhaps Alexandria *ca.*150 CE and the *Acts of Peter* perhaps to Rome between 180–190 CE.

70 *Acts of Peter*, Papyrus Berolinensis 8502, p. 132,1–4 (Brashler and Parrott, 'The Act of Peter, BG, 4: 128,1–141,7', pp. 482–83).

function as an instrument through which harm would be done.[71] When the girl is ten, a rich man, Ptolemy, sees her bathing with her mother and desires to marry her.[72] The combination of her female beauty and her young age evidently arouses his desire. Given that Ptolemy's subsequent behaviour does not evince much concern for whether the girl is 'available' or under someone else's authority, and noting that the text has no direct interest in denying sexual attraction to Peter's wife, whom Ptolemy also has seen bathing, one may reasonably conclude that the girl's young age was not the only, but nevertheless was a significant factor in creating a situation that led to unwanted advances and that eventually led to her physical oppression. Further, the girl's youthfulness was a necessary element in creating a constellation in which adult male desire and parental authority came into conflict.

Once Ptolemy's sexual desires are aroused, he insists on marrying the girl. Although her mother 'was not persuaded',[73] a comment that creates the impression that the mother's judgement of the marriage proposal was given some weight, Peter's daughter receives no opportunity to speak on her own behalf.[74] How Peter responds, or rather reacts, will become obvious in a moment.

Following a lacuna of two pages,[75] the text depicts Peter and his wife finding their daughter left at the door outside their home, likely by Ptolemy's men-servants.[76] She appears 'with one whole side of her body from her toes to her head, paralysed and withered'.[77] Quite clearly, physical harm had been done to her. Yet who is responsible?

Despite the Coptic fragment's lacuna, Augustine's comments preserved in his anti-Manichaean treatise *Against Adimantus* permit a plausible reconstruction of the girl's stay with Ptolemy. This wealthy man seems to have abducted the girl from her parents' home. Yet when he physically was about to 'take her for his wife',[78] his attempts were frustrated by Peter's assertion of parental authority. Augustine attests that 'Peter's daughter had been made a paralytic through [her] father's prayers'

71 *Acts of Peter*, Papyrus Berolinensis 8502, pp. 131,13–132,5 (Brashler and Parrott, 'The Act of Peter, BG, 4: 128,1–141,7', pp. 482–83).

72 *Acts of Peter*, Papyrus Berolinensis 8502, p. 132,7–17 (Brashler and Parrott, 'The Act of Peter, BG, 4: 128,1–141,7', pp. 482–85).

73 *Acts of Peter*, Papyrus Berolinensis 8502, p. 132,17–18 (Brashler and Parrott, 'The Act of Peter, BG, 4: 128,1–141,7', pp. 484–85).

74 Whether or not the lost section, which follows the scene in which Ptolemy demanded to marry the girl, contained any description of a reaction on the part of the girl, or on the part of Peter for that matter, cannot be determined. Given the description at the end of p. 132, where negotiation is presented as having taken place between Ptolemy and the mother only, and where these negotiations come to an end that frustrated Ptolemy, it may very well have been the case that the mother's refusal being sufficient, Ptolemy realized that he would have no chance at getting the girl without recourse to physical force.

75 Page 133 and most of page 134 are missing. See Brashler and Parrott, 'The Act of Peter, BG, 4: 128,1–141,7', p. 484.

76 Of *Acts of Peter*, Papyrus Berolinensis 8502, fol. 134, only half a line remains that contains the words 'ⲛ̄ⲣⲱⲙⲉ ⲙ̄', which Brashler and Parrott understand as '[t]he men-servants of' (Brashler and Parrott, 'The Act of Peter, BG, 4: 128,1–141,7').

77 *Acts of Peter*, Papyrus Berolinensis 8502, 135,6–9 (Brashler and Parrott, 'The Act of Peter, BG, 4: 128,1–141,7', 484–85).

78 *Acts of Peter*, Papyrus Berolinensis 8502, p. 132,16–17 (Brashler and Parrott, 'The Act of Peter, BG, 4: 128,1–141,7', 484–85), where his intent is stated.

(*Petri filiam paralyticam factam precibus patris*).[79] When in a later scene the Coptic fragment presents Peter as healing and then withdrawing healing from his daughter, his words are not identified as prayer. An act in which the girl is made a paralytic through her father's prayer in a strict sense of the word is not contained in the Coptic fragment. Augustine's remark therefore most likely refers to the description of a scene when the girl initially becomes paralysed in response to her father's prayer, a scene arguably depicted on the missing pages.[80] The participial *factam* describes the beginning of the girl's status as a paralytic in the past, not her reintroduction into that state later on.

Whether or not Peter specifically prays that his daughter become paralysed so that she would no longer be an object of Ptolemy's desires requires further exploration. Peter may have prayed for a precise plan of action – Augustine's report neither supports nor denies this possibility – or, he may have prayed for protection for his daughter in more general terms, leaving to God the choice of what form that help ought to take.

Augustine is primarily interested in the fact that Peter prays, and that the Manichaeans who accepted the *Acts of Peter* acknowledge the power of the apostle's prayer.[81] Whether he would have seen any problem with a father praying for his child to become diseased, if that condition allowed the child and so the family to escape the defilement of the family's honour through rape, is unclear. The author or redactor of the Coptic fragment seems to have had no second thoughts regarding such an incident. Stories of physical violence done to a young female's body to preserve her from shame, even to the point of death, as mentioned above, were well known in Antiquity. Again, Lucretia suffices as an example.[82] Such stories also had their followers in Christian circles, although some do question whether violence leading to death could validly be inflicted on the girls, even by the girls themselves.[83]

79 Augustine of Hippo, *Contra Adimantum* 17 (Joseph Zycha [ed.], *Sancti Aureli Augustini De utilitate credendi, De duabus animabus, Contra Fortunatum, Contra Adimantum, Contra Epistulam Fundamenti, Contra Faustum* [Corpus Scriptorum Ecclesiasticorum Latinorum, 25; (sect. 6, pars 1) [Prague, Vienna, and Leipzig: F. Tempsky and G. Freytag, 1891], 170, l. 12): *et ipsius Petri filiam paralyticam factam precibus patris*.

80 His subsequent comment on the girl known from the *Epistle of Pseudo-Titus* likewise presents what he thought was the crucial point of the story. We might call Augustine's comment yet another 'multiform' of the base narrative. In such a case, however, its value as a witness to the content of the missing folios in the Coptic fragment of the *Act of Peter* would be diminished. For discussion of the relationships of different versions of a given story element or story to one another as well as to their respective, reconstructed 'base narrative' see Thomas, 'Revivifying Resurrection Accounts'.

81 Augustine of Hippo, *Contra Adimantum* 17 (Zycha [ed.], *Sancti Aureli Augustini ... Contra Adimantum*, 170, ll. 15–16): *tamen ad preces apostolic factum esse non negant*.

82 See also above, n. 40.

83 See, for example, Augustine of Hippo, *De civitate Dei* 1.16–19 (Bernardus Dombart and Alphonsus Kalb [eds.], *Sancti Aurelii Augustini De civitate Dei libri I–X* [CCSL 47: Aurelii Augustini Opera Pars XIV, 1; Turnholti: Typographi Brepols Editores Pontificii, 1955], pp. 17–22, see especially ch. 19 on pp. 20–22 for discussion of Lucretia's case), where he is concerned to distinguish carefully between voluntary death and martyrdom and clearly states that anyone who kills him- or herself, no matter what the circumstances, has broken the sixth commandment. For the acceptance of the necessity of the death of girls to preserve virginity, see also Eusebius of Emesa, *De martyribus* (ed. É.M. Buytaert, *Eusèbe d'Émèse. Discours conserves en latin, t. 1. La Collection de Troyes (Discours I á XVII)* [Spicilegium Sacrum Lovaniense. Etudes et documents 26; Louvain:

Against the background of acceptance, in principle, of at least limited harm done to a female person's body,[84] in cases where presumed higher goods were seen as requiring preferential consideration, one might reconsider the likelihood of a more explicit prayer on Peter's part. Indeed, the seed for Peter's praying for a physical deformation of his daughter's body could have been planted early on.

As noted above, the Coptic fragment of the *Act of Peter* tells that at the time of his daughter's birth, Peter receives a vision concerning the harm she would bring to others were her body not afflicted. Like any father who takes delight in his baby, Peter initially is reluctant to set body against soul, the physical against the spiritual. He first seems to think that the vision had 'mocked' (ⲤⲰⲂⲈ) him.[85] Eventually, however, he recognizes his daughter's potential as a stumbling-block (ⲢⲤⲔⲀⲚⲆⲀⲖⲒⳒⲈ ⲈⲂⲞⲖ ⳅⲒ ⲦⲞⲞⲦⲤ) for men.[86] From siding with his child without any reservations and against all odds, Peter changes to taking on the perspective of the threatened male suitor, and he finds such confidence in this role that he becomes one who 'smiled' (ⲤⲰⲂⲈ)[87] at those who do not understand that his daughter had to be deprived of her health.

Initially, when his daughter is born, Peter doubts that God would take away her physical well-being. Yet in the scene that frames the whole of the story recounted in the Coptic fragment, Peter hides himself behind God as the one to whom alone 'it [was] apparent ... why her body [was] not healthy'.[88] In between these two different expressions of attitudes, Peter becomes not only the instrument (through his prayer) but also the architect (through the suggestion expressed in his prayer) of the change in his daughter's physical condition. Consequently, the ten-year-old girl loses her father. She becomes subjected to the consequences that result from the transformation of a father willing to side with her against heaven when her physical integrity is at stake, into a father whose authority and power merge with that of the divine realm. She gains a father who has come to consider her and her body from multiple angles and who thus has come to consider the value of her well-being from multiple perspectives. Now her physical loss of virginity has to be weighed against other physical infringements of her bodily integrity, paralysis included. The latter would bring harm only to her; the former would damage everyone involved: herself, her suitor's soul, and her parents' honour. Peter's decision to seize control and direct,

---

Spicilegium Sacrum Lovaniense, 1953]), pp. 151–74; See also D. Amand de Mendieta, 'La virginité chez Eusèbe d'Émèse et l'ascétisme familial dans la première moitié du IVᵉ siècle', *Revue d'Histoire Ecclésiastique* 50 (1955), pp. 777–820. Martyrdom in the ancient world continues to arouse scholarly interest. See for example Arthur J. Droge and James D. Tabor, *A Noble Death: Suicide and Martyrdom among Christians and Jews in Antiquity* (San Francisco: HarperSanFrancisco, 1992); Daniel Boyarin, *Dying for God: Martyrdom and the Making of Christianity and Judaism* (Stanford, CA: Stanford University Press, 1999); and Elizabeth A. Castelli, *Martyrdom and Memory: Early Christian Culture Making* (New York: Columbia University Press, 1994).

84 Any harm that may have affected a girl's emotional well-being generally is not considered.

85 *Acts of Peter*, Papyrus Berolinensis 8502, p. 132,7 (Brashler and Parrott, 'The Act of Peter, BG, 4: 128,1–141,7', pp. 482–83).

86 See *Acts of Peter*, Papyrus Berolinensis 8502, p. 132,10–11 (Brashler and Parrott, 'The Act of Peter, BG, 4: 128,1–141,7', 482–83).

87 *Acts of Peter*, Papyrus Berolinensis 8502, p. 129,9 (Brashler and Parrott, 'The Act of Peter, BG, 4: 128,1–141,7', pp. 480–81).

88 *Acts of Peter*, Papyrus Berolinensis 8502, p. 129,10–12 (Brashler and Parrott, 'The Act of Peter, BG, 4: 128,1–141,7', pp. 480–81).

or redirect, the unavoidable harm to be done to his daughter's body in fact may not have been such a difficult one.

According to the Coptic fragment of the *Act of Peter*, Peter's parental control continues beyond his praying that his daughter might be afflicted with paralysis. This control encompasses the girl's entire life, both physical and material. Indeed, of the parcel of land that Ptolemy bequeathed her, she apparently sees no revenue. Rather, Peter decides that it would be best for all involved to sell the property and give the proceeds to the poor.[89] When people who gathered around Peter to benefit from his healing ministry demand he also heal his daughter, he displays, at least temporarily, absolute power over his daughter's body again, by making the girl get up who was 'lie[ing] crippled there in the corner',[90] a place and situation to which her life had been reduced. He makes her walk about without anyone's help except that of Jesus.[91] Yet in the end, he orders her again to sit down and return to her prior state of paralysis. The miracle is intended to please the crowds and increase their faith in God's power. Its purpose is not to benefit the girl.

At the outset of the scene, an onlooker describes the girl as one 'who has believed in the name of God'.[92] In the story that provides the framework, Peter's daughter experiences her father as subjecting her again to physical infirmity, now through words not explicitly formulated as prayers and without any need on his part to decide against her well-being as the smaller evil of two. On top of it all, Peter states twice, first to his daughter directly, and then to the crowds, that it is 'beneficial for her and me' [i.e. Peter] that she become paralysed again.[93] Even were one to acknowledge any benefit deriving from this situation, Peter's statement does not appear grounded in selfless interest in his daughter's well-being, here limited to a spiritual well-being. He assumes he would benefit from her miserable situation as well.

Whatever perceived benefit may have derived from preferring the mutilation of a girl's body, it is impossible to see any element of a child's experience of liberation in this account. Too tight is the net of authority of the *paterfamilias* joined with the authority of the apostle as representative of God. That net held down any life that may have sprung up in this young girl. Whether she continues to believe in God, despite the manifold acts of oppression and repression to which she is subjected, remains an open question. Whereas Thecla's estrangement from her mother leads to greater freedom and helps turn her into an example for other children, the account of Peter's daughter sublimates the process of estrangement in a way that merely leads to the girl's greater oppression, at least on the physical level. While 1 Corinthians 7 seems to have opened up ways for fathers to provide for the liberating possibility

---

89 *Acts of Peter*, Papyrus Berolinensis 8502, p. 139,6–17 (Brashler and Parrott [eds. and trans.], 'The Act of Peter, BG, 4: 128,1–141,7', 490–91).

90 *Acts of Peter*, Papyrus Berolinensis 8502, p. 129,4–5 (Brashler and Parrott [eds. and trans.], 'The Act of Peter, BG, 4: 128,1–141,7', 478–79).

91 *Acts of Peter*, Papyrus Berolinensis 8502, p. 130,3–6 (Brashler and Parrott [eds. and trans.], 'The Act of Peter, BG, 4: 128,1–141,7', 480–81).

92 *Acts of Peter*, Papyrus Berolinensis 8502, pp. 128,19–129,1–2 (Brashler and Parrott [eds. and trans.], 'The Act of Peter, BG, 4: 128,1–141,7', 478–79).

93 *Acts of Peter*, Papyrus Berolinensis 8502, p. 129,4–5 (Brashler and Parrott [eds. and trans.], 'The Act of Peter, BG, 4: 128,1–141,7', 478–79).

of a life of virginity for their marriageable daughters,[94] the way Peter went about realizing such a possibility in the *Act of Peter* reduces such virginity to a necessity for salvation, of oneself and others.

Did early Christian children and young girls in particular look also to Peter's daughter as a model for imitation? The answer is both yes and no as the following, concluding section discusses. The retelling of her case in the hagiography of Petronilla shows how at times the story of Peter's daughter was appropriated as one of the possible models of idealized female martyrdom, while the case of the Gardener's Daughter shows rejection of virginity when it comes at the price of the loss of physical well-being.

(Not) Responding to Children's Oppression: Petronilla and the Gardener's Daughter as Alternatives

Various representations of suffering and martyrdom depicted in the Apocryphal Acts of the Apostles have been the subject of investigation. Caroline Schroeder considers how the language of erotic passions, sometimes expressed in the terminology of suffering, in these texts functions to further the expression of philosophic-religious enquiry. Françoise Morard investigates the various ways in which depictions of the suffering of a given figure point towards the suffering of Christ on the cross, the model that early Christian martyrs strove to imitate.[95] Female figures are clearly among the topics studied in these contexts. An examination of the story of Peter's daughter that is not only interested in solving the puzzle of the redaction history of the *Acts of Peter*, but that is also seeking to understand the images and potential realities available to, employed by, and created by the ancient authors must at least raise the problem of children's suffering.

In the Coptic fragment of the *Act of Peter*, visitors to Peter's house are shown to have been concerned about the sick girl's fate. Although the person demanding her healing is cast as Peter's opponent,[96] at least this one voice expresses some awareness of the injustice of her deplorable state. When Peter healed his daughter and then reversed the healing, 'the whole crowd wept and begged' him for her health.[97] Whether they are satisfied with the course of events upon learning from Peter that the girl had fallen into paralysis already as a young child and likely through God's response to his prayers, and particularly when they heard Peter's laconic response

---

94 See Horn and Martens, *'Let the Little Ones Come to Me'*, Chapter 8.

95 See Caroline T. Schroeder, 'Embracing the Erotic in the *Passion of Andrew*. The Apocryphal *Acts of Andrew*, the Greek novel, and Platonic philosophy', in Jan N. Bremmer (ed.), *The Apocryphal Acts of Andrew* (Leuven: Peeters, 2000), pp. 110–26; and Françoise Morard, 'Souffrance et Martyre dans les Actes Apocryphes des Apôtres', in François Bovon *et al.* (eds.), *Les Actes Apocryphes des Apôtres*, pp. 95–108. See also Caroline T. Schroeder's article in this volume.

96 'He became bold to speak to Peter.' *Acts of Peter*, Papyrus Berolinensis 8502, p. 128,7–8 (Brashler and Parrott [eds. and trans.], 'The Act of Peter, BG, 4: 128,1–141,7', pp. 478–79).

97 *Acts of Peter*, Papyrus Berolinensis 8502, p. 131,9–10 (Brashler and Parrott [eds. and trans.], 'The Act of Peter, BG, 4: 128,1–141,7', pp. 482–83).

that it is 'beneficial for her and me'[98] that his daughter remained paralysed, is never revealed in the text.

Of the many possible responses to a girl's parentally and divinely inflicted, lifelong suffering, ancient witnesses preserve at least four possible ones.[99] The following discussion considers these responses with a view towards their concerns with the image of the suffering child and the related issue of parental or adult authority. After a brief revisit of Augustine's assessment, this discussion engages *Papyrus Berolinensis 8502*, the *Acts of Nereus and Achilleus*, and finally the *Epistle of Pseudo-Titus*.

Augustine highlights the centrality of the power of the apostle's prayer. Concerned with apostolic authority, he does not seem to see the problem of Peter's daughter's lifelong bodily suffering. Likewise, he reduces the relation between adult and suffering child to one that was considered only from the perspective of the power of the adult.

The rationale behind the decision of the writer or copyist of the Nag Hammadi codex *Papyrus Berolinensis 8502* to include the *Act of Peter* deserves exploration. The length of the *Act of Peter*, which just about fits onto the few pages at the end of the manuscript, is one plausible reason why the copyist includes this text and not another.[100] Schmidt sees the text's encratite message as a reason for inclusion.[101] Douglas Parrott considers the possible connection between the *Act of Peter* and the content of the treatise *Sophia of Jesus Christ*, which immediately precedes it in the codex.[102] Specifically, he sees 'the rich possibilities for allegorization [which] this story [i.e. the *Act of Peter*] would have presented to the Gnostics' as 'the sufficient reason' for why it was included.[103] Yet how exactly that allegory is intended to be resolved remains unclear. Parrott regards the figure of Ptolemy as an allegory of the soul – attracted to the world's beauty, which is represented by Peter's daughter – lost in ignorance had Christ's light and voice not brought true knowledge. The daughter's paralysis 'could have represented the power of divine knowledge over the powers of this world'. Alternatively, Parrott also is willing to see in the girl 'a type of the fallen Sophia',[104] yet he does not elaborate on how prototype and type match up. Conflating Parrott's distinctions, Christine Thomas sees Ptolemy's figure as the dominant one in

---

98 *Acts of Peter*, Papyrus Berolinensis 8502, p. 131,14 (Brashler and Parrott [eds. and trans.], 'The Act of Peter, BG, 4: 128,1–141,7', pp. 482–83).

99 The context to and healing of Charitine in *Acts of Philip* IV.4–6 will not be considered here. The text is edited and translated in François Bovon, Bertrand Bouvier and Frédéric Amsler, *Acta Philippi: Textus* (CCSA 11; Turnhout: Brepols, 1999), pp. 122–31. For commentary, see Frédéric Amsler, *Acta Philippi: Commentarius* (CCSA 12; Turnhout: Brepols, 1999), pp. 201–204.

100 Schmidt, *Die alten Petrusakten*, 2: 'Der Grund, weshalb der Schreiber den kleinen Text am Schluss angefügt hat, liegt offensichtlich darin, dass ihm noch eine Reihe Blätter von der letzten Papyruslage übriggeblieben waren, die er nicht unbeschrieben lassen wollte.'

101 Schmidt, *Die alten Petrusakten*, 13: 'Der innere Grund der Auslösung liegt in dem stark enkratitischen Charakter der Erzählung, die für gnostische Leser ein besonderes Interesse hatte.'

102 For the edition of *Sophia of Jesus Christ* contained in Papyrus Berolinensis 8502, see Douglas M. Parrott, *Nag Hammadi Codices III,3–4 and V,1 with Papyrus Berolinensis 8502,3 and Oxyrhynchus Papyrus 1081, Eugenostos and the* Sophia of Jesus Christ (The Coptic Gnostic Library, NHS 27; Leiden, New York, København, and Köln: E. J. Brill, 1991), uneven pages, right columns.

103 Brashler and Parrott [eds], 'The Act of Peter, BG, 4: 128,1–141,7', 476.

104 Brashler and Parrott [eds], 'The Act of Peter, BG, 4: 128,1–141,7', 476.

a possible allegorical interpretation and as functioning as 'a human allegory of the fall of Sophia'.[105]

Problems with such allegorical readings can be discerned at least on two levels. As Thomas herself notes, neither of these connections between the two texts can be shown with sufficient certainty to be grounded in the letter of the text.[106] Thus any assumptions as to whether or not Gnostics intended to read the *Act of Peter* as an allegory either of the whole or of part of the preceding text must remain tentative. In addition, except for Parrott – who considers it possible to see in Peter's daughter the type of Sophia – for other allegorical connections between the two texts, the suffering and absolute subjection to authority of Peter's daughter plays no role. If such a position corresponds with the writer or copyist's intentions, then the Gnostic treatment of the girl is no different from Augustine's. Yet if one assumes a correlation between Sophia and Peter's daughter, the precise nature of which would require further exploration, it would also be necessary to examine what kind of relationship may have been seen to exist between Peter's daughter and the Mary-figure in the *Gospel of Mary*, the first of the three major texts in the Berlin codex.[107] For a codex in which the first text features conflicts over authority and power of speech between male apostles, particularly Peter and Mary,[108] a concluding narrative illustrating how Peter in the end gained absolute control over a female figure may have been deemed fitting. If there is a compositional logic behind the assembling of the whole of the codex, the choice of the *Act of Peter* may have been made to show Peter's regained authority over his household, perhaps signifying the *oikos* of the Christian community, or, to stay with feminized imagery, the *ekklesia*.[109] In such a reading, Peter's daughter could become an embodiment of the community of believers as child of the one who was apostle, father and representative of God.

Although both Augustine and the Gnostic copyist of the *Act of Peter* employ the figure of Peter's daughter, arguably even in a manner that was central to their respective purposes, neither attempts to counteract the message that it was or could be advisable to inflict suffering on one's dependants, especially on one's children; rather it may be 'beneficial' to do so, because it serves higher purposes.[110] The fifth- or sixth-century *Acts of Nereus and Achilleus* offers a presentation of Peter's daughter that in a limited way could be considered as less offensive.

The *Acts of Nerseus and Achilleus* erases any overt references to the girl's young age. Instead, the text presumes the readers' familiarity with her earlier story by

---

105 Thomas, *The* Acts of Peter, *Gospel Literature, and the Ancient Novel*, p. 20.

106 Thomas, *The* Acts of Peter, *Gospel Literature, and the Ancient Novel*, p. 20.

107 For the Coptic text and an English translation of as well as a brief introduction to the *Gospel of Mary*, see R. McL. Wilson and George W. MacRae, 'The Gospel according to Mary. BG, 1:7,1–19,5', in *Nag Hammadi Codices V, 2–5 and VI with Papyrus Berolinensis 8502,1 and 4*, NHS XI (Leiden: E.J. Brill, 1979), pp. 453–71.

108 See *Gospel of Mary*, Papyrus Berolinensis 8502, p. 129,4–5 (Brashler and Parrott [eds. and trans.], 'The Act of Peter, BG, 4: 128,1–141,7', pp. 478–79.

109 The control Peter exercises over the crowd in the introductory scene of the healing and reversal of the healing of his daughter also fits in very well with such a reading of the evidence.

110 Augustine explicitly highlighted the argument of the beneficial character of Peter's prayer, afflicting paralysis in one case and death in another. See *Contra Adimantum* 17 (Zycha [ed.], *Sancti Aureli Augustini ... Contra Adimantum*, 170, ll. 13–15): *et respondent, quod hoc eis expediebat, ut et illa solveretur paralysi et illi moreretur.*

simply calling to mind that 'Peter's daughter Petronilla ... had become one who was bound to her bed (κλινήρης) through the will of the apostle Peter.'[111] The text also identifies the disciple Titus as the one who requested Peter heal 'Petronilla the paralytic' (τὴν Πετρωνίλλαν παραλυτικήν).[112] Also in this retelling, Peter 'forced (ἐκέλευσεν) her again onto her bed', thus creating great 'fear of God' among his audience, and the text leaves no doubt that the girl's paralysis continued until the end of her life.[113] Different from the account in the Coptic fragment of the *Act of Peter*, in the *Acts of Nereus and Achilles* no early childhood suitor had to be overcome. Rather, a certain *comes* Flaccus demands Petronilla's hand in marriage.[114] Different from the nameless and voiceless daughter in the *Act of Peter*, Petronilla counters her suitor's advances on her own. Asking for three days for consideration, she manages to die before the allotted time was up.[115] Turning the virgin into a defender of her virginity against a pagan aggressor much in the way of ancient confessors, the *Acts of Nereus and Achilles* also makes sure to mention the site of her commemoration, likely the church of Petronilla, built by Siricius after 390.[116] A fragmentary painting located in a *cubiculum* attached to the apsis depicts Petronilla as a youthful, unveiled figure.[117] She served as patroness to a certain Aurelia Petronilla, whose sarcophagus, now lost, carried as inscription: *Aureliae Petronillae filiae dulcissimae*.[118]

While the late fourth-century Roman cult of Petronilla evidences officially supported female piety that respected Peter's daughter as a saintly and youthful figure, a powerful female mediator on the way to paradise,[119] the hagiographical tradition of the *Acts of Nereus and Achilleus* sends mixed messages regarding Petronilla's reception. A feminist reading of the *Acts of Peter* will welcome some aspects of its treatment of her character; yet it will find others problematic.

111 *Acta SS. Nerei et Achillei* 15 (Hans Achelis [ed.], *Acta SS. Nerei et Achillei. Text und Untersuchung* (Texte und Untersuchungen zur Geschichte der altchristlichen Literatur 11.2; Leipzig: J. C. Hinrichs'sche Buchhandlung, 1893], 14, ll. 7 and 10–11).

112 *Acta SS. Nerei et Achillei* 15 (Achelis [ed.], *Acta SS. Nerei et Achillei*, 14, ll. 13–14). The reference to Titus in the *Acts of Nereus and Achilles* may be related to the fact that the scene of the gardener's daughter, discussed below, is included in the *Epistle of Pseudo-Titus*.

113 *Acta SS. Nerei et Achillei* 15 (Achelis [ed.], *Acta SS. Nerei et Achillei*, 14, ll. 19–21).

114 *Acta SS. Nerei et Achillei* 15 (Achelis [ed.], *Acta SS. Nerei et Achillei*, 14, ll. 24–26).

115 *Acta SS. Nerei et Achillei* 15 (Achelis [ed.], *Acta SS. Nerei et Achillei*, 15, ll. 3 and 6–7).

116 *Acta SS. Nerei et Achillei* 17 (Achelis [ed.], *Acta SS. Nerei et Achillei*, 17, l. 30). See also Achelis (ed.), *Acta SS. Nerei et Achillei*, 40 and 66.

117 Achelis (ed.), *Acta SS. Nerei et Achillei*, 40. For a colour reproduction of the painting, see Norbert Zimmermann, *Werkstattgruppen römischer Katakombenmalerei* (Jahrbuch für Antike und Christentum, Ergänzungsband 35; Münster, Westfalen: Aschendorff Verlag, 2002), plate XLVII, fig. 216. See also Wolfgang Braunfels and Engelbert Kirschbaum, *Lexikon der christlichen Ikonographie; vol. 8: Ikonographie der Heiligen* (Rome, Freiburg, Basel, Vienna: Herder, 1976), p. 158, for a black and white photograph.

118 Achelis (ed.), *Acta SS. Nerei et Achillei*, 41.

119 Achelis (ed.), *Acta SS. Nerei et Achillei*, 41, who interprets the depiction of Petronilla as a guide to paradise. On Petronilla, see also Philippe Pergola, '*Petronella Martyr*: une évergète de la fin du IVᵉ siècle?', in Eugenio Alliata, Theofried Baumeister, and Fabrizio Bisconti (eds.), *Memoriam sanctorum venerantes: miscellanea in onore di Monsignor Victor Saxer* (Studi di Antichità Cristiana 48; Città del Vaticano: Pontificio Instituto di Archeologia Cristiana, 1992), pp. 627–36, for whom the tomb has nothing to do with Peter's daughter Petronilla, as known through the *Acts of Nereus and Achilles*, but who also does not analyse the wall-painting.

Among the positive features is the simple fact that Peter's daughter receives a name.[120] Whether the name 'Petronilla' sufficiently distinguishes her as her own person or merely spells out her identity by way of a dependent relationship upon her father is a different matter. In the end, one may settle for the more balanced recognition of her figure in the latter account. That both she and her father have names places them more on a par.

The *Acts of Nereus and Achilleus* also gives Petronilla voice. When trying to counteract Flaccus's proposal, Petronilla speaks for herself.[121] At the same time, the text extinguishes any traces of prior traditions displayed of identifying her young age.[122] It even seems that the two factors of power of speech and age go hand in hand. Almost by virtue of her young age, in the *Acts of Peter* the apostle's daughter has no voice at all, while her mother, also a female person, is reported as having expressed her will. Also the figure of Petronilla still suffers from the threat of sexual aggression, and similar to the *Acts of Peter* also the *Acts of Nereus and Achilleus* establishes a connection between the threat to her sexual self-determination and her escape at the price of her physical well-being. Petronilla dies in order to escape the threat. Her bodily integrity, however, which in both stories is destroyed through paralysis, is disconnected from the endangering of her sexual status in the later retelling. In the *Acts of Nereus and Achilleus*, even more so than in the *Act of Peter*, control over her paralysis is handed over to her father. Peter 'forced' her to return to her sickness. As in the *Acts of Peter*, also in the *Acts of Nereus and Achilleus* Peter uses her temporary healing for his own purposes. Whether or not one should see Peter's calling upon her for service in the latter text as more of a sign of the father's exploitation of his daughter remains undetermined. In the *Acts of Peter*, the fact that his daughter walked about certainly functioned for Peter as a means of crowd control. Yet to see Petronilla's service to her father and Titus simply as an even more exploitative move on Peter's part might not get at the full meaning of the text.

In the *Acts of Nereus and Achilleus*, Petronilla's temporary healing is modelled on that of Peter's (or Simon's) mother-in-law in Lk. 4.39 and Mk 1.31, insofar as the

120 The lack of personal names of many of the women featured in ancient texts and its crippling impact on attempts to reconstruct women's history has been recognized. For the realm of canonical biblical literature, the recent reference work by Carol Meyers, Toni Craven and Ross S. Kraemer (eds.), *Women in Scripture: A Dictionary of Named and Unnamed Women in the Hebrew Bible, the Apocryphal/Deuterocanonical Books, and the New Testament* (Boston: Houghton Mifflin, 2000) constitutes a laudable effort towards countering and overcoming this problem. There is a need to address the same problem within the realm of extra-canonical, post-biblical and even more broadly early and late ancient Christian literature. The study of children in canonical and extra-canonical biblical literature is impacted by the same phenomenon, especially with regard to attempts at reconstructing the history of female children. Megan McKenna, *Not Counting Women and Children. Neglected Stories from the Bible* (Maryknoll, NY: Orbis Books, 1994), with Chapter 3 focusing on children, does not systematically address the problem of unnamed children in the texts. Yet the title of her book points in the right direction.

121 *Acta SS. Nerei et Achillei* 15 (Achelis [ed.], *Acta SS. Nerei et Achillei*, 14, ll. 27–31).

122 The principle established above that an unmarried girl is likely to be regarded as still of young age holds in the context of early Christian literature of the first two to three centuries, yet after the massive rise of asceticism from the third century on cannot be applied with the same certainty. Thus, in a fifth- or sixth-century text like the *Acts of Nereus and Achilleus*, a virgin is not necessarily to be regarded as a young girl.

text identifies as its purpose the subsequent service (διακόνησον ἡμῖν, διηκόνει) of a group of people, Peter and Titus. In all three cases, as well as in Mt. 8.15, healing enables the healed person to serve men. Some feminist readings of the healing of Peter's mother-in-law have seen the service she provides to Jesus as parallel to the angels ministering to him (οἱ ἄγγελοι διηκόνουν αὐτῷ) (Mk 1.13),[123] or as a model of discipleship.[124] One might also see it as Scripture's first instance of diaconal ministry.[125] When the late fourth-century painting in the church of Petronilla depicted Peter's daughter as patroness and guide for the lady buried in the shrine, this interpretation also acknowledges Petronilla's service and instructive authority. The arcosole painting depicts a youthful girl, who with her left hand is pointing to depictions of scrolls, possibly an indication of the written record of her story. Thus through the record of her sufferings and her smart defence of her virginity against pagan sexual desire Petronilla emerges as a youthful embodiment of ministry within the *ekklesia*.

Still, the question remains: Is there really anything redeeming about Peter's healing of his paralysed daughter, seemingly for the sole purposes of serving him and his companion, and then sending her back to her bed to remain crippled forever? Whereas the *Act of Peter* argued that it is 'beneficial' for Peter's daughter to remain paralysed, and while Augustine repeats that sentiment, the *Acts of Nereus and Achilleus* explains Petronilla's suffering as empowering her prayers to bring salvation and healing to many.[126] The miracle of her healing and its reversal also is seen as bringing about 'great fear of God'.[127] Thus, not only during the short period when she is healed, but again afterwards, Petronilla is 'at the service' of people. She brings benefits to people through her suffering, but in the end has little choice to do otherwise. However much one may be willing to see her empowerment for service as a sign of liberation, in the *Acts of Nereus and Achilleus* more than in the earlier texts, Petronilla is not only deprived of her childhood, she also is more obviously instrumentalized for a cause she is free neither to choose nor to refuse.

What remains distinct in the *Acts of Nereus and Achilleus* is Petronilla's transformation into a saint, a move which some women and men a century or so earlier interpreted as an act of heavenly liberation from oppression and as a sign of her power over her enemies. These women and men placed onto the altar of sainthood a suffering girl cheated of healing that had been available to her. It will have to be left to the reader to decide whether and to what extent this decision contributed to a justification for acts of violence against women and girls.

Peter's daughter's various embodiments do not constitute the only alternative response to Thecla. The *Acts of Peter* likely contained another variation on the theme that might shed some light on how girls in the ancient world resisted suffering imposed upon them through higher or parental authorities and how at least

123 Tolbert, 'Mark', p. 354.
124 Fander, 'Frauen in der Nachfolge Jesu', pp. 417–18; see also Joanna Dewey, 'The Gospel of Mark', in Elisabeth Schüssler Fiorenza (ed.), *Searching the Scriptures. Volume Two: A Feminist Commentary*, pp. 470–509 (476).
125 Especially if one assumes that Peter's mother-in-law prepared food for them and thus waited on them at the table. See Acts 6.1–2.
126 *Acta SS. Nerei et Achillei* 15 (Achelis [ed.], *Acta SS. Nerei et Achillei*, 14, ll. 22–23).
127 *Acta SS. Nerei et Achillei* 15 (Achelis [ed.], *Acta SS. Nerei et Achillei*, 14, l. 20).

some Christian girls did not see virginity as their only option. The example to be considered last is the story of the girl known as the Gardener's Daughter.

Escaping the οἶκος: The Gardener's Daughter

According to Augustine's *Contra Adimantum*, apocryphal texts that the Manichaeans accepted also contained a story of a gardener's daughter who dies because of Peter's prayers.[128] Given both that this comment immediately follows the one on Peter's daughter and that Peter is said to have been instrumental in both instances – namely, in bringing paralysis to the one girl and death to the other – the two episodes may once have been part of the same text, the *Acts of Peter*.[129]

Like the story of Peter's daughter, the account of the daughter of the gardener is not preserved in the extant *Acts of Peter*. In 1908, Dom Donatien De Bruyne published what he identified as fragments of an apocryphal text in Latin, entitled *Epistola Titi discipuli Pauli, De dispositione sanctimonii*,[130] found in the eighth-century *Codex Burchardi*, a manuscript kept in Würzburg, Germany.[131] Seventeen years later, De Bruyne edited and published the complete Latin text of this *Epistle of Pseudo-Titus*, which contains the account of the Gardener's Daughter on fol. 85v.[132]

A gardener who had only one (*una*) child, a relatively young (*puella*) virginal daughter (*filiam virginem*), asked Peter for his prayers on her behalf. The text does not provide a reason for the father's request, although since his daughter was his only child and he was already an older man (*ille senex*),[133] he may have been concerned both about her well-being and his own need to have a helper. Shortly after the apostle completed his prayer and assured the father that God would do whatever was best

---

128 Augustine, *Contra Adimantum* 17 (Zycha [ed.], *Sancti Aureli Augustini … Contra Adimantum*, 170, l. 13): *hortulani filiam ad precem ipsius Petri esse mortuam*.

129 Thomas, *The Acts of Peter, Gospel Literature, and the Ancient Novel*, pp. 18 and 127–28, n. 32, successfully refutes Andrea Molinari's challenge to such a reading of the evidence, also with regard to the story of the Gardener's Daughter.

130 For a German translation, see Aurelio de Santos Otero, 'Der Pseudo-Titus-Brief', in Wilhelm Schneemelcher (ed.), *Neutestamentliche Apokryphen in deutscher Übersetzung, II. Band: Apostolisches, Apokalypsen und Verwandtes* (Tübingen: J.C.B. Mohr [Paul Siebeck], 1989), pp. 50–70 (52–70). The story of the gardener is on pp. 54–55. Thomas, *The* Acts of Peter*, Gospel Literature, and the Ancient Novel*, p. 68, provides a translation of the story of the Gardener's Daughter into English. For studies of this treatise, see Giulia Sfameni Gasparro, 'L'Epistula Titi discipuli Pauli de dispositione sanctimonii e la tradizione dell'enkrateia', *ANRW* II.25.6 (1988), pp. 4551–64; Aurelio de Santos Otero, 'Der Apokryphe Titusbrief', *ZKG* 74 (1963), pp. 1–14; H. Kock, 'Zu Ps. Titus, De dispositione sanctimonii', *ZNW* 32 (1933), pp. 131–44; and Adolf von Harnack, 'Der apokryphe Brief des Paulusschülers Titus "De dispositione sanctimonii"', in *Sitzungsberichte der Berliner Akademie der Wissenschaften, Phil.-hist. Klasse* 17 (1925), pp. 180–213.

131 P. Domitien de Bruyne, 'Nouveaux Fragments des Actes de Pierre, de Paul, de Jean, d'André, et de l'Apocalypse d'Élie', *Revue Bénédictine* 25 (1908), pp. 149–60.

132 P. Domitien de Bruyne, '*Epistula Titi, Discipuli Pauli, De dispositione Sanctimonii*', *Revue Bénédictine* 37 (1925), pp. 47–72 (50, ll. 83–93). See also De Bruyne, 'Nouveaux Fragments', pp. 151–152. De Bruyne also suggested identifying another passage from ms Cambrai 254 (thirteenth century) as a complementary part of the story ('Nouveaux Fragments', pp. 152–53).

133 De Bruyne, '*Epistula Titi*', p. 50, l. 89, reads *ille senes*, without further comment. That reading may reflect a Medieval Latin variation.

for his daughter's soul, the girl died (*puella iacuit mortua*).[134] That was not quite what the father had had in mind. Unlike Peter, the gardener saw no 'divine benefit' (*beneficia divina*) in harm done to his child.[135] Rather, he implored the apostle to restore his only daughter (*unicam filiam*) to life.[136] In this narrative, the parent shows concern over the loss of his daughter, confronts apostolic authority, and seemingly is successful because the girl indeed is restored to life. The division between the interests of the parent and those of the divinely sanctioned apostolic figure works itself out in continuing a 'normal' household situation in which all family members experience physical well-being and are of service to each other. Parental emotions rather than spiritually informed assumptions are presented as what best guarantees the physical well-being of children. Yet such an interpretation again pays insufficient attention to the girl herself.

A few days after the daughter's resurrection at Peter's hand a man rushes into the gardener's house and remains for a while.[137] The fragment that likely was part of the *Acts of Peter* speaks of the visitor ruining the girl (*perdiditque puellam*).[138] While the expression could refer to the girl's loss of her virginity, it can also describe an exchange of new ideas, possibly of a religious nature. The visitor is described as *homo vinctus fidelis*,[139] either a Christian slave or someone who pretended to be a Christian[140] and thus either a non-Christian or an adherent of a sect that differed from the one to which Peter and the gardener's household belonged. The secondary interpretation in the *Epistle of Pseudo-Titus* clearly understands the *perdidit* in the sense of sexual corruption, since it comments on it via the imagery of adultery (*qui enim adulterat suum corpus*).[141] The story of the Gardener's Daughter concludes with the comment that neither the girl nor the visitor ever appeared again, suggesting that both had left behind any influence which apostolic teaching may have had on them. As the girl's father confronts apostolic authority from inside the normal workings of family life, the gardener's young daughter confronts apostolic influence by choosing to follow other teachings.

Unlike Petronilla, the Gardener's Daughter does not allow herself to be completely instrumentalized, either by an apostle or by her father. Unlike Peter's daughter whom the Coptic fragment repeatedly identifies as one who believes in God but who does not question what happens to her, the gardener's young daughter either gives up on the Christian faith as she may have become seduced by new teachings or she may have been moved by her quite traumatic experience to take greater responsibility for which faith she wanted to follow. The story of the Gardener's Daughter in the *Epistle of Pseudo-Titus* may very well be a multiform of the story of Peter's daughter, as Christine Thomas noted.[142] Yet the necessity of preserving one's virginity as a

---

134 De Bruyne, '*Epistula Titi*', p. 50, l. 87.

135 De Bruyne, '*Epistula Titi*', p. 50, l. 90.

136 De Bruyne, '*Epistula Titi*', p. 50, ll. 90–91.

137 De Bruyne, '*Epistula Titi*', p. 50, ll. 90–91.

138 De Bruyne, '*Epistula Titi*', p. 50, l. 93.

139 De Bruyne, '*Epistula Titi*', p. 50, l. 92.

140 See de Santos Otero, 'Der Pseudo-Titus-Brief', p. 55, n. 20, who refers to Harnack and Ficker respectively as those who first suggested the varying translations.

141 De Bruyne, '*Epistula Titi*', p. 50, ll. 93–94.

142 Thomas, *The* Acts of Peter, *Gospel Literature, and the Ancient Novel*, p. 67.

condition of salvation here more clearly is enhanced by the threat of apostasy which might go hand in hand with bonding between male and female. From the perspective of the apostle, preventing either is best served at the price of physical incapacity, even if that might mean the girl's death. While the girl's father merely resists such a conclusion that comes at the price of his daughter's life, the girl's response is more comprehensive. Like Thecla, the Gardener's Daughter decides to move outside familial bonds. Yet unlike Thecla, she does not necessarily reject constructions of family life as such. Rather, she appears to have decided to create new ones. To what extent class may have been a factor in bringing about these different reactions cannot here be discussed at length.[143] It seems that within lower classes, the perpetuation of family life was seen, and understood also by the young, as a natural task of life that was not to be dismissed. As a girl from a more humble background, the Gardener's Daughter clearly is not opposed to family bonds. While she rejects connections to her family of origin, she likely continues life in a real, physical family, yet now in one of her own choosing.

This investigation of Apocryphal Acts material, which adopts from feminist methodology the concern for the marginalized and seemingly insignificant, children, has highlighted different characters whose child-dimensions thus far have been neglected. It also demonstrates that Apocryphal Acts do more than merely feature children. They offer children not a monolithic message, but at times rather contradictory, alternative models for imitation. It is quite in keeping with the study of women in these apocryphal texts that of the three girls considered as models for children here, two clearly challenge and ultimately break the bonds of family life to pursue their own ideals, while one remains strictly and unquestionably within her family of origin. It is that one also who dies. Clearly, not only fathers but also spiritual fathers determined which girls they wanted to promote as saints and on whose memory it seemed preferable to cast suspicion.

---

143 For a recent consideration of class as a factor of sexual politics in the AAA, see also Andrew S. Jacobs, 'A Family Affair: Marriage, Class, and Ethics in the Apocryphal Acts of Apostles', *JECS* 7 (1999), pp. 105–38.

ANSWERS TO THE PLIGHTS OF AN ASCETIC WOMAN NAMED THECLA

MAGDA MISSET-VAN DE WEG

In the fourth century CE, a woman named Egeria undertook a pilgrimage that also brought her to the city '*quae appellatur Seleucia Hisauriae*',[1] where she finds, in the church situated in the midst of a monastic complex, the beautiful *martyrium* of Thecla. Egeria, who kept a journal of her travels, mentions that she prays in the *martyrium* and reads there the Acts of the holy Thecla (*et lectio omni actu sanctae Teclae*).[2]

Together with evidence from the reception and tradition history, archaeological monuments, iconographic representations and the many translations, Egeria's travel report is a witness to the importance and the popularity (the *Acts of*) *Thecla* once enjoyed.[3] However, in the sixth century CE, the *Acts of Thecla*, which came to be incorporated in the *Acts of Paul*, was rejected by ecclesiastical authorities and branded as apocryphal.[4] Nevertheless it 'survived' and at present the interest for this and other hidden treasures of the apocryphal and repudiated literature is still growing.

To perceive the hidden treasures or the 'mysteries' of the apocryphal texts is – as Eric Junod wrote – often a complicated matter; the readers need to find keys to unlock these mysteries.[5] In one article not each and every hidden treasure can be dug up. So I chose two keys, namely magic and patronage, which I will use in an

---

1 Pierre Maraval, *Égérie: Journal de Voyage (Itinéraire) Itinerarium et lettre sur la B^{se} Égérie*: Introduction, texte et traduction par M.C. Díaz y Díaz (Sources Chrétiennes 296; Paris: Éditions du Cerf, 1982; repr. 1997), 23, 5.

2 *Égérie: Journal de Voyage*, 23,26.

3 See for example: Ruth Albrecht, *Das Leben der heiligen Makrina auf dem Hintergrund der Thekla-Traditionen: Studien zu den Ursprüngen des weiblichen Mönchtums im 4. Jahrhundert in Kleinasien* (Forschungen zur Kirchen- und Dogmengeschichte 38; Göttingen: Vandenhoeck & Ruprecht, 1986); Karl Holzhey, *Die Thekla-Akten: Ihre Verbreitung und Beurteilung in der Kirche* (München: Lentner, 1905); Éric Junod and Jean-Daniel Kaestli, *L'histoire des Actes apocryphes des Apôtres du IIIe au IXe siècle: Le cas des Actes de Jean* (Cahiers de la Revue de Théologie et de Philosophie, 7; Genève, etc.: s.n., Fonds National Suisse de la Recherche Scientifique, 1982); Dennis R. MacDonald and Andrew D. Scrimgeour, 'Pseudo-Chrysostom's *Panegyric* to Thecla: The Heroine of the *Acts of Paul* in Homily and Art', *Semeia* 38 (1986), pp. 151–59; Claudia Nauerth and Rüdiger Warns, *Thekla: Ihre Bilder in der frühchristlichen Kunst* (Göttinger Orientforschungen 2/3; Wiesbaden: Otto Harrassowitz, 1981); Willy Rordorf, 'Sainte Thècle dans la tradition hagiographique occidentale', *Augustinianum* 24 (1984), pp. 73–81.

4 The 'Liber qui appellatur *Actus Theclae et Pauli*' was, together with other apocryphal works, condemned in the *Decretum Gelasianum*.

5 Éric Junod, 'Le mystère apocryphe ou les richesses cachées d'une littérature méconnue', in Jean-Daniel Kaestli and Daniel Marguerat (eds.), *Le mystère apocryphe: Introduction à une littérature méconnue* (Essais Bibliques 26; Genève: Labor et Fides, 1995), pp. 1–25.

attempt to clarify some aspects of this narrative.[6] This focus will allow me to bring to the fore historical backgrounds that can shed light on the puzzling and intriguing relation between Thecla, the daughter and her mother Theocleia as well as between Thecla, the Christian ascetic and the queen Tryphaena. My focus will also help to clarify how women cope with the reaction of and confrontation with the society at large concerning their choice against marriage, and how miraculous events function to validate such a choice.

Magic and Miracles

In many or most respects, formative Christianity did not differ or distance itself from the worlds in which it originated. For instance, with people from every level of society Christians shared belief in the 'reality' of miracles or the fear of magic, and either admired or feared the *magos*.[7] Not surprisingly therefore, miracles were a noticeable feature of Christianity from its very inception and occur in profusion in both canonical and extra-canonical traditions.[8] Like their contemporaries, Christians

6 For other 'keys', such as initiation as a thread that holds the narrative together, see Magda Misset-van de Weg, *Sara & Thecla. Verbeelding van vrouwen in 1 Petrus en de Acta Theclae* (Ph.D. diss. Utrecht University, Utrecht, 1998).

7 On the subject, see for example D.E. Aune, 'Magic in Early Christianity', *ANRW* II.23.2 (1980), pp. 1507–57, esp. 1518–19; Elisabeth Schüssler Fiorenza, 'Miracles, Mission, and Apologetics: An Introduction', in *eadem* (ed.), *Aspects of Religious Propaganda* (University of Notre Dame Center for the Study of Judaism and Christianity in Antiquity 2; Notre Dame, IN and London: University of Notre Dame Press, 1976), pp. 1–25, esp. 6; Paul J. Achtemeier, 'Jesus and the Disciples as Miracle Workers in the Apocryphal New Testament', in Schüssler Fiorenza (ed.), *Aspects of Religious Propaganda*, pp. 149–86, esp. 152–53 and 173–74; Gérard Poupon, 'L'accusation de magie dans les Actes apocryphes', in François Bovon, *et al.* (eds.), *Les Actes apocryphes des apôtres: Christianisme et monde païen* (Genève: Labor et Fides, 1981), pp. 71–85, esp. 80–82. In this article I shall not concern myself with or pretend to contribute to paradigm or terminology debates on 'magic' or any other (larger) subjects in the same field, such as the dichotomy between magic and religion. A considerable number of studies have been published on these subjects. See, for example Aune, 'Magic in Early Christianity'; H.S. Versnel, 'Some Reflections on the Relationship Magic–Religion', *Numen* 38 (1991), pp. 177–97; H.D. Betz, 'Magic and Mystery in the Greek Magical Papyri', in Christopher A. Faraone and Dirk Obbink (eds.), *Magika Hiera: Ancient Greek Magic and Religion* (New York/Oxford: Oxford University Press, 1991), pp. 244–59; A.F. Segal, 'Hellenistic Magic: Some Questions of Definition', in Roelof van den Broek, *et al.* (eds.), *Studies in Gnosticism and Hellenistic Religions Presented to Gilles Quispel* (Leiden: Brill, 1981), pp. 349–75; and cf. Mary Douglas, *Purity and Danger: An Analysis of the Concepts of Pollution and Taboo* (repr. London/New York: Routledge 1992), pp. 18,19 and 58; Fritz Graf, 'Prayer in Magic and Religious Ritual', in Faraone and Obbink (eds.), *Magika Hiera*, pp. 188–213; Fritz Graf, *Gottesnähe und Schadenzauber: Die Magie in der griechisch-römischen Antike* (München: Beck, 1996); Peter Schäfer and Hans G. Kippenberg (eds.), *Envisioning Magic: A Princeton Seminar and Symposium* (Leiden and New York: Brill, 1997). For an overview of the different connotations of the term *magos* and, among others, the development of its use in a derogatory sense, including further references, see Albert F. de Jong, *Traditions of the Magi: Zoroastrianism in Greek and Latin Literature* (Leiden: Brill, 1997), pp. 387–403.

8 On magic and miracles in the literary canon and even in historical reports, see for example Richard Reitzenstein, *Hellenistische Wundererzählungen* (Darmstadt: Wissenschaftliche Buchgesellschaft, 1963), p. 16: 'Daneben dringt die Wundererzählung, und zwar gerade diejenige, welche lehrenden, d.h. religiösen Zweck verfolgt, auch in die große Literatur und strebt nach prunkvoller Form'; G.W.H. Lampe, 'Miracles and Early Christian Apologetic', in C.F.D. Moule (ed.), *Miracles:*

translated social concerns and problems into miracle stories, and such tales also functioned as a means of propaganda or as a sanctioning device when faced with competition and slanderous attacks. Christian apologists emphasized the superiority of the miracles performed by Jesus and relegated pagan miracles to the realm of evil spirits.[9] Of course not everybody was convinced. Celsus, for example, depicted Jesus as a magician who had a bewitching hold on his followers,[10] and he called the New Testament miracles 'monstrous tales', as well as 'the practices of wicked men possessed by an evil daemon'.[11] From the standpoint of the accuser the miracle worker could be considered to be in league with 'wrong' powers or the demonic, while from the standpoint of the supporter, miracle-workers sanctioned the 'right' powers. In other words, the labelling was relative and depended upon who was responding to whom.

Because for most ancient persons the question was not whether miracles were possible, but who was able to perform them and what the source of their power was, conflicts over magic were usually not dominated by believers versus rationalists; rather, they were often related to social tensions and the asymmetry of power. The accusation of the practice of magic was used as a means to exert social control, and a *magos* was often condemned on primarily social grounds. Literary sources in which the charge of magic appears often reveal such primarily polemical programmes.[12]

In the *Acts of Thecla* we encounter examples of both the ambiguous attitude towards 'magic' and the strategy of labelling someone as a morally suspect *magos* in order to get rid of him.

On Fetters and What They Unleash

The main event of the opening scene of the *Acts of Thecla* is the arrival of the apostle Paul in Iconium. He is warmly received by Onesiphorus, an Iconian Christian, his two children Simmias and Zeno and his wife Lectra, who escort him to their house. The mention of this family indicates that the Christian community in Iconium did

---

Cambridge Studies in Their Philosophy and History (London: A.R. Mowbray & Co, 1965), pp. 203–18, who notes that even 'serious' authors reproduce legends, for example Eusebius (*H.E.* I.13).

9 Outperformance of non-Christian miracle-workers is not an issue in the *Acts of Thecla*. For a striking example thereof, see the controversy between Simon Magus and the apostle Peter in the *Acts of Peter*. On the aspect of propaganda see for example, Elisabeth Schüssler Fiorenza (ed.), *Aspects of Religious Propaganda*, and J.-M. van Cangh, 'Miracles évangéliques – Miracles apocryphes', in F. Van Segbroeck, *et al.* (eds.), *The Four Gospels 1992. Festschrift Frans Neirynck* III (Leuven: Leuven University Press, 1992), pp. 2277–2319, esp. 2279.

10 Margaret Y. MacDonald, *Early Christian Women and Pagan Opinion. The Power of the Hysterical Woman* (Cambridge, UK: Cambridge University Press, 1996), p. 175.

11 That is to say, Origen records Celsus saying these words in his apologetic work *Contra Celsum* I.6 and II.32.

12 See Eric R. Dodds, *Pagan and Christian in an Age of Anxiety* (Cambridge, UK: Cambridge University Press, 1965), p. 124; Aune, 'Magic in Early Christianity', pp. 1518–19, 1522; Anne-Marie Tupet, 'Rites magiques dans l'antiquité romaine', *ANRW* II.16.3 (1986), pp. 2591–675; Poupon, 'l'Accusation de Magie', p. 83; C.R. Phillips III, '*Nullum Crimen sine Lege*: Socioreligious Sanctions on Magic', in Faraone and Obbink (eds.), *Magika Hiera*, pp. 260–76, esp. 261 and his 'The Sociology of Religious Knowledge in the Roman Empire to A.D. 284', *ANRW* II.16.3 (1986), pp. 2677–73, esp. 2719, where he refers to later developments when ostensibly Christian practices of which the institutional Church did not approve were labelled as 'magic'.

not exclude marriage or procreation, but it did propagate an ascetic form of marriage as a male prerogative.[13] Lectra, who remains in the shadow of her family throughout the narrative, can be said to represent the category of women who are indispensable but invisible.

While Paul speaks 'the word of God concerning self-control and resurrection' (*Acts of Thecla* 5, 6) in the ἐκκλησία gathered together in the house of Onesiphorus, Thecla – who is introduced as a παρθένος, i.e. a young unmarried woman – listens to him from her window.[14] She becomes fascinated by his words and longs to see Paul in person. In the meantime Theocleia, Thecla's mother, becomes increasingly worried because of her daughter's fascination. Seeking the help of Thamyris, Thecla's fiancé, she relates to him how her daughter is completely mesmerized, confused, 'bound (δεδεμένη) to the window like a spider by his words' (9), and how a strange passion seems to have a hold on her, in short how a spell has been cast on her.

For my purpose it is significant that Theocleia's reference to Paul as a stranger (ξένος) seems to be the first, still implicit, allegation that this man is a *magos* in her eyes.[15] Besides, her interpretation of her daughter's emotional state suggests both the notion of the 'wonderful' power or irrational impact of speech (λόγος), which was believed to stir passions and to deceive,[16] and, more important, the notion of erotic magic. It is especially the theme of 'binding' (δέω) and connotations of the related terms πρόσκειμαι and κρατέω which carry this suggestion of erotic magic.[17] On the symbolic level this theme continually surfaces and colours the narrative.

When Thamyris and Theocleia have tried to convince Thecla to turn away from her fascination, but to no avail, Thamyris – a prominent man (πρῶτος) – goes after the man who seduced his Thecla. After the crowd, in step with Thamyris, has demanded 'Away with the *magos* for he has seduced all our wives' (15), Paul is brought before the governor, bound and sent to prison. Thecla, who until that moment is depicted as rather 'motionless', gets up and becomes active. 'But Thecla during the night,

13 Cf. the beatitude: 'blessed are those who have wives as not having them; they shall be heirs of God' [5].

14 On the relation between self-control and resurrection, see Willy Rordorf, 'Quelques jalons pour une interprétation symbolique des *Actes de Paul*', in David H. Warren, Ann Graham Brock and David W. Pao (eds.), *Early Christian Voices: In Texts, Traditions, and Symbols. Essays in Honor of François Bovon* (Boston/Leiden: Brill, 2003), pp. 251–92, esp. 252: 'la continence (sexuelle) est une force qui s'apparente à celle de la résurrection, une personne continente anticipe en quelque sorte l'état de la résurrection, elle personifie le paradis retrouvé'.

15 The status of the magician as a 'stranger' was a known concept that did not represent a xenophobic reaction but corresponded to the social status of the *magos*, who 'is always the other, not us'; see F. Graf, 'How to Cope with a Difficult Life', in Schäfer and Kippenberg, *Envisioning Magic*, pp. 93–114, esp. 112. Of course not every ξένος was considered a *magos*.

16 Jacqueline de Romilly, *Magic and Rhetoric in Ancient Greece* (Cambridge, MA: Harvard University Press, 1975), esp. 75–88, argues how the old alliance between magic and rhetoric was revived in the first two centuries CE. It concerns (sublime) speech that produces enchantment and ecstasy, startles and acquires an influence and power that is irresistible.

17 Erotic magic formulas (κατάδεσμοι) and rituals for seducing a girl or a woman (against her will), or for binding her to a man, are known both from the magical papyri and as literary motifs. See, for example, Poupon, 'L'accusation de Magie', p. 73. On fettering and unfettering, see Walter Burkert, *Creation of the Sacred: Tracks of Biology in Early Religions* (Cambridge, MA: Harvard University Press, 1996), pp. 118–21; and see the magic song of the Erinyes (ὕμνος δέσμιος) and the magic formulas (κατάδεσμα), better known as *defixiones*.

having taken off her bracelets, gave them to the doorkeeper. And when the door had been opened for her she went to the prison. And giving a mirror made of silver to the jailer she went in to Paul. And sitting at his feet ... her faith increased and she kissed his fetters' (18). Both the gestures and the items symbolize that Thecla severs the ties that bind her to her family and everything that 'mirrors' the world (κόσμος), including marriage.[18] The original value of the items is transformed into the means of opening doors to a new situation and the stepping stone to a new life. At the same time doors close, not least because she is transgressing the conventional boundaries, stepping into the male world, and thus provoking disapproval, hostility and suspicion.[19] Thecla, who obviously belonged to the elite social stratum, is from now on a social outcast, as is also suggested by her position in the prison and will be underscored later in the story.

The binding symbolism is at its height when, sitting at Paul's feet, Thecla kisses his fetters and thus embraces new ties, binding herself to Paul and the Christian faith. This is followed by another suggestion of erotic magic, again connected with binding, in the announcement that Thecla's family find Thecla and Paul 'as it were bound together (συνδεδέμενην) in loving affection' (19).

It is at this point that readers might either conclude that the *magos* has reached his goal or look closer and adjust to other (over)tones, such as the message that Thecla is bound by faith (7), becomes Paul's pupil (sitting at his feet), and experiences a growing faith (18).

Binding occurs one last time when in the second episode Thecla is bound by her feet between bulls. By then fire surrounds her and consumes the ropes, and Thecla is as one unbound (35). But this happens later, and the Iconium episode must still be rounded off.

After Thecla and Paul are found together in the prison they are both put on trial. Whereas the grounds for Paul's verdict are not mentioned, it seems likely that the governor meets the demands of Thamyris and the crowd – 'He is a *magos*, away with him' (20) – which would mean that Paul is indeed punished as the *magos* who seduced the women of Iconium and Thecla in particular. However, it appears that the Iconian authorities are disturbed less by the male *magos* than by the female adherent of a life of celibacy: for, although the *magos* does not get away scot-free, Thecla, his 'victim', is condemned to death for committing the crime of discarding the customs of the Iconians.

As the verdict is instigated by the mother, the question arises as to what could possibly have prompted such a distressing scene in which a screaming mother demands that her daughter be burned to death. A possible answer might be that, in Antiquity, marriage (together with procreation), was considered of vital importance

18 Jewellery used to be part of a dowry. An (adorned) mirror was, among other things, known as a gift of a lover; as the attribute of the love goddess Aphrodite and as a symbol of worldly things. See J. Evans Grubbs, '"Pagan" and "Christian" Marriage: The State of the Question', *JECS* 2 (1994), pp. 361–412; J.N. Bremmer, *Greek Religion* (New Surveys in the Classics 14; Oxford: Oxford University Press, 1994), p.14.

19 Cf. Virginia Burrus, *Chastity as Autonomy: Women in the Stories of Apocryphal Acts* (Studies in Women and Religion, 23; Lewiston, NY and Queenston, Ont: Edwin Mellen Press, 1987), pp. 87–93.

for the welfare of families, the city and in fact humanity.[20] The refusal to be married was therefore regarded as breaking a fundamental law.[21] Because in the *Acts of Thecla* a *paterfamilias* and other male relatives are conspicuously absent, Theocleia – whom the readers must therefore regard as either a widow or an unwed mother – would have been responsible for maintaining any social rules and obligations, such as raising her daughter and arranging her marriage. Consequently she would be held accountable for the unruly behaviour of a daughter that would bring shame on her family and affect anyone related to her family, such as a fiancé. All this explains not only why Theocleia called for the help of Thamyris, whose interests – his honour and his love – were at stake as well,[22] but also Theocleia's assessment of Paul, amounting to her allegation that he is a magician, which reverberates throughout the entire episode. Her interpretation of what happened to her daughter might reflect a known mechanism to save the face and even more the honour of her family.[23] The claim that a *magos* made a girl elude parental control might alleviate the social tragedy and a fall in the family's fortunes.[24]

It will not make it any better for twenty-first-century eyes, but Theoclecia's very disturbing reaction might thus be seen as the attempt of a desperate woman trying to salvage what she can. Narratively speaking it is remarkable that Theocleia had already distanced herself from and even mourned her daughter's social death.[25] And so this mother is now, in view of the family honour, demanding Thecla's physical death as a warning sign for other women. The reason she supplies might also serve her own rehabilitation, because the Iconians would interpret it as laudable indication that she has the well-being of the city at heart, which is after all the goal for which each and every citizen ought to strive.

20 On marriage legislation in a time and society with a population 'grazed thin by death', see, for example, Peter Brown, *The Body and Society: Men, Women and Sexual Renunciation in Early Christianity* (New York: Columbia University Press, 1988; repr. London/Boston: Faber and Faber, 1990), p. 5, and Sarah B. Pomeroy, *Goddesses, Whores, Wives, and Slaves: Women in Classical Antiquity* (New York: Dorset Press, 1975), p. 166.

21 On the dramatization in myths of the refusal of marriage and how this was considered as a matter regarding a wider circle, see Louise Bruit Zaidman, 'Pandora's Daughters and Rituals in Grecian Cities', in Pauline Schmitt Pantel (ed.), *A History of Women in the West I: From Ancient Goddesses to Christian Saints* (Cambridge, MA/London: The Belknap Press of Harvard University Press, 1992), pp. 338–76, esp. 362.

22 Thamyris is notably absent in the conviction scene. He is last 'seen' when he roams the streets looking for his fiancée. At the end of the narrative, when Thecla returns to Iconium, he is dead. He is like a literary conventional victim of love for whom a *remedium amoris* could not be found and so who withered away and died. See J.J. Winkler, 'The Constraints of Eros', in Faraone and Obbink (eds.), *Magika Hiera*, pp. 214–43, who refers to classical examples like Phaedra and Chariton's Callirhoe.

23 The importance and pervasiveness of the honour/shame concept could not be lingered upon within the framework of this article.

24 The last paragraph of the *Acts of Thecla* suggests an awareness of possible financial conse-quences for parents (in this case a mother) whose daughters chose an ascetic life: Thecla tells her mother, 'if it is money you desire, the Lord shall give it to you through me'.

25 For the intervention of the fiancé, the appeal to the concept of shame, the mourning, etc., see *Acts of Thecla* 10.

Metamorphosis and the Power of Prayer

Following the trial the governor and the crowd immediately leave for the theatre to await the spectacle, but: 'Thecla, like a lamb in the wilderness looks around for the shepherd, so she was seeking Paul, and when she was looking at the crowd she saw the Lord sitting there in the shape of Paul' (21). An account of metamorphosis is a well-known element of Hellenistic magical belief and a recurring feature in Greek literature of old. As a theme it surfaces frequently in the Apocryphal Acts.[26] Jesus appears in many different forms, for example as one of the apostles, as a child or as a sailor.[27] In the *Acts of Thecla* the appearance of Jesus is clearly meant to strengthen Thecla, who thereby receives her first reward for choosing the ascetic lifestyle: 'Blessed are the pure in heart, for they shall see God.'[28] The effect is amazing: she is transformed into a woman radiating inner strength (δύναμις):[29] 'when she was brought in naked, the governor wept and marvelled at her inner strength … And she, assuming the shape of the cross mounted the pyre' (22).[30]

The second miraculous event occurs after Thecla has mounted the pyre and the fire blazes. At that moment God makes the earth rumble and causes hail and rain to come down in large quantities, so that the fire is extinguished. Many people die as a result of this violent event – after all, the miracle not only saves; it kills as well – but Thecla is saved. God is undoubtedly the agent of this miracle. However, in the ensuing episode in the open tomb, much of the credit for salvation goes to Paul, for even though Thecla praises God for saving her, her rescue is also described as the answer to Paul's prayers: 'And when he stood up Paul saw her and said, "God, knower of hearts, the Father of our Lord Jesus Christ, I praise you because you hastened to grant me what I asked"' (24). This surprising turn underscores that Paul is a true apostle.[31] He is not a *magos* who seduces women, but he is what he claimed to be: the teacher of the things revealed to him by the living God who sent him to Iconium to carry out that task.

26 On aspects of metamorphosis in the Apocryphal Acts, see Pieter J. Lalleman, 'Polymorphy of Christ', in Jan N. Bremmer (ed.), *The Apocryphal Acts of John* (Studies on the Apocryphal Acts of the Apostles, 1; Kampen: Kok Pharos, 1995), pp. 97–118.

27 See for example the *Acts of Andrew* 47; the *Acts of Peter* 22; the *Acts of Thomas* 11.

28 As has been pointed out by Sheila E. McGinn, 'The Acts of Thecla', in Elisabeth Schüssler Fiorenza (ed.), *Searching the Scriptures II: A Feminist Commentary* (2 vols.; New York: SCM Press, 1994), pp. 800–28, esp. 815.

29 Δύναμις can mean power, the ability to do anything, authority, but has also spiritual connotations, such as magical power and the manifestation of divine power (see Mt. 11.20–21).

30 For the connotation of triumph in assuming the shape of the cross, see Jan N. Bremmer, 'Magic, Martyrdom and Women's Liberation in the Acts of Paul and Thecla', in *idem* (ed.), *The Apocryphal Acts of Paul and Thecla* (Studies on the Apocryphal Acts of the Apostles 2; Kampen: Kok Pharos, 1996), pp. 36–59, esp. 49. Praying with outstretched arms and open palms was also a known gesture expressing praise (the opposite of kneeling as an attitude of penitence). See, however, P. Cox Miller's admonition, in her 'Desert Asceticism and "The Body from Nowhere"', *JECS* 2/2 (1994), pp. 137–53, to weigh theologically motivated interpretations which associate 'one of the least comprehensible forms of ascetic display with a most orthodox Christian theology of the cross' (p. 145).

31 The view that the performance of miracles is one of the signs of the true apostle can also be deduced from the New Testament letters of Paul. See Judah Goldin, 'The Magic of Magic and Superstition', in Schüssler Fiorenza (ed.), *Aspects of Religious Propaganda*, pp. 115–47, esp. 122–23; Achtemeier, 'Jesus and the Disciples', pp. 150–52.

Miracles in a Christian context were considered as acts performed through God's power and indeed through prayer, and the invocation of the name of God or Jesus is considered as the empowering act.[32] The prayers of Thecla and Tryphaena in the Antioch episode can and ought to be appreciated in the same manner. Like Paul, the women perform this empowering act, and, judging from the results, have been granted the same saving powers, for Phalconilla is saved, transferred to the place of the righteous, or as is summarized later, raised from the dead![33] And Thecla is saved a second time, a rescue preceded by Tryphaena's prayer: 'God of Thecla, my child, help Thecla'(30). Thecla's thanksgivings to God, on the other hand, communicate the conviction maintained throughout the narrative: it is ultimately God who works all miracles via others (24; 31; 42).

Another important message conveyed by the miracle that saved Thecla from the pyre is that Thecla's choice not to marry Thamyris, to break with her family, and thereby break the law of the Iconians, is divinely sanctioned. In short: women who choose an ascetic lifestyle may have to endure the consequences, they may have to suffer and their family may declare or wish them dead, but God will be on their side.

The Magical Power of Baptism

After first Paul and finally Thecla have been driven out of Iconium (26) and are reunited in an open tomb, Thecla announces that she wishes to follow the apostle. He will not have it because, he says, there is wickedness all around and she is beautiful. His additional remark that she might not be able to resist another temptation debases this young woman who just bore the worst test. He not only refuses to credit Thecla with integrity, but ignoring her extraordinary achievements, he reduces her to the classical tropes of woman and/or beauty – that is, sexuality and so seduction – and thus he turns women's option for an ascetic life into a matter of the body which is equated with her sexuality. Underlying Paul's reaction might be the tendency to keep control over the bodies of women and the fear of women invading the male domain.[34] But sure enough, a woman like Thecla does not let herself be put off. Trying another approach in answer to the stereotypical gender-biased reaction she says: 'Just give me the seal in Christ and no trial will touch me' (25).[35] Paul tells her to have patience. The suggestion of the magical protective power of baptism resounds here, but Paul's reaction may indicate a rejection of this notion. The narrative will prove him wrong. In the following episode in Antioch, Thecla amply demonstrates that she is not

---

32 See, for example, Achtemeier, 'Jesus and the Disciples', pp. 170, 174.

33 Whereas the story is explicit about what happens to Thecla, the readers receive only implicit information regarding Phalconilla's fate, namely when Tryphaena says: 'Now I believe that the dead are raised, now I believe that my child lives' (39).

34 Cf. Eva Cantarella, *Pandora's Daughters: The Role and Status of Women in Greek and Roman Antiquity* (trans. Maureen B. Fant; Baltimore/London: The Johns Hopkins University Press, 1987), p. 97.

35 On the meaning of σφραγίς in Antiquity and Christianity, see Franz Joseph Dölger, *Sphragis: Eine altchristliche Taufbezeichnung in ihren Beziehungen zur profanen und religösen Kultur des Altertums* (Studien zur Geschichte und Kultur des Altertums 5/3–4; Paderborn, 1909; repr. New York: Johnson Reprint Company, 1967), pp. 70, 98. On baptism as protection, see for example the *Acts of Thomas* 49.

only quite capable of resisting temptation; further, it is shown that once Thecla has baptized herself nothing can touch her. A second time God then sends fire, which surrounds and protects Thecla from raging bulls.[36] Moreover, 'her nakedness can no longer be seen' (34); in other words, her body is no longer public property.

Women Working Miracles

For reasons unknown, Paul takes Thecla to Antioch after all. Upon their arrival a prominent citizen named Alexander, who falls in love with Thecla at first sight, offers Paul money and presents because he wants to have her. The answer of this apostle, who has been sent by God to draw people away from corruption and immorality (17), is: 'I do not know the woman of whom you speak, nor is she mine' (26). Explanations that Paul's reaction is a narrative ploy to set things in motion, or that it confirms his worry that she will be tempted, do not exclude other perspectives. On the one hand Paul may confirm his own statement that Thecla belongs to God (24); on the other hand, he most certainly knows who Thecla is, despite his reference to her as 'the woman'. Moreover, he is the one who refused her the protection of the seal she requested. In other words: the apostle fails her.

As a result of Paul's attitude, Alexander, the man of power (26), apparently feels free to accost Thecla right then in the middle of the street. Thecla 'however did not put up with it …' (26). She appeals to her status as a prominent citizen of Iconium and to her rights as a stranger and as a servant of God (δούλη τοῦ θεοῦ), but to no avail.[37] She debases the man and is brought before the governor, who finds her guilty of sacrilege and condemns her to be thrown to the wild animals.

The women of Antioch react immediately. Shocked, they protest most vehemently against this appalling and unholy judgement (27). But the women are not 'heard'. As Thecla and Paul have barely arrived in Antioch, and as their new Christian identity has not been brought up in any way, it may very well be that the women are reacting against a non-consensual boundary violation that strips the victim of her dignity, that is deeply shameful, dehumanizing and status reducing, and that could have lasting harmful effects.[38] Part of the women's protest may also have been directed against the obfuscation of the reality that Thecla acted in self-defence or even the flagrant double-standard that women were not protected by the law in the same way men were.

Whatever their rationale, the women of Antioch do not abandon Thecla. Refusing to bow to their position of social disadvantage and lack of authority they resort to their own means of power.[39] Throughout the episode they remain present, ventilating

---

36 For symbolic meanings of water and fire in the context of baptism, see Wolf D. Berner, *Initiationsriten in Mysterienreligionen, im Gnostizismus und im antiken Judentum* (Ph.D. diss., University of Göttingen, 1972).

37 She may have appealed to her status as a guest-friend (ξένη), based upon a treaty or tie of hospitality between Iconium and Antioch, and/or to the status of the inspired servants who observed a rule of chastity and were a widespread, recognized phenomenon.

38 See Lyn M. Bechtel, 'Boundary Issues in Genesis 19.1–38', in Harold C. Washington, *et al.* (eds.), *Escaping Eden: New Feminist Perspectives on the Bible* (The Biblical Seminar 65; Sheffield: Sheffield Academic Press, 1998), pp. 22–40.

39 For useful definitions of authority and power see N. Steinberg, 'Israelite Tricksters, Their Analogues and Cross-Cultural Study', *Semeia* 42 (1988), pp. 1–13, esp. 6.

their protests, lamenting or rejoicing loudly and profoundly, and throwing herbs
into the arena with the miraculous result that all the animals are anesthetized but
are neither harmed nor killed.[40] The women's conspicuously non-violent action is in
marked contrast with the violence instigated by Alexander and supported by other
men.

Non-violence also characterizes the action of the lioness who does not attack
but licks Thecla's feet and lays herself down there – later, however, the lioness kills
a she-bear while defending Thecla – and especially the interventions of the queen
Tryphaena.[41] This woman appears when Thecla begs the governor that she may
'remain pure' (27). Like other convicted women, Thecla had to await the fight with
the animals in prison where she would have been in danger of being raped.[42] It is
most likely that Thecla begs the governor to spare her precisely this ordeal. Her wish
is granted: the queen Tryphaena takes her into *custodia libera*.[43] Another reason for
taking Thecla into her home is that her deceased daughter, Phalconilla, appears to her
mother in a dream-vision and tells her: 'Mother you shall have Thecla, the desolate
stranger, in my place, that she may pray for me and I may be transferred to the place
of the righteous' (28).[44]

Tryphaena had tried to safeguard Thecla by verbally frightening away Alexander
(30), whereupon the governor sent soldiers (!) to fetch Thecla. Even then Tryphaena
still 'did not shrink away' (31). She resorts to supporting Thecla by escorting her to
the arena – a most unusual act for a queen to perform. And finally, analogous to the
action of the lioness, the queen too lays herself down, so to speak. Whereas neither
the actions of the women, nor the divine protection in the form of a cloud/flame of
fire impresses the authorities or induces them to put a stop to the fight, Tryphaena's
fainting, in combination with the ploy of her handmaidens who declare that she died,
terminates the ordeal (36). It is tempting to explain this last event by drawing an
analogy between the actions of Tryphaena and her handmaidens and the so-called
trickster-paradigm. Trickery is behaviour to which individuals resort under certain

---

40 A sophisticated command of drug compounding was common. It was not unusual for women
(and men!) to know the magic or religious connotations of plants or herbs. Drugs were even
considered to function as 'the hands of the gods'; see J. Scarborough, 'The Pharmacology of Sacred
Plants, Herbs, and Roots', in Faraone and Obbink (eds.), *Magika Hiera*, pp. 138–74, esp. 163. A
comparison can be made with Medea who used herbs to lull the guardian reptile of the golden fleece
(Apollonius of Rhodes, *Argonautica* IV.156–8). Thus, I do not endorse Achtemeier's conclusion in
his 'Jesus and the Disciples as Miracle Workers', pp. 169–70, that the Apocryphal Acts never so
much as hint at the use of herbs, incantations or magical devices in the description of the miracles.
Apparently he does not consider the actions of the women to be magical acts, which might be due
to his focus on the apostles as the mighty men of wonders.

41 For symbolic meanings of the animals in the *Acts of Thecla*, especially the lion(ess), see
Rordorf, 'Quelques jalons pour une interprétation symbolique des *Actes de Paul*'.

42 On the subject of condemned female prisoners who dreaded rape or placement in a brothel,
see Anne Jensen, *Gottes selbstbewusste Töchter*, Frauenemanzipation im Fruhen Christentum
(Freiberg: Herder, 1992), pp. 185–95, who concludes her chapter on 'die traurigen Fakten der
römischen Christenverfolgung' by recalling that 'wenig später auch Christen in der Verfolgung
Andersdenkender mit sexuellem Sadismus gegen Frauen vorgegangen sind'.

43 A privilege that was mostly granted to criminals of the upper class.

44 On visions and dreams as miracles, see, for example, Reitzenstein, *Hellenistische
Wundererzählungen*, p. 9.

social conditions, often but not necessarily when they lack authority; tricksters, whether male or female, are persons who 'resort to strategies which allow them to achieve their goals and gain compliance with their wishes'.[45] The most fascinating and culturally valuable aspect of the trickster is his or her paradoxical status. Their function is characterized by both deception and at the same time promotion of the welfare of the/a community.[46] Because in the *Acts of Thecla* the 'deception' is used as a means of power by women, who do not have access to legitimate means of power, and because the well-being of those who lack authority is promoted, the 'deception' of Tryphaena and the handmaidens might be designated as a form of trickery. However, in order to avoid annexation of a complex paradigm as well as a too easy identification of women with morally ambivalent trickery, another suggestion might be to consider the actions of the women as prompted by their wit, understood as the intelligence and understanding to make the right decision or take the right action in a particular situation.[47] Either way, the women are the ones who finally bring Alexander to his knees and save Thecla.

Patronage

I turn now to the framework and elements of the pervasive cultural phenomenon of patronage. The relationship between the two women, or the largesse of the queen and the reciprocal activities of Thecla, reflect an early Christian form of this practice.[48]

In the first centuries of the Christian era, patronage permeated Mediterranean society from top to bottom.[49] This highly complex and hierarchically organized

45 Steinberg, 'Israelite Tricksters', p. 6, who adds on the same page: 'I understand trickery to be a kind of power available to persons in a subordinate position vis-à-vis another individual.'

46 Mieke Bal, 'Tricky Thematics', *Semeia* 42 (1988), pp. 133–55 (136–37).

47 Female wit recalls the quality called μῆτις, the cunning intelligence that is, for example, Odysseus's heroic characteristic. See S. Murnaghan, 'Penelope's *Agnoia*: Knowledge, Power, and Gender in the *Odyssey*', in M. Skinner (ed.), *Rescuing Creusa. New Methodological Approaches to Women in Antiquity*. A Special Issue of *Helios*, n.s. 13/2 (1987), pp. 103–15, esp. 104.

48 The comfort and support Tryphaena lends Thecla can also indicate that she adopts Thecla, becomes her new mother and thus incorporates Thecla into a new family: the Christian community. Others suggest that Tryphaena simply takes a liking to the girl and/or finds in her a substitute for her deceased aughter. See Léon Vouaux, *Les Actes de Paul et ses lettres apocryphes* (Paris: Librairie Letouzey et Ané, 1913), p. 221, n. 3 ; Albrecht, *Das Leben der heiligen Makrina*, p. 264; Dennis R. MacDonald, *The Legend and the Apostle. The Battle for Paul in Story and Canon* (Philadelphia, PA: Westminster Press, 1983), p. 51. Anne Jensen, *Thekla-Die Apostelin: Ein apokrypher Text neu entdeckt* (Frauen-Kultur-Geschichte 3; Freiburg: Herder, 1995), p. 92.

However, even though there are moments in the narrative which seem to suggest an adoption or a mother–daughter relation between Tryphaena and Thecla, the adoption thesis is open to a number of objections: until the third century CE, women could not adopt a child; the fact that Tryphaena acted as a mother towards Thecla is in keeping with patronage; to early Christian ascetics family ties were of no importance since they wanted to be totally free, mentally and physically, in order to be able to serve Christ. For further explanations, see Magda Misset-van de Weg, 'A wealthy woman named Tryphaena: patroness of Thecla of Iconium', in Bremmer (ed.), *The Apocryphal Acts of Paul and Thecla*, pp.16–35, esp. 32–34.

49 Richard P. Saller, *Personal Patronage Under the Early Empire* (Cambridge, UK: Cambridge University Press, 1982), p. 194. See also Paul Veyne, *Le pain et le cirque: Sociologie historique d'un pluralisme politique* (Paris: Édition du Seuil, 1976), p. 271, who states that the imperial period was 'incontestablement l'âge d'or de l'évergétisme'.

tentacular network functioned as the prime mechanism in the allocation or channelling of scarce resources of all sorts and at every level of society. On the level of interpersonal exchange and interaction, it functioned as an elementary structure of social life with discrete, yet universal, characteristics. On a broader level, patronage functioned as an important means of controlling and legitimizing the social order and for reproducing the major social institutions of power.[50] The two levels must be considered against a background in which the public and the private were inextricably linked and scarcely distinguishable.[51]

Patronage was not a well-defined, smoothly operating system following predictable and inevitable rules, but a flexible and dynamic system that could be adapted to changing social circumstances.[52] Core-characteristics of the patron-client nexus were:[53]

- *Reciprocity*, involving exchanges of services over time between two parties.
- Access to resources was predominantly mediated by *personalized relationships*.[54]
- The relations were *asymmetrical*, i.e. between parties of different/unequal social status, which gave rise to an exploitative tendency in the relationship.[55]
- Relations were *voluntary*, i.e. not legally enforceable or at least not fully legal or contractual. However, even if individual relationships were voluntary, there is nothing voluntary about a social system that succeeds in perpetuating inequalities.[56]
- The relation was based on *solidarity*, often closely related to conceptions of personal identity, especially of personal honour and obligations. Some, even if ambivalent, personal 'spiritual' attachment could exist between patron and clients.[57]

In theory the system of patronage functioned in a mutual manner; both subject and object benefited. Benefactions could consist of, for example, distribution of food,

50 Terry Johnson and Christopher Dandeker, 'Patronage: relation and system', in Andrew Wallace-Hadrill (ed.), *Patronage in Ancient Society* (London/New York: Routledge, 1989), pp. 219–41, esp. 220–21. Cf. Wallace-Hadrill's introductory remarks, pp. 5–6 in the volume as well as his included essay, 'Patronage in Roman society: from Republic to Empire', pp. 63–88, esp. 65 and 72. Patronage was not only appreciated in a positive way. On aversion of patronage, see Paul Millet, 'Patronage and its avoidance in classical Athens', in Wallace-Hadrill (ed.), *Patronage in Ancient Society*, pp. 15–48, esp. 33. Saller, *Personal Patronage*, pp. 11–15, quotes from Cicero (*Off.* 2.69): 'some Romans think it as bitter as death to have accepted a patron or to be called clients'.

51 Cf. David Braund, 'Function and dysfunction: personal patronage in Roman imperialism', in Wallace-Hadrill (ed.), *Patronage in Ancient Society*, pp. 137–52, esp. 140–42.

52 Wallace-Hadrill, 'Patronage in Roman society', pp. 71, 78.

53 The characteristics are based on the tripartite definition offered by Boissevain, endorsed by Saller and others, and complemented by Garnsey & Woolf and Millett. See Wallace-Hadrill, *Patronage in Ancient Society*, pp. 3–4; Millett, 'Patronage and its avoidance', p. 16.

54 Johnson and Dandeker, 'Patronage: relation and system', p. 226.

55 Millet, 'Patronage and its avoidance', p. 16. See also S.N. Eisenstadt and Louis Roniger, 'Patron-Client Relations as a Model of Structuring Social Exchange', *Comparative Studies in Society and History* 22 (1980), pp. 42–77, esp. 49–50.

56 Wallace-Hadrill, *Patronage in Ancient Society*, p. 8.

57 Cf. Eisenstadt and Roniger, 'Patron-Client Relations', p. 50.

building of temples, baths, financing of festivals and entertainment. In return the benefactors could receive or secure senatorial magistracies, public and religious offices, privileges,[58] political support and influence,[59] loyalty and honour, all of which would have a positive influence on the prestige of the benefactors and their families.

The above already indicates that different forms of patronage can be identified. Besides 'status-raising' on the level of political patronage, cities relied to a great extent on the wealthy elite trying 'to outdo each other in lavish benefactions ... stimulated by an elaborate complex of honours emanating from the city'.[60] Down the societal ladder the poor, as in all historical periods, depended to a significant degree on the quality of their relationships with more fortunate members of society for the satisfaction of vital needs, such as food, clothing and shelter.[61]

The above also shows that the system could create the well-being or even the upward mobility of a client and enhance the social status and/or political stature of the patron and his or her family. Yet, it was also a highly ambiguous system, because patronage presupposes inequality or at least asymmetry and maintains it.[62] Inequality and solidarity do not go together well and the same applies to coercion and choice, mutual obligations and a voluntary relationship. Therefore, even though one might conclude that the euergetic system was for the good of 'the people' who received real benefits in return for giving honour, the true purpose of giving was not (always) to receive honour, but (often) to maintain power and wealth.[63]

Patronesses

Inscriptions provide numerous examples of women's benefactions and the honour bestowed upon them.[64] Many of these inscriptions record that women, in return for their largesse, were assigned functions such as ἀρχή, δημιουργός, γυμνασίαρχος (in most cases for the provision of oil), κτίστρια, δεκάπρωτος, ἱεροφάντις and

---

58 Varying from a front seat in the theatre to the right to own land.

59 Patrons could expect support from their clients when standing for election, and so could their friends and/or members of their family (see for example White, 'Social Networks', pp. 23–36).

60 Riet van Bremen, 'Women and Wealth', in Averil Cameron and Amélie Kuhrt (eds.), *Images of Women in Antiquity* (London/Canberra: Croom Helm, 1983), pp. 223–42, esp. 224. According to Ramsay MacMullen, *Roman Social Relations: 50 B.C. to A.D. 284* (New Haven, CT and London: Yale University Press, 1974), pp. 25–26, villages too probably kept up connections with rich and influential patrons, who could be counted on to pay for a public building or social occasions, but there is little information on the subject.

61 See Peter Garnsey and Greg Woolf, 'Patronage of the rural poor in the Roman world', in Wallace-Hadrill (ed.), *Patronage in Ancient Society*, pp. 153–70, esp. 158. For several other forms of patronage see Pomeroy, *Goddesses, Whores, Wives, and Slaves*, p. 200.

62 Eric R. Wolf, 'Kinship, Friendship, and Patron-Client Relations in Complex Societies', in Michael Banton (ed.), *The Social Anthropology of Complex Societies* (A.S.A. Monographs; London: Tavistock Publications, 1968), pp. 1–22, esp. 16.

63 Cf. Richard Gordon, 'The Veil of Power: emperors, sacrificers and benefactors', in Mary Beard and John North (eds.), *Pagan Priests: Religion and Power in the Ancient World* (Ithaca, NY: Cornell University Press, 1990) pp. 201–31, esp. 224; Richard Saller, 'Patronage and friendship in early imperial Rome: drawing the distinction', in Wallace-Hadrill (ed.), *Patronage in Ancient Society*, pp. 49–62.

64 For examples, see Ross S. Kraemer (ed.), *Maenads, Martyrs, Matrons, Monastics: A Sourcebook on Women's Religions in the Greco-Roman World* (Philadelphia, PA: Fortress Press, 1988), p. 207.

ἀγωνοθέτης. The fact that women held such positions seems a striking phenomenon in a world known from literary sources for the traditional view of woman's place and for a strict division between the male and the female domain, or between the public and the private world. How can this ambiguity be explained?

To start with, gender was not a determinative factor as far as patronage was concerned, whereas wealth and social class were. So, even though wealthy women played a prominent public role in the cities long before the period of decay,[65] they became more visible as patronesses in this period of degeneration of political life and economic downturn. Municipal life thereupon started to depend on wealthy women to underwrite the costs of public buildings, festivals, baths and other types of benefaction.[66] As women exercised no *actual* power, their appointment to various positions was a painless way for cities to gain money and glitter.[67] The emergence of benefactresses in the striking capacities, therefore, did not necessarily mean a shift in the social power of women in general, nor in the traditional view of women as such.[68] The functions women held were largely ceremonial and/or nominal and lay outside the political or commercial spheres. Furthermore, women were praised for typically female virtues, such as φιλανδρία, φιλοτεκνία and σωφροσύνη (love for a husband, love of one's children and temperance), in carefully constructed language that mirrored the traditional ideas about women in the Hellenistic and Roman literary and philosophical sources.[69]

While traditional ideas concerning women seem to have changed little in the course of the Hellenistic and Roman periods,[70] shifts in the system of patronage created conditions that made women's presence increasingly visible and constantly felt. The inscriptions were an effective way of affirming the superiority of the ruling class, but at the same time these conspicuous inscriptions and monuments reminded the inhabitants of the cities constantly of the largesse and activities of many women. To some extent the hegemonic paradigm was thus breached, and the women (and the men) were presented with alternative models of identification.[71]

Patronage in the Acts of Thecla

In the *Acts of Thecla* the terminology of patronage is not overtly present, but absence of explicit terminology does not necessarily mean absence of patronage.[72] In the *Acts*

65 Van Bremen, 'Women and Wealth', pp. 233–34.

66 Veyne, *Le pain et le cirque*, p. 357 n. 261: 'les magistratures féminines s'expliquaient toujours par des raisons d'argent'.

67 M.T. Boatwright, 'Plancia Magna of Perge: Women's Roles and Status in Roman Asia Minor', in Sarah B. Pomeroy (ed.), *Women's History and Ancient History* (Chapel Hill: University of North Carolina Press, 1991), pp. 249–77, esp. 258–60. See also Gordon, 'The Veil of Power', p. 230.

68 Van Bremen, 'Woman and Wealth', pp. 231–33.

69 Elizabeth P. Forbis, 'Women's Public Image in Italian Honorary Inscriptions', *American Journal of Philology* 111 (1990), pp. 493–512, esp. 496–97, has pointed out and illustrated that the Italians commemorated their benefactresses in a different way. They either ignored or minimized the benefactress's domestic duties: 'Not only did the Italians honor aristocratic women for their public munificence, but they also praised them accordingly.'

70 Van Bremen, 'Women and Wealth', p. 237.

71 Cf. Van Bremen, 'Women and Wealth', pp. 236–37 and Boatwright, 'Plancia Magna of Perge', p. 263.

72 Millet, 'Patronage and its avoidance', pp. 15–16.

of Thecla we do find the epithet βοηθος and references to God as σωτήρ (cf. resp. 42, 6, 17, 37, 38) which might reflect an understanding of God and Jesus as benefactors.[73] The ambivalent attitude of the governors during the trial, especially of Castelius, the governor of Iconium, might reflect embeddedment in the patronage system. Castelius is interested in what Paul has to say, he sympathizes with Thecla, as did his colleague from Antioch – they even shed tears – but after having taken council (!), and even though he is extremely vexed, he orders Paul to be flogged and condemns Thecla to be burned (17–21). Behind this may lie the actuality of the patronage network. For a steady rise to power within that system it was essential to maintain a good relationship with the emperor as the supreme patron. To that end governors also needed a good relationship with the people they governed, including the local elite. The support of local notables could, for example, be needed to protect a governor from complaints about maladministration that would obstruct his career.[74]

Alexander also seems to fit the pattern of the patron. He is introduced as someone 'doing many things in this city during his office' (26); he appears to be crowned, an honour conferred upon a person who was found to be fine and noble and well-disposed to the city;[75] and he is the one arranging the fight – which could refer to the title ἀγωνοθέτης (30). The narrative may be said to give his role a twist so that he becomes – at least for Christians – the model for the wrong kind of benefactor, 'wrong' in the sense that he provides the city with worldly things and because he uses patronage as a means for revenge and restoration of his honour. The implicit message could thus be that Christians – or the ascetic community – should no longer turn to and/or depend on benefactors like Alexander nor desire his kind of benefactions.

In marked contrast with Alexander, Tryphaena represents the right model. She is equally, or even more so, a prominent woman, but her benefactions are indeed of a different kind. She takes a 'desolate stranger',[76] a handmaiden of God, under her wings. By doing so, she safeguards Thecla's 'honour' and this is of extreme importance. Whereas the honour of men could be injured but also restored, the honour of women, which was connected with their sexuality, could not be gained, only lost.[77] The fact that 'remaining pure' constitutes an inclusio of the episode in Tryphaena's house (cf. 27 and 31) underlines the importance of Tryphaena's *custodia libera*.[78]

---

73 Cf. Stephen Charles Mott, 'Greek Ethics and Christian Conversion: The Philonic Background of Titus II 10–14 and III 3-7', *NovT* 20 (1978), pp. 22–48, esp. 43–46.

74 Cf. John K. Chow, *Patronage and Power. A Study of Social Networks in Corinth* (JSNTSS 75; Sheffield: Sheffield Academic Press, 1992), p. 51.

75 See Bruce W. Winter, 'The Public Honouring of Christian Benefactors: Romans 13.3–4 and 1 Peter 2.14–15', *JSNT* 34 (1988), pp. 87–103, esp. 89–90; Veyne, *Le pain et le cirque*, p. 276 and p. 357 n. 261, on 'στεφανηφόρος'.

76 Even though Tryphaena is not primarily portrayed in this specific role, we may find here an echo of patronage as a mechanism by which newcomers were incorporated with the patron as sponsor as new citizens, cf. Wallace-Hadrill, 'Patronage in Roman Society', pp. 76–77.

77 Cf. Karen Jo Torjesen, 'In Praise of Noble Women: Gender and Honor in Ascetic Texts', *Semeia* 57 (1993), pp. 41–64, esp. 56.

78 The words μισθός, ἁγνός/ἁγνεία and τηρέω also link Thecla's words/request with one of the main themes: remaining pure/chaste, which will be rewarded with eternal bliss. See the beatitudes, esp. the second and last one in (5) and (6); and see (7), (9) and (12). The close correspondence between (6) and (31) might indicate that remaining pure and helping someone to remain pure are equally important.

Tryphaena's patronage finds further expression in the manner in which she offers hospitality (39), comfort (27), compassion (29), and support (28; 30; 31), and is instrumental in securing Thecla's freedom. By assigning 'all that is hers' to Thecla, she enables Thecla to lead an independent and autonomous life (39). Finally, she gives so much that enough is left to minister to the poor (41). Consequently, not only is she Thecla's personal benefactress, but the Christian community profits from her benefactions as well.

The *do ut des* principle, or the characteristic of reciprocity, is not absent in the story. In return for Tryphaena's 'favours', Thecla prays for Tryphaena's daughter and for Tryphaena herself (31). The Christians gathered in the house of Hermeios also remember Tryphaena in their prayers (41).

What also emerges in the narrative is a shift in the manner in which honour is bestowed on the patron(ess). Tryphaena – ultimately a Christian patroness – is to give freely in recognition of spiritual benefits and without expecting the honour and loyalty which were the normal responses to patronage. As such her patronage is an example of Christian benefaction where the *gratia*, due as honour, worship and loyalty, is and must be directed to Christ.[79] However, a Christian patroness might also have deduced from the *Acts of Thecla* that a Christian patroness may receive at least some *gratia* in and precisely through narrative as a form of remembrance and thus also of honour and celebration. The *Acts of Thecla* shows how this particular narrative might even (partially) function as a monument to a queen among women.[80] This brings me to the didactic or normative side of this kind of 'remembrance'. The *Acts of Thecla*, just like inscriptions and other monuments, could and was possibly meant to encourage and motivate rich, potential patron(esse)s to follow a good example.[81] Patronage was after all of vital importance for (ascetic) Christian communities. Patron(esse)s often provided meeting places in their homes; their money was much needed for the construction of the communities as well as for their charity operations such as care of the poor and the widows;[82] and their prestige could be

79 Robert Stoops, 'Christ as Patron in the Acts of Peter', *Semeia* 56 (1992), pp. 143–57, esp. 152, 154,158.

80 Whether or not Christian benefactors always settled for recognition in the form of, for example, remembrance in prayers is an intriguing question, especially when it concerns women. In the following centuries Jerome lavishes praise on benefactresses such as Melania and Paula. However, Jerome stereotypically praises them for their private virtues: chastity and humility. Although it is difficult to believe that none of these extremely wealthy ladies, who founded monasteries, did claim a function/religious office in return, a deafening silence reigns. Because 'women's authority was problematic only if it was being exercised in the public arena', it seems a reasonable assumption that these women may have claimed functions in the relatively closed (monastic) communities. Cf. W. Cotter, 'Women's Authority Roles in Paul's Churches: Countercultural or Conventional?', *NovT* 36/4 (1994), pp. 350–72, esp. 368–9. On the silence surrounding Christian benefactresses, see Torjesen, 'In Praise of Noble Women', pp. 50–53, and Elizabeth A. Clark, 'Piety, Propaganda, and Politics in the *Life of Melania the Younger*', in *eadem* (ed.), *Ascetic Piety and Women's Faith: Essays on Late Ancient Christianity* (Studies in Women and Religion, 20; Lewiston, NY and Queenston, Ont.: Edwin Mellen Press, 1986), pp. 61–94.

81 On the subject, see Veyne, *Le pain et le cirque*, p. 235.

82 Cf. Jan N. Bremmer, 'Why did Early Christianity Attract Upper-class Women', in Antonius A.R. Bastiaensen, *et al.* (eds.), *Fructus Centesimus. Mélanges offerts à Gerard J.M. Bartelink à l'occasion de son soixante-cinquième anniversaire* (Instrumenta patristica 19; Steenbrugis/ Dordrecht: In Abbatia S. Petri/Kluwer Academic Publishers, 1989), pp. 37–47, esp. 41, 47; Elizabeth

of importance for survival and expansion in a hostile environment.[83] Eventually the retreat to private space – the homes of benefactors – even became a necessity for proscribed Christian groups/movements.[84]

A Few Remarks in Conclusion

The *Acts of Thecla* dramatize and may mirror what it might have meant for a second-century woman to become an ascetic Christian in a society in which the institution of marriage (and procreation) was of fundamental importance. From the perspective of non-believers she may be bewitched, lack shame or may even be found lawless, and will therefore find herself in violent confrontation with her family and society. Moreover, judging from the reaction of the apostle and the absence of positive support from the side of the Christian community in the *Acts of Thecla*, the ascetic community too might initially bestow suspicion and fear on her. In short: she will be on her own and suffer. Nonetheless, the story conveys, she may endure and survive. God will be on her side: women as God's agents work miracles and/or offer (mental and material) support. All of this might lead to what is told in the last paragraphs of the *Acts of Thecla*. Thecla, representing such a woman, is validated by the civil and religious authorities (i.e. the governor and the apostle) as the δούλη τοῦ θεοῦ she herself claimed to be (27), and confirmed and commissioned to teach the word of God.[85]

How comforting or empowering could this kind of survival have been to second-century women? How comforting can relying on supernatural intervention be even when and if mediated by women? And are the acts of the women not simply placed in a framework of reproduction of clichés of women as the weaker sex who are incapable of resorting to rational means in order to alter their situation?

As to the first question: even though reliance on the 'miraculous' for gaining religious power remains questionable, the supernatural intervention might also be translated into faith in and reliance on the miraculous sympathy, solidarity, care and intelligence of women, which might be sorely needed in a hostile and mistrusting (Christian) environment.

Of the framework of clichés, which is undeniably visible, it may be said that at several moments the stereotypical is exploded: Thecla leaves her home and family, Thecla resists Alexander's abuse, the women engage in fierce protests, the queen challenges the governor. Such moments express a form of autonomy and may offer the encouragement that women are indeed capable of detaching themselves from the societal norms/values they are expected to embody.

A. Clark, 'Ideology, History, and the Construction of "Woman" in Late Ancient Christianity', *JECS* 2 (1994), pp. 155–84, esp. 178–79, and Jan N. Bremmer, 'Pauper or Patroness. The Widow in the Early Christian Church', in Jan N. Bremmer and Lourens van den Bosch (eds.), *Between Poverty and the Pyre: Moments in the History of Widowhood* (London/New York: Routledge, 1995), pp. 31–57.

83 Stoops, 'Christ as Patron', p. 151.

84 H.O. Maier, 'Religious Dissent, Heresy and Households', *VC* 49 (1989), pp. 49–52, describes and illustrates the retreat to private space, where asceticism as well as other ideas were promoted, and became for the representatives of the ecclesiastical establishment 'maddeningly uncontrollable'.

85 'Confirmed' is the right term, because just as she made her own choice, unlocked doors for herself, defended herself, and baptized herself, she already taught the word of God and made converts (39).

THECLA 'TRIED AND TRUE' AND THE INVERSION OF ROMANCE

SUSAN A. CALEF

The stories about women in the Apocryphal Acts have been the object of interest in recent years. The *Acts of Paul and Thecla*, in particular, has attracted considerable attention due to its intense focus on a single female character.[1] A consensus regarding its presentation of women, however, has yet to emerge. For some interpreters, this and other Apocryphal Acts attest to women seeking autonomy by commitment to a chastity that liberates them from the patriarchal household, hence, to what has been termed 'proto-feminism'.[2] Others conclude, 'Although Thecla is the leading character of the story, she exists only as an extension of Paul's influence and personality ... The document marks a retreat from the affirmation of womanhood into the by-ways of self-abnegation.'[3]

Recent studies by Kate Cooper and Judith Perkins which compare the rhetoric of the Apocryphal Acts to that of the ancient Greek novel or romance seek to isolate the narrative strategies and ideologies of both genres, and in so doing, offer a new

---

1 On the relationship of the *Acts of Paul and Thecla* to the larger work (*Acts of Paul*), see Willy Rordorf, 'Tradition and Composition in the *Acts of Thecla*. The State of the Question', *Semeia* 38 (1986), pp. 43–52; Sheila McGinn, 'The Acts of Thecla', in Elisabeth Schüssler Fiorenza (ed.), *Searching the Scriptures*, Vol. II. *A Feminist Commentary* (New York: Crossroad, 1994), pp. 800–28, esp. 800–806. Some prefer the title *Acts of Thecla* in recognition of Thecla's centrality in the narrative; e.g. Ross Kraemer, *Her Share of the Blessings. Women's Religions among Pagans, Jews, and Christians in the Greco-Roman World* (New York and Oxford: Oxford University Press, 1992), p. 238. Although my reading confirms Thecla's centrality to the narrative, hence the appropriateness of this preference, because I read the narrative as an ancient novel or romance, I prefer the title *Acts of Paul and Thecla*, which parallels a number of the romances (*Chaereas and Callirhoe, Daphnis and Chloe*).

2 Most notably, Virginia Burrus, 'Chastity as Autonomy: Women in the Stories of the Apocryphal Acts', *Semeia* 38 (1986), pp. 101–17; *eadem, Chastity as Autonomy: Women in the Stories of Apocryphal Acts* (Lewiston, NY and Queenston, Ont.: Edwin Mellen Press, 1987); *eadem*, 'Word and Flesh. The Bodies and Sexuality of Ascetic Women in Christian Antiquity', *JFSR* 10 (1992), pp. 27–51; Kraemer, *Her Share*, pp. 150–55; *eadem*, 'The Conversion of Women to Ascetic Forms of Christianity', *Signs: Journal of Women in Culture and Society* 6 (1980), pp. 298–307; John Petropoulos, 'Transvestite Virgin With a Cause: *The Acta Pauli et Thecla* and Late Antique Proto-feminism', in B. Berggreen and N. Marinatos (eds), *Greece and Gender* (Bergen, Norway: Norwegian Institute at Athens, 1995), pp. 125–39.

3 Margaret Howe, 'Interpretations of Paul in the Acts of Paul and Thecla', in D. Hagner and M. Harris (eds), *Pauline Studies. Essays Presented to Professor F.F. Bruce on his 70th Birthday* (Grand Rapids, MI: Paternoster/W. Eerdmans, 1980), pp. 33–49; see p. 46. See also Peter Dunn, 'Women's Liberation, the *Acts of Paul*, and other Apocryphal Acts of the Apostles', *Apocrypha* 4 (1993), pp. 245–61. For a valuable summary of recent developments in the interpretation of the *Acts of Paul and Thecla*, see Shelly Matthews, 'Thinking of Thecla: Issues in Feminist Historiography', *JFSR* 17 (2001), pp. 39–55.

perspective on the role of their female protagonists.[4] The novels, on Cooper and Perkins's reading, prescribe or 'script' for ancient readers a sociosexual identity in the figures of the elite couple, whose spontaneous desire for one another, while potentially disruptive of the social order, is in the end harnessed to its needs through marriage, the conventional happy ending and telos of the romance plot. Thus, 'the romance legitimated the prevailing [patriarchal] social order and the [civic] elite's position in it'.[5] The Apocryphal Acts preserve the erotic script of the romance but, by means of strategic revisions, turn it and the social order that it underwrites upside down, thereby subverting the ideology of eros inscribed in the romance.[6] On this reading the Apocryphal Acts are not about sexual continence per se but a contest for power and authority between men, an itinerant apostle and a high-status householder who is the romance hero. In their contest for a woman's allegiance, the apostle, armed with his message of sexual continence, triumphs over the traditional house-holder by means of persuasive speech. The attractive, aristocratic young virgin or wife is thus cast in the supporting role of 'ideal listener, straining after truth', whose attentiveness reflects glory on the heroic apostle.[7] The female protagonist of the Acts is, then, in Cooper's words, 'icon of obedience to the apostolic word'.[8]

These studies of the texts' rhetoric demonstrate the benefit of reading the romances and Apocryphal Acts in relation to each other, and they yield new insights into both genres.[9] However, in the effort to isolate the narrative patterns and strategies common to the multiple works of each genre, elements unique to a particular narrative that would nuance its reading are ignored. The *Acts of Paul and Thecla* is a case in point. The characterization of the female protagonist of the Apocryphal Acts as a listener and 'icon of obedience to the apostolic word', although apt for the majority of the women depicted in the Acts, hardly does justice to Thecla, a woman who does far more than listen. The bulk of the narrative, in fact, consists of adventures in which she, like her romance counterparts, undergoes dreadful trials and ordeals, which she endures and from which she emerges unscathed.

---

4 Kate Cooper, *The Virgin and the Bride: Idealized Womanhood in Late Antiquity* (Cambridge, MA: Harvard University Press, 1996); Judith Perkins, *The Suffering Self. Pain and Narrative Representation in the Early Christian Era* (London and New York: Routledge, 1995), esp. pp. 41–76.

5 Perkins, *Suffering Self*, p. 52. Elsewhere Perkins observes, 'these works, focused on the testing and endurance of a social relationship, celebrate the revitalized social identity of the Greek urban elite' (p. 44). Cooper and Perkins detect in the romance's sympathetic portrayal of the curial class and concern for the marriage of the socially compatible an elite perspective; see Cooper, *Virgin*, pp. 20–44; Perkins, *Suffering Self*, p. 52. On the subordination of spontaneous desire to the social order, see Perkins, *Suffering Self*, pp. 62, 65, 71; Cooper, *Virgin*, p. 37.

6 See Cooper, *Virgin*, pp. 66–67, 45; Perkins, *Suffering Self*, esp. pp. 41–76; also Melissa Aubin, 'Reversing Romance? The *Acts of Thecla* and the Ancient Novel', in R. Hock, Bradley Chance and Judith Perkins (eds), *Ancient Fiction and Early Christian Narrative* (SBL Symposium Series; Atlanta: Scholars Press, 1998), pp. 257–72.

7 Cooper, *Virgin*, pp. 55, 64.

8 Cooper, *Virgin*, p. 64.

9 For demonstration of the value of reading an ancient Jewish narrative in light of the ancient romance, see also Richard I. Pervo, 'Aseneth and Her Sisters. Women in Jewish Narrative and in the Greek Novels', in Amy-Jill Levine (ed.), *'Women Like This': New Perspectives on Jewish Women in the Greco-Roman World* (Early Judaism and Its Literature, I; Atlanta: Scholars Press, 1991), pp. 145–60.

This essay sets forth a reading of the *Acts of Paul and Thecla* in relation to the erotic script of the romance which, by giving due attention to the trials and ordeals that feature prominently in the narrative, affords a fresh perspective on one prominent woman of the Apocryphal Acts.[10] I propose to read these episodes in light of an ancient interpretive model, that of the test. It is my contention that variations on the test which occur in the ancient Greek romance and in ancient Jewish and Christian texts guide readers, ancient or modern, to construe Thecla's experience as a test or trial akin to those of romance heroines and so, too, of the afflicted righteous of biblical tradition. On this reading, Thecla is surely more than an obedient listener to the apostolic word. By her endurance in face of mortal affliction, this virgin convert proves 'tried and true', worthy of divine approval and deliverance, and so, too, of an apostolic commission to teach the word of God

'Test' as Interpretive Model or Convention

The notion of 'testing' is what anthropologists call an 'interpretive model' or 'interpretive convention', that is, a pattern or construct, current in a given culture, that guides members of the culture in interpreting diverse events or circumstances. That the interpretive model of 'the test' enjoyed currency in Graeco–Roman culture and in the contemporaneous Jewish and Christian sub-cultures has been demonstrated by Susan Garrett.[11] The model is based on a recurring narrative pattern observable in the literature of these culture groups. The pattern consists of a protagonist in pursuit of a culturally approved goal, and an antagonist or agent of testing intent to impede progress towards that goal or deflect the protagonist from the goal entirely. As the words 'protagonist' and 'antagonist' suggest, the testing involves a struggle in which the protagonist either perseveres despite the antagonist's efforts or succumbs to them. One variation on the model, not discussed by Garrett but which I consider

10 In the larger project of which this essay is a part (*A New Desire and A Fearful Passion: The Politics of Desire in the Acts of Paul and Thecla*), I read the *Acts of Paul and Thecla* in relation to the erotic script of the ancient romance, the nearest sibling genre of the Apocryphal Acts in the Late Antique literary environment. That project entails detailed comparison of the narrative to the romance script and quite explicitly engages recent research on the ancient romance, including the work of Cooper and Perkins on the inversion of romance that occurs in the Apocryphal Acts. My objective is to set forth a reading that makes sense of the narrative in its entirety, including the seemingly peculiar, even problematic, dynamics between Thecla and Paul that have been noted by recent interpreters.

11 My description of the interpretive model of the test draws on her work, albeit with abbreviation and adaptations. On interpretive models of testing, see S. Garrett, *The Temptations of Jesus in Mark's Gospel* (Grand Rapids, MI: Eerdmans, 1998); on interpretive models of affliction, see *eadem*, 'Paul's Thorn and Cultural Models of Affliction', in L. Michael White and O. Larry Yarbrough (eds), *The Social World of the First Christians: Essays in Honor of Wayne A. Meeks* (Minneapolis, MN: Fortress Press, 1995), pp. 82–99; *eadem*, 'The God of This World and the Affliction of Paul, 2 Cor. 4.1–12', in David Balch *et al.* (eds), *Greeks, Romans, and Christians. Essays in Honor of Abraham J. Malherbe* (Minneapolis, MN: Fortress Press, 1990), pp. 99–117. Some scholars object to the recent trend in early Christian studies of assuming commensurability between the modern societies upon which social-scientific models are based and the societies of the ancient Graeco–Roman world. Distinct from this trend, Garrett constructs her models not on studies of modern societies but on 'perceived patterns in ancient texts'; on this point see her *Temptations*, p. 172, n. 1; also 'Paul's Thorn', p. 86, n. 15.

to be pertinent to the Thecla narrative, appears in the Greek romances to which the Apocryphal Acts are temporally and thematically related.[12]

'Test' in the Ancient Romance

Interpreters of the ancient romance agree that, for all their 'manifest variety', these narratives share a basic plot schema: a young man and woman of privileged status and noble beauty meet unexpectedly, usually in the context of a religious festival, and experience love at first sight. Their desire for one another, however, is frustrated by separation that leads to symptoms of lovesickness. After numerous trials of their fidelity to the object of their desire, they are eventually reunited and their reciprocal desire consummated in marriage.[13] Structurally, then, all action in this patently erotic script unfolds between two poles of plot movement: the initial flaring of mutual desire and the eventual happy ending, union in marriage.[14]

Interpreters further agree that at the core of this erotic script is a test of the heroic couple, hence, the alternate designation of the romance as 'adventure novel

12 The precise date of the emergence of the romances is not settled. Scholars generally date their appearance to the first centuries BCE or CE. Those extant seem to come from the first to third centuries CE; see David Konstan, *Sexual Symmetry. Love in the Ancient Novel and Related Genres* (Princeton, NJ: Princeton University Press, 1994), p. 3. Most of the Apocryphal Acts are dated to the second and third centuries CE; see Wilhelm Schneemelcher, 'Second and Third Century Acts of Apostles', in Edgar Hennecke and Wilhelm Schneemelcher (eds), *New Testament Apocrypha*, vol. 2 (Philadelphia, PA: Westminster/John Knox Press, rev. edn, 1992), pp. 75–86. The *Acts of Paul*, of which the *Acts of Paul and Thecla* is a part, is commonly dated to the late second or early third century; see Schneemelcher, *New Testament Apocrypha*, Vol. 2, pp. 233, 235; also E. Plümacher, 'Apokryphe Apostelakten', *RE*, Suppl. 15 (Stuttgart: Druckenmüller, 1978), pp. 26–30.

13 On their 'manifest variety', see Konstan, *Sexual Symmetry*, p. 60. For a fuller discussion of the variations among the romances, see Konstan, *Sexual Symmetry*, pp. 60–98. My understanding of the romance is based on study of the five extant Greek texts and the secondary literature in ancient romance research, in particular, M. Bakhtin, 'Forms of Time and of the Chronotope in the Novel', in *idem, The Dialogic Imagination. Four Essays by M.M. Bakhtin* (trans. Caryl Emerson and Michael Holquist; ed. Michael Holquist; Austin and London: University of Texas Press, 1981), pp. 84–110; B. Egger, 'Women and Marriage in the Greek Novels: The Boundaries of Romance', in J. Tatum (ed.), *The Search for the Ancient Novel* (Baltimore, MD and London: The Johns Hopkins University Press, 1994), pp. 260–80; *eadem*, 'Zu den Frauenrollen im griechischen Roman. Die Frau als Heldin und Leserin', in H. Hofmann (ed.), *Groningen Colloquia on the Novel* I (Groningen: Egbert Forster, 1988), pp. 33–66; *eadem*, 'Women in the Greek Novel: Constructing the Feminine' (Ph.D. diss., University of California, Irvine; Ann Arbor: UMI, 1990); T. Hägg, *The Novel in Antiquity* (Berkeley: University of California Press, 1983); Konstan, *Sexual Symmetry*; *idem*, 'Acts of Love: A Narrative Pattern in the Apocryphal Acts', *JECS* 6 (1998), pp. 15–36; G. Schmeling (ed.), *The Novel in the Ancient World* (Leiden: E.J. Brill, 1996); J. Tatum (ed.), *The Search for the Ancient Novel* (Baltimore, MD and London: The Johns Hopkins University Press, 1994). An edition of the Greek novels in English translation is now available: B.P. Reardon (ed.), *Collected Ancient Greek Novels* (Berkeley: University of California Press, 1989). Unless otherwise noted, citation of romance texts follows the titles, numbering and pagination of the Reardon edition.

14 Bakhtin ('Forms of Time', p. 89) further observes, 'the pivot around which content is organized is the main characters' love for each other and those internal and external trials to which this love is subjected. All other events have meaning in the novel only by virtue of their relationship to this pivot' (p. 109). On marriage as the literary happy ending, see Perkins, *Suffering Self*, pp. 41–76; Egger, 'Women and Marriage', esp. pp. 260–62.

of ordeal'.[15] The testing, in this instance, involves two protagonists, a male and a female, both of whom, in their passionate desire to be united, must overcome numerous obstacles and contend with a variety of antagonists, including rival suitors whose actions and intentions threaten their mutual fidelity. Thus, the adventures upon which the protagonists embark are, as one commentator observes, 'not simply the occasion for thrills and excitement, but constitute the test and exhibit the essence of conjugal loyalty. True fidelity, while inspired by eros, overcomes time, distance, and adversity.'[16] The testing of the romance protagonists often entails legal procedures that 'sum up the adventures of the heroes and provide a legal and judicial affirmation of their identity, especially in its most crucial aspect – the lovers' fidelity to each other'.[17] It is not simply the separate adventures, however, that are organized as tests of the protagonists but the novel as a whole. 'The result of this whole lengthy novel', Bakhtin observes, 'is that the hero marries his sweetheart. And yet people and things have gone through something ... something that did verify and establish their identity, their durability and continuity. The hammer of events ... tries the durability of an already finished product. And the product passes the test.'[18]

'Test' in Early Jewish and Christian Texts
The admonition 'My child, when you come to serve the Lord, prepare yourself for testing' (Sir. 2.1) expresses a conviction frequently encountered in early Jewish and Christian literature. Those who strive to walk in the way of the Lord can expect to be sorely tested.[19] The agent (God, Satan, hostile enemies), purpose (investigation, discipline, chastisement), and means or mode of testing (seduction, affliction) are variables in this highly flexible narrative pattern. Of the multiple variations on the

15 Bakhtin considered the test to be the basic compositional or organizing motif of these narratives ('Forms of Time', pp. 105-6), hence, his designation of them as 'adventure novels of ordeal' (p. 86). Similarly, R.M. Rattenbury maintains that the main object of the romance authors was 'to subject their characters to the greatest tests of endurance, and to proclaim their triumph; to make their difficulties apparently insuperable, and so, to enhance the value of their victory' ('Chastity and Chastity Ordeals in the Ancient Greek Romances', *Proceedings of the Leeds Philosophical and Literary Society* 1 [1926], pp. 59–71; see p. 62). Perkins observes, 'These romances narrated the testing and survival of the loyalty and commitment holding between a married couple and displayed the durability not simply of a personal attachment, but of a social unity' (*Suffering Self*, p. 67). See also I. Stark, 'Strukturen des griechischen Abenteuer- und Liebesromans', in H. Kuch (ed.), *Der antike Roman: Untersuchungen zur literarischen Kommunikations und Gattungsgeschichte* (Berlin: Akademie-Verlag, 1989), pp. 82–106, esp. p. 83.

16 Konstan, *Sexual Symmetry*, p. 58.

17 Bakhtin, 'Forms of Time', p. 109. He further observes, 'the shaping force of the idea of trial stands out with extraordinary clarity in the Greek romance – in fact, the general theme of trial literally takes on judicial and legal expression' (p. 106). See, e.g. the legal battle over custody of Callirhoe (Chariton, *Chaereas and Callirhoe* 5–6) and the trial to which Charikleia is subjected (Heliodorus, *An Ethiopian Story* 8.9).

18 Bakhtin, 'Forms of Time', pp. 106–107.

19 For a review of traditions of testing in the Hebrew Bible, later Judaism, and early Christianity, see Garrett, *Temptations*, pp. 19–49; also, H. Seesemann, 'πεῖρα/ πειράω/ πειράζω', *TDNT* 6, pp. 23–36. The Greek word-group expressive of the testing motif includes πειράζω, δοκιμάζω, πυρόω, ἀγονίζομαι, παιδεύω; see Schuyler Brown, *Apostasy and Perseverance in the Theology of Luke* (Rome: Pontifical Biblical Institute, 1969), pp. 10–35.

model, it is the test or trial by affliction that is of principal interest for the present study.

The model is readily summarized. The protagonist (the people Israel, a righteous individual, the Christian community) seeks to walk the straight and narrow path marked out by God. Some form of tribulation tempts the protagonist to stray from the way of the Lord and/or threatens to undermine the protagonist's confidence in God. By endurance, variously understood as holding fast to God the Deliverer and/or perseverance in walking the straight and narrow path, the protagonist gains divine approval and reward.[20]

Interpretation of the experience of hardship or affliction as a πειρασμός, translated 'test', 'trial', or 'temptation',[21] is amply attested in early Jewish and Christian literature.[22] It is embodied narratively in figures lauded for their exemplary endurance under duress, most notably Job, paragon of endurance in his trial by affliction, and the Maccabean martyrs, who persevered in faith despite the mortal threats of the tyrant Antiochus Epiphanes.[23] Early Christians, heirs to Jewish interpretive traditions, likewise construe their founder's experience in terms of the testing model. The Synoptic Gospels, for example, depict Jesus as tested by Satan in the wilderness (Mk 1.12–13; Mt. 4.1–11; Lk. 4.1–13). The Gospel of Mark portrays Jesus as undergoing a series of trials that climax when he is handed over to death for the final testing of his flesh. By his endurance in the face of mortal affliction, Jesus proved to be the truly obedient Son of God and so, in a sign of divine approval and vindication, was raised up.[24]

The pattern of Jesus' test – affliction, endurance unto death, divine approval and vindication – became the predominant interpretive model for Christians' own experience of affliction. Paul, in order to demonstrate his superiority to his opponents, uses hardship lists to cast himself in the role of afflicted righteous one

---

20 On endurance in biblical traditions, see F. Hauck, 'ὑπομένω, ὑπομονή', *TDNT* 4, pp. 581–88.

21 Garrett, noting the tendency of English speakers to interpret suffering as a 'test' but seductive persons as 'temptations', observes that Jewish and early Christian use of the Greek noun πειρασμός and its cognates suggests that they regarded 'tests' and 'temptations' as integrally related. For her summary of the ancient perspective see *Temptations*, p. 5. In the ancient texts relevant to the present study, it seems clear that affliction or hardship is πειρασμός in all three senses of the word. It is a 'test' or 'trial' insofar as it tries and proves the integrity of one's commitment and faith; furthermore, insofar as it seduces one to abandon the appointed path in order to avoid the suffering, i.e. tempts one to infidelity and/or apostasy, the experience of affliction is also 'temptation'.

22 For pertinent texts, see Garrett ('God of This World', p. 100) who cites e.g. *Pss. Sol.* 16.14–15; *T. Jos.* 2.7; 4 Macc. 17.11–16; Wis. 3.5–6; Sir. 2.1–5; Jdt. 8.25–27; 1 Pet. 1.6–9. For hardships as a 'test' in the writings of pagan moralists, see Garrett, 'God of This World', p. 100, n. 7.

23 Job's endurance is emphasized in the *Testament of Job*; also Jas. 5.11. On the endurance of the Maccabean martyrs, see esp. 2 and 4 Maccabees. That their experience is construed as a 'test' is evident in 4 Macc. 9.7–9; 17.11–16 where the Greek vocabulary for test occurs (πείραζε, 9.7; δοκιμάζουσα, 17.12).

24 In Mark, Jesus, like predecessors in Jewish tradition (e.g. Abraham, Job), is tested more than once and by various antagonists (Satan, 1.12–13; earthly adversaries, 8.11–13; 10.2; 12.13–17; his disciples, 8.27–33); thus, Garrett demonstrates that the Markan narrative tells the story of Jesus as tested through what he suffered (*Temptations*, pp. 59–60). On Jesus as tempted, see Seesemann, 'πεῖρα', pp. 33–36; also Garrett, *Temptations*, pp. 51–135; J.H. Korn, *PEIRASMOS. Die Versuchung des Glaübigen in der gr. Bibel* (Stuttgart: W. Kohlhammer Verlag, 1937), pp. 76–88.

(1 Cor. 4.9–13; 2 Cor. 4.8–11).[25] Among the experiences which early Christians, like their Jewish predecessors, frequently construed as πειρασμός, was persecution by hostile enemies. In Revelation, for example, the Son of Man speaking through the prophet John warns the church of Smyrna, 'Beware, the devil is about to throw some of you into prison, that you may be tested, and for ten days you will have affliction', then exhorts to endurance in hope of divine approval and reward, 'Be faithful until death, and I will give you the crown of life' (2.10; NRSV).[26] Similarly, the author of 1 Peter interprets persecution as test or trial which, insofar as it affords an opportunity to share in Christ's sufferings, ought to be embraced with joy: 'Beloved, do not be surprised at the fiery ordeal that is taking place among you to test you, as though something strange were happening to you. But rejoice insofar as you are sharing in Christ's sufferings' (1 Pet. 4.12-13; NRSV).[27]

The purpose of the test or trial by affliction in both Jewish and Christian traditions is suggested by its frequent metaphoric association with refining metal,[28] a process which, by use of severe heat to eliminate the worthless dross, purifies, and so proves the metal of true or genuine worth. Analogously, affliction, a metaphoric 'trial by fire', purifies and proves the genuinely righteous, hence, their worthiness of divine approval or acceptance.[29]

Testing and the Inversion of Romance in the Acts of Paul and Thecla

'A New Desire and A Fearful Passion' and the πειρασμός *of the Virgin Thecla*
The influence of the ancient Greek romance on the Apocryphal Acts has long been recognized.[30] That the *Acts of Paul and Thecla* bears striking resemblance to the

---

25 Paul combines elements from a Stoic view of the endurance of hardships with a more typically Jewish portrayal of himself as a suffering righteous one; on this see Garrett, 'Paul's Thorn', p. 86. On Paul's use of the literary portrait of the afflicted sage, see also *eadem*, 'God of Affliction', p. 117. On Paul's use of peristasis-catalogues or hardship lists, see also John T. Fitzgerald, *Cracks in an Earthen Vessel: An Examination of the Catalogues of Hardships in the Corinthian Correspondence* (SBLDS, 99; Atlanta: Scholars Press, 1988).

26 The author of Revelation urges endurance as the proper attitude of believers in face of present trials, asserting that salvation depends on perseverance to the end (Rev. 2.2–3; cf. Rev. 3.10–12). Similarly, James, which refers to the tests (1.2; 1.12) that come upon Christians, includes an exhortation to endurance at both beginning (1.2–4) and end (5.7–11) and promises blessing and crown of victory to those who endure (1.12; 5.11).

27 For a similar sentiment, see Phil. 1.29–30. Hebrews, addressed to a community that evidently experienced persecution (10.32) and must endure it again (10.36), encourages its recipients to fix their gaze on Christ whose death is construed in terms of the virtue endurance: 'let us run with perseverance (ὑπομονῆς) the race that is set before us, looking to Jesus the pioneer and perfecter of our faith, who for the sake of the joy that was set before him endured (ὑπέμεινεν) the cross, disregarding its shame, and has taken his seat at the right hand of the throne of God' (Heb. 12.1b–2, NRSV; cf. 1 Pet. 2.21). Early Christians taught that followers of Jesus should not only expect trials, but embrace them joyfully (Jas 1.2; 1 Pet. 1.6–7).

28 See e.g. Wis. 3.1–6; Sir. 2.1–6; 1 Pet. 1.6–7.

29 On the metaphoric association of testing with refining metal, see Brown, *Apostasy*, p. 20.

30 Beginning with E. von Dobschütz, 'Der Roman in der altchristlichen Literatur', *Deutsche Rundschau* 111 (1902), pp. 87–106. Rosa Söder drew connections between the individual motifs of the Apocryphal Acts and the ancient romance in her *Die apokryphen Apostelgeschichten und die romanhafte Literatur der Antike* (Stuttgart: W. Kohlhammer, 1932; repr. Darmstadt:

erotic script of the romance needs little demonstration. Thecla, smitten with desire, exhibits symptoms of the lovesickness that typically afflicts romance heroes and heroines alike: sitting transfixed at the window, she neglects to eat and drink, causing her mother to describe her as 'sorely troubled' (3.8) and her fiancé to be fearful of her 'distraction' (3.10).[31] Throughout the narrative her attention is fixed upon her hero when he is on the scene; when adversity separates her from the apostle, she seeks him out at every turn in hope of reunion.[32] Structurally, the narrative unfolds around two poles of plot movement parallel to those in the romance: an initial encounter that enflames desire and an eventual happy ending; as in the romance, the hiatus between these two poles is filled with trials and ordeals.

These trials and ordeals constitute two major episodes, each comprised of the same three-part sequence of events: Thecla's rejection of a high-status male; her arrest, trial and condemnation to death; the attempt to execute her. That Thecla's experience constitutes a test or trial is indicated by a pivotal scene, the conversation between Paul and Thecla that occurs between the two episodes. Thecla, having been delivered from the first execution, rejoins Paul at his rural hideout, where she proposes to follow him wherever he goes (3.25). The apostle, however, hesitating, observes, 'The season is unfavourable, and you are beautiful. May no other temptation (πειρασμός) come upon you, worse than the first, and you not endure and play the coward' (3.25).[33] In view of the trial and ordeal from which she escaped in the preceding episode, the thrust of Paul's comment is that because Thecla is nobly beautiful, other men will surely desire her and thereby tempt her to abandon, by test or trial, her commitment to 'the word of purity' (3.7) that quickened desire in her.[34] The reference 'and you not endure (οὐχ ὑπομείνῃς) and play the coward' indicates that Thecla's capacity to endure in this new faith is at issue.

Wissenschaftliche Buchgesellschaft, 1969). Cooper and Perkins (n. 4 above) are among the first to read the two genres in relation to each other.

31 In ancient romance, both the hero and heroine are depicted as 'lovesick', and so, as relatively passive. See, for example, the love sickness of Chaereas and Callirhoe (Chariton, *Chaereas and Callirhoe* 1.1.8–10) and that of Anthia and Habrocomes (Xenophon, *An Ephesian Tale* 1.4–5). On lovesickness in ancient literature, see Peter Toohey, 'Love, Lovesickness, and Melancholia', *Illinois Classical Studies* 17 (1992), pp. 265–86. For an edition of the Greek text of the *Acts of Paul and Thecla*, see R. Lipsius (ed), *Acta Apostolorum Apocrypha* (Hildesheim: Georg Olms Verlagsbuchhandlung, 1959), pp. 90–104. The English translation cited here is that of Schneemelcher, *Acts of Paul*, in Hennecke and Schneemelcher, *New Testament Apocrypha*, Vol. 2, pp. 239–46. Citations follow the numbering of the Schneemelcher edition.

32 Cooper recognizes in Thecla's pursuit of the elusive apostle echoes of the long searches endured by hero and heroine in ancient romances (*Virgin*, p. 50). The elite status of the major characters – Thecla, Thamyris, Alexander, Tryphaena – also evokes the ancient romance, in which the main characters are often the most prominent in their cities; see A. Scarcella, 'Social and Economic Structures of the Ancient Novels', in G. Schmeling (ed.), *The Novel in the Ancient World* (Leiden: E.J. Brill, 1996), pp. 221–76.

33 On the multiple meanings of πειρασμός, see above n. 21. The πειρασμός to which Paul here refers could also be translated, rightly in my estimation, 'trial' or 'test'.

34 The content of Paul's preaching is summarized in two phrases: first, 'the word of God concerning continence and resurrection' (λόγος θεοῦ περὶ ἐγκρατείας καὶ ἀναστάσεως, 3.5), and shortly thereafter, 'the word of purity' (τὸν περὶ ἁγνείας λόγον, 3.7).

'Trial by Fire'

The first of Thecla's trials is precipitated by her initial encounter with Paul, an encounter that disrupts the type of erotic relationship that the romance script celebrates. When Paul arrives in Iconium, Thecla and her fiancé Thamyris are in their proper 'romance place': Thecla, 'among the Iconians ... one of the first' (3.26) is betrothed to 'the first man of this city' (3.11). These 'darlings of the provincial elite' are on the verge of assuming their proper role as householders in the civic order, thereby maintaining the stability of the society.[35] Things do not proceed according to romance script, however, thanks to Paul's preaching. Stunningly, the weak and unappealing 'stranger', by 'the word of purity' (3.7), triumphs over, and so usurps the place of 'the first man of this city' in this elite woman's affections,[36] deflecting her desire to a new and transcendent object – the word of the one God, who lives in heaven (3.43) – and a new end, not marriage but baptism into the household of God and an apostolic commission to teach the word.[37] Thecla's reorientation, which causes her to reject Thamyris, is, in the perspective of her family and social order, a

35 In Cooper's words, 'The chaste hero and heroine stand for the social order's regeneration, because it is understood that their triumph over obstacles and their rejection of alternate sexual partners will find its natural end in marriage, and in the consequent householding and production of progeny' (*Virgin*, p. 38).

36 Short, bald, bowlegged, with hooked nose and eyebrows that meet (*Acts of Paul and Thecla* 3.3), Paul is, even by ancient canons, physically unappealing and weak (cf. 2 Cor. 10.10), the antithesis of romance heroes who are invariably described as possessing potent eye appeal, often tall with a good head of hair (see e.g. Theagenes in Helidorus, *An Ethiopian Story* 2.34–35; 3.3–4; 7.10; Dionysius, a major character although not the protagonist, in Chariton, *Chaereas and Callirhoe* 2.5). The physical beauty of the romance protagonists confirmed their noble status; see Perkins, *Suffering Self*, 53. Much recent scholarship construes the portrait of Paul in the *Acts of Paul and Thecla* as an idealization (Paul as general; heroic Herakles; virile male and ideal citizen); however, see Janos Bollok, 'The description of Paul in the *Acta Pauli*', in Jan Bremmer (ed.), *The Apocryphal Acts of Paul and Thecla* (Kampen: Kok Pharos, 1996), pp. 1–15, with whom I concur that Paul's features are unflattering by ancient standards, although we arrive at our conclusions by different routes. I read the physical description in relation to the erotic script of the ancient romance in 'Romancing the Body: The Description of Paul "in the flesh" in the *Acta Pauli*', presented at the AAR/SBL Rocky Mountain Regional Meeting, 19 April 2002.

37 Although Paul usurps the place of the romance hero in Thecla's affections, the nature of the relationship between Paul and Thecla is hardly that of the romance heroes and heroines. Above all, it is not symmetrical or reciprocal, as in the ancient romance; Paul, after all, shows no sign of being smitten by Thecla, her beauty and noble status notwithstanding. Rather, when he intercedes on her behalf in prayer, he implores, 'Father of Christ, let not the fire touch Thecla, but be merciful to her, for *she is yours*' (3.24; emphasis mine). Nor is Thecla 'in love' with Paul in the same way Anthia is 'in love' with Habrocomes (*Ephesian Tale*) or Callirhoe with Chaereas (*Chaereas and Callirhoe*); for, whereas the romance is dominated by an erotics of the gaze, in which love arises at first sight of the noble beauty of a social equal and inspires a desire for sexual union, the love with which Thecla is smitten has nothing to do with sight. In the narrative, when Thecla is 'smitten' she has yet to lay eyes on Paul; thus, her desire is based solely on hearing him preach (3.7). Paul, then, is not the true object of Thecla's desire. Rather, as privileged recipient of revelation (3.1; 3.17), who has eyes only for the goodness of Christ (3.1), Paul is an intermediary between heaven and earth, and so, between Thecla and the God to whom she now belongs. The apostle is the object of her attention insofar as he is the source of the word of God which has quickened desire in her and to which she longs to devote herself.

manifestation of what her mother Theocleia deems a 'new desire and fearful passion' (3.9).[38]

The fearfully antisocial nature of Thecla's new desire is evidenced by the appalled reactions of various characters. Theocleia complains, 'Thamyris, this man is upsetting the city of the Iconians, and your Thecla in addition; for all the women and young people go in to him, and are taught by him' (3.9). In his public confrontation with Paul the jilted Thamyris hurls the charge, 'You have destroyed the city of the Iconians, and my betrothed, so that she will not have me' (3.15), to which the crowd joins in chorus, 'Away with the sorcerer! For he has corrupted all our wives!' (3.15). The governor interrogates Thecla, 'Why do you not marry Thamyris according to the law of the Iconians?' The threat that her daughter's refusal to marry poses to the civic order is made dramatically clear in Theocleia's cry, 'Burn the lawless one (τὴν ἄνομον)! Burn her that is no bride' (τὴν ἄνυμφον), and the reference to deterrence with which it concludes, 'that all women who have been taught by this man may be afraid' (3.20).

The stance of these characters reflects the ancient Greek ethos according to which the female was required to pass from the undomesticated status of παρθένος to that of γυνή, thereby harnessing her sexuality to the demands of the social order.[39] By her flagrant disregard of the sociosexual imperative of her culture, she who is 'first' has become a deviant, a body out of place. A 'new desire and fearful passion' indeed! Members of the civic aristocracy, however, will have none of this. Thamyris and Thecla's family, rallying a crowd about them, report her transgression to the governor (3.19); hence, the ensuing trial and ordeal that sorely try the virgin's new allegiance.

When hauled before the governor at the judgement seat, remarkably Thecla shows no sign of fear or intimidation at the prospect of an encounter with public authority. Rather, 'she went off with joy exulting' (3.20); to the governor's query, 'Why do you not marry Thamyris?' she gives no answer but 'stood there looking steadily at Paul' (3.20). Not even her mother's shocking call for her daughter's execution 'Burn the lawless one!' penetrates the hold that desire has upon her.[40] Thecla's attention remains firmly fixed on Paul throughout the trial (3.21). Just as she was unmoved by her household's mourning at loss of her (3.10), she is strangely untouched by the threat that this powerful man and proceedings pose to her. The governor, cognizant

---

38 Ironically, it is a minor villain of the narrative who provides what is, on my reading, an apt designation of the revised erotic script of our narrative, for we have here desire of a new and fearful kind, one which, in effect, subverts the socially conservative romance script.

39 In Greek to be a woman (γυνή) is to be a wife (γυνή), and every female was 'bound to bleed', be it by defloration or first parturition. On this point, see esp. Helen King, 'Bound to Bleed: Artemis and Greek Women', in A. Cameron and A. Kuhrt (eds), *Images of Women in Antiquity* (Detroit, MI: Wayne State University Press, 1983), pp. 109–27; *eadem*, 'Sacrificial Blood: The Role of the Amnion in Ancient Gynecology', *Helios* 13 (1987), pp. 117–26. On the connection between marriage and sacrifice, see Helene Foley, 'Marriage and Sacrifice in Euripides' Iphigenia in Aulis', *Arethusa* 15 (1982), pp. 159–80. Perkins notes that each of the romance protagonists sacrifices her/himself to the social covenant exemplified in marriage (*Suffering Self*, p. 65).

40 The larger project of which this essay is a part argues that the narrative representation of Thecla's experience replicates the pattern of Jesus' passion. On the accusation of lawlessness, see Luke 22.37.

of the subversive import of her deviance, hence, the need for deterrence, sentences her to the pyre (3.21).

Death by fire was among the aggravated or ultimate punishments (*summa supplicia*) meted out by Roman authorities upon those guilty of especially heinous crimes.[41] Because one function of the death penalty in the ancient context was deterrence, public executions were calculated to humiliate the offender. The element of humiliation, in addition to deterring others from similar crimes, served to distance onlookers from the condemned and thereby reduced the likelihood of a sympathetic response.[42] Otherwise put, death in the arena was a form of political theatre in which the performance reinforced the existing political and social order by reducing transgressors to the level of an object.[43] To that end punitive spectacles were carefully scripted rituals in which a series of events was carried out in a particular order and the audience expected to witness behaviour of a consistent type. As one commentator observes, 'They expected to see penitence and terror in the condemned, they expected to hear them scream, and they expected to see the terror in their faces as they confronted the beasts or the other savage forms of execution which were employed in the arena.'[44]

The account of Thecla's execution reflects the ancient ritual. The performance is staged in the theatre where the pyre is prepared, fittingly, by the very group, 'young men and virgins' (3.22), upon whom the death of this recalcitrant virgin must have its deterrent effect. The drama commences with the condemned paraded naked onto the 'stage'. From this point on, however, the spectators do not see what they expect. Thecla offers no scream of protest or display of fear. Rather, with startling composure, silently she mounts the pyre and by a single resolute gesture – 'making the sign of the cross' – speaks her new allegiance (3.22). Thus, it is not degradation and impotence that the audience witnesses; instead, the one whom the social order would render powerless appears, even to the eye of the presiding authority, powerful

---

41 Death by fire, crucifixion and exposure to the beasts were classified as *summa supplicia*, forms of punishment in which the condemned had no hope of escaping a gruesome end. Execution by fire, which became more common under the Empire, was mostly for slaves and those of the lower orders (*humiliores*) convicted of arson, desertion, magic and treason, and it was an especially common punishment for Christians; see Donald Kyle, *Spectacles of Death in Ancient Rome* (London and New York: Routledge, 1998), p. 53.

42 On the deterrent function of public executions, see Keith Hopkins, *Death and Renewal. Sociological Studies in Roman History* (Cambridge: Cambridge University Press, 1983), pp. 27–29; K.M. Coleman, 'Fatal Charades: Roman Executions Staged as Mythological Enactments', *JRS* 80 (1990), pp. 47–73 (48–49). On the necessity of humiliation in executions, see Coleman, 'Fatal Charades', pp. 46–47; on the uses of violence to reinforce the social order, see Hopkins, *Death and Renewal*, pp. 11, 29; Kyle, *Spectacles of Death*, p. 7.

43 On this point see David Potter, 'Martyrdom As Spectacle', in Ruth Scodel (ed.), *Theater and Society in the Classical World* (Ann Arbor: University of Michigan Press, 1993), pp. 53–88, esp. 65; Hopkins, *Death and Renewal*, p. 11; Kyle, *Spectacles of Death*, p. 7.

44 Potter, 'Martyrdom as Spectacle', p. 53; on the behaviour expected of the condemned, see his discussion of reliefs and mosaics depicting executions (pp. 68–69); also Shelby Brown, 'Death as Decoration: Scenes from the Arena on Roman Domestic Mosaics', in Amy Richlin (ed.), *Pornography and Representation in Greece and Rome* (NY and Oxford: Oxford University Press, 1992), pp. 180–211.

by her endurance: upon witnessing the spectacle, 'the governor wept and marvelled at the power (δύναμιν) that was in her' (3.22).

Thecla's steadfast endurance in the midst of her fiery ordeal is met with a gesture of divine approval and vindication that makes for an extraordinary sight: 'although a great fire blazed up the fire did not touch her' (3.22).[45] Moved, apparently, by her perseverance, God engineers a rainstorm so that 'the fire was quenched and Thecla saved' (3.22).[46] Sorely afflicted, Thecla endured and so is delivered. The execution did not proceed according to script. Thanks to the divinely orchestrated meteorological display, the condemned is neither debased nor reduced to death but raised up, while the civic authorities, impotent to move her will or touch her body, are brought low. The spectacle of death becomes a spectacle of salvation, a display of superior power literally from 'on high'.

The Ordeal of the Beasts

After her marvellous deliverance, Thecla is reunited with Paul. She proposes to follow him in his apostolic journeys, only to be rebuffed as the apostle cites concern that she face a 'πειρασμός worse than the first' (3.25). Undaunted by Paul's hesitation, Thecla counters with a proposal that speaks for the strength of her desire and her faith in the power of the baptismal seal: 'Only give me the seal in Christ, and temptation (πειρασμός) shall not touch me' (3.25). Paul, thinking apparently that baptism at this point would be premature, counsels, 'Have patience, Thecla, and you shall receive the water' (3.25).[47]

The apostle's reservations prove well founded. No sooner do Paul and Thecla arrive in Antioch than a restaging of the πειρασμός occurs: 'Alexander, one of the first of the Antiochenes, seeing Thecla fell in love with her' (3.26). When this 'powerful' man (δυνάμενος) discovers that Paul is not her guardian, he is determined

---

45 That the ancient audience would likely construe the act in terms of divine approval and/or vindication is further suggested by comparison with a parallel scene in the romance. In Heliodorus, *An Ethiopian Story* 8.9.11–16, Charikleia – having been found guilty of poisoning – is condemned to the pyre but, miraculously, the flames do not touch her, whereupon the spectators see in this deliverance the hand of God and declare her innocent. The principle of ordeal, Rattenbury observes, is that God will defend the right ('Chastity and Chastity Ordeals', p. 64). The account of the fiery ordeal of Shadrach, Meshach and Abednego (Daniel 3) further attests the tendency to construe miraculous rescues in terms of divine deliverance and vindication of the righteous.

46 This divine intervention on behalf of Thecla is parallel to what later happens to Paul in the *Acts of Paul* 7, where a hailstorm delivers the apostle from death by the beasts.

47 The feminist estimation of Paul as villainous in this narrative owes much to his refusal to baptize her. His refusal to do so, however, is consistent with 1 Cor. 1.14–17, 'for Christ did not send me to baptize but to proclaim the gospel' (v. 17). That this Pauline conviction is the basis for the refusal is further suggested by a later narrative development; after her self-baptism, Thecla says to Paul, 'God worked with you for the gospel and with me for the bath' (3.40). Also, it should be noted that Paul's refusal is accompanied by the counsel, 'have patience, Thecla, and you will receive the water' (3.25). This suggests that it is not yet time but that it will happen if she has patience, which in fact it does. In the later scene of Thecla's self-baptism, she realizes, 'Now is the time for me to wash' (3.34). The Greek here – νῦν καιρός – recalls Paul's earlier reference to 'the unfavourable time' (ὁ καιρὸς αἰσχρός, 3.25). The hiatus between the unfavourable time to which Paul refers and the eventual bath is filled with the ordeals that constitute the test of her desire. I presented an alternative feminist reading of the Thecla–Paul dynamics in 'Paul as Villain in the *Acts of Paul and Thecla*: A Reappraisal', AAR/SBL Rocky Mountain Regional Meeting, 2001.

to have his way with her and accosts her on the open street (3.26).[48] His sexual assault upon her body poses a fearsome threat to the purity to which Thecla desires to devote herself, and so, constitutes a πειρασμός indeed 'worse than the first'.

Thecla, however, like the heroines of the romance, proves capable of resolute action when untoward sexual advances jeopardize her purity. In the name of her new allegiance as 'handmaid of God' (τὴν τοῦ θεοῦ δούλην, 3.26),[49] she vehemently resists the assault and launches an effective counter-attack, ripping Alexander's cloak and knocking the crown off his head. Remarkably, the 'powerful man' who would have his way with her proves ineffectual; he does not, after all, get his way. Worse yet, he is made a laughing stock, a public spectacle, and this at the hands of a woman.[50] In the ancient context, for a woman to humiliate a man in public was a grievous assault on his honour. Thecla's transgression is doubly so, insofar as she assaults not just any male but a priest of the imperial cult, upon whose head sat a crown bearing the image of the emperor.[51] Utterly disgraced by her public assault

48 In ancient Greek culture respectable women were not to appear in public unaccompanied by a male guardian. The ancient novels reflect this cultural expectation. Egger observes that in the ancient novels 'the outside is dangerous. As soon as she [a woman] is seen in public, she is threatened by male desire and aggression. The message is: do not travel alone – you will get raped; you need a house to hide in and a man to protect you' ('Women in the Greek Novel', p. 275).

49 In her own voice Thecla asserts her new identity, 'force not the stranger, force not the handmaid of God'. Thecla is indeed 'stranger' (ξένη), not citizen, of the city of Antioch; moreover this self-identification replicates that of Paul who is repeatedly branded 'stranger' (ξένος) throughout the narrative (3.8, 13, 19). Likewise, Thecla's self-designation – δούλην, servant or slave – replicates Paul's self-identification as δοῦλος of Christ (Rom. 1.1; Gal. 1.10). Both self-designations thus serve to establish a parallel between Paul and Thecla's identities. By the end of the narrative, Thecla will be the female counterpart to Paul, an itinerant apostolic witness to 'the word of God concerning continence and resurrection' (3.5).

50 Bakhtin's concept of the carnivalesque serves as a useful heuristic tool for illumining the subversive import of the episode. In brief, the carnivalesque involves transgression of bodily barriers, inversion of hierarchy, and degradation of the sacred. Elsewhere ('Games Gone Carnivalesque: The World Turned Upside Down in the *Acts of Paul and Thecla*', AAR/SBL Rocky Mountain Regional Meeting, 2000) I have identified ways in which the episode of the ordeal of the beasts includes 'carnivalesque' elements, e.g. the status reversals experienced by the two central characters, the condemned Thecla and the cultic Alexander; the references to three body parts that figure in the shifting scenes of the episode – head (on which sits a crown), male genitals (of the bulls), and feet (bound feet, licked feet, characters at feet); the degradation of the sacred by means of Alexander's decrowning. The rhetorical effect of these 'games gone carnivalesque' is unmistakable: the audience witnesses a startling spectacle that demonstrates the superiority of the Christian economy over the imperial.

51 Crowns formed part of the costume of civic leaders, and so, at the very least Alexander is a civic official. Gold crowns decorated with the busts of emperors and empresses were de rigueur for priests of the imperial cult (Riet Van Bremen, *The Limits of Participation. Women and civic life in the Greek East in the Hellenistic and Roman periods* [Amsterdam: J.C. Gieben, 1996], p. 143), and so, it is also possible that Alexander is an imperial priest. S.R.F. Price (*Rituals and Power: The Roman Imperial Cult in Asia Minor* [Cambridge: Cambridge University Press, 1984], p. 124) argues that Thecla is punished in the theatre for damaging the imperial image of the priest's crown; similarly, Aubin ('Reversing Romance', p. 268) cites the Armenian text of the *Acts of Thecla*, in which Thecla 'tore off the golden crown of the figure of Caesar, which he had on his head and dashed it to the ground'. That Alexander was probably a priest of the imperial cult is further suggested by his sponsorship of games which, as L. Robert has established, were closely connected with emperor-worship in the eastern provinces (*Les gladiateurs dans l'Orient grec* [Paris: E. Champion, 1940]). His status as an imperial priest would

upon him and upon the imperial order, Alexander has her charged with 'sacrilege'.[52] The priest, if not entirely defrocked, is 'decrowned', to use Bakhtin's term, and quite literally in this case.

Again, however, Thecla is undaunted in the face of imperial authority. When brought before the governor, she forthrightly confesses that she had done the things of which he accused her (3.27), and so, is condemned to the beasts (*damnatio ad bestias*). She responds to the dreadful sentence with none of the expressions of terror or protest one would expect at the prospect of such a terrible death. In fact, she voices concern, not for her death, but for her purity. Evidently foreseeing the possibility of sexual assault while awaiting execution, 'Thecla asked of the governor that she might remain pure (ἁγνή) until she was to fight the beasts' (3.27), to which the governor responds by remanding her to the custody of a rich widow Tryphaena (3.27) who becomes her protectress.

A ritual procession intended to humiliate the condemned immediately follows the sentencing: bound to a fierce lioness, Thecla is paraded naked before the public eye, the verdict 'Guilty of Sacrilege' branded on a superscription.[53] The performance, however, does not proceed according to script, as the spectators witness not degradation but a bizarre reversal in which Thecla rides triumphant: 'Thecla sat upon her back, the lioness licked her feet, and all the crowd was amazed' (3.28).[54] In the absence of humiliation, sympathy for the victim is aroused, as the women with their children, daring to voice their criticism from the seats farthest from both the spectacle and the social hierarchy it was meant to preserve,[55] invoke divine attention to the city's action: 'O God, an impious judgment is come to pass in this city!' (3.28). These initial departures from script are an ominous presage of things to come, and the subsequent proceedings continue to unravel.

Thecla's sentence is to be carried out the following day in the midst of the games

---

explain the charge of sacrilege for which Thecla is condemned to the beasts. There is no indication in the narrative that Alexander's attempted assault on Thecla is an actionable offence.

52 In the ancient context, one function of trial and punishment was restoration of the status of the wronged; see Coleman, 'Fatal Charades', p. 46, citing Gellius, *NA* 7.14.3: 'That reason for punishment exists when the dignity and the prestige of the one who is wronged must be maintained, in case the omission of punishment should bring him into contempt and diminish the esteem in which he is held.' Thus, restoration of the imperial priest's status and with it the reaffirmation of imperial religion are at stake in Thecla's punishment.

53 Criminals were led into the arena almost or fully naked, with a rope or chain around their necks, sometimes bearing the verdict (*titulus*) attached to them. Their condemnation was proclaimed, and, tied to posts or without weapons, they were exposed to the beasts. Beasts were a common penalty for slaves, foreign enemies and freemen guilty of a few heinous offences, but Severan sources show more frequent use for rustling, murder and, as here, for sacrilege. See Kyle, *Spectacles of Death*, p. 53.

54 On the use of female animals in the execution of women so that 'their sex might be matched to that of the beast', see David Potter, 'Performance, Power, and Justice in the High Empire', in W.J. Slater (ed.), *Roman Theater and Society. E. Togo Salmon Papers* I (Ann Arbor: University of Michigan Press, 1996), pp. 129–59, esp. p. 129.

55 The tiered seating at the arenas was reflective of the social hierarchy. Women and the poorest men could sit or stand only in the top tier, farthest from the action (Suetonius, *Augustus* 44); see Hopkins, *Death and Renewal*, pp. 17–18; Kyle, *Spectacles of Death*, p. 3; Coleman, 'Fatal Charades', p. 72.

that Alexander is sponsoring.[56] Games and other *spectacula* were sponsored by leading citizens as a crucial means of status maintenance and enhancement, hence, Goffman's term for them, 'status blood-baths'.[57] The execution of this 'sacrilegious one' as the featured performance affords Alexander the opportunity both to restore his status diminished by Thecla's assault and to reaffirm imperial religious values. Things begin badly for him, however, when at dawn his attempt to take charge by escorting the condemned to his games is foiled by Tryphaena whose cries cause him to flee. The soldiers subsequently dispatched to retrieve Thecla fare no better when Tryphaena, refusing to turn her over, 'taking her by the hand herself led her up' (3.31).

The two women arrive at the arena to 'a tumult, and roaring of the beasts, and a shouting of the male assembly (τοῦ δημοῦ) and of the women' (3.32), and the ritual of humiliation begins conventionally enough: 'Thecla was taken out of Tryphaena's hands and stripped, then given a girdle and flung into the stadium' to face certain death as 'lions and bears were set upon her' (3.33). But then, the world is turned upside down: the fierce beasts do not attack the defenceless woman; instead, beast turns against beast, and females unite across the human/beast boundary as a fierce lioness runs to and lies down at Thecla's feet, then defends her against the assault of the other beasts (3.33). When one of Alexander's own male lions, one 'trained against humans', is set loose to do the deed, 'the lioness grappled with the lion' (3.33), and marvellously, the male does not triumph over the female; rather, both perish. The boundaries that define beast and human, male and female, are thus confounded.

The conduct of the condemned, likewise, defies expectation. Thecla does not flee, cry out, or cower in fear of a dreadful death. In the midst of the violent swirl of activity she models composure and faith, her attention directed not to the assaulting beasts but to the heavens: 'she stood and stretched out her hands and prayed' (3.34).[58] As she anticipates that she will die by the beasts, the sight of a pool of water prompts her realization, 'Now is the time for me to wash' (3.34). Fearful not of death but that she will die without baptism, to the horror of the spectators who expect that she will be killed by the seals in the pool, Thecla takes the plunge, declaring, 'In the name of Jesus Christ I baptize myself on the last day!' At sight of this, the governor 'wept that such beauty should be devoured by seals' (3.34).[59] The condemned is no gruesome spectacle, as the execution script prescribes; she appears, rather, even to the eye of the governor, as a spectacle of beauty.

Thecla's self-baptism receives what one commentator aptly terms 'stereophonic divine approbation',[60] as a selectively fatal lightning-strike kills the seals but spares Thecla (3.34); so, in another stunning reversal, it is not Thecla who dies, as both

56 Although capital sentences were supposed to be executed promptly, a delay was permitted in cases of condemnation to the beasts, due to the cost involved and the need to procure and prepare the animals; see Coleman, 'Fatal Charades', p. 57.

57 Hopkins, *Death and Renewal*, pp. 9, 13. See also Kyle, *Spectacles of Death*, p. 35.

58 A gesture parallel to that of Paul immediately prior to martyrdom; see *Acts of Paul* 11.5.

59 In amphitheatres the basins used for aquatic displays often were stocked with fish. The use of seals in aquatic displays in amphitheatres is attested by Calpurnius Siculus 7.65–68. See K.M. Coleman, 'Launching into History: Aquatic Displays in the Early Empire', *JRS* 83 (1993), pp. 48–74, esp. 57.

60 McGinn, 'Acts of Thecla', p. 818.

she and the audience expect, but the seals.[61] The ritualized display of power in support of the social order is short-circuited by divinely orchestrated pyrotechnics. Thecla's virgin body remains pure – not even the penetrating gaze of the spectators allowed to touch it – for 'there was about her a cloud of fire, so that neither could the beasts touch her nor could she be seen naked' (3.34).[62] More terrible beasts are set loose to finish the task but fail, thanks to the women, whose intervention with 'botanical weapons' of petals, nard, cassia and amomum produces a bizarre sight: ferocious beasts 'overpowered' by petals and spices, small and delicate but packed with sedative potency (3.35).[63] Inspired by Thecla's noble endurance, a divine and female conspiracy has rallied to her cause. Unarmed victims, male or female, were not expected to survive an encounter with the beasts; yet this audience, assembled for its spectacle of death, witnesses a spectacle of life, in which Thecla, centre-stage, is not debased but beautiful.

Not even this astonishing turn of events, however, causes Alexander, whose status has yet to be restored, to relent. As a last resort he proposes to bind Thecla to his own fierce bulls.[64] The sexual overtones of her last, climactic ordeal are unmistakable: naked she is bound by the feet between bulls, and red-hot irons are placed against the bulls' genitals 'that being the more enraged they might kill her' (3.36).[65] In this brutal scene the bulls, goaded to gore Thecla's body, are proxy for the enraged Alexander whose sexual advances this woman had dared to reject. However, in this last desperate attempt to have his way with her, Alexander again proves impotent: Thecla

61 The ancient audience might have sensed something especially extraordinary in this display. According to Pliny (*Nat. Hist.* 2.56), the seal was thought immune to lightning strikes; thus, Augustus, who was terrified of thunder, always carried a seal-skin around him *pro remedia* (Suetonius, *Augustus* 90). On this point, see J.M.C. Toynbee, *Animals in Roman Life and Art* (Ithaca, NY: Cornell University Press, 1973), p. 206.

62 Note that the 'cloud of fire' serves to protect her from the physical touch of the beasts and from the penetrating gaze of the arena audience. In biblical tradition, the cloud is a frequent symbol of God's presence, protection and faithfulness; see e.g. Neh. 9.18; Pss. 78.14; 105.39. The combination of cloud and fire is especially prominent in the Exodus traditions, e.g. Exod. 13.21; 14.19–20, 24; 40.38; Num. 9.16.

63 This is but one of numerous references to female supporters who rally to Thecla's cause during her ordeals. At Antioch an anonymous group of women protest the governor's condemnation of Thecla, declaring, 'An evil judgment! A godless judgment' (3.27), and thereafter serve as a kind of female chorus of Thecla-sympathizers. When she is led in procession to the arena, women cry out, 'O God, an impious judgment is to come to pass in this city!' (3.28), then implore her not to cast herself into the pool of seals (3.34) and later throw their potent petals into the arena (3.35). The rich and imperially connected Tryphaena befriends her, providing on the eve of her encounter with the beasts a refuge that protects her from any further threat to the purity that Thecla wishes to preserve (3.27–31). This remarkable depiction of female solidarity includes a wild animal, as the lioness on which Thecla rides in procession licks her feet and later dies in defence of her (3.28, 33).

64 For a North African terracotta depicting a condemned woman tied to a bull, see Kyle, *Spectacles of Death*, p. 93.

65 Noted by Petropoulos, 'Transvestite Virgin', p. 135. Wild beasts were stimulated if necessary by firebrands; see Hopkins, *Death and Renewal*, p. 11; also Brown, 'Death as Decoration', p. 185. Bulls could be pursued with flares to stir them to fury; see Toynbee, *Animals*, p. 149. In the ancient world power and sexuality coalesce in the figure of the bull. On the association of the bull with male sexual potency, see e.g. Horace, *Epode* 12, cited by Diana E.E. Kleiner and Susan B. Matheson (eds), *I Claudia. Women in Ancient Rome* (New Haven, CT: Yale University Art Gallery, 1996), p. 134.

is delivered from harm by still more amazing means: a beneficent fire burns the ropes that bind her to the bulls and sets her free.[66] Things then go from bad to worse for Alexander. Tryphaena, upon witnessing her beloved Thecla's ordeal, faints, evoking her maidservants' cry, 'The queen Tryphaena is dead!' Alexander, fearful of Caesar's reprisal when he hears of his relative's death, is brought literally to his knees by this turn of events. Assuming the posture of a supplicant at the feet of the governor, he begs for mercy and, in a public reversal, requests that his offender be set free (3.36). Tryphaena, of course, is not really dead, and so the joke is on Alexander.[67] This 'first man of Antioch' is twice humiliated, twice the public spectacle, and this time at his own games!

The final and climactic spectacle of the performance, however, belongs to Thecla, as the governor, astounded that she remains untouched by the beasts, summons her and asks, 'Who are you? And what have you about you that not one of the beasts touched you?' (3.37). Thecla's answer is boldly confessional: 'I am a handmaid (δούλη) of the living God. As to what I have about me, I have believed in him in whom God is well pleased, His Son ... he alone is the goal of salvation and the foundation of immortal life ... whoever does not believe in him shall not live, but die for ever' (3.37). Moved, apparently, by what he has seen and now heard, the governor, halting the execution, orders that garments be brought and tells Thecla to put them on. Thecla dares to have the last word in their exchange, declaring, 'He who clothed me when I was naked among the beasts shall clothe me with salvation in the day of judgment' (3.38). Only after this defiant affirmation that her body and spirit belong not to him but to a higher authority does Thecla accept the garments and dress.[68]

The dual appearances of Alexander and Thecla before the governor present pointedly contrasting images: Alexander, on his knees and full of fear, begging for mercy; Thecla, standing fearless, using the governor's summons as a pulpit from which to proclaim her faith in the living God, the ultimate source of salvation. The drama has played out as a startling reversal in these games 'gone carnivalesque'. It is Thecla who is raised up, as the governor, in a retraction of the earlier judgement 'guilty of sacrilege', pronounces her 'pious handmaid of God' (τὴν τοῦ θεοῦ δούλην τὴν θεοσεβῆ) and releases her (3.38); conversely, the powerful first man of the city and imperial priest is brought to his knees at his own 'status blood-bath'. In contrast to Alexander's impotence, Thecla's bold witness in the final scene proves powerful, its effects on others immediate and startling. Upon the governor's reversal of the sentence, the women in unison shake the city with an acclamation of Thecla's God as the source of salvation: 'One is God, who has delivered Thecla!' (3.38). Likewise, Tryphaena, revived from her exquisitely timed swoon, upon hearing 'the good news', affirms, 'Now I believe that the dead are raised up! Now I believe that my child lives!' (3.39), a declaration that, in its explicit reference to resurrection, signals her

---

66 Readers familiar with biblical traditions might well interpret this marvellous deliverance in terms of the promise of divine protection from the beasts that is made to those who place their hope and trust in God; see esp., Psalm 91. Also, on God's deliverance of the righteous out of their distress see e.g. Pss. 9.9–11; 31.2–9; 33.18–22; 34.5–11,18–23; 37.39–40; 91.15.

67 As observed by Aubin, 'Reversing Romance', p. 270.

68 As noted by Margaret Miles, *Carnal Knowing: Female Nakedness and Religious Meaning in the Christian West* (Boston: Beacon Press, 1989), p. 58; also Burrus, 'Word and Flesh', pp. 29–30.

conversion to Christianity, in which she is later joined by her maidservants when they hear Thecla instruct Tryphaena in the word of God (3.39).

Subsequent to her marvellous deliverance and release, Thecla is reunited with Paul at Myra where the last element of the plot comes to resolution. Earlier Paul had rebuffed Thecla for fear that she fall to a 'trial (πειρασμός) worse than the first' (3.25). But now he encourages her, 'Go forth and teach the word of God' (3.41). The apostle's change of heart follows Thecla's report of her baptism and account of 'everything (that had happened)' (3.40–41), that is, her trial and ordeal in Antioch. By this testimony Paul learns that Thecla had faced a worse πειρασμός, endured, and been delivered; moreover, she had received the baptismal seal, which, according to the thought-world that informs this narrative, rendered one immune to the touch of temptation (πειρασμός).[69] Because Thecla has proved her devotion to the word and received the seal, Paul no longer has reason to fear for her exposure to the world in the itinerant apostolic life. As one whose untouchablity is now guaranteed by the baptismal seal, Thecla can teach the word of continence and resurrection to a world that, in its aversion to that word, poses trials to its apostolic representatives.[70] After a brief return to her home in Iconium, the apostle Thecla departs for Seleucia, where she, like Paul, 'encouraged many with the word of God' (3.43).

Conclusion

I have read the *Acts of Paul and Thecla* as a romance or adventure novel of ordeal in which the betrothed Thecla is seized by 'a new desire and a fearful passion' for 'the word of God concerning continence and resurrection'. That desire is sorely tested by a series of trials and ordeals. Consistent with the pattern of testing in Jewish and Christian traditions, she is sorely afflicted, endures in face of death, and gains divine approval and vindication; like her romance counterparts she remains steadfast in single-hearted devotion to the object of her desire, Jesus Christ, Son of the Living God. Once tried and proved true, Thecla's desire consummates not in marriage, as

---

69 Recall Thecla's earlier request, 'only give me the seal in Christ and temptation (πειρασμός) shall not touch me', to which Paul responds, 'have patience, Thecla, and you shall receive the water' (3.25). The understanding of the seal here appears to reflect 2 Cor. 1.21–22: 'it is God who establishes us with you in Christ, and has commissioned us; he has put his seal upon us and given us his Spirit in our hearts as a guarantee' (RSV), which is influenced by Old Testament traditions about signs set by God upon the elect to mark them as his own and to protect them from destruction. In the ancient context, seals, as marks of ownership, are frequently used for soldiers and for slaves, both of whom are bound to the service of a master. In our narrative, Thecla, who twice identifies herself as a handmaiden or slave of God (3.26; 3.37), requests the seal that will not only identify her but also protect her. On the pagan and Jewish cult-practices which form the background of Paul's metaphorical use of 'seal' (σφραγίς), see Chapter 1 in G.W.H. Lampe, *The Seal of the Spirit. A Study in the Doctrine of Baptism and Confirmation in the New Testament and the Fathers* (2nd edn; London: SPCK, 1967), esp. pp. 10–18.

70 That Thecla's trials and ordeals do not cease with her baptism is significant. On my reading, the ordeal of the bulls that follows her baptism functions to prove her untouchability, now guaranteed by the baptismal seal. Note that it is the spectacle of Thecla's untouchability that raises for the governor the question of Thecla's identity (Who are you?), in response to which Thecla boldly confesses her identity as 'handmaid of the living God' and her faith in that God as source of her salvation, that is, safety.

in the romance, but in baptism and an apostolic commission to teach that socially subversive word of God that had caused her to reject the first man of Iconium.

Reading the narrative as an adventure novel of ordeal has the effect of highlighting Thecla's bold initiatives on behalf of the divine 'word of continence and resurrection' to which she devotes herself: rejecting Thamyris, her fiancé; repulsing the sexual advances of a priest of the imperial cult; requesting of the governor that she might remain pure until she fights the beasts; finally, with the realization that death is imminent, baptizing herself in the name of Jesus Christ. It also foregrounds Thecla's unconventional virtues: not σωφροσύνη or chastity, the virtue proper to a devoted and fertile wife and valorized in the romance,[71] but continence (ἐγκράτεια), a virtue antithetical to the measured sexual expression within marriage that the romance script endorses; endurance or perseverance (ὑπομονή), the virtue par excellence of the biblical righteous and counted among the pre-eminent virtues in the Graeco–Roman world;[72] and purity (ἀγνεία), which the virgin Thecla embodies. This reading also has the effect of spotlighting Thecla's power. After successfully defying the cultural imperative that she marry a social equal, she resists the sexual assault of a powerful priest of the imperial cult and then, in the narrative climax, her testimony before the governor brings the women of Antioch to confess the one God as source of salvation and a queen with connections to the emperor to profess faith in the resurrection. In the spectacles of death to which she is condemned, Thecla in effect 'steals the show', becoming, even to the eyes of a governor, a spectacle of power.

Significantly, Thecla's initiative, virtues and power, on this reading, have little to do with Paul. He is conspicuously, some would say notoriously, absent when Thecla undergoes her trials. It is, rather, Thecla and the one God, whose 'word concerning continence and resurrection' quickened desire in her, who play the leads in this drama, with Paul cast in the supporting role of intermediary: preaching the word that mediates her encounter with the one God (3.5–7), praying for her when she is condemned to the pyre (3.24), counselling her to patience when she desires the baptismal seal (3.25), and in the end, encouraging her to 'go forth and teach the word of God' (3.41).[73] Moreover, Thecla is as central as Paul to the inversion of romance. No man succeeds in putting the upstart back in her proper romance place; nor does any civic or imperial authority manage to expel this deviant female from the social order by execution. It is Thecla's own trials and ordeals that occasion a series of stunning reversals by which the patriarchal social order, headed by its elite male householders and its imperial priests, is turned upside down and trumped by the

---

71 On this point, see Cooper, *Virgin*, p. 56.

72 See Hauck, 'ὑπομένω, ὑπομονή', pp. 581–83.

73 Although the narrative does not attribute Thecla's achievements to Paul, it reflects Pauline convictions that Thecla, like Paul, embodies; e.g. Paul considered endurance of hardship, including persecution and threat of death, as a hallmark of the apostolic life (1 Cor. 4.9–13; 2 Cor. 4.7–12; 6.4–10; cf. Phil. 1.29–30), regarding such hardships and affliction as opportunities for the demonstration of power (2 Cor. 12.9–10). In this narrative, the beleaguered and steadfast Thecla meets the Pauline standard for the apostolic life: endurance of suffering and hardship in imitation of the crucified Christ (2 Cor. 11–12).

Christian οἰκονομία, with its supremely powerful God in the heavens and its 'tried and true' apostles, male and female, wooing the world.[74]

As a feminist interpreter, I am interested not simply in illuming the meaning of a text in its original context, as I have sought to do here, but also in assessing its potential impact on the consciousness and lives of contemporary women. In conclusion, then, one must ask, is this Christian adventure novel of ordeal worthwhile reading for contemporary women, especially women who identify with the Christian tradition? Constraints of space permit brief remarks regarding its reception history, which attest its value for previous generations of women, and its representation of Thecla, which contemporary women are seeing in new ways.

For centuries the figure of Thecla enjoyed a remarkable 'afterlife'.[75] As the focus of a vibrant and widespread cult, Thecla attained a celebrity status rivalling that of Mary, mother of Jesus, with the ascetically inclined Methodius, Gregory of Nyssa and Gregory of Nazianzus counted among her admirers.[76] By means of the stories told about them, revered ascetic women such as Thecla in effect blazed a trail on which subsequent generations of Christian women, rejecting their 'manifest destiny' to the patriarchal marriage bed, pursued intellectual and spiritual interests that the conventional path of marriage and motherhood would have denied them.[77] Thecla's story even inspired some to claim authority to teach and baptize, much to the chagrin of Tertullian and, we may suspect, others.[78] Apparently, they interpreted the narrative, as I have done here, as far more than the story of a woman's conversion to Christianity by Paul's preaching. Rather, the example of this 'tried and true' female apostle authorized their own aspirations to leadership roles in their communities and can continue to do so. At the narrative's end, this female heroine, unlike Perpetua, is very much alive, on the move, and actively teaching the word of God. In preserving her story the tradition affords contemporary women an encouraging exemplar for their own aspirations to ministry of the word.[79] At a time when women in some churches continue to be excluded from ordained ministry, the example of

74 Among the ways in which the narrative reflects Pauline thought, note here the conception of Christians as citizens not of this world but of a heavenly πολίτευμα (Phil. 3.17–21).

75 I refer to the figure of Thecla to make clear that I make no claims regarding the historicity of the narrative. Cognizant that one cannot presume mimetic relationships between text and reality, in my work on the *Acts of Paul and Thecla* I have chosen to bracket the historical questions that preoccupy feminist historiography. In focusing on the narrative as text rather than document, I am not, however, entirely disinterested in historical questions. I am, for example, interested in the text's reception history and the impact of textual representations on the lives and consciousness of real women.

76 See Stephen J. Davis, *The Cult of Saint Thecla: A Tradition of Women's Piety in Late Antiquity* (Oxford Early Christian Studies; Oxford: Oxford University Press, 2001).

77 On ascetic renunciation among early Christian women, see esp. Burrus, 'Word and Flesh'; Elizabeth A. Castelli, 'Virginity and Its Meanings for Women's Sexuality in Early Christianity', *JFSR* 2 (1986), pp. 61–88; Elizabeth A. Clark, 'Ascetic Renunciation and Feminine Advancement: A Paradox of Late Ancient Christianity', in *eadem, Ascetic Piety and Women's Faith: Essays in Late Ancient Christianity* (New York: Edwin Mellen Press, 1986), pp. 175–208.

78 In his treatise *On Baptism*, written *ca.* 200 CE, Tertullian criticizes those who cite the 'example of Thecla' (*exemplum Theclae*) in order to 'defend the liberty of women to teach and baptize' (*ad licentiam mulierum docendi tinguendique defendere, De bapt.* 17).

79 Extant sources suggest, however, that Thecla, like Mary Magdalene whose apostolic witness has long been obscured by the image of the penitent prostitute, was revered primarily for her virginity (her flesh) rather than her apostolic witness (her speech).

Thecla belies the rationale for the exclusion, namely, that men more appropriately 'image' Christ. Thecla not only embodies the word of God, which in this case is 'the word of God concerning continence and resurrection'; the pattern of her experience conforms to that of Christ. Like Jesus, she undergoes a 'passion' that tries her fidelity, and she perseveres, as he did. Moreover, her story features a remarkable depiction of female solidarity, as women, even a lioness, rally to her cause. Their voiced and visible protest affords, for women of any era, a spectacle that might yet inspire defiant solidarity in protest of current injustices in church and state.

While previous generations of Christian women have seen in Thecla an example to be revered and emulated, many feminist interpreters, viewing her through the lens of critical theory, now find her story wanting when measured by canons of subjectivity, agency and autonomy.[80] It has been objected, for example, that Thecla is far less subject than object in the narrative. As Paul's virgin convert, she is primarily object of his will and activity; as Thamyris's betrothed and target of Alexander's roving eye, she is sexual object of men's desiring; as condemned, naked and on display in the arena, she is object of the public gaze. The violent scenes in which Thecla is paraded naked before the eyes of the arena audience, which includes those of us seated in the farthest seats outside the narrative arena, beg scrutiny through the lens of feminist film criticism, which is alert for the pornographic in representations of women.[81]

Granted, in the context of the larger work known as *Acts of Paul*, the Thecla narrative reads as a kind of side-bar about Paul's premier convert, and so redounds above all to the glory of Paul. The spotlight in the *Acts of Paul and Thecla* itself, however, is squarely on Thecla, and not as mere object of conversion. For various characters in the narrative she is, indeed, object to be desired, seized or cast out. Thecla, however, rejects and resists their desires. Instead she actively, and successfully, pursues the object of her own desire – Jesus Christ, Son of the Living God. She is, then, a desiring subject, whose desire, once 'consummated', enables her to assume the role of itinerant apostolic witness. By the narrative's end, the converted becomes the converter, Tryphaena and her household being the first (3.39) among the many who were enlightened by Thecla teaching the word of God (3.43).

This is not to conclude, however, that the representation is entirely unproblematic. Thecla is, after all, presented as a woman whose virginal bodily state – untouched and unpenetrated – becomes at the narrative's climax the primary focus of attention. Given the role that woman's identification with body has played in the subjugation of women throughout history, this focus on Thecla's bodily state calls for critical scrutiny. In addition, although Thecla rejects what was woman's fate in the ancient world, namely, to become the sexual property of a husband, her willingness to identify herself as 'handmaid' or 'slave' of God is a less than appealing ideal for those of us

---

80 For a valuable summary of the dilemmas that structuralist and poststructuralist thought pose for feminist historiography, see Elizabeth A. Clark, 'The Lady Vanishes: Dilemmas of a Feminist Historian after the "Linguistic Turn"', *Church History* 67 (1998) pp. 1–31; also, see her 'Women, Gender, and the Study of Christian History', *CH* 70 (2001) pp. 395–426.

81 For demonstration of the value of such a project, see e.g. Blake Leyerle, 'John Chrysostom on the Gaze', *JECS* 1 (1993), pp. 159–74. The advisability of the task in relation to the Thecla narrative is confirmed by recent work exposing the pornographic dimensions of the ancient romance, e.g. Helen E. Elsom, 'Callirhoe: Displaying the Phallic Woman', in Amy Richlin (ed.), *Pornography and Representation in Greece and Rome*, pp. 212–30.

increasingly critical of traditional theological language and cognizant of its detrimental impact on the lives of Christian women.[82] Furthermore, Cooper's compelling argument, that the Apocryphal Acts are really about a contest between men, raises the question, do we have here simply a variation on the 'traffic in women',[83] one in which, in this case, perpetual virgins are the currency by which Christian men claim the superiority of their alternative οἰκονομία?

It has also been objected that Thecla is heroine only insofar as she becomes in some sense 'male', cutting her hair and dressing like a man; furthermore, the standard of heroism by which she is measured remains androcentric – willingness to suffer, even die, for the word of God as Jesus did and as male apostles like Paul do, in other words, in imitation of men. Thus, she is heroine, 'saint', because this woman can do what men do.[84] Much about her representation – e.g. her lack of terror in the arena, her physical assertiveness against Alexander – undermines ancient cultural assumptions regarding the weakness of women, as does the series of ordeals that she endures. Indeed, the test or trial (πειρασμός) highlighted in this essay prompts further questions. What, if anything, does her test have to do with her being a woman? Is the point of her πειρασμός to prove her manliness? Answers to these questions require a more lengthy exposition than can be offered here. Elsewhere I argue that the significance of Thecla's πειρασμός is not unrelated to the politics of desire inscribed in the ancient romance and in the *Acts of Paul and Thecla*.[85]

Last, although the Thecla narrative turns upside down and trumps the patriarchal social order, headed by its elite male householders and its imperial priests, it does not dismantle, even seriously challenge, that social order. Its rhetoric is content, rather, to persuade for an 'other-worldly' and, so it claims, superior alternative for an elite few; and so the 'romance world' and its patriarchal politic[86] remain intact,

82 Metaphors of servanthood and slavery, as traditional language of Christian identity, are used for men as well as women. In his extant letters, Paul, for example, refers to himself as slave of Christ Jesus (Rom. 1.1; Gal. 1.10). It can be argued, however, that within patriarchal churches, the traditional language of servanthood and slavery has had and continues to have very different consequences in the lives of women than in those of men.

83 A cultural pattern identified by anthropologist Gayle Rubin; see Gayle Rubin, 'The Traffic in Women', in Rayna Rapp Reiter (ed.), *Toward an Anthropology of Women* (New York: Monthly Review, 1975), pp. 157–210.

84 Virginia Burrus's characterization of Thecla and other second-century women figures as virile and masculinized is apt indeed. On the literary transformation of these 'manly' women – *viragines* – into feminine, docile *virgines*, see Burrus, 'Reading Agnes: The Rhetoric of Gender in Ambrose and Prudentius', *JECS* 3 (1995), pp. 25–46. On virilization of women in early Christian literature, see also Elizabeth A. Castelli, '"I Will Make Mary Male": Pieties of the Body and Gender Transformation of Christian Women in Late Antiquity', in Julia Epstein and Kristina Straub (eds), *Body Guards: The Cultural Politics of Ambiguity* (New York: Routledge, 1991), pp. 29–49.

85 The politics of desire, including the constructions of gender and sexuality that are constitutive elements of the politics, are the focus of Chapter 3 of my current project (*A New Desire and a Fearful Passion: The Politics of Desire in the Acts of Paul and Thecla*).

86 By 'romance world' I mean the world as represented in the ancient romance, including its politics of desire. It is a world in which women are vulnerable and in need of confinement to private space and/or male supervision and protection in public space. See note 48 above. In our narrative, Thecla, as object of male desire (e.g. Alexander), is vulnerable when not under male guardianship; she lives in a world in which a woman's 'assault' on a priest's crown, with its imperial image, is punishable by death but the priest's sexual assault upon that woman's body is not.

as untouched as Thecla's virgin body. The ideals of womanhood envisioned by the ancient romance and the Apocryphal Acts remain but two, perpetual virgin or bride within a patriarchal household, neither of which represents an attractive ideal to many women today.[87]

Thecla is one of the precious few women-figures among the predominantly male ranks of early heroes of the Christian faith; yet, she is little known beyond circles of scholars. Today Christian women in increasing numbers want to know more about women of the tradition and are seeking ways to interpret its texts in ways that empower rather than demean women. Study of Thecla is, I believe, a good place to begin. Her story in the *Acts of Paul and Thecla* proves especially instructive for exercises in feminist criticism by which women can develop the skills to become agents, not mere recipients, of interpretation, able to assess for ourselves the promise and the perils that texts of the tradition hold for us.[88] Early Christian men, Peter Brown alerts us, used women to think with.[89] All the more reason for women to 'think with' women, real and representational. I, for one, am not yet finished 'thinking with' Thecla.

87 Likewise, the two rival ideals set before women in early Christian tradition – Mary, perpetually virgin mother, and divinely protected perpetual virgin Thecla – are unattainable and, for the vast majority of Christian women, undesirable. For forthright and insightful comment on the ideal of virginity from the perspective of a Christian woman, see 'What's So Great About Being a Virgin?' in Renita Weems, *Showing Mary. How Women Can Share Prayers, Wisdom, and the Blessings of God* (West Bloomfield, MI: Warner Books, 2002), pp. 41–53.

88 The Thecla narrative is required reading in the primer of exercises with which I teach feminist criticism. It has proved to be especially useful for an exercise in what I term 'the feminist gaze', the subject-stance in which the interpreter, conscious of the politics of representation, exerts her/his power in relation to another's representation. My experiment with 'the feminist gaze' is informed by Susanne Kappeler's analysis of the politics of representation; see her *The Pornography of Representation* (Minneapolis: University of Minnesota Press, 1986); also John Berger, *Ways of Seeing* (Harmondsworth: Penguin, 1972). The need to develop a strategy for viewing representations of women in literature and film is based on the recognition that the vast majority of such representations are products and producers of the dominant male gaze.

89 See Peter Brown, *The Body and Society: Men, Women, and Sexual Renunciation in Early Christianity* (Lectures on the History of Religion, 13; New York: Columbia University Press, 1988), p. 153, where Brown acknowledges that he adopts the phrase 'using women to think with' from Claude Lévi-Strauss's *Structural Anthropology* (2 vols.; trans. Claire Jacobson and Brooke Grundfest Schoepf; New York: Basic Books, 1963). For critical comment regarding the implications of Brown's observation for feminist historiography, see Matthews, 'Thinking of Thecla', esp. pp. 46–51.

Buying the Stairway to Heaven:
Perpetua and Thecla as Early Christian Heroines

Gail P.C. Streete

> There's a sign on the wall,
> But she wants to be sure
> 'Cause you know sometimes words have two meanings
> Led Zeppelin, 'Stairway to Heaven'

The representatives of evil, armed with the power to kill, demanded a confession of faith from their young female victim: 'Do you believe?' When she replied in the affirmative, they put her to death. Soon, her story was told and retold until it became a symbol of courage supplied by faith in the confrontation between good and evil, God and the devil, of a frail female in the face of armed male intimidation, an inspiration to the Christian world. 'Her peers made her a saint who died to redeem them,' as one contemporary account of her legend put it.[1]

The martyrdom of Cassie Bernall, the teenager who met death at the hands of the young trench-coated killers of Columbine High School, has become a best-selling book entitled *She Said Yes*.[2] According to some accounts, it was the 17-year-old Rachel Scott who replied to the question in the affirmative, either instead of Cassie or in a variation of Cassie's story that makes it appear as though confessing Christians were the target of the anti-Christian killers.[3] Rachel's story is similarly celebrated in a memorial book illustrated with her own drawings and containing excerpts from her diary;[4] it is celebrated as well by her pastor Bruce Porter in *The Martyr's Torch* (2000), which claims for Rachel the exemplary role of one who bore 'a torch that was stained by the blood of the martyrs from the very first day of the Church's existence in the world 2,000 years ago'.[5] Cassie Bernall was a young woman who had been very much like the teen who eventually murdered her, one who fantasized about killing her parents and other authorities. Her story was transformed into an account

---

1 Hanna Rosin, 'Columbine girl who really said "Yes" shuns fame', *Times-Picayune* (Saturday 17 October 1999), p. A-23. Original article appeared in *Washington Post* (Wednesday 14 October 1999), p. C1.

2 Misty Bernall and Madeline L'Engle, *She Said Yes: The Unlikely Martyrdom of Cassie Bernall* (Farmington, PA: Plough Publishing House, 1999).

3 Various versions of this account have been cited in Justin Watson, *The Martyrs of Columbine: Faith and the Politics of Tragedy* (New York: Palgrave Macmillan, 2002), e.g. p. 15.

4 Beth Nimmo and Darrell Scott (Rachel's parents) with Steve Rabey, *Rachel's Tears: The Spiritual Journey of Columbine Martyr Rachel Scott* (Nashville: Thomas Nelson, 2000).

5 Bruce Porter, pastor of Celebration Christian Fellowship, at Rachel Scott's funeral service, cited in Watson, *Martyrs*, p. 53, n. 7.

of a born-again Christian who fearlessly claimed her new-found faith in the face of death. Rachel, an evangelical Christian teen who was universally remembered as 'nice' to everyone, even to her eventual killers,[6] nevertheless also claimed in capital letters on the back of her journal, found with her at her death, the possibly prophetic words, 'I WON'T BE LABELLED AS AVERAGE'.[7] The problem is that the young woman who really said 'Yes', Valeen Schnurr, lived, and lived to tell what should have been an equally inspiring story, but she tells it reluctantly, infrequently and often to disbelief and anger. Of the thirteen fatalities from Columbine High School, there are only two – Cassie and Rachel – who are the subjects of books – and only four, including Cassie and Rachel, who have websites. Of these four, three are female, but of the three, the website of Kelly Fleming is small, not maintained, and does not even have the dates of her birth. The website of Daniel Mauser, put up by his parents, advocates gun control, but its most 'current news' is from 1999. Further, it is now known as most likely that of the three 'confessors', Valeen was the proven one and that the account of Rachel's 'confession' is the most tenuous.[8]

The stories of Cassie and Rachel illustrate an ironic good about martyrs: while they stay safely dead, their stories can be told and retold, remodelled through the transforming power of the imagination to suit contemporary religious ideals and aspirations, until they assume a mythic truth quite independent of the actual events. The most potent form of 'witness' (μάρτυς), the original meaning of the word 'martyr', is one that stands at the boundary between life and death, social and sexual norms and eternal absolutes, and crosses over it. Thus, while the dead martyr herself is beyond changing, her story may be subject to reshaping to reflect changing values. The stories of martyrs serve the theological, social and political ends of the living, even if the martyrs themselves, while living, did not. The duplicate narratives of Cassie and Rachel, coupled and contrasted with that of Valeen, are tales of dead and living martyrs which offer a fascinating entrée into the way in which martyrologies take shape. Their stories also help to shed some light upon the way in which early Christian martyrologies – themselves the mould in which Cassie's and Rachel's stories have been cast – both furnished ideal examples for Christian behaviour in the face of persecution and functioned as encapsulations of communal religious and social attitudes that might be variously interpreted and edited by different Christian communities to suit their own spiritual needs.

More often than not, just as in the Columbine examples, female martyrs seem to have been preferred to males as narrative vehicles for the expression of these attitudes and needs. As Sebastian Brock and Susan Ashbrook Harvey note in the cases of Syrian women martyrs, men usually tell stories *about* women to men and women.[9] This assertion is amply borne out by the stories of the Columbine martyrs;

---

6 Watson, *Martyrs*, pp. 66–67.

7 See the 'Official website', n.p. [cited 20 June 2005] online: http://www.rachelscott.com.

8 'Triumph over Tragedy', by Valeen Schnurr as told to Janna R. Graber, from *Stories for a Teen's Heart* (Sisters, OR: Multnomah Publishers, 1999), n.p. [Cited 23 June 2005] Online: http://www.jannagraber.com/triumph_over_tragedycolumbine.htm. See also Watson, *Martyrs*, pp. 115–47. Misty Bernall allows the possibility that all three young women confessed their faith, including Valeen, who 'miraculously survived' (Bernall, *She Said Yes*, p. 132).

9 *Holy Women of the Syrian Orient*, translated with an introduction by Sebastian P. Brock and Susan Ashbrook Harvey (Berkeley: University of California Press, 1987), p. 25.

despite the involvement of mothers in writing both Cassie's and Rachel's stories, the tales were most frequently employed by *male* evangelical Christian preachers, writers and politicians to appeal to young men and women.[10] What makes women more 'attractive' than men as subjects of martyrologies? As 'marginal' persons to begin with, bounded with a number of socially validated restrictions including sexual ones, women can be used symbolically as 'liminal' or 'threshold' figures that can stand outside society either to critique it or to bring its values more sharply into focus. Female characters may be shown in extreme situations in which they transgress the boundaries of ordinarily appropriate gendered behaviour, only to make the boundaries that much clearer. They may also be placed in situations where the values of the dominant society are represented as an evil with which there can be no compromise, even at the cost of life. In such situations, the non-dominant (in this case, gender) must defy the dominant one. Because such situations are extreme, however, they call for unusual behaviour: the martyrology is not offered as a mandate for continued transgression.

An important and unvarying subtext to these martyrologies and perhaps another reason for the attraction of stories of female martyrs is that of sexuality. The stories of women martyrs are frequently accompanied by accounts of their resolute chastity and references to their female bodies exposed and graphically tortured, references that are usually absent from accounts of male martyrs.[11] Thus, the stories of Cassie Bernall and Rachel Scott and to a lesser extent of Valeen Schnurr, like those of Perpetua and Thecla, fit into the same mould – that of martyrdom. The stories of Cassie and Rachel (and again, to a lesser extent, that of Valeen) validate acceptable, if not dominant, social norms and familial values, fidelity to an accepted religion, and obedience to political authority, while those of Perpetua and Thecla appear either to critique or to invalidate these categories. And yet, each can be and has been counted as a story of a martyr. If we look more closely, however, we will see that all these stories, despite their differences and modifications, originate in and resonate with groups that perceive themselves as prescribing ideals of what they deem Christian behaviour.

In what follows, I briefly treat the stories of the two early Christian female saints, both dating roughly from the early third century of the Common Era. The first, *The Martyrdom of Saints Perpetua and Felicity*, is the story of two young Christian women, one relatively upper class and the other a slave, who died in North Africa about 203 CE. What makes this story remarkable is that it consists, in large part, of a 'prison diary' containing the narratives, visions and reflections of the more

---

10 See Watson, *Martyrs*, especially 'The Politics of Tragedy', pp. 79–113.

11 *Holy Women*, p. 25. Cassie Bernall's conversion apparently involved conversion to sexual purity. One of her friends, Cassandra, is quoted as saying Cassie did not get 'caught up looking for a boyfriend' because she 'felt that only God was going to be able to fulfill her' (Bernall, *She Said Yes*, p. 112). Her youth pastor, Dave McPherson, claimed that she was 'married' to Jesus in heaven (Watson, *Martyrs*, p. 46). Rachel Scott also reportedly turned away from romantic relationships because it would interfere with her relationship with God (Nimmo, Scott and Rabey, *Rachel's Tears*, p. 106). Both martyrs' stories illustrate 'the themes of sexual purity and an eroticized love of God', according to Watson, *Martyrs*, p. 74. Valeen Schnurr's story has no such account of sexual renunciation.

prominent character, Perpetua.[12] So powerful was her story among Christians of the third century and later that the prominent Carthaginian writer Tertullian, her contemporary – who elsewhere asserted that women, for the sin of Eve, bore eternal shame as 'the Devil's gateway' (*Cult fem.* 1.1.12) – praised Perpetua as 'the most heroic martyr', one who was guaranteed to enter the gateway to Paradise closed to Eve by the flaming sword. As an example for all those who would follow her into heaven at the cost of 'their own heart's blood' (*An.* 51.6), Perpetua reverses Eve's trajectory. The date of her martyrdom and that of Felicity became a feast-day in the Church, appearing in the Western (Philocalian) calendar of 354; the bishop of the North African Church in Hippo, Augustine, preached most likely between 401–412 three sermons on the annual observance of their martyrdom. Perhaps following a rhetorical trope established in the account of the martyred mother of 4 Maccabees, the woman with the 'same mind as Abraham' (4 Macc. 14.20, NRSV) with whom Felicity has sometimes been conflated,[13] Augustine particularly emphasizes the 'virile spirit' (*virilis animus*) in these women's fragile bodies and observes how fitting it was that a woman should vanquish the enemy (*inimicum*) who had deceived the original woman and helped her to deceive the first man (*Serm.* 281.1.1–2; 2.2).[14]

The second story, the apocryphal *Acts of Paul and Thecla*, recounts the tale of a young noblewoman from Iconium. Converted by the apostle Paul to Christianity of a severely ascetic kind, Thecla casts off her mother, her fiancé and her household. She endures several near-martyrdoms but miraculously escapes until, self-baptized, she achieves Paul's approval. Then like him she lives the life of an apostle by preaching, teaching and working miracles until she finally meets a peaceful death, 'having enlightened many' (*Acts of Paul and Thecla*, 43). Yet while Tertullian held Perpetua up as a model of Christian virtue and female heroism, the very same writer rejected the story of Thecla as a forgery and condemned its use by Christian women to justify their claims to the clerical authority to preach, teach and baptize (*Bapt.* 17.5).[15] On the other hand, the Eastern Christian writer Methodius (260–312) employed the

---

12 Åke Fridh has posed the question of whether the *Martyrdom of Perpetua and Felicity*, including the visions of Perpetua and Saturus, is a literary fiction, but in the end concludes that Perpetua's account, however edited, goes back to a historical source, namely Perpetua. See Åke Fridh, *Le problème de la passion des Saintes Perpétue et Félicité* (Studia Graeca et Latina Gothoburgensia XXVI; Göteburg: Almqvist & Wiksell, 1968), pp. 8, 55, 83.

13 A fifth-century Christian version of the *passio* of the seven Maccabean brothers names Felicity as the otherwise unnamed mother (Catholic Information Network, CIN, 'St. Felicity and the Seven Holy Brothers,' n.p. [cited 7 July 2000]; online: http://www.cin.org/saints/felicity.html).

14 Nonetheless, Augustine trod a fine line between the Donatist exhortation to martyrdom and what he deemed the appropriate role of the martyrs in the Church. When he built a shrine to house the relics of the proto-martyr Stephen in his cathedral, he was symbolically corralling the veneration of the saint within the church. See Maureen A. Tilley, 'Harnessing the Martyrs' (paper presented at the annual meeting of the North American Patristic Society, Chicago, 30 May, 1998), pp. 1–8. Cited 24 June 2005; online: http://divinity.library.vanderbilt.edu/burns/chroma/saints/martilley.html.

15 But what was the forgery? If, as Tertullian claims, the 'presbyter of Asia' who claimed to have admitted the forgery did so 'out of love of Paul', the motive would seem highly unlikely given that in the *Acts of Thecla*, Paul appears ineffectual or even cowardly, as his denial of Thecla when she is threatened by the Antiochene noble, Alexander, demonstrates.

figure of Thecla as a substitute Socrates,[16] the leader of a Christianized version of Plato's *Symposium* called *The Banquet of the Ten Virgins*, in which ten noble young women, not a group of drunken Greek men, conduct a dialogue on the virtues of virginity rather than a discourse on erotic attraction. In this dialogue, which consists of a series of interpretations of Scripture on the subject of virginity, Thecla interprets the figure of the 'woman clothed with the sun' in Rev. 12.1–6 as the church (*ekklesia*), the 'spiritual Zion' of Isa. 66.7–8 whose bearing of a male child suggests that all Christians through baptism are reborn 'a masculine people' (λαόν τὸν ἄρσενα) who forsake 'the passions of women' (τῶν γυναικείων παθῶν) (Methodius, *Symp.* 8.7). Thecla is praised by her comrades because she has appeared in the 'chief contests of the martyrs' (τοῖς μεγάλοις καὶ πρώτοις ἄθλοις ... τῶν μαρτύρων) a 'bodily strength' (τὴν ῥώμην τοῦ σώματος) that matches the height of her advice (*Symp.* 8.17). By the fifth century, Thecla's tomb in Seleucia had become a destination for pilgrimage, the alleged site of miracles, and the centre of a monastic order of virgins led by a deaconess (Egeria, *Pilgrimage*, 23). The fact that Thecla was not, technically speaking, a martyr, since she had not died at the hands of her persecutors but miraculously escaped through the strength of her faith, bothered her devotees not at all.[17] Yet while Perpetua is still considered a martyr-saint in the Western Church, Thecla's name was removed from its canon of saints in 1969,[18] presumably for reasons of historicity, although Jerome as early as the beginning of the fifth century, referring to Tertullian, had called the story a 'fable' (*fabula*) and counted it apocryphal (*Vir. ill.* 7.1014). Thecla does, however, remain a venerated saint, virgin, martyr and teacher in Eastern Orthodox Churches.

Clearly, both stories had something important and powerful to say to various groups of Christians over time, and the fact that both centred on persecuted heroines is not the least part of their significance. Further, 'like all representations, especially [those of] heroines', these images are 'susceptible to manipulation by [their] interpreters'.[19] Martyrdom provides an opportunity not only to the martyr (to confess her faith) but to the martyrologist (who decides what aspect of the 'faith' she is confessing). Just

---

16 Peter Brown, *The Body and Society: Men, Women, and Sexual Renunciation in Early Christianity* (Lectures on the History of Religions, 13; New York: Columbia University Press, 1988), p. 184.

17 Léonie Hayne, 'Thecla and the Church Fathers', *VC* 48 (1994), pp. 209–18 (212). This situation is different than the contested martyrdoms of Valeen Schnurr, Cassie Bernall and Rachel Scott. As Justin Watson and others note, it is the manner of the deaths of Cassie and Rachel, the 'crucible of martyrdom', that highlights their lives and the way in which they were lived (Watson, *Martyrs*, p. 157).

18 Paul VI, in his apostolic letter *Mysterii paschalis*, suggests that several saints were removed from the calendar because 'with the passage of centuries', the faithful had observed so many special devotional days that 'the principal mysteries of redemption have lost their proper place' (Rome: Vatican Polyglot Press, 14 February, 1969), n.p. Cited 24 June 2005; online: http: // www.catholic-forum.com/saints/day0923.htm.

19 Francine Cardmon, 'Women, Ministry and Church Order in Early Christianity', in Ross Shepard Kraemer and Mary Rose D'Angelo (eds.), *Women and Christian Origins* (New York: Oxford University Press, 1999), pp. 300–29 (302). As Justin Watson suggests of the martyrs of Columbine, who have frequently been compared to the earlier Christian martyrs, 'Martyrs of course have always been at the mercy of martyrologists – those who tell, interpret, and preserve the story of the martyr' (Watson, *Martyrs*, p. 115).

as the 'Columbine martyrs' Cassie and Rachel (but not the 'confessor' Valeen, who lived) 'challenge the legitimacy' of 'ideological secularism', sexual promiscuity and the 'community of the political Left',[20] both Perpetua and Thecla functioned as models of and for particular virtues valued by Christianity during its formative period, the second century until the early fifth. These early Christian women became associated with virtues that were regarded by their contemporaries as 'masculine' virtues: courage, which in and of itself meant 'manliness' (*virtus*, ἀνδρεία) and its accompanying virtue of self-control or self-mastery (*continentia*, ἐγκράτεια). These virtues could be portrayed both positively and negatively when applied to women, whose distinctive virtues were normally seen as modesty and chastity or *pudicitia*/ἁγνεία. When women sought power within the Church, not merely moral and spiritual authority but institutional authority and clerical office, they were castigated for appropriating these feminine examples. The stories of Perpetua and Thecla portray heroines who possess extraordinary power that ironically evidences divine sanction for their often antisocial and transgressive behaviour. In the case of Perpetua, this power enables her and those like her to gain access to heaven and even to intercede on behalf of the living and the dead, but not necessarily to gain access to earthly institutional authority. In Thecla's case, it enables her to ward off her persecutors, who represent the corruption of pagan society, and it authorizes her eventually to take on the apostolic authority of her role model, Paul. But as will be seen, her story is later interpreted as that of a valiant virgin who models chaste obedience to God for both men and women. In both narratives, appropriate and inappropriate conduct for men and women, pagan and Christian, is constructed and given either divine approbation or condemnation.

The Martyrdom of Perpetua and Felicity consists of two main parts. The first is the framework, which itself consists of an introduction and the account of the martyrdom of Perpetua, Felicity and their fellow-Christians. The second part of the martyrology which has been of most interest – much of it revived thanks to feminist historians of early Christianity – is Perpetua's 'prison diary', wherein she recounts the events that led to her arrest by the pagan Roman authorities, her imprisonment, and the four visions or dreams she had while in prison.[21] According to the framework, the story of Perpetua and her fellow sufferers is evidence that God's spirit is being revived within the Christian community in the form of visions and martyrdoms. That Perpetua and Felicity are both women and that the latter is a slave are important factors for the narrator because the two are offered as proof that the end-time prophecy of Joel (2.28–32), first quoted in a Christian context in the book of Acts (2.16–17), is coming true after a delay of a century or more. 'For in the last days, God declares, I will pour out my Spirit upon all flesh and their sons and daughters shall prophesy and on my manservants and maidservants I will pour my Spirit, and the young men shall see visions, and the old men shall dream dreams.'[22] Because of its deliberate references

---

20 Watson, *Martyrs*, pp. 26–27.

21 Attached to Perpetua's diary is the account of a vision by her comrade Saturus, in which Perpetua also appears, but which is much shorter than her story and has not attracted nearly as much interest.

22 Translation from 'A Christian Woman's Account of Her Persecution', in Ross Shepard Kraemer (ed.), *Maenads, Martyrs, Matrons and Monastics* (Philadelphia, PA: Fortress Press, 1988), p. 96. The critical Latin text is found in C.J.M. van Beek, *Passio Sanctarum Perpetuae et Felicitatis*

to this prophecy as embedded in Acts, *The Martyrdom of Perpetua and Felicity* could be considered a type of 'apocryphal' Act, despite the absence of any named (male) apostle. The bestowal of the spirit, then, transgresses boundaries of gender, class and age. Perpetua's narrative and her visions reinforce the truth of that erasure of boundaries. They also show how a society like that of the Roman empire – whose cosmos, in the dual meaning of both 'world' and 'order', depends upon the very maintenance of those boundaries – must regard anyone who deliberately crosses them as an intolerable threat. As Daniel Boyarin has demonstrated, women martyrs like Perpetua are perceived as 'aggressively masculinized', moving into an unacceptably (to the dominant) combative role while men martyrs forfeit masculinity by their willingness to submit their bodies to be broken by the dominant male authorities.[23]

Yet Perpetua's transgression of those boundaries, as her own narrative shows, is deliberate, and it enables her at least symbolically to break down other boundaries in the construction of a new, uniquely 'Christian' identity that belongs to a new family and that is neither male nor female while simultaneously both. The story begins with the arrest of Vibia Perpetua, 'a newly married woman (*matrona*) of good family and upbringing' (*Martyrdom*, 2.1), whose parents and one brother are still living, and who, at the time of her arrest, is nursing an infant son. Except for the fact that she has been arrested, and that in the company of slaves, Perpetua seems to exemplify up to this point the contemporary Roman matronly ideal. She comes from a good family and has done the expected thing by marrying and producing a son. The absence of any appearance of a husband is not, in the context, strange, since a young Roman married woman's father played a more decisive role in her life than her spouse did.[24]

Indeed, it is Perpetua's father (her mother is mentioned in *Martyrdom*, 2.2, but never appears or speaks) who precipitates her transgression of expected social roles. He attempts to persuade her not to persist in her allegiance to Christianity, upon which she replies that she cannot 'be called anything other than' a Christian (3.2). Although he is angry enough to attempt to strike her, in the end she rejoices that he is 'vanquished along with his diabolical arguments' (3.3). Having conquered one representative of the devil, Perpetua suits ritual to word and is baptized as a Christian. Since she now truly has 'the name' whose mere possession is a crime (3.5; 6.2), this act marks the beginning of her assumption of a new identity eventually realized in her death, the crossing of the final boundary. Gradually, she sheds her old identity, assisted in the process by visions of the other world which she is 'greatly privileged' to be granted (4.1) and which she shares as revelations of their heavenly future with

---

(Nijmegen: Dekkers and Van de Vegt, 1936). See the recent English translation and commentary by Maureen A. Tilley, 'The Passion of Saints Perpetua and Felicity', in Richard Valantasis (ed.), *Religions of Late Antiquity in Practice* (Princeton Readings in Religion; Princeton, NJ and Oxford: Princeton University Press, 2000), pp. 387–97.

23 Daniel Boyarin, *Dying for God: Martyrdom and the Making of Christianity and Judaism* (Stanford, CA: Stanford University Press, 1999), p. 75.

24 Gillian Clark, *Women in Late Antiquity: Pagan and Christian Lifestyles* (Oxford: Clarendon Press, 1993), p. 15. Some later orthodox interpreters of her story were so shocked by the absence of a husband that they supplied one, but Daniel Boyarin (*Dying for God,* p. 82) suggests that for some others, Perpetua's 'continued marital life is interpreted as sexual violation'. Carolyn Osiek both tidies up and complicates the story by suggesting that Perpetua's fellow martyr Saturus was her husband ('Perpetua's Husband', *JECS* 10 (2002), pp. 287–90 [290]).

her fellow-prisoners. For the Christian reader after the legalization of Christianity, this story becomes on the one hand prophetic, since the 'demonic' pagan government is not the ultimate commonwealth, but on the other might possibly be dangerous or at least problematic if the 'government' itself is Christian; witness the changing fates of the Book of Revelation.

In her first vision, Perpetua climbs up a narrow, dangerous ladder or staircase, to which are attached sharp metal weapons intended to mangle the flesh of those who do not concentrate on the path. Another terror is a great dragon, an obvious representation of Satan (cf. Rev. 12.3–9), upon whose head, with the 'name of Christ Jesus' Perpetua steps (4.6). With another manifestation of Satan defeated, she enters an expansive garden, symbolic of paradise in the Christian repertoire. There, 'a grey-haired man (*hominem canem*) in shepherd's garb' (4.8), the substitute heavenly father for her earthbound father and his 'diabolical arguments' (cf. 6.3), gives her sweet sheep's milk cheese to eat, perhaps symbolizing her spiritual rebirth and infancy.[25] The dream convinces her that 'from now on', she and her fellow prisoners could have no hope 'in this life' (4.10). Figuratively, she has already turned heavenward, and the identity she will now be constructing, like that of the Christians in the last days (Acts 2.16–17), will be spiritual, no longer bound to earth.[26]

Perpetua's earthly father continues to attempt to dissuade her from her climb of the symbolic ladder of martyrdom that leads to heaven and a transformed identity. He appeals to her with all of her earthly ties, with pity for him and the love he has shown her 'above all your brothers' (5.2), a plea that is not a common one in a society that might expose its daughters at infancy, but that is not entirely unknown, given Cicero's affection for his daughter Tullia and his grief at her death.[27] He appeals to her not to disgrace her family publicly, and he subtly points to its prominence by flattering her with the honorific title of 'lady' (*domina*, 5.5), designating the female head of a household, rather than 'daughter' (*filia*), one who can be commanded. (Perhaps here she has symbolically if not actually taken the place of her own mother, the 'head female' of the household.) He appeals to her a final time to have pity on her infant son and sacrifice to the emperor. Perpetua, though pitying her father, remains adamant. When he refuses to return her baby – perhaps because she has in his eyes forfeited her status as mother, perhaps because of the baby's potential as a male heir – Perpetua's last tie to familial roles on earth is severed. As she relates it, she has no more anxiety on the baby's account and all mention of him fades from her story. Symbolically, her last 'hope in this life' (cf. 4.10) is truly gone – possibly well gone.

Felicity's motherhood throughout provides a subtle counterpoint for Perpetua's. Because Felicity is a slave-woman, neither her family nor her child's father (like Perpetua's husband, absent, but in her case more expectedly) would necessarily provide significant ties that she needs to break; rather, they have broken with her. Nor is Felicity considered 'greatly privileged', even in this extreme situation. It is

---

25 See Patricia Cox Miller, *Dreams in Late Antiquity: Studies in the Imagination of a Culture* (Princeton, NJ: Princeton University Press, 1994), pp. 156–57.

26 Miller, *Dreams in Late Antiquity*, pp. 156–57.

27 Cicero refers to Tullia in a letter to his wife Terentia as '*lux nostra*' (our light) (*Ad familiares 14.5*) and is inconsolable at her death (*Ad familiares 4.5*, To Servius Sulpicius).

not unusual for a slave to be considered a criminal; it is for a free woman or man to be considered so. Her pregnancy plays a more complicated role. On the one hand, it serves to limit her to the expected role of a slave-woman, to bear children (presumably for the master). On the other, she eventually succeeds in 'overcoming' her role's limitations. Perpetua is later also to help Felicity to her feet in the arena (20.6); they stand together in their martyrdom, thus pointedly demonstrating the solidarity of Christians as well as their rejection of socially mandated class roles.

Perpetua's next two visions concern a dead member of her family, her brother Dinocrates. In the first vision, Perpetua sees Dinocrates suffering in a 'dark hole' where he is 'hot and thirsty' and unable to relieve his distress (7.7). Troubled by her vision, Perpetua prays for him daily until she receives a second vision in which her brother is 'clean, well-dressed, and refreshed', and has enough water to drink (8.1–3). Her power to transform Dinocrates's extraterrestrial state comes from the fact that she has been imprisoned and is about to die in a fight with the beasts. In other words, from her liminal but blessed status between earth and heaven, she is able to grant release for Dinocrates, who is also in a liminal, although less blessed state. In a similar vein, Thecla is to deliver the Antiochene noblewoman Tryphaena's dead daughter Falconilla in repayment for Tryphaena's 'keeping her chaste' before her final trials in the arena in Antioch (*APTh* 8.1–2). In both stories, the power of the confessor, already on the border between life and death, can better enhance the afterlife of the dead. Once more, as in the case of the Columbine martyrs, the martyr 'dies to redeem' those who could not or did not confess the martyr's faith.

Perpetua's final transformation is yet to come. With her biological family, living and dead, now behind her, she dreams that she is led into an arena where her clothing is stripped off – the symbol of a shocking loss of modesty for a matron, with the suggestion of sexual violation.[28] But ultimately her nakedness does not matter since suddenly she becomes a man, a gladiator being prepared in typical fashion by stripping (the torso alone remained naked), girding of the loins and oiling for combat with an Egyptian, who Perpetua later realizes is yet another manifestation of the devil (*me ... contra diabolum esse pugnaturam*). In the contest, she/he bests the Egyptian by aggressively kicking his face and finally by treading on his head as she trod upon the head of the serpent in her first vision. Triumphant, she/he begins to walk towards the 'Gate of Life', the gate for those victorious in the arena (10.5–13). Perpetua's diary ends here with the words, 'About what happened at the contest [martyrdom] itself let him write of it who will' (10.15).[29]

In the account of the contest, often attributed to Tertullian, Perpetua is portrayed as acting 'as if she were already treading on the Egyptian's head' (18.7), that is, with *virtus* (literally, 'manliness') or courage, in the masculine identity of her dream. Boldly, she instructs the others to stand fast and show no weakness. Ironically,

---

28 Eusebius, *HE* 9.1 claims that in the martyrdoms at Thebais under Diocletian, women were hanged 'head downward, their bodies completely naked without a morsel of clothing, presenting thus the most shameful, brutal, and inhuman of all spectacles to everyone watching' (Eusebius, *The History of the Church from Christ to Constantine*, translated and with an introduction by G.A. Williamson [New York: New York University Press, 1966], p. 337).

29 This last sentence almost irresistibly invites the hermeneutically suspicious reader to conjecture that the author of Perpetua's martyrdom claims that he is willed to write it by the martyr herself, again raising doubts about the authenticity of the diary.

however, the narrator (presumably male) also draws attention to her femaleness. She is called the 'wife (*matrona*) of Christ, the beloved (*dilecta*) of God' (18.2).[30] When she is matched along with Felicity in a contest with a 'wild heifer', they are both stripped naked (20.1–2). While Perpetua clearly takes the leading role here, as she has throughout the account – a quasi-Apocryphal Act – she is paired with Felicity, who appears here not as slave but as her equal, once again demonstrably fulfilling the prophecy of Joel 2.28–32 quoted in Acts 2.16–17. Martyrdom appears to level all status indicators. Unlike the male public nakedness appropriate for combat, such as that of the gladiator of her dream, the public nudity of the women in the arena clearly is intended to emphasize and humiliate their sex. The brutal crowd is horrified at what even they recognize as a shameful sight and demand that the women be clothed (20.2–3). When Perpetua (reclothed) is tossed by the heifer, she thinks 'more about her modesty than of her pain' (20.4); she is concerned about the rip in her tunic and about her dishevelled hair, indications of a woman who is not 'modest' and therefore not virtuous. Finally, as Perpetua is about to be dispatched by a young gladiator who cannot control his trembling arm, she guides his sword to her throat, in a classic theatrical gesture of brave but womanly death.[31]

Tertullian, Perpetua's contemporary, pointed to the final vision of 'this most heroic martyr' as evidence of his contention that only through martyrdom, the public shedding of blood, could a Christian enter Paradise before the second coming (*An.* 51.6). For some Christians, members of the 'New Prophecy' or Montanists to which sect Tertullian later converted, Perpetua's story illustrated three significant beliefs. First, persecution would increase as a sign of the end-times and the envisioned return of Christ; second, prophetic visions and dreams would also increase. Finally and perhaps most controversial, the 'new world', also known as the Kingdom of God or Kingdom of Heaven, was symbolized by the 'unity of male and female in Christ, a world in which Christ appeared to them in the form of a woman as well as in the form of a man'.[32]

Because of these beliefs, women – who were also considered more 'open' to prophetic ecstasy than men, as Perpetua's story illustrates – could hold leading positions within those Churches that accepted the validity of the New Prophecy. Furthermore, it was widely held by Christian authorities that persons imprisoned for the faith ('confessors') who later died for it (the true 'martyrs') were granted 'extraordinary power', the 'power of the keys' (cf. Mt. 16.19) to 'forgive the sins

---

30 Thomas Heffernan, *Sacred Biography* (New York: Oxford, 1988), p. 190, says that this is the earliest instance of the *topos* of Christ as the 'Bridegroom of the Saint'. It may thus be that Christ is the substitute for Perpetua's missing husband, just as the grey-haired shepherd (God) substitutes for her unsatisfactory father.

31 Nicole Loraux, *Tragic Ways of Killing a Woman* (trans. Anthony Forster; Cambridge, MA: Harvard University Press, 1987), pp. 49–65.

32 Frederick C. Klawiter, 'The Role of Martyrdom and Persecution in Developing the Priestly Authority of Women in Early Christianity', *CH* 49.3 (September, 1980), pp. 251–61 (260). Nevertheless, one might also read Perpetua's story showing the heroic martyrdom of a woman, carefully paired with that of a man – Saturus – and one that gains her the respectability in heaven as *matrona Christi* and the *dilecta Dei* that she had in life. By her martyrdom (albeit from the 'right' authority) she recovers the gender roles she forsook in life. Dead, she can be employed to support either position. Like Cassie Bernall and Rachel Scott, she has forfeited earthly marriage for higher, heavenly marriage.

of those who had lost the faith', or conversely not to readmit them to communion, a power traditionally given to the two top levels of clerical authority, bishops and presbyters. Before the end of the second century, a male confessor released from prison had the status and authority of a presbyter.[33] Already by the mid-100s, whether women had that status, as well as the honour accorded to such 'voluntary' martyrs and to prophets and visionaries, was a source of sharp dissension within Christian Churches holding to the New Prophecy and those who called themselves Orthodox. Both groups 'as late as the fifth century claimed Perpetua's example' when there was no longer any danger of persecution by the pagan state.[34] A further complicating factor in North Africa was the Donatist imitation of the martyrs in resisting imperial authority.[35] Nevertheless, female martyrs and confessors, while revered by the faithful as representing the suffering Christ, were given no 'concrete authority' by the pre-Constantinian Orthodox Church that eventually suppressed the New Prophecy as a heresy: that authority was reserved for the male bishop as Christ's institutional embodiment on earth.[36] In this development, the great Orthodox bishop Augustine might have the last, rather ambiguous word. In his first sermon on the feast-day of the martyrdom of Perpetua and Felicity (7 March), he writes, 'What, then, is more glorious than these women, whom men more easily admire than imitate ...? According to the inner human, they are found neither male nor female; so that even in those who are feminine in body, their manliness of mind might leave behind the sex of their flesh' (*Serm.* 281.1.1, *Patrologia latina* 38:1281). Climbing the stairway to heaven is possible only for women who have become men, but only in death; such authority is an ironic impossibility in the world.[37]

While martyrdom as confessing the faith before a hostile world was no longer possible for Christians after the Edict of Toleration in the fourth century, Christian male writers like John Chrysostom, Gregory of Nyssa, Ambrose and Augustine himself tended to portray abstinence from the flesh, the struggle to overcome 'carnal lust and the world', as an effective substitute for martyrdom.[38] Thus one might really 'buy', albeit negatively through renunciation, the stairway to heaven. This is not really so surprising since, as Maureen A. Tilley convincingly shows, the already widespread ascetic practices of pre-Constantinian Christianity had allowed the martyrs to 'reconfigure their bodies as battleground'. The multiple renunciations of asceticism 'made possible the renunciation of mortal life itself'.[39] Yet women

33 Klawiter, 'The Role of Martyrdom', p. 254.

34 Klawiter, 'The Role of Martyrdom', p. 254.

35 J. Patout Burns, 'Authority and Power: The Role of the Martyrs in the African Church in the Fifth Century', n.p. (cited 24 June 2005; online: http://divinity.library.vanderbilt.edu/burns/chroma/saints/martburn.html).

36 Ann Jensen, *God's Self-Confident Daughters: Early Christianity and the Liberation of Women* (trans. O.C. Dean; Louisville, KY: Westminster/John Knox, 1996), p. 120.

37 For a discussion of the gaining of power by early Christian women, including Perpetua and Thecla, through assuming male roles, see Gail Paterson Corrington (Gail Corrington Streete), *Her Image of Salvation: Female Saviors and Formative Christianity* (Gender and the Biblical Tradition; Louisville, KY: Westminster/John Knox Press, 1992), pp. 24–25.

38 Gillian Cloke, *This Female Man of God: Women and Spiritual Power in the Patristic Age, AD 350–450* (London and New York: Routledge, 1995), p. 33.

39 Maureen A. Tilley, 'The Ascetic Body and the (Un)making of the World of the Martyr', *JAAR* 59.3 (1991), pp. 467–79.

who chose the ascetic path did not do so merely as the result of patristic rhetoric; quite possibly they followed an empowering model of their own, like Thecla. The ground, however, had already been prepared by examples like that of Perpetua, whose rejection of earthly familial roles is a kind of athletic training or *askesis* that culminates in her role as the victorious gladiator.

The story of Thecla is a rather complex one, unlike that of Perpetua, probably because she proved to be a much more ambiguous character, at least for the orthodox Western Church that failed to 'domesticate' her and that rejected as a forgery and later declared heretical the *Acts of Paul and Thecla* (Tertullian, *Bapt.*, 17). Dennis R. MacDonald contends that the account of Thecla, incorporated with an apocryphal *Acts of Paul*, originated from stories told by and to ascetic women who used Thecla's story to legitimate their own claims to ministry, particularly to baptism and teaching, within the institutional Church.[40] As such, it represents, as does the *Martyrdom of Perpetua and Felicity*, a struggle over an appropriate understanding of the division between a society and its values viewed as 'worldly', and a religion oriented 'against this world'. A rejection of 'this world and its social norms may be all very well when the world is defined as anti-Christian, but when it becomes defined as a Christian world in which the norms rejected are Roman social norms that have been Christianized, a very different story emerges. As Daniel Boyarin observes, 'No longer simply the victorious, valorous, virilized gladiator, à la Perpetua, the fourth-century [i.e. post-Constantine] virgin martyr was now partially rewritten via the intertexts as a model of passive, female virtue.'[41] The definition of sexuality and of its application to gender become part of the rhetoric of this struggle.

The story of Thecla begins, like that of Perpetua, with an upper-class young woman as its heroine. Thecla, a 'noble virgin of Iconium', is mesmerized, even enchanted, when she hears the charismatic word of the celibate life preached by the apostle Paul (*Acts of Paul and Thecla* 7 [2.2]).[42] Night and day she sits in the window of her house, literally on the borderline between the appropriate sphere for a respectable unmarried woman (inside the house) and the sphere in which she should not appear (outside), hanging on Paul's every word. In every respect, she appears like the lovesick maiden of a romance. Indeed, she is described as 'a spider bound at the window' (9 [2.8]) by her mother, Theocleia, who worries, with an irony that could not escape an ascetic Christian reader, that 'so modest' a virgin can be so troubled by her passion for 'one single God only and ... a pure [i.e. celibate] life' (9 [2.7]). Thecla's fiancé, Thamyris, tries to dissuade Thecla, as Perpetua's father had tried to dissuade

---

40 Dennis R. MacDonald, *The Legend and the Apostle: The Battle for Paul in Story and Canon* (Philadelphia, PA: Westminster Press, 1983), pp. 34–37.

41 Boyarin, *Dying for God*, pp. 75–76.

42 Translation and numbering taken from Kraemer (ed.), *Maenads, Martyrs*, pp. 280–88, which prints only the portion of the *Acts of Paul and Thecla* in which Thecla herself appears, a portion sometimes referred to as the *Acts of Thecla* (e.g. Bart D. Ehrman, *After the New Testament: A Reader in Early Christianity* [New York and Oxford: Oxford University Press, 1999], pp. 278–84). Numbers in brackets represent alternative numbering taken from the longer English translation by W. Hone, *The Apocryphal New Testament* (London, 1820), pp. 99–111, in the St Pachomius Orthodox Library, n.p. (cited September/October, 1995; online: http://www.ocf.org/Orthodox page//reading/ St. Pachomius/index.html). Greek text is R.A. Lipsius and M. Bonnet, *Acta Apostolorum Apocrypha* (Darmstadt: Wissenschaftliche Buchgesellschaft, 1959), Vol. 1, pp. 235–72.

her, out of love. Yet this loyalty of the lover, a staple of the Greek romance, indicates in this Christian anti-romance the lust of a pagan male. Unmoved and unspeaking, Thecla turns away from her earthly lover and concentrates, not on Paul himself, but on his word, whereupon Thamyris weeps 'for the loss of a wife', Theocleia 'for a daughter', and the female slaves 'for a mistress' (10 [2.11]). Like Perpetua, Thecla while living has chosen to become dead to her family and hence to the social roles that familial status requires of women. When Paul is arrested and imprisoned for preaching against marriage, Thecla violates norms of respectable female conduct by going out of her house alone at night and by bribing the jailer so that she may visit and talk to Paul, a male 'stranger' and not a family member (18 [4.10–11]). When she too is arrested, largely because of her immodest and abnormal behaviour, she 'head[s] off, joyfully exulting' (20 [5.5]); when the governor asks her why she does not marry Thamyris, 'according to the law of the Iconians' (20 [5.7]), she refuses to answer and so shows public disrespect for male social and governmental authority. So 'unnatural' and threatening is her behaviour that her own mother demands that the 'un-bride' be burned as an example lest other women follow this strange teaching and avoid marriage (20 [5.8]). We have no satisfactory explanation of the cause of Theocleia's violent reaction, but one explanation might be that the mother hopes to hold onto, or perhaps improve, her status as one of the 'first citizens' of Iconium by a strategic marriage that is thwarted by this strange, illegitimate and cult-like teaching.[43] Thecla has thus nullified her status as a woman of whom marriage might legitimately be expected.

As if to reinforce the fact that Thecla's behaviour is immodest and shameless, the narrative depicts her as brought into the arena naked to be burned, and thus publicly exposed in a shameful and shaming act. Such is Thecla's 'power' (22 [5.13]),[44] however, that God causes a hailstorm, the fire is put out, and Thecla is saved. Thecla (quite wisely) leaves Iconium to look for Paul, whom she eventually finds; she tells him that she will cut her hair short (so that she will look like a man and presumably not be accosted as a woman) and follow him wherever he goes. Rather uncourageously, ignoring Thecla's suggestion for defusing her lust potential, Paul says that she is too beautiful, possibly for her own good, and might encounter another 'temptation' (25 [7.13]). Again, the irony of this statement cannot be lost: Paul's own appearance is far from that of the beautiful young men of the Greek romances. Earlier the narrative describes him as short, balding and bandy-legged with a hooked nose ([1.7]). There is little surface beauty to tempt Thecla: might it be that her beauty would tempt Paul? Certainly in both the Iconian and Antiochene parts of the story Paul assiduously avoids her, perhaps because he represents the kind of Christian male for whom a woman who chooses itinerancy – albeit as an encratite – will be a problem. When she begs him to 'give her the seal' of baptism as a defence against temptation, the kind of Christian force-field that protects virgins in

43 The parallel is not a complete one, but Theocleia's reaction suggests that of Misty Bernall when she finds out that her daughter is first engaged in activities that appear to make her 'unreachable' (Bernall, *She Said Yes*, p. 63) and later when she meets the evangelical Jamie, 'not my idea of a nice Christian girl' (p. 82).

44 Thecla's 'power', like that of many other women in the Apocryphal Acts, comes from her steadfast celibacy. See Corrington (Streete), *Her Image*, pp. 182–83.

brothels in countless Christian stories (25 [6.14–15]),[45] he refuses and urges her to 'have patience', presumably to endure other trials until she has proven herself worthy. This entire exchange is fraught with gender irony and perhaps even satire in that Paul is supposed to be the one whose manly self-control would make him impervious to temptation and whose recognized authority might quell any advances on Thecla's part. Why would anyone want to satirize Paul? Perhaps to use him as an example of male claims against the fitness of women to be prophets, teachers and apostles; Paul is the reluctant male authority who is an unworthy foil for Thecla's worth.

Paul's behaviour towards Thecla becomes even more cowardly and hence 'unmanly'. When Thecla follows him to Antioch, the 'first man of the Antiochenes' (26 [7.2]), an official named Alexander, seeks to seduce her. Perhaps thinking that Paul is her pimp, Alexander tries to bribe him, whereupon Paul, in what may be a deliberate parody of Peter's betrayal of Christ (Mk 14.66–72; Mt. 26.69–75; Lk. 22.54–62; Jn 18.15–18, 25–27), claims, 'I don't know the woman of whom you speak, nor is she mine' (26 [7.3]). When Alexander, thinking that she is a loose woman after Paul denies her, tries to embrace her on the public street, boldly, Thecla stands upon her own public authority as 'the first woman of the Iconians' (26 [7.4]) and no low-status woman to be abused. Thecla's actual status is not apparent to Alexander because it is at variance with the expected; he sees her only as someone connected to Paul (wife? mistress? daughter?) until Paul corrects him, thus exposing Thecla as sexual prey. She defends herself by ripping his cloak and taking his crown, symbol of his authority as a Roman official, off his head, thus shaming him publicly, 'making him a laughingstock' (26 [7.5]). Symbolically, Thecla the woman, who should be the submissive object of his desire, unmans Alexander, the authoritative man. The power of the Christian virgin is more than a match for that of a lustful pagan male.

At this point we move from the world of Iconium, Thecla's hometown, dominated by the male values of female enclosure, modesty and marriage, to the female-dominated world of Antioch, which decries and opposes these values even before the conversion of its women to Christianity. Margaret P. Aymer proposes that the discrepancy between these two stories represents the work of an editor responding to the very different ways in which the early Church viewed Thecla. The orthodox world praised her virginity as an example of the celibate life for women, but only at the instigation and under the authority of men; the heterodox world continued to allow independent charismatic authority to unmarried women who led the ascetic life. She suggests that Iconium and Antioch are the foci of two originally separate stories about Thecla, the Iconian story being the 'orthodox' version and the Antiochene story perhaps the original.[46] Regardless of which story was first, it seems that the combined version allows a tension between the two to stand. Thecla's choice in the redacted version is both instigated and approved by Paul, the male authority.

In the Antiochene story, women take on power and achieve the justice for Thecla that was turned on her in Iconium. Male lust remains unsatisfied and male authority defused, events that in Iconium took an act of God to accomplish, since both men and women, young and old, were complicit in the attempt to punish Thecla for

---

45 Boyarin, *Dying for God*, p. 87.

46 Margaret P. Aymer, 'Hailstorms and Fireballs: Redaction, World Creation, and Resistance in the *Acts of Paul and Thecla*', *Semeia* 79 (1997), pp. 45–62 (56).

defying the sanctioned norm. In Antioch, Alexander, seeking to recover from the disgrace to his male honour, orders Thecla to be put to the beasts, whereupon the leading women, including the wealthy and prominent 'queen' Tryphaena – who is later to substitute for Thecla's rejecting mother as Thecla substitutes for Tryphaena's dead daughter – cry out, 'An evil judgment! An impious judgment!' (27 [8.1]). At Thecla's request, which Alexander inexplicably grants (perhaps he has no power to resist), Tryphaena is given care of Thecla in order that she be kept 'pure' (27 [8.1]) until her battle in the arena. Tryphaena's dead daughter, Falconilla, appears to her in a vision and intimates that Tryphaena should adopt Thecla as her daughter so that with the imprisoned martyr's power, as Perpetua did for Dinocrates, she might intercede for Falconilla 'to be translated to the place of the righteous' (28 [8.5]). There is also the possibility that Thecla's prayer for Falconilla has a greater chance to be granted because of Tryphaena's righteous deed in helping preserve Thecla's purity.

In the ensuing scene in the arena, the women of Antioch keep crying out against the injustice of the event. Even the beasts take on the male vs. female conflict: Thecla is spared by a lioness that attacks and kills the male lion that was set upon her.[47] Finally, seeing a ditch with ravening seals into which the governor has prepared to throw her, Thecla seizes the initiative and throws herself in, declaring, 'I baptize myself on the last day!' (34 [9.7]),[48] whereupon the seals are blasted by lightning. As if this were not enough, Thecla is clothed with a divine 'cloud of fire' (34 [9.9]) recalling the epiphany of God in a pillar of fire in Exod. 13.21–22. No beasts can touch her through this protective cloud and – perhaps more important, remembering that this is a public arena and recalling the example of Perpetua – no one can see her naked. Next, Alexander the scorned suitor begs that more beasts be summoned. They are no match for the women, who bombard them with flowers and sweet perfumes so that they are drugged. Still undaunted, Alexander tries to kill Thecla by tying her between bulls whose testicles are goaded with red-hot irons. (It takes little imagination to figure out the symbolism here!)[49] Miraculously, the fire burns through the ropes, and Thecla once more is saved, but Tryphaena, who does not possess the power of Thecla's determined virginity, faints. Alarmed because Tryphaena is the emperor's relative,[50] the governor, who is now justifiably fearful of Thecla's demonstrated power, releases her.

After converting the household of the now-revived Tryphaena and assuming a masculine guise (as she had previously offered to do in order to follow Paul) by

47 Boyarin, *Dying for God*, p. 74, points out that Thecla's presentation of her 'vital parts' to the (male) lions is an 'obvious eroticized displacement of the offer of her sexual parts' to her rejected male pagan partner. Obviously also, the ravening beasts are a trope representing male sexual lust and an intended violation of the woman's body even more serious than the rending of flesh in torture (so Ambrose of Milan's *De virginibus*). Ambrose further claims that the male lion about to tear Thecla apart turned into a female and thus spared her (Boyarin, *Dying for God*, p. 75).

48 The Hone translation in the St Pachomius Orthodox Library makes this passive – 'I am this last day baptized' – perhaps to avoid giving any impression of a woman's baptizing herself.

49 Cf. Ross Shepard Kraemer, *Her Share of the Blessings: Women's Religions Among Pagans, Jews, and Christians in the Greco-Roman World* (New York and Oxford: Oxford University Press, 1992), p. 152.

50 There is an historical queen, Antonia Tryphaena, mother of Polemo II, king of Pontus, who was a relative of the emperor Claudius. But it is unlikely that this is that Tryphaena. Perhaps the name is borrowed to lend a note of verisimilitude to the story.

sewing her woman's garments into a man's cloak, Thecla sets off to find Paul. At first, not having the perception to take her male disguise as indicative of her 'male' nature, Paul is still suspicious of her, but when she asserts that she has 'taken the bath' (i.e. been baptized, 40 [10.2]) with the aid of Christ, and announces her intention of going back to Iconium, he (probably with relief) gives her his blessing, 'Go and teach the word of God' (41 [10.4]). Reaching Iconium, Thecla finds Thamyris dead and does not bother about his posthumous salvation as she did for Falconilla at Tryphaena's request, but converts her mother, Theocleia. Iconium, like Antioch, has been transformed into a manifestation of the virgin power of Thecla, now having assumed the identity of the male apostle. After that, she 'headed off to Seleucia, where, after enlightening many with the word of God, she slept with a fine sleep' (43).[51]

Another, longer version of the *Acts of Thecla*, detached from the *Acts of Paul* and incorporated by Pseudo-Basil of Seleucia into his *Life and Miracles of St Thecla* (fifth century),[52] continues the list of triumphs and tribulations out of which she always emerges victorious, casting out demons and healing the sick (primarily women). Finally, escaping from the hands of 'wicked and unreasonable men' who attempt to rape her, she takes refuge in a cave, which miraculously closes to shut her in. There she leads the celibate life of an enclosed anchorite until 'the Lord translated her' across the boundary to heaven (*Acts of Paul and Thecla* 11.8–15).[53]

Unlike the story of Perpetua, that of Thecla had a mixed reception, perhaps from its very first circulation in folktales and oral traditions. On the one hand, virginity and the ascetic life, the main subject of the *Acts of Paul and Thecla*, were for many Christians, male and female, the preferred way to live in yet out of this world.[54] In this regard, many Christian women, particularly those who made up the aristocracy post-Constantine, 'took as their apostolic model the legendary St. Thecla, apocryphal disciple of St. Paul, who was heavily drawn on in this period in writings directed at women'.[55] Some prominent churchmen also praised Thecla. Ambrose, Augustine's mentor and bishop of Milan, of which city Thecla was the patron saint, praised Thecla and Mary of Nazareth, mother of Christ, as ideals of Christian virginity, to his sister Marcellina: 'Therefore let Saint Mary inform you of the discipline for life; let Thecla teach you how to die' (*Virg.* 2.19–21). Ambrose illustrates the mode of Thecla's 'dying' by her 'offering up' her sexual organs to the lion, a rather unusual way to demonstrate virginity, although his point is that it is better to be eaten by

51 Thus ends the more commonly accepted version. In the longer version (*Acts of Paul and Thecla* 10.9–11, 17 in the Hone version) Theocleia 'gave no credit to the things which were said by the martyr Thecla, and Thecla perceived that she had discoursed to no purpose' [10.9–10].

52 Willi Rordorf, 'Tradition and Composition in the *Acts of Thecla*: The State of the Question', *Semeia* 38 (1986), pp. 43–52 (51–52).

53 Hone translation.

54 Here I disagree with Boyarin (*Dying for God*, p. 122) who cites Virginia Burrus, 'Word and Flesh: The Bodies and Sexuality of Ascetic Women in Christian Antiquity', *JFSR* 10 (1994), pp. 27–51 and Elizabeth Castelli, 'Imperial Reimaginings of Christian Origins: Epic in Prudentius's Poem', in *eadem* and Hal Taussig (eds.), *Reimagining Christian Origins: A Colloquium Honoring Burton L. Mack* (Valley Forge, PA: Trinity Press International, 1996), pp. 173–84 to claim that the 'powerful eroticization of Christian martyrology' is a product of fourth-century Christianity. Both Perpetua and Thecla's martyrdoms – written in the early third and late second centuries, respectively – are heavily eroticized.

55 Cloke, *This Female Man of God*, pp. 165–66.

lions than submit to men's lust.[56] The Christian teacher Jerome, whose friends and patrons included many aristocratic and ascetic women, praised one of them, Melania the Elder, as 'the new Thecla' (*Chron.* 329) and in a letter to a young woman, Eustochium, whom he was encouraging to adopt the virgin life, said that she would meet Thecla and Mary in heaven, together with her heavenly Bridegroom, Christ (*Ep.* 22.41).[57]

Yet Thecla was scarcely accorded the honour in the Western Churches that she had in the Eastern. The Latin father Tertullian, in a treatise on baptism against the teacher Quintilla, excoriates her use of the example of Thecla as a model to claim clerical authority for women:

> The impudence, moreover, of a woman who has appropriated [the office of] teaching, when not even the right of baptism is permitted to her! ... But if these practices [of allowing women to teach and baptize] are falsely ascribed to Paul, and they defend the example of Thecla for the license of women to teach and baptize, let them know that there is a presbyter in Asia, who fabricated that writing, heaping up works under his own name as if under Paul's, but being convicted and having confessed that he did it for the love of Paul, he was removed from his place. For what seems more credible, that the one would give a woman the power to teach and baptize, who assuredly did not even permit a woman to learn? [Cf. 1 Cor. 14.33–35; 1 Tim. 2.11–15][58]

Ambrose himself appears rather than Thecla to have preferred another, uniquely Roman martyr, Agnes, who has the advantage of Thecla in that supposedly she was not only was a virgin, but, unlike Thecla, she actually met her death by burning during the reign of the emperor Domitian.[59] Jerome, who broke with Melania the Elder, his 'new Thecla', over her support of a rival doctrine, was sceptical about the authenticity of the *Acts of Paul and Thecla*, as previously noted, and eventually substituted Agnes for Thecla as a model for virgins.[60] This ambivalent attitude of the Western fathers towards Thecla may have been the result of their concern 'lest the

---

56 This idea of 'dying daily' in devotion to God is emphasized by Dave McPherson, Cassie Bernall's youth minister, in Bernall, *She Said Yes*, pp. 136–37: 'The world looks at Cassie's "yes" of April 20, but we need to look at the daily "yes" she said day after day, month after month, before giving that final answer.'

57 Hayne, 'Thecla and the Church Fathers', pp. 210–11.

58 Tertullian, *Bapt.*, PL 1: 1326–29. Translation mine. While Tertullian's polemic against the *Acts of Paul and Thecla* is widely cited as evidence of its fraudulence, it seems likely that in an age widely known for pseudonymous works and with different standards for authenticity than our own, the allegation appears more an attack on a specific part of its content than on the manner of its composition. Although the North African Church Father Cyprian, who was bishop of Carthage in 248, within fifty years after Tertullian was writing and in the same city, mentions 'the devil baptizing through a woman' (*Ep.* 75.11; Hayne, 'Thecla and the Church Fathers,' p. 210), he does not specifically call its composition into question. The other Church Fathers who accepted the historicity of Thecla and her *Acts* do not mention the baptism either positively or negatively; it may be possible that in one version of the story (no longer extant) Thecla baptized others in addition to herself.

59 Cf. Hayne, 'Thecla and the Church Fathers', p. 211. Although Agnes is named (along with Thecla and others) in the *Depositio martyrum* of Rome (354), her martyrology was not written until the fifth century. Unlike Thecla, Agnes is still acknowledged in the West as a saint.

60 Hayne, 'Thecla and the Church Fathers', p. 211.

choice of a celibate life for women guarantee their equality with men'.[61] The Western Church seems to have endorsed this gradual 'cooling' towards the saint by removing her from the Roman calendar of the saints in 1969, along with other revered saints like Ursula and Barbara, whose stories were regarded as purely fictional.[62] In the Eastern Churches, on the other hand, Thecla and her story seem to have flourished. A 'vibrant' Thecla cult survived well into the late fifth century and beyond.[63] The fifth-century tourist, Egeria, describes the *martyrium* or shrine of St Thecla in the city of Seleucia, the home of an enclosed monastic community of men and women 'ruled' by her friend Marthana, 'a deaconess'. Egeria confesses herself thrilled with being at the site: 'When I had come there in the name of God, prayer was made at the shrine and the reading was from the *Acts of Thecla*. I gave thanks to God who deigned to fulfill all my desires ...'[64] What is curious about Egeria's account is that, like the story of Thecla in Antioch, the atmosphere seems to be mainly female. The *Acts* themselves are not referred to as the *Acts of Paul and Thecla*, but only *of Thecla*, a fact that may indicate the existence of an independent Thecla cycle revered by women and giving them warrant for a celibate lifestyle led by women rather than subject to regulation by male clerics. Just as there is no Paul to legitimate Thecla, there is no male to legitimate Marthana's authority over women and men. So attractive was the cult of Thecla to women that, like Egeria, two Syrian 'virgins', Marna and Cyra, walked fasting over two hundred miles to visit the shrine and convent.[65] Another apocryphal book of Acts featuring women, the *Acts of Xanthippe, Polyxena and Rebecca*, refers to Thecla as an example (*Acts*, 36) and uses the model of her converts.[66]

The Cappadocian Fathers Gregory of Nazianzus, who spent time in the convent at Seleucia, and Gregory of Nyssa also revere Thecla as a model for female conduct. The latter's reverential *Life* of his sister Macrina portrays her discoursing learnedly on the resurrection life, much in the same way as Methodius portrays Thecla discoursing on virginity, as a philosopher. In the *Life of St Macrina*, moreover, Gregory relates how his mother, pregnant with Macrina, had a vision of Thecla, and so that Thecla became both Macrina's 'secret name' and the model of her way of life.[67] A reverential *Life and Miracles of St Thecla*, produced in the fifth century, the heyday of Thecla-worship, has been attributed to no less a person than Basil, bishop of Seleucia. In it, according to Léonie Hayne, Thecla is both the evangelist and apostle of the *Acts*

61 Gail Corrington Streete, *The Strange Woman: Power and Sex in the Bible* (Louisville, KY: Westminster John Knox Press, 1997), p. 165.

62 Some saints removed from the Roman calendar, including Christopher, Philomena (1961) and Joan of Arc, are still venerated locally or regionally, according to the apostolic letter (*Mysterii paschalis*) of Paul VI. See above, n.17.

63 Sheila E. McGinn, 'The Acts of Thecla', in Elisabeth Schüssler Fiorenza (ed.), *Searching the Scriptures: A Feminist Commentary* (2 vols; New York: Crossroad, 1994), 2, pp. 800–28 (820).

64 Egeria, *Pilgrimage*, 23, in Patricia Wilson-Kastner (ed.), *A Lost Tradition: Women Writers of the Early Church* (Washington, DC: University Press of America, 1981), p. 77.

65 MacDonald, *Legend*, p. 93, citing Theodoret, *Hist. eccl.* 29.

66 MacDonald, *Legend*, p. 95.

67 Gregory of Nyssa, *Vita Macrinae* 960–62, cited by Hayne, 'Thecla and the Church Fathers', p. 213.

(which are incorporated into the *Life*), but also the champion of orthodoxy, even after her death.[68]

What, then, can explain the appeal to Thecla both to advocates of the female-dominated New Prophecy and heterodox exponents of the ascetic lifestyle that authorized its women to teach and baptize, and to champions of orthodoxy like Methodius, Gregory of Nazianzus and Gregory of Nyssa? What explains its simultaneous condemnation by Church authorities like Tertullian and the consignment of her story to extra-canonical and heretical status by the early sixth century? Insofar as Christian communities increasingly from the fourth century onward advocated celibacy and the ascetic life as virtuous, Thecla's refusal of marriage (especially marriage to a non-Christian) and resolute virginity could be praised. Thecla's popularity as a model for ascetic women is amply documented by the examples of real women like Egeria, Marna and Cyra, and Macrina. Her use as an icon for virginity by the Church Fathers, however, has a different motivation. When in the fifth century Thecla is transformed by Pseudo-Basil of Seleucia into a 'quasi-goddess' whose role as a model for virginity is simply '*the* virgin',[69] she is also transformed from a counter-cultural heroine who defies male civic and sexual authority, who does not need a male apostle in order to be baptized, and who carries out an independent preaching and teaching apostleship, into an advocate of Christian orthodoxy, a critic of Gnostics (whose theology allowed for women to be full equals within the Church), and a supporter of another revered virgin, Mary, the *Theotokos* or 'mother of God', who eventually replaces her as *the* virgin, in a kind of hierarchy of unattainability.[70] Mary is the one who once more embodies the ancient 'feminine' ideals of modesty and chastity and who adds one more: obedience. As long as no woman lays claim to preach, teach or baptize in Thecla's name, and as long as Thecla assists orthodoxy while supporting its ideal of female virginity, she serves the function as the Church-approved role model. Like Perpetua, she has figuratively 'bought' (and paid for) the stairway to orthodox heaven by becoming enshrined as a martyr rather than as an example for living women. As the varied accounts of Cassie Bernall, Rachel Scott and Valeen Schnurr show, the meaning given to the tragic deaths of a Cassie or a Rachel by their chroniclers robs the life of a Valeen of its utility, since it cannot be used to promote a specific ideological agenda. Although it has been made abundantly clear since the Columbine shooting that 'the girl who said yes' was Valeen, and although, as noted by her interviewer, *Washington Post* journalist Hanna Rosin, 'It's frustrating to see someone else canonized for your miracle', Valeen herself is reluctant to confront 'an American Christian community that's found its most effective symbol in decades'.[71]

68 Hayne, 'Thecla and the Church Fathers,' pp. 213–14. The way in which Thecla is portrayed as a champion of orthodox Christianity is similar to the way in which the Columbine martyrs, Cassie and Rachel, are used to defend evangelical Christianity.

69 Jensen, *God's Self-Confident Daughters*, p. 80. 'Quasi-goddess' is her term, which she does not explain, but perhaps what is meant here is a female personality that is unattainable by any human female; this explanation would be consonant with Jensen's characterizing of Pseudo-Basil's *Life and Miracles of St Thecla* as 'misogynistic' (80).

70 Cf. Hayne, 'Thecla and the Church Fathers', pp. 214–25; Jensen, *God's Self-Confident Daughters*, p. 80.

71 Rosin, 'Columbine girl', p. A-23.

The myth of the dead martyrs, especially Cassie, had become that strong, despite the fact that Valeen's response to the question, 'Do you believe in God?' is characterized by her in terms reminiscent of Perpetua's response to her father, that she cannot be called anything other than Christian (*Martyrdom* 3.2): 'I don't think of it as bravery. I think of it as what I said because it's true, because it's just me. What else was I going to say?'[72] The 'Columbine martyrs' were promoted as models for appropriate Christian behaviour, and according to one account written by a sceptical 15-year-old young woman, Rachel Williams, the story 'sparked ... a Christian-sanctified death wish', leading one sophomore woman to remark, 'God has laid it on my heart that I'm going to be martyred ... When I told one of my friends, he said, "That's awesome, I wish it could happen to me."'[73] Once again, she who buys the stairway to heaven must be prepared to pay for it by putting her life at the mythologizing disposal of others for whom 'truth is a trifle'.[74] But as a model for women's behaviour, the stairway to heaven may prove too costly a trifle.[75]

72 Rosin, 'Columbine girl', p. A-23.
73 Rachel Williams, 'Rachel's Other Page: Truth Doesn't Matter', n.p. (cited 26 June 2005; dated 24 October 1999; Online: http://members.tripod.com/rachelw2/rotruth.html).
74 Rosin, 'Columbine girl,' p. A-23.
75 This article was completed without knowledge of and before the publication of Elizabeth Castelli's *Martyrdom and Memory: Early Christian Culture Making* (New York: Columbia University Press, 2004), which treats some of the same subjects, particularly the Columbine martyrdoms.

Sexual Defence by Proxy: Interpreting Women's Fasting in the *Acts of Xanthippe and Polyxena*[1]

Jill C. Gorman

And since (Melania) feared that one of them might fall out of pride in excessive mortification, she said, 'Of all the virtues, fasting is the least. Just as a bride, radiant in every kind of finery, cannot wear black shoes, but adorns even her feet along with the rest of her body, so also does the soul need fasting along with all the other virtues. If someone is eager to perform the good deed of fasting apart from the other virtues, she is like a bride who leaves her body unclothed and adorns only her feet.' (*Life of Melania the Younger*, 43)

Anthropologists suggest that one of the main reasons people perform religious fasts is to communicate self-empowerment; this power exists in the form of control over one's own body, or in effecting power over the environment surrounding a person's body.[2] Certainly this was the case in Late Antique ascetic Christianity where the key to salvation was a conscious and steady control over the self and the desire for bodily pleasures.[3] However, as in any ideological system, this Christianity found itself in heated contestations over competing claims about what constituted 'proper' asceticism.[4] As the epigraph attributed to the fifth-century holy woman Melania implies, fasting was seen as a cause for holiness, but excessive fasting could be construed as prideful arrogance. The late fourth- or early fifth-century *Acts of Xanthippe and Polyxena* (*AXP*) offer multiple ideas of both what fasting could protect and how excessive fasting may have provided women with a form of empowerment that was perceived by the men in the community as a threatening bid for authority.

The *AXP* recounts the adventures of two women, Xanthippe and Polyxena. Xanthippe is a dutiful Christian ascetic who has renounced her marriage to her

---

1 I would like to thank all those people who have contributed to the development and growth of this paper, including Vasiliki Limberis, Laura Levitt and Steve Davies. I would also like to thank A.-J. Levine for her meticulous and substantive suggestions. While this paper reflects their suggestions and comments, the deficiencies within remain my own.

2 See Bruce Malina, *Christian Origins and Cultural Anthropology: Practical Models for Biblical Interpretation* (Atlanta: John Knox Press, 1986), pp. 200–204. For explanation of the efficacy of women's religious fasting in the Middle Ages and its emphasis on female piety, see Carolyn Walker Bynum, *Holy Feast and Holy Fast: The Religious Significance of Food to Medieval Women* (Berkeley: University of California Press, 1987).

3 For a comprehensive study of various approaches to studying asceticism, see Vincent Wimbush and Richard Valantasis (eds.), *Asceticism* (Oxford: Oxford University Press, 1995).

4 Just three books in the list of increasing scholarship devoted to this subject would include Virginia Burrus, *The Making of a Heretic: Gender, Authority, and the Priscillianist Controversy* (Berkeley: University of California Press, 1995); David Brakke, *Athanasius and the Politics of Asceticism* (Oxford: Clarendon Press, 1995); and Elizabeth A. Clark, *Reading Renunciation: Asceticism and Scripture in Early Christianity* (Princeton, NJ: Princeton University Press, 1999).

husband Probus upon the advice of the visiting apostle, Paul.[5] Polyxena is her Christian sister who is abducted by a 'cruel magician' in the middle of the tale, experiences numerous perilous misfortunes, and yet manages to return home to Xanthippe as a virgin.[6] During the reunion of the two women, Xanthippe reveals that she has maintained a forty-day fast on behalf of Polyxena so that her virginity would not be taken away. Having made this statement, Xanthippe dies, and Polyxena, we are told, 'remains by Paul the rest of her days in fear of her temptations' (42).

Though many approaches to the final scene could be taken,[7] this study attends to the depiction of Xanthippe's ascetic forty-day fast. My argument proceeds as follows. First, relying primarily on the study on fasting by Teresa Shaw, I situate Xanthippe's actions within the context of Late Antiquity's notions about the relationship between fasting and the regulation of sexual desire. Second, demonstrating in what ways this text is unique in its historical milieu, I argue that whereas fasting was commonly believed to be not only effective, but, indeed, necessary for protecting one's own sexual boundaries, the *AXP* offers an example of one woman fasting with the expressly stated purpose of defending another woman's sexual integrity. In short, I argue that the *AXP* gives us a woman who believes she performs a 'sexual defence by proxy'. Finally, I show how the *AXP* ultimately condemns Xanthippe's proxy fast; in so doing, it suggests that a proxy fast might have been viewed as threatening to male authority. This analysis of the representation of fasting in the *AXP* seeks to add to our understanding of the diverse ways in which fasting was viewed within the ascetic imagination in Late Antiquity.

Relating Fasting and Sexuality: The Legacy of Galen in the AXP

The *AXP* builds upon the common Late Antique notions concerning the efficacy of fasts in taming sexual desires: specifically, the representation of Xanthippe's proxy fast implies her belief that fasting can control such desire. In her solid study of the interlinking world of fasting and sexuality in Late Antiquity,[8] historian Teresa Shaw

---

5 I have argued elsewhere that the *AXP* demonstrates a transition in the way Christian ascetics represented themselves. The text sits between the second- and third-century Apocryphal Acts of the Apostles and the increasingly popular *vitae* of the fourth and fifth centuries. See Jill C. Gorman, 'Reading and Theorizing Women's Sexualities: The Representation of Women in the *Acts of Xanthippe and Polyxena*' (Ph.D. diss.,Temple University, 2003). An English translation of the *AXP* can be found in W.A. Craigie, 'The Acts of Xanthippe and Polyxena', in A. Menzies (ed.), *The Ante-Nicene Fathers*, Vol. 10 (10 vols.; Grand Rapids, MI: Eerdmans, 1980), pp. 203–17.

6 Though the text does not specifically state whether there is a biological relationship between these two women, the implicit evidence indicates that there is none. When Polyxena is returned to Spain and the women are reunited, Xanthippe refers to her as 'my true sister' (γνήσια ἀδελφή σοι). This emphasis on 'true' is consistent with the Christian notion of one who has a new family upon Christian conversion. It is for this reason that such familial appellations are common throughout early Christian literature, e.g. husbands and wives refer to each other as 'sister' and 'brother'.

7 For an approach to the final scene that is read within the context of the Greek romances, see Jill C. Gorman, 'Producing and Policing Female Sexuality: Thinking With and About "Same-Sex Desire" in the *Acts of Xanthippe and Polyxena*', *Journal of the History of Sexuality* 10.3–4 (2001), pp. 416–41.

8 Teresa M. Shaw, *The Burden of the Flesh: Fasting and Sexuality in Early Christianity* (Minneapolis, MN: Fortress Press, 1998).

re-examines scholarly notions that ancient ascetics were dualistic thinkers who engaged in 'self-denial' practices in an attempt to separate themselves from their bodies. Arguing that Antiquity had no divisions among medicine, philosophy, ethics and religion, Shaw shows that corporeal fasting was directly integrated with the ascetic's philosophical and ethical goals.

From the writings of medical authors such as Galen and theologians such as Basil of Caesarea and Evagrius of Pontus, Shaw demonstrates that fasting provided a link between the spiritual and the corporeal. For example, the second-century physician Galen believed that the soul had a corporeal nature, and thus he concluded that a person's virtue could be linked to his or her physical regimen. That is, control of bodily practices affected ethical formation. Galen writes: 'The character of the soul is corrupted by poor habits in food, drink, exercise, sights, sounds, and all the arts. Therefore the one pursuing health should be practiced in all these things, and should not think that it is proper only for the philosopher to shape the character of the soul.'[9] As Shaw demonstrates, Galen's integration of the corporeal with the intellectual and spiritual affected Christian thought. For example, Pseudo-Athanasius writes that fasting 'cures disease, dries up the body's humors, puts demons to flight, (and) gets rid of evil thoughts'.[10]

The *AXP* similarly reflects this normative understanding of self-protective fasts. In the first half of the tale, both prior to and after her conversion to Christianity, Xanthippe performs constant fasts, and because of this bodily preparation she is able to ward off potential sexual encounters. For example, in addition to withdrawing from sexual relations with her husband, Xanthippe twice encounters demons that desire to tempt her sexually. First, as Xanthippe is on her way to visit the apostle Paul in the middle of the night, 'demons with fiery torches and lights' pursue her. Lest the reader be confused about the intention of these demons, Xanthippe makes it clear when she complains, 'What has happened to you now, wretched soul? You have been deprived of your (sexual) desire.'[11] The second example occurs after Probus's conversion. Xanthippe arranges a celebratory feast but of course does not partake of it; rather, she retires to her bedroom. On her way, she encounters a 'demon coming in the likeness of one of the actors'. Alarmed, Xanthippe screams in anger, 'Many a time have I said to him that I no longer care for toys, yet he (still) despises me as a woman.' She then picks up an iron lamp and, hurling it at the demon's face, crushes its features. The demon responds with equal alarm, 'O violence, from this destroyer even women have received power to strike us' (23).

Such demonic attacks fit well within Late Antiquity's ascetic worldview. Ascetic thinkers believed that what individuals could not conquer in their minds would manifest itself and attack them from the outside. For example, Evagrius of Pontus, in *On the Various Evil Thoughts*, argues that the nature of demons is to attack in a systematic fashion; just as a person overcomes one of the eight vices, demons will

---

9 Galen, *De sanitate tuenda* 1.8 (in Galen, *Opera Omnia*, D.C.G. Kuhn [ed.], [20 vols.; Leipzig: C. Knoblochii, 1821–33], 6, p. 40), trans. Shaw, *Burden of the Flesh*, p. 48.

10 Pseudo-Athanasius, *De Virginitate* 7, trans. Shaw, *Burden of the Flesh*, p. 226.

11 The word here is ἐπιθυμία which has an explicit sexual connotation. See Dale Martin, *The Corinthian Body* (New Haven, CT: Yale University Press, 1995), p. 37.

attack in the form of the next.[12] Given this scenario, Xanthippe's attack by demons demonstrates that she has not reached perfection.

In its depiction of demons, the *AXP* offers an innovative construction of women's asceticism. In her discussion of women and demonic interaction in Late Antique ascetic literature, Elena Giannarelli argues that while male literature posits Satan and demons to be real forces external to the protagonist, in women's literature Satan is 'above all an interior voice'. She continues, 'As far as I know, no text presents Satan disguised as a handsome boy in order to provoke a girl who has devoted herself to God.' Here, however, a demon attempts to tempt Xanthippe sexually.[13]

Although Xanthippe fasts to rid herself of her sexual desires, the *AXP*, like other ascetic texts directed to women, still emphasizes her sexual nature. The connection is in part medical. As noted above, Galen remarks on the perceived link between a woman's dietary regimen and her sexual desire. Further, he states both that the female produced seed and that without a certain release of that seed to maintain health, hysteria might result.[14] This connection of seed, hysteria and the necessary function of sexual intercourse receives attention in the *AXP*. For example, the narrative seems to acknowledge that sexual activity has its merits (albeit in a fully metaphoric manner), for it discusses the relationship between the virgin Xanthippe and Christ in terms of sexual imagery. When praying, Xanthippe bemoans that God has 'shown to me, humble and unworthy, the ever-living and abiding seed (though my ignorance permits me not to receive it)' (13). The connotation is that knowledge of Christ is the equivalent of the reception of God's 'seed'. In sum, even though the *AXP* highlights Xanthippe's fast as effective in battling her own earthly sexual desires, the tale continues to embody Xanthippe as a sexual being in the service of God.

This reading is further supported by what Xanthippe proclaims after she receives baptism and the Eucharist. Thanking God, she proclaims that she is 'compelled to speak, for someone inflames and sweetens me within'. This association of sexual desire with heat appears as well in Galen's work: he writes that warm *pneuma* is generated by sexual urges.[15] While Xanthippe struggles to maintain continent, the *AXP* economizes on the sexual desire aroused by and culminated in God.

Such sexual imagery resonates with other Late Antique writings. Basil of Ancyra writes that the virgin's body is the bridal chamber in which Christ will lie as bridegroom.[16] Likewise, Jerome writes to the young virgin Eustochium that the receipt of Christ will occur '(w)hen sleep overtakes you (and) He will come behind and put His hand through the hole of the door, and your heart shall be moved for Him'.[17] Similarly, patristic authors differentiated between the eyes that saw pleasure in this world and the eyes that were able to see Christ. According to Evagrius, these

---

12 Evagrius Pontus, *De diversis malignis cogitationibus* 1 (PG 79.1200D–1201A), trans. Shaw, *Burden of the Flesh*, pp. 144–45.

13 Elena Giannarelli, 'Women and Satan in Christian Biography and Monastic Literature (IVth–Vth Centuries)', *Studia Patristica* 30 (1995), pp. 196–201.

14 Galen, *De loc. Aff.* 6.5 (Kuhn 8:413–36).

15 Galen, *De usu partium*, 14.1–2 (Kuhn 4:142–44).

16 Basil of Ancyra, *De virg.* 27 (PG 30.725B).

17 Jerome, *Ep.* 22.25 (CSEL 54:178–180).

original eyes were ones of mind or intellect;[18] Basil of Ancyra notes that it was the 'eyes of desire' that caused Adam to fall.[19] It was fasting, though, that could enable ascetics to redirect their sight and, in so doing, Evagrius continues, they might be able to see God with their original 'intellectual eyes'.[20] The *AXP* displays this view when Xanthippe, after her fasts, receives a vision. Using language similar to that of Evagrius, she proclaims when Christ appears in her room that her own 'intellectual eyes' have been opened (13).

Fasting to Protect Another

In addition to Xanthippe's defence and elevation of her spiritual self, the *AXP* has Xanthippe understanding that she can defend the sexual integrity of her lost sister. Initially taken from her bedroom in a city in Spain, Polyxena – exchanged among men seven times – experiences abduction by pagans and rescue by Christians. Consistently, the non-Christian men kidnap Polyxena because of their own sexual desire.[21] Back at home, Xanthippe, unsure of her sister's fate, begins a new form of ascetic ritual through prayer and fasting in seclusion. The reader, however, is not made aware of her efforts until the very end when Polyxena returns. Xanthippe describes the proxy defence: 'I, my true sister, Polyxena, did not come out at all for forty days, excessively begging the loving God *in your defence*, purposefully so that *your virginity might not be stolen*' (41).

Though Xanthippe's description of her efforts to save Polyxena is brief, the reader has been trained to understand Xanthippe's self-induced seclusion. Her zealous devotion to ascetic prayer is frequently emphasized. From the moment Xanthippe hears Paul's message, she begins 'wasting herself away with waking and abstinence and other austerities' (2). She is 'seized with great faintness from lack of food' and is 'greatly exhausted by abstinence and the vision and want of sleep and other austerities'. Such austerities are presented as endangering her health early on; Probus asks his friends to check 'whether she still lives, for it's been twenty-nine days since she has tasted anything'; he continues, her face looked 'as of one ready to die' (18).

Legislating the World of Fasting

Though the *AXP* presents a Xanthippe quite confident in her proxy ascetic effort, the larger message in the *AXP* suggests some unease about it. The *AXP* admonishes Xanthippe's ascetic zeal both through its fashioning of Polyxena's understanding of her predicament and through the 'male position' in the tale.

Whereas Xanthippe is adamant about the effectiveness of her ascetic performance, Polyxena feels that her sexual status is, at best, precarious. Again relying upon

18 Evagrius, *Ep. Ad. Mel* 6 [Parmentier, 13 (English translation); Frankenberg, 619 (Greek retranslation from the Syriac)].

19 Basil of Ancyra, *De virg.*, 44, trans. Shaw, *Burden of the Flesh*, p. 81.

20 Evagrius of Pontus, *Keph.Gn.* 1.50, trans. Shaw, *Burden of the Flesh*, p. 200.

21 Abduction often served as a form of marriage. The woman's marital value would vanish because all would assume that her virginity had been taken during her abduction. For more on the motivations behind and legal ramifications of abduction marriages, see Judith Evans Grubbs, '"Pagan" and "Christian" Marriage: The State of the Question', *JECS* 2 (1994), pp. 361–412.

the trope of demonic sexual temptation, the narrative presents Polyxena, in the wilderness, crying, 'Woe is me, who at one time showed myself not even to my servants, but now display myself to demons' (xxvi).[22] Believing that prayer affords some measure of sexual defence, she states while imprisoned in the governor's bedroom: 'Woe is me ... (for) I understand now how the devil hates virginity, but O Lord, because I *dare not beg you on my own behalf*, I bring to you the prayers of your holy preacher Paul so that *you might not allow my virginity to be destroyed* by anyone' (37).

Polyxena's plea here is remarkably and, I would argue, purposefully similar to Xanthippe's closing statement. First, they both emphasize God's ultimate control over Polyxena's virginity. Second, both statements describe their communication with God as one of 'begging': Polyxena states, 'I dare not beg you myself' and Xanthippe states that she 'begged God excessively'.[23]

The third similarity is that both prayers promote the idea of proxy prayer[24] just as both call attention to Polyxena's inability to pray in her own defence. However, each woman promotes a different proxy. Polyxena's statement showcases Paul as the proper intercessory. Conversely, Xanthippe's statement highlights the effectiveness of her own intercession. In other words, there is a purposeful tension created over who is best suited to protect Polyxena's virginity given her own ability to do so.

The *AXP* posits Xanthippe's understanding of her ascetic performance over and against the understanding of Paul and Probus. After explaining the nature of her ascetic performance to her sister, Xanthippe continues: 'And Paul, the preacher of God, said to me, "Her virginity will not be taken away, and she will come (home) quickly". Even Probus said to me, "It was assigned to her by God to be thus afflicted. Do you see how by many devices God saves many?"'(42).

Here the division becomes evident. Xanthippe's understanding of the efficacy and necessity of her asceticism is at conflict with the understanding of the two Christian men. Though Xanthippe felt that her steadfast prayer and fasting would protect her sister, she informs Polyxena in this final statement that Paul had advised her differently. According to Paul: God was looking out for Polyxena, and her trials were intended for a purpose. This point is anticipated a few lines earlier when Polyxena, asking Paul to protect her from any further abductions, receives the reply, 'Thus must we be troubled my daughter that we may realize our defender, Jesus Christ.' While Paul's responses to Polyxena and Xanthippe emphasize the nature and usefulness of divine providence, the text offers Xanthippe as one who not only boldly offers her own prayers to God instead of Paul's, but, additionally, disbelieves Paul's assurances and continues to act in spite of them.

This construction should be read not as a move to discredit Paul but rather as a teaching about the error of Xanthippe's actions.[25] To argue that the apostle is the

22 The term here for 'display' is θεατρίζω, which means to 'put on a show or sexual show'. See H.G. Liddell and R. Scott (eds.), *Greek-English Lexicon* (Oxford: Clarendon Press, 1996), p. 380.
23 The Greek used in each case δέομαι to describe the nature of the prayer.
24 I thank A.-J. Levine for making this similarity clearer to me.
25 Similar ambivalent responses to representations of Paul can be found in scholarship on the second-century *Acts of Paul and Thecla*. Paul has been criticized by some for abandoning Thecla in her times of need. Others read Paul's actions toward Thecla as empowering her. For a sampling of these views, see Ross S. Kraemer, *Her Share of the Blessings: Women's Religions Among Pagans,*

approved authority figure, one need only look at the earlier episode, wherein upon realizing Polyxena has been called by God, Xanthippe immediately runs to inform Paul (24). Likewise, it is Paul whom Xanthippe seeks upon hearing that Probus decided to convert.

The textual admonition of Xanthippe's ascetic performance is reinforced by Probus himself. His response to Xanthippe's seclusion echoes the theocentric perspective: he, too, believes that it is through suffering and trials that one can come to know and understand God as the 'true' protector, and thus Polyxena's suffering must be understood in terms of divine will. Further, Probus sees this suffering as being for Polyxena's edification. Certainly, this theodical understanding has precedent as far back as Job. But highlighted here is Paul's response and the position of moderate asceticism that he embodies. In sum, then, the 'male response' to Xanthippe's fasting in Polyxena's defence is not only that it is unnecessary, but, further, that Xanthippe actually embodies ignorance of God's purpose.

This textual dismissal is continued through Xanthippe's *narrative fate*. Xanthippe tells her sister one last thing, 'Now, my beloved sister, having unexpectedly seen your face, now I shall pleasantly die.' In addition to demonstrating Xanthippe accepting her death, this statement also demonstrates the uncertainty she had about her sister's return. Probus and Paul announced that Polyxena was divinely guaranteed to return home, but Xanthippe appears to have doubted their assurances. Finally, this victory of male authority over women's ascetic performances finds ultimate vindication in Polyxena's fate. She chooses to remain by Paul the rest of her days precisely because she remains afraid. Paul's authority has been secured, once and for all.

While most texts, including the *AXP*, present the view that strictly controlling what went into one's mouth would have a prophylactic effect on what went into one's other bodily orifices, the *AXP* further suggests that such control might protect the orifices of others. Xanthippe's fasting for her own sexual defence against her husband and demons would have resonated with an audience accustomed to the advice of Pseudo-Athanasius or Gregory Nazianzus. However, her performance of a sexual defence by proxy was presumably less familiar to this same audience, a point supported by the *AXP*'s resolution.

Adding the AXP *to our Understanding of Late Antique Asceticism*

Why does the *AXP* give Xanthippe such a revolutionary notion of fasting only to undermine it through her death? Xanthippe learns no lesson about the futility of her ascetic performance; she dies quite happily, and, further, she dies only after she sees with her own eyes Polyxena's safe return.

To be sure, the text is ambiguous about the cause of Polyxena's return. Although Paul and Probus voice their opinions about why she suffered, and although Xanthippe offers her own, different, version, the text does not explicitly state who was right.

Jews, and Christians in the Greco-Roman World (Oxford: Oxford University Press, 1992); *eadem* (ed.), *Women's Religions in the Greco-Roman World: A Sourcebook* (Oxford and New York: Oxford University Press, 2004), and Melissa Aubin, 'Reversing Romance? The *Acts of Thecla* and the Ancient Novel', in Ronald F. Hock, J. Bradley Chance and Judith Perkins (eds.), *Ancient Fiction and Early Christian Narrative* (SBL Symposium Series; Atlanta, GA: Scholars Press, 1998), pp. 257–72.

One could argue that Xanthippe's death provides a textual verdict. However, there remains very little evidence outside the *AXP* either to support or to dissuade the notion of proxy ascetical performances.

One possible reference occurs in a fourth-century homily by John Chrysostom. Mursillo writes concerning his praise of Mary in Rom. 16.8: 'For Mary is one "who bestowed much labour on us", that is, not on herself only, nor upon her own advancement (for this many women of the present day do, by fasting and sleeping on the floor) but *upon others also.*'[26] It is possible that Chrysostom's reference to proxy performances is an allusion to 'golden days past' when such acts, he implies, were popular. Further, he valorizes those actions in the golden days in order to polemicize against his contemporaries who fast precisely 'for their *own* advancement'.

A second possible reference to proxy ascetic performance, though recorded in the sixth century, appears in the story of Bishop Aravatius by Gregory of Tours. According to Gregory, this bishop fasted and prayed to 'save Gaul from the invasion of the Huns'.[27] Aravatius, feeling that his fast was ineffective, travels to Rome and receives a vision that Gaul will indeed fall, but he will not see it happen. Happily, he returns home and, sure enough, he dies within days. While this example contains proxy ascetical fasting, the *final* saving effect turns out to be in terms of the bishop's own self; it is he who dies, not Gaul that is saved. Yes, the extreme prayer and fast works, and, yes, like Xanthippe, Aravatius *believes* that his fast can work, but, for Aravatius, it doesn't work except insofar as that it secures his own death.

The tension in the *AXP* between the efficacy and admonishment of proxy fasting evinces *different* historical concerns. Though the dichotomy between zealous ascetical performance embodied in Xanthippe and the more moderate approach embodied in Paul and Probus's response comfortably fits within the Late Antique debate over extreme asceticism and episcopal 'orthodoxy', the *AXP* reveals not only the tendency for women to perform excessive asceticism, but also the male concern over the relationship of asceticism to issues of authority. The precise enactment of this link between zealous fasting and authority is embodied in the juxtaposition of Xanthippe, undeniably and demonstrably the best faster in town, and Paul and Probus, the male authority figures in Xanthippe's life.

This concern is voiced elsewhere in Late Antique patristic texts. Basil of Caesarea, for example, warns that 'Abstinence and all bodily mortification have some value, but if one follows one's own impulses, and does what is pleasing, and is not persuaded by the superior who gives counsel, then the harm done will be greater than the virtuous action.'[28] The *AXP*, too, subordinates Xanthippe's independent fast through her death.

Along with ascetic prescriptions for fasting exist equally consistent warnings about the dangers of *excessive* fasting. Pseudo-Chrysostom writes that God esteems meekness and self-control over virginity, fasting, contempt of wealth and almsgiving.

---

26 John Chrysostom, *Homilies on the Epistle of St. Paul to the Romans*, in *Nicene and Post-Nicene Fathers*, vol. 11 (Grand Rapids, MI: Eerdmanns, 1973).

27 Lewis Thorpe (ed. and trans.), *The History of the Franks* (Baltimore, MD: Penguin, 1974), p. 114.

28 For a discussion of Pseudo-Chrysostom, see Shaw, *Burden of the Flesh*. For Basil of Caesarea, see *Serm. Asc.*, 2.2 (PG 31.888A–B), trans. Shaw, *Burden of the Flesh*, p. 230.

Cyril of Jerusalem counsels his disciples that fasting is permitted, but the ascetic should not lose sight of the true purpose of asceticism. He advises, 'Let the body be nourished by food so it may continue to *live* and give unimpaired service.' In what could be a direct response to Xanthippe's ascetic performance, and in an argument quite consistent with Paul's response to the fast, Cyril reinforces the idea that fasting could end up doing more harm than good. One of the likely explanations of the opposition between Xanthippe, one who fasts for forty days, and the 'male perspective' embodied by Paul and Probus, is that the *AXP* reflects the common notion that fasting a little bit is necessary but fasting too much is dangerous not only to one's health, but also to one's soul.

Aline Rousselle has demonstrated that in contrast to the ubiquitous prescriptions to monks about the dangers of sexual temptations, the ascetic prescriptions for, and quotes attributed to, women focus more on the dangers of pride.[29] For example, in the fifth century, Amma Theodora said that 'neither asceticism, nor vigils of any kind or suffering are able to save, *only true humility can do that'*.[30] Likewise, Melania the Younger counsels her disciples that they should not be boastful of their ascetic endeavours or they could fall victim to the Devil. She warns, 'We fast, but he eats nothing at all ... Let us thus hate arrogance since it was through this fault that he fell down from the heavens and by it he wishes to carry us down with him.'[31] The way that the debate over Xanthippe's excessive fasting is framed in the *AXP* – a contest between a zealous woman ascetic versus the male apostle – indicates that some of the concern for ascetic pride in women carried over into claims of authority and legitimacy in ascetic communities.

The body became a site of empowerment, punishment and legislative property in Late Antiquity. Xanthippe fasts because it was the only mechanism an elite woman had for protecting an abducted sister. Peter Brown writes that ascetic women fasted because they lacked other opportunities to excel spiritually: 'Deprived of the clear boundary of the desert, their energies less drained by hard physical labor and unable to expose themselves far from their place of residence for fear of sexual violence, virgins frequently defined themselves as separate from the world through an exceptionally rigid control of their diet.'[32]

In this respect, Xanthippe's fast is a very powerful, proactive move. Further, as Shaw demonstrates, many ascetic women felt that fasting was a way to get closer to God; Shaw summarizes much of this thought when she writes that '(f)asting and virginity are ... ways of imitating the original blessed human condition in paradise before the fall and life in the paradise to come'.[33] But, as the *Acts of Xanthippe and*

29 Aline Rousselle, *Porneia: On Desire and the Body in Antiquity* (Oxford and Cambridge: Blackwell, 1988), pp. 136–73.

30 Amma Theodora, Saying 6, in Ross Kraemer (ed. and trans.), *Maenads, Martyrs, Matrons, and Monastics* (Philadelphia, PA: Fortress Press, 1988), p. 124.

31 *Life of Melania*, 43, in Elizabeth A. Clark (ed. and trans.), *The Life of Melania the Younger: Introduction, Translation and Commentary* (Studies of Women in Religion, 14; New York: Edwin Mellen Press, 1984).

32 Peter Brown, *The Body and Society: Men, Women, and Sexual Renunciation in Early Christianity* (Lectures on the History of Religions 13; New York: Columbia University Press, 1988), p. 269.

33 Shaw, *Burden of the Flesh*, p. 25.

Polyxena demonstrates, while this was an opportunity for women to excel, perhaps even to excel above their male counterparts, a woman's sense of the potential power afforded by fasting was something that, like all other aspects of women's asceticism, would inevitably be legislated by male authorities.[34]

34 For more on the legislation of women's ascetic communities by male authorities, see Susanna Elm's '*Virgins of God': The Making of Asceticism in Late Antiquity* (Oxford: Clarendon Press, 1994).

THINKING WITH VIRGINS: ENGENDERING JUDAEO-CHRISTIAN DIFFERENCE*

DANIEL BOYARIN

'The glory of women is always twisted.'[1]

Nicole Loraux

'Charlotte, we're Jewish,' says Cher in the opening scene of *Mermaids*, as she passes her adolescent daughter, Wynona Ryder, genuflecting ecstatically at her private shrine to St Perpetua. Charlotte abandons her worship of the martyr, with a rather dramatic effect on her nascent sex life. What might it be about a young Christian woman tortured to death in the arena in third-century North Africa that would so attract an American Jewish teenager as a model and ego ideal?

In fact, virginity and martyrdom have been intimately connected in Christianity from the fourth century on, and the virgin girl is a topos in both Judaism and Christianity for thinking about male bodies and their spiritual states. Here, I will investigate the figure of the virgin girl in the traditions of both rabbinic Jews and Christians in Late Antiquity, first as an ego ideal for men, and then as one for women, with strikingly different conclusions to the two analyses.[2]

Virgin Rabbis; or, the Empire as Brothel

At the end of the story about Rabbi Eli^cezer and the disciple of Jesus,[3] the Rabbi declares that his sin was violating the injunction encapsulated in a verse of Proverbs to stay far away from sectarian heresy, namely, Christianity. When the Talmud cites this story, the text continues directly with a halakhic passage that draws on the

---

* Reprinted from *Dying for God: Martyrdom and the Making of Christianity and Judaism* with permission of the publishers, Stanford University Press, 1999 by the Board of Trustees of the Leland Stanford Junior University.

1 Nicole Loraux, *Tragic Ways of Killing a Woman* (trans. Anthony Foster; Cambridge, MA: Harvard University Press, 1987), p. 29.

2 Perpetua herself was, of course, not a virgin, but, in fact a mother. One of the arguments of Virginia Burrus in 'Reading Agnes: The Rhetoric of Gender in Ambrose and Prudentius', *JECS* 3 (1995), pp. 25–46, however, is that the relevance of the figure of the virgin was coming to the fore in the fourth century. See also, however, Burrus, 'Word and Flesh: The Bodies and Sexuality of Ascetic Women in Christian Antiquity', *JFSR* 10 (1994), pp. 27–51, p. 30 n. 8: 'the distinction between virginal and nonvirginal ascetic women is of relatively little use for understanding women's asceticism from a female point of view'. The relevant distinction from 'the female point of view' was sexual domination by a man or not, and in that sense, Perpetua is as relevant as a virgin.

3 See 'The Close Call: Or, Could a Pharisee Be a Christian?' in Boyarin, *Dying for God*, pp. 22–41 (27); *Tosefta Hullin* 2.24.

citation from Proverbs that was used in the story about Rabbi Eli^cezer: 'Keep her ways far away from you, and do not come near to the opening of her door' (Prov. 5.8). The issue begins with a typical midrashic exploration of the precise referent of 'her' in the verse:

> 'Keep her [the 'Strange Woman's'] ways far away from you!' – This [refers] to sectarianism.
> 'And do not come near to the opening of her door' – This is the government.
>
> There are those who say: 'Keep her ways far away from you!' – This is sectarianism and the government. 'And do not come near to the opening of her door' – This is the prostitute. How far [must one keep away from the prostitute's door]? Rav Ḥisda said: 'four cubits'.
>
> (*Babylonian Talmud Avoda Zara* 17a[4])

From here until the end of the text, these three themes, heresy, collaboration and prostitution will be intertwined. Sectarian heresy, prostitution and collaboration with Roman power had become associated in the cultural 'unconscious' of rabbinic Judaism, no doubt at least in part simply because all three are seductive and dangerous.[5] The seemingly literal reading, that one must be wary of the sexual lure of the 'strange woman', is tacked on here, almost as an afterthought. However, as we shall see, there are overtones to this nexus that go far beyond this rather obvious and trivial observation. The association of negative Jewish behaviour with the lust of the male customer of the prostitute is crucial to the main theme of the text, the transformation of the chaste Jewish male – and indeed the Jewish people – into female virgin as the one most fit to resist such sexualized enticements.[6]

The gendering of sectarian heresy, which here is Christianity, is supported by the fact that in the Proverbs verse what one is enjoined to keep away from is 'her

---

4 Note that this is the same distance the Rabbis took from the 'heretic' Rabbi Eli^cezer on his death bed (Boyarin, *Dying for God*, p. 37; *TB Sanhedrin* 68a) creating one more resonance between heresy and whores.

5 Marcel Simon makes the interesting point that by the time of this text, in fact, 'sectarianism', that is, Christianity, and the Roman government were themselves 'twins', indeed, according to a sequel in this same talmudic passage, the two daughters of Gehenna:

> 'The leech has two daughters: Give! and Give!' (Prov. 30.15): Said Rav Ḥisda, said Mar Uqba,
> 'The voice of two daughters cries out from Hell and says in this world "Give! Give!" And what are they? – heresy and the government.' There is another version: Said Rav Ḥisda, said Mar Uqba, 'The voice of Hell cries out and says, "Bring me two daughters that say in this world, 'Give! Give!'" [And what are they? – heresy and the government].'

See Simon, *Verus Israel: A Study of the Relations Between Christians and Jews in the Roman Empire (135–425)* (trans. H. McKeating; The Littman Library of Jewish Civilization; Oxford: Oxford University Press, 1986), p. 187. Cf. Athanasius's representation of Arianism as 'the daughter of the devil' (Burrus, 'Word and Flesh', p. 37).

6 An important source for this image is, to be sure, to be found in the Bible, for in Ezekiel 16 there is an explicit figure of Israel as a female infant, then nubile maiden, and God as her lover. The transfer of this image of the nation as virgin to each individual male Israelite as female virgin is accomplished via the liturgy of the circumcision, in which the verse 'I said to you when you were in your blood, Live; I said to you when you were in your blood, Live' (Ezra 16.6) is applied to the newly circumcised male infant. See also Ilana Pardes, *The Biography of Ancient Israel* (Berkeley: University of California Press, 1999), chapter 2.

ways'.[7] The literal subject of the verse is the seductive 'strange woman', whose lips drip honey, but whose aftertaste is bitter. It is important to recognize here a major metaphorical shift. For the Prophets, the dominant metaphor is of a female Israel gone awhoring with myriad lovers, while here, we find Israel figured as a lustful male tempted sorely by a seductive female. This shift of the metaphor of a straying Israel from female to male is accomplished by repeatedly reading figures of sexual danger from Proverbs as if they were allegories for religious temptations and dangers. Foreign whores and seductive daughters are transformed, as we shall see below, into heresies and seductions of collaboration, thus rendering the errant Jews their illicit male partner.[8]

At first glance, this claim may seem strange, since I and others have been arguing so strenuously that the Rabbis saw themselves as feminized.[9] However, on further reflection, there is no paradox here at all. If the negative, the abjected image of self is the lustful male, the valorized image is the virgin female. We can find an explicit modern pendant for this theory in Ramakrishna's exhortation to his disciples to 'become woman' in order to transcend their own sexual desire to be with women: 'A man can change his nature by imitating another's character. By transposing on to yourself the attributes of woman, you gradually destroy lust and the other sensual drives. You begin to behave like women.'[10] By the time we reach the end of the talmudic narrative, we shall see that the female virgin is indeed an object of identification for the Rabbis, in much the same way that Virginia Burrus has taught us that the virgin performed symbolically for contemporary Christians such as the fourth-century Bishop Ambrose of Milan. As we shall see below through a reading

7 Naturally, Christians at this time were gendering 'Judaism' as feminine in almost exactly the same way, especially via the associations between Arianism and 'Judaizing'. Virginia Burrus, *Begotten Not Made: Conceiving Manhood in Late Antiquity* (Stanford, CA: Stanford University Press, 2000), Chapter 2. And, in general, 'heresy' is gendered in the same way. Burrus, '"Equipped for Victory": Ambrose and the Gendering of Orthodoxy', *JECS* 4 (1996), pp. 461–75.

8 In the rabbinic text, the 'foreign woman' of Proverbs, almost a perennial source of sexual excitement in many human cultures, becomes the primary metaphor for all that is exotic and thus alluring to Jews, whether as political power or seductive foreign cults. Jews are faced with the dual temptations of collaboration with oppressors or of assimilation into the dominant cultural forms. Either of those seductive options provides an escape from the sometimes unbearable tensions of difference. They provide two means of being like all the other nations. On my reading, it is precisely the allure of these two avenues of flight from the tensions of diasporized Jewish existence that is central to the text, and it is these diversions that are thematized as being similar to the forms of escape that sexual pleasure provides, as well.

9 Daniel Boyarin, *Unheroic Conduct: The Rise of Heterosexuality and the Invention of the Jewish Man* (Berkeley: University of California Press, 1997).

10 *The Gospel of Sri Ramakrishna* (trans. Swami Nikhilananda; New York: Ramakrishna-Vivekananda Center, 1985), p. 176, quoted in Parama Roy, *Indian Traffic: Identities in Question in Colonial and Postcolonial India* (Berkeley: University of California Press, 1998). As Parama Roy remarks, 'This feminine identification was quite compatible with a marked gynophobia.' Alice Jardine also reminds us that Daniel Schreber's desire to become a woman was an attempt to transcend sexual desire. Schreber wrote: 'When I speak of my duty to go deeper into voluptuous pleasures, I never mean by that sexual desires towards other human beings (women) and even less sexual commerce, but I imagine myself man and woman in one person in the process of making love to myself', upon which Jardine comments: 'The desire to be both woman and spirit ... may be the only way to avoid becoming the object of the *Other's* (female's) desire' (Alice A. Jardine, *Gynesis: Configurations of Woman and Modernity* [Ithaca, NY: Cornell University Press, 1985], pp. 98–99).

of her work, at a time contemporaneous with the Rabbis, Ambrose also urged self-feminization as an antidote to the perceived evils of the male psyche. In both late ancient Christianity and Judaism, ideal male identity was secured in part via cross-gender identification with female virgins. Affinities run strong and deep.

Following this small bit of halakhic discourse, the Talmud goes on with stories of tricksters and martyrs, and I wish now to interpret a part of the Talmudic martyrology. Immediately after describing the punishments of the three members of Rabbi Ḥanina's family, the text explains why God has allowed them to be so mistreated:

> Him to burning, for he used to pronounce the Holy Name literally. How is it possible that he did such a thing?! For we have a tradition that Abba Shaul says that also one who pronounces the Holy Name literally has no place in the World to Come. He did it for the purpose of self-instruction, for as another tradition says: '"Do not learn to do" [pronouncing God's name; Deut. 18.9], but you may learn in order to understand and to teach.' [If that is the case], why was he punished? Because he used to pronounce the Holy Name literally in public, and it says 'This is my eternal name' (Ex. 3.15), but the word 'eternal' לעולם is spelt as if it meant 'for hiding' לעלם.
>
> And his wife for execution [by the sword], because she did not censure him.
>
> And his daughter to sit in a prostitute's booth, for Rabbi Yoḥanan said: She was once walking among the great of Rome, and they said, 'How beautiful are the steps of this maiden!' And she immediately became more meticulous about her steps.

This narrative explains the punishments of the three members of the martyr's family and provides a version of a theodicy. The explanations of the punishment of the Rabbi and of his daughter are doublets and highly gendered in their implications. Rabbi Ḥanina himself was condemned for doing something in public that he should have done in private. The two explanations for his punishment, the 'realistic' one, that the Romans had arrested him for illegally teaching Torah in public and the theodical one, that God had arrested him for revealing his name to the public, have to be read as comments upon each other.

It was appropriate, indeed, for him to be pronouncing God's name as it is written and together with its vowels in order to instruct himself, but this activity needed to be carried in private, just as his study and teaching of Torah ought to have been in private, according to Rabbi Yose the son of Kisma. God's name was given for hiding, not for public exposure to the eyes of the hostile Romans. In other words, the text is proposing a homology between the reasons for Rabbi Ḥanina's capture by the Romans at both the pragmatic and the theological levels. God has meant the teaching of Torah to be a private, internal activity for the Jewish people in a hostile world, a 'hidden transcript', and not a matter of provocation and defiance, just as a chaste maiden is meant to keep herself hidden from the eyes of lustful males and certainly not to encourage and wilfully attract their gazes. The Torah is a bride for the Rabbis: 'Rabbi Ḥiyya taught: Anyone who studies Torah in front of the one of the "people of the land" is like one who has intercourse with his fiancée in front of them' (*TB Pesaḥim* 49b).[11] By teaching Torah in public, therefore, Rabbi Ḥanina was engaged in an act as provocative and as immodest as that of his daughter.

---

11 In addition, however, to the question of gender and power vis-à-vis Rome that is most actively mobilized by this text, there is perhaps another sub-theme of public and private that is also lurking

Resistance, according to this view – the trickster party in rabbinic Judaism – consists of doing what we do without getting into trouble and using evasiveness in order to keep doing it. Interestingly enough, in defying the Romans and thus courting a martyr's death, Rabbi Ḥanina was behaving in a way culturally intelligible to the Romans[12] – behaving like a 'real man', a muscle Jew – while Rabbi Yose the son of Kisma through deceptive, 'womanish' complicity with the Romans, *resisted* their cultural hegemony.[13]

---

under its surface, one that has to do with internal power relations within Jewish society between different sects or competing elites. The 'people of the land' certainly represent such competing groups, Abraham Oppenheimer, *The Am Ha-ʾAretz: A Study in the Social History of the Jewish People* (Leiden: E.J. Brill, 1977); Tessa Rajak, 'The Jewish Community and Its Boundaries', in Judith Lieu, John North and Tessa Rajak (eds.), *The Jews Among Pagans and Christians in the Roman Empire* (London: Routledge, 1992), pp. 9–28 (13)). Cynthia Baker has argued persuasively that for the Rabbis, the Bet-Hamidrash, Study House, functioned as private space in another sense, a sense internal to Jews and not only in the conflict between Jews and Romans, for the Study House was the quintessential place for the formation of rabbinic identity over against these Others who are Jews, the *ʿAm Ha-ʾAretz* ('Neighbor at the Door or Enemy at the Gate? Notes Toward a Rabbinic Topography of Self and Other', paper presented at the American Academy of Religion, New Orleans, 1996). See also Dan Urman, 'The House of Assembly and the House of Study: Are They One and the Same?' *Journal of Jewish Studies* 44.2 (Autumn 1993), pp. 236–57. Since one who studies Torah in the presence of these Jewish Others is compared to one who has sexual intercourse with his fiancée in their presence, this continues as a commonplace rabbinic metaphor of Torah study as the act of love, the Torah as bride for the Rabbis, and the *privacy* that such a relationship connotes – as well, of course, as marking clearly once again the gender of those who have exclusive access to Torah. In addition, then, to provoking Rome, Rabbi Ḥanina may have been inviting the wrath of the other Rabbis by convening congregations and teaching Torah in public spaces analogous to the Synagogues ('congregations'), which were still, at this early time, in the control of the nonrabbinic parties among the Jews, or even worse, in the virtual equivalent of the marketplace, that site of 'social intercourse at its most chaotic and uncertain, and therefore most dangerous' (Cynthia Baker, 'Bodies, Boundaries, and Domestic Politics in a Late Ancient Marketplace', *Journal of Medieval and Early Modern Studies* 26.3 [Fall 1996], pp. 391–418 (405)). This interpretation of Torah as virtually esoteric knowledge, almost as a mystery, is strongly supported by the doubling in the text, whereby convening of public congregations for the teaching of Torah is made analogous to the revealing of God's Holy Name in public.

12 Glen W. Bowersock, *Martyrdom and Rome* (The Wiles Lectures Given at the Queen's University of Belfast; Cambridge, UK: Cambridge University Press, 1995), pp. 63–64. See Chapter 4, 'Whose Martyrdom Is This, Anyway?' in Boyarin, *Dying for God*, pp. 67–92.

13 See Peter Brown, *Power and Persuasion in Late Antiquity: Towards a Christian Empire* (Madison: University of Wisconsin Press, 1992), p. 65, on Ammianus's admiration of Christian martyrs because 'they had put their bodies "on the line" by facing suffering and death'. And see also Carlin Barton, *Roman Honor: The Fire in the Bones* (Berkeley: University of California Press, 2001). '[The Roman] looked for the contest when one proclaimed one's *Nomen* or identity. The Romans, for instance, recognized that the man or woman who proclaimed *Christianus sum* or *Judaios eimi* were doing so as challenges.' Rabbinic texts, on the other hand, counselled Jews to disguise themselves as non-Jews in order to avoid being martyred (Jehuda Theodor and Hanoch Albeck [eds.], *Genesis Rabbah* [Jerusalem: Wahrmann, 1965], p. 984). See also Saul Lieberman, 'The Martyrs of Caesarea', *Annuaire de l'institut de philologie et d'histoire orientales et slaves* 7 (1939–1944), pp. 395–446 (416 and especially 423). On the other hand, in a compelling reading, using both Scott's notion of the 'hidden transcript' (James C. Scott, *Domination and the Arts of Resistance: Hidden Transcripts* [New Haven, CT: Yale University Press, 1985]) and Bhabha's 'colonial mimicry' (Homi K. Bhabha, *The Location of Culture* [London: Routledge, 1994]), Joshua Levinson shows how adoption of the gladiatorial model for the martyrs constitutes a fundamental

As I have suggested, however, Rabbi Ḥanina's own sin, the sin of public exposure of the Torah to the gaze of outsiders, whether Jewish or Roman, is doubled by the sin of his daughter, which then enables us to interpret the father's transgression. She, like the Torah 'bride' of her father, reveals herself in that same marketplace.[14] Exposed to the predatory male gaze, ethnicized as both 'Roman' and the province of the powerful males of Rome, she does not evade the gaze, but seeks to enhance her object status further.[15] Having thus rendered herself a sexual object, she is punished by being turned into a whore, the ultimate depersonalized sexual object. Although the text is couched in the form of a critique of the woman here, and that (unfair) judgement, that blaming of the victim if you will, ought not to be papered over in our reading, at the same time, there is also encoded here a critique of the male gaze itself. It is no accident that it is the important men of Rome who are represented at this moment. They are the proverbial (or stereotypical) 'construction workers' in this text. And Rashi comments, citing the biblical verse: 'A respectable king's daughter remains indoors', at one and the same time a 'sexist' demand for a kind of purdah for women and, since the daughter of the king is Israel, a comment on the proper behaviour of Jews in general in the world. The daughter's story then doubles the critique of her father's provocative behaviour. Through this doubling, the approved practice for Jews is gendered feminine, while the behaviour of Romans is gendered masculine. The violence of their gaze is congruous with the greater violence of their bloodshed, and the resistance of the Jews is to be veiled: 'eternal' through being 'in hiding', as the double meaning of the verse implies. 'Remain indoors. Continue to live, continue to maintain Jewish practice, but do not behave in ways that draw attention to us or provoke the hostile intervention of the ruling powers. It is God who has sent them to rule.' Thus the text once more seemingly endorses the view of Rabbi Yose the son of Kisma (and the practice of Rabbi El'azar ben Perata, as well) that the trickster is to be preferred over the martyr, but it does not by any means entirely erase or delegitimate the way of Rabbi Ḥanina, either.

The end of the daughter's story reprises the issue of hidden transcripts and trick-sterism, this time, however, firmly gendering it by incorporating it in a version of the folktale of the virgin in the brothel. In her ultimate redemption, and via the mode by which she preserves herself, this girl will be installed as an archetypical female virgin, as a positively marked, valorized model for Jewish masculinity:

---

subversion of Roman values – precisely, that is, what it claims to be (Joshua Levinson, 'The Athlete of Piety: Fatal Fictions in Rabbinic Literature' [Hebrew], *Tarbiz* 68 (1999), pp. 61–86). This results in quite a different reading of the gendering of martyrdom, as well. For Levinson, the subversiveness of the martyr is most exquisitely encapsulated in the transformation of feminine submissiveness, including the death blow to the neck for the defeated gladiator, into a moment of triumph according to a hidden transcript. See, however, Carlin Barton ('Savage Miracles: The Redemption of Lost Honor in Roman Society and the Sacrament of the Gladiator and the Martyr', *Representations* 45 [Winter 1994], pp. 41–71), who reads this as a moment of triumph, of recovered honour, for the gladiator himself. This has interesting implications for the reading of Burrus, 'Reading Agnes', as well, I think. For Rabbi Yose the son of Kisma, see Boyarin, *Dying for God*, pp. 57–63.

14 Baker, 'Bodies, Boundaries'.

15 Carlin Barton has written, 'It is important to understand that, in ancient Rome, looking was not passive but active. To look was a challenge. The *spectator* was inspector, judge and connoisseur' (*Roman Honor*, p. 60).

Beruria, the wife of Rabbi Me'ir was the daughter of Rabbi Ḥanina. She said to him: It is painful to me that my sister is sitting in a prostitute's booth. He took a *tarqeva* of dinars and went, saying if she has done nothing wrong [i.e. if she is sexually innocent], there will be a miracle, and if not, there will be no miracle. He dressed up as a soldier and solicited her. She said: I am menstruating. He said: I can wait. She said: There are many here more beautiful than I. He said: I understand from this that she has done nothing wrong. He went to her guard: Give her to me! The guard said: I am afraid of the king. He [Me'ir] took the *tarqeva* of dinars, and gave it to him, and said: Take the *tarqeva* of dinars. Keep half and use half for bribing anyone who comes. He [the guard] said: What shall I do when they are gone? He [Me'ir] said: Say 'God of Me'ir save me' and you will be saved. He [guard] said: How do I know that this will be so? He [Me'ir] said: [Now you will see.] There came some dogs that eat people.[16] He shouted to them, and they came to eat him. He said: 'God of Me'ir save me', and they let him go.

He let her go.

In contrast to a Polyxena or a Perpetua, the archetypal Graeco–Roman–Christian martyrs for chastity, the daughter of Rabbi Ḥanina does not stand up to her oppressors and defend her virtue in a demonstrative way, thus bringing upon her their wrath and her death. Rather, she tricks her way out of the situation through lies and wiles (rather like the Three Billy Goats Gruff and their troll from European folklore).

---

16 Ruth Clements has suggested to me a riveting parallel here. Psalm 22 has been read, of course, as a virtual allegory of the Crucifixion, or better, the Passion narratives are a midrash on the Psalm. One of the few verses in that text that has not been given a paschological reading is 21: 'Deliver my life from the sword; my soul from the power of the dog.' Given the Crucifixion motif further on in the story, and the miraculous delivery of the soldier from the cross, contrasting – perhaps parodying – Elijah's 'failure' to remove Jesus from the Cross in Mark, the possibility becomes very seductive that this text is a sort of anti-gospel or folktale dialogue with a gospel or with anti-Jewish polemics based on a paschological midrash on this psalm. Fascinatingly, the talmudic story might even preserve a bit of Christian lore, a bit of gospel tradition in the form of a midrash on Ps. 22.21 otherwise unknown, to the best of my knowledge (Naomi Koltun-Fromm, 'Psalm 22's Christological Interpretive Tradition in Light of Christian Anti-Jewish Polemic', *JECS* 6 (1998), pp. 37–57). Clements suggests to me a slightly different possibility, writing:

> I think there is another way of reading the significance of the presence of biting dogs (and I freely admit that this comes partially of my unease with pushing it to be a 'lost Gospel' tradition). You are postulating a situation in which Rabbis and Christians have a good deal of intimacy with each other (with which I concur). The notion of a Gospel parody testifies to intimate Jewish knowledge of Christian texts and prooftexts, and what we know from Origen's witness implies that Jews and Christians argued about these most important texts all the time. Psalms 21/22, unlike Isaiah 53, must have been even a greater stumper for the Rabbis, precisely because so many of the narrative features of the psalm are worked into the earliest versions of the Passion narrative itself. What neater way to expose the literarily contrived nature of the actual Passion narratives than to take one of the few details of the psalm which is absolutely unable to be fit into the passion narrative as a 'true fact' and use it as the pivot to show the miraculous power of God when invoked by R. Meir. In other words, in this reading, it is precisely because this detail in the psalm was an embarrassment for Christian prophecy that it shows up here in the rabbinic parody. (Personal letter to the author.)

There is another possible echo of Christian midrash on Psalm 22, as well, namely, the fact that its opening verse is read in the Palestinian Talmud as a reference to the slow unfolding of the redemption.

All that is necessary for God to perform miracles and for her to be saved, however, is that she succeed at the task. The 'dishonourable' means are totally irrelevant. At the same time, though, the text is thematizing the vulnerability of the people without power. Without the miracle, they would be eaten alive by the 'dogs'.

Lest we think that the counsel of tricksterism is intended only for women, the text immediately goes on to disable such a reading:

> The matter became known in the house of the king. They brought him [the guard] and crucified him. He said 'God of Me'ir save me,' and they took him down and asked: What was that?[17] He told them: This is how the events took place. They wrote it on the gates of the city, and they engraved Rabbi Me'ir's face on the gates of Rome and said: If a man who looks like this comes, arrest him! When Rabbi Me'ir came there, they wished to arrest him. He ran away from them and *went into a whorehouse*. Elijah came in the guise of a whore and embraced him. *Some say that he put his hand in Gentile foods and tasted them*. They [the Romans] said: God forfend! If that were Rabbi Me'ir he wouldn't do such a thing.[18] Because of these events [Rabbi Me'ir] ran away to Babylonia.

The most striking aspect of this sequence is, of course, the escape via entering into the whorehouse and, moreover, disguising himself, once more, as a customer of the prostitutes. This time, however, it is not to test the chastity of someone else, but to save his own skin. Just as it was considered by the Jewish text entirely proper for the young woman to pretend to acquiesce in prostitution in order to preserve her life, so it is entirely proper for Rabbi Me'ir to disguise himself and pretend to (or maybe actually) violate the Jewish law in order to keep himself alive, in accord with the principle that the commandments are given to live by, and not to die by. The trickster option is reopened, and Rabbi Me'ir runs away to Babylonia, a safer place for the study of Torah, and not so incidentally the place where this story was formulated.

In the end, then, there is a perfect analogy between the male Rabbi and the young female Jew, and the thematic material of the entire text is brought together in a culminating fashion. The association between the Roman government and its blandishments and dangers and the house of prostitution is reprised, and the text opens up to its final moral and nearly allegorical meanings in which the Jewish people are figured no more as a man, Jacob, even a feminized man, but as a woman.[19] It is now Rabbi Me'ir, the paragon of male virtue, who preserves his chastity in the

---

17 This is plausibly read as a parody of Jesus' 'My God, my God, why hast thou forsaken me', itself a midrash on Ps. 22.2, for which there are other parodic parallels in this narrative.

18 This continuation contains a whole series of Gospel parallels, including the *answered* call from the Cross, the inscription on the Cross, and a virtual *ecce homo*.

19 See also Amy-Jill Levine, 'Diaspora as Metaphor: Bodies and Boundaries in the Book of Tobit', in J. Andrew Overman and Robert S. MacLennan (eds), *Diaspora Jews and Judaism: Essays in Honor of and, in Dialogue with, A. Thomas Kraabel* (South Florida Studies in the History of Judaism; Atlanta: Scholars Press, 1992), pp. 105–18.

whorehouse.[20] As Laurie Davis has phrased it, 'the rabbis see themselves as virgins in a brothel'.[21]

Virgin Fathers; or, Androgyny and the Lion

In this collection of martyr stories from the Talmud *Avoda Zara*, a text that insists on the representation of the Christian heresy as a beautiful prostitute who tempts the male Jewish people away from God, the Rabbis seem very close to those Christian ascetics who at exactly the same period also were using the female virgin as *their* most valorized exemplar.[22] The harlot, moreover, was a privileged metaphor for heresy among fourth-century Christians, as well.[23] These Christians were tangled up with power and prestige in the Empire in highly complex and nuanced ways that have been explored by Virginia Burrus: 'To state the thesis in general terms: post-Constantinian Christianity lays claim to the power of classical male speech; yet at the same time late ancient Christian discourse continues to locate itself in paradoxical relation to classic discourse through a stance of feminizing ascesis that renounces public speech.'[24] As Burrus here unveils, within the discourse of such figures as the late fourth-century Christian writers Ambrose and Prudentius, there are knotty and intricate elements of resistance to the dominant (Roman) discourse of masculinity, and of masculine sexuality in particular. This resistance or reconception of masculinity is achieved in no small measure by 'thinking with' virgins.

For example, in Ambrose's *On Virgins*, we find such countermasculinity thematized and symbolized in a story that issues in an array of paradoxical gender identifications. In one crucial episode, Thecla, the apocryphal female associate of Paul, has entered the martyrological ring. She is the proverbial Christian who has been thrown to the lions. As Ambrose structures his recounting of this episode, the lion 'initially represents the sexual violence signalled by both the "rage" of Thecla's would-be husband and the "immodest eyes" of the male onlookers who gaze upon the spectacle of her nakedness'.[25] The would-be martyr, Thecla, voluntarily presents to the lion her 'vital parts', an obvious eroticized displacement of the offer of her sexual parts

---

20 It has been suggested to me that Rabbi Me'ir is not approbated in this story, but condemned, and that his flight to Babylonia is a sort of punishment. This seems to me not the case because of the intervention of Elijah the Prophet as divine intercessor and miracle maker for him, just as in the case of El'azar ben Perata discussed in chapter 2 of the book. Divine intervention on behalf of someone can be reliably read, I suggest, as evidence of the narrator's approval of the character and his other actions. Cf. Susan Sered and Samuel Cooper, 'Sexuality and Social Control: Anthropological Reflections on the Book of Susanna', in Ellen Spolsky (ed.), *The Judgment of Susanna: Authority and Witness* (Atlanta: Scholars Press, 1996), pp. 43–55 (45).

21 Laurie Davis, 'Virgins in Brothels: A Different Feminist Reading of Beruriah', paper presented at the Graduate Theological Union, Berkeley, CA, 1994.

22 See also Averil Cameron, *Christianity and the Rhetoric of Empire: The Development of Christian Discourse* (Berkeley: University of California Press, 1991), p. 147, on Thecla as a model in the writings of Methodius, Gregory of Nyssa and Jerome. It is ambiguous in Cameron's context, however, whether Thecla was being held up as a model for men or only for women.

23 Burrus, 'Word and Flesh', pp. 36–45.

24 Burrus, 'Reading Agnes', p. 44. See also her concise description of the relevant political conditions for the shifts in Christian representations of virginity. 'Reading Agnes', p. 44.

25 Burrus, 'Reading Agnes', p. 32.

to her rejected fiancé. Male sexuality is figured as devouring of the woman, and the lion represents the rapacity of a husband, as well as that of the Empire.[26] As Gillian Clark has written, 'Christians inherited a discourse of sexuality as invasive and violent.'[27] The text draws an explicit analogy between the hunger of the male lion to eat the virgin's flesh and the lust of her husband to consummate the marriage. Even the lion, a mere beast, however, is led to transform its bestial and violent maleness in the presence of the virgin martyr, and by her example.

We find an important shift taking place in fourth-century Christian discourse. As is well known by now, earlier Christian texts frequently represented the possibility of a virilization of the female, whether as a martyr, Perpetua, or as apostle, Thecla.[28] It could be argued, indeed, that in the earliest periods of Christianity, there was a radical critique of Graeco–Roman gender discourses and sexual dimorphism *tout court*. This critique is represented in large part through 'gender-bending' attacks on female subordination such as the famous early story in which Jesus promises to make Mary male.[29] Although, obviously, we should be very chary of ascribing 'feminist' motives to such representations, it seems that the stance of drastic alienation from the Roman world and all its works, including marriage, led to at least this burst of imagination, this envisioning of female power and autonomy.[30]

26 Interestingly enough, the Rabbis also used the lion as a symbol for a violent male sexuality, saying that 'the ignorant man is like the lion who tramples and then devours its prey', while they used the courting routine of the rooster as a positive example of the husband who plays, dallies with, and arouses his wife before intercourse. For the lion as an image of violent male sexuality in Roman literature, see the text of Martial cited in Amy Richlin, *The Garden of Priapus: Sexuality and Aggression in Roman Humor* (2nd edn; New York: Oxford University Press, 1992), p. 137. For the persistence of the lion in this guise, see James Joyce's *Ulysses*, in which Bloom remarks, 'the lion reek of all the male brutes that have possessed [a prostitute]' (*Ulysses* [1914; New York: Random House, 1961], p. 409).

27 Gillian Clark, 'Bodies and Blood: Late Antique Debate on Martyrdom, Virginity and Resurrection', in Dominic Montserrat (ed.), *Changing Bodies, Changing Meanings: Studies on the Human Body in Antiquity* (London: Routledge, 1998), pp. 99–115 (107). I part company, however, from her statement that 'this fitted very neatly with the story of the Fall in the book of Genesis, in which sexual awareness was the first sign that humans had acquired knowledge of evil'. It has been adequately demonstrated by now that is neither the 'original' nor an ineluctable construction of the Genesis narrative. See Ilana Pardes, 'Beyond Genesis 3', *Hebrew Studies in Literature and the Arts* 17 (1989), pp. 161–87, and Gary Anderson, 'Celibacy or Consummation in the Garden? Reflections on Early Jewish and Christian Interpretations of the Garden of Eden', *HTR* 82.2 (1989), pp. 121–48.

28 Elizabeth A. Castelli, '"I Will Make Mary Male": Pieties of the Body and Gender Transformation of Christian Women in Late Antiquity', in Julia Epstein and Kristina Straub (eds), *Body Guards: The Cultural Politics of Ambiguity* (New York: Routledge, 1991), pp. 29–49. While in earlier work, scholars read these representations as manifesting 'genuine' spaces of autonomy for women in early Christian culture (e.g. Burrus, *Chastity as Autonomy: Women in the Stories of Apocryphal Acts* [Studies in Women and Religion; New York: Edwin Mellen Press, 1987]), more recently, these same scholars are inclined to see male representations of self via complex and contradictory identifications with female figures. See Burrus, 'Reading Agnes', and '"Equipped for Victory"'.

29 Marvin W. Meyer, 'Making Mary Male: The Categories "Male" and "Female" in the Gospel of Thomas', *NTS* 31 (1985), pp. 554–70.

30 Burrus, *Chastity as Autonomy*. Joyce Salisbury effectively contrasts the martyrdom in the first- or second-century Jewish 4 Maccabees with that of Perpetua. In 4 Maccabees, the martyred woman is martyred as a mother, and 'this martyrdom was about preserving family identity and piety in the

In the second century, we find Perpetua, who is marked as the Christian resister to the Roman culture of gender through her 'ability to stare directly back into the faces of her persecutors, not with the elusive demeanour of a proper *matrona*', but with a returned gaze that, in Brent Shaw's words, 'broke with the normative body language in a way that signalled an aggressiveness that was not one of conventional femininity'.[31] Slightly before her, there is Blandina, whose 'fortitude and endurance were compared to those of a victorious male athlete'.[32] In contrast to these virile, masculinized female martyrs of the second century, in the fourth century, we have a much more complex structure of gender in which both the masculinized aggressivity of the female martyr as *virago* and an almost contradictory feminized passivity as *virgo* are produced simultaneously.[33] In the *Acts of Paul and Thecla*, Thecla is saved by a *female* lion and serves as a powerful icon not only of resistance to the family values of the ancient city, but of female autonomy and solidarity.[34] In Ambrose's narrative, the male lion 'becomes female' and abandons his attack on the girl.[35] In other words, what was once unambiguously countercultural and subversive with respect to Rome and its gendered hierarchies and representations had now become highly ambiguous, almost fluid in its meanings. No longer simply the victorious,

---

face of oppression'. In the martyrdom of Perpetua, after some ambivalence, the milk in Perpetua's breast dries up, and 'the baby had no further desire for the breast'. Salisbury remarks: 'This seeming evidence of divine approval in the text reinforced the notion that martyrdom was incompatible with maternity. The time of the Maccabean mothers was over; martyrdom was a matter of private conscience, not family ties' (Joyce Salisbury, *Perpetua's Passion: The Death and Memory of a Young Roman Woman* [New York: Routledge, 1997], pp. 88, 91).

31 B.D. Shaw, 'The Passion of Perpetua', *Past and Present* 139 (May 1993), pp. 3–45 (4).

32 Shaw, 'The Passion of Perpetua', p. 19. In that same text, we note the transformation of the female slave, Biblis, first thought 'unmanly and easily broken', who then 'comes to her senses' and is martyred. For a discussion, see Burrus, 'Torture and Travail: Producing the Christian Martyr', in A.-J. Levine (ed.), *Feminist Companion to Patristic Literature* (London: Continuum, forthcoming). For a subtly and interestingly different take on Perpetua's gaze, see Salisbury, *Perpetua's Passion*, p. 138. For Salisbury, this represents the 'pride of a Roman matron'. On the whole, Shaw's interpretation of this seems to me more convincing. Barton, *Roman Honor*, refers to her dismissal of her father's entreaties as exemplary of Roman *virtus*, a *virtus*, that, as Barton makes clear, was available in the early Roman culture to both men and women.

33 Burrus, 'Reading Agnes', p. 41. According to Barton's argument, the shift is part and parcel of a shift in Roman culture, even apart from its Christianization, as Burrus's work also indicates. Burrus shows how martyrdom itself is rather slippery with respect to its complicated dialectics of defiances and passivity. But, in a sense, this is the intertextual transformation of a much earlier textual practice, for Loraux marks also that 'women in tragedy died violently. More precisely, it was in this violence that a woman mastered her death, a death that was not simply the end of an exemplary life as a spouse. It was a death that belonged to her totally.' Loraux, *Tragic Ways of Killing a Woman*, p. 3. Indeed, but we should not forget that this is a death that robs her of a life that would belong to her, if only partially. It is the constant transformation of the intertext, the transgression and remaking of the signifying practices, that constitutes cultural history, and Burrus's work here equips us with an exemplary case of such processes. One could say, perhaps, that the most strikingly new thing about the signifying practice called 'Christianity' was that within it, virgins were more autonomous than wives, while in 'classical' culture, and rabbinic Judaism within that, '(virgins) have less autonomy than wives'. Loraux, *Tragic Ways of Killing a Woman*, p. 31.

34 Burrus, *Chastity as Autonomy*, p. 59.

35 See Burrus, 'Word and Flesh', p. 48 for a further discussion.

valorous, virilized gladiator, à la Perpetua, the fourth-century virgin martyr was now partially rewritten via the intertexts as a model of passive, female virtue.[36]

Burrus traces the discursive modes through which is achieved 'the literary transformation of would-be "manly" women – *viragines* – into femininely docile *virgines*'.[37] The most vivid example of this is in her reading of Prudentius's poem on the death of the martyr Agnes. In this text, the virgin presents her breast to the persecuting executioner's sword, but in the end is executed by decapitation. This is a highly marked shift, as Burrus argues, employing the work of Nicole Loraux. Death by sword to the breast is a masculine death, the death of a warrior; death by sword to the neck is a feminine death, the death of a sacrificial victim.[38] Loraux has shown how shifting versions of the story of the death of the Trojan virgin Polyxena from Euripides through Virgil differently construct this symbol.[39] In various of these versions, Polyxena is either given the choice of the virile death by sword to the breast or denied that choice and forced to accept the feminine death. Burrus demonstrates how the variations of the death of this virgin as it moves from Euripides through Ovid and Seneca are vital for understanding its Christian version in Prudentius. In the Greek, Polyxena offers the executioner the manly breast or the womanly throat, and the latter chooses the throat. Ovid and Seneca, on the other hand, 'unlike Euripides, are willing to grant the virgin at least the outward sign of a noble and manly death, admittedly still controlled by bridal and sacrificial interpretations'. Prudentius's variation, however, is even more chilling than Euripides's because this virgin offers only the manly breast, but the text has her killed nevertheless via the suppliant bend of the neck for decapitation.

As Burrus concludes: 'Prudentius does not fail to exploit the exaggerated boldness of the Latin Polyxena as she shapes his portrait of Agnes, but like the Greek tragedian he compromises his portrayal of manly womanhood at the final, fatal moment. Refocusing the narrative gaze on the vulnerability of the female neck, Prudentius provides Agnes with the place of death which for him, as for ancient Greek tragedy, reestablishes her essential femininity in sexualized subjugation. But the message

36 Reading Burrus (and the other scholars whom she cites, as well), one realizes that '*the* fourth-century virgin martyr' is a nearly exact designation, since we have really one story that is split, recombined, doubled. Burrus's, 'it was a favorite story in the post-Constantinian church' is thus a precise formulation. Thecla is supplemented by the virgin of Antioch, who then becomes merged in part with Agnes, who is then split into Agnes and Eulalia, and so on. The point of this is to emphasize that this figure is an ideologically charged symbol of this particular moment, a symbol of a very tensely poised balance between an assertion of female audacity ('not much' remarks Burrus – but that's still some) and its 'firm restraint'. Burrus, 'Reading Agnes', p. 25.

37 Burrus, 'Reading Agnes', p. 26.

38 Strictly speaking, it is death by piercing or slashing the throat that is marked as 'feminine'. Loraux, *Tragic Ways of Killing a Woman*, pp. 49–65, and see B.D. Shaw, 'Body/Power/Identity: Passions of the Martyrs', *JECS* 4 (1996), pp. 269–312 (273 n. 10). But surely, in the contrast between the manly death place of the breast and the womanly death place of the throat, this distinction would hardly have been determinative. Although, if Shaw's interpretation that this piercing of the throat is a symbolic oral rape, a forced *irrumatio*, is accepted, then the distinction would make more of a difference. Shaw, 'Body/Power/Identity', p. 305. It is not clear, however, that his interpretation is ineluctable, particularly given the antecedents in tragedy. Loraux, *Tragic Ways of Killing a Woman*, p. 41.

39 Loraux, *Tragic Ways of Killing a Woman*, pp. 56–61.

now rings more harshly. Euripides's Polyxena offers both breast and throat only to die by the more feminine death of the throat. But Prudentius's still more virile Agnes offers *only her breast*, so that it is in complete and chilling disregard of her words that her *neck* is severed. More violently even than Euripides's Polyxena, the Christian Agnes must be wrenched back into her womanly place.'

'She is not after all audacious *virago* but docile *virgo*',[40] not, that is, triumphant warrior, but sacrificed virgin. There is, however, yet one more wrinkle to be added to this analysis, for the submissive neck for decapitation does not carry precisely the meaning of the feminine death via piercing the throat, either, but suggests rather the reclaiming of a variety of masculinized honour, like the submission to death of a defeated gladiator. Thus all the ambiguities of gendering, honour and death remain in play while clearly restraining the audacity, the representation of female martyr as *victorious* gladiator, as *virago*, that characterized the second-century texts.[41] As Burrus concludes, 'Perhaps we should resist the temptation to seek a "final word" which would resolve the tensions and ambiguities of the late fourth-century tale into one all-too-neat judgment.'[42]

The female martyr remained a highly charged symbol, owing to her subversions of sexuality and gender, but she functioned now most readily as an example for the male ascetic. As virilized woman, she could have functioned as an ego ideal for Christian women, an ideal that conduces to the overturning of gendered hierarchies and even of gender itself, as signified by Thecla's lioness and her own androgynous mien.[43] Burrus shows that as passive virgin, mirrored by the feminized male lion Thecla is no longer primarily a figure for the virilized female, but rather for the feminized male, the male who upon perceiving her is inspired, like the lion, to a complete renunciation of his 'naturally' violent, leonine, male sexuality – which is not to say that he achieves it. The masculinization and pluralization of the lions in the Ambrose version is significant of their transformation into an icon of the audience watching the martyrdom (and the audience reading the martyrology), at least insofar as these are male.[44] This audience (and the writers/readers) are thus called upon to identify both with the lion and with the victim of that lion, with both the figure of an oppressive male and that of a resistant virgin. One way of saying this would be that in the earlier version, one could imagine at least a female subjectivity in some sense behind the text. The implied author *could* be female.[45] The implied author of

40 Burrus, 'Reading Agnes', pp. 38–41.

41 I am grateful to an anonymous reader for Stanford Press for pointing out this distinction to me. See Barton, 'Savage Miracles', and also Burrus, 'Torture and Travail'.

42 Burrus, 'Reading Agnes', pp. 42–43.

43 Burrus, 'Reading Agnes', pp. 46–47.

44 Burrus, 'Reading Agnes', pp. 46–47; Burrus, 'Word and Flesh', p. 48.

45 Burrus, *Chastity as Autonomy*, pp. 53–57; Dennis Ronald MacDonald, *The Legend and the Apostle: The Battle for Paul in Story and Canon* (Philadelphia, PA: Westminster Press, 1983), pp. 34–53; Burrus, 'Word and Flesh', p. 45.

Ambrose's text is unambiguously, if complexly, gendered male.[46] Thus, the virgin becomes available for male identification.[47]

Burrus sums up her reading of this passage by remarking that 'through the manipulation of the figure of the lion, the subjugating force of male sexual violence has not been defeated so much as sublimated. On one reading at least, the lion's averted, feminized gaze continues paradoxically to restrain the virgin; the very gesture of honouring her – indeed of freely mirroring her feminine subjugation – becomes itself the vehicle of her constraint.'[48] In the era of 'imperial Christianity', the resistance to male sexuality, understood as 'naturally' violent because of its cultural construction within the dominant Roman formation to which most Christians had belonged, remained an important part of Christian male self-construction, but it no longer could accommodate such resistance through figurations of female 'achievement' of maleness.[49] Gender hierarchy had to be preserved, but not at the cost of reinstating an ideal of invasive phallic maleness. The point was to 'sublimate' it. Subjugation was to be retained, but without violence. This is the moment that Burrus refers to as 'the veiling of the phallus'. A paradoxical relation of these men to their own male selves is paralleled in their paradoxical relation to classical discourse (figured as 'male') and even to Roman imperial power itself. It is precisely through their stance of self-feminization that the Fathers produced and maintained their discourses of subjugating women.

In this respect too, the Fathers are quite similar to both early Rabbis and later rabbinic tradition. These also subjugated women through a discourse of self-feminization.[50] Both early rabbinic Jews and early Christians performed resistance to the Roman imperial power structure through 'genderbending' – males consciously renouncing the markers of masculinity and adopting practices that signified them as female within the economy of Roman gender models – thus marking their own understanding that gender itself is implicated in the maintenance of political power. Various symbolic enactments of 'femaleness' – as constructed within a particular

46 'Several factors seem crucial to understanding the fourth-century sexualized textualization of female bodies: first, the introduction of a decisively male-dominated political model for Christian community.' Burrus, 'Word and Flesh', p. 44. 'But Ambrose's voice was not the only voice of his time. We can well imagine that some of the ascetic women he addressed were telling versions of Thecla's story which remained disturbingly close to the second-century "original".' 'Word and Flesh', p. 48.

47 Burrus, 'Reading Agnes', p. 32. This female lion in the earlier text, I would argue, supports the earlier readings of the Apocryphal Acts as narratives of female autonomy and perhaps as even female-authored narratives (Stevan L. Davies, *The Revolt of the Widows: The Social World of the Apocryphal Acts* [Carbondale: Southern Illinois University Press, 1980]). See especially Burrus, *Chastity as Autonomy*, in this regard. In my opinion, the retreat from this position has been too precipitous. Cf. for instance, Kate Cooper, 'Apostles, Ascetic Women, and Questions of Audience: New Reflections on the Rhetoric of Gender in the *Apocryphal Acts*', paper presented at the Society of Biblical Literature/American Academy of Religion, Atlanta, 1992.

48 Burrus, 'Reading Agnes', p. 33.

49 Richlin, *The Garden of Priapus*.

50 Boyarin, *Unheroic Conduct*, pp. 151–85. Burrus has remarked on this similarity. 'Reading Agnes', p. 44 n. 54. See also Sered and Cooper, 'Sexuality and Social Control', pp. 54–55, on the way in which the feminized figure of Daniel in the Book of Susanna serves to reinforce male control of female sexuality by robbing women of the trickster role.

system of genders – among them asceticism, submissiveness, retiring to private spaces, (ostensible) renunciation of political power, exclusive devotion to study and self-castration[51] were adopted variously by Christians or rabbinic Jews as acts of resistance against Roman culture and the masculinist exercise of power.

This point is made by Burrus about early Christianity: 'For men, the pursuit of Christian ascesis entailed the rejection of public life and therefore of the hierarchies of office and gender; in this respect, their opponents were not far off the mark when they insinuated that male ascetics were "feminized" through their rejection of the most basic cultural expressions of male identity.'[52] Sulpicius Severus, a Gallic ascetic synchronous with our talmudic text, like Ambrose, his contemporary and associate explicitly identifies women, and especially virginal women, as his models for the ascetic life of retirement and withdrawal from public exposure and activity. 'Sulpicius's special interest in virginal women is in large part attributable, I think, to the fact that it is women in general and virginal women in particular who traditionally model the life of complete retirement and avoidance of public exposure', Burrus writes. Thus, 'Sulpicius puts forth the radical suggestion that the male must indeed "become female" through his ascetic renunciation of public life' and 'presents the virgin as an ideal of which Martin [of Tours, the soldier-monk who brought Christianity to much of fourth-century Gaul] acknowledges himself to fall short, compromised by his Episcopal office and also, I would add, by his very maleness.'[53] The male must become female in order to escape the moral dangers of his masculine state.

This parallels the becoming female of the Rabbis through their ascetic renunciations of intercourse with alluring Christianity or participation in the Roman state. The Rabbis, as well, adopted distinctly feminized stances of renunciation of political power.[54] In the talmudic text, the Rabbis are close, *mutatis mutandis*, to those ascetics for whom the virgin was a model for a life of withdrawal from public exposure – *mutatis mutandis*, for the withdrawal of a Roman aristocrat from the public could not be identical to the withdrawal of a Jewish Sage. Insofar as the female virgin was being utilized by male cultural products as a mode of negotiation of their critical, resisting, accommodating, alienated, envious and other stances towards Roman power and cultural prestige, different positionings with respect to 'Rome' would result in different virgins.

As a tentative hypothesis, I would offer the following: Identification with the

51 Condemned, of course (for clerics), at Nicaea, in the very first of the canons, as Willis Johnson has reminded me. Peter L'Huillier, *The Church of the Ancient Councils: The Disciplinary Work of the First Four Ecumenical Councils* (Crestwood, NY: St. Vladimir's Seminary Press, 1996), pp. 31–32.

52 Virginia Burrus, *The Making of a Heretic: Gender, Authority, and the Priscillianist Controversy* (Berkeley: University of California Press, 1995), p. 14.

53 Virginia Burrus, 'The Male Ascetic in Female Space: Alienated Strategies of Self-Definition in the Writings of Sulpicius Severus', paper presented at the Society of Biblical Literature/American Academy of Religion, San Francisco, CA, 1992. It should be noted for clarity that the quotation marks around 'become female' are not meant to indicate a quotation of Sulpicius, but rather precisely the appropriation of another culture's terms to interpret his practice. The admiration of both Sulpicius and Ambrose for Paulinus of Nola, a wealthy and cultivated poet – and disciple of Ausonius – who renounced his wealth, together with his wife, and retired to rural Italy, is emblematic of this position (Robert A. Markus, *The End of Ancient Christianity* [Cambridge, UK: Cambridge University Press, 1990], p. 36).

54 Boyarin, *Unheroic Conduct*, pp. 81–126.

female virgin was a mode for both Rabbis and Fathers of disidentification with a 'Rome' whose power was stereotyped as a highly sexualized male. Both groups were engaged in complex, tangled and ambivalent negotiations of self-fashionings in response to their attraction and repulsion from that Rome. Each, however, occupied a different space within the economies of power and ethnic emplacement in the Empire. Christian writers, even as late as the fourth or fifth centuries, frequently were former Roman 'pagans', sons of power and prestige in imperial society who were highly educated and who identified with classical culture. It is telling that both Ambrose and Prudentius were former provincial governors.[55] Their renunciation of such identification and certain forms of power and prestige is thus both more dramatic (for being voluntary and 'expensive'[56]) and more ambivalent than that of the Rabbis, who were always already outsiders to a certain extent by virtue of birth into a minority ethnic and religious group and by virtue of socialization into a different language and literary tradition.

Christian culture, with its powerful, but by no means univocal critique of marriage, continued to represent a much more radical rejection of Roman cultural values than did that of the Rabbis. I find here, nevertheless, a remarkable example of sharp cultural convergence. This is analogous, in Burrus's subtle readings, of the ways that power and prestige were both subverted and maintained, even by such ascetic figures as Sulpicius (a fortiori by bishops such as Ambrose) through their rhetorics of seclusion, withdrawal and 'feminizing ascesis'.[57]

This analysis of Burrus's proves strikingly productive, therefore, for our under-standing of the rabbinic text, as well, for parallel to the development of a discourse of male identification with female virgins among the Fathers, a similar discourse was developing among the Rabbis. The Rabbis also obviously stood in a highly ambivalent position vis-à-vis their version of 'Rome'. As we have seen, for them, being male represented a species of danger, danger of being 'seduced' into pursuing one of two prostitutes, heretical sectarianism in the form of Christianity (which was becoming the dominant religion of the Empire) or collaboration with Roman power.[58] Thus, also for them, the female virgin was to become symbolic of a virtual ego ideal.

Another way of saying this would be to mark the gap between the explicit and implicit meanings of the rabbinic text. On the explicit level, the text represents the purity of rabbinic culture, its efforts to remain entirely different and other from Christianity. However, at the same time, via its use of the figure of the female virgin to symbolize its valorized male self – the self that resists Christianization – it is indicating, at this distance at least, the convergence of rabbinic culture with that

---

55 Burrus, 'Reading Agnes', p. 34.

56 Brown, *The Cult of the Saints: Its Rise and Function in Latin Christianity* (The Haskell Lectures on History of Religions; Chicago, IL: University of Chicago Press, 1981), pp. 63–64.

57 This lack of univocity is very important to the conclusion of my argument. Kate Cooper (*The Virgin and the Bride: Idealized Womanhood in Antiquity* [Cambridge, MA: Harvard University Press, 1996]) has been very important for the development of my thinking here. Her book is another extended exploration of the ways that figures of idealized women are used within Late Antique culture in the rhetorical struggles *between men* for prestige and power.

58 In a text that I have discussed elsewhere, such collaboration is explicitly marked as becoming leonine. Boyarin, *Unheroic Conduct*, p. 88, and 'feminine' stealth is recommended as the antidote.

of the Christians, or, perhaps better put, their common cultural history and development. In her habitation of 'private' indoor spaces, the talmudic virgin is the figure who is construed as most able to resist the 'sexual' seductions of both sectarianism and accommodation to Roman power. To reprise: It is behaving as a male with respect to the 'female' blandishments of heresy or collaboration that gets one into trouble. Behaving as a 'female', then, would get one out of it.

Virgin Brides, Virgin Martyrs

For all this convergence, however, there are differences, as well. As Burrus has written: 'Both the continuity and the "otherness" of rabbinic Judaism in relation to Christianity are revealing, as Jewish and Christian men are seen to deploy strikingly different rhetorics of sexuality for the construction of counter-masculinities within the context of late ancient Greco-Roman culture.'[59] One source of such differences, I would suggest, is that the use of the virgin as male identificatory symbol is highly dependent on the posture of a given society towards actual virgin girls, and this was crucially different for the Rabbis and for the Fathers of the fourth-century Church. Up until now, I have focused entirely on the identification of the Rabbis with the female virgin in the brothel as a symbol of their tricky resistance, their playing of the hidden transcript, within the brothel of the Empire.[60] As such, my strategy has been to downplay the gendered differences of the text, emphasizing instead the ways that the genders are homologized in the narrative, that Rabbi Meʾir doubles the daughter of Rabbi Ḥanina, who doubles Rabbi Elʿazar ben Perata in his trickster escape, who doubles Rabbi Eliʿezer in his. All these males are feminized figures finally metaphoricized as the virgin in the brothel. The tricksterism of the virgin daughter thus at one level reprises and spotlights the openness of the talmudic text on the question of tricksters versus martyrs. Even in the very narrative in which martyrdom is being valorized, there is a favoured instance as well of tricky escape. But even this is compromised by the fact that both the daughter and Rabbi Yose ben Kisma seem engaged in pleasing 'the great men of Rome'. Both the defiance of the father and the trickster escape of the daughter seem equally valorized, or at any rate once more, the text just won't settle down to a univocal position on the acts of the tricksters and the martyrs.

However, if we reread its ending, now emphasizing gendered differences rather than disavowing them, we will find very different meanings emerging from the text. In other words, if we look at the virgin as a representative of Jewish female subjectivity, rather than as a transgendered symbol of identification for the Rabbis and for the people of Israel, we suddenly discover not a narrative that opens options for Jewish *people*, but a narrative that shuts them down for Jewish *women*.

To put it bluntly: In the rabbinic world, there can be no virgin martyrs.[61] The

---

59 Burrus, 'Reading Agnes', p. 44 n. 55.

60 This locution was originally applied to the talmudic story by Rachel Adler, 'The Virgin in the Brothel and Other Anomalies: Character and Context in the Legend of Beruriah' (*Tikkun* 3.6 [1988]), pp. 28–32. For other parallels, see Martha Malamud, *A Poetics of Transformation: Prudentius and Classical Mythology* (Ithaca, NY: Cornell University Press, 1989), pp. 157, 166–67.

61 The story of Miriam bat Tanḥum and the martyrdom of the wife of Rabbi Ḥanina here demonstrate this rule, since in both cases, the martyrdom is simply an appendix to the martyrdom of the men in their lives, and in neither case do we have much more than a mere mention of the death of the woman. Moreover, both are certainly not virgin martyrs. Indeed, they are martyred mothers.

daughter has to escape from the brothel, not only to reopen and revalorize the trickster option, but also because she must not die a virgin. The female virgin provided a highly valued model of rabbinic and patristic resistance to certain 'Roman' cultural values and practices, as we have seen. But this Jewish virgin, insofar as she is a girl and not a mere device for the exploration of male selves,[62] is subtly different from her Christian sisters.[63] She escapes her fated sexual violation, not through open resistance, resistance that ultimately costs her her life, like the second-century Perpetua, whose continued marital life is interpreted as sexual violation, or even like the fourth-century Agnes, but instead through the use of trickster methods, 'feminine' wiles, which allow her to escape both fates, rape as well as death. If the paradigmatic virgin for the fourth-century Fathers was the virgin martyr, the paradigmatic virgin for the Rabbis was the virgin in the brothel, who will, in the end, be a virgin bride.[64]

The sequel to the story of Thecla in Ambrose forms a remarkable parallel to the talmudic story that we have just read and will help sharpen this point dramatically.[65]

'Eroticized self-sacrificial death' (Burrus, 'Reading Agnes', p. 32), remained only for men. In part, this is simply a reflection of different gender/body politics in the two religious communities. The female roles of wife and mother were so highly honoured in the rabbinic world, in which sexuality and procreation were central values, that women were practically excluded from all other possibilities, including those, notably the teaching of Torah, that would lead to martyrdom. The emblem of saintly womanhood for traditional Judaism has been Rachel, wife of Rabbi Akiva, whose martyrdom consisted of waiting for him in poverty and chastity for twenty-four years while he was off studying in the Yeshiva. Amy-Jill Levine has remarked to me in a letter than the intertextual models for women heroes in Judaeo-Greek literature are always chaste wives or widows, the only virgin being Sarah in the Book of Tobit. This acute observation only sharpens the question of why this should be so. To get a sense of the significance of this difference between rabbinic Judaism and Christianity in the third and fourth centuries, one need only pay close attention to the struggles Christian writers had in valorizing married female martyrs in the fifth century, as documented recently in Cooper, *The Virgin and the Bride*, pp. 119–27. This, then, provides a direct contrast with the intertextual models mobilized in non-Christian Jewish circles.

In medieval Jewish female martyrology, the two instances of public and dangerous female heroism that are usually focused upon are attendance at the ritual bath (following menstruation and prior to the resumption of sexual relations) and attending to the circumcision of sons, exemplary practices, of course, of the married woman. For the former, see Charlotte Fonrobert, *Menstrual Purity: Rabbinic and Christian Reconstructions of Biblical Gender* (Stanford, CA: Stanford University Press, 2000).

62 Kate Cooper, 'Insinuations of Womanly Influence: An Aspect of the Christianization of the Roman Aristocracy', *JRS* 82 (1992), pp. 150–64.

63 For an extended exploration of the idea that rabbinic Judaism and Christianity are two different systems of sex/gender, see Daniel Boyarin, 'Gender', in Mark C. Taylor (ed.), *Critical Terms for the Study of Religion* (Chicago: University of Chicago Press, 1998), pp. 117–35.

64 Ambrose, in *On Virgins*, book I, chapter 4 (15), explicitly distinguishes between the permanent virginity espoused by the Church and temporary chastity, such as that of the Vestals, a fortiori also that of Jewish girls or the heroines of Greek novels. Note that even in Ambrose's version of 'virgin in the brothel' story, the virgin ends up in the arena, a martyr.

65 Virginia Burrus both called my attention to this text and its significance as a parallel to the talmudic story and suggested the direction of interpretation of it as a cross-gendering narrative that I adumbrate below and that will be much more fully developed in her own work on this. I am grateful to her, also, for sharing with me her work in progress, which has taught me so much about these texts. As long ago as 1987, Burrus had pointed out the relevance of the talmudic Rabbi Me'ir story for the Ambrose text, and had pointed to several other Christian and at least one non-Christian

It is so close to the talmudic narrative that it must clearly count as a variant of the same folktale type, but, the differences between the two culturally localized versions (ecotypes) are as instructive as the similarities. Since the text is rather long, I will paraphrase it, quoting only excerpts.

Ambrose tells of a virgin in Antioch who avoided being seen in public and who, knowing of the desire of many men for her, declared herself a perpetual virgin, whereupon 'she was no longer loved, instead she was betrayed'. The virgin, insisting on her chastity and not afraid of death, prepares herself for it. However, her persecutors have a more nefarious plan. They will allow her neither the crown of martyrdom nor virginity. After she refuses to sacrifice to the emperor, they send her, like Rabbi Ḥanina's daughter, to a brothel:

> At this the young woman, not in doubt about her religion but fearing for her chastity, said to herself: 'What shall I do? Today I shall be either a martyr or a virgin. One of the two crowns is begrudged us. But the title of virginity has no meaning where the author of virginity is denied.'

Virginity itself is worthless unless it is virginity of God. She will not sacrifice in order to preserve her chastity, any more than she would to preserve her life. Rather than risking giving up her religion, she chooses to enter the brothel, assuming that, like Rahab, she will be forgiven for this. Ambrose continues:

> All at once my discourse is ashamed and fears, as it were, to enter upon and relate the wicked course of events. Stop your ears, virgins of God: a young woman of God is being led to a brothel. But open your ears, virgins of God: a virgin can be made to prostitute herself but she cannot be made to commit adultery. Wherever a virgin of God is, there is a temple of God. Brothels not only do not bring chastity into disrepute, but chastity even does away with the disrepute of a place.
>
> A huge crowd of curiosity seekers surged towards the bordello. (Learn the miracles of the martyrs, holy virgins, but unlearn the vocabulary of these places.) The dove was shut up inside, while outside the hawks were loud, contending among themselves as to who would be the first to seize the prey.

In an echo of the lions, who were metaphorical representations of male sexual desire in the Thecla sequence, here we find the desiring male represented as a raptor. The virgin prays, invoking the miracle that saved Daniel from the lion's den, and indeed, God vouchsafes her a miracle in the form of a trickster:

> She had hardly completed the prayer when all of a sudden a man with the appearance of a fearsome soldier burst in. How the virgin trembled before him ... 'A sheep too may lie hidden in this lair of wolves. Christ, who even has legions (cf. Mt. 26.53), has his soldiers as well. Or perhaps the executioner has come in.[66] Do not be afraid, my soul: he is used to making martyrs.' O Virgin, 'your faith has saved you' (Lk. 8.48).

Roman version (Seneca) of the tale type. Burrus, *Chastity as Autonomy*, p. 65 n. 29. Revealingly, in Seneca's story, the virgin preserves her chastity by killing a man with his own sword, which is quite different from both our Jewish and Christian female and male tricksters, for all their internal differences, as well.

66 That is, someone who will kill her, not take her chastity.

The virgin here considers the possibility that the fierce soldier who has come in is not a lustful customer, but her potential executioner. Perhaps she will be saved by her faith, granted the two crowns of virginity and martyrdom after all. But not quite, for

> the soldier said to her: 'I beg you not to fear, my sister. I have come here as your brother to save my soul, not to destroy it. Heed me, so that you may be spared. Having come in as an adulterer, I shall, if you wish, go out a martyr. Let us exchange our clothing; yours fits me and mine fits you, but both fit Christ. Your garb will make me a true soldier; mine will make you a virgin. You will be clothed well and I shall be stripped better, so that the persecutor may recognize me. Put on the garment that will hide the woman and hand over the one that will consecrate the martyr.' ... While saying this he removed his cloak, which was a garment· that until this time was suspected of being that of a persecutor and an adulterer ... When she had changed her clothing the maiden flew out from the snare, but no longer with her own wings, inasmuch as she was borne by spiritual wings. And – what had never been seen before – she left the brothel a virgin, but Christ's.

Ambrose's rhetoric here is very deft. The virgin in the brothel, so far from being a sight that the ages never had seen, is practically a topos in this type of literature, but Ambrose (with a wink and a nudge) informs us that this was a sight that never had been seen before.[67] The blind and rapacious audience cannot see the *thauma edestai* that there is before their eyes, an intact virgin leaving the brothel:

> Those, however, who were looking with their eyes but did not see (cf. Mt. 13.13), were like wolves overpowering a lamb, raging at their prey. One who was less modest went in. But when with his eyes he had grasped the situation he said: 'What is this? A maiden went in but a man is here. This is not that famous story of the hind substituted for the virgin.[68] Rather it is a case of a maiden transformed into a soldier. I had heard and did not believe that Christ changed water into wine (cf. Jn 2.1–10), but now he has begun to change sexes as well. Let us get out of here while we still are what we were. Have I myself, who see something else

67 One wonders at the Ambrose who is so sophisticated a folklorist that he can refer to the parallel tale of a virgin turned into a hind (in the next paragraph), not being aware that here also he is dealing with a virtual tale type. His insistence on the uniqueness of this event could be seen, therefore, as a bit of highly effective rhetorical flourish. Alternatively, it would be seen as a very part of the topos itself, as Virginia Burrus has commented to me.

68 For this tale type, see Antti Aarne and Stith Thomson, *The Types of the Folktale: A Classification and Bibliography* (2nd edn; Folklore Fellows Communications, 3; Helsinki: Suomalainen Tiedeakatamia, 1987), p. 131. I am grateful to Galit Hasan-Rokem for this information. Boniface Ramsey, *Ambrose* (The Early Church Fathers; New York: Routledge, 1997) p. 222 n. 21, suggests that this is an allusion to the story of Iphigenia. She, however, was translated into a goat, not a hind, so I think rather that we have here a very ancient form of a folktale otherwise attested only in much later sources. Another shared theme between Christian and Jewish legends in this period is the topos of the robber or the prostitute reformed. For the Christian texts, see inter alia, Benedicta Ward, *Harlots of the Desert: A Study of Repentance in Early Monastic Sources* (Cistercian Studies Series, 106; Kalamazoo, MI: Cistercian Publications, 1987); Susanna Elm, *'Virgins of God': The Making of Asceticism in Late Antiquity* (Oxford Classical Monographs; Oxford: Clarendon Press and New York: Oxford University Press,1994), pp. 258, 318. Derwas J. Chitty, *The Desert a City: An Introduction to the Study of Egyptian and Palestinian Monasticism Under the Christian Empire* (1966; Crestwood, NY: St. Validimir's Seminary Press, 1995), p. 53. For Jewish parallels, see Daniel Boyarin, 'Homotopia: The Feminized Jewish Man and the Lives of Women in Late Antiquity', *differences* 7 (1995), pp. 41–71.

than I can believe, been changed too? I came to a brothel, I see a pledge.[69] And yet I shall depart changed, I shall go out chaste – I who came in unchaste.'[70]

Here are more violent figures for male desire, but it is also a very clever moment, indeed. The shameless pagan who went in sees a woman changed into a man and fears that he, too, will be transformed. His sex will change, and he will exit the brothel a female virgin – that is, a Christian. Once more, Ambrose has produced the virgin girl as the type of the Christian male.

The Christian soldier disguised as virgin gets caught, of course: 'He who had been seized in place of the virgin was condemned in place of the virgin. Thus it was not just a virgin but martyrs who came out of the brothel.' Here we have another effective rhetorical move in which the identification of the female virgin as male role model is made explicit. The folkloristic figure of the man disguised as woman is explicitly thematized as an appropriation of the name 'virgin' by the male martyr, an appropriation that is doubled by the identification of the Fathers with female virgins, both martyred and not. In other words, the male Christian cross-dressed as a Roman soldier and then once again cross-dressed as a virgin martyr produces the same effect of identification with a virgin for a male audience as that produced through the cross-gendering of the lion/ess in Ambrose's retelling of Thecla's story. The transformation of the second customer makes a perfect double of the transformation of the lion. He also goes in as a hypermale predator – a wolf – and is transformed into a celibate, feminized Christian. The point of identification is made even more palpable here, however, and thus serves as a further interpretive key, guaranteeing Burrus's reading, for the 'female' object, the 'virgin' who produces this second conversion, is, in fact, this time literally, a cross-dressed man.

The story goes on to report that the escaped maiden, however, returns to the place of punishment. The virgin insists that she must be martyred, also, using the very reasonable argument that it was chastity she sought, and her chastity is equally in danger now. Moreover, if the soldier is martyred in her place, then she would be guilty of his blood. 'A virgin has a place to bear a wound, even if she had no place to bear an affront ... I have changed my clothing, not my profession. If you snatch death from me, you have not saved me but circumvented me.'[71] In the end, of course, both achieve the crown of martyrdom together.[72]

The typological connection, perhaps even the genetic connection, between this story and the story of Rabbi Me'ir's martial disguise is palpable. In both cases, the male rescuer disguises himself as a Roman soldier, a typical customer of the prostitute's, in order to reveal himself to her as her rescuer. The stories have very different endings, however. Rabbi Me'ir's sister-in-law escapes, and that is the end of her story. The narrative of the virgin of Antioch, however, reprises the by now

---

69 Ramsey notes here: 'The "pledge" (*vadimonium*) refers to the fact that as the following paragraph explains, the soldier is a bondsman or guarantee for the virgin. The man in whose mouth these words has been placed has inexplicably grasped the situation.' Ramsey, *Ambrose*, p. 222 n. 22.

70 Ramsey, *Ambrose*, pp. 96–101.

71 I have substituted 'circumvented' from the NPNF translation for Ramsey's 'defrauded'.

72 Ambrose, *On Virgins*, pp. 2, 19–20. Ramsey, *Ambrose*, pp. 96–101.

familiar Christian plot of the escaped martyr who returns to fulfil his or her destiny as martyr.

The virgin of Antioch is, indeed, not circumvented by being rescued. We have here, then, a narrative of female autonomy: she gets to choose her fate, the double crown of virginity and martyrdom. However, we also have here a narrative of the most extreme form of social control. As Burrus elucidates, the function of the narrative of the virgin of Antioch is to 'obscur[e] the awkward narrative fact of Thecla's triumphant survival of persecution. It is by juxtaposing Thecla's story with that of the Antiochene martyr that Ambrose brings Thecla directly ... under the control of the late fourth-century tale of the virgin martyr, with its necessary fatal conclusion.'[73] Conversely, the rescue of the rabbinic virgin is as necessary in terms of the rabbinic discourse of gender as the death of the patristic one is for theirs, for were the Jewish virgin to die then, her calling as woman would have been destroyed, not preserved. Whereas for much of the Christian tradition the perpetual virgin girl is perfection itself, for the Rabbis, she is a chrysalis, not fully formed. As Chrysostom well put it: 'The Jews disdained the beauty of virginity ... The Greek admired and revered the virgin, but only the Church of God adored her with zeal.'[74] For Chrysostom, by the fourth century, rabbinic Judaism, with its anti-ascetic tendency, simply *is* Judaism.

For Ambrose, the primary issue in the symbolization of the virgin as ego ideal is precisely her virginity – her literal continence, interpreted as a model for male celibates, that is, as an abiding sign of Christian resistance to the regimes of heteronormativity and natalism of the Graeco–Roman world.[75] Rabbinic Judaism, in contrast, for all its alienation from certain aspects of late classical culture, strongly accepted and identified with the ideologies favouring marriage and childbearing that were current in their time in the Roman world.

Early Christianity, it could fairly be argued, was in large part a powerful resistance movement to this facet of Roman culture. In the Ambrose text about Thecla, her near martyrdom is caused entirely by her resistance to the dominant Roman cultural norm of marriage and procreation. There is virtually nothing in the story about her belief in Christ, her rejection of pagan gods, or even her rejection of emperor worship that leads her into the ring with the lions. To be sure, her commitment to virginity was generated by her conversion to Christianity, but the content of that conversion is seemingly more about virginity than about any other religious practice or belief.[76]

This is typical of virgin-martyr acts in general. As Elizabeth Castelli has characterized this type of text, 'The formulaic character of many of the accounts suggests not an audience expecting novelty, but one finding a compelling spiritual idiom in the repetitions of the triumph of virginal virtue over scurrilous and scandalous male

---

73 Burrus, 'Reading Agnes', p. 31.

74 Chrysostom, *On Virginity*, I, I.

75 For a slightly different interpretation of the meaning of 'virginity' in Alexander and Athanasius of Alexandria, namely, as a Douglas-like symbolic representation of the 'definition and enforcement of communal and doctrinal boundaries', see Burrus, 'Word and Flesh', pp. 35–45. This is more like the symbolic functioning of female chastity in some earlier Jewish texts such as the Book of Tobit. Amy-Jill Levine, 'Diaspora as Metaphor'.

76 Burrus, *Chastity as Autonomy*, pp. 43–33.

desire',[77] including, I would add and emphasize, the scurrilous and scandalous desire of 'legitimate' husbands.[78] To be fair, this text comes from Ambrose's treatise 'On Virginity', so it is not entirely surprising that this should be the focus, but the story as it appears in the apocryphal *Acts of Paul and Thecla* is not all that different in content, although told not nearly so well there.

Early Christian sainthood, I wish to suggest, is as much about sexuality and about the resistance to, critique of, and oppositional positioning with respect to a certain regime of power/knowledge about sex as it is about anything else. That regime is found in the discourse shared by both pagans and Jews in the late antique city: the foundation of human good is the formation of reproductive families. Rabbi Ḥanina is the perfect model of a family man, and in every respect, other than his commitment to the study of Torah, a fine support for the Late Antique city. The virginity of his daughter, preserved miraculously in the brothel to which she was sent, will certainly fit her by the end of that story for a proper marriage to a scholar of Talmud, just like her father (although perhaps a more prudent one).[79]

The Rabbi's daughter cannot, therefore, die a virgin.[80] Although there are, of course, stories within the Jewish and even the rabbinic traditions of youths and maidens who commit suicide rather than sacrifice their chastity to Gentile oppressors, the point about reproductive families is, in fact, strengthened by that very narrative because the fact that they die unmarried is considered to add to the tragedy of the situation, not as, in itself, a religious triumph.[81] Another extraordinary story has a large group

77　Elizabeth A. Castelli, *Visions and Voyeurism: Holy Women and the Politics of Sight in Early Christianity*, vol. 2 of Christopher Ocker (ed.), *Protocol of the Colloquy of the Center for Hermeneutical Studies, New Series* (Berkeley, CA: Center for Hermeneutical Studies, 1995), p. 10.

78　In the discussion of Castelli's *Visions and Voyeurism* at the Center for Hermeneutical Studies, Steven Knapp remarked, 'One could have the impression reading both the paper and the responses that the prospective women martyrs were mainly concerned on the eve of their martyrdom with the question of whether to accept or resist the male gaze, rather than with the fact that they were about to be tortured to death in the name of their religious beliefs', thus missing the point that the resistance to the male gaze (and even more) was precisely the significant content of their belief. Castelli, *Visions and Voyeurism*, p. 51.

79　Of course, we do not literally have the sequel to the story of Rabbi Ḥanina's daughter, and therefore my claim that she will end up married has something of the flavour of 'How many children had Lady Macbeth?' about it. I think that I can make the case stronger by referring to a parallel instance. Both rabbinic and Christian cultures in the fourth and fifth centuries told tales of reformed and converted prostitutes. It seems highly significant to me that in the Christian versions, these women end up ascetic, nuns and even cross-dressed monks (see Ward, *Harlots of the Desert*). In the rabbinic versions, however, otherwise very closely parallel to the Christian ones, the erstwhile harlot ends up the wife of a Rabbi. *Sifre to Numbers* 15.37, *TB Menaḥot* 44a. The point that I am making about the ideological difference between the two cultures therefore seems well taken. For Christian family martyrdoms, see G.W. Clarke (trans. and ed.), *Letters 1–27*, vol. 1 of *The Letters of St. Cyprian of Carthage* (Ancient Christian Writers: The Works of the Fathers in Translation, 46; New York: Newman Press, 1986), p. 195.

80　Sered and Cooper, 'Sexuality and Social Control', p. 54.

81　*TB Gittin* 57b. Similarly, already in the Bible, the girls gather yearly to cry over the virginity of the Daughter of Jephta, that is, to mourn the fact that she died a virgin. Chrysostom knew what he was talking about. The theme of mass suicide to avoid sexual humiliation goes back at least to the Danaids in Aeschylus, who sought death to avoid marriage. Loraux, *Tragic Ways of Killing a Woman*, p. 10. Once again, the contrasts, as well as the comparisons between various forms of the motif are what make cultural difference and cultural history.

of married Jewish couples who have been separated for purposes of sexual exploitation and die bloodily rather than violate their marriage vows. In the story, the blood of the husbands and the blood of the wives join into one stream.[82] Thus, even though we don't literally have the end of the story, by all normative rabbinic traditions, the Rabbi's daughter in the story we have been reading will have to end up a bride.[83]

Were this all there were to say about the issue, we would simply have two exactly equally violent systems of oppression of women: one dictating marriage for all, and one dictating universal virginity. Indeed, one could argue that the very *longuer* of the Ambrosian narrative is generated by its necessity to transform a trickster-escape tale into a tale of a virgin martyr. By the time of Ambrose's writing, however, the Christian girl could choose to be a virgin or a bride, for all that the virgin remained more honoured.[84]

Thus, although the Rabbi's daughter cannot die a virgin because she must end up a bride, the Christian girl has two choices open to her: bride or virgin.[85] In this respect, early Christianity, even in its post-Constantinian phase, reflects a much more radical revision of Graeco–Roman mores than does rabbinic Judaism. Kate Cooper has written: 'The romance of late antiquity takes [among Christians] the form of a saint's life, in which the chaste desire of the legitimately married hero and heroine has metamorphosed into the otherworldly passion by which a Christian saint embraces a childless death.'[86] If we accept the current view that one major function of the Greek novels was to reinforce marriage and the reproductive family as the foundation of civic society, as has been argued by Cooper, among others,[87] and that the Apocryphal Acts, including especially the *Acts of Paul and Thecla*, were about parodying and resisting that romantic ideology, then the rabbinic text – even this rabbinic martyrology – is ideologically closer to those Hellenistic novels than it is to the Apocryphal Acts. As Judith Lieu has describe them, these last 'create a world in sharp conflict with contemporary social structures, rejecting marriage and family life, anticipating and valuing suffering and death'.[88] One would hardly describe rabbinic culture in these terms.

82 I thank my friends Menahem Hirshman and Galit Hasan-Rokem for reminding me of these texts from the Palestinian midrash on the book of Lamentations.

83 In a similar thematic vein, Christian stories of reformed prostitutes end with the repentant a nun (or sometimes a monk, as Pelagia/Pelagius), while such stories among the Rabbis end in a marriage. Ward, *Harlots of the Desert*.

84 As Ambrose emphasizes over and over in the letter to his sister Marcellina that constitutes his tractate *On Virgins*, he is not condemning marriage. 'From the time of Jovinian Catholic writers had to acknowledge the good of marriage or face a charge of heresy.' Cooper, *The Virgin and the Bride*, p. 116 and see her p. 97 as well.

85 Elm, *'Virgins of God'*, pp. 337–38.

86 Cooper, *The Virgin and the Bride*, p. 44.

87 Cooper, *The Virgin and the Bride*, p. 44. See also Judith Perkins, *The Suffering Self: Pain and Narrative Representation in the Early Christian Era* (London and New York: Routledge, 1995), p. 26, and David Konstan, 'Acts of Love: A Narrative Pattern in the Apocryphal Acts', *JECS* 6 (1998), pp. 15–36. Not all, to be sure, read the novels in quite this way. One recent scholar would see in these works precisely what would praise 'the idea of young people – teenagers – standing up for what they wanted' and even suggests that 'this was not Roman, but it was what the young Perpetua did when she defied her family to follow Christ'. Salisbury, *Perpetua's Passion*, p. 47.

88 Judith Lieu, *Image and Reality: The Jews in the World of the Christians in the Second Century* (Edinburgh: T&T Clark, 1995), p. 17.

Elizabeth Clark, and with her, several other feminist scholars, have emphasized that the 'otherworldly passion' represented a real, if also direly compromised avenue of autonomy for early Christian girls and women.[89] Castelli has made the point that 'in a tradition where self-representation is a virtual impossibility for women, [Blandina's martyrdom] stands as a remarkable moment of spiritual assertion and refusal to be fully defined by the terms she did not accept'.[90] Even this sort of highly compromised option did not exist for our Talmudic virgin, however. Her escape is not only an escape from oppression but also, an oppressive escape, signified in that she has to pass a chastity test before even being deemed worthy of rescue by Rabbi Me'ir. Her escape is not a sign of her freedom. She is constrained to escape precisely because her virginity is being preserved, like that of Leucippe, *for* her husband, while the Antioch virgin's telos is rendered with compelling eroticism. Miracles prevent her from being sexually violated, but none will circumvent her desire for martyrdom. As the executioner approaches her, she speaks:

> I revel more a wild man comes,
> A cruel and violent man-at-arms,
> Than if a softened youth came forth,
> Faint and tender, bathed in scent,
> To ruin me with chastity's death.
> This is my lover, I confess,
> A man who pleases me at last!
> I shall rush to meet his steps
> So I don't delay his hot desires.
> I shall greet his blade's full length
> Within my breast; and I shall draw
> The force of sword to bosom's depth.
> As bride of Christ, I shall leap over
> The gloom of sky, the aether's heights.
> Eternal King, part Heaven's gates,
> Barred before to earth-born folk,
> And call, O Christ, a virgin soul,
> A soul that aims to follow thee,
> Now a sacrifice to Father God.[91]

89 Elizabeth A. Clark, 'Ascetic Renunciation and Feminine Advancement: A Paradox of Late Ancient Christianity', in *eadem*, *Ascetic Piety and Women's Faith: Essays in Late Ancient Christianity* (New York: Edwin Mellen Press, 1986), pp. 175–208; Burrus, *Chastity as Autonomy*; Elizabeth A. Castelli, 'Virginity and Its Meaning for Women's Sexuality in Early Christianity', *JFSR* 2 (1986), pp. 61–88.

90 Castelli, *Visions and Voyeurism*, p. 19. Cf. the point made by Loraux about the tragic deaths of women: 'With its solid bolts that have to be forced back for the dead woman to be reached – or rather the dead body from which the woman has already fled – this room reveals the narrow space that tragedy grants to women for the exercise of their freedom. They are free enough to kill themselves, but they are not free enough to escape from the space to which they belong.' Loraux, *Tragic Ways of Killing a Woman*, p. 23. Blake Leyerle has pointed out to me that the topos continues even unto Thelma and Louise [Reader's report]. Of these too, it could be said, that 'women's glory in tragedy was an ambiguous glory'. Loraux, *Tragic Ways of Killing a Woman*, p. 28.

91 Prudentius, *The Poems of Prudentius* (trans. M. Clement Eagen; The Fathers of the Church: A New Translation; Washington, D.C.: Catholic University of America Press, 1962), p. 277. I have used here the far more beautiful translation found in Elizabeth A. Clark, *Women in the Early Church*, p. 112. See also Burrus, 'Reading Agnes', pp. 36–38 for a discussion. The 'wild man' is, as Burrus

At the point of Prudentius's writing, however, Christian women were hardly being martyred anymore. The virgin martyr was now the model and type of the ascetic life of the Bride of Christ, the nun,[92] while, of course, the option of carnal marriage also was available for women.[93]

Burrus paraphrases this text: 'Invoking a potential tale of liberation only to subvert that narrative, the poet compromises Agnes's rescue from sexual violation and indeed undermines her very resistance through his spectacular scripting of her climactic speech.'[94] There is no escape offered from male domination.[95] At the same time, however, the power of the virgin martyr never can be completely eclipsed: 'Only by explicitly problematizing female audacity can the tale of the virgin martyr attempt to restrain the heroism of women. And because the tale must therefore become engaged in the construction and contemplation of the heroic *virago*, its message of virginal docility always carries with it the potential for its own subversion.'[96] If, moreover, we remember that medieval Christianity did offer intellectual and spiritual vocations for religious women, however much under the hierarchical superiority of males, while medieval Judaism offered none, then we can, again following Burrus, see this as an incompletely subverted potential tale of liberation (or a partially subverted tale of

---

notes, both executioner and Christ bridegroom, but the last lines of the speech add yet another wrinkle, for now the virgin soul identifies herself with Christ as a sacrifice to the Father. The plays of identification and desire are as complex as any neo-Freudian could possibly want.

92 John Petruccione, 'The Portrait of St. Eulalia of Mérida in Prudentius' *Peristephanon*', *Analecta Bollandiana* 108 (1990), pp. 81–104 (86); Elizabeth A. Castelli, 'Imperial Reimaginings of Christian Origins: Epic in Prudentius's Poem', in *eadem* and Hal Taussig (eds.), *Reimagining Christian Origins: A Colloquium Honoring Burton L. Mack* (Valley Forge, PA: Trinity Press International, 1996), pp. 173–84; Markus, *The End of Ancient Christianity*, p. 24.

93 Cooper's chapter 'The Imprisoned Heroine' comprises a study of how this tension between virginal ideal and a valorization of marriage was textualized and to a certain degree resolved in the *Gesta* of the Roman martyrs, a genre of fictional martyrology roughly contemporaneous with Prudentius, *The Virgin and the Bride*, pp. 116–43. This was done in part by 'encouraging married women to imagine themselves as the spiritual heirs of the pre-Constantinian martyrs'. *The Virgin and the Bride*, p. 139. I will be forgiven seeming cynical, however, if I suggest that the example of Agnes or Eulalia (especially Eulalia) was more likely to encourage young women to be nuns than wives. Even Anastasia's exemplum, as discussed at length by Cooper, would hardly inspire women to marriage. Nevertheless, it is clear that the Catholic Church was powerfully engaged in a struggle to validate the spirituality of both the virgin and the bride by the fifth century. It is important to note that Cooper's thesis is that an ancient Christian tradition of validation of the chastity of the *matrona* was threatened by the rise of the ascetic movement in the fourth century, while my instinct, not nearly as educated as Cooper's of course, suggests that the needs of the post-Constantinian Church would require a greater emphasis on the spiritual vocations of those who were the pillars of everyday society. Thus, I would be inclined to lean a priori to the option that the 'emphasis on the spirituality of the *matrona* in the *Liber* and the *Passio* (of St. Anastasia)' finds its 'context in the battle between orthodoxy and Manichaeism of fifth-century Rome', as opposed to the option that they 'represent a last flicker of the traditionalism of late fourth-century senatorial Christians', Cooper, *The Virgin and the Bride*, p. 140. I would argue that Cooper's own argument with respect to the contrast between 'the frenzied craving for continence of the heroines of the *Apocryphal Acts*' and the '*pudor* of the honorable wife Anastasia' strongly leads in the direction of the first option. Cooper herself, it seems, leans in this direction. *The Virgin and the Bride*, pp. 142–43, if I have read her correctly.

94 Burrus, 'Reading Agnes', pp. 37–38.

95 Sered and Cooper, 'Sexuality and Social Control', pp. 53–54.

96 Burrus, 'Reading Agnes', p. 42.

virginal docility), and not one that is unequivocally compromised and undermined. As Burrus writes, '[Agnes] is not after all audacious *virago* but docile *virgo*', but insofar as she is an ego ideal for Christian girls, she presents the possibility of choosing a life path, however compromised, however limited, that rabbinic society had shut down completely.[97]

Only a naive, highly apologetic, or triumphalist voice – of which there are unfortunately many – would claim that Christianity bears a feminist message vis-à-vis a misogynist Judaism.[98] To be sure, it is a caricature that regards the lives of Jewish wives in Antiquity as peculiarly worse than those of their Christian or traditionalist Graeco–Roman sisters, or that sees early Christianity as a 'feminist' movement, or ignores the 'patriarchal' control of even religious women in the church.[99] As Charlotte Fonrobert has argued: 'We have to ask whether in a discourse which builds up an elite of sexual renunciation, in which women are allowed or even encouraged to participate, married women might perhaps fare worse than in a culture in which everybody is required to marry.'[100] And Fonrobert further remarks that 'because of its focus on doctrinal questions on the one hand, and on sexual *akesis* primarily for the Christian leadership, on the other, early Christian discourse often neglected to consider the everyday life of those who failed to rise to prominence as hailed ascetics', that is, to produce a Christian sexual ethic for them.[101] She maintains that observance of 'Jewish' menstrual-purity rules provided an avenue of spiritual fulfilment, of *akesis*, analogous to virginity for the Christian married women of the community of the *Didascalia*.[102]

This is a different Christian solution to the problem than emphasis on marriage as a form of martyrdom and suggests different interpretations of possible meanings of menstrual purity for rabbinic Jewish women, as well. The use of a claim of menstruation as a means of 'self-defence' in the story of Beruriah's sister above suggests this motive also, a motive that goes back as far as Rachel claiming to be menstruating in order to trick her father out of his household gods in the Bible.[103] Fonrobert's discussion of the *Didascalia* suggests as well that perhaps the exclusion of women from the study of Torah among rabbinic Jews was not as total as imagined. There is a passage from the Tosefta, also preserved in the Palestinian Talmud, that reads: 'gonnorheics, menstruants and parturients are permitted to read the Torah, to study Mishna, midrash, religious law and aggada, but men who have had a seminal

97 For the extent to which choice of the virginal option was or was not a free-will decision in at least one fourth-century Christian environment, see Elm, *'Virgins of God'*, pp. 139–40.

98 Katharina von Kellenbach, *Anti-Judaism in Feminist Religious Writings* (American Academy of Religion; Atlanta: Scholars Press, 1994).

99 Kathleen Corley, 'Feminist Myths of Christian Origins', in Castelli and Taussig (eds.), *Reimagining Christian Origins,* pp. 51–67; von Kellenbach, *Anti-Judaism in Feminist Religious Writings*.

100 Charlotte Fonrobert, 'Women's Bodies, Women's Blood: Politics of Gender in Rabbinic Literature' (Ph.D. diss., Graduate Theological Union, 1995; microfilm).

101 Fonrobert, 'Women's Bodies, Women's Blood'.

102 Charlotte Fonrobert, 'The Didascalia Apostolorum: A Mishnah for the Disciples of Jesus', *JECS* 9 (2001), pp. 483-509.

103 I am grateful to Amy-Jill Levine for calling this last point to my attention, although I have 'processed' it somewhat differently than her formulation. Note the highly charged concatenation of menstruation as a space for some female autonomy and the trickster role as well.

emission may not' (*Berakhot*, ch. 2, para. 12). Even those who have taken this passage seriously as an original halakhic text have understood it as reflecting only a utopian possibility, not a reality of woman studying Torah in antiquity.[104] However, the converted Jewish women of the *Didascalia* openly claim that they are not allowed to study Scripture when they are menstruating, suggestive at least, of the possibility that their practice represents another halakhic tradition, the one that the Tosefta speaks against, and that we thus have some real evidence that at least some Jewish women did study Torah in Antiquity. The *Didascalia*, it should be emphasized, is almost exactly contemporaneous with the Tosefta.[105]

This is surely the other side of the coin.[106] It nevertheless remains the case that Perpetua, Thecla, Agnes and Eulalia paved the way for Hildegard, Julian and Teresa, all of whom, in medieval Jewish society, would have been only someone's wife and somebody's mother. They also could have been prominent businesswomen, of course, like Glikl, or my great grandmother, but not abbesses, writers, theologians or poets.[107] As Castelli has written, 'the decision to remain a virgin and to renounce marriage and the world did provide some virgins with an opportunity to pursue intellectual and spiritual activities which would otherwise have been unavailable to them. Especially among educated aristocratic women who wished to pursue a life of study, the life of ascetic renunciation was the only institutionally established means of pursuing intellectual work.'[108] It is not entirely surprising, therefore, that Cher's American Jewish daughter, Charlotte, might have fixed on Perpetua as a heroine and model of female spiritual self-realization.[109]

It would seem, then, that in contrast to the dilemma of the trickster and the martyr, where the Christian text seemed to feel it necessary to provide only one honoured road, while the Jewish text left both ways open, in the matter of the virgin and the bride, it is the Christian text that permits two life paths, neither, of course, presenting anything like full autonomy for women, while the rabbinic text firmly shuts the gate in front of perhaps the only way available in Antiquity for females to achieve any measure of spiritual or intellectual autonomy at all.

Rabbinic Judaism and Christianity thus can perhaps be most richly read as complexly related subsystems of one religious polysystem, well into Late Antiquity and even beyond. I am inspired here, as frequently before, by the words of Mieke Bal. 'Dichotomies have two inevitable consequences: They subsume all relevant phenomena under only two categories, thus restricting the possibilities and paralysing the imagination, their centripetal quality. And they turn hierarchical, shedding off one pole as negative in favor of the other, which needs to establish its value, their

---

104 Daniel Boyarin, *Carnal Israel: Reading Sex in Talmudic Culture* (The New Historicism: Studies in Cultural Poetics, vol. 25; Berkeley: University of California Press, 1993), pp. 180–81.

105 Phillip Sigal, 'Early Christian and Rabbinic Liturgical Affinities: Exploring Liturgical Acculturation', *NTS* 30 (1984), pp. 63–90 (66).

106 On this point, see also the discussion in Elm, *'Virgins of God'*, pp. 160–61 n.71, 171–83.

107 Daniel Boyarin, *Unheroic Conduct*, pp. 158–62.

108 Castelli, 'Virginity and Its Meaning', p. 82. See also Joyce Salisbury, *Church Fathers, Independent Virgins* (London: Verso, 1991); Salisbury, *Perpetua's Passion*.

109 In my previous work, I referred to spiritual coverture in medieval and early modern Judaism, in contrast to the economic and sexual coverture of the general European culture.

centrifugal quality.'[110] Such is the dichotomy between a reified Judaism and a reified Christianity. Unsettling this binary opposition and upsetting the almost ineluctable invidiousness accompanying dichotomies is thus not only a matter of rectifying the historical record, but also of mobilizing new ways to imagine and conceive of well-known texts and cultural events.

---

110 Mieke Bal, *Murder and Difference: Gender, Genre, and Scholarship on Sisera's Death* (Indiana Studies in Biblical Literature; Bloomington: Indiana University Press, 1988), p. 9.

BIBLIOGRAPHY

Aarne, A., and S. Thomson, *The Types of the Folktale: A Classification and Bibliography* (2nd edn; Folklore Fellows Communications, 3; Helsinki: Suomalainen Tiedeakatamia, 1987).

Achelis, H., (ed.), *Acta SS. Nerei et Achillei. Text und Untersuchung* (Texte und Untersuchungen zur Geschichte der altchristlichen Literatur 11.2; Leipzig: J. C. Hinrichs'sche Buchhandlung, 1893).

Achtemeier, P.J., 'Jesus and the Disciples as Miracle Workers in the Apocryphal New Testament', in Elisabeth Schüssler Fiorenza (ed.), *Aspects of Religious Propoganda* (University of Notre Dame Center for the Study of Judaism and Christianity in Antiquity, 2; Notre Dame, IN and London: University of Notre Dame Press, 1976), pp. 149–86.

Adak, M., 'Claudia Anassa – eine Wohltäterin aus Patara', *Epigraphica Anatolica* 27 (1996), pp. 127–42.

Adamik, T., 'Eroticism in the *Liber de miraculis beati Andrea apostoli* of Gregory of Tours', in Bremmer (ed.), *Acts of Andrew*, pp. 35–46.

Adler, R., 'The Virgin in the Brothel and Other Anomalies: Character and Context in the Legend of Beruriah', *Tikkun* 3.6 (1988), pp. 28–32.

Adrados, F.R. (ed.), *Diccionario Griego-Español* V (Madrid: Consejo Superior de Investigaciones Científicas, Instituto 'Antonio de Nebrija', 1997).

Adrados, F.R. (ed.), *Diccionario Griego-Español* V (5 vols.; Madrid: Consejo Superior de Investigaciones Científicas, Instituto 'Antonio de Nebrija', 1997).

Albrecht, R., *Das Leben der heiligen Makrina auf dem Hintergrund der Thekla-Traditionen: Studien zu den Ursprüngen des weiblichen Mönchtums im 4. Jahrhundert in Kleinasien* (Forschungen zur Kirchen- und Dogmengeschichte 38; Göttingen: Vandenhoeck & Ruprecht, 1986), pp. 239–319.

Alton, E.H., D.E.W. Wormell and E. Courtney (eds), *P. Ovidi Nasonis Fastorum Libri Sex* (Leipzig: BSB B.G. Teubner Verlagsgesellschaft, 1978).

Amand de Mendieta, D., 'La virginité chez Eusèbe d'Émèse et l'ascétisme familial dans la première moitié du IVe siècle', *Revue d'Histoire Ecclésiastique* 50 (1955), pp. 777–820.

Amsler, F., *Acta Philippi: Commentarius* (CCSA 12; Turnhout: Brepols, 1999).

Andersen, R., *The Power and the Word: Language, Power and Change* (London: Paladin Grafton Books, 1988).

Anderson, G., 'Celibacy or Consummation in the Garden? Reflections on Early Jewish and Christian Interpretations of the Garden of Eden', *HTR* 82 (1989), pp. 121–48.

Arjava, A., 'Paternal Power in Late Antiquity', *JRS* 88 (1998), pp. 147–65.

— *Women and Law in Late Antiquity* (Oxford: Clarendon Press, 1996).

Armstrong, A.H. (ed. and trans.), *Plotinus* (7 vols.; LCL; Cambridge, MA: Harvard University Press, 1966–88).

Aubin, M., 'Reversing Romance? The *Acts of Thecla* and the Ancient Novel', in Ronald F. Hock, Bradley Chance and Judith Perkins (eds), *Ancient Fiction and*

Early Christian Narrative (SBL Symposium Series, 6; Atlanta: Scholars Press, 1998), pp. 257–72.

Aune, D.E., 'Magic in Early Christianity', *ANRW* II.23.2 (1980), pp. 1507–57.

— (ed.) *The Westminster Dictionary of New Testament and Early Christian Literature and Rhetoric* (Louisville, KY: Westminster/John Knox Press, 2003), pp. 2–3.

Aymer, M.P., 'Hailstorms and Fireballs: Redaction, World Creation, and Resistance in the *Acts of Paul and Thecla*', *Semeia* 79 (1997), pp. 45–62.

Baker, C., 'Bodies, Boundaries, and Domestic Politics in a Late Ancient Marketplace', *Journal of Medieval and Early Modern Studies* 26 (1996), pp. 391–418.

— 'Neighbor at the Door or Enemy at the Gate? Notes Toward a Rabbinic Topography of Self and Other', paper presented at the American Academy of Religion, New Orleans, 1996.

Bakhtin, M., 'Forms of Time and of the Chronotope in the Novel', in *idem*, *The Dialogic Imagination. Four Essays by M.M. Bakhtin* (trans. Caryl Emerson and Michael Holquist; ed. Michael Holquist; Austin and London: University of Texas Press, 1981), pp. 84–110.

Bakke, O.M., *When Children Became People. The Birth of Childhood in Early Christianity* (trans. Brian McNeil; Minneapolis, MN: Fortress Press, 2005).

Bal, M., 'Tricky Thematics', *Semeia* 42 (1988), pp. 133–55.

— *Murder and Difference: Gender, Genre, and Scholarship on Sisera's Death* (Indiana Studies in Biblical Literature; Bloomington: Indiana University Press, 1988).

Balch, D.L., and Carolyn Osiek (eds), *Early Christian Families in Context. An Interdisciplinary Dialogue* (Religion, Marriage, and Family series; Grand Rapids, MI and Cambridge, UK: Eerdmans, 2003).

Barnes, T.D., 'The Composition of Cassius Dio's *Roman History*', *Phoenix* 38 (1984), pp. 240–55.

Barns, J., 'A Coptic Apocryphal Fragment in the Bodleian Library', *JTS* n.s. 11 (1960), pp. 70–76.

Barton, C., *Roman Honor: The Fire in the Bones* (Berkeley: University of California Press, 2001).

— 'Savage Miracles: The Redemption of Lost Honor in Roman Society and the Sacrament of the Gladiator and the Martyr', *Representations* 45 (Winter 1994), pp. 41–71.

Bechtel, L.M., 'Boundary Issues in Genesis 19.1–38', in Harold C. Washington, *et al.* (eds), *Escaping Eden: New Feminist Perspectives on the Bible* (The Biblical Seminar 65; Sheffield: Sheffield Academic Press, 1998), pp. 22–40.

Berger, J., *Ways of Seeing* (Harmondsworth, UK: Penguin, 1972).

Berger, P. *The Social Reality of Religion* (Harmondsworth, UK: Penguin Books, 1967).

Bernall, M., and Madeline L'Engle, *She Said Yes: The Unlikely Martyrdom of Cassie Bernall* (Farmington, PA: Plough Publishing House, 1999).

Berner, W.D., *Initiationsriten in Mysterienreligionen, im Gnostizismus und im antiken Judentum* (Ph.D. diss., University of Göttingen, 1972).

Betz, H.D., *Galatians: A Commentary on Paul's Letter to the Churches in Galatia* (Hermeneia Series; Philadelphia, PA: Fortress Press, 1979).

— 'Magic and Mystery in the Greek Magical Papyri', in Christopher A. Faraone and Dirk Obbink (eds), *Magika Hiera: Ancient Greek Magic and Religion* (New York/Oxford: Oxford University Press, 1991), pp. 244–59.

Bhabha, H.K., *The Location of Culture* (London: Routledge, 1994).

Bielman, A., and R. Frei-Stolba, 'Les flaminiques du Culte impérial: contribution au rôle de la femme dans l'empire romain', *Études de Lettres* 1994, pp. 114–26.

Blake, W.E. (ed.), *De Chaerea et Callirhoe Amatoriarum Narrationum Libri Octo* (Oxford: Clarendon Press, 1938).

Boatwright, M.T., 'Plancia Magna of Perge: Women's Roles and Status in Roman Asia Minor', in Sarah B. Pomeroy (ed.), *Women's History and Ancient History* (Chapel Hill: University of North Carolina Press, 1991), pp. 249–77.

Boissevain, U.P. (ed.), *Cassii Dionis Cocceiani Historiarum Romanarum Quae Supersunt* (5 vols.; Berlin: Weidmann, 1895–1931).

Boswell, J., *Same-Sex Unions in Premodern Europe* (New York: Villard Books, 1994).

Boughton, L.C., 'From Pious Legend to Feminist Fantasy: Distinguishing Hagiographical License from Apostolic Practice in *Acts of Paul/Acts of Thecla*', *Journal of Religion* 71 (1991), pp. 362–83.

Bourdieu, P., 'Marriage Strategies as Strategies of Social Reproduction', in Robert Forster and Orest Ranum, *Family and Society: Selections from the Annales, Economies, Sociétés, Civilisations* (trans. Elborg Forster and Patricia Ranum; Baltimore, MD: The Johns Hopkins University Press, 1976).

Bovon, F., 'Byzantine Witnesses for the Apocryphal Acts of the Apostles', in François Bovon, Ann Graham Brock and Christopher R. Matthews (eds), *The Apocryphal Acts of the Apostles* (Harvard Divinity School Studies; Cambridge, MA: Harvard University Press, 1999), pp. 87–98.

— 'The Words of Life in the *Acts of the Apostle Andrew*', *HTR* 87 (1994), pp. 139–54.

Bovon, F., and Eric Junod, 'Reading the Apocryphal Acts of the Apostles', *Semeia* 38 (1986), pp. 161–71.

Bovon, F., *et al.* (eds), *Les Actes Apocryphes des Apôtres: Christianisme et monde païen* (Geneva: Labor et Fides, 1981).

Bovon, F., B. Bouvier and Frédéric Amsler, *Acta Philippi: Textus* (CCSA 11; Turnhout: Brepols, 1999).

Bovon, F., Bertrand Bouvier and Frédéric Amsler, *Acta Philippi: Textus* (CCSA 11; Turnhout: Brepols, 1999).

Bowers, P., 'Paul and Religious Propaganda in the First Century', *NovT* 22 (1980), pp. 316–23.

Bowersock, G.W., *Martyrdom and Rome* (The Wiles Lectures Given at the Queen's University of Belfast; Cambridge, UK: Cambridge University Press, 1995).

Bowie, E., 'The novels and the real world', in B. Reardon (ed.), *Erotica Antiqua* (Bangor: University College of North Wales, 1994).

Bowie, E., 'The Readership of Greek Novels in the Ancient World', in Tatum, *The Search for the Ancient Novel*, pp. 435–59.

Boyarin, D., *Carnal Israel: Reading Sex in Talmudic Culture* (The New Historicism: Studies in Cultural Poetics, vol. 25; Berkeley: University of California Press, 1993).

— *Dying for God: Martyrdom and the Making of Christianity and Judaism* (Stanford, CA: Stanford University Press, 1999).

— 'Gender', in Mark C. Taylor (ed.), *Critical Terms for the Study of Religion* (Chicago: University of Chicago Press, 1998), pp. 117–35.

— 'Homotopia: The Feminized Jewish Man and the Lives of Women in Late Antiquity', *differences* 7.2 (summer 1995), pp. 41–71.

— *A Radical Jew: Paul and the Politics of Identity* (Berkeley: University of California Press, 1994).

— *Unheroic Conduct: The Rise of Heterosexuality and the Invention of the Jewish Man* (Berkeley: University of California Press, 1997).

Brakke, D., *Athanasius and the Politics of Asceticism* (Oxford: Clarendon Press, 1995).

Brashler, J., and D.M. Parrott (trans.), 'Acts of Peter', in E. Hennecke and W. Schneemelcher (eds), *New Testament Apocrypha* (2 vols.; trans. R. McL. Wilson; Philadelphia, PA: Westminster/John Knox Press, rev. edn, 1992), pp. 271–321.

Brashler, J., and Douglas M. Parrott (eds and trans.), 'The Act of Peter, BG, 4: 128,1–141,7', in *Nag Hammadi Codices V, 2–5 and VI with Papyrus Berolinensis 8502,1 and 4*, NHS XI (Leiden: E.J. Brill, 1979), pp. 473–93.

Braund, D., 'Function and dysfunction: personal patronage in Roman imperialism', in Wallace-Hadrill (ed.), *Patronage in Ancient Society*, pp. 137–52, esp. 140–42.

Braunfels, W., and Engelbert Kirschbaum, *Lexikon der christlichen Ikonographie; vol. 8: Ikonographie der Heiligen* (Rome, Freiburg, Basel, Vienna: Herder, 1976).

Breckenridge, J.D., 'Apocrypha of Early Christian Portraiture', *Byzantinische Zeitschrift* 67 (1974), pp. 101–109.

Bremmer, J.N. (ed.), *The Apocryphal Acts of Andrew* (Louvain: Peeters, 2000).

— (ed.), *The Apocryphal Acts of John* (Kampen: Kok Pharos, 1995).

— (ed.), *The Apocryphal Acts of Paul and Thecla* (Studies on the Apocryphal Acts of the Apostles; Kampen: Kok Pharos, 1996).

— (ed.), *The Apocryphal Acts of Peter* (Louvain: Peeters, 1998).

— (ed.), *The Apocryphal Acts of Thomas* (Louvain: Peeters, 2001).

— 'The Apocryphal Acts: Authors, Place, Time and Readership', in *idem* (ed.), *The Apocryphpal Acts of Thomas* (Leuven: Peeters, 2001), pp. 149–70.

— 'Aspects of the Acts of Peter: Women, Magic, Place and Date', in *idem* (ed.), *The Apocryphal Acts of Peter: Magic, Miracles and Gnosticism* (Leuven: Peeters, 1998), pp. 1–20.

— 'Correspondences Between the Ancient Novel and the Christian Apocryphal Acts: Place, Time and Readership', *Groningen Colloquia on the Novel* 9 (1998), pp. 157–80.

— *Greek Religion* (New Surveys in the Classics 14; Oxford: Oxford University Press, 1994).

— 'Magic, Martyrdom and Women's Liberation in the Acts of Paul and Thecla', in *idem* (ed.), *The Apocryphal Acts of Paul and Thecla* (Studies on the Apocryphal Acts of the Apostles 2; Kampen: Kok Pharos, 1996), pp. 36–59.

— 'Man, Magic, and Martyrdom in the *Acts of Andrew*', in *idem* (ed.), *Acts of Andrew*, pp. 15–34.

— 'Marginalia Manichaica', *Zeitschrift für Papyrologie und Epigraphik* 39 (1980), pp. 29–34.

— 'Oedipus and the Greek Oedipus Complex', in *idem* (ed.), *Interpretations of Greek Mythology* (London: Routledge, 1988), pp. 49–51.

— 'Pauper or Patroness: the Widow in the Early Christian Church', in J.N. Bremmer and L. van den Bosch (eds), *Between Poverty and the Pyre. Moments in the History of Widowhood* (London and New York: Routledge, 1995), pp. 31–57.

— 'The Novel and the Apocryphal Acts: Place, Time and Readership', in H. Hofmann and M. Zimmerman (eds), *Groningen Colloquia on the Novel* IX (Groningen: Egbert Forsten, 1998), pp. 157–80.

— 'The Old Women of Ancient Greece', in J. Blok and P. Mason (eds), *Sexual Asymmetry. Studies in Ancient Society* (Amsterdam: Gieben, 1987), pp. 191–215.

— 'Why Did Early Christianity Attract Upper-class Women?', in Antonius A.R. Bastiaensen, *et al.* (eds), *Fructus Centesimus. Mélanges offerts à Gerard J.M. Bartelink à l'occasion de son soixante-cinquième anniversaire* (Instrumenta patristica, 19; Steenbrugis/Dordrecht: In Abbatia S. Petri/Kluwer Academic Publishers, 1989), pp. 37–47.

Brock, A.G., 'Political Authority and Cultural Accommodation: Social Diversity in the *Acts of Paul* and the *Acts of Peter*', in François Bovon, Ann Graham Brock and Christopher R. Matthews (eds), *Apocryphal Acts of the Apostles* (Harvard Divinity School Studies; Cambridge, MA: Harvard University Press, 1999), pp. 145–69.

Brock, S.P., and S.A. Harvey, *Holy Women of the Syrian Orient* (Berkeley: University of California Press, 1987).

Brooten, B.J., 'Der lange Schatten der Sklaverei im Leben von Frauen und Mädchen', in Frank Crüsemann, Marlene Crüsemann, Claudia Janssen, Rainer Kessler and Beate Wehn (eds), *Dem Tod nicht glauben. Sozialgeschichte der Bibel. Festschrift für Luise Schottroff zum 70. Geburtstag* (Gütersloh: Gütersloher Verlagshaus, 2004), pp. 488–503.

— *Love Between Women: Early Christian Responses to Female Homoeroticism* (Chicago: The University of Chicago Press, 1996).

Brown, P., *The Body and Society: Men, Women, and Sexual Renunciation in Early Christianity* (Lectures on the History of Religions 13; New York: Columbia University Press, 1988; repr. London/Boston: Faber and Faber, 1990).

— *Power and Persuasion in Late Antiquity: Towards a Christian Empire* (Madison: University of Wisconsin Press, 1992).

— *The Cult of the Saints: Its Rise and Function in Latin Christianity* (The Haskell Lectures on History of Religions; Chicago: University of Chicago Press, 1981).

Brown, Shelby, 'Death as Decoration: Scenes from the Arena on Roman Domestic Mosaics', in Amy Richlin (ed.), *Pornography and Representation in Greece and Rome* (New York and Oxford: Oxford University Press, 1992), pp. 180–211.

Brown, Shugler, *Apostasy and Perseverance in the Theology of Luke* (Rome: Pontifical Biblical Institute, 1969).

Buckley, J.J., 'An Interpretation of Logion 114 in *The Gospel of Thomas*', *NovT* 27 (1985), pp. 245–72.

— *Female Fault and Fulfillment in Gnosticism* (Chapel Hill: University of North Carolina Press, 1986).

Burke, K., 'Definition of Man', in idem (ed.) *Language as Symbolic Action* (Berkeley: University of California Press, 1996), pp. 3–24.

— '(Nonsymbolic) Motion/(Symbolic) Action', *Critical Inquiry* 4 (1978), pp. 809–38.

— *The Philosophy of Literary Form* (Berkeley: University of California Press, 1973 [1941]).

Burkert, W., *Creation of the Sacred: Tracks of Biology in Early Religions* (Cambridge, MA: Harvard University Press, 1996).

Burns, J.P., 'Authority and Power: The Role of the Martyrs in the African Church in the Fifth Century' (cited 24 June 2005; online: http://divinity.library.vanderbilt.edu/burns/chroma/saints/martburn.html).

Burrus, V., *Begotten Not Made: Conceiving Manhood in Late Antiquity* (Stanford, CA: Stanford University Press, 2000).

— 'Chastity as Autonomy: Women in the Stories of the Apocryphal Acts', *Semeia* 38 (1986), pp. 101–17.

— *Chastity as Autonomy: Women in the Stories of the Apocryphal Acts* (Studies in Women and Religion, 23; Lewiston/Queenston: Edwin Mellen Press, 1987).

— '"Equipped for Victory": Ambrose and the Gendering of Orthodoxy', *JECS* 4 (1996), pp. 461–75.

— *The Making of a Heretic: Gender: Authority, and the Priscillianist Controversy* (Berkeley: University of California Press, 1995).

— 'The Male Ascetic in Female Space: Alienated Strategies of Self-Definition in the Writings of Sulpicius Severus' (paper presented at the Society of Biblical Literature/American Academy of Religion, San Francisco, CA, 1992).

— 'Reading Agnes: The Rhetoric of Gender in Ambrose and Prudentius', *JECS* 3 (1995), pp. 25–46.

— *The Sex Lives of Saints: An Erotics of Ancient Hagiography* (Divinations Series; Philadelphia: University of Pennsylvania Press, 2003).

— 'Torture and Travail: Producing the Christian Martyr', in A.-J. Levine (ed.), *Feminist Companion to Patristic Literature* (London: Continuum, forthcoming).

— 'Word and Flesh: The Bodies and Sexuality of Ascetic Women in Christian Antiquity', *JFSR* 10 (1994), pp. 27–51.

Buytaert, É.M. (ed.), *Eusèbe d'Émèse. Discours conserves en latin, t. 1. La Collection de Troyes (Discours I á XVII)* (Spicilegium Sacrum Lovaniense. Etudes et documents 26; Louvain: Spicilegium Sacrum Lovaniense, 1953).

Bynum, C.W., *Holy Feast and Holy Fast: The Religious Significance of Food to Medieval Women* (Berkeley: University of California Press, 1987).

Calef, S., 'Games Gone Carnivalesque: The World Turned Upside Down in the *Acts of Paul and Thecla*', AAR/SBL Rocky Mountain Regional Meeting, 2000.

— 'Paul as Villain in the *Acts of Paul and Thecla*: A Reappraisal' AAR/SBL Rocky Mountain Regional Meeting, 2001.

— 'Romancing the Body: The Description of Paul "in the flesh" in the *Acta Pauli*', presented at the AAR/SBL Rocky Mountain Regional Meeting, 19 April 2002.

Cameron, A., 'Ascetic closure and the End of Antiquity', in V.L. Wimbush and R. Valantasis (eds), *Asceticism* (Oxford: Oxford University Press, 1995), pp. 147–61.

— *Christianity and the Rhetoric of Empire: The Development of Christian Discourse* (Berkeley: University of California Press, 1991).

Cantarella, E., *Pandora's Daughters: The Role and Status of Women in Greek and*

Roman Antiquity (trans. Maureen B. Fant; Baltimore, MD and London: The Johns Hopkins University Press, 1987).

Cardman, F., 'Women, Ministry and Church Order in Early Christianity', in Ross Shepard Kraemer and Mary Rose D'Angelo (eds), *Women and Christian Origins* (New York: Oxford University Press, 1999), pp. 300–329.

Cartlidge, D.R., 'Transfigurations of Metamorphosis Traditions in the *Acts of John, Thomas*, and *Peter*', *Semeia* 38 (1986), pp. 53–66.

Castelli, E.A., '"I Will Make Mary Male": Pieties of the Body and Gender Transformation of Christian Women in Late Antiquity', in Julia Epstein and Kristina Straub (eds), *Body Guards: The Cultural Politics of Ambiguity* (New York: Routledge, 1991), pp. 29–49.

— 'Imperial Reimaginings of Christian Origins: Epic in Prudentius's Poem', in *eadem* and Hal Taussig (eds), *Reimagining Christian Origins: A Colloquium Honoring Burton L. Mack* (Valley Forge, PA: Trinity Press International, 1996), pp. 173–84.

— *Martyrdom and Memory: Early Christian Culture Making* (New York: Columbia University Press, 1994).

— 'Virginity and Its Meaning for Women's Sexuality in Early Christianity', *JFSR* 2 (1986), pp. 61–88.

— *Visions and Voyeurism: Holy Women and the Politics of Sight in Early Christianity*, vol. 2 of Christopher Ocker (ed.), *Protocol of the Colloquy of the Center for Hermeneutical Studies, New Series* (Berkeley, CA: Center for Hermeneutical Studies, 1995).

Catholic Information Network (CIN), 'St. Felicity and the Seven Holy Brothers', n.p. (cited 7 July 2000); online: http://www.cin.org/saints/felicity.html.

Cazzaniga, E. (ed.), *S. Ambrosii Mediolanensis Episcopi De virginibus libri tres* Corpus Scriptorum Latinorum Paravianum 1; Aug. Taurinorum, Mediolani, Patavii, Florentiae, Romae, Neapoli, Panormi: In Aedibus Io. Bapt. Paraviae et Sociorum, 1948.

Chadwick, H., *Origen: Contra Celsum* (Cambridge, UK: Cambridge University Press, 1965).

Charlesworth, J.H., 'From the Philopedia of Jesus to the Misopedia of the Acts of Thomas', in Hugh Nibley, John M. Lundquist and Stephen David Ricks (eds), *By Study and also by Faith: Essays in Honor of Hugh W. Nibley on the Occasion of his Eightieth Birthday, 27 March 1990* (Salt Lake City and Provo, UT: Deseret Book and the Foundation for Ancient Research and Mormon Studies, 1990), pp. 46–66.

Chitty, D.J., *The Desert a City: An Introduction to the Study of Egyptian and Palestinian Monasticism Under the Christian Empire* (1966; Crestwood, NY: St. Validimir's Seminary Press, 1995).

Chow, J.K., *Patronage and Power. A Study of Social Networks in Corinth* (JSNTSS 75; Sheffield: Sheffield Academic Press, 1992).

Clark, E.A., 'Antifamilial Tendencies in Ancient Christianity', *Journal of the History of Sexuality* 5 (1995), pp. 356–80.

— *Ascetic Piety and Women's Faith: Essays in Late Ancient Christianity* (Studies in Women and Religion, 20; Lewiston, NY and Queenston, Ont.: Edwin Mellen Press, 1986).

— 'Ideology, History, and the Construction of "Woman" in Late Ancient Christianity', *JECS* 2 (1994), pp. 155–84.

— 'The Lady Vanishes: Dilemmas of a Feminist Historian after the "Linguistic Turn"', *CH* 67 (1998), pp. 1–31.

— *The Life of Melania the Younger. Introduction, Translation, and Commentary* (Studies in Women and Religion, 14; New York and Toronto: Edwin Mellen, 1984).

— *The Origenist Controversy: The Cultural Construction of an Early Christian Debate* (Princeton, NJ: Princeton University Press, 1992).

— *Reading Renunciation: Asceticism and Scripture in Early Christianity* (Princeton, NJ: Princeton University Press, 1999).

— 'Women, Gender, and the Study of Christian History', *CH* 70 (2001), pp. 395–426.

Clark, G., 'Bodies and Blood: Late Antique Debate on Martyrdom, Virginity and Resurrection', in Dominic Montserrat (ed.), *Changing Bodies, Changing Meanings: Studies on the Human Body in Antiquity* (London: Routledge, 1998), pp. 99–115.

— 'The Fathers and the Children', in Diana Wood (ed.), *The Church and Childhood: Papers Read at the 1993 Summer Meeting and the 1994 Winter Meeting of the Ecclesiastical History Society* (Studies in Church History, 31; Oxford and Cambridge, MA: Blackwell, 1994), pp. 1–27.

— 'Women and Asceticism in Late Antiquity: The Refusal of Status and Gender', in V.L. Wimbush and R. Valantasis (eds), *Asceticism* (Oxford: Oxford University Press, 1995), pp. 33–48.

— *Women in Late Antiquity: Pagan and Christian Lifestyles* (New York: Oxford University Press, and Oxford: Clarendon Press, 1993).

Clarke, G.W., (trans. and ed.), *Letters 1–27*, vol. 1 of *The Letters of St. Cyprian of Carthage* (Ancient Christian Writers: The Works of the Fathers in Translation, 46; New York: Newman Press, 1986).

Cloke, G., *This Female Man of God: Women and Spiritual Power in the Patristic Age, AD 350–450* (London and New York: Routledge, 1995).

Cohen, S.J.D. (ed.), *The Jewish Family in Antiquity* (BJS, 289; Atlanta: Scholars Press, 1993).

Cole, S.G., 'Could Greek Women Read and Write?', in H. Foley (ed.), *Reflections of Women in Antiquity* (New York and London: Gordon and Breach, 1981), pp. 219–45.

Coleman, K.M., 'Fatal Charades: Roman Executions Staged as Mythological Enactments', *JRS* 80 (1990), pp. 44–73.

— 'Launching into History: Aquatic Displays in the Early Empire', *JRS* 83 (1993), pp. 48–74.

Conway, R.S., and C.F. Walters (eds), *Titi Livi Ab Urbe Condita, t. 1, libri I–V* (Oxonii: E typographeo Clarendoniano, 1914).

Cook, J.G., 'In Defence of Ambiguity: Is There a Hidden Demon in Mark 1.29–31?' *NTS* 43 (1997), pp. 184–208.

Cooper, K., 'Apostles, Ascetic Women, and Questions of Audience: New Reflections on the Rhetoric of Gender in the *Apocryphal Acts*', paper presented at the Society of Biblical Literature/American Academy of Religion, Atlanta, 1992.

— 'Insinuations of Womanly Influence: An Aspect of the Christianization of the Roman Aristocracy', *JRS* 82 (1992), pp. 150–64.

—*The Virgin and the Bride: Idealized Womanhood in Late Antiquity* (Cambridge, MA: Harvard University Press, 1996).

Corley, K., 'Feminist Myths of Christian Origins', in E. Castelli and H. Taussig (eds), *Reimagining Christian Origins*, A Colloquium Honoring Burton L. Mack (Valley Forge, PA: Trinity Press International, 1996), pp. 51–67.

Corrington, G.P. (Gail P.C. Streete), 'The "Divine Woman"? Propaganda and the Power of Chastity in the New Testament Apocrypha', *Helios* 13 (1986), pp. 151–62.

— *Her Image of Salvation: Female Saviors and Formative Christianity* (Gender and the Biblical Tradition; Louisville, KY: Westminster/John Knox Press, 1992).

Cothenet, E., 'Le Protévangile de Jacques: origine, genre et signification d'un premier midrash chrétien sur la Nativité de Marie', *ANRW* II.25.6 (1988), pp. 4252–69.

Cotter, W., 'Women's Authority Roles in Paul's Churches: Countercultural or Conventional?', *NovT* 36/4 (1994), pp. 350–72.

Craigie, W.A., 'The Acts of Xanthippe and Polyxena', in A. Menzies (ed.), *The Ante-Nicene Fathers*, Vol. 10 (10 vols.; Grand Rapids, MI: Eerdmans, 1980), pp. 203–17.

Crossan, J.D., *The Historical Jesus: The Life of a Mediterranean Jewish Peasant* (San Francisco, CA: HarperSanFrancisco, 1991).

Curtius, E.R., *European Literature and the Latin Middle Ages* (trans. Willard R. Trask; Bollingen Series 36; New York: Bollingen Foundation, Inc. by Pantheon Books, 1953; repr. Princeton, NJ: Princeton University Press, 1990).

Dalmeyda, G. (ed.), *Les Éphésiaques ou Le Roman d'Habrocomès et d'Anthia* (Paris: Editions Belles Lettres, 1926).

Danker, F.W., *A Greek-English Lexicon of the New Testament and other Early Christian Literature* (3rd edn; Chicago and London: University of Chicago Press, 2000).

Davies, S.L., *The Revolt of the Widows: The Social World of the Apocryphal Acts* (Carbondale: Southern Illinois University Press, 1980), pp. 95, 105–107.

— 'The Social World of the Apocryphal Acts' (Ph.D. diss., Temple University, Ann Arbor, MI: University Microfilms Int., 1978).

— 'Women in the Third Gospel and the New Testament Apocrypha', in A.-J. Levine (ed.), *'Women Like This': New Perspectives on Jewish Women in the Greco-Roman World* (Early Judaism and Its Literature, 1; Atlanta: Scholar's Press, 1991), pp. 185–97.

Davis, L., 'Virgins in Brothels: A Different Feminist Reading of Beruriah', paper presented at the Graduate Theological Union, Berkeley, CA, 1994.

Davis, Stephen J., *The Cult of St Thecla: A Tradition of Women's Piety in Late Antiquity* (Oxford Early Christian Studies; Oxford and New York: Oxford University Press, 2001), pp. 8–18, 28–29.

De Boeck, F., and R. Devisch, 'Ndembu, Luunda and Yaka Divination Compared: From Representation and Social Engineering to Embodiment and Worldmaking', *Journal of Religion in Africa* 24.2 (1994), pp. 98–133.

De Bruyne, P.D., *'Epistula Titi, Discipuli Pauli, De dispositione Sanctimonii'*, *Revue Bénédictine* 37 (1925), pp. 47–72.

254   *A Feminist Companion to the New Testament Apocrypha*

— 'Nouveaux Fragments des Actes de Pierre, de Paul, de Jean, d'André, et de l'Apocalypse d'Élie', *Revue Bénédictine* 25 (1908), pp. 149–60.

De Jong, A.F., *Traditions of the Magi: Zoroastrianism in Greek and Latin Literature* (Leiden: Brill, 1997).

Dekkers, D.E. (ed.), *Tertulliani Opera*, I (CCSL, 1; Turnhout: Brepols, 1953).

De la Vega, J.H., 'Mujeres, carisma y castidad en el cristianismo primitivo', *Gerón* 11 (1993), pp. 229–44.

De Mendieta, D.A., 'La virginité chez Eusèbe d'Émèse et l'ascétisme familial dans la première moité du IVᵉ siècle', *Revue d'Histoire Ecclésiastiques* 50 (1955), pp. 777–820.

De Romilly, J., *Magic and Rhetoric in Ancient Greece* (Cambridge, MA: Harvard University Press, 1975).

De Santos Otero, A., 'Der Apokryphe Titusbrief', *ZKG* 74 (1963), pp. 1–14.

— 'Der Pseudo-Titus-Brief', in Wilhelm Schneemelcher (ed.), *Neutestamentliche Apokryphen in deutscher Übersetzung, II. Band: Apostolisches, Apokalypsen und Verwandtes* (Tübingen: J.C.B. Mohr [Paul Siebeck], 1989), pp. 50–70.

De Ste Croix, G.E.M., *The Class Struggle in the Ancient Greek World from the Archaic Age to the Arab Conquests* (Ithaca, NY: Cornell University Press, 1981).

De Strycker, E., *La Forme la Plus Ancienne du Protévangile de Jacques* (Subsidia Hagiographica, 33; Brussels: Société des Bollandistes, 1961).

Den Boeft, J., and J.N. Bremmer, 'Notiunculae Martyrologicae III', *VC* 39 (1985), pp. 110–30.

Dewey, J., 'The Gospel of Mark', in Elisabeth Schüssler Fiorenza (ed.), *Searching the Scriptures. Volume Two: A Feminist Commentary* (2 vols; New York: Crossroad, 1994), pp. 470–509.

Dixon, S., *The Roman Family* (Oxford: Clarendon Press, 1997).

— 'The Sentimental Ideal of the Roman Family', in Rawson, *Marriage, Divorce and Children*, pp. 99–113.

Dodds, E.R., *Pagan and Christian in an Age of Anxiety* (Cambridge, UK: Cambridge University Press, 1965).

Dölger, F.J., *Sphragis: Eine altchristliche Taufbezeichnung in ihren Beziehungen zur profanen und religösen Kultur des Altertums* (Studien zur Geschichte und Kultur des Altertums 5/3–4; Paderborn, 1909; repr. New York: Johnson Reprint Company, 1967).

Dombart, B., and Alphonsus Kalb (eds), *Sancti Aurelii Augustini De civitate Dei libri I–X* (CCSL 47: Aurelii Augustini Opera Pars XIV, 1; Turnholti: Typographi Brepols Editores Pontificii, 1955).

Dönni, G., *Der alte Mensch in der Antike* (Bamberg: Difo Druck, 1996).

Douglas, M., *Purity and Danger: An Analysis of the Concepts of Pollution and Taboo* (repr. London/New York: Routledge, 1992).

Dragon, G., with Marie Dupré la Tour, *Vie et miracles de sainte Thècle, texte grec, traduction, et commentaire* (Subsidia hagiographica 62; Brussels: Société des Bollandistes, 1978).

Droge, A.J., and James D. Tabor, *A Noble Death: Suicide and Martyrdom among Christians and Jews in Antiquity* (San Francisco: HarperSanFrancisco, 1992).

Dunn, P.W., 'Women's Liberation, the *Acts of Paul*, and other Apocryphal Acts of the Apostles', *Apocrypha* 4 (1993).

Eagen, M.C. (trans.), *The Poems of Prudentius* (The Fathers of the Church: A New Translation; Washington, D.C.: Catholic University of America Press, 1962).

Edwards, C., *The Politics of Immorality in Ancient Rome* (Cambridge, UK: Cambridge University Press, 1993), pp. 35–38, 53–58.

Egger, B., 'Looking at Chariton's Callirhoe', in J.R. Morgan and R. Stoneman (eds), *Greek Fiction. The Greek Novel in Context* (London and New York: Routledge, 1994), pp. 31–48.

— 'Women and Marriage in the Greek Novels: The Boundaries of Romance', in J. Tatum (ed.), *The Search for the Ancient Novel* (Baltimore, MD and London: The Johns Hopkins University Press, 1994), pp. 260–80.

— 'Women in the Greek Novel: Constructing the Feminine' (Ph.D. diss., University of California, Irvine; Ann Arbor: UMI, 1990).

— 'Zu den Frauenrollen im griechischen Roman. Die Frau als Heldin und Leserin', in H. Hofmann (ed.), *Groningen Colloquia on the Novel* I (Groningen: Egbert Forsten, 1988), pp. 33–66.

Ehrman, B.D., *After the New Testament: A Reader in Early Christianity* (New York and Oxford: Oxford University Press, 1999).

Eisenstadt, S.N., and Louis Roniger, 'Patron-Client Relations as a Model of Structuring Social Exchange', *Comparative Studies in Society and History* 22 (1980), pp. 42–77.

Elliott, J.K., *The Apocryphal New Testament: A Collection of Apocryphal Christian Literature in an English Translation* (Oxford: Clarendon Press, 1993).

Elliott, J.K., *The Apocryphal New Testament: A Collection of Apocryphal Christian Literature in an English Translation based on M. R. James* (Oxford: Clarendon Press, 1993).

Elm, S., *'Virgins of God': The Making of Asceticism in Late Antiquity* (Oxford Classical Monographs; Oxford: Clarendon Press and New York: Oxford University Press, 1994).

Elsom, H.E., 'Callirhoe: Displaying the Phallic Woman', in Amy Richlin (ed.), *Pornography and Representation in Greece and Rome* (New York and Oxford: Oxford University Press, 1992), pp. 212–30.

Eltrop, B., *Denn solchen gehört das Himmelreich. Kinder im Matthäusevangelium. Eine feministisch-sozialgeschichtliche Untersuchung* (Stuttgart: Ulrich E. Grauer, 1996).

— 'Kinder im Neuen Testament: Eine sozialgeschichtliche Nachfrage', in Martin Ebner *et al.* (eds), *Jahrbuch für Biblische Theologie: Gottes Kinder*, vol. 17 (Neukirchen-Vluyn: Neukirchener Verlag, 2002), pp. 83–96.

— 'Problem Girls: A Transgressive Reading of the Parable of the Ten Virgins (Matthew 25.1–13)', in Claudia Janssen, Ute Ochtendung and Beate Wehn (eds), *Transgressors: Toward a Feminist Biblical Theology* (trans. Linda M. Maloney; Collegeville, MN: Liturgical Press, 2002), pp. 163–71.

Engelmann, H., 'Ephesos und die Johannesakten', *Zeitschrift für Papyrologie und Epigraphik* 103 (1994), pp. 297–302.

Engelmann, H., H. Wankel and R. Merkelbach, *Die Inschriften von Ephesus* (Bonn: Habelt, 1979–84).

Evans Grubbs, J., *'The Virgin and the Bride: Idealized Womanhood in Late Antiquity,'* *Classical Philology* 93 (1998), pp. 201–209.

Eyben, E., *Restless Youth in Ancient Rome* (London and New York: Routledge, 1993).

Fander, M., 'Frauen in der Nachfolge Jesu: die Rolle der Frau im Markusevangelium', *EvTh* 52 (1992), pp. 413–32.

Faraone, C.A., and D. Obbink, *Magika Hiera: Ancient Greek Magic and Religion* (New York: Oxford University Press, 1991).

Fitzgerald, J.T., *Cracks in an Earthen Vessel: An Examination of the Catalogues of Hardships in the Corinthian Correspondence* (SBLDS, 99; Atlanta: Scholars Press, 1988).

Foley, H., 'Marriage and Sacrifice in Euripides' Iphigenia in Aulis', *Arethusa* 15 (1982), pp. 159–80.

Fonrobert, C., 'The Didascalia Apostolorum: A Mishnah for the Disciples of Jesus', *JECS* 9 (2001), pp. 483–509.

— *Menstrual Purity: Rabbinic and Christian Reconstructions of Biblical Gender* (Stanford, CA: Stanford University Press, 2000).

— 'Women's Bodies, Women's Blood: Politics of Gender in Rabbinic Literature' (Ph. D. diss., Graduate Theological Union, 1995; microfilm).

Forbis, E.P., 'Women's Public Image in Italian Honorary Inscriptions', *American Journal of Philology* 111 (1990), pp. 493–512.

Foss, F.K., and C.L. Griffin, 'A Feminist Perspective on Rhetorical Theory: Toward a Clarification of Boundaries', *Western Journal of Communication* 56 (1992), pp. 330–49.

Foucault, M., *History of Sexuality* (3 vols, trans. Robert Hurley; New York: Vintage Books, 1986).

— *History of Sexuality*, I (Harmondsworth, UK: Penguin, 1978).

— *History of Sexuality*, 2 (Harmondsworth, UK: Penguin, 1985).

Francis, J., *Subversive Virtue: Asceticism and Authority in the Second-Century Pagan World* (University Park: Pennsylvania State University Press, 1995).

Fridh, Å, *Le problème de la passion des Saintes Perpétue et Félicité* (Studia Graeca et Latina Gothoburgensia XXVI; Göteburg: Almqvist & Wiksell, 1968).

Frilingos, C., '"For My Child, Onesimus": Paul and Domestic Power in Philemon', *JBL* 119 (2000), pp. 91–104.

Frischer, B., *The Sculpted Word* (Berkeley, Los Angeles and London: University of California Press, 1982).

Gardner, I. *et al.*, *Coptic Documentary Texts from Kellis* I (Oxford, Oxbow, 1999).

Gardner, J.F., *Women in Roman Law and Society* (Bloomington: Indiana University Press, 1986), p. 57.

Garnaud, J.-P. (ed.), *Le Roman de Leucippé et Clitophon* (Paris: Editions Belles Lettres, 1991).

Garnsey, P., 'Sons, Slaves – and Christians', in Beryl Rawson and Paul Weaver (eds), *The Roman Family in Italy. Status, Sentiment, Space* (Oxford: Clarendon Press; Canberra: Humanities Research Centre, 1997), pp. 101–21.

Garnsey, P., and Greg Woolf, 'Patronage of the rural poor in the Roman world', in Wallace-Hadrill (ed.), *Patronage in Ancient Society*, pp. 153–70.

Garrett, S., 'The God of This World and the Affliction of Paul, 2 Cor. 4.1–12', in David Balch *et al.* (eds), *Greeks, Romans, and Christians. Essays in Honor of Abraham J. Malherbe* (Minneapolis, MN: Fortress Press, 1990), pp. 99–117.

— 'Paul's Thorn and Cultural Models of Affliction', in L. Michael White and O. Larry Yarbrough (eds), *The Social World of the First Christians: Essays in Honor of Wayne A. Meeks* (Minneapolis, MN: Fortress Press, 1995), pp. 82–99

— *The Temptations of Jesus in Mark's Gospel* (Grand Rapids, MI: Eerdmans, 1998).

Gasparro, G.S., 'L'Epistula Titi discipuli Pauli de dispositione sanctimonii e la tradizione dell'enkrateia', *ANRW* II.25.6 (1988), pp. 4551–64. Aurelio.

Gerö, S., 'Infancy Gospel of Thomas: A Study of the Textual and Literary Problems', *NovT* 13.1 (1971), pp. 46–80.

Giannarelli, E., 'L'infanzia nella biografia cristiana', *Studia Patristica* 18.2 (1989), pp. 217–21.

— 'Women and Satan in Christian Biography and Monastic Literature (IVth–Vth Centuries)', *Studia Patristica* 30 (1995), pp. 196–201.

Ginestet, P., *Les organizations de la jeunesse dans l'Occident Romain* (Brussels: Latomus Revue d'Études Latines, 1991).

Gnilka, C., *Aetas spiritalis. Die Überwindung der natürlichen Altersstufen als Ideal frühchristlichen Lebens* (Theophaneia 24; Bonn: P. Hanstein, 1972).

Goehring, J.E., 'Libertine or Liberated: Women in the So-called Libertine Gnostic Communities', in K.L. King (ed.), *Images of the Feminine in Gnosticism* (Philadelphia, PA: Westminster Press, 1988), pp. 329–44, repr. in D.M. Scholer (ed.), *Women in Early Christianity* (New York and London: Garland, 1993), pp. 183–98.

Goessler, L., *Plutarchs Gedanken über die Ehe* (Zürich: Buchdruckerei Berichthaus, 1962).

Golden, M., '*Pais*, "Child," and "Slave"', *L'Antiquité Classique* 54 (1985), pp. 91–104.

Goldhill, S., *Foucault's Virginity: Ancient Erotic Fiction and the History of Sexuality* (Cambridge: Cambridge University Press, 1995).

Goldin, J., 'The Magic of Magic and Superstition', in E. Schüssler Fiorenza (ed.), *Aspects of Religious Propaganda* (London and Notre Dame, IN: University of Notre Dame Press, 1976), pp. 115–47.

Gorce, D. (ed.), *Vie de Sainte Mélanie* (Sources Chrétiennes 90; Paris: Les Éditions du Cerf, 1962).

Gordon, R., 'The Veil of Power: emperors, sacrificers and benefactors', in Mary Beard and John North (eds), *Pagan Priests: Religion and Power in the Ancient World* (Ithaca, NY: Cornell University Press, 1990) pp. 201–31.

Gorman, J.C., 'Producing and Policing Female Sexuality: Thinking With and About "Same-Sex Desire" in the *Acts of Xanthippe and Polyxena*', *Journal of the History of Sexuality* 10.3–4 (2001), pp. 416–41.

— 'Reading and Theorizing Women's Sexualities: The Representation of Women in the *Acts of Xanthippe and Polyxena*' (Ph.D. diss., Temple University, 2003).

Graf, F., *Gottesnähe und Schadenzauber: Die Magie in der griechisch-römischen Antike* (München: Beck, 1996).

— 'How to Cope with a Difficult Life', in Schäfer and Kippenberg, *Envisioning Magic*, pp. 93–114.

— 'Prayer in Magic and Religious Ritual', in Faraone and Obbink (eds), *Magika Hiera*, pp. 188–213.

Gregory of Nyssa, *Life of Macrina*, in Pierre Maraval (ed. and trans.), *Grégoire de Nysse. Vie de Sainte Macrine* (Sources Chrétiennes 178; Paris: Les Éditions du Cerf, 1971).

Grubbs, J.E., *Law and Family in Late Antiquity: The Emperor Constantine's Marriage Legislation* (Oxford: Clarendon Press, 1995), pp. 96–98, 102.

— '"Pagan" and "Christian" Marriage: The State of the Question', *JECS* 2 (1994), pp. 361–412.

Guillaumont, A., *Les "Kephalaia Gnostica" d'Evagre le Pontique et l'histoire de l'Origénisme chez les Grecs et chez les Syriens* (Patristica Sorbonensia 5; Paris: Editions du Seuil, 1962).

Hägg, T., *The Novel in Antiquity* (Berkeley: University of California Press, 1983).

Hauck, F., 'ὑπομένω, ὑπομονή', *TDNT* 4, pp. 581–88.

Havelaar, H., 'Sofia en Maria Magdalena. Twee vrouwenfiguren in gnostische teksten', in D. van Paassen and A. Passenier (eds), *Op zoek naar vrouwen in ketterij en sekte* (Kampen: Kok Pharos, 1993), pp. 25–40.

Hayne, L., 'Thecla and the Church Fathers', *VC* 48 (1994), pp. 209–18.

Heffernan, T., *Sacred Biography* (New York: Oxford, 1988).

Hennecke, E., and W. Schneemelcher (eds), *New Testament Apocrypha* (2 vols; trans. R. McL. Wilson; Philadelphia, PA: Westminster/John Knox Press, rev. edn, 1992).

Henry, R. (ed.), *Photius. Bibliothèque. Tome II ('Codices' 84–185)* (Collection Byzantine; Paris: Société d'Édition 'Les Belles Lettres', 1960).

Herbert, M., and M. McNamara, *Irish Biblical Apocrypha. Selected Texts in Translation* (Edinburgh: T&T Clark, 1989).

Hidalgo de la Vega, J., 'Mujeres, carisma y castidad en el cristianismo primitivo', *Gerión* 11 (1993), pp. 229–44.

Hilhorst, A., 'Tertullian on the Acts of Paul', in Bremmer, *The Acts of Paul and Thecla*, pp. 150–63.

— 'The Text of the *Actus Vercellenses*', in Jan N. Bremmer (ed.), *The Apocryphal Acts of Peter. Magic, Miracles and Gnosticism* (Leuven: Peeters, 1998), pp. 148–60.

Hilhorst, A., and P.J. Lalleman, 'The *Acts of Andrew and Matthias*: Is It Part of the Original *Acts of Andrew*?', in Bremmer (ed.), *Acts of Andrew*, pp. 1–14.

Hock, R.F., *The Infancy Gospels of James and Thomas* (The Scholars Bible, 2; Santa Rosa, CA: Polebridge Press, 1995).

Holzhey, K., *Die Thekla-Akten: Ihre Verbreitung und Beurteilung in der Kirche* (München: Lentner, 1905).

Hone, W., *The Apocryphal New Testament* (London, 1820).

Hopkins, K., 'The Age of Roman Girls at Marriage', *Population Studies* 18 (1965), pp. 309–27.

— *Death and Renewal. Sociological Studies in Roman History* (Cambridge: Cambridge University Press, 1983).

Horn, C.B., 'The Depiction of Children and Young People as Literary Device in the Canonical and Apocryphal Acts', in Pierluigi Piovanelli (ed.), *Proceedings of the Apocrypha and Pseudepigrapha Section of the SBL International Meeting Held in Groningen, The Netherlands, 25–28 July 2004* (Turnhout: Brepols, forthcoming).

Horn, C.B., and John W. Martens, *'Let the Little Ones Come to Me': Children in the Early Christian Community* (Baltimore, MD: The Johns Hopkins University Press, forthcoming).

Howe, M., 'Interpretations of Paul in the Acts of Paul and Thecla', in D. Hagner and M. Harris (eds), *Pauline Studies. Essays Presented to Professor F.F. Bruce on his 70th Birthday* (Grand Rapids, MI: Paternoster/W. Eerdmans, 1980), pp. 33–49.

Jacobs, A.S., 'A Family Affair: Marriage, Class, and Ethics in the Apocryphal Acts of the Apostles', *JECS* 7 (1999), pp. 105–38.

— '"Let Him Guard *Pietas*": Early Christian Exegesis and the Ascetic Family', *JECS* 11 (2003), pp. 265–81.

— 'Writings Demetrias: Ascetic Logic in Ancient Christianity', *CH* 69 (2000), pp. 719–48.

Jacobs, A.S., and Rebecca Krawiec, 'Fathers Know Best? Christian Families in the Age of Asceticism', *JECS* 11 (2003), pp. 257–63.

Jakab, A., '*Actes de Jean*: État de la recherche (1892–1999)', *Rivista di Storia e Letteratura Religiosa* 36 (2000), pp. 299–334.

Janssen, C., *Elisabet und Hanna – zwei widerständige alte Frauen in neutestamentlicher Zeit. Eine sozialgeschichtliche Untersuchung* (Mainz: Matthias-Grünewald Verlag, 1998).

Jardine, A.A., *Gynesis: Configurations of Woman and Modernity* (Ithaca, NY: Cornell University Press, 1985).

Jenkins, G., 'Papyrus 1 from Kellis. A Greek text with affinities to the Acts of John', in Bremmer, *Apocryphal Acts of John*, pp. 197–216.

Jensen, A., *God's Self-Confident Daughters: Early Christianity and the Liberation of Women* (trans. O.C. Dean; Louisville, KY: Westminster/John Knox, 1996).

— *Gottes selbstbewusste Töchter. Frauenemazipation im frühen Christentum* (Freiburg: Herder, 1992).

— *Thekla-Die Apostelin: Ein apokrypher Text neu entdeckt* (Frauen-Kultur-Geschichte 3; Freiburg: Herder, 1995), p. 92.

Johnson, T., and Christopher Dandeker, 'Patronage: relation and system', in Andrew Wallace-Hadrill (ed.), *Patronage in Ancient Society* (London/New York: Routledge, 1989), pp. 219–41.

Jones, C.P., *Culture and Society in Lucian* (Cambridge, MA: Harvard University Press, 1986), pp. 117–32.

Joyce, J., *Ulysses* (1914; New York: Random House, 1961).

Jung, L.S., 'Autonomy as Justice: Spatiality and the Revelation of Otherness', *Journal of Religious Ethics* 14.1 (1986), pp. 157–83.

Junod, E., 'Le mystère apocryphe ou les richesses cachées d'une littérature méconnue', in Jean-Daniel Kaestli and Daniel Marguerat (eds), *Le mystère apocryphe: Introduction à une littérature méconnue* (Essais Bibliques 26; Genève: Labor et Fides, 1995), pp. 1–25.

Junod, E., and J.-D. Kaestli, *Acta Iohannis* (2 vols.; CCSA 1–2; Turnhout: Brepols, 1983).

— *L'Histoire des Actes Apocryphes des Apôtres du IIIe au IXe Siècle: Le Cas des Actes de Jean* (Cahiers de la Revue de Théologie et de Philosophie, 7; Genève, Lausanne, and Neuchâtel: Fonds National Suisse de la Recherche Scientifique, 1982).

Kaestli, J.-D., 'Fiction littéraire et réalité sociale: que peut-on savoir de la place des femmes dans le milieu de production des actes apocryphes des apôtres?', *Apocrypha* 1 (1990), pp. 279–302.

— 'Les Actes apocryphes et la reconstitution de l'histoire des femmes dans le christianisme ancien', *Cahiers bibliques de Foi et Vie* 28 (1989), pp. 71–79.

— 'L'utilisation des Actes Apocryphes des apôtres dans le Manichéism', in M. Krause (ed.), *Gnosis and Gnosticism* (NHS 8; Leiden: Brill, 1977), pp. 107–16.

— 'Response to Burrus', *Semeia* 38 (1986), pp. 119–31.

Kappeler, S., *The Pornography of Representation* (Minneapolis: University of Minnesota Press, 1986).

King, H., 'Bound to Bleed: Artemis and Greek Women', in A. Cameron and A. Kuhrt (eds), *Images of Women in Antiquity* (Detroit, MI: Wayne State University Press, 1983), pp. 109–27.

— *Hippocrates' woman: Reading the female body in Ancient Greece* (London & New York: Routledge, 1998), p. 23.

— 'Sacrificial Blood: The Role of the Amnion in Ancient Gynecology', *Helios* 13 (1987), pp. 117–26.

Klawiter, F.C., 'The Role of Martyrdom and Persecution in Developing the Priestly Authority of Women in Early Christianity', *CH* 49.3 (September, 1980), pp. 251–61.

Kleijwegt, M., *Ancient Youth. The Ambiguity of Youth and the Absence of Adolescence in Greco-Roman Society* (Amsterdam: J.C. Gieben, 1991).

Kleiner, D.E.E., and Susan B. Matheson (eds), *I Claudia. Women in Ancient Rome* (New Haven, CT: Yale University Art Gallery, 1996).

Klijn, A.F.G., *The Acts of Thomas: Introduction, Text, Commentary* (Leiden: E.J. Brill, 1962).

Kloppenborg, J.S., 'The Formation of Q and Antique Instructional Genres', *JBL* 105 (1986), pp. 443–62.

— *The Formation of Q: Trajectories in Ancient Wisdom Collections* (Studies in Antiquity and Christianity; Philadelphia, PA: Fortress Press, 1987).

Kock, H., 'Zu Ps. Titus, De dispositione sanctimonii', *ZNW* 32 (1933), pp. 131–44.

Koester, H., *Ancient Christian Gospels: Their History and Development* (Philadelphia, PA: Trinity Press International, 1990).

— *Introduction to the New Testament* (2 vols.; Philadelphia, PA: Fortress Press, 1982).

Kolb, F., 'Die Sitzordnung von Volksversammlung und Theaterpublikum im kaiserzeitlichen Ephesos', in H. Friesiner and F. Krinzinger (eds), *100 Jahre Österreichische Forschungen in Ephesos* (Vienna: Verlag der Österreichischen Akademie der Wissenschaften, 1999), pp. 101–105.

Koltun-Fromm, N., 'Psalm 22's Christological Interpretive Tradition in Light of Christian Anti-Jewish Polemic', *JECS* 6 (1998), pp. 37–57.

Konstan, D., 'Acts of Love: A Narrative Pattern in the Apocryphal Acts', *JECS* 6 (1998), pp. 15–36.

— *Sexual Symmetry: Love in the Ancient Novel and Related Genres* (Princeton, NJ: Princeton University Press, 1994).

Korn, J.H., *PEIRASMOS. Die Versuchung des Glaübigen in der gr. Bibel* (Stuttgart: W. Kohlhammer Verlag, 1937).

Kosack, G., 'Christianisierung – Ein Schritt zur Emanzipation? Die Bedeutung der Religion für die Mafa-Frauen (Nordkamerun)', *Anthropos* 90 (1995), pp. 206–17.

Kraemer, R.S. 'The Conversion of Women to Ascetic Forms of Christianity', *Signs: Journal of Women in Culture and Society* 6 (1980), pp. 298–307.
— *Her Share of the Blessings: Women's Religions among Pagans, Jews, and Christians in the Greco-Roman World* (New York and Oxford: Oxford University Press, 1992).
— 'Women's Authorship of Jewish and Christian Literature in the Greco-Roman Period', in Levine, *'"Women Like This"'*, pp. 221–42.
— (ed.), *Maenads, Martyrs, Matrons, Monastics: A Sourcebook on Women's Religions in the Greco-Roman World* (Philadelphia, PA: Fortress Press, 1988).
— (ed.), *Women's Religions in the Greco-Roman World: A Sourcebook* (Oxford: Oxford University Press, 2004).
Krause, D., 'Simon Peter's Mother-in-Law – Disciple or Domestic Servant? Feminist Biblical Hermeneutics and the Interpretation of Mark 1.29-31', in Amy-Jill Levine (ed.), *A Feminist Companion to Mark* (Feminist Companion to the New Testament and Early Christian Writings, 2; Sheffield: Sheffield Academic Press, 2001), pp. 37–53.
Krause, J.-U., *Witwen und Waisen im Römischen Reich* (4 vols; Stuttgart: Steiner, 1994–95).
Kuhn, D.C.G. (ed.), *Opera Omina* (20 vols.; Leipzig: C. Knowblochii, 1821–33).
Kyle, D., *Spectacles of Death in Ancient Rome* (London and New York: Routledge, 1998).
L'Huillier, P., *The Church of the Ancient Councils: The Disciplinary Work of the First Four Ecumenical Councils* (Crestwood, NY: St. Vladimir's Seminary Press, 1996), pp. 31–32.
La Tour, M.D., *Vie et miracles de sainte Thècle, texte grec, traduction, et commentaire* (Subsidia hagiographica 62; Brussels: Société des Bollandistes, 1978).
Laes, C., 'Desperately Different? *Delicia* Children in the Roman Household', in Balch and Osiek (eds), *Early Christian Families*, pp. 298–324.
Laistner, M.L.W. (trans.), *Christianity and Pagan Culture in the Later Roman Empire together with an English Translation of John Chrysostom's Address on Vainglory and the Right Way for Parents to Bring Up Their Children* (Ithaca, NY: Cornell University Press, 1951; repr. 1967).
Lakoff, G., *Women, Fire and Dangerous Things* (Chicago: University of Chicago Press, 1987).
Lalleman, P.J., *The Acts of John: a two-stage initiation into Johannine Gnosticism* (Louvain: Peeters, 1998).
— 'Polymorphy of Christ', in J.N. Bremmer (ed.), *The Apocryphal Acts of John* (Studies on the Apocryphal Acts of the Apostles, 1; Kampen: Kok Pharos, 1995), pp. 97–118.
Lambdin, T.O., 'The Gospel of Thomas', in Bentley Layton (ed.), *Nag Hammadi Codex II, 2–7 Together with XIII.2*, Brit. Lib. Or. 4926 (1), and pOxy. 1, 654, 655* (2 vols.; NHS, 20; Leiden: E.J. Brill, 1989), I, pp. 52–93.
Lampe, G.W.H., 'Miracles and Early Christian Apologetic', in C.F.D. Moule (ed.), *Miracles: Cambridge Studies in Their Philosophy and History* (London: A.R. Mowbray & Co, 1965), pp. 203–18.
— *A Patristic Greek Lexicon* (Oxford: Clarendon Press, 1961).
— *The Seal of the Spirit. A Study in the Doctrine of Baptism and Confirmation in the New Testament and the Fathers* (2nd edn; London: SPCK, 1967).

Lampe, P., *Die stadtrömischen Christen in den ersten beiden Jahrhunderten* (Tübingen: Mohr, 1989).

Lane-Fox, R., 'Literacy and power in early Christianity', in A.K. Bowman and G. Woolf (eds), *Literacy and Power in the Ancient World* (Cambridge: Cambridge University Press, 1994), pp. 126–48.

— *Pagans and Christians* (Harmondsworth, UK: Allen Lane, 1986).

Lautman, F., 'Differences or Changes in Family Organization', in Robert Forster and Orest Ranum (eds), *Family and Society: Selections from the Annales: Economies, Sociétés, Civilisations* (trans. Elborg Forster and Patricia Ranum; Baltimore, MD: The Johns Hopkins University Press, 1976), pp. 251–61.

Lee, A.G., 'Ovid's Lucretia', *Greece and Rome* 22 (1953), pp. 107–18.

Lefkowitz, M., 'Did Ancient Women Write Novels?', in Levine, *'Women Like This'*, pp. 199–219.

Letoublon, F., *Les lieux communs du roman. Stéréotypes grecs d'aventure et d'amour* (Leiden: Brill, 1993).

Leutzsch, M., *Die Wahrnehmung sozialer Wirklichkeit im 'Hirten des Hermas'* (Göttingen: Vandenhoeck & Ruprecht, 1987).

Levine, A.-J., 'Diaspora as Metaphor: Bodies and Boundaries in the Book of Tobit', in J. Andrew Overman and Robert S. MacLennan, *Diaspora Jews and Judaism: Essays in Honor of, and in Dialogue with, A. Thomas Kraabel* (South Florida Studies in the History of Judaism; Atlanta: Scholars Press, 1992), pp. 105–18.

— 'Theological Education, the Bible, and History: Détente in the Culture Wars', in *Early Christian Families in Context* (Religion, Marriage, and Family; Grand Rapids, WI: Eerdmans, 2003), pp. 327–36.

—*'Women Like This': New Perspectives on Jewish Women in the Greco-Roman World* (Early Judaism and Its Literature, 1; Atlanta: Scholars Press, 1991).

Levinson, J., 'The Athlete of Piety: Fatal Fictions in Rabbinic Literature' [Hebrew] *Tarbiz* 68 (1999), pp. 61–86.

Lévi-Strauss, C., *Structural Anthropology* (2 vols.; trans. Claire Jacobson and Brooke Grundfest Schoepf; New York: Basic Books, 1963).

Leyerle, B., 'Appealing to Children', *JECS* 5.2 (1997), pp. 243–70.

— 'John Chrysostom on the Gaze', *JECS* 1 (1993), pp. 159–74.

— *Theatrical Shows and Ascetic Lives: John Chrysostom's Attack on Spiritual Marriage* (Berkeley: University of California Press, 2001).

Liddell, H.G., and R. Scott (eds), *Greek-English Lexicon* (Oxford: Clarendon Press, 1996).

Lieberman, S., 'The Martyrs of Caesarea', *Annuaire de l'institut de philologie et d'histoire orientales et slaves* 7 (1939–1944), pp. 395–446.

Lieu, J., *Image and Reality: The Jews in the World of the Christians in the Second Century* (Edinburgh: T & T Clark, 1996).

Lipsius, R.A., and M. Bonnet (eds), *Acta Apostolorum Apocrypha* (2 vols.; Darmstadt: Wissenschaftliche Buchgesellschaft, 1959; Hildesheim: Georg Olms, 1959).

Lipsius, R.A., and M. Bonnet (eds), *Acta Apostolorum Apocrypha* (2 vols.; Hildesheim: Georg Olms, 1959).

Lock, M., and N. Scheper-Hughes, 'A Critical Interpretive Approach in Medical Anthropology: Rituals and Routines of Discipline and Dissent', in T.M. Johnson and C.F. Sargent (eds), *Medical Anthropology: Contemporary Theory and Method* (New York: Praeger, 1990), pp. 47–72.

Loraux, N., *Tragic Ways of Killing a Woman* (trans. Anthony Forster; Cambridge, MA: Harvard University Press, 1987).

MacDonald, D.R., *The Acts of Andrew and the Acts of Andrew and Matthias in the City of the Cannibals* (Texts and Translations 33; Christian Apocrypha 1; Atlanta: Scholars Press, 1990).

— *Christianizing Homer:* The Odyssey, *Plato and* The Acts of Andrew (New York: Oxford University Press, 1994).

— *The Legend and the Apostle. The Battle for Paul in Story and Canon* (Philadelphia, PA: Westminster Press, 1983).

— 'The Role of Women in the Production of the Apocryphal Acts', *The Iliff Review* 41 (1984), pp. 21–38.

— 'The Shipwrecks of Odysseus and Paul', *NTS* 45 (1999), pp. 88–107.

— *There Is No Male and Female: The Fate of a Dominical Saying in Paul and Gnosticism* (Harvard Dissertations in Religion, 20; Philadelphia, PA: Fortress Press, 1987).

MacDonald, D.R., and Andrew D. Scrimgeour, 'Pseudo-Chrysostom's *Panegyric* to Thecla: The Heroine of the *Acts of Paul* in Homily and Art', *Semeia* 38 (1986), pp. 151–59.

MacDonald, M.Y., *Early Christian Women and Pagan Opinion. The Power of the Hysterical Woman* (Cambridge, UK: Cambridge University Press, 1996).

Mack, B.L., *The Lost Gospel: The Book of Q and Christian Origins* (San Francisco, CA: HarperSanFrancisco, 1993).

MacMullen, R., *Changes in the Roman Empire* (Princeton, NJ: Princeton University Press, 1990).

— *Roman Social Relations: 50 B.C. to A.D. 284* (New Haven, CT and London: Yale University Press, 1974).

Maier, H.O., 'Religious Dissent, Heresy and Households', *VC* 49 (1989), pp. 49–52.

Malamud, M., *A Poetics of Transformation: Prudentius and Classical Mythology* (Ithaca, NY: Cornell University Press, 1989).

Malherbe, A., 'The Apologetic Theology of the *Preaching of Peter*', *Restoration Quarterly* 13 (1970), pp. 205–23.

Malina, B., *Christian Origins and Cultural Anthropology: Practical Models for Biblical Interpretation* (Atlanta: John Knox Press, 1986).

Malingrey, A.-M. (ed. and trans.), *Jean Chrysostom. Sur la vaine glore et l'éducation des enfants* (Sources Chretienes, 188; Paris: Les Éditions du Cerf, 1972).

Malitz, J. (ed. and trans.), *Nikolaos von Damaskus. Leben des Kaisers Augustus* (Texte zur Forschung, 80; Darmstadt: Wissenschaftliche Buchgesellschaft, 2003).

Maraval, Pierre, *Égérie: Journal de Voyage (Itinéraire) Itinerarium et lettre sur la B^{se} Égérie*: Introduction, texte et traduction par M.C. Díaz y Díaz (Sources Chrétiennes 296; Paris: Éditions du Cerf, 1982; rep. 1997), 23, 5.

Markus, R.A., *The End of Ancient Christianity* (Cambridge, UK: Cambridge University Press, 1990).

Martin, D.B., 'The Construction of the Ancient Family: Methodological Considerations', *JRS* 86 (1996), pp. 40–60.

— *The Corinthian Body* (New Haven, CT: Yale University Press, 1995).
— 'Slave Families and Slaves in Families', in Balch and Osiek (eds), *Early Christian Families*, pp. 207–30.
— *Slavery as Salvation: The Metaphor of Slavery in Pauline Christianity* (New Haven, CT: Yale University Press, 1990), pp. 147–49.

Matthews, S., 'Thinking of Thecla: Issues in Feminist Historiography', *JFSR* 17 (2001), pp. 39–55.

McGinn, S.E., 'The Acts of Thecla', in Elisabeth Schüssler Fiorenza (ed.), *Searching the Scriptures. Vol. 2: A Feminist Commentary* (2 vols.; New York: Crossroad, 1994), pp. 800–28.

McKenna, M., *Not Counting Women and Children. Neglected Stories from the Bible* (Maryknoll, NY: Orbis Books, 1994).

Meeks, W., *The First Urban Christians: The Social World of the Apostle Paul* (New Haven, CT: Yale University Press, 1983), pp. 53–55, 214–15.
— 'The Image of the Androgyne: Some Uses of a Symbol in Earliest Christianity', *History of Religions* 13 (1973–74), pp. 165–208.

Methuen, C., 'Widows, Bishops, and the Struggle for Authority in the *Didascalia Apostolorum*', *Journal of Ecclesial History* 46 (1995), pp. 197–213.

Meyer, M.W., 'Making Mary Male: The Categories "Male" and "Female" in the Gospel of Thomas', *NTS* 31 (1985), pp. 554–70.

Meyers, C., Toni Craven and Ross S. Kraemer (eds), *Women in Scripture: A Dictionary of Named and Unnamed Women in the Hebrew Bible, the Apocryphal / Deuterocanonical Books, and the New Testament* (Boston: Houghton Mifflin, 2000).

Miles, M., *Carnal Knowing: Female Nakedness and Religious Meaning in the Christian West* (Boston: Beacon Press, 1989).

Millar, F., *A Study of Cassius Dio* (Oxford: Clarendon Press, 1964).

Miller, P.C., 'Desert Asceticism and "The Body from Nowhere"', *JECS* 2/2 (1994), pp. 137–53.
— *Dreams in Late Antiquity: Studies in the Imagination of a Culture* (Princeton, NJ: Princeton University Press, 1994).

Millet, P., 'Patronage and its avoidance in classical Athens', in Wallace-Hadrill (ed.), *Patronage in Ancient Society*, pp. 15–48.

Milner, N.P., *An Epigraphical Survey in the Kibyra-Olbasa Region Conducted by A.S. Hall* (Ankara: British Institute of Archaeology at Ankara, 1998).

Misset-van de Weg, M., 'A wealthy woman named Tryphaena: patroness of Thecla of Iconium', in Jan N. Bremmer (ed.), *The Apocryphal Acts of Paul and Thecla* (Studies on the Apocryphal Acts of the Apostles; Kampen: Kok Pharos, 1996), pp. 16–35.
— *Sara & Thecla. Verbeelding van vrouwen in 1 Petrus en de Acta Theclae* (Ph.D. diss., Utrecht University, Utrecht, 1998).

Molinari, A.L., 'Augustine, *Contra Adimantum, Pseudo-Titus*, BG 8502.4 and the *Acts of Peter*: Attacking Carl Schmidt's Theory of an Original Unity Between the *Act of Peter* and the *Acts of Peter*' (SBLSP 38; Atlanta: Society of Biblical Literature, 1999), pp. 426–47.
— *I Never Knew the Man: the Coptic Act of Peter (Papyrus berolinensis 8502.4): Its Independence from the Apocryphal Acts of Peter, Genre and Legendary Origins* (Bibliothèque copte de Nag Hammadi. Section 'Etudes' 5, Québec: Presses de l'Université Laval; and Louvain: Editions Peeters, 2000).

Mommsen, T., and Paul Kruegger (eds), *The Digest of Justinian* (3 vols.; trans. Alan Watson; Philadelphia, PA: University of Pennsylvania Press, 1985).

Moore, C.H., and J. Jackson (trans.), *Histories* (4 vols.; LCL; Cambridge, MA: Harvard University Press, 1969).

Morard, F., 'Souffrance et Martyre dans les Actes Apocryphes des Apôtres', in François Bovon *et al.* (eds), *Les Actes Apocryphes des Apôtres. Christianisme et Monde Païen* (Publications de la Faculté de Théologie de l'Université de Genève N° 4; Genève: Editions Labor et Fides, 1981), pp. 95–108.

Mott, S.C., 'Greek Ethics and Christian Conversion: The Philonic Background of Titus II 10–14 and III 3–7', *NovT* 20 (1978), pp. 22–48.

Moxnes, H. (ed.), *Constructing Early Christian Families: Family as Social Reality and Metaphor* (London and New York: Routledge, 1997).

Murnaghan, S., 'Penelope's *Agnoia*: Knowledge, Power, and Gender in the *Odyssey*', in M. Skinner (ed.), *Rescuing Creusa. New Methodological Approaches to Women in Antiquity*. A Special Issue of *Helios*, n.s. 13/2 (1987), pp. 103–15.

Musurillo, H., *The Acts of the Christian Martyrs* (Oxford: Clarendon Press, 1972).

Nasrallah, L.S., '"She Became What the Words Signified": The Greek *Acts of Andrew*'s Construction of the Reader-Disciple', in François Bovon *et al.* (eds), *The Apocryphal Acts of the Apostles: Harvard Divinity School Studies* (Cambridge, MA: Harvard University Press, 1999), pp. 233–58.

Nathan, G.S., *The Family in Late Antiquity: The Rise of Christianity and the Endurance of Tradition* (London and New York: Routledge, 2000).

Nauerth, C., 'Nachlese von Thekla-Darstellungen', in Guntram Koch (ed.), *Studien zur spätantiken und frühchristlichen Kunst und Kultur des Orients* (Wiesbaden: Otto Harrassowitz, 1982), pp. 14–18.

— 'Zweifelhafte Isaak-Bilder in der koptischen Kunst', in *Studien zur frühchristlichen Kunst II*, pp. 1–5.

Nauerth, C., and Rüdiger Warns, *Thekla: Ihre Bilder in der frühchristlichen Kunst* (Göttinger Orientforschungen 2/3; Wiesbaden: Otto Harrassowitz, 1981).

Newsom, C.A. and S.H. Ringe (eds), *The Women's Bible Commentary* (Louisville, KY: Westminster/John Knox Press, 1992; rev. edn, 1998).

Neyrey, J.H., *Paul, In Other Words: A Cultural Reading of His Letters* (Louisville, KY: Westminster/John Knox Press, 1990).

Ng, E.Y.L., '*Acts of Paul and Thecla*: Women's Stories and Precedent?' *JTS* n.s. 55 (2004), pp. 1–29.

Nimmo, B., and Darrell Scott with Steve Rabey, *Rachel's Tears: The Spiritual Journey of Columbine Martyr Rachel Scott* (Nashville, TN: Thomas Nelson, 2000).

Nock, A.D., *Essays on Religion and the Ancient World* II (ed. Z. Stewart; 2 vols.; Oxford: Oxford University Press, 1972).

Norden, E., *Agnostos Theos. Untersuchungen zur Formgeschichte religiöser Rede* (Leipzig: Teubner, 1913; reprint Darmstadt, 1974), pp. 313–14.

Nürnberg, R., 'Non decet neque necessarium est, ut mulieres doceant. Überlegungen zum altkirchlichen Lehrverbot für Frauen', *Jahrbuch für Antike und Christentum* 31 (1988), pp. 57–73.

Oppenheimer, A., *The Am Ha-ʾAretz: A Study in the Social History of the Jewish People* (Leiden: E.J. Brill, 1977).

Osiek, C., 'Perpetua's Husband', *JECS* 10 (2002), pp. 287–90.

Osiek, C., and David L. Balch, *Families in the New Testament World: Households and House Churches* (The Family, Religion, and Culture series; Louisville, KY: Westminster/John Knox Press, 1997).

Pardes, I., 'Beyond Genesis 3', *Hebrew Studies in Literature and the Arts* 17 (1989), pp. 161–87.

— *The Biography of Ancient Israel* (Berkeley: University of California Press, 1999).

Parrott, D.M. (ed.), *Nag Hammadi Codices III,3–4 and V,1 with Papyrus Berolinensis 8502,3 and Oxyrhynchus Papyrus 1081, Eugenostos and the* Sophia of Jesus Christ (The Coptic Gnostic Library, NHS 27; Leiden, New York, København, and Köln: E. J. Brill, 1991).

— (ed.), *Nag Hammadi Codices V, 2–5 and VI with Papyrus Berolinensis 8502, 1 and 4* (NHS 11; Leiden: E.J. Brill, 1979), pp. 473–93.

Patterson, C., 'Plutarch's "Advice on Marriage": Traditional Wisdom through a Philosophical Lens', *ANRW* II.33.6 (1992), pp. 4709–23.

Patterson, S.J., *The Gospel of Thomas and Jesus* (Sonoma, CA: Polebridge, 1993).

Paul IV, *Mysterii paschalis* (Rome: Vatican Polyglot Press, 14 February 1969), n.p., cited 24 June 2005; online: http://www.catholic-forum.com/saints/day0923.htm.

Pearson, B.A., *The Emergence of the Christian Religion: Essays on Early Christianity* (Harrisburg, PA: Trinity Press International, 1997).

Perelman, C., and L. Olbrechts-Tyteca, *The New Rhetoric: A Treatise on Argumentation* (Notre Dame, IN: University of Notre Dame Press, 1969).

Pergola, P., '*Petronella Martyr*: une évergète de la fin du IVe siècle?', in Eugenio Alliata, Theofried Baumeister and Fabrizio Bisconti (eds), *Memoriam sanctorum venerantes: miscellanea in onore di Monsignor Victor Saxer* (Studi di Antichità Cristiana 48; Città del Vaticano: Pontificio Instituto di Archeologia Cristiana, 1992), pp. 627–36.

Perkins, J., 'The Apocryphal Acts of the Apostles and Early Christian Martyrdom', *Arethusa* 18 (1985), pp. 211–30.

— *The Suffering Self: Pain and Narrative Representation in the Early Christian Era* (London and New York: Routledge, 1995), pp. 41–76.

Pervo, R.I., 'Aseneth and Her Sisters. Women in Jewish Narrative and in the Greek Novels', in Amy-Jill Levine (ed.), *'Women Like This': New Perspectives on Jewish Women in the Greco-Roman World* (Early Judaism and Its Literature, I; Atlanta: Scholars Press, 1991), pp. 145–60.

— *Profit with Delight: The Literary Genre of the Acts of the Apostles* (Philadelphia, PA: Fortress Press, 1987).

Peterson, E., *Frühkirche, Judentum und Gnosis* (Freiburg: Herder, 1959).

Petropoulos, J., 'Transvestite Virgin With a Cause: *The Acta Pauli et Thecla* and Late Antique Proto-feminism', in B. Berggreen and N. Marinatos (eds), *Greece and Gender* (Bergen, Norway: Norwegian Institute at Athens, 1995), pp. 125–39.

Petruccione, J., 'The Portrait of St. Eulalia of Mérida in Prudentius' *Peristephanon*', *Analecta Bollandiana* 108 (1990), pp. 81–104.

Pfister, F., in E. Hennecke (ed.), *Neutestamenliche Apokryphen* (Tübingen: Mohr, 1924), p. 169.

Pfisterer-Haas, S., *Darstellungen alter Frauen in der griechischen Kunst* (Frankfurt: Peter Lang, 1989).

Phillips III, C.R., '*Nullum Crimen sine Lege*: Socioreligious Sanctions on Magic', in Faraone and Obbink (eds), *Magika Hiera*, pp. 260–76.

— 'The Sociology of Religious Knowledge in the Roman Empire to A.D. 284', in *ANRW* II.16.3 (1986), pp. 2677–73.

Philsy, S., 'Diakonia of Women in the New Testament', *Indian Journal of Theology* 32 (1983), pp. 110–18.

Pinault, J.R., 'The Medical Case for Virginity in the Early Second Century C.E.: Soranus of Ephesus, "Gynecology" 1.32', *Helios* 19 (1992), pp. 123–39.

Plato, *Phaedo* 9, 13, in *Plato*, ed. and trans. Harold North Fowler, LCL; 7 vols (Cambridge, MA: Harvard University Press, 1914, repr. 1982).

Plümacher, E., 'Apokryphe Apostelakten', *RE* Suppl. 15 (Stuttgart: Druckenmüller, 1978), pp. 26–30.

— 'Apostolische Missionsreise und statthalterliche Assisetour. Eine Interpretation von Acta Iohannis c. 37.45 und 55', *ZNW* 85 (1994), pp. 259–78.

— 'Wirklichkeitserfahrung und Geschictsschreibung bei Lukas. Erwägungen zu den Wir-Stücken der Apostelgeschite', *ZNW* 68 (1977), pp. 1–22.

Pomeroy, S.B., *Goddesses, Whores, Wives, and Slaves: Women in Classical Antiquity* (New York: Dorset Press, 1975).

Potter, D., 'Martyrdom As Spectacle', in Ruth Scodel (ed.), *Theater and Society in the Classical World* (Ann Arbor: University of Michigan Press, 1993), pp. 53–88.

— 'Performance, Power, and Justice in the High Empire', in W.J. Slater (ed.), *Roman Theater and Society. E. Togo Salmon Papers* I (Ann Arbor: University of Michigan Press, 1996), pp. 129–59.

Poupon, G., 'L'accusation de magie dans les Actes apocryphes', in François Bovon, *et al.* (eds), *Les Actes apocryphes des apôtres: Christianisme et monde païen* (Genève: Labor et Fides, 1981), pp. 71–85.

— 'Les "Actes de Pierre" et leur remaniement', *ANRW* II.25.6 (1988), pp. 4363–83.

— 'Encore une fois: Tertullien, *De baptismo* 17.5', in D. Knoepfler (ed.), *Nomen Latinum. Mélanges A. Schneider* (Neuchâtel and Geneva: Faculté des Lettres and Droz, 1997), pp. 199–205.

Price, S.R.F., *Rituals and Power: The Roman Imperial Cult in Asia Minor* (Cambridge: Cambridge University Press, 1984).

Prieur, J.-M. (ed. and trans.), *Acta Andreae* (CCSA 5–6 Turnhout: Brepols, 1989).

Prieur, J.-M., and W. Schneemelcher, 'The Acts of Andrew', in W. Schneemelcher (ed.), *New Testament Apocrypha* (2 vols.; trans. R. McL. Wilson; Cambridge, UK: James Clarke & Co., 1992), vol. 2, pp. 101–118.

Puech, B., 'Prosopographie des amis de Plutarque', *ANRW* II.33.6 (1992), pp. 4831–93.

Puelma, M., 'Die Dichterbegegnung in Theokrits Thalysien', *Museum Helveticum* 17 (1960), pp. 144–64.

Quass, F., *Die Honoratiorenschicht in den Städten des griechischen Ostens* (Stuttgart: Steiner, 1993).

Radway, J.A., *Reading the Romance: Women, Patriarchy, and Popular Literature* (Chapel Hill: University of North Carolina Press, 1991).

Raepsaet-Charlier, M.Th., 'La vie familiale des élites dans la Rome impériale: le droit et la pratique', *Cahiers du Centre G. Glotz* 5 (1994), pp. 165–97.

Rajak, T., 'The Jewish Community and Its Boundaries', in Judith Lieu, John North and Tessa Rajak (eds), *The Jews Among Pagans and Christians in the Roman Empire* (London: Routledge, 1992), pp. 9–28.

Rajak, T., and D. Noy, '*Archisynagogoi*: Office, Title and Social Status in the Greco-Jewish Synagogue', *JRS* 83 (1993), pp. 75–93.

Ramakrishna, S., *The Gospel of Sri Ramakrishna* (trans. S. Nikhilananda, S.; New York: Ramakrishna-Vivekananda Center, 1985).

Ramsey, B., *Ambrose* (The Early Church Fathers; New York: Routledge, 1997).

Rattenbury, R.M., 'Chastity and Chastity Ordeals in the Ancient Greek Romances', *Proceedings of the Leeds Philosophical and Literary Society* 1 (1926), pp. 59–71.

Rattenbury, R.M., and T.W. Lumb (eds), *Les Éthiopiques: Théagène et Chariclée* (3 vols.; Paris: Editions Belles Lettres, 1935–43).

Rawson, B. (ed.), *Marriage, Divorce, and Children in Ancient Rome* (Oxford: Clarendon Press, 1991).

Reardon, B. (ed.), *Erotica Antiqua* (Bangor: University College of North Wales, 1994).

Reardon, B.P. (ed.), *Collected Ancient Greek Novels* (Berkeley: University of California Press, 1989).

— (ed.), *Erotica Antiqua* (Bangor: University College of North Wales, 1994).

Rebhorn, W.A., 'Baldesar Castiglione, Thomas Wilson, and the Courtly Body of Renaissance Rhetoric', *Rhetorica* 10.6 (1993), pp. 241–74.

Reiter, R.R. (ed.), *Toward an Anthropology of Women* (New York: Monthly Review, 1975).

Reitzenstein, R., *Hellenistische Wundererzählungen* (Darmstadt: Wissenschaftliche Buchgesellschaft, 1963), p. 16.

Riccobono, S., *et al.* (eds), *Fontes Iuris Romani Antejustiniani* (3 vols.; Florence: S.A.G. Barbèra, 1968).

Richlin, A., *The Garden of Priapus: Sexuality and Aggression in Roman Humor* (2nd edn; New York: Oxford University Press, 1992), p. 137.

Robert, L., *Les gladiateurs dans l'Orient grec* (Paris: E. Champion, 1940).

— *Le martyre de Pionios, prêtre de Smyrne* (Washington, D.C.: Dumbarton Oaks, 1994).

Robinson, J.M., 'LOGOI SOPHON: On the Gattung of Q', in James M. Robinson and Helmut Koester (eds), *Trajectories through Early Christianity* (Philadelphia, PA: Fortress Press, 1971), pp. 71–113.

Rodman, R.C., 'Who's on Third? Reading *Acts of Andrew* as a Rhetoric of Resistance', *Semeia* 79 (1997), pp. 27–44.

Rolfe, J.C. (trans.), *Suetonius: The Lives of the Caesars*, vol. I: *Julius, Augustus, Tiberius, Gaius, Caligula* (LCL; Cambridge, MA: Harvard University Press, 1969).

Rolfe, J.C. (trans.), *Suetonius: The Lives of the Caesars: Julius, Augustus, Tiberius, Gaius, Caligula* (LCL; Cambridge, MA: Harvard University Press, 1969).

Rordorf, W., 'Quelques jalons pour une interprétation symbolique des *Actes de Paul*', in David H. Warren, Ann Graham Brock and David W. Pao (eds), *Early Christian Voices: In Texts, Traditions, and Symbols. Essays in Honor of François Bovon* (Boston/Leiden: Brill, 2003), pp. 251–92.

— 'Sainte Thècle dans la tradition hagiographique occidentale', *Augustinianum* 24 (1984), pp. 73–81.

— 'Tradition and Composition in the *Acts of Thecla*: The State of the Question', *Semeia* 38 (1986), pp. 43–52.

— 'Tradition et composition dans les Actes de Thècle. Etat de la question', *TZ* 41 (1985), pp. 272–83.

Rosin, H., 'Columbine girl who really said "Yes" shuns fame', *Times-Picayune* (Saturday, 17 October 1999), p. A-23. Original article appeared in *Washington Post* (Wednesday, 14 October, 1999), p. C1.

Rouselle, A., 'The Family Under the Roman Empire: Signs and Gestures', in André Burguière *et al.* (eds), *A History of the Family*. I. *Distant Worlds, Ancient Worlds* (2 vols.; Cambridge, MA: The Belknap Press of Harvard University Press, 1996), pp. 269–310.

— 'Personal Status and Sexual Practice in the Roman Empire', in M. Feher *et al.* (eds), *Fragments for a History of the Human Body*, I (New York: Urzone, 1989), pp. 300–33.

— *Porneia: On Desire and the Body in Antiquity* (Cambridge & Oxford: Blackwell, 1988).

Roy, P., *Indian Traffic: Identities in Question in Colonial and Postcolonial India* (Berkeley: University of California Press, 1998).

Rubin, G., 'The Traffic in Women', in Rayna Rapp Reiter (ed.), *Toward an Anthropology of Women* (New York: Monthly Review, 1975), pp. 157–210.

Sahin, S., *Die Inschriften von Arykanda* (Bonn: Habelt, 1994).

Saïd, S., 'The City in the Greek Novel', in J. Tatum (ed.), *The Search for the Ancient Novel* (Baltimore, MD: The Johns Hopkins University Press, 1994), pp. 216–36.

Salisbury, J., *Church Fathers, Independent Virgins* (London: Verso, 1991).

— *Perpetua's Passion: The Death and Memory of a Young Roman Woman* (New York: Routledge, 1997).

Saller, R., 'Patronage and friendship in early imperial Rome: drawing the distinction', in A. Wallace-Hadrill (ed.), *Patronage in Ancient Society* (Leicester-Nottingham Studies in Ancient Society, 1; London: Routledge, 1989), pp. 49–62.

Saller, R.P., *Personal Patronage Under the Early Empire* (Cambridge, UK: Cambridge University Press, 1982).

Saller, R.P., and B. Shaw, 'Tombstones and Roman Family Relations in the Principate: Civilians, Soldiers, and Slaves', *JRS* 74 (1984), pp. 124–56.

Scarborough, J., 'The Pharmacology of Sacred Plants, Herbs, and Roots', in Faraone and Obbink (eds), *Magika Hiera*, pp. 138–74.

Scarcella, A., 'Social and Economic Structures of the Ancient Novels', in G. Schmeling (ed.), *The Novel in the Ancient World* (Leiden: E.J. Brill, 1996), pp. 221–76.

Schäfer, P., and Hans G. Kippenberg (eds), *Envisioning Magic: A Princeton Seminar and Symposium* (Leiden and New York: Brill, 1997).

Schäferdiek, K., 'Herkunft und Interesse der alten Johannesakten', *ZNW* 74 (1983), pp. 247–67.

Schlarb, C., 'Die (un)gebändigte Witwe', in M. Tamcke *et al.* (eds), *Syrisches Christentum weltweit* (Münster: LIT, 1995), pp. 36–75.

Schmeling, G. (ed.), *The Novel in the Ancient World* (Leiden: E.J. Brill, 1996).

Schmidt, C., 'Die alten Petrusakten im Zusammenhang der apokryphen Apostellitteratur nebst einem neuentdeckten Fragment', in *TU* 24.1, N.F. 9.3 (Leipzig: J. C. Hinrichs'sche Buchhandlung, 1903), pp. 3–7.

— 'Studien zu den alten Petrusakten', *ZKG* 43 (1924), pp. 321–48.

Schneemelcher, W., 'XV. Apostelgeschichten des 2. und 3. Jahrhunderts. Einleitung', in *idem* (ed.), *Neutestamentliche Apokryphen in deutscher Übersetzung, II. Band: Apostolisches, Apokalypsen und Verwandtes* (Tübingen: J.C.B. Mohr [Paul Siebeck], 1989), pp. 71–93.

— 'Paulusakten', in *idem* (ed.), *Neutestamentliche Apokryphen in deutscher Übersetzung, II. Band: Apostolisches, Apokalypsen und Verwandtes* (2 vols.; Tübingen: J.C.B. Mohr [Paul Siebeck], 1989), vol. 2, pp. 193–241.

— 'Second and Third Century Acts of Apostles', in Edgar Hennecke and Wilhelm Schneemelcher (eds), *New Testament Apocrypha*, vol. 2 (Philadelphia, PA: Westminster/John Knox Press, rev. edn, 1992), pp. 75–86.

— (ed.) *New Testament Apocrypha* (2 vols.; trans. R. McL. Wilson; Cambridge, UK: James Clarke & Co., 1992).

Schneemelcher, W. and K. Schäferdiek, 'Introduction, Second and Third-Century Acts of the Apostles', in W. Schneemelcher (ed.), *New Testament Apocrypha* (2 vols., trans. R. McL. Wilson; Cambridge, UK: James Clarke & Co., 1992), 2, pp. 75–100.

Schneider, P., *The Mystery of the Acts of John* (San Francisco, CA: Mellen Research University Press, 1991).

Schnurr, V., 'Triumph over Tragedy', as told to Janna R. Graber, *Stories for a Teen's Heart* (Sisters, OR: Multnomah Publishers, 1999).

Schroeder, C.T., 'Embracing the Erotic in the *Passion of Andrew*. The Apocryphal *Acts of Andrew*, the Greek Novel, and Platonic Philosophy', in Jan N. Bremmer (ed.), *The Apocryphal Acts of Andrew* (Leuven: Peeters, 2000), pp. 110–26.

Schüssler Fiorenza, E. (ed.), *Aspects of Religious Propaganda* (University of Notre Dame Center for the Study of Judaism and Christianity in Antiquity 2; Notre Dame, IN and London: University of Notre Dame Press, 1976).

— *In Memory of Her: A Feminist Theological Reconstruction of Christian Origins* (New York: Crossroad, 1983).

— 'Miracles, Mission, and Apologetics: An Introduction', in *eadem* (ed.), *Aspects of Religious Propaganda* (University of Notre Dame Center for the Study of Judaism and Christianity in Antiquity 2; Notre Dame, IN and London: University of Notre Dame Press, 1976), pp. 1–25.

— (ed.), *Searching the Scriptures: A Feminist Introduction and Commentary* (2 vols.; New York: Crossroad, 1993, 1994).

— 'Word, Spirit and Power: Women in Early Christian Communities', in Rosemary Ruether and Eleanor McLaughlin (eds), *Women of Spirit: Female Leadership in the Jewish and Christian Traditions* (New York: Simon & Schuster, 1979), pp. 29–70.

Schwahn, W., 'Strategos', *RE* Suppl. 6 (1954), pp. 1112–13.

Schwarz, G., '"Er berührte ihre Hand"? (Matthäus 8,15)', *Biblische Notizen* 73 (1994), pp. 33–35.

Scott, J.C., *Domination and the Arts of Resistance: Hidden Transcripts* (New Haven, CT: Yale University Press, 1985).

Scott, J.W., *Gender and the Politics of History* (rev. edn; New York: Columbia University Press, 1999).

Scott, R.L., 'On Viewing Rhetoric as Epistemic', in B.L. Brock *et al.* (eds), *Methods of Rhetorical Criticism: A Twentieth-Century Perspective* (Detroit: Wayne State University Press, 1989), pp. 134–43.

Scott-Kilvert, I., *Cassius Dio: The Roman History. The Reign of Augustus* (London: Penguin Books, 1987).

Seesemann, H., 'πεῖρα, πειράω, πειράζω', *TDNT* 6, pp. 23–36.

Segal, A.F., 'Hellenistic Magic: Some Questions of Definition', in Roelof van den Broek, *et al.* (eds), *Studies in Gnosticism and Hellenistic Religions Presented to Gilles Quispel* (Leiden: Brill, 1981), pp. 349–75.

Seim, T.K., 'The Gospel of Luke', in E.S. Schüssler Fiorenza (ed.), *Searching the Scriptures II: A Feminist Commentary* (2 vols.; New York: Crossroad, 1994), pp. 728–62.

Sered, S., and S. Cooper, 'Sexuality and Social Control: Anthropological Reflections on the Book of Susanna', in Ellen Spolsky (ed.), *The Judgment of Susanna: Authority and Witness* (Atlanta: Scholars Press, 1996), pp. 43–55.

Settis, S., 'Severo Alessandro e i suoi Lari (S.H.A., S.A., 29, 2–3)', *Athenaeum* 50 (1972), pp. 237–51.

Shaw, B.D., 'The Age of Roman Girls at Marriage: Some Reconsiderations', *JRS* 77 (1987), pp. 30–46.

— 'Body/Power/Identity: Passions of the Martyrs', *JECS* 4 (1996), pp. 269–312.

— 'The Family in Late Antiquity: The Experience of Augustine', *Past and Present* 115 (1987), pp. 3–51.

— 'The Passion of Perpetua', *Past and Present* 139 (May 1993), pp. 3–45.

Shaw, T.M., *The Burden of the Flesh: Fasting and Sexuality in Early Christianity* (Minneapolis, MN: Fortress Press, 1998).

Sigal, P., 'Early Christian and Rabbinic Liturgical Affinities: Exploring Liturgical Acculturation', *NTS* 30 (1984), pp. 63–90.

Simon, M., *Verus Israel: A Study of the Relations Between Christians and Jews in the Roman Empire (135-425)* (trans. H. McKeating; The Littman Library of Jewish Civilization; Oxford: Oxford University Press, 1986).

Sissa, G., 'Subtle Bodies', in M. Feher *et al.* (eds), *Fragments for a History of the Human Body* (New York: Urzone, 1989), vol. 3, pp. 132–56.

Smolenaars, J.J., *Statius Thebaid VII: a commentary* (Leiden: Brill, 1994).

Söder, R., *Die apokryphen Apostelgeschichten und die romanhafte Literatur der Antike* (Stuttgart: W. Kohlhammer, 1932; repr. Darmstadt: Wissenschaftliche Buchgesellschaft, 1969).

Stark, I., 'Strukturen des griechischen Abenteuer- und Liebesromans', in H. Kuch (ed.), *Der Antike Roman: Untersuchungen zur literarischen Kommunikations und Gattungsgeschichte* (Berlin: Akademie-Verlag, 1989), pp. 82–106.

Steinberg, N., 'Israelite Tricksters, Their Analogues and Cross-Cultural Study', *Semeia* 42 (1988), pp. 1–13.

Stephens, S.A., 'Who read ancient novels?', in Tatum, *The Search for the Ancient Novel*, pp. 405–18.

Stoneman, R., 'The *Alexander Romance*: From History to Fiction', in J.R. Morgan and Richard Stoneman (eds), *Greek Fiction: The Greek Novel in Context* (London: Routledge, 1994), pp. 117–29.

Stoops, R., 'Christ as Patron in the Acts of Peter', *Semeia* 56 (1992), pp. 143–57.

Strange, W.A., *Children in the Early Church: Children in the Ancient World, the New Testament and the Early Church* (Carlisle, UK: Paternoster Press, 1996; repr. Eugene, OR: Wipf and Stock, 2004).

Streete, G.P.C., *The Strange Woman: Power and Sex in the Bible* (Louisville, KY: Westminster John Knox Press, 1997).

Stroumsa, G.A.G., '*Caro salutis cardo*: Shaping the Person in Early Christian Thought', *History of Religions* 30.1 (1990), pp. 25–50.

— *Another Seed: Studies in Gnostic Mythology* (NHS, 24; Leiden: E.J. Brill, 1984).

Sullivan, L.E. , 'Body Works: Knowledge of the Body in the Study of Religion', *History of Religions* 30.1 (1990) pp. 86–99.

— '"Seeking an End to the Primary Text" or "Putting an End to the Text as Primary"', in F.E. Reynolds and S.L. Burkhalter (eds), *Beyond the Classics? Essays in Religious Studies and Liberal Education* (Atlanta: Scholars Press, 1990), pp. 41–58.

Synek, E.M., 'In der Kirche möge sie schweigen', *Oriens Christianus* 77 (1993), pp. 151–64.

Tatum, J. (ed.), *The Search for the Ancient Novel* (Baltimore, MD and London: The Johns Hopkins University Press, 1994).

Tatum, W.B., 'Did Jesus Heal Simon's Mother-in-law of a Fever?' *Dialogue* 27 (1994), pp. 148–58.

Theissen, G., *Sociology of Early Palestinian Christianity* (trans. John Bowden; Philadelphia, PA: Fortress Press, 1978).

— *Soziologie der Jesusbewegung* (Munich: Kaiser Verlag, 1977).

— *Urchristliche Wundergeschichten* (Gütersloh: Gerd Mohn, 1974).

Theodor, J., and H. Albeck (eds), *Genesis Rabbah* (Jerusalem: Wahrmann, 1965).

Thomas, C.M., *The* Acts of Peter, *Gospel Literature, and the Ancient Novel: Rewriting the Past* (Oxford and New York: Oxford University Press, 2003).

— 'Revivifying Resurrection Accounts: techniques of composition and rewriting in the *Acts of Peter* cc. 25-28', in J.N. Bremmer (ed.), *The Apocryphal Acts of Peter: Magic, Miracles and Gnosticism* (Leuven: Peeters, 1998), pp. 65–83.

Thorpe, L. (ed. and trans.), *The History of the Franks* (Baltimore, MD: Penguin, 1974).

Till, W.C., and Hans-Martin Schenke, *Die gnostischen Schriften des koptischen Papyrus Berolinensis 8502*, in *TU* 60 (2nd rev. and enlarged edn; Berlin: Akademie Verlag, 1972).

Tilley, M.A., 'The Ascetic Body and the (Un)making of the World of the Martyr', *JAAR* 59.3 (1991), pp. 467–79.

— 'Harnessing the Martyrs', paper presented at the annual meeting of the North American Patristic Society, Chicago, 30 May 1998.

— 'The Passion of Saints Perpetua and Felicity', in Richard Valantasis (ed.), *Religions of Late Antiquity in Practice* (Princeton Readings in Religion; Princeton, NJ and Oxford: Princeton University Press, 2000), pp. 387–97.

Tissot, Y., 'Encratisme et Actes Apocryphes', in François Bovon *et al.* (eds), *Les Actes Apocryphes des Apôtres. Christianisme et Monde Païen* (Publications de la Faculté de Théologie de l'Université de Genève N° 4; Genève: Editions Labor et Fides, 1981), pp. 109–19.

Tolbert, M.A., 'Mark', in Carol A. Newsom and Sharon H. Ringe (eds), *Women's Bible Commentary; Expanded Edition with Apocrypha* (Louisville, KY: Westminster/ John Knox Press, 1998), pp. 350–62.

Toohey, P., 'Love, Lovesickness, and Melancholia', *Illinois Classical Studies* 17 (1992), pp. 265–86.

Torjesen, K.J., 'In Praise of Noble Women: Gender and Honor in Ascetic Texts', *Semeia* 57 (1993), pp. 41–64.

— 'Tertullian's "Political" Ecclesiology and Women's Leadership', *Studia Patristica* 21 (1989), pp. 277–82.

Toynbee, J.M.C., *Animals in Roman Life and Art* (Ithaca, NY: Cornell University Press, 1973).

Treggiari, S., *Roman Marriage: Iusti Coniuges from the Time of Cicero to the Time of Ulpian* (Oxford: Clarendon Press, 1991).

Tribby, J., 'Body/Building: Living the Museum Life in Early Modern Europe', *Rhetorica* 10.2 (1992), pp. 139–62.

Tupet, A.-M., 'Rites magiques dans l'antiquité romaine', *ANRW* II.16.3 (1986), pp. 2591–675.

Urman, D., 'The House of Assembly and the House of Study: Are They One and the Same?' *Journal of Jewish Studies* 44.2 (Autumn 1993), pp. 236–57.

Valantasis, R., 'Constructions of Power in Asceticism', *JAAR* 58 (1995), pp. 775–821.

— 'Is the Gospel of Thomas Ascetical? Revisiting an Old Problem with a New Theory', *JECS* 7 (1999), pp. 55–81.

— *The Gospel of Thomas* (London: Routledge, 1997).

— 'The Nuptial Chamber Revisited: The *Acts of Thomas* and Cultural Intertextuality', SBLSP 34 (1995), pp. 380–93.

Van Beek, C.J.M., *Passio Sanctarum Perpetuae et Felicitatis* (Nijmegen: Dekkers and Van de Vegt, 1936).

Van Bremen, R., *The Limits of Participation. Women and civic life in the Greek East in the Hellenistic and Roman periods* (Amsterdam: J.C. Gieben, 1996).

— 'Women and Wealth', in Averil Cameron and Amélie Kuhrt (eds), *Images of Women in Antiquity* (London/Canberra: Croom Helm, 1983), pp. 223–42.

Van Cangh, J.-M., 'Miracles évangéliques – Miracles apocryphes', in F. Van Segbroeck, *et al.* (eds), *The Four Gospels 1992. Festschrift Frans Neirynck* III (Leuven: Leuven University Press, 1992), pp. 2277–319.

Van der Horst, P.W., *Hellenism-Judaism-Christianity. Essays on Their Interaction* (Kampen: Kok Pharos, 1994).

— 'Images of Women in Ancient Judaism', in R. Kloppenborg and W.J. Hanegraaff (eds), *Female Stereotypes in Religious Traditions* (Leiden: Brill, 1995), pp. 43–60.

Van Kampen, L., *Apostelverhalen* (Ph.D. diss., University of Utrecht: Merweboek, 1999).

Versnel, H.S., 'Some Reflections on the Relationship Magic-Religion', *Numen* 38 (1991), pp. 177–97.

Veyne, P., 'La famille et l'amour sous le Haut-Empire romain', *Annales ESC* 23 (1978), pp. 35–63.

— *Le pain et le cirque: Sociologie historique d'un pluralisme politique* (Paris: Édition du Seuil, 1976).

— 'The Roman Empire', in P. Veyne, Philippe Ariès and Georges Duby (eds), *A History of Private Life*, I. *From Pagan Rome to Byzantium* (trans. A. Goldhammer; Cambridge, MA: Harvard University Press, 1987), pp. 5–234.

Von Dobschütz, E., 'Der Roman in der altchristlichen Literatur', *Deutsche Rundschau* 111 (1902), pp. 87–106.

Von Harnack, A., 'Der apokryphe Brief des Paulusschülers Titus "De dispositione sanctimonii"', *Sitzungsberichte der Berliner Akademie der Wissenschaften, Phil.-hist. Klasse* 17 (1925), pp. 180–213.

— *Die Mission und Ausbreitung des Christentums* (1902; Leipzig: Hinrich, 1924).

Von Kellenbach, K., *Anti-Judaism in Feminist Religious Writings* (American Academy of Religion; Atlanta: Scholars Press, 1994).

Vorster, J.N., 'Construction of Culture Through the Construction of Person: The *Acts of Thecla* as an Example', in Stanley E. Porter and Thomas H. Olbricht (eds), *The Rhetorical Analysis of Scripture. Essays from the 1995 London Conference* (JSNTSS, 146; Sheffield: Sheffield Academic Press, 1997), p. 445–73.

— 'The Blood of the Female Martyrs as the Sperm of the Early Church', *Religion and Theology* 10.1 (2003), pp. 66–99.

Vouaux, L., *Les Actes de Paul et ses lettres apocryphes* (Paris: Librairie Letouzey et Ané, 1913).

Wagener, K.C., '"Repentant Eve, Perfected Adam": Conversion in *The Acts of Andrew*' (SBLSP 30; Atlanta: Scholars Press, 1991), pp. 348–56.

Wallace-Hadrill, A. (ed.), *Patronage in Ancient Society* (Leicester-Nottingham Studies in Ancient Society, 1; London: Routledge, 1989).

Ward, B., *Harlots of the Desert: A Study of Repentance in Early Monastic Sources* (Cistercian Studies Series, 106; Kalamazoo, MI: Cistercian Publications, 1987).

Warns, R., 'Weitere Darstellungen der heiligen Thekla', in Guntram Koch (ed.), *Studien zur spätantiken und frühchristlichen Kunst und Kultur des Orients II* (Wiesbaden: Otto Harrassowitz, 1986), pp. 75–131.

Watson, J., *The Martyrs of Columbine: Faith and the Politics of Tragedy* (New York: Palgrave Macmillan, 2002).

Weems, R., 'What's So Great About Being a Virgin?', in *eadem, Showing Mary. How Women Can Share Prayers, Wisdom, and the Blessings of God* (West Bloomfield, MI: Warner Books, 2002), pp. 41–53.

Weinreich, O., *Antike Heilungswunder* (Giessen: Töpelmann, 1909).

— *Religionsgeschichtliche Studien* (Darmstadt: Wissenschaftliche Buchgesellschaft, 1968).

Wesseling, B., 'The Audience of the Ancient Novel', in Hofmann, *Groningen Colloquia* I, pp. 67–79.

— *Leven, Liefde en Dood: motieven in antieke romans* (Ph.D. diss., University of Groningen, 1993: privately printed).

Wiedemann, T.E.J., *Adults and Children in the Roman Empire* (New Haven, CT: Yale University Press, 1989).

Williams, M.A., *The Immovable Race: A Gnostic Designation and the Theme of Stability in Late Antiquity* (NHS, 29; Leiden: E.J. Brill, 1985).

— *Rethinking 'Gnosticism': An Argument for Dismantling a Dubious Category* (Princeton, NJ: Princeton University Press, 1996).

Williams, R., 'Rachel's Other Page: Truth Doesn't Matter', n.p. (cited 26 June 2005; dated 24 October 1999; online: http://members.tripod.com/rachelw2/rotruth. html).

Williamson, G.A., (trans.), *The History of the Church from Christ to Constantine* (New York: New York University Press, 1966).

Wilson, R. McL., and George W. MacRae, 'The Gospel according to Mary. BG, 1:7,1–19,5', in *Nag Hammadi Codices V, 2–5 and VI with Papyrus Berolinensis 8502,1 and 4*, NHS XI (Leiden: E.J. Brill, 1979), pp. 453–71.

Wilson-Kastner, P. (ed.), *A Lost Tradition: Women Writers of the Early Church* (Washington, D.C.: University Press of America, 1981).

Wimbush, V., and R. Valantasis (eds), *Asceticism* (Oxford: Oxford University Press, 1995).

Winkler, J.J., 'The Constraints of Eros', in Faraone and Obbink (eds), *Magika Hiera*, pp. 214–43.

— 'The Invention of Romance', in James Tatum (ed.), *The Search for the Ancient Novel* (Baltimore and London: The Johns Hopkins University Press, 1994), pp. 23–38.

Winter, B.W., 'The Public Honouring of Christian Benefactors: Romans 13.3–4 and 1 Peter 2.14–15', *JSNT* 34 (1988), pp. 87–103.

Wolf, E.R., 'Kinship, Friendship, and Patron-Client Relations in Complex Societies', in Michael Banton (ed.), *The Social Anthropology of Complex Societies* (A.S.A. Monographs; London: Tavistock Publications, 1968), pp. 1–22.

Wood, D. (ed.), 'The Fathers and the Children', in *The Church and Childhood: Papers Read at the 1993 Summer Meeting and the 1994 Winter Meeting of the Ecclesiastical History Society* (Studies in Church History, 31; Oxford and Cambridge, MA: Blackwell, 1994), pp. 1–27.

Wrede, H., 'Matronen im Kult des Dionysos', *Römische Mitteilungen* 88 (1991), pp. 164–88.

Wright, W. (ed.), *Apocryphal Acts of the Apostles*, vol. I: *The Syriac Texts* (Amsterdam: Philo Press, 1968).

Wyke, M., 'Woman in the Mirror: The Rhetoric of Adornment in the Roman World', in Léonie J. Archer, Susan Fichler and Maria Wyke (eds), *Women in Ancient Societies: An Illusion of the Night* (New York: Routledge, 1994), pp. 134–51.

Zaidman, L.B., 'Pandora's Daughters and Rituals in Grecian Cities', in Pauline Schmitt Pantel (ed.), *A History of Women in the West I: From Ancient Goddesses to Christian Saints* (Cambridge, MA/London: The Belknap Press of Harvard University Press, 1992), pp. 338–76.

Zanker, P., *Die trunkene Alte* (Frankfurt: Fischer, 1989).

Zimmermann, N., *Werkstattgruppen römischer Katakombenmalerei* (Jahrbuch für Antike und Christentum, Ergänzungsband 35; Münster, Westfalen: Aschendorff Verlag, 2002).

Zycha, J. (ed.), *Sancti Aureli Augustini ... Contra Adimantum*, 170, ll. 15–16: *tamen ad preces apostolic factum esse non negant*.

— (ed.), *Sancti Aureli Augustini De utilitate credendi, De duabus animabus, Contra Fortunaturm, Contra Adimantum, Contra Epistulam Fundamenti, Contra Faustum* (Corpus Scriptorum Ecclesiasticorum Latinorum, 25; Prague, Vienna and Leipzig: F. Tempsky and G. Freytag, 1891).

INDEX OF REFERENCES

INDEX OF AUTHORS